German Combat Planes

DOUBLEDAY & COMPANY, INC., GARDEN CITY, NEW YORK, 1971

German Combat Planes

RAY WAGNER

AND

HEINZ NOWARRA

Library of Congress Catalog Card Number 71–125035

Printed in the United States of America
First Edition

Contents

MESSERSCHMITT ME 262

Introduction

German Combat Planes provides the reader with the first history of all warplanes built by Germany from World War I's beginning in 1914 to World War II's end in 1945.

Photographs and technical data are provided for every combat plane of those times, and the narrative describes each plane's role in the two great wars. Prototype aircraft that influenced or demonstrate design development are included, as well as the mass production types that made such a great impression on history.

While books on German World War One aircraft are available, as well as others on the Second World War, they limit themselves to an alphabetical type catalogue without integrating the story of each aircraft with the others and with the wars themselves. Our narrative is historical, introducing each type as it made its impact, large or small, on the times.

An advantage of joining both wars has been that the aircraft of Germany's secret military aviation between the wars can be described, often for the first time in any detail. This book also has the opportunity to use newly discovered information to correct or fill in gaps in earlier works, even on the more famous types.

Combining so many aircraft in one book requires a concise narrative centered on the most important facts and to wartime history. The photos tell much of the story themselves. Our annotated bibliography will guide readers wishing further information about any particular phase of this history. Official German designation forms are followed, but the *umlaut* and extra periods have been omitted, for the comfort of American readers.

Research in German military history presents a difficulty not found in the American and British fields. Original records were largely destroyed, and what remains is quite spotty. For example, aircraft delivery records have been preserved for certain months in 1936 and 1940, but not in between. An inventory of aircraft types at the front in 1914–18 is available, but not an accounting of how many of each type was produced.

H. J. Nowarra supplied most of the data and photographs used here, while Ray Wagner wrote the text and utilized other sources available in America. Peter Grosz supplied much World War I data, including the lists of planes at the front, loaned many photos, and contributed much as a critical reader of the first four parts. Others who provided individual photos are hereby given our thanks. The bibliography cites the published works which were of enormous assistance, especially those of Peter Gray, William Green, and the late Gert Heumann and A. R. Weyl. The project was helped by Ron Bulinski's loan of his German aviation collection, and above all completed by Mary Wagner's patient typing.

ALBATROS DV

World War I

Part 1 Workhorses of the War: The Two-seaters

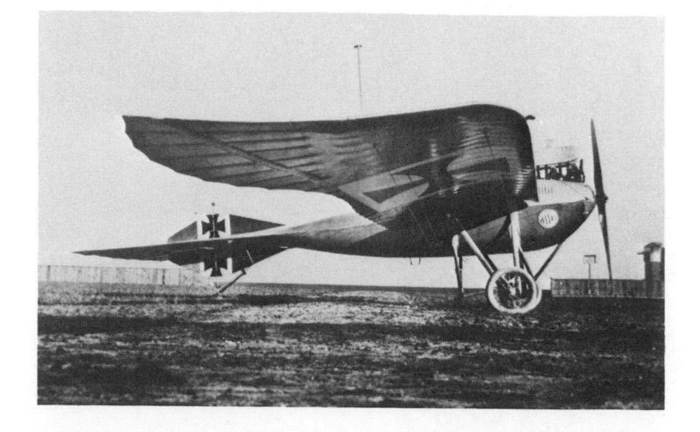

GERMANIA TAUBE

1.

A and B Types, 1914–15

When the First World War began in August 1914, Germany's Military Aviation Service had 246 aircraft, a number quickly increased by new production and impressment.[1] None of these planes had guns, for they were intended only for reconnaissance duties. But while not, strictly speaking, combat planes, they soon found themselves involved in fighting and so these designs set the patterns for two generations of German combat types.

Type designation of 1914 German aircraft was quite simple; A for monoplanes and B for biplanes. Nearly all were two-seaters with an observer in front and the pilot in the second cockpit. No armament was fitted, but a carbine or rifle could be added to the airmen's pistols.

The aircraft were distributed among 33 flying sections, or *Feldfliegerabteilung* (*Feld Fl. Abt.*) with six aircraft each, and four-plane flights (*Festungsflieger Abteilungen*) attached to eight fortress cities.[2] There was no attempt to standardize aircraft types within a flight, and even aircraft of the same type varied a good deal in rigging.

Most of the A types were the famous *Taube* (Dove) monoplanes. These were a delight to the eye of Americans then accustomed to the pioneer box-kite Wright and Curtiss biplanes. The *Tauben* had bird-like, sweptback wing tips, long fan-shaped, one-piece elevator, and split rudders like tail pennants. Control was by warping the wing tips with a wire and pulley system.

The *Taube* had originally been developed in 1910 from Professor Ahlborn's basic idea by Igo Etrich, who sold the manufacturing rights to the Rumpler firm at Johannisthal, Berlin. Besides the *Tauben* built by Rumpler from 1911 to 1914, fourteen companies including Albatros, Gotha, and Halberstadt also built them for the Army. These two-seaters had fabric-covered wooden frames with a 100 hp water-cooled, six-cylinder inline Mercedes, Benz, or Argus as the usual powerplant. The Jeannin *Taube*, however, had a steel-tube fuselage and Argus engine. These monoplanes had a flight duration of about four hours.

Tauben were frequently seen over the front lines in the opening weeks of the war, the most famous exploits including the discovery of a Russian advance at the Battle of Tannenberg, and the "Five O'Clock" *Taube* that regularly visited Paris in August 1914, dropping little (6.6 lb.) bombs, and even a demand that the city surrender. On August 31, 1914, there were 44 monoplanes with front-line flying sections, including 16 Gotha, 10 Rumpler, nine Jeannin, five Albatros, and one Hirth type. These include aircraft behind the lines at depots, but not those at training fields.

Our photos contrast Gotha *Taube* A 69, delivered October 16, 1914, with split rudders, with a Roesner-designed Gotha having conventional tail and nose radiator. Other *Tauben* illustrated are the Jeannin Rumpler, and a rare Germania.

Not all the A monoplanes were *Tauben*, however. Anthony Fokker's A I, built at Schwerin in Mecklenburg, had conventional straight wire-braced wings, but employed wing warping for control. This two-seater featured a fuselage of welded steel tubing, cockpit sides cut down, comma-shaped rudder, and a light air-cooled 80 hp Oberursel rotary, actually a license-built Gnome engine.

The A I appeared in October 1914 with the factory label M 8, and the famous Dutchman built about

[1] According to Gray, but *Die Militarluftfahrt bis 1914* said 325 usable aircraft. The Army organization fits 246 more closely, and 261 were known to be at the front on August 31, 1914.

[2] Deployment of these 1914 units is given in H. J. Nowarra, *Eisernes Kreuz und Balkenkreuz*, Verlag Dieter Hoffman, Mainz 1968 p. 32–34 in English text. Data from *Mobilmachung, Aufmarsch und erster Einsatz der deutschen Lufstreitkrafte in August 1914, Kriegsgeschichtliche Einzelschriften der Luftwaffe*, Berlin, 1939. See also, *The German Fliegertruppe and Luftschiffertruppe at Mobilization—August 1914*, Horst Reh (Cross and Cockade Journal, Vol. 3, Number 4, Winter 1962, p. 367.)

GOTHA A 69/14 (LE 3)
Mercedes D I, 100 hp
DIMENSIONS: Span 14.5 m. (47'7"), Lg. 10 m. (32'9½"), Wing Area 33.5 qm. (360 sq. ft.)
WEIGHT: Empty 690 kg. (1518 lb.), Gross 1062 kg. (2332 lb.)
PERFORMANCE: Speed—Max. 96 km/hr (60 mph), Climb 800 m. (2624)/12 min.

GOTHA A (LE 4)

JEANNIN A
Argus As II, 120 hp
DIMENSIONS: Span 14 m. (45'11"), Lg. 10.2 m. (33'5"), Wing Area 36 qm. (387.50 sq. ft.)
WEIGHT: Empty 650 kg. (1430 lb.), Gross 850 kg. (1870 lb.)
PERFORMANCE: Speed—Max. 115 km/hr (71 mph)

RUMPLER A

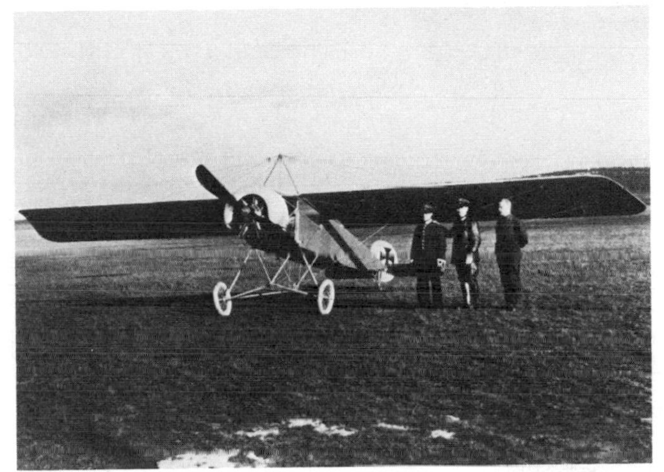

FOKKER M 8
Oberursel U I, 100 hp
DIMENSIONS: Span 9.52 m. (31'3"), Lg. 7.2 m. (23'7½"), Wing Area 16 qm. (172 sq. ft.)
WEIGHT: Empty 363 kg. (800 lb.), Gross 645 kg. (1290 lb.)
PERFORMANCE: Speed—Max. 135 km/hr (84 mph), Service ceiling 3000 m. (9840')

60 for the German Army, with another batch license-built by Halberstadt as the Halb. A II. Some of Fokker's similar M 5 single-seat monoplanes were also obtained as the A II (long-span wings) and A III (short-span wings). The latter type will be met later as the first E I fighter.

German monoplanes at the front had increased to a high of 65 in February 1915, including 23 Fokkers and five Halb. A IIs, as well as 16 Jeannin, seven Albatros, six Gotha and six Kondor *Tauben*.

A third type of monoplane was the parasol with the wing placed above to afford an excellent view of the ground below. In Germany this was exemplified by the Pfalz A I, which was actually a copy of the Morane-Saulnier Model L built under license at Speyer on the Rhine and powered by the 80 hp Oberursel.

PFALZ A I
Oberursel UO, 80 hp
DIMENSIONS: Span 11.2 m. (36′9″), Lg. 6.9 m. (22′8″), Ht. 3.4 m. (11′2″), Wing Area 18 qm. (193.68 sq. ft.)
WEIGHT: Empty 365 kg. (805 lb.), Gross 595 kg. (1310 lb.)
PERFORMANCE: Speed—Max. 135 km/hr (84 mph), Climb 800 m./6 min. (2642′/6 min.) 3000 m./30 min. (9840′/30 min.)

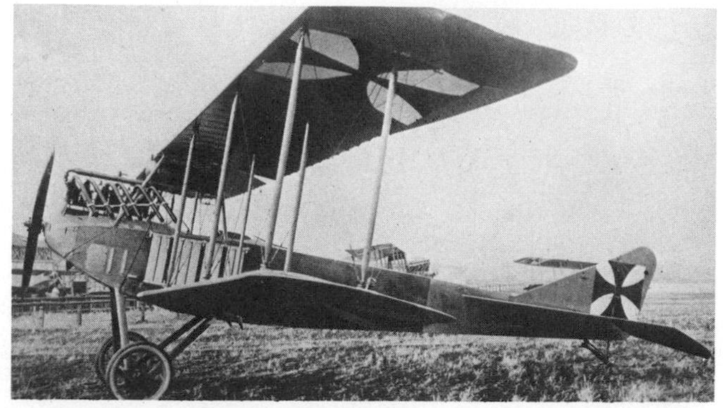

ALBATROS B I
Mercedes D I, 100 hp (or Benz Bz II)
DIMENSIONS: Span 14.48 m. (47′6″), Lg. 8.55 m. (28′½″), Ht. 3.15 m. (10′4″), Wing Area 43 qm. (462.85 sq. ft.)
WEIGHT: Empty 725 kg. (1595 lb.), Gross 1165 kg. (2563 lb.)
PERFORMANCE: Speed—Max. 110 km/hr (68 mph), Cruising speed 100 km/hr (62 mph), Climb 800 m./10 min. (2624′/10 min.), Range 650 km. (400 miles)

PFALZ A II
Oberursel UI, 100 hp
DIMENSIONS: Span 11.2 m. (36′9″), Lg. 6.9 m. (22′8″), Ht. 3.4 m. (11′2″), Wing Area 18 qm. (193.68 sq. ft.)
WEIGHT: Empty 420 kg. (924 lb.), Gross 674 kg. (1483 lb.)
PERFORMANCE: Speed—Max. 135 km/hr (84 mph), Cruising speed 110 km/hr (68 mph), Climb 3000 m./25 min. (9840′/25 min.)

After the war broke out, 60 Pfalz A Is were purchased for Bavarian flying units of the German Army. A few fitted with the 100 hp Oberursel became the A II, and later the E III.

Germany built over 300 A type aircraft in 1914, and only 13 in 1915, because the B type biplanes were considered sturdier and better suited for frontline service. These B ships were also unarmed two-seaters, with 1054 produced in 1914. Although most were withdrawn from the front in 1916 due to the change to armed C types, the B biplanes continued to serve at home as trainers, and 4770 were produced from 1915 to the end of production in 1918.

The most widely used B types were those produced by Albatros at Johannisthal. The first of these, the Albatros B I designed by Ernst Heinkel in April 1913, was powered either by a 100 hp Mercedes or a 110 hp Benz. The water radiator was originally mounted above the cylinder heads protruding up from the nose. Later the radiators were placed on each side of the fuselage and the six exhaust pipes pointed down to the left. The fuselage was built of slab sides of plywood on four main longerons, while the wings were a fabric-covered wooden frame. The original low tail fin was made higher on later ships.

Heinkel also designed the Albatros B II before the war; a smaller and faster version, with two bays (two pairs of struts on each side) instead of the three usual on the B I. The "Rhino horn" exhaust manifolds seen pointing up from the exposed cylinders in the photos are just two of many exhaust shapes provided for the Mercedes or Benz engines. On all these ships, the observer sat in the front seat sandwiched in between the top and bottom wings with rather poor visibility and a limited field of fire for his occasional carbine or rifle.

There were 157 Albatros B I and 27 B IIs at the front on April 30, 1915, and on October 31, of a total of 597 B types at the front, there were 90 Albatros B I and 212 B IIs. After the B types were withdrawn from the front, the Albatros B II continued in production as a trainer by seven other companies. The B IIa, produced in large quantities through 1918, had dual controls for a student pilot, minor structure changes, and had its radiator on the leading edge of the top wing, instead of alongside the fuselage.

Robert Thelen and Rudolf Schubert designed the Albatros B III or "Blue Mouse," which was used in 1914–15 by both Army and Navy units. It was smaller and faster than the earlier ships, and used various Mercedes, Benz and Argus engines.

ALBATROS B II
Mercedes D I (Benz Bz II), 100 hp (110 hp)
DIMENSIONS: Span 12.80 m. (42′), Lg. 7.76 m. (25′5½″), Ht. 3.15 m. (10′4″), Wing Area 40.12 qm. (433 sq. ft.)
WEIGHT: Empty 723 kg. (1591 lb.), Gross 1071 kg. (2356 lb.)
PERFORMANCE: Speed—Max. 120 km/hr (74 mph), Cruising speed 110 km/hr (68 mph), Rate of climb 800 m./10 min. (2624 ft./10 min.), Range 700 km. (434 mph), Service ceiling 3000 m. (9840′)

ALBATROS B III
Mercedes (Benz), 100 or 120 hp (150 or 120 hp)
DIMENSIONS: Span 11 m. (36′1″), Lg. 7.80 m. (25′7″), Ht. 2.80 m. (9′2″)
WEIGHT: Empty 600 kg. (1320 lb.), Gross 960 kg. (2112 lb.)
PERFORMANCE: Speed—Max. 140 km/hr (87 mph), Cruising speed 120 km/hr (74 mph), Climb 3000 m./20 min. (9840′/20 min.), Range 560 km. (347 miles)

While the Albatros B II was considered the best of the 1914's B types, some 18 other German companies produced designs to the same two-place biplane formula. Today this seems a remarkably wasteful duplication of effort, but in 1914 trial and error engineering was the rule, prototypes cost little, and the government was generous with contracts and uninterested in standardization. This situation accounts for the bewildering variety of wartime types. Not until later in the war did standardization become the thing at the front.

The most widely used biplane at the beginning of the war was the LVG B I. Quite similar to the Albatros, it was a double-bay biplane with slightly sweptback wings. The 100 hp Mercedes D I had an exhaust pipe pointed downward on the starboard side, but a few B Is had a 110 hp Benz with the exhaust pipe on the port side.

This general purpose two-seater had been designed in 1913 by Franz Schneider, a Swiss engineer with Luft-Verkehrs Gesellschaft at Johannisthal, near Berlin. Originally, the B I had a skid on the undercarriage to prevent propeller damage on nose overs. The fuselage was a wire-braced spruce structure covered with fabric except for a metal deck over the engine.

An improved B II appeared at the front late in 1914, with the 120 hp Mercedes and various refinements, including a cutout in the upper wing's trailing edge to improve visibility from the rear cockpit. The radiators were moved from the cylinder heads to the sides. There were 165 at the front by October 1915, including a few built by Otto. The B II was gradually relegated to training fields, and Schutte-Lanz also produced the trainer version in 1917–18.

Of 173 B type aircraft at the front on August 31, 1914, 30 had been Albatros, 47 Aviatik, and 84 LVG biplanes, with a sprinkling of AEG (3), DFW (2), Euler (5), Fokker (1), and Rumpler (1) types. A year later, 1915 front-line strength reached 580 B planes, including 267 Albatros, 196 LVG, 65 Aviatik, 17 Rumpler, nine AEG, eight Euler, eight Otto, six Halberstadt, and four Fokker two-seater biplanes.

Most of the 1914 biplanes look so much alike that only a sharp eye can tell them apart. The Aviatik B I had a slight sweepback with both two and three bay wings, while the Rumpler 4A13 and smaller B I had more rounded tips on the upper wing. Most distinctive wing shape was that of the "Flying Banana," the DFW B I with its curved, sweptback wings, and a little gravity tank above the center section.

While 17 DFW B Is were at the front in October 1914, the type soon disappeared, as did the few Euler B I and Hansa-Brandenburg B I two-seaters.

LVG B I (D4)
Benz Bz II or Mercedes D I, 110 or 100 hp
DIMENSIONS: Span 14.5 m. (47′6½″), Lg. 7.81 m. (25′7″) Ht. 3.2 m. (10′6″)
WEIGHT: Not available
PERFORMANCE: Speed—Max. at sea level 100 km. (62 mph)

LVG B II
Mercedes D II, 120 hp
DIMENSIONS: Span 12.12 m. (39′9″), Lg. 8.30 m. (27′3″), Ht. 2.93 m. (9′7″), Wing Area 35.42 qm. (381 sq. ft.)
WEIGHT: Empty 726 kg. (1597 lb.), Gross 1074 kg. (2363 lb.), Fuel 173 liters (46 gal.)
PERFORMANCE: Speed—Max. 105 km/hr (65 mph), at 1000 m. (3280′), Climb 1000 m./12 min. (3280′/12 min.), Range duration 4 hours

AVIATIK B I
Mercedes D I, 100 hp
DIMENSIONS: Span 14 m. (45′11″), Lg. 7.93 m. (26′2″), Ht. 3.05 m. (10′2″)
WEIGHT: Empty 668 kg. (1470 lb.), Gross 1090 kg. (2400 lb.)
PERFORMANCE: Speed—Max. 100 km/hr (62 mph) at sea level, Rate of climb 1000 m./15 min. (3280′/15 min.) Range duration 4 hours

RUMPLER 4A13
Mercedes D I, 100 hp
DIMENSIONS: Span 14.5 m. (47′6½″) Lg. 8.5 m. (27′10″), Ht. 3.2 m. (10′6″)
WEIGHT: Empty 780 kg. (1716 lb.), Gross 1060 kg. (2332 lb.)
PERFORMANCE: Speed—Max. 145 km/hr (90 mph) at sea level, Cruising speed 120 km/hr (74 mph)

DFW B I (MD 14)
Mercedes D I, 100 hp
DIMENSIONS: Span 14 m. (45′11″), Lg. 8.4 m. (27′6½″), Wing Area 40 qm. (430.56 sq. ft.)
WEIGHT: Empty 650 kg. (1430 lb.), Gross 1015 kg. (2233 lb.)
PERFORMANCE: Speed—Max. 120 km/hr (74 mph), Cruising speed 100 km/hr (62 mph)

The Eulers were modified LVGs with 100 hp Mercedes, while the Brandenburgs had a 110 hp Benz and resembled the Albatros B II previously designed by the same Ernst Heinkel.

In 1915, the Rumpler B Is on hand increased to 41 on April 30, joined by eight new AEG B IIs. Fitted with a 120 hp Mercedes and two-bay wings, the trim B II replaced 1914's 100 hp, three-bay AEG B I. Similar changes were made in the Aviatik B II, which increased from one in June to 38 in October 1915.

A Gotha LD 2 acquired August 31, 1914, by the Army was another three-bay biplane and led to an LD 6 and an LD 6a tested early in 1915 with two-bay wings and a 150 hp Benz. While nine LD 1a and ten LD 5 biplanes delivered in spring 1915 were Gotha trainers with Oberursel rotarics, the heavier LD 7 designed by Burkhard for recon work became the Army's Gotha B I. Eighteen, including five sent to Turkey, were delivered with the 120 hp Mercedes from August to November 1915.

Most B types had the typical water-cooled engine, but Fokker's small B series had the features of his monoplanes; the air-cooled Oberursel rotary, steel-tube fuselage frame and comma-shaped rudder. Fokker's biplanes began in January 1915 with a few M 7 sesquiplanes (bottom wing much shorter than the top, which went to German Navy shore stations. This type was strengthened as the M 10E (single-bay) of June 1915, and the M 10Z (two-bay) biplanes which were sold to Austria as the B I and B II. Only a few B Is were accepted for front-line service by Germany, of about 50 built.

An 80 hp Oberursel rotary also powered the Halberstadt B I, which appeared in June 1915, but the Halberstadt B II had the more usual 100 hp Mercedes and a B III a 120 hp Mercedes. Halberstadts at the front on October 31, 1915, included four B I, three

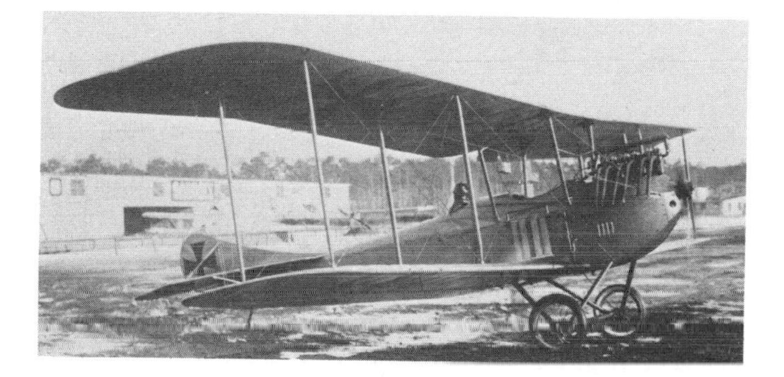

RUMPLER B I (4A)
Mercedes D I, 100 hp
DIMENSIONS: Span 13 m. (42′8″), Lg. 8.4 m. (27′6½″), Ht. 3.1 m. (10′2″)
WEIGHT: Empty 750 kg. (1650 lb.), Gross 950 kg. (2090 lb.)
PERFORMANCE: Speed—Max. 145 km/hr (90 mph), Cruising speed 120 km/hr (74 mph)

EULER B I (B 413/14)

HANSA-BRANDENBURG B I (Fd)

AEG B II (B 260/14)

AVIATIK B II (B 558/15)

HALBERSTADT B I (B 125/15)

GOTHA LD 2 (B 458/14 in original form)
Mercedes D I, 100 hp
DIMENSIONS: Span 12.55 m. (41′2″), Lg. 8.4 m. (27′7″), Wing Area 36 qm. (389 sq. ft.)
WEIGHT: Empty 525 kg. (1155 lb.), Gross 935 kg. (2057 lb.)
PERFORMANCE: Speed—Max. 120 km/hr (75 mph), Range 450 km. (280 miles)

GOTHA B I (LD 7)
Mercedes D II, 120 hp
DIMENSIONS: Span 12.4 m. (40′8″), Lg. 8.4 m. (27′7″), Wing Area 39.5 qm. (425 sq. ft.)
WEIGHT: Empty 900 kg. (1985 lb.), Gross 1465 kg. (2930 lb.)
PERFORMANCE: Speed—Max. 126 km/hr (78 mph), Service ceiling 2000 m. (6560′)

OTTO B
Mercedes D I, 100 hp
DIMENSIONS: Span 14.9 m. (48′10½″), Lg. 10/8 m. (35′5″)
WEIGHT: Data not available
PERFORMANCE: Speed—Max. 110 km/hr (68 mph), Cruising speed 90 km/hr (56 mph)

HALBERSTADT B II

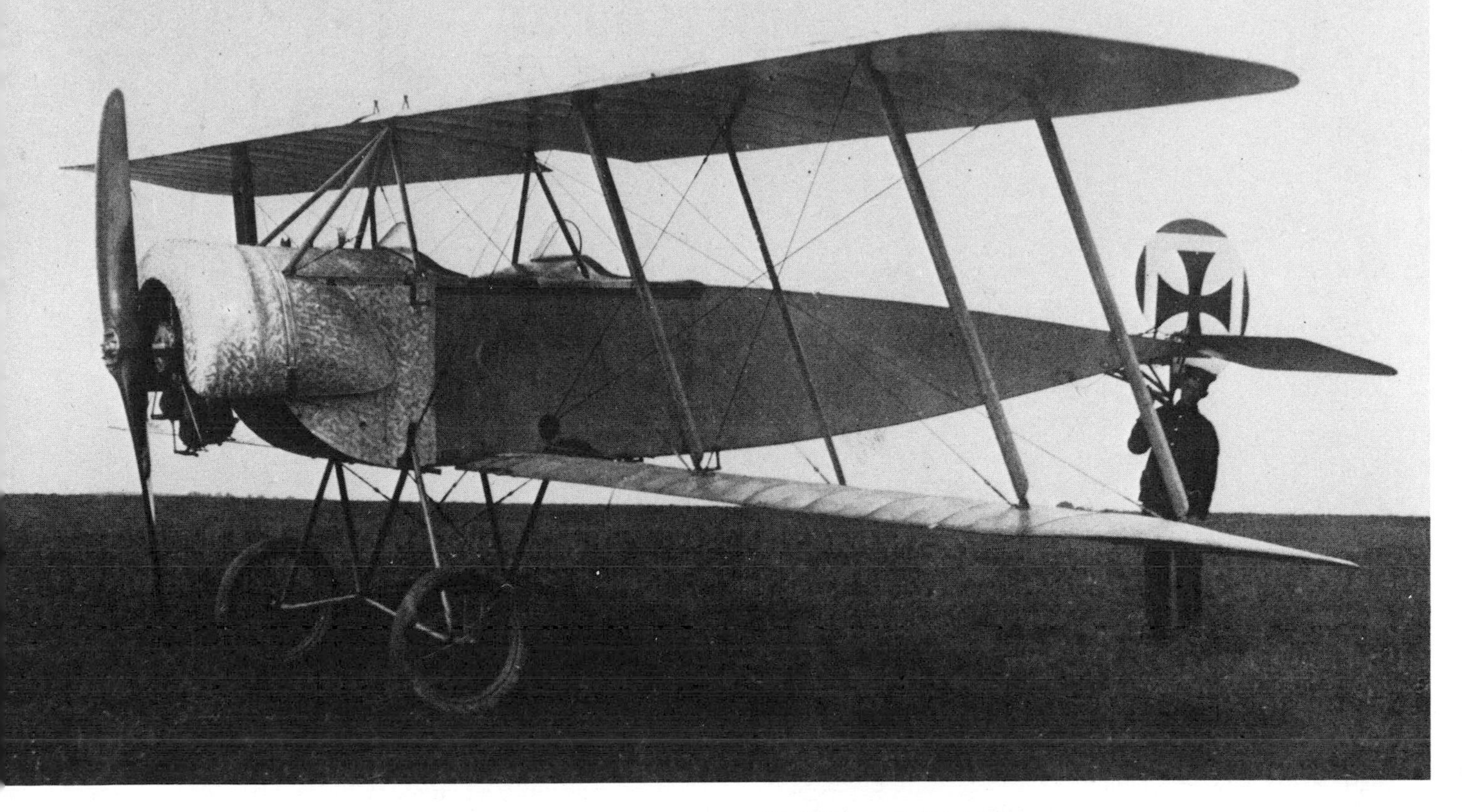

FOKKER B II (M 10Z)
Oberursel UO, 80 hp
DIMENSIONS: Span 8.75 m. (28′8″), Lg. 6.4 m. (21′), Ht. 2.45 m. (8′½″), Wing Area 48 qm. (193.68 sq. ft.)
WEIGHT: Data not available
PERFORMANCE: Speed—Max. 90 km/hr (56 mph) at sea level

B II and five B III models. Smaller German firms offering B designs included Germania, Goedecker, Jeannin NFW, Kondor, Rex, and Siemens-Schuckert, but these biplanes added little to production totals and nothing in original design features.

Unique among the B types was the Otto biplane pusher built in Munich. The crew had a clear view forward because the Mercedes faced backward, and the tail was supported on an open frame. Thanks to the Bavarian War Ministry's preference for local products, the Otto pusher achieved production both in Munich and under license by Pfalz. They served Bavarian flights, and a Pfalz-built version in East Africa was converted to a floatplane to spot for the cruiser *Koenigsberg*. The Otto pusher had a poor climb, and was often mistaken for the French pusher aircraft and shot at all the time. Otto then produced LVG B IIs and a few tractor B types of its own.

The front-line usefulness of the unarmed A and B types was gradually ended by the increasingly aggressive behavior of enemy aircraft. As early as August 26, 1914, Hauptmann Kerksiek, of Fl. Abt. 5, was killed by pistol shots from two French biplanes over Nancy. A Voisin pusher with a Hotchkiss machine gun shot down an Aviatik on October 5, 1914, and later incidents involved Frenchmen firing carbines from their two-seaters. But the real doom of the unarmed aircraft on the front came on April 1, 1915, when Garros destroyed his first Albatros by firing a Hotchkiss through the propeller of his Morane monoplane.

PFALZ-OTTO pusher

PFALZ-OTTO as seaplane in Africa

PARABELLUM GUN ON ALBATROS CI

2.

Armed C Types, 1914–18

Combat with enemy aircraft created a requirement for the C type, the two-seat biplane armed to protect itself from enemy planes.

These two-seaters became the workhorses of the air force, scouting enemy positions, directing artillery fire, and flying whatever photography, infantry contact, or even light bombing missions that seemed necessary. Of 46,583 German military aircraft produced from 1915 thru 1918, 25,057, over half, were the type C two-seaters.

The first generation of Cs appeared at the front in April 1915 and were simply B type biplanes with a more powerful engine, and a movable machine gun mounted on the observer's cockpit. They were first distributed singly to the various flight sections and were used to escort the unarmed B types. Their usefulness was limited because they had to turn away to allow the observer's gun to fire. Credit for the first C type is usually given to LVG (Luft-Verkehrs Gesellschaft), who began with the advantages of a B type second only to the Albatros in the quantity being produced, and the Swiss, Franz Schneider, as their chief designer. He had obtained a patent on a machine gun synchronized with the propeller as early as July 1913, and on September 16, 1914, patented a rotating ring mount for a Parabellum light machine gun. It was this ring mount that was fitted in 1915 to the LVG C I and many later German aircraft with flexible guns.

The LVG C I had the pilot in the front seat and the observer in the rear, where he had a better field of fire. Aside from this reversal of the observer and pilot's positions, and a 150 hp Benz instead of the 110 hp engine in the B, the LVG C I was nearly identical to the B I. Sixty were at the front on August 31, 1915, but were soon superseded by the Mercedes-powered LVG C II, which was based on the LVG B II.

The LVG C II's fuselage was a wooden box girder braced with wires and covered with metal around the 160 hp Mercedes, plywood around the cockpits and fabric over the remainder. The two-bay fabric-covered straight wings had "kinked" ailerons, with a radiator on the upper center section leading edge and a fuel tank below and slightly to the left.

There was only a single LVG C III, which was a C II with the observer back in the front cockpit, but 255 LVG C IIs were at the front by June 30, 1916. The most famous LVG exploit was the first raid on London, made on November 28, 1916, by a single C II carrying six 10 kg. (22 lb.) bombs. In 1917–18, AGO and Otto built LVG C IIs as training planes.

The most popular, C class biplanes of 1915 were those made by Albatros, the most prolific builder of German warplanes. The Albatros C I, designed by Thelen and Schubert, closely resembled the B II, with its double-bay wings, plywood-covered fuselage, and side radiators, but the observer sat in the rear with his ring-mounted machine gun. Small bombs could be carried in vertical drums between the cockpits.

The prototype used a 150 hp Benz Bz III, but most production ships had the 160 hp Mercedes. When fitted with an 180 hp Argus As III and radiator on the top wing's center section, the type became the C Ia trainer. Built in large numbers, the C I was flown by Boelcke and Richthofen before they became fighter pilots. The number of Albatros C Is at the front increased from one on April 30, 1915, to 349 in February 1916. These included license-built OAW and Roland versions, although the later BFW and Mercur (C Ib) versions were only trainers.

An experimental pusher type was also built by Albatros as the C II, using C I wings and landing gear, and a 150 hp Benz. This company also owned the Ostdeutsche Albatros-Werke (OAW) at Schneidemuehl (now Pila, Poland), whose designer Groh-

LVG C I (D4)
Benz Bz III, 150 hp
DIMENSIONS: Span 14.5 m. (47'7"), Lg. 7.81 m. (25'7"), Ht. 3.2 m. (10'6"), Wing Area 41.5 qm. (457.3 sq. ft.)
WEIGHT: Empty 835 kg. (1837 lb.), Gross 1373 kg. (3021 lb.)
PERFORMANCE: Speed—Max. 100 km/hr (62 mph)

LVG C I with added gun mount on top wing

LVG C II
Mercedes D III, 160 hp
DIMENSIONS: Span 12.68 m. (41'7"), Lg. 8.7 m. (28'6"), Ht. 2.93 m. (9'7"), Wing Area 37.6 mm. (404.58 sq. ft.)
WEIGHT: Empty 845 kg. (1859 lb.), Gross 1405 kg. (3091 lb.)
PERFORMANCE: Speed—Max. 130 km/hr (81 mph) at sea level, Cruising speed 110 km/hr (68 mph), Endurance 4 hours

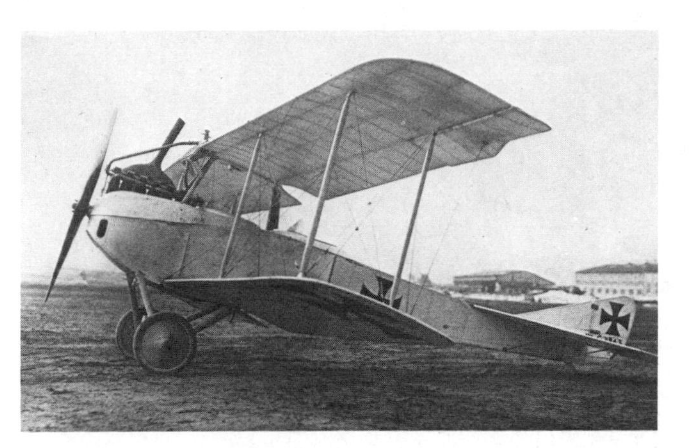

LVG C III

ALBATROS C I
Mercedes D III, 160 hp (also Benz 150 hp, and Argus 100 hp)
DIMENSIONS: Span 12.9 m. (42'4"), Lg. 7.85 m. (25'0"), Ht. 3.14 m. (10'4"), Wing Area 40.4 qm. (437 sq. ft.)
WEIGHT: Empty 875 kg. (1925 lb.), Gross 1190 kg. (2618 lb.)
PERFORMANCE: Speed—Max. 132 km/hr (82.5 mph) at sea level, Climb 1000 m./9.75 min. (3280'/9.75 min.), Endurance 2½ hours

ALBATROS C I

ALBATROS C II

mann produced a three-bay biplane with a 150 hp Benz designated Albs. C I (OAW) and a two-bay biplane with a 220 hp Mercedes and four-bladed propeller, designated Albs. C II. (OAW). An unusual double cockpit was featured, but only the experimental aircraft were made.

Albatros' most widely used two-seater was the C III, a smaller, faster and refined successor to the C I, that used the B III's graceful tail. Although the C I engines remained; a Benz on the first ships, the Mercedes on most, the radiator was moved up in front of the leading edge. The usual flexible Parabellum gun on the Schneider mount was later joined by a synchronized Spandau gun on the right side of the cowl. The fixed forward gun was soon adopted by all C types being built.

The number of C IIIs at the front increased from 12 at the end of 1915 to 354 on August 31, 1916. Albatros was joined in C III production by OAW, BFW, DFW, Hansa, Linke-Hofmann, Siemens-Schuckert, and even their rival LVG, whose machines had a higher vertical tail. License-built machines were built until 1918 for training.

The Albatros C IV of 1916 had a 160 hp Mercedes, C III fuselage and tail, thick, single-bay Madelung wings, and gun rails in the front cockpit. Only test examples were built.

By the end of 1915, C types had become the most important element of German air strength, with 660 at the front, including 290 Albatros and 184 LVG types. Other companies contributing C I types to the total were Aviatik (81), AEG (26), DFW (25),

ALBATROS C I (OAW)

ALBATROS C II (OAW)

Rumpler (29), AGO (16) and one Otto. Flight sections at the front still did not standardize on one type, but often operated several different designs, since they had to perform a variety of missions.

The Aviatik C I was an orthodox development of the firm's B II two-seater. Powered by a 160 hp Mercedes with side radiators, the Aviatik's unusual

feature was that the observer still sat in the front seat. His machine gun was fired from a Geyer mount; two racks at the sides of the cockpit, with the gun switched back and forth as the gunner needed. His field of fire was blocked by his own wings and struts.

Later Aviatiks, however, did have the observer in the rear cockpit with a normal ring mount, and had the radiator moved to above the engine.[1] Hannover built 146 Aviatik C Is under license. A 220 hp Benz Bz IV was used on the Aviatik C II, which omitted the vertical fin ahead of the rudder, and was first reported in August 1915.

The design was considerably refined in the C III which reached the front by the summer of 1916. The type could be recognized by the streamlined nose and spinner for the 160 hp Mercedes. The first of these still had the observer in front, but finally he was put in the rear with a ring mount.

The first Aviatik C I had arrived at the front in April 1915, and their number increased to 219 on June 30, 1916. By February 1917, there were 63 C Is, 62 C IIs, and 20 C IIIs, but despite the new models, Aviatiks were withdrawn from the front in 1917. The next Aviatik two-place design known is the C V, an unusual Vee-strutted gull-winged biplane with an 180 hp Argus As III. While it failed to win acceptance,

[1] Aviatiks with ring mounts are called C Ia in some books.

ALBATROS C III

Mercedes D III, 160 hp or Benz Bz III, 150 hp

DIMENSIONS: Span 11.69 m. (38′4″), Lg. 8 m. (26′3″), Ht. 3.1 m. (10′2″), Wing Area 36.91 qm. (397 sq. ft.)

WEIGHT: Empty 851 kg. (1872 lb.), Gross 1353 kg. (2976 lb.)

PERFORMANCE: Speed—Max. 140 km/hr (87 mph), Climb 1000 m./9 min. (3280′/9 min.)

ALBATROS C III

FRONT GUN ON ALBATROS C III

ALBATROS C III (LVG)

ALBATROS C IV

AVIATIK C I
Mercedes D III, 160 hp
DIMENSIONS: Span 12.5 m. (41′), Lg. 7.92 m. (26′), Ht. 2.95 m. (9′8″), Wing Area 43 qm. (462.68 sq. ft.)
WEIGHT: Empty 750 kg. (1650 lb.), Gross 1242 kg. (2732 lb.)
PERFORMANCE: Speed—Max. 142 km/hr (89 mph) at sea level, Climb 1000 m./12 min. (3280′/12 min.), Endurance 3 hours, Service ceiling 3500 m. (11,480′)

AVIATIK C I with Geyer gun mount

AVIATIK C I with gun ring

AVIATIK C II

AVIATIK C III
Mercedes D III, 160 hp
DIMENSIONS: Span 11.8 m. (38′8″), Lg. 8.20 m. (26′10″), Ht. 2.9 m. (9′6″), Wing Area 35 qm. (377 sq. ft.)
WEIGHT: Empty 925 kg. (2035 lb.), Gross 1340 kg. (2948 lb.)
PERFORMANCE: Speed—Max. 160 km/hr (99 mph) at sea level, Climb 1000 m./7 min. (3280′/7 min.), Range 480 km. (3000 miles), Service ceiling 4500 m. (14,760′)

AVIATIK C V

AEG C I (KZ 9)
Benz Bz III, 150 hp
DIMENSIONS: Span 13 m. (42′8″), Lg. 7.8 m. (25′7″), Wing Area 41 qm. (441 sq. ft.)
WEIGHT: Empty 710 kg. (1562 lb.), Gross 1125 kg. (2475 lb.)
PERFORMANCE: Speed—Max. 130 km/hr (81 mph), Climb 1000 m./4.5 min. (3280′/4.5 min.)

AEG C II
Mercedes D III, 160 hp
DIMENSIONS: Span 13 m. (42′8″), Lg. 7.9 m. (25′11″), Wing Area 41 qm. (441 sq. ft.)
WEIGHT: Empty 680 kg. (1496 lb.), Gross 1200 kg. (2640 lb.)
PERFORMANCE: Speed—Max. 135 km/hr (84 mph), Service ceiling 3500 m. (11,480′)

they went into production with the Aviatik C VI, which was actually the DFW C V built under license.

AEG, which stood for the *Allgemeine Elektrizitats Gesellschaft* (General Electric Company) aviation branch in Hennigsdorf, Berlin, produced two-place biplanes designed by Georg Koenig. Constructed largely of steel tubing with fabric covering, they were recognized by a pointed metal nose with two louvers on each side, and had radiators alongside the front cockpit and the fuel tank in the upper wing. A pair of center section struts sloped back from the upper wing to the rear cockpit.

The AEG C I was a strengthened B II with a 150 hp Benz and a ring mount for the rear seat observer's Parabellum. A 160 hp Mercedes, however, was used on the similar C II.[2] While the C I appeared at the front in June 1915, the total of AEGs in front-line service was only 34 C Is and one C II by April 30, 1916, after which both types nearly disappeared.

An experimental development of 1915 was the AEG C III, whose deep fuselage completely filled the gap between the wings. Since the upper wing was no longer in the way, the gunner could be placed in the front cockpit, and the pilot in the rear.

The Deutsche Flugzeugwerke (DFW) of Leipzig, produced an armed version of Oelerich's "Flying Banana" as the C I with a 150 hp Benz. The observer remained in the front cockpit, and the version shown here has him standing to fire his Parabellum gun from a gun ring raised above the curved wings. Others had the gun in the cockpit itself.

[2] A Benz Bz III, according to Gray.

AEG C III
Benz Bz III, 150 hp
DIMENSIONS: Span 12 m. (39′4″), Lg. 6.5 m. (21′4″)
WEIGHT: Empty 687 kg. (1511 lb.), Gross 1237 kg. (2721 lb.)
PERFORMANCE: Speed—Max. 158 km/hr (99 mph) at sea level

DFW C I (KD 15)
Benz Bz III, 150 hp
DIMENSIONS: Span 14 m. (45′11″), Lg. 8.4 m. (27′6½″), Wing Area 40 qm. (430.56 sq. ft.)
PERFORMANCE: Speed—Max. 130 km/hr (81 mph)

Although about 100 C Is were said to have been built, only 25 were at the front at the end of 1915. DFW did offer a C II and a C III design with the same Benz engine, but neither went into production. The C II was a conventional two-bay biplane with the observer in the rear seat and the radiator moved from the fuselage sides to below the upper wing's leading edge. The C III is obscure while the C IV was a single-bay development of the C II.

While the Rumpler C I arrived at the front late in 1915, it soon became third behind Albatros and LVG in use. Of composite construction in wood, metal, and fabric, it had two-bay wings swept back five degrees, with rounded wing tips, rudder and elevators. A semicircular radiator was placed at the upper wing's center section leading edge. The usual Parabellum gun in the rear cockpit was later joined by a fixed Spandau gun on the left side of the cylinders.

The C I was made by Rumpler at Johannisthal, as well as by Germania, Markische Flugzeug-Werft, Hansa-Brandenburg, and Albert Rinne Flugzeugwerke. These ships used the 160 hp Mercedes, while those built by Bayerische Rumpler-Werke had a 150 hp Benz Bz III, and Hannover's later C Ia (387 built) used the 180 hp Argus As III. By October

DFW C II
Benz Bz III, 150 hp
DIMENSIONS: Span 11.2 m. (36'9"), Lg. 7.2 m. (23'7"), Wing Area 33 qm. (355.21 sq. ft.)
WEIGHT: Empty 725 kg. (1595 lb.), Gross 1235 kg. (2717 lb.)
PERFORMANCE: Speed—Max. 140 km/hr (87 mph), Service ceiling 4000 m. (13,120')

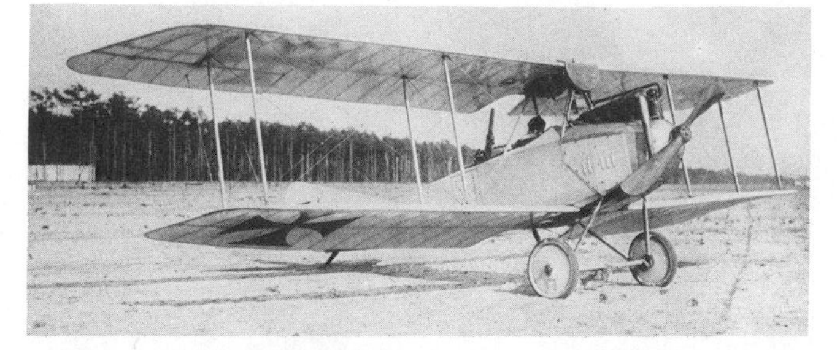

RUMPLER C I (5A 2)
Mercedes D III, 160 hp
DIMENSIONS: Span 12.15 m. (39'10"), Lg. 7.85 m. (25'9"), Ht. 3.06 m. (10'½"), Wing Area 30.7 qm. (330 sq. ft.)
WEIGHT: Empty 793 kg. (1744 lb.), Gross 1330 kg. (2933 lb.), Fuel 240 liters (63 gallons)
PERFORMANCE: Speed—Max. 152 km/hr (94 mph) at sea level, Range 600 km. (372 miles)

DFW C IV (T 25)
Benz Bz III, 150 hp
DIMENSIONS: Span 11.2 m. (36'9"), Lg. 7.2 m. (23'7"), Wing Area 33 qm. (355.21 sq. ft.)
WEIGHT: Empty 720 kg. (1584 lb.), Gross 1230 kg. (2706 lb.)
PERFORMANCE: Speed—Max 135 km/hr (84 mph), Cruising speed 115 km/hr (71 mph), Range 400 km. (248 miles)

31, 1915, there were 231 C Is and two C Ias at the front, with 55 C Is and 162 C Ias on June 30, 1916. License-built trainer versions remained in production to 1918.

Most unusual C types in production were those made by AGO (Aerowerke Gustav Otto) of Johannisthal, near Berlin. Designed by the Swiss engineers Haefeli and Schorpf, these biplanes had the two crewmen in a center nacelle ahead of the engine and pusher propeller, and unique twin wooden fuselages supporting twin rudders.

The first model, the AGO C I had a 150 hp Benz, side radiators and twin nose wheels below the observer's front cockpit. His Parabellum had a clear forward field of fire, the pusher's advantage. While the Army's C Is had two bays of struts, a 220 hp Mercedes with a wing radiator and three-bay wings distinguished the few AGO C IIs.

A little smaller, the AGO C III appeared with single-bay struts, and although the first example had nose wheels, these were eliminated on a later model which used a 160 hp Mercedes engine. The only pusher C types used in combat by the Germans, the well-liked AGOs appeared at the front in the summer of 1915, and by February 1916, 22 C Is, one C II and one C III were on hand.

Munich's Otto company also turned out a twin-boomed pusher with a Benz, kinked ailerons, and nose wheels. Apparently three to seven Otto C Is were built in 1915, with most going to Bulgaria and one to Flt. Abt. 35. Otto's C II, however, was a completely conventional 1917 two-seater trainer with a 150 hp Mercedes. This company became BFW in 1916.

That completes the list of C types at the front in 1915, but there were several efforts by other firms that did not pass the experimental stage. Euler and Germania simply modified their very conventional B Is by adding a gun ring at the rear pit. A stronger 150 hp Benz Bz III was used on the Germania C type, while Euler, who had been building LVG B Is under license, simply labeled one batch C I when a 120 hp Mercedes and gun ring were fitted in 1915.

Euler also built a pusher two-seater whose pilot sat forward with a fixed gun, like Euler's earlier "airship destroyer," while the observer stood up behind him to fire another Parabellum that could be rotated completely around to shoot over the top wings and twin rudders attached to a strut frame. A fairing had been added on our second photo. Powered by a 160 hp Mercedes, it appears designed more for fighting than observation work, despite its large size.

RUMPLER C I with 25 kg. (55 lb.) bombs

RUMPLER C Ia

AGO C I (DH 6)
Benz Bz III, 150 hp
DIMENSIONS: Span 14.5 m. (47'6½"), Lg. 7 m. (22'11½")
WEIGHT: Empty 800 kg. (1760 lb.), Gross 1320 kg. (2904 lb.)
PERFORMANCE: Speed—Max. 145 km/hr (90 mph), Cruising speed 130 km/hr (81 mph), Climb 3000 m./30 min. (9840'/30 min.), Range 500 km. (310 miles), Service ceiling 4500 m. (14,760')

AGO C II (DH 7)
Mercedes D IV, 220 hp
DIMENSIONS: Span 18.3 m. (60½"), Lg. 7 m. (22'11½")
WEIGHT: Empty 1360 kg. (2992 lb.), Gross 1946 kg. (4281 lb.)
PERFORMANCE: Speed—Max. 145 km/hr (90 mph)

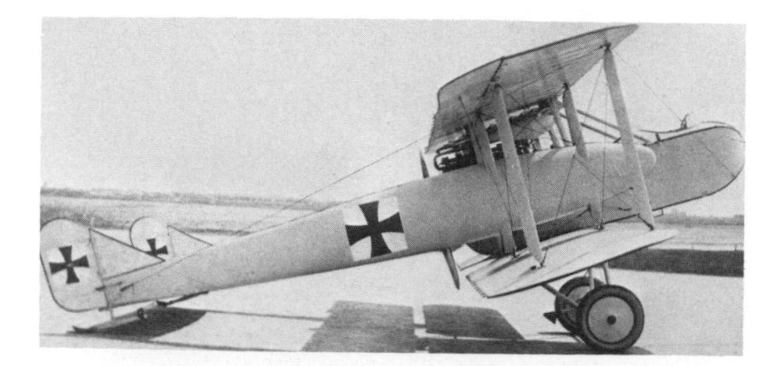

AGO C III
Mercedes D III, 160 hp
DIMENSIONS: Span 11 m. (36′), Lg. 7 m. (22′ 11½″)
WEIGHT: Not available
PERFORMANCE: Speed—Max. 145 km/hr (90 mph)

GERMANIA C type

OTTO C I
Benz Bz III, 150 hp
DIMENSIONS: Span 14.5 m. (47′6½″)
WEIGHT: Empty 915 kg. (2013 lb.), Gross 1500 kg. (3300 lb.)
PERFORMANCE: Speed—Max. 150 km/hr (93 mph) at sea level

OTTO C II
Mercedes D III, 160 hp
DIMENSIONS: Span 13.4 m. (43′11½″)
WEIGHT: Empty 829 kg. (1824 lb.), Gross 1329 kg. (2924 lb.)
PERFORMANCE: Not available

EULER C I

EULER 1915 Pusher
Mercedes D III, 160 hp
DIMENSIONS: Span 14.8 m. (48′7″), Lg. 9.3 m. (30′6″), Ht. 3.2 m. (10′6″), Wing Area 52.6 qm. (566 sq. ft.)
WEIGHT: Empty 492 kg. (1082 lb.)
PERFORMANCE: Not available

EULER Pusher with fairing

EULER pusher (revised)

HALBERSTADT C I

The only 1915 experimental C type with an air-cooled engine was the Halberstadt C I, an armed version of their B I with a 100 hp Oberursel rotary engine instead of the usual water-cooled type. This type's performance and history are unknown, but the photo shows a small double-bay biplane with a single cockpit for both crewmen and an unbraced, finless rudder.

Designer Ernst Heinkel had left Albatros in 1914 to join Hansa and Brandenburgische Flugzeugwerke, where he produced very successful seaplanes. His multipurpose landplanes, however, were not accepted by the Army, and were actually designed for production by affiliates in Austria-Hungary.

Heinkel's DD biplane had a 150 hp Mercedes in front, a gunner in a basket mount raised above the top wing, and a third man facing the rear with another gun. The Hansa-Brandenburg DD established an altitude record in September 1915, by carrying four passengers to 4760 meters (15,618 feet). Developed into the conventional LDD two-seater, the design was built under license by UFAG and Phoenix for the Austrian Army as the Brandenburg C I.

Hansa-Brandenburg also offered two pusher two-seaters with a 150 hp Benz facing backwards, and a flexible gun for the observer in the nose. The MLD of 1915 had a strut frame holding the twin tail assembly, but the smaller KF of 1916 had twin nacelles running back to the rudders, and was designed with fighting in mind. Neither type was accepted.

Another pusher two-seater was designed on official

HANSA-BRANDENBURG DD

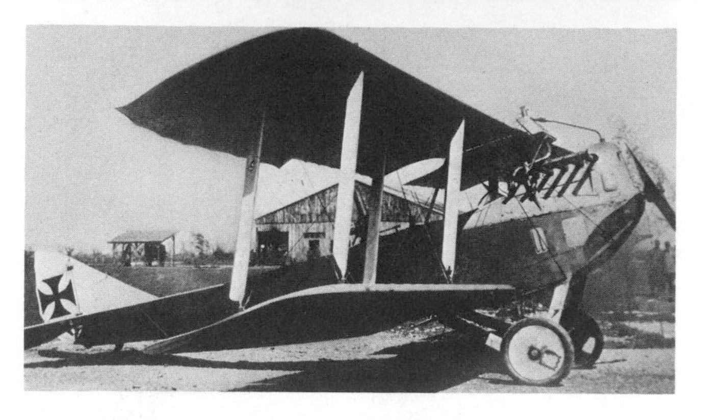

HANSA-BRANDENBURG C I (LDD)
Mercedes or Avstro-Daimler, 160 hp
DIMENSIONS: Span 13.12 m. (43′½″), Lg. 8.20 m. (26′10½″), Wing Area 43.46 qm. (467.62 sq. ft.)
WEIGHT: Empty 770 kg. (1694 lb.), Gross 1270 kg. (2794 lb.)
PERFORMANCE: Speed—Max. 120 km/hr (87 mph), Service ceiling 4000 m. (13,120′)

HANSA-BRANDENBURG KF
Benz Bz III, 150 hp
DIMENSIONS: Span 11.60 m. (38′½″), Lg. 8.48 m. (27′10″), Wing Area 38.60 qm. (415.33 sq. ft.)
WEIGHT: Empty 760 kg. (1672 lb.), Gross 1290 kg. (2838 lb.)
PERFORMANCE: Not available

SCHUTTE-LANZ C

DFW C type pusher

request in early summer 1915 by Schutte-Lanz, a firm that later was preoccupied building AGO and LVG two-seaters under license. Powered by a 160 hp Mercedes D III, the C I had a short nacelle attached to the top wing, giving the flexible front gun a good field of fire. Development was abandoned when the German Army decided against further production of pushers. This decision also doomed an obscure DFW pusher C with four-wheeled landing gear.

Fastest C type of 1915 was the remarkably streamlined Roland C II, called the *Walfisch* (Whale). Luftfahrzeug Gesellschaft (LFG) at Adlershof, near Berlin, had chosen the trade name Roland to distinguish itself from the LVG company. During 1915 the factory was occupied with the production of Albatros B II and C I two-seaters, until its designer, Tantzen, conceived the Roland C II as a radical improvement on the standard types.

The fuselage shape had emerged from wind tunnel tests as an oval cross-section, rounded from the carefully cowled 160 hp Mercedes to the tail. This body filled the gap between the wings, which were joined by a pair of streamlined I struts. The two crewmen had a clear view above the aircraft, a pylon was installed ahead of the pilot, and small windows provided the cockpits with light and an emergency exit. Thin plywood covered the first mass-produced semi-momocoupe fuselage; strong, but slow to build.

The *Walfisch* made a good combat ship, but its worst weakness was the lack of visibility forward and down, which caused many bad crashes to less experienced pilots.

An engine failure caused the prototype's destruction on its first flight in October 1915, but the first production examples were accepted in March 1916. Linke-Hofmann also began producing the type in November, although slow production and attrition limited *Walfisch* strength at the front to but 64 on December 31, 1916.

The C IIa designation appeared at the front in

August 1916, and seems to refer to provision of a fixed Spandau gun for the pilot in addition to the gunner's Parabellum, racks for four 12.5 kg. (27 lb.) bombs, and some wing modifications. The Rolands remained at the front until about July 1917.

Roland built an improved version of the *Walfisch,* the C III, which had a 200 hp Benz and ordinary two-bay wings, but the prototype was destroyed in a September 1916 factory fire and not rebuilt.

A rather streamlined nose was also seen in the experimental Kondor W 2C designed by Westphal, but today the only thing known about this obscure type is that it was said to be the first aircraft flown with the 220 hp, eight-cylinder Mercedes D IV, and achieved an altitude record in spring 1916.

SECOND GENERATION C TYPES

A second generation of C types emerged in 1916 as a result of the more powerful engines available, and 660 C types at the front at the year's start grew to 1508 on December 31, 1916.

Over half of these were Albatros designs. Older C I and C III types were joined by the Mercedes-powered C V, the C VI with an Argus engine, and the more successful C VII with a Benz powerplant. The first of these had a 220 hp Mercedes D IV with eight cylinders and reduction gearing enclosed in the long metal-covered nose, with only the water expansion tank and the "rhino horn" exhaust exposed. A large spinner covered the propeller and "ear" radiators protruded from the fuselage sides. The ply-

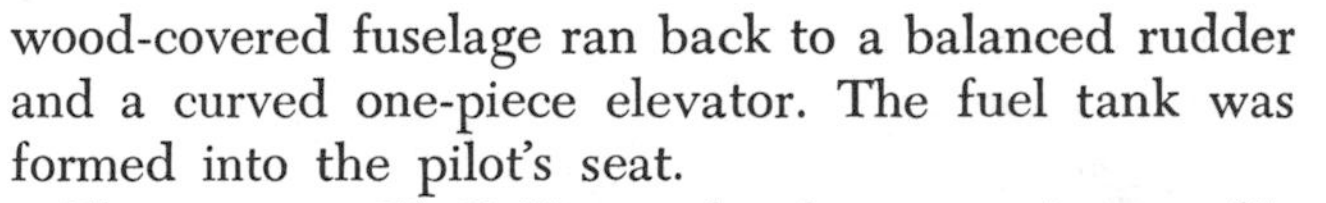

wood-covered fuselage ran back to a balanced rudder and a curved one-piece elevator. The fuel tank was formed into the pilot's seat.

There were 65 C Vs at the front on August 31, 1916, but trouble with the new engine soon reduced their numbers. Next year, an improved version appeared, unofficially called the C V/17 (the earlier design was then labeled C V/16). This version had its radiator on the upper wing, and its exhaust pipe pointed sideways. Balances were added to the ailerons and to the elevator, and the lower wing tips

ROLAND C II
Mercedes D III, 160 hp
DIMENSIONS: Span 10.33 m. (33′10½″), Lg. 7.52 m. (24′8″), Ht. 2.89 m. (9′6″), Wing Area 27.96 qm. (300.85 sq. ft.)
WEIGHT: Empty 789 kg. (1736 lb.), Gross 1309 kg. (2880 lb.)
PERFORMANCE: Speed—Max. 165 km/hr (102 mph), Climb 1000 m./7 min. (3280′/7 min.) Range 825 km. (511 miles), Endurance 4 hours, Service ceiling 4000 m. (13,120′)

ROLAND C III

KONDOR W 2C

ALBATROS C V (1916)

ALBATROS C V
Mercedes D IV, 220 hp
DIMENSIONS: Span 12.78 m. (41′11″), Lg. 8.95 m. (29′4″), Ht. 4.50 m. (14′9″), Wing Area 43.4 qm. (468 sq. ft.)
WEIGHT: Empty 1069 kg. (2352 lb.), Gross 1585 kg. (3487 lb.)
PERFORMANCE: Speed—Max. 170 km/hr (105 mph), Cruising speed 150 km/hr (93 mph), Climb 1000 m./8 min. (3280′/8 min.), Range 550 km. (340 miles), Endurance 3 hours 15 min.

ALBATROS C VI
Argus As III, 180 hp
DIMENSIONS: Span 11.70 m. (38′4½″), Lg. 7.90 m. (25′11″), Ht. 3.20 m. (10′6″), Wing Area 19 qm. (204.44 sq. ft.)
WEIGHT: Empty 830 kg. (1826 lb.), Gross 1343 kg. (2955 lb.)
PERFORMANCE: Speed—Max. 145 km/hr (90 mph), Climb 3000 m./35 min. (9840′/35 min.), Range 650 km. (403 miles), Service ceiling 4000 m. (13,120′)

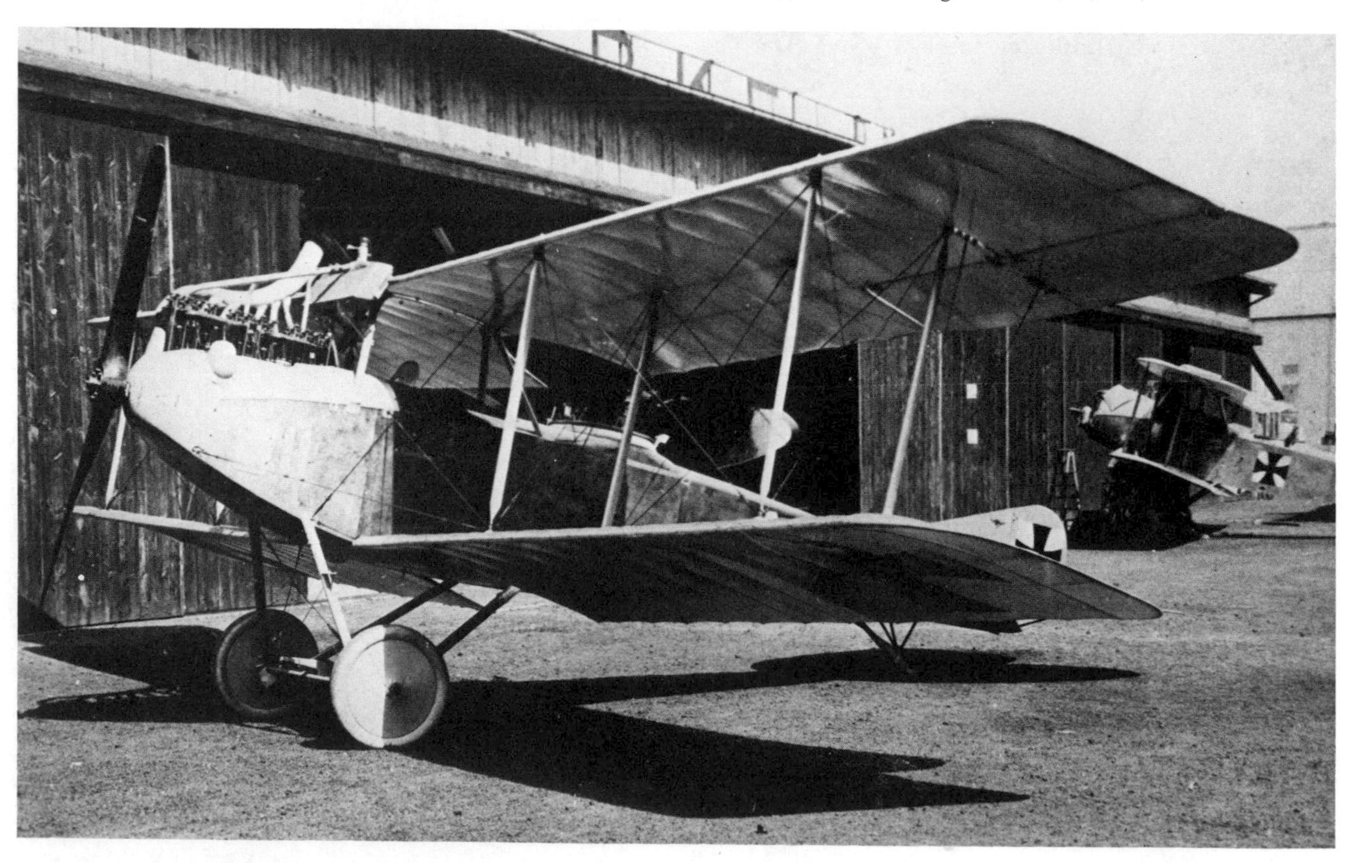

ALBATROS C VII
Benz Bz IV, 200 hp
DIMENSIONS: Span 12.78 m. (41′11″), Lg. 8.70 m. (28′6″), Ht. 3.60 m. (11′9½″), Wing Area 43.4 qm. (468 sq. ft.)
WEIGHT: Empty 1034 kg. (2275 lb.), Gross 1550 kg. (3410 lb.)
PERFORMANCE: Speed—Max. 170 km/hr (105.5 mph), Cruising speed 150 km/hr (93 mph), Climb 1000 m. 5½ min. (3280′/5½ min.), Range 550 km. (340 miles), Endurance 31/3 hours, Service ceiling 5000 m. (16,400′)

were tapered. Although handling qualities were improved, engine problems limited front-line use.

The 180 hp Argus As III engine was used on the Albatros C VI, which, while built at the same time as the C V, actually retained the C III design with its exposed cylinders, and unbalanced controls. On the other hand, the widely used Albatros C VII was introduced in the fall with most of the C V components, and the reliable 200 hp Benz Bz IV's six cylinders and exhaust protruding upward. The ear radiators and the lower wings were those of the C V/16, but the balanced ailerons and elevator presaged those of the C V/17. By February 28, 1917, Albatros types at the front included 52 C I, 214 C III, 50 C V, 111 C VI, and 372 C VII models. Some C VIIs were built by BFW.

Their rival LVG lost ground during this period, for their only offering was the LVG C IV, which also used the troublesome 220 hp Mercedes D IV. As Franz Schneider's last design in production, it had the same squared-off lines as the LVG C II, enlarged for the heavier engine. A balanced rudder distinguished it from earlier LVGs. At the end of 1916, LVG had 155 C II and 76 C IV planes at the front, after which the numbers declined.

AEG's contribution to 1916 C type production was Georg Koenig's C IV, which retained the 160 hp Mercedes D III. Its construction was fabric-covered steel tubing, with 16 mm. diameter longerons, and 40 mm. spars. The side louvers in front, the short fuselage, box radiator under the center section and unbalanced control surfaces distinguished the AEG from its rivals.

LVG C IV (D 11)
Mercedes D IV, 220 hp
DIMENSIONS: Span 13.6 m. (44′7″), Lg. 8.5 m. (27′11″), Ht. 3.1 m. (10′2″), Wing Area 38.2 qm. (411 sq. ft.)
WEIGHT: Empty 1050 kg. (2310 lb.), Gross 1600 kg. (3520 lb.)
PERFORMANCE: Not available

AEG C IV
Mercedes D III, 160 hp
DIMENSIONS: Span 13 m. (42′8″), Lg. 6.3 m. (20′8″), Wing Area 39 qm. (419.64 sq. ft.)
WEIGHT: Empty 800 kg. (1760 lb.), Gross 1120 kg. (2464 lb.)
PERFORMANCE: Speed—Max. 158 km/hr (98 mph), Cruising speed 140 km/hr (87 mph), Climb 1000 m./6 min. (3280′/6 min.), Service ceiling 5500 m. (18,040′)

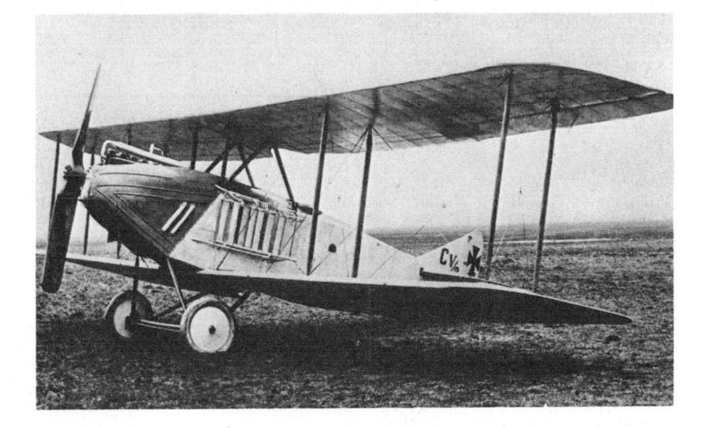

AEG C V
Mercedes D IV, 220 hp
DIMENSIONS: Span 13.2 m. (43′3½″), Lg. 7.6 m. (24′11″), Wing Area 41.5 qm. (446.70 sq. ft.)
WEIGHT: Empty 900 kg. (1980 lb.), Gross 1432 kg. (3150 lb.)
PERFORMANCE: Speed—Max. 165 km/hr (103 mph), Climb 1000 m./5 min. (3280′/5 min.)

AEG C VII

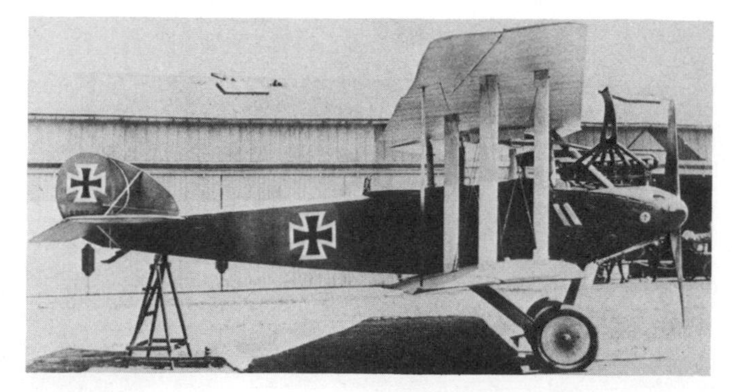

AGO C IV
Benz Bz IV, 220 hp
DIMENSIONS: Span 12 m. (39'4"), Lg. 7.5 m. (24'7"), Ht. 3.5 m. (11'6"), Wing Area 37.5 qm. (403.5 sq. ft.)
WEIGHT: Empty 900 kg. (1980 lb.), Gross 1330 kg. (2932 lb.)
PERFORMANCE: Speed—Max. 190 km/hr (119 mph), Time of climb 3000 m./22 min. (9840'/22 min.), Range 750 km. (465 miles), Service ceiling 5500 m. (18,040')

AEG C VIII (as biplane)
Mercedes D III, 160 hp
DIMENSIONS: Span 9.5 m. (31'2"), Lg. 6.9 m. (22'8")
WEIGHT: Empty 800 kg. (1760 lb.), Gross 1160 kg. (2552 lb.)
PERFORMANCE: Speed—Max. 170 km/hr (106 mph) at sea level, Climb 1000 m./3.8 min. (3280'/3.8 min.)

AGO C IV

AEG C VIII Triplane

By June 30, 1917, 127 were at the front and Fokker, to his chagrin, had to build under license 250 AEG C IVs ordered February 1917, and his deliveries began in August for home use. None of several attempts to improve the AEG design succeeded. They included the C V of February 1916 with a 220 hp Mercedes D IV, the C VI with a 200 hp Benz, and the C VII of December 1916, which had the 160 hp Mercedes with single-bay wings. More daring was the AEG C VIII of July 1917, which had a single pair of the I interplane struts. In December this two-seater reappeared as a triplane with two pairs of I struts. Since none of these efforts achieved production, the C IV was the last AEG C type in combat.

AGO also offered a C IV design in 1916, but the design by Letsch utilized the 220 hp Benz Bz IV in a neat metal nose. The most unusual feature was the two-bay wings, which had sharply tapered square tips, with the forward inner struts removed to give the observer a shot forward if needed. The usual forward-firing Spandau for the pilot was concealed under the cowl.

The C IVs were also made under license by Schutte-Lanz (250) and Rathgeber (10) and 90 of the AGO-designed two-seaters were at the front by August 31, 1917. AGO attempted to improve the design, but only unsuccessful prototypes emerged. Among them were the C V with 220 hp Benz and N struts, the C VII with the Benz and straight double-box wings, and a C VIII with a 260 hp Mercedes.

The most successful two-seater of this period was

AGO C V

AGO C VII

the DFW C V. A fairly conventional biplane, it had a plywood-covered fuselage, ear radiators and heart-shaped balanced elevators. This design by Heinrich Oelerich had originated with unbalanced tail controls, but evolved into the C V with the 220 hp Benz Bz IV. A larger version with the Bz IVa was developed in 1918 as the C VI, but did not pass prototype stage.

The DFW C V appeared at the front in the fall of 1916, and 42 were on hand by year's end. As license-built Aviatik, LVG and Halberstadt copies came off the line, the number increased until August 31, 1917, when of 2061 C types at the front, 1057 were DFW CVs. This type remained the most widely used C type at the front until the end of the war. License-built aircraft were first known as the Aviatik C VI, LVG C VI until March 23, 1917, and Halb. C I to February 9, 1917, becoming the DFW V (Av), (LVG), and (Halb.).

Last of the 1916 crop of two-seaters to enter service was the Rumpler C III (6A 5), which had a 220 hp Benz, with prop spinner, and the pilot and observer in a single long cockpit. Other recognition features were the balanced control surfaces, and the "comma" rudder without a vertical fin.

The missing fin was this type's weakness, for insufficient stability caused some deadly crashes. There was one C III at the front at the end of 1916, and 42 on February 28, 1917, but after that the Rumpler C IV rapidly replaced it in service.

AGO C VIII

AGO C Experimental

DFW C V (T 29)
Benz Bz IV, 220 hp
DIMENSIONS: Span 13.3 m. (43′7½″), Lg. 7.9 m. (25′11″), Ht. 3.3 m. (10′10″)
WEIGHT: Empty 970 kg. (2134 lb.), Gross 1430 kg. (3146 lb.)
PERFORMANCE: Speed—Max. 155 km/hr (96 mph), Cruising speed 140 km/hr (87 mph), Rate of climb 1000 m./4 min. (3280′/4 min.) Time of climb 3000 m./25 min. (9840′/25 min.), Range 500 km. (310 miles), Endurance 3½ hrs. Service ceiling 4000 m. (13,120′)

DFW C V (TA 9)

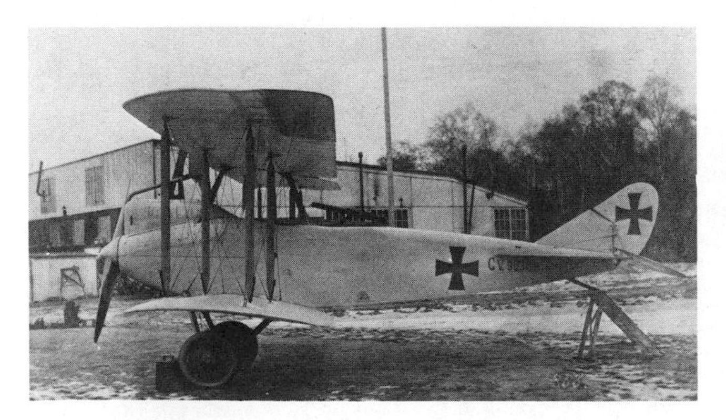

RUMPLER C IV (6A 7)
Mercedes V IV, 260 hp
DIMENSIONS: Span 12.66 m. (41′6″), Lg. 8.4 m. (27′6½″), Ht. 3.25 m. (10′8″), Wing Area 34.8 qm. (374.44 sq. ft.)
WEIGHT: Empty 1050 kg. (2310 lb.), Gross 1630 kg. (3586 lb.)
PERFORMANCE: Speed—Max. 170 km/hr (106 mph), at 500 m. (1640′), 150 km/hr (93 mph) at 5000 m. (16,400′), Time of climb 5000 m./30 min. (16,400′/30 min.) Range 585 km. (362 miles), Service ceiling 6800 m. (22,300′)

RUMPLER C IV (6A 7)

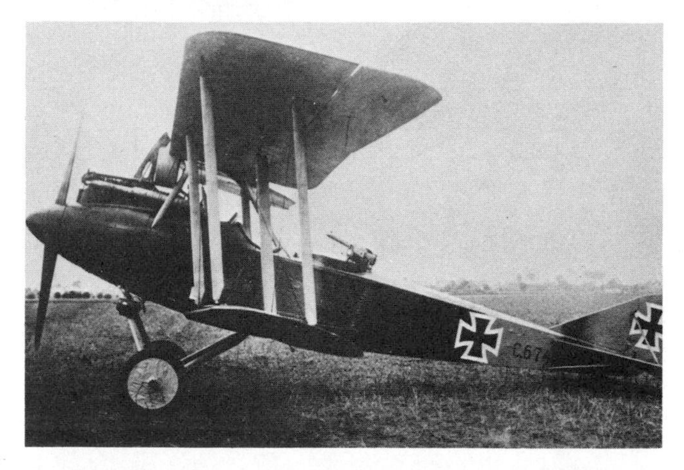

ALBATROS C IX
Mercedes D III, 160 hp
DIMENSIONS: Span 10.40 m. (34′1″), Lg. 6.22 m. (20′5″), Ht. 2.73 m. (9′)
WEIGHT: Empty 790 kg. (1738 lb.), Gross 1150 kg. (2530 lb.)
PERFORMANCE: Speed—Max. 155 km/hr (96 mph), Climb 1000 m./5 min. (3280′/5 min.), 4000 m./30 min. (13,120′/30 min.), Range 385 km. (238.7 miles)

RUMPLER C III (6A 5)
Benz Bz IV, 220 hp
DIMENSIONS: Span 12.66 m. (41′6″), Lg. 8.2 m. (26′11″), Ht. 4.57 m. (14′6″), Wing Area 34.8 qm. (374.45 sq. ft.)
WEIGHT: Empty 839 kg. (2250 lb.), Gross 1264 kg. (3390 lb.)
PERFORMANCE: Speed—Max. 136 km/hr (85 mph) at 2000 m. (6560′), Time of climb 2000 m./16 min. (6560′/16 min.), Range 480 km. (300 miles), Service ceiling 4000 m. (13,120′)

Sometimes considered the best long-range reconnaissance type of 1917, the Rumpler C IV (6A 7) began a new series by introducing the 260 hp Mercedes D IVa six-cylinder engine. All four wings had about 2½ degrees of sweep, with the top wing staggered forward, while the lower wings had a dragonfly shape ("Libellen") suggested by the designer, Budig. Construction was of wooden framework with fabric covering, except for some metal and plywood forward, and a belly trapdoor was made for the camera. Armament included the usual two guns, as well as four 25 kg. bombs on external racks.

The C IV appeared at the front in March 1917, and with the aid of production sub-contracted to Rumpler's Bavarian branch (Bayru) and to Pfalz (as the Pfalz C I), the total at the front increased to 257 by the end of August.

Albatros rapidly lost their leading position among the C plane builders, despite several new models introduced in 1917. The Albatros C VIIIN and C IX both used the 160 hp Mercedes, but were of opposite sizes. The former had big three-bay wings for night bombing, and so is shown later in the section on N ships.

Short single-bay wings were used on the Albatros C IX, which was actually a predecessor of the CL type two-seat fighters. Only three were built, arriving

ALBATROS C X
Mercedes D IVa, 260 hp
DIMENSIONS: Span 14.37 m. (47′1½″), Lg. 9.15 m. (30′), Ht. 3.40 m. (11′1½″), Wing Area 42.7 qm. (459.62 sq. ft.)
WEIGHT: Empty 1088 kg. (2394 lb.), Gross 1668 kg. (3669 lb.)
PERFORMANCE: Speed—Max. 175 km/hr (109 mph), Cruising speed 150 km/hr (93 mph), Climb 1000 m./5 min. (3280′/5 min.) 5000 m./55 min. (16,400′/55 min.) Range 600 km. (372 miles), Endurance 3 hours 25 min., Service ceiling 5000 m. (16,400′)

at the front in August 1917, and one was used as a personal transport by Baron Manfred von Richthofen.

The 260 hp Mercedes D IVa first was used on an Albatros in the C X design that appeared about March 1917. It was basically a larger C VII with typical Albatros lines, but ailerons were provided on all four double-bay wings. This model was quickly followed by the Albatros C XII, which used the same engine, but had a new fuselage and perhaps the most elegant appearance of any wartime two-seater. The C XII could be told from the C X by addition of a plywood underfin and an exhaust pipe pointing to the right instead of the older "rhino horn."

Despite additional production by subcontractors like Linke-Hofmann, OAW, Roland and BFW, these Albatros types did not reach the front in large numbers, but were used for training. On June 30, 1917, there were 98 C X and 41 C XII planes at the front, and two months later there were 47 C X and 93 C XII planes there. After that the number declined, partly due to the C XII's tendency to break its back on hard landings.

Actually, the C XII was the last Albatros two-seater to reach production, for the remainder failed to pass the experimental stage. The Albatros C XIII was actually a two-seat version of the D V fighter, with a single pair of Vee struts and the 160 hp Mercedes D III, but only one example of this 1917 aircraft was built.

The elimination of Albatros two-seaters from front-line units was rapid. At the beginning of 1917, they had been a majority of the C types, but at the end of the year, out of 1861 C types, Albatros contributed only 66 C XII's and 35 survivors of six older models. The most widely used types on December 31, 1917, were 845 of the DFW C Vs described earlier, 446 LVG C Vs and 364 of the various Rumpler models.

LVG had obtained a new designer, Sabersky-Mussigbrod, in 1917, and he developed the LVG C V. Powered by the 200 hp Benz Bz IV, it was in appearance rather like the DFW C V that LVG had been building under license. Unlike previous LVG designs, the C V had plywood, instead of fabric covering, the balanced elevator was in one piece and the ailerons had overhanging balances.

ALBATROS C XII
Mercedes D IVa, 260 hp
DIMENSIONS: Span 14.37 m. (47'1½"), Lg. 8.85 m. (29'), Ht. 3.25 m. (10'8"), Wing Area 42.7 qm. (459.62 sq. ft.)
WEIGHT: Empty 1059 kg. (2330 lb.) Gross 1639 kg. (3605 lb.)
PERFORMANCE: Speed—Max. 175 km/hr (109 mph), Cruising speed 150 km/hr (93 mph), Climb 1000 m./5 min. 5000 m./45 min. (16,400'/45 min.), Range 600 km. (372 miles,) Service ceiling 5000 m. (16,400')

ALBATROS C XIII
Mercedes D III, 160 hp
DIMENSIONS: Span 10 m. (32'10"), Lg. 7.80 m. (25'7"), Ht. 2.71 m. (8'11"), Wing Area 11.77 qm. (123.64 sq. ft.)
WEIGHT: Empty 700 kg. (1540 lb.), Gross 1060 kg. (2332 lb.)
PERFORMANCE: Speed—Max. 165 km/hr (103 mph), Climb 1000 m./4 min. (3280'/4 min.) 5000 m./47 min. (16,-400'/47 min.), Range 415 km. (257 miles), Endurance 2½ hours

LVG CV
Benz Bz IV, 220 hp
DIMENSIONS: Span 13.62 m. (44'8"), Lg. 7.24 m. (23'9"), Wing Area 42.7 qm. (459.62 sq. ft.)
WEIGHT: Empty 985 kg. (2167 lb.), Gross 1505 kg. (3311 lb.), Fuel 249 liters (66 gal.)
PERFORMANCE: Speed—Max. 175 km/hr (109 mph), 164 km/hr (102 mph) at 2000 m. (6560'), Cruising speed 150 km/hr (93 mph), Climb 4000 m./35 min. (13,-120'/35 min.) Service ceiling 5500 m. (18,040')

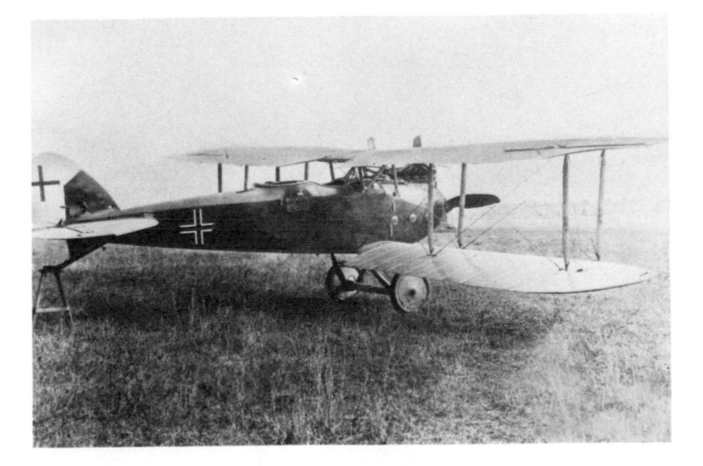

LVG CVI
Benz Bz IV, 220 hp
DIMENSIONS: Span 12.85 m. (42′1½″), Lg. 8.1 m. (26′6½″), Wing Area 37 qm. (398 sq. ft.)
WEIGHT: Empty 930 kg. (2046 lb.), Gross 1390 kg. (3058 lb.)
PERFORMANCE: Speed—Max 190 km/hr (118 mph), Climb 1000 m./4 min. (3280′/4 min.) Endurance 3½ hours, Service ceiling 6000 m. (19,680′)

Appearing at the front in the summer of 1917, the LVG C V was so successful that one was credited with destroying four British scouts in a fight on May 23, 1918. There were 565 of this type at the front on April 30, 1918, but the following month production shifted to the improved C VI type.

The LVG C VI improved visibility with large cut-outs at the wing roots, and by staggering the top wing forward. The prop spinner and overhanging aileron balances were eliminated, and lighter construction improved performance. The box radiator ahead of the leading edge was replaced by one inserted into the wing center section, or sometimes by ear radiators on the side. There were 133 LVG Vs and 400 LVC VIs at the front on August 31, 1918, and production of the latter is said to have amounted to nearly 1000 aircraft by the war's end.

While the DFW and LVG types were used primarily for artillery spotting and other such short-range, low-altitude work, the Rumplers were assigned to high-altitude, long-range penetrations of enemy air-space. The successful C IV was joined in the closing months of 1917 by four new Rumpler designs.

The Rumpler C V had the same 260 hp Mercedes and wings of the popular C IV, although the prototype reverted to the "comma" rudder and curved fuselage deck of the older C III. While the C V arrived at the front in October 1917, only nine were on hand at the year's end.

More successful was the Rumpler C VII using the 245 hp Maybach Mb IVa, a six-cylinder high-compression engine yielding its power at high altitudes (2000 m. or 6560′).[3] Appearing at the front in December 1917, they differed from the C IV only in details, such as the exhaust manifold turned sideways instead of up, no spinner and unbalanced elevators.

Parallel to this model was the *Rubild* (Rumpler photographic) which appeared in October 1917 with the front gun and extra weight removed to carry oxygen generators, electric flying suits and a special camera, known as the *Reihenbilder*. This fixed camera made running shots during flight to completely cover a long strip of territory; a great improvement on previous hand-held models. While the first *Rubilds* were begun as C VI models with Mercedes engines, they were joined in 1918 by the *Rubild* Mb, actually the Maybach-powered C VII fitted with the special equipment.

The front gun was retained in the standard Rumpler C VII, together with a radio. Considered the best of Germany's long-range reconnaissance planes, these Rumplers could do about 100 mph at 20,000 feet, an altitude beyond the effective reach of most fighters.

[3] The Mb IVa was listed as a 260 hp engine in German publications so that it would not seem inferior to the Mercedes D IV.

RUMPLER C V

RUMPLER C VI (*Rubild*)

RUMPLER C VII
Maybach Mb IV, 260 hp
DIMENSIONS: Span 12.7 m. (41′8″), Lg. 8.4 m. (27′6½″), Ht. 3.2 m. (10′6″) Wing Area 34.8 qm. (374.44 sq. ft.)
WEIGHT: Empty 1057 kg. (2325 lb.), Gross 1435 kg. (3157 lb.)
PERFORMANCE: Speed—Max. 175 km/hr (109 mph) at 1000 m. (3280′), Climb 1000 m./2.3 min. (3280′/2.3 min.) 5000 m./21.5 min. (16,400′/21.5 min.), Range 585 km. (362.7 miles), Endurance 3½ hours, Service ceiling 7300 m. (23,944′)

RUMPLER C VIII (6A 8)
Argus As III, 180 hp
DIMENSIONS: Span 12.22 m. (40′1″), Lg. 7.9 m. (25′11″), Wing Area 35.7 qm. (384.13 sq. ft.)
WEIGHT: Empty 870 kg. (1914 lb.), Gross 1370 kg. (3014 lb.)
PERFORMANCE: Speed—Max 170 km/hr (105 mph), Cruising speed 140 km/hr (87 mph)

RUMPLER 6 A2

By June 30, 1918, Rumpler had 182 C IV, four C V, 112 C VII, five C IX, 39 *Rubild* and 79 *Rubild* Mb models at the front.

Although bearing the C designation, the Rumpler C VIII (6A 8) introduced in November 1917, was actually a lighter aircraft intended only for advanced training and fitted with a more economical 180 hp Argus. The Rumpler C IX, however, had a 245 hp Maybach and like the C IV with extra tankage for 5½ hours flight. Twenty C IXs were at the front on December 31, 1917.[4]

Rumpler tried several experiments during this period, including development of a single-bay biplane series of two-seater fighters. This work began with a 6A 2 powered by 160 hp Mercedes. After a crash during tests, odd X struts were replaced by a standard pair, but the aircraft was destroyed in another crash. The same engine and single-bay arrangement was used on the 7C 1 of 1917, which had a streamlined fuselage and I struts. The original finless rudder was later replaced by a more modern tail, but the design was unsuccessful.

Rumpler's last effort was the C X (8C 14) of 1918, which had a 240 hp Maybach and a single pair of X struts. Only one such plane seems to have been built.

The last German firm to introduce C types at the front was the Halberstadter Flugzeug-Werke from the city of that name. Their first effort in that class had been the obscure Halberstadt C I, the armed development of the rotary-powered B I that was tested in 1915. This same C I designation was also briefly applied in 1917 to the license-built DFW C V (Halb.). Halberstadt's next C type was the Mercedes-powered

[4] This conventional looking C IX has been confused with the Rumpler 7C 1 fighter prototype.

RUMPLER 7C 1
Mercedes D III, 160 hp
DIMENSIONS: Wing span 8.2 m. (26′11″), Lg. 5.9 m. (19′4″), Ht. 2.6 m. (8′6″)
WEIGHT: Not available
PERFORMANCE: Speed—Max. 165 km/hr (102 mph), Cruising speed 150 km/hr (93 mph), Service ceiling 6500 m. (21,320′)

RUMPLER 7C 1 (Modified)

RUMPLER C X (8C 14)
Maybach Mb IV, 240 hp
DIMENSIONS: Span 10.5 m. (34′5½″), Lg. 6.9 m. (22′8″), Ht. 3.12 m. (10′4″), Wing Area 29 qm. (312 sq. ft.)
WEIGHT: Empty 950 kg. (2090 lb.), Gross 1385 kg. (3047 lb.)
PERFORMANCE: Speed—Max. 195 km/hr (121 mph), Cruising speed 170 km/hr (105 mph), Climb 6000 m./27 min. (19,680′/27 min.), Range 625 km. (387.5 miles) Endurance 3½ hours

HALBERSTADT C III
Benz Bz IV, 200 hp
DIMENSIONS: 12.20 m. (40′), Lg. 7.40 m. (24′3″)
WEIGHT: Empty 850 kg. (1870 lb.), Gross 1310 kg. (2882 lb.)
PERFORMANCE: Speed—Max. 160 km/hr (99 mph), Cruising speed 140 km/hr (87 mph), Range 485 km. (300 miles)

HALBERSTADT C V
Benz Bz IV, 200 hp
DIMENSIONS: Span 13.60 m. (44′7″), Lg. 6.90 m. (22′8″), Ht. 3.36 m. (11′) Wing Area 43 qm. (462.68 sq. ft.)
WEIGHT: Empty 930 kg. (2046 lb.), Gross 1360 kg. (2992 lb.)
PERFORMANCE: Speed—Max. 170 km/hr (105 mph), Climb 5000 m./23 min. (16,400′/23 min.), Range 600 km. (372 miles)

single-bay CL II which was successful in 1917 and was followed by the CL IV. Since both were ground attackers, rather than reconnaissance aircraft, they had the CL designation and are covered in the next section of this book.

Strictly for long-range reconnaissance was the larger Halberstadt C III of 1917. With two-bay wings and a 200 hp Benz, the C III's most outstanding feature was a keel between the fuselage and lower wing to increase gap.

While only six C IIIs were built, they led to the C V which had the same 200 hp Benz, plywood fuselage and graceful tail of the earlier Halberstadt ships, but had wide double-bay wings and separate cockpits. The Halberstadt C V was tested in March 1918, and by June was at the front as a long-range reconnaissance type, manufactured as well by Aviatik, BFW and DFW. Four Halberstadts produced in 1918 failed to pass the test stage. The C VI was reportedly a modified CL IV fighter with an 150 hp Benz, while the C

HALBERSTADT C VI

VII was a C V with a 245 hp Mayback Mb IVa. The Maybach engine was also used on the single C VIII, which was a larger single-bay combination of CL IV and C V features tested in October 1918. Finally, the Halberstadt C IX was a C V fitted with an Austrian 230 hp Hiero.

Exact figures on the German strength in C ships at the end of the war is unavailable, but the data for August 31, 1918, shows the types in use in the closing months. There were 1787 C type aircraft at the front: including 620 DFW C Vs, 533 LVG C Vs and C VIs, 177 *Rubilds*, 110 Rumpler C IVs, and 85 C VIIs, 192 Halberstadt C Vs, 34 AEG C IVs, only 15 Albatros C XIIs, and a scattering of older machines.

The roster of C types at the front has been completed, but passing mention may be made of the numerous prototypes offered since 1917. In most cases, these were "one only" aircraft which vanished into obscurity, and little is remembered of them.

Albatros produced a new C type in 1918, using the 220 hp Benz Bz IVa and, for the first time for Albatros, staggered wings. Originally, one had unbalanced ailerons and was called the C XIV, then production ships were fitted with balanced ailerons, slightly enlarged, and designated C XV. None of the few built seem to have reached the front, but one used after the war was said to be the fastest German mailplane.[5]

Aviatik produced the C VIII of 1917, a more conventional single-bay type with a 160 hp Mercedes D III that may have been intended as a fighter. In 1918, Aviatik offered the double-bay C IX with a 200 hp Benz, but it too was rejected, and the factory

[5] Albatros landplanes were redesignated "L" after the war, beginning retroactively with the B I as L 1, and surviving C XVs became L 47s.

HALBERSTADT C VIII
Maybach Mb IVa, 260 hp
DIMENSIONS: Span 12 m. (39'4"), Lg. 7.35 m. (24'1"), Ht. 2.95 m. (9'8½"), Wing Area 33 qm. (355 sq. ft.)
WEIGHT: Empty 928 kg. (2046 lb.), Gross 1363 kg. (3005 lb.)
PERFORMANCE: Speed—Max. 180 km/hr (111 mph), Climb 7000 m./58 min. (22,960'/58 min.), Service ceiling 8000 m. (26,240')

ALBATROS C XV
Benz Bz IVa, 220 hp
DIMENSIONS: Span 11.80 m. (38'8½"), Lg. 7.48 m. (24'6"), Ht. 3.30 m. (10'10") Wing Area 18.75 qm. (201.75 sq. ft.)
WEIGHT: Empty 890 kg. (1958 lb.), Gross 1320 kg. (2904 lb.)
PERFORMANCE: Speed—Max. 185 km/hr (115 mph), Climb 1000 m./3.4 min. (3280'/3.4 min.) 5000 m./23 min. (16,400'/23 min.), Range 580 km. (360 miles), Endurance 3 hours

devoted its production to license-built DFW, Gotha and Halberstadt designs.

DFW offered a C VI two-seater in 1918, which used the same Benz engine as the popular C V, but added balances to the ailerons. Only one example was completed. It was followed by the C VII, also powered by the Benz. Only three were built, but after the war, the third aircraft was fitted with a 185 hp BMW and called the F 37. On November 5, 1919, the F 37 reached an altitude of 7600 meters (24,900') but this world's record was not acknowledged by the FAI because of armistice regulations.

Anthony Fokker made his only effort in the C category, the V 38, which was actually a two-seat, enlarged version of the famous D VII. Powered by a 185 hp BMW IIIa, it had the main fuel tank between the wheels. Although the prototype was rejected by the German Army, Fokker undertook 60 production ships as the Fokker C I. After the war Fokker moved these C Is to Holland and sold them to the Dutch

AVIATIK C VIII

AVIATIK C IX

HALBERSTADT C IX

DFW C VI

DFW C VII (F 37)
Benz Bz IVa, 200 hp
DIMENSIONS: Span 13.6 m. (44′7″), Lg. 7 m. (22′11½″), Ht. 2.8 m. (9′2″), Wing Area 38 qm. (408.88 sq. ft.)
WEIGHT: Empty 800 kg. (1760 lb.), Gross 1230 kg. (2706 lb.)
PERFORMANCE: Speed—Max. 175 km/hr (109 mph), Climb 1000 m./3 min. (3280′/3 min.) Service ceiling 6000 m. (19,680′)

FOKKER V 38 (C I)
BMW IIIa, 185 hp
DIMENSIONS: Span 10.49 m. (34′5″), Lg. 7.21 m. (23′8″), Ht. 2.84 m. (9′4″)
WEIGHT: Empty 701 kg. (1881 lb.), Gross 806 kg. (2161 lb.)
PERFORMANCE: Speed—Max. 175 km/hr (109 mph) at sea level, Climb 5000 m./21.5 min. (16,500′/21.5 min.)

GERMANIA C I

GERMANIA C II

LFG ROLAND C V

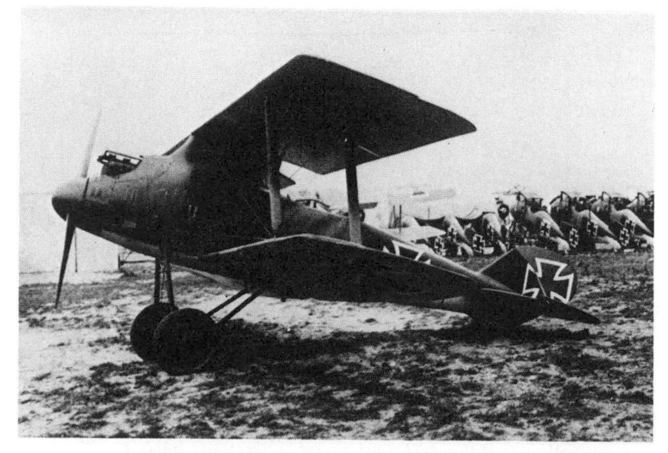

Army, for whom they may have been intended in the first place. The type was also produced later in Holland and examples were sold to the United States and to Russia.

Germania was less successful, offering their 1918 C I with its two pairs of I struts. Probably powered by the 220 hp Benz, it was followed by a Germania C II with staggered wings, but only the prototypes were made, the factory continuing production of the Rumpler C 1a trainer.

LFG Roland attempted a C V design in 1917, a single-bay two-seat development of their D II fighter, but nothing is known of its specifications. The same obscurity cloaks the Roland C VIII, with a 260 hp Mercedes and a peculiar humped rear cockpit.

More is known about the LVG C VIII, which was a refinement of the C VI with a car-type radiator in front of the Benz engine, and an unbalanced tail control. Several prototypes were made, about August 1918.

Sablatnig was a Berlin firm best known for their seaplanes, but they did venture into the two-seat landplane category. The first C I was developed into the N I of 1917, and is described in the following

LFG ROLAND C VIII

LVG C VIII
Benz Bz IVa, 200 hp
DIMENSIONS: Span 13 m. (42′8″), Lg. 7 m. (22′11½″), Ht. 2.8 m. (9′2″), Wing Area 35.7 qm. (384 sq. ft.)
WEIGHT: Empty 900 kg. (1980 lb.), Gross 1380 kg. (3036 lb.)
PERFORMANCE: Speed—Max. 165 km/hr (102 mph), Endurance 4 hours

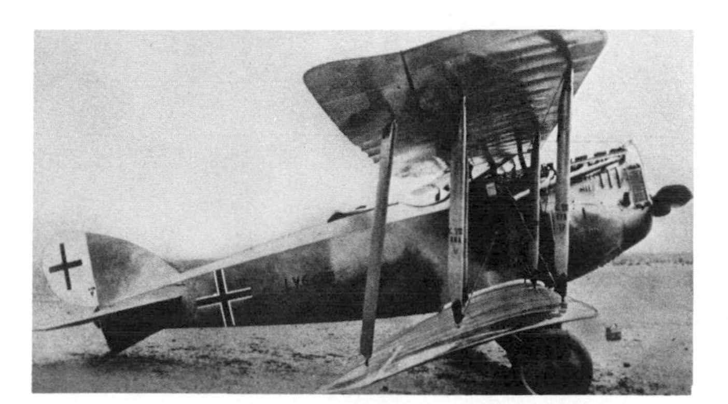

SABLATNIG C II
Maybach Mb IV, 200 hp
DIMENSIONS: Span 12.5 m. (41′), Lg. 8.3 m. (27′3″), Ht. 3.2 m. (10′6″)
WEIGHT: Empty 1080 kg. (2376 lb.), Gross 1590 kg. (3498 lb.)
PERFORMANCE: Speed—Max. 150 km/hr (93 mph), Climb 1000 m./4.5 min. (3280′/4.5 min.), 4000 m./20 min. (13,120′/20 min.), Range 525 km. (325 miles), Service ceiling 7100 m. (23,280′)

SABLATNIG C II with modified struts

SABLATNIG C III
Maybach Mb IVa, 245 hp
DIMENSIONS: Span 13.60 m. (44′7½″), Lg. 8.70 m. (28′6½″) Wing Area 30 qm. (323 sq. ft.)
WEIGHT: Empty 1026 kg. (2257 lb.), Gross 1326 kg. (2917 lb.)
PERFORMANCE: Speed—Max. 160 km/hr (99 mph), Climb 3000 m./10 min. (9840′/10 min.)

ZEPPELIN-LINDAU C I

ZEPPELIN-LINDAU C II
Maybach Mb IV, 240 hp
DIMENSIONS: Span 12 m. (39′4″), Lg. 7.85 m. (25′9″), Ht. 3.62 m. (11′11″), Wing Area 36.25 qm. (390 sq. ft.)
WEIGHT: Empty 1050 kg. (2310 lb.), Gross 1485 kg. (3267 lb.)
PERFORMANCE: Climb 1000 m./2.8 min. (3280′/2.8 min.), 5000 m./24.8 min. (16,400′/24.8 min.), Service ceiling 7500 m. (24,600′)

ZEPPLIN-LINDAU C I

section. In 1918, the Sablatnig C II had a Maybach engine, plywood fuselage and two pairs of I struts. Later prototypes also tried the usual parallel struts, as well as an X strut version.

Most remarkable prototype in this class the Sablatnig C III, which was a low-wing monoplane, the wing being braced by cables attached to the fuselage top near the turn-over pylon. The powerplant was a 245 hp Maybach Mb IVa, and a single flexible gun was provided. This advanced aircraft was not completed until after the Armistice.

Concluding this section are the biplanes designed by Paul Jaray at the Zeppelin works at Friedrichshafen. All-metal construction was intended, but the two C I prototypes were made of wood and a fabric. The first Zeppelin C I was flown on October 17, 1917, but later lost to apparent sabotage.

Six metal-framed, fabric-covered C IIs followed, one competing at Adlershof on May 6, 1918. Powered by the 245 hp Maybach, it had a single pair of V struts between the wings. Twenty more were not in time for delivery to German forces, but 19 were sold to the Swiss Army, which they served for many years. A Zeppelin C III remained a paper project, while the C IV was an enlarged C II whose fuselage is still stored at the Musée de l'Air in France.

ARMORED JUNKERS J I attack

3.

Specialized Two-Seaters

While the C types were general purpose machines whose main duty was reconnaissance, Germany developed three classes of two-seaters in 1917 for specialized work; the CL two-seat fighters, the J class for ground attack, and the N class for night bombing. Later, the CLS and S ground attack classes were added.

Agile and fast, the small CL planes were designed for the *Schutzstaffeln* (Protection Flights) intended to escort the regular C planes. Later, these units were designated *Schlachtstaffeln* (Battle Flights) as ground strafing and close support duties were added to their mission.

The first such type to go into action was the Halberstadt CL II, which reached the front in August 1917, and on September 6, 1917, 24 Halberstadts made a successful strafing attack on British troops crossing Somme bridges. Powered by a 160 hp Mercedes D III, the CL II was armed with one Spandau gun by the engine, a Parabellum gun for the observer and four 10 kg. (22 lb.) bombs. One CL II gunner was actually credited with 12 victories, an unheard-of score for a rear-seat crewman.[1]

For close cooperation the crewmen sat in a single cockpit with a gun ring for the observer, and grenade racks outside. The small wings were single bay with the upper wing staggered forward and fitted with balanced ailerons. The curved rudder was balanced, and a one-piece elevator was used.

After prototype tests in May 1917, CL II production was ordered in July 1917, with contracts for 679 going to Halberstadt and 100 to BFW. By the year's end, 170 were at the front, with 342 there by April 30, 1918, and production still underway on additional orders. One example was tested in February 1918 with a 185 hp BMW IIIa, but production aircraft had to be content with the Mercedes D III.

The Halberstadt CL IV differed from the CL II in having a shorter fuselage, balanced elevator, and a blunter nose without a spinner. Arriving at the front in July 1918, the CL IV had better climb and maneuverability. Some CL IVs were built under license by Roland, and there were 175 CL IIs and 136 CL IVs at the front on August 31, 1918, the last date for which figures are available. A smaller and lighter version, the Halberstadt CLS I, was tested in October 1918; too late for production.

Companions to the Halberstadts were the deep-bodied two-seaters built by the Hannoversche Waggonfabric A.G. This firm's aircraft activity began in 1915 with license production of 146 Aviatik C Is, followed by 387 Rumpler C Ias. The next numeral was given to Hermann Dorner's CL II design (Light C class) for Hannover in 1917.

A biplane tail was the most distinctive design feature of the Hannover planes, along with a deep ply-

[1] Vfw. Ehmann of *Schlachtstaffel* 15.

HALBERSTADT CL II
Mercedes D III, 160 hp
DIMENSIONS: Span 10.77 m. (35'4"), Lg. 7.3 m. (23'11"), Ht. 2.75 m. (9'), Wing Area 27.5 qm. (296 sq. ft.)
WEIGHT: Empty 773 kg. (1700 lb.), Gross 1133 kg. (2493 lb.)
PERFORMANCE: Speed—Max. 165 km/hr (103 mph), Cruising speed 150 km/hr (93 mph), Climb 1000 m./5 min. (3280'/5 min.) Range 480 km. (300 miles)

wood body and upper wing so close to the fuselage that the gunner had a good field of fire. The CL II appeared with a 180 hp Argus As III engine, and was built under license by LFG Roland as the CL IIa (Rol.). It was followed in March 1918 by the CL III with a 160 hp Mercedes D III. A shortage of Mercedes engines led to restoration of the Argus engine on the CL IIIa. Armament was comprised of one fixed and one flexible machine gun and grenades.

The Hannover CL II appeared at the front in October 1917, and by the following February 28, they were 295 at the front. They were formidable in combat, although said to catch fire easily. On June 30, 1918, the *Schlachtstaffeln* had 72 CL II, 67 CL III, and 159 CL IIIa Hannovers, and on August 31, the 604 CL planes at the front included 31 Hannover CL IIs, 29 CL IIIs, and 233 CL IIIas. Total production to the end of the war included 439 CL IIs, 80 CL IIIs and 573 CL IIIas.

Another 138 CL IIIa aircraft were completed in 1918 after the November 11 Armistice. Legally the war wasn't over until the peace treaty, so many German factories continued production into 1919.

Hannover built the larger CL IV with the 245 hp Maybach and a different strut arrangement. A BMW engine and I struts were used on the smaller CL V which appeared first with the biplane tail, and later had only the lower surface. Five CL IV and

HALBERSTADT CL IV
Mercedes D III, 160 hp
DIMENSIONS: Span 10.74 m. (35'3"), Lg. 6.58 m. (21'7"), Ht. 2.67 m. (8'9"), Wing Area 27 qm. (290.52 sq. ft.)
WEIGHT: Empty 728 kg. (1602 lb.), Gross 1068 kg. (2350 lb.)
PERFORMANCE: Speed—Max. 165 km/hr (103 mph), Cruising speed 150 km/hr (93 mph), Climb 500 m./32 min. (16,400'/32 min.), Range 500 km. (310 miles)

HALBERSTADT CLS I
Mercedes D III, 160 hp
DIMENSIONS: Wing span 9.70 m. (31'10"), Lg. 6.95 m. (22'9½"), Ht. 3.05 m. (10'), Wing Area 26.4 qm. (284 sq. ft.)
WEIGHT: Empty 670 kg. (1474 lb.), Gross 1190 kg. (2618 lb.)
PERFORMANCE: Speed—Max. 185 km/hr (115 mph), Cruising speed 160 km/hr (99 mph), Climb 4500 m./36 min. (14,760'/36 min.), Range 370 km. (230 miles)

HANNOVER CL II
Argus As III, 180 hp
DIMENSIONS: Span 12 m. (39′4″), Lg. 7.8 m. (25′7″), Wing Area 33.8 qm. (363 sq. ft.)
WEIGHT: Empty 750 kg. (1650 lb.), Gross 1110 kg. (2442 lb.)
PERFORMANCE: Speed—Max. 165 km/hr (103 mph), Cruising speed 140 km/hr (87 mph), Service ceiling 7500 m. (24,600′)

HANNOVER CL II (Rol.)

HANNOVER CL III
Mercedes D III, 160 hp
DIMENSIONS: Span 11.85 m. (38′10″), Length 7.8 m. (25′7″), Wing Area 33.1 qm. (356.15 sq. ft.)
WEIGHT: Empty 734 kg. (1615 lb.), Gross 1074 kg. (2362 lb.)
PERFORMANCE: Speed—Max. 165 km/hr (103 mph), Cruising speed 150 km/hr (93 mph), Service ceiling 7500 m. (24,600′)

HANNOVER CL IIIa
Argus As III, 180 hp
DIMENSIONS: Span 11.7 m. (38′5″), Lg. 7.58 m. (24′10½″), Ht. 2.8 m. (9½′), Wing Area 32.7 qm. (352 sq. ft.)
WEIGHT: Empty 717 kg. (1577 lb.), Gross 1081 kg. (1732 lb.)
PERFORMANCE: Speed—Max. 165 km/hr (103 mph), at 5000 m. (16,400′), Climb 1000 m./5.3 min. (3280′/5.3 min.), Endurance 3 hours

HANNOVER CL IV
Maybach Mb IV, 245 hp
DIMENSIONS: Wing span 12.5 m. (41′), Lg. 7.8 m. (25′7″), Wing Area 33.6 qm. (361.53 sq. ft.)
WEIGHT: Empty 900 kg. (2112 lb.), Gross 1395 kg. (3009 lb.)
PERFORMANCE: Speed—Max. 160 km/hr (99 mph), Service ceiling 8000 m. (26,240′)

HANNOVER CL V
BMW IIIa, 185 hp
DIMENSIONS: Span 10.4 m. (34'1"), Lg. 7.1 m. (23'3½"), Ht. 2.9 m. (9'6"), Wing Area 28.5 qm. (306.66 sq. ft.)
WEIGHT: Empty 720 kg. (1584 lb.), Gross 1080 kg. (2376 lb.)
PERFORMANCE: Speed—Max. 185 km/hr (115 mph), at 2000 m. (6560'), Climb 1000 m./3.3 min. (3280'/33 min.) 4000 m./15 min. (13,120'/15 min.), Service ceiling 9000 m. (29,520')

BFW CL II

BFW CL I

46 CL V Hannovers were built before the Armistice and five more CL IVs and 57 CL Vs afterward.

Bayerische Flugzeug-Werke (BFW) or Bay, of Munich attempted to develop a two-seat fighter, from their Halberstadt CL II experience. It appeared in April 1918 as the BFW CL I with I struts and a 160 hp Mercedes, reappeared in revised form in May 1918 as the CL II, with a 175 hp Man III and had a Mercedes in the CL III prototype.

Claude Dornier's two-seaters designed for Zeppelin-Lindau were unique in their all-metal construction, with the fuselage covered with stressed sheet alloy, and fabric over the metal wing spars. Powered by a 160 hp Mercedes, the Zeppelin CL I was tested in March 1918, with a radiator in the center section of the wing. A plan to build 300 was canceled. The Zeppelin CL II, which was first flown on August 17, 1918, had the same single-bay wings, but with increased gap and a car-type nose radiator.

The most modern design of all the German two-seaters was the Junkers CL I, an all-metal monoplane with a corrugated dural fuselage. Other prominent features were the nose radiator and a turn-over safety pylon between the cockpits. Armament was the usual one fixed and one flexible gun. The prototype appeared as the Junkers J 8 early in January 1918, and was followed in March by the production version with the company designation J 10, and Army designation CL I. The J 8's large aileron overhung balances were deleted, and the original 160 hp Mercedes retained. Forty-three Junkers CL Is were completed by the war's end. Appearing only singly on the Western front, they were used after the Armistice in the Baltic area by the *Sachsenberg Geschwader,* and for civil operations.

The J class two-seaters were armored biplanes intended for infantry contact patrols, which involved flying low over the front lines to maintain contact with the positions of the friendly and enemy forces. They appeared at the front in the summer of 1917, the first such type being the AEG J I.

Basically, this was an enlarged C IV provided with a 200 hp Benz, ailerons on all four wings, and 860 lb. of five mm. steel armor from the engine back to the rear of the second cockpit. Armament usually consisted of the observer's ring-mounted Parabellum and two Spandau guns on the floor of the rear cockpit pointed 45 degrees forward and down for strafing.

In the spring of 1918, the AEG J II appeared, adding overhung balances on the rudder, elevators, and

BFW CL III

DORNIER (ZEPPELIN) CL I
Mercedes D III, 160 hp
DIMENSIONS: Span 10.5 m. (34′5″), Lg. 7.6 m. (24′11″), Ht. 2.84 m. (9′4″), Wing Area 27.12 qm. (292 sq. ft.)
WEIGHT: Empty 730 kg. (1606 lb.) Gross 1070 kg. (2354 lb.)
PERFORMANCE: Speed—Max. 162 km/hr (101 mph), Climb 1000 m./4.5 min. (3280′/4.5 min.), Service ceiling 5000 m. (16,400′)

DORNIER (ZEPPELIN) CL II
Mercedes D III, 160 hp
DIMENSIONS: Span 10.5 m. (43′5″), Lg. 7.46 m. (24′6″), Ht. 2.95 m. (9′8″), Wing Area 28.12 qm. (302.57 sq. ft.)
WEIGHT: Empty 730 kg. (1610 lb.), Gross 1070 kg. (2360 lb.)
PERFORMANCE: Speed—Max. 165 km/hr (103 miles), Service ceiling 5300 m. (17,380′)

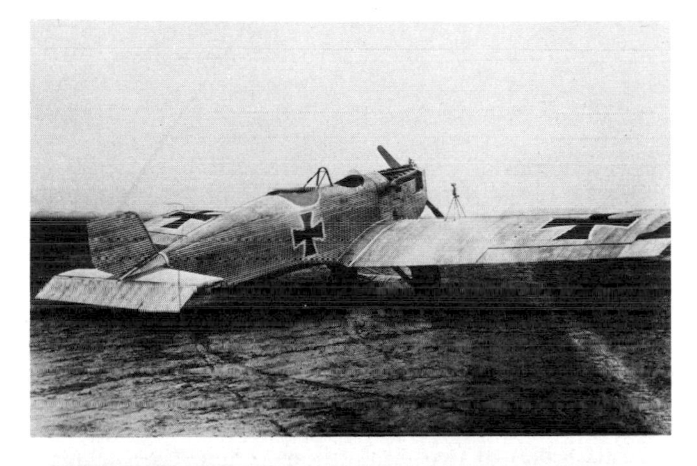

JUNKERS CL I (J 8)
Mercedes D III, 160 hp
DIMENSIONS: Span 12.95 m. (42′6″), Lg. 7.9 m. (25′11″), Ht. 2.7 m. (8′7″), Wing Area 23.4 qm. (251.78 sq. ft.)
WEIGHT: Empty 710 kg. (1562 lb.), Gross 1050 kg. (2310 lb.)
PERFORMANCE: Speed—Max. 180 km/hr (112 mph)

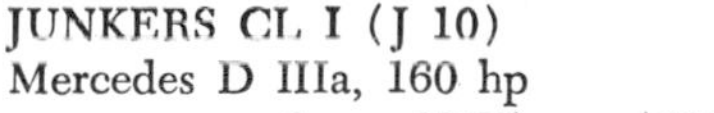

JUNKERS CL I (J 10)
Mercedes D IIIa, 160 hp
DIMENSIONS: Span 12.25 m. (40′2″), Lg. 7.9 m. (25′11″), Ht. 3.1 m. (10′2″) Wing Area 27.7 qm. (298 sq. ft.)
WEIGHT: Empty 735 kg. (1620 lb.), Gross 1155 kg. (2541 lb.)
PERFORMANCE: Speed—Max. 190 km/hr (118 mph), Climb 3000 m./14 min. (9840′/14 min.), Range 950 km. (590 miles) Service ceiling 5200 m. (17,060′)

AEG J I
Benz Bz IV, 200 hp
DIMENSIONS: Span 13 m. (42′8″), Lg. 7.2 m. (23′7″), Ht. 3.3 m. (10′10″), Wing Area 33 qm. (355 sq. ft.)
WEIGHT: Empty 1450 kg. (3190 lb.), Gross 1730 kg. (3806 lb.), Fuel 187 liters (49 gal.)
PERFORMANCE: Speed—Max. 150 km/hr (93 mph), Cruising speed 130 km/hr (81 mph), Climb 1000 m./16 min. (3280′/6 min.) 3000 m./30 min. (9840′/30 min.), Range 375 km. (232 miles), Service ceiling 4500 m. (14,760′)

upper ailerons. By April 30, 1918, AEG had 66 J Is and 15 J IIs at the front, and the following June 30, there were 43 J Is and 65 J IIs. Production of AEG J types is said to have reached 609, including those built after the war.

The remainder of the 184 J types at the front in June 1918 were 51 Albatros J Is and 25 Junkers J Is. The Albatros type appeared late in 1917, using the C XII wing and tail, the Benz engine, and had 490 kg. (1078 lb.) of five mm. armor around the cockpits. Armament was the same as that of the AEG type, although both makers sometimes tried experimental rigs, even including a 20 mm. Becker gun and a flame thrower device. The Albatros J II was similar, but added balances to the upper ailerons and additional armor around the engine. There were 16 Albatros J Is and 19 J IIs at the front on August 30, 1918. Too much dead weight made a long takeoff and poor climb.

The most advanced of these close support types was the Junkers J I, an unusual biplane of all-metal construction. The forward fuselage was a 1034 lb. shell of 5 mm. sheet steel armor, and the rear fuselage was a fabric-covered alloy tube frame. The wings had 2 mm. corrugated dural skin riveted to a framework of dural tube spars. The usual 200 hp Benz was completely enclosed in an armored shell, and armament again began with the ring-mounted Parabellum and two guns in the floor. As aiming these weapons from low altitudes proved impractical, Junkers later changed to two synchronized Spandaus in the nose.[2]

[2] While angle-mounted guns were good for trench-strafing, forward-firing guns were better for the mobile warfare in the East.

AEG J II
Benz Bz IV, 200 hp
DIMENSIONS: Span 13 m. (42′8″), Lg. 7.9 m. (25′11″), Ht. 3.3 m. (10′10″), Wing Area 33 qm. (355 sq. ft.)
WEIGHT: Empty 1480 kg. (3256 lb.), Gross 1760 kg. (3872 lb.)
PERFORMANCE: Speed—Max. 150 km/hr (93 mph), Climb 1000 m./6 min. (3280′/6 min.), Range 375 km. (232 miles), Endurance 2½ hours, Service ceiling 4500 m. (14,760′)

ALBATROS J I
Benz Bz IV, 200 hp
DIMENSIONS: Span 14.28 m. (46′10″), Lg. 8.83 m. (28′11½″), Ht. 3.21 m. (10′6″), Wing Area 42.7 qm. (459.45 sq. ft.)
WEIGHT: Empty 1398 kg. (3076 lb.), Gross 1808 kg. (3977 lb.)
PERFORMANCE: Speed—Max. 140 km/hr (87 mph), Cruising speed 120 km/hr (74 mph), Climb 1000 m./11.4 min. (3280′/11.4 min.) 3000 m./55 min. (9840′/55 min.), Range 350 km. (217 miles), Service ceiling 3000 m. (9840′)

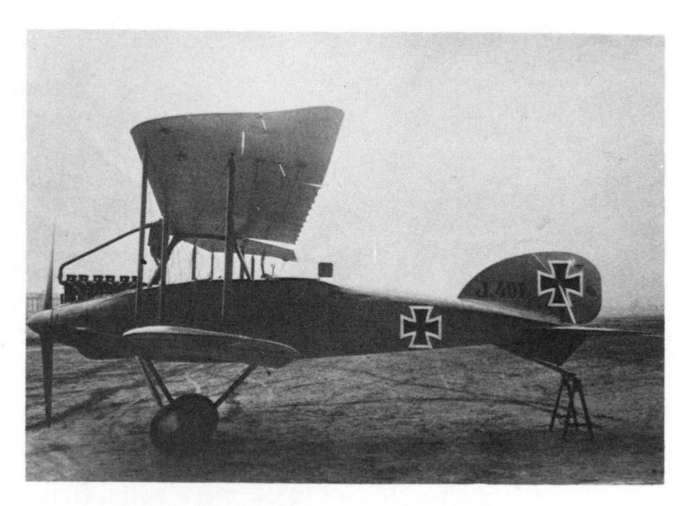

ALBATROS J II
Benz Bz IVa, 220 hp
DIMENSIONS: Span 13.55 m. (44′5″), Lg. 8.43 m. (27′8″), Ht. 3.38 m. (11′1″), Wing Area 43.2 qm. (464.83 sq. ft.)
WEIGHT: Empty 1517 kg. (3337 lb.), Gross 1927 kg. (4239 lb.)
PERFORMANCE: Speed—Max. 140 km/hr (87 mph) at sea level, Cruising speed 120 km/hr (74.4 mph), Climb 1000 m./8.7 min. (3280′/8.7 min.) 1500 m./19.6 min. (4920′/19.6 min.), Endurance 2½ hours, Service ceiling 2500 m. (8200′)

JUNKERS J I (J.4)
Benz Bz IV, 200 hp
DIMENSIONS: Span 16 m. (52′6″), Lg. 9.1 m. (29′10″), Ht. 3.4 m. (11′2″), Wing Area 48.5 qm. (521.86 sq. ft.)
WEIGHT: Empty 1766 kg. (3885 lb.), Gross 2176 kg. (4787 lb.)
PERFORMANCE: Speed—Max. 155 km/hr (96 mph), Cruising speed 120 km/hr (74 mph), Climb 2000 m./32 min. (6560′/32 min.), Endurance 2 hours, Range 310 km. (192 miles)

Bearing both the company label Junkers J 4 and the Army designation J I, the prototype made its first flight on January 28, 1917. Production ships, the first all-metal aircraft built in quantity, differed by the addition of overhung aileron balances. While one Junkers was reported at the front as early as August 1917, late armor deliveries delayed quantity production until February 1918. By the war's end, 227 armored two-seaters had been built. Sixty were at the front on August 31, 1918, along with 91 AEGs and 35 Albatros J types.

This review of the armored low-level attack planes concludes with mention of the AGO S I, an obscure two-seat, double-bay biplane. Few details of the two prototypes are known, but an armor hood protected the pilot and three to seven mm. plate the gunner. Engine was a 260 hp Basse and Selve BuS III, and armament was said to have included two Spandau guns and a 20 mm. flexible cannon (or two machine guns) fired thru a floor opening by the gunner, who also had a gun ring on top for defense. Flown in 1919, it was destroyed by Allied order.

Least known and least used among the German two-seaters were the N types; wide-span biplanes designed for night bombing. Most of these were AEG N Is, a development of the C IV with three pairs of interplane struts. The added wing area was to enable slower landing speeds and the capacity for carrying

JUNKERS J I (J.4)

JUNKERS J II

AGO S I

AEG N I (C IVN)
Benz Bz III, 150 hp
DIMENSIONS: Span 15.3 m. (50′2″), Lg. 7.3 m. (23′11″), Ht. 3.3 m. (10′10″)
WEIGHT: Empty 880 kg. (1945 lb.), Gross 1400 kg. (3090 lb.)
PERFORMANCE: Speed—Max. 142 km/hr (89 mph) at sea level, Climb 3000 m./50 min. (9840′/50 min.), Range 410 km. (355 miles), Service ceiling 4000 m. (13,120′)

SABLATNIG C I
Argus As III, 180 hp
DIMENSIONS: Span 16 m. (52′6″), Lg. 8.7 m. (28′6½″)
WEIGHT: Empty 1050 kg. (2310 lb.), Gross 1540 kg. (3388 lb.)
PERFORMANCE: Speed—Max. 120 km/hr (74 mph), Climb 1000 m./9 min. (3280′/9 min.) 2000 m./20 min. (6560′/20 min.)

SABLATNIG N I
Benz Bz IV, 200 hp
DIMENSIONS: Span 16 m. (52′6″), Lg. 8.7 m. (28′6½″), Ht. 3.2 m. (10′6″)
WEIGHT: Empty 1100 kg. (2420 lb.), Gross 1800 kg. (3960 lb.)
PERFORMANCE: Speed—Max. 125 km/hr (78 mph), Climb 1000 m./10 min. (3280′/10 min.) 4000 m./59 min. (13,120′/59 min.), Range 500 km. (310 miles), Service ceiling 4000 m. (13,120′)

ALBATROS C VIII N
Mercedes D III, 160 hp
DIMENSIONS: Span 16.74 m. (54′11″), Lg. 7.34 m. (24′1″)
WEIGHT: Not available
PERFORMANCE: Speed—Max. 145 km/hr (90 mph) at sea level, Climb 1000 m./5 min. (3280′/5 min.)

BFW DrN I

FRIEDRICHSHAFEN N I

six 50 kg. (110 lb.) bombs. Other features of this otherwise conventional type were the Benz engine and single Parabellum gun.

One hundred AEG N Is ordered in December 1916, first reached the front in October 1917, and by February 28, 1918, there were 37 at the front. On August 31, 1918, there were only four AEG N Is left, along with nine of the newer Sablatnig N Is.

Sablatnig's design began in 1917 as the C I, a double-bay biplane with an 180 hp Argus. Only a few were built before development into the Sablatnig N I, which had a blunter nose for the 200 hp Benz. Although 50 were ordered in the 1918 production plan, only a few reached the front by June 1918. The N I also had six 50 kg. bombs and was protected by one Spandau fixed and one Parabellum flexible gun.

Albatros offered a night bomber in October 1916, the C VIII N. A three-bay biplane powered by a 160 hp Mercedes, and armed like the Sablatnig craft, the Albatros C VIII N did not reach production status.

Two other N I prototypes used the 260 hp Mercedes, but also failed to reach production. The BFW DrN I was a triplane claiming to lift 744 kg. (1636 lb.) of bombs, while Friedrichshafen's N I was a biplane with a pronounced wing sweep.

Part 2 Single-seat Fighters

4.

E Type Monoplanes, 1914–15

The German fighter plane began as a defensive weapon against the increasing menace of French aircraft armed with machine guns. Roland Garros, in particular, had armed his Morane monoplane with a Hotchkiss gun that fired thru the propeller. Steel wedges deflected those bullets that did not miss the whirling wooden blades.

Garros shot down his first enemy on April 1, 1915, and on the same day Navarre and Robert downed a German with carbine fire. Other victories for Garros followed, until April 19, when a rifle shot from the ground brought him down behind German lines.

With the French secret in their hands, the Germans tried to copy it, only to find their chrome bullets shattered the propeller. The problem was then given to twenty-five-year-old Anthony Fokker, who took a Parabellum machine gun to his works at Schwerin. Less than a week later, a mechanical interrupter gear was produced that allowed firing through the propeller without hitting it. Single-seaters so armed were designated E types in 1915.

How much credit should go to Fokker for this development has always been disputed. A synchronization device had been patented by LVG's Franz Schneider in July 1913, and Schneider did win a court suit against Fokker, but only after the war. Interested readers may wish to compare the account in Fokker's autobiography with those in the Hegener and the critical Weyl books cited in the bibliography.

In any case, it is clear that the Fokker *Eindecker* (monoplane) was the first German fighter actually used in combat, and the first used anywhere with a synchronized gun.

The story of this plane begins with the appearance in 1913 of the French Morane monoplane. This machine aroused great interest in Germany, and several efforts were made to copy it. Bruno Hanuschke built a single-seater quite like it, but with a different control system, and on the outbreak of war six Hanuschke monoplanes were obtained by the German Navy. It was said their purpose was to defend Zeppelin hangars, although how an unarmed aircraft could do this is not clear.

Anthony Fokker had purchased a secondhand Morane Type H for only 500 marks ($125) and overhauled it at Schwerin in January 1914. This experience led to the design of the Fokker M 5 (M for Military). Prepared by the young engineer Martin Kreutzer and welder Reinhold Platz, the M 5 had

HANUSCHKE
Gnome, 80 hp
DIMENSIONS: Span 10 m. (32′10″), Lg. 7 m. (22′11½″), Wing Area 17 qm. (182.92 sq. ft.)
WEIGHT: Gross 300 kg. (660 lb.)
PERFORMANCE: Speed—Max. 130 km/hr (80 mph)

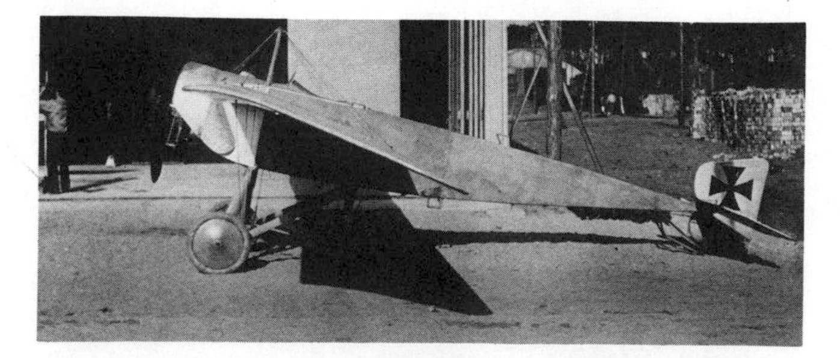

FOKKER 5K/MG

Fokker E I
Oberursel U. 0, 80 hp
DIMENSIONS: Span 8.95 m. (29'3"), Lg. 7.31 m. (22'2"), Ht. 9.14 m. (10'5"), Wing Area 16 qm. (172 sq. ft.)
WEIGHT: Empty 350 kg. (770 lb.), Gross 560 kg. (1235 lb.), Fuel 70 liters (18 gal.)
PERFORMANCE: Speed—Max. 130 km/hr (81 mph), Climb 1000 m./7 min. (3280'/7 min.), Endurance 1½ hours, Service ceiling 3000 m. (9840')

the same 50 hp Gnome rotary engine and monoplane design as the Morane, but added several improvements. These included a welded steel-tube structure for the fuselage instead of the wooden box girder, a new structure for the wire-braced wing, and a wide track undercarriage.

After test flights in April 1914, the M 5 prototype was joined by a second prototype fitted with longer wings. This became known as the M 5L (*Lang* or long) while the first was the M 5K (*Kurz* or short). The second model also introduced the comma-shaped rudder that characterized Fokker planes of the 1914–17 period. When Oberursel got its license-built 80 hp seven-cylinder Gnome into production, this rotary (known as the U. 0) replaced the French ones on the prototypes, and was used with an aluminum cowl on production ships.

About ten M 5Ls were built for the Army, beginning in June 1914, but when the war began in August, the Army hastily ordered all aircraft available from the little shop. A new two-seat M 8 monoplane became the A I, the single-seat M 5L became A II, and the M 5K the A III, on military records. These unarmed A types were known as "cavalry spotters."

There were seven A Is, 13 A IIs and one A III at the front on April 30, 1915, while Fokker went ahead with his first gun project. Probably his M 5K had been chosen because it was the best model available.

The first gun installed was a 7.9 mm. Parabellum LMG 14, designed for the C type two-seaters. The aircraft involved was M 5K/MG factory no. 216, which later became the Fokker E I 1/15 (the first *Eindecker* armed monoplane, ordered in 1915). Later E I machines standardized the more reliable LMG 08. Firing 600 rounds per minute, the 7.9 mm. weapon was called by Allied writers the Spandau, after the location of the arsenal that produced it.

The first and third E Is were taken on a tour of Army airfields by Fokker for demonstrations beginning May 23. His autobiography tells the famous story of how he was sent out to demonstrate the weapon in actual combat, but this version has been rejected by critical authorities. Nor is it still accepted that the victory by Max Immelmann on August 1, 1915, was the first with a Fokker.

Flying E I serial 2/15, one of four then at the front, Lieutenant Kurt Wintgens scored his first victory on July 1, 1915, over Lunéville, a month before Immelmann's victory at Douai. Several fatal training crashes about this time delayed the widespread use of the Fokker, however, and it was not until winter that they began making a real impact.

In the meantime, Fokker developed improvements, the first being the E II which appeared in July 1915 with a 100 hp nine-cylinder Oberursel U. I, and shorter wings. Fokker reverted to wider wings on the main model, the E III that came out in August. All three E types were built and used at the front at the same time.

By November, a 160 hp twin-row Oberursel U. III was available for the first E IV (Fokker M 15). Most Fokkers had but one gun, but a few E IIIs and the E IV had two, while an E IV built specially for Immelmann had three. Shortages of the unreliable engines limited the number of E IVs completed, while E IIIs were used as test beds for various engines, including captured French ones.

By the end of 1915, there were 26 E Is, 14 E IIs, 40 E IIIs, and six E IVs at the front, scattered in ones and twos among the 72 field aviation sections. Allied fliers spoke of the "Fokker Scourge," and despaired of finding an Allied weapon to counter it. The Germans failed to make best use of their advantage, for they did not concentrate their fighter

FOKKER E III (M14)
Oberursel 100 hp
DIMENSIONS: Span 9.52 m. (31'3"), Lg. 7.2 m. (23'7¼"), Ht. 2.4 m. (7'10"), Wing Area 16 qm. (172 sq. ft.)
WEIGHT: Empty 390 kg. (858 lb.), Gross 670 kg. (1475 lb.)
PERFORMANCE: Speed—Max. 140 km/hr (87 mph), Climb 1000 m./5 min. (3280'/5 min.) 3000 m./30 min. (9840'/30 min.), Endurance 1½ hours, Service ceiling 3000 m. (9840')

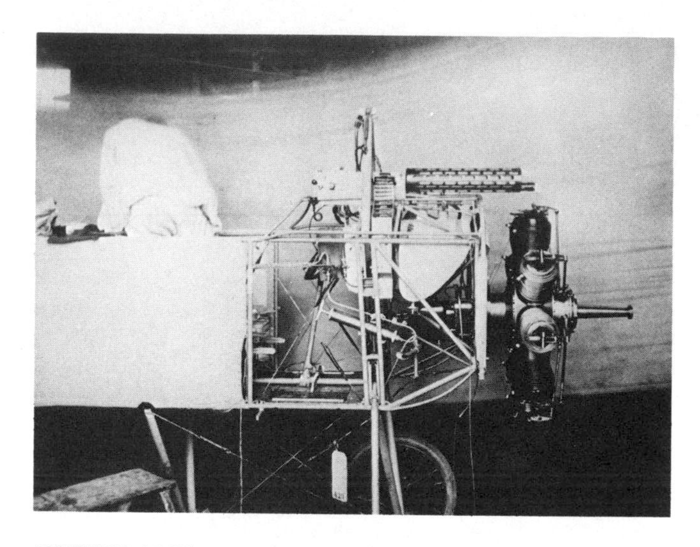

FOKKER M.15
Oberursel U. III, 160 hp
DIMENSIONS: Span 10 m. (32'10"), Lg. 7.5 m. (24'7"), Ht. 2.77 m. (9'1"), Wing Area 16 qm. (172 sq. ft.)
WEIGHT: Empty 460 kg. (1012 lb.), Gross 720 kg. (1584 lb.)
PERFORMANCE: Speed—Max. 160 km/hr (99 mph), Climb 4000 m./25 min. (13,120'/25 min.), Range 240 km. (148.8 miles), Service ceiling 4000 m. (13,120')

FOKKER E II

PFALZ E I
Oberursel U. 0, 80 hp
DIMENSIONS: Span 9.26 m. (30'5"), Lg. 6.3 m. (20'8"), Ht. 2.55 m. (8'4"), Wing Area 14 qm. (151 sq. ft.)
WEIGHT: Empty 345 kg. (759 lb.), Gross 535 kg. (1177 lb.)
PERFORMANCE: Speed—Max. 145 km/hr (90 mph), Climb 2000 m./12 min. (2620'/12 min.), Endurance 1½ hours

PFALZ E I

force, and forbade the pilots to cross the front lines. Somehow, the Army held to a concept of an air blockade, an impractical hope that a few fighters could prevent enemy air operations over their own territory.

There were 173 Fokker fighters (22 E Is, 13 E IIs, 110 E IIIs, and 28 E IVs) on April 30, 1916, the zenith of *Eindecker* strength at the front. By that time the Allies, despite their lack of synchronized guns, had superior fighters of their own, such as the Nieuport 11, D.H. 2, and F.E. 2b.

An E III that did cross the lines was captured on April 8, 1916, and the synchronization secret was out. This aircraft is still exhibited in London's Science Museum, and is the only genuine Fokker E extant. After Immelmann was killed in an E III on July 18, 1918, the Fokker monoplanes were seldom used on the Western front, although they continued on the Eastern front, and on training fields. In the West, they had been swept from the sky by the Nieuports.

Of 647 E types built in 1915–16, over two-thirds were Fokkers, including at least 56 E Is, and 258 E IIIs. About 20 went to Austria-Hungary, and a few to Turkey and to the German Navy. Fokker had established a permanent place in history as builder of the first fighters to use a synchronized gun in combat.

Fokker's fame obscured the presence at the front of the Pfalz monoplanes, nearly identical in appearance but for the rudder shape and straight wheel axle. Actually, the Pfalz E I was a licensed copy of the Morane Type H, for which Pfalz had obtained a manufacturing license before the war.[1] Retaining the usual wooden box-girder fuselage construction, its

[1] Full license fees were paid to Morane in 1919 for all such aircraft built by Pfalz during the war.

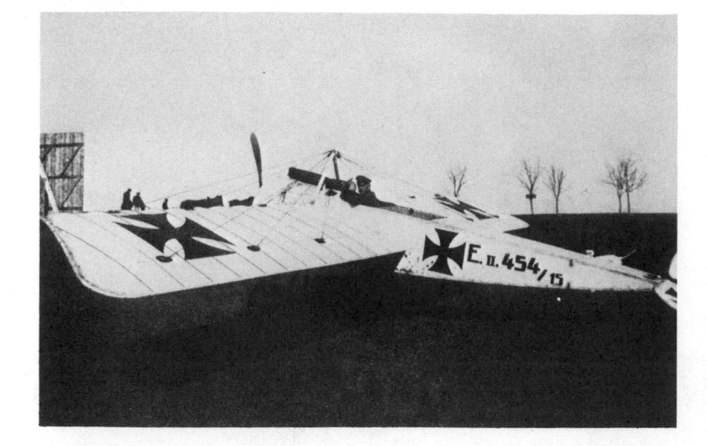

PFALZ E II
Oberursel U I, 100 hp
DIMENSIONS: Span 10.2 m. (33'5½"), Lg. 6.45 m. (21'2"), Ht. 2.55 m. (8'4"), Wing Area 16 qm. (172 sq. ft.)
WEIGHT: Empty 410 kg. (902 lb.), Gross 577 kg. (1270 lb.)
PERFORMANCE: Speed—Max. 130 km/hr (81 mph), Climb 2000 m./9.75 min. (6560'/9.75 min.), Endurance 1½ hours, Service ceiling 3000 m. (9840')

PFALZ E III (from A II)
Oberursel U I, 100 hp
DIMENSIONS: Span 11.2 m. (36'9"), Lg. 6.85 m. (22'5½"), Ht. 3.4 m. (11'2") Wing Area 18 qm. (193.68 sq. ft.)
WEIGHT: Empty 445 kg. (979 lb.), Gross 705 kg. (1551 lb.)
PERFORMANCE: Speed—Max. 150 km/hr (92 mph), Climb 3000 m./23 min. (9840'/23 min.), Service ceiling 3000 m. (9840')

wire-braced wings had no ailerons, but had flexible trailing edges that were warped for control.

The first E I passed its acceptance tests in September 1915, and appeared at the front the next month. Like the parallel Fokker, it had a single gun and 80 hp Oberursel. By December the E II was at the front with a 100 hp Oberursel rotary.

Some Pfalz A II parasol monoplanes were armed with a synchronized gun and redesignated E III, but it's not certain whether or not the second seat was retained. These few Pfalz E IIIs were the only high-wing fighters on the German side before 1918.

A twin row 160 hp Oberursel rotary and twin guns were used on the Pfalz E IV, which had its *Typen-Pruefung* (acceptance tests) in January 1916. An unreliable engine and an unstable aircraft made a poor combination, so only 24 E IVs were built at the Speyer factory.

There were 27 E Is, 20 E IIs, four E IIIs, and five E IVs at the front on April 30, 1916, when monoplane fighter strength was greatest. The Pfalz ships were favored by Bavarian flying sections, and also operated in Palestine, but most served as trainers.

A water-cooled Mercedes of 100 hp distinguished the Pfalz E V, but only 20 were ordered. Three were at the front on June 30, 1916, along with 13 E I, 30 E II, and eight E III types. By this time, the sturdier biplane designs were replacing the mono-

PFALZ E IV
Oberursel U III, 160 hp
DIMENSIONS: Span 10.2 m. (33'5½"), Lg. 6.66 m. (21'8"), Ht. 2.55 m. (8'4½"), Wing Area 16 qm. (172 sq. ft.)
WEIGHT: Empty 471 kg. (1036 lb.), Gross 694 (1527 lb.)
PERFORMANCE: Speed—Max. 160 km/hr (99 mph) at sea level, Climb 800 m./2 min. (2625'/2 min.) 2000 m./8.5 min. (6560'/8.5 min.) Endurance 1 hour

PFALZ E V
Mercedes D I, 100 hp
DIMENSIONS: Span 10.2 m. (33′5½″), Lg. 6.6 m. (21′8″), Ht. 2.6 m. (8′6″), Wing Area 16 qm. (172 sq. ft.)
WEIGHT: Empty 510 kg. (1122 lb.), Gross 696 kg. (1531 lb.)
PERFORMANCE: Speed—Max. 165 km/hr (103 mph), Endurance 2 hours

SIEMENS Bulldog (Sh 1)

planes with the fighter squadrons. Pfalz did build 20 E VIs also, but these were trainer developments of the E IIs with larger rudders and 100 hp Oberursels.

Quite similar to the Pfalz and Fokker types except for a more streamlined plywood-covered fuselage, the Siemens-Schuckert E I was designed by Bruno and Franz Steffen. This company had made the curious Forssman "Bulldog" monoplane in 1914 for the Crown Prince, building one with a 110 hp Siemens-Halske Sh I rotary, and another with a 100 hp inline Mercedes. While neither aircraft was accepted by the Army, the builders went on to use the rotary engine on the E I of 1915, armed with the usual single synchronized gun.

Twenty E Is were ordered in November 1915, and were completed without the prop spinner seen on the prototype. Only five were at the front on October 31, 1916, so the type was probably used mainly for training and hack work.

One Siemens-Schuckert E II was built, using a 120 hp Argus As II, but in June 1916 it was destroyed in a crash, killing co-designer Franz Steffen. A 100 hp Oberursel powered six E IIIs built the same year.

Unique among these monoplanes was the LVG E designed by Franz Schneider, a two-seater with both a pilot's synchronized gun and an observer's flexible gun on a ring mount. It had a 120 hp water-cooled Mercedes D II and used ailerons, instead of the wing-warping control of previous monoplanes. The design was advanced, but the single prototype aircraft was destroyed accidently on the way to the front.

The most advanced monoplane concept of this period was that of Professor Hugo Junkers, who produced the world's first all-metal aircraft. The new strength offered by this construction enabled use of an internally braced, cantilever wing. "Are you so tired of life, then, that you fly a plane without bracing wires?" a test pilot was asked.

SIEMENS Bulldog (Mercedes)

SIEMENS E I
Siemens Sh I, 110 hp
DIMENSIONS: Span 10 m. (32′10″), Lg. 7.1 m. (23′4″), Wing Area 473 qm. (1041 sq. ft.)
WEIGHT: Empty 473 kg. (1041 lb.), gross 673 kg. (1481 lb.)
PERFORMANCE: Speed—Max. 140 km/hr (87 mph), Service ceiling 3000 m. (9840′)

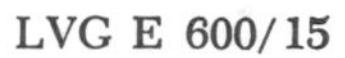
LVG E 600/15

SIEMENS E II

JUNKERS J 2 (E II)
Mercedes D II, 120 hp
DIMENSIONS: Span 11 m. (36′1″), Lg. 7.5 m. (24′7″), Ht. 3.13 m. (10′3″), Wing Area 19 qm. (204.44 sq. ft.)
WEIGHT: Empty 920 kg. (2028 lb.), Gross 1165 kg. (2569 lb.)
PERFORMANCE: Speed—Max. 205 km/hr (127 mph), Range 615 km. (382 miles), Service ceiling 4500 m. (14,760′)

JUNKERS J 1
Mercedes D II, 120 hp
DIMENSIONS: Span 12.95 m. (42′6″), Lg. 8.60 m. (28′4″), Ht. 3.17 m. (10′5″), Wing Area 24.3 qm. (261.47 sq. ft.)
WEIGHT: Empty 900 kg. (1980 lb.), Gross 1080 kg. (2376 lb.)
PERFORMANCE: Speed—Max. 170 km/hr (105 mph)

JUNKERS J 2 (E II)

NFW E I
Oberursel U. I, 80 hp
DIMENSIONS: Span 10 m. (32'10"), Lg. 6.5 m. (21'4"), Wing Area 15.72 qm. (169 sq. ft.)
WEIGHT: Empty 428 kg. (641 lb.), Gross 620 kg. (1364 lb.)
PERFORMANCE: Speed—Max. 156 km/hr (97 mph), Climb 1300 m./6 min. (4260'/6 min.)

NFW E II
Mercedes D III, 160 hp
DIMENSIONS: Span 12 m. (39'4"), Wing Area 17 qm. (182.92 sq. ft.)
WEIGHT: Empty 558 kg. (1228 lb.), Gross 768 kg. (1689 lb.)
PERFORMANCE: Speed—Max. 180 km/hr (112 mph), Climb 2900 m./6.3 min. (9510'/6.3 min.)

Construction of the Junkers J 1 began as a private venture in June 1915, and the pioneer "Tin Donkey" was first flown at Dessau on December 12, 1915. Powered by a 120 hp Mercedes, the J 1 was a clean, square-cut monoplane covered with two mm. sheet steel welded to the girder framework. An open cockpit accommodated the pilot, and if needed, an observer.

Although built entirely as an unarmed research vehicle, Junkers' first aircraft was brought to the Army's test field at Doeberitz to evaluate its military potential. Despite its sluggish climb, the strong construction and high speed suggested a possible fighter.

Six examples of a fighter version were ordered, with the company name of J 2 and the military designation E II. Armed with one fixed gun, this single-seater was smaller than its predecessor and used the same engine. Unfortunately, it also proved to be heavier, and its first flight trials in July 1916 showed a climb rate too poor for combat service.

The third J 2 appeared in September with a longer fuselage, but was destroyed in a crash. The Army showed no further interest in the design, and Junkers would have to develop a structure of lighter metal before he could revive interest in his style of aircraft.

Another cantilever monoplane, with wooden construction, was built by NFW (National Flugzeug-Werke, formerly Jeannin). This E I was flown April 15, 1916, with an Oberursel rotary and plywood-covered wings whose two spars passed through the fuselage, the pilot sitting between them under a roll bar. A heavier Mercedes-powered E II was built the following year, but neither type saw production.

5.

Biplane Fighters to 1917

Biplanes were stronger and more maneuverable in those early days of the war, and so in 1916 the E types were replaced by D (*Doppeldecker*) types. From the Halberstadt D I to the famous Fokker D VII, these single-seat biplanes fought the Allies for control of the sky over the front.

Before these types went into production, several single-seat biplanes were tested by the Germans; prototypes so obscure that today neither specifications or aircraft history have survived. The first of these, and apparently the first German aircraft with a machine gun, was the Euler *Gelber Hund* (Yellow Dog). As early as 1912, August Euler had patented (Nr. 248601) an "Airship-Destroyer"; a pusher biplane with a machine gun mounted in front of the pilot. His first such single-seater appeared in 1915 with a 100 hp Mercedes, and twin rudders on outrigger struts. Such a pattern was successful on the British DH 2, but now Germany had the Fokker synchronization gear, and thought the pusher style undesirable. Nevertheless, Fokker paid a royalty to Euler for the idea of a fixed forward-firing gun.

Another single-seat pusher was the little Schwade of 1915. Powered by an 80 hp Stahlherz rotary, it supported a large tail with a strut framework. It is not certain when the later Bergmann LMG 15 shown in our photo was installed, but the aircraft design was poor.

Schwade, an Erfurt firm, tried again in 1915 with another pusher single-seater. This one had 100 hp and twin rudders on twin booms, but did not make the grade either. Failure was probably due to the unreliability of the Stahlherz rotaries.

Several single-seat tractor (propeller in front) biplanes appeared early in the war. In 1914 the German Navy acquired three AGO DV 3s, a conventional double-bay machine with an 80 hp Gnome rotary. More original was the Albatros ME designed by Hermann Dorner, with thick wings connected over a wide gap by a single pair of thin struts, and a 100 hp water-cooled Mercedes. Both aircraft were considered cavalry spotters, rather than fighters.

Schutte-Lanz offered a single-seater with Sopwith lines and a 100 hp Gnome in summer 1915, and designer Hillmann later claimed it was the first true D plane. Provisions had been made for two synchronized guns. It was not accepted as officials thought at that time that biplanes were less suitable for fighting than monoplanes because their upper wing blocked visibility.

The peculiar DFW T28 "Flea" had the upper wing joined to the deep fuselage, which gave good visibility upward, but a bad view down. A crash during tests late in 1915 ended its chances.

Halberstadter Flugzeug-werke produced the first series of biplane fighters used at the front. The most distinctive feature of Halberstadt D I was the tall rudder supported only by two steel struts and the rudder post; otherwise construction was the usual fabric-covered wood framework, with two pairs of wire-braced steel struts on each side between the wings, and ailerons only on the upper wings. To the left of the 100 hp Mercedes was mounted a syn-

ALBATROS D III

EULER "Gelbe Hund"

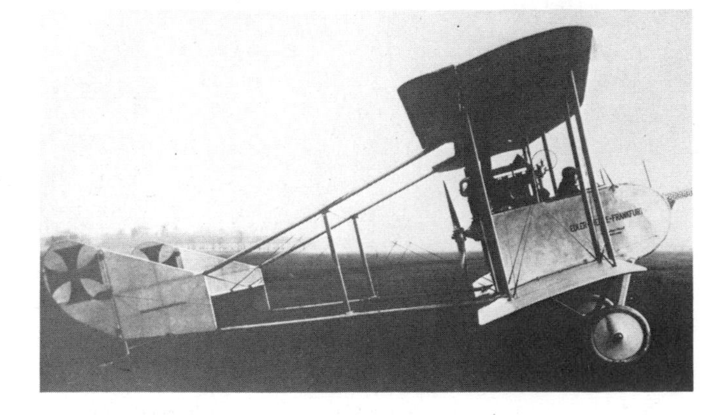

SCHWADE Pusher

SCHWADE Pusher No. 2

AGO DV 3

chronized 7.9 mm. LMG 08/15, which replaced the LMG 08 in May 1916. A water radiator was fitted into the top-wing center section alongside a gravity fuel tank.

This model was followed by the D II which had a 120 hp Mercedes, and was also produced under license as the Aviatik D I (later Halb. D II Av.), and by Hannover as the Halb. D II (Han.). A radiator in front was tried on a test aircraft, while a 120 hp Argus was used on the D III. A 150 hp Benz and single bay struts denoted the two-gun D IV, which was not put into production.

Final version was the Argus-powered D V which appeared at the front in October 1916, with a single machine gun, balanced ailerons and reverted to a double-bay strut arrangement. The D V was also used in Turkey.

SCHUTTE LANZ D I
Gnome, 100 hp
DIMENSIONS: Span 7.5 m. (24'7"), Lg. 5.4 m. (17'8½")
Other data unavailable

DFW T 28
Benz Bz III, 150 hp
DIMENSIONS: Span 6.2 m. (20'4"), Lg. 4.5 m. (14'9"), Wing Area 15 qm. (161.40 sq. ft.)
WEIGHT: Empty 420 kg. (924 lb.), Gross 650 kg. (1430 lb.)
PERFORMANCE: Not available

ALBATROS ME

HALBERSTADT D I

HALBERSTADT D II
Mercedes D II, 120 hp
DIMENSIONS: Span 8.8 m. (28′10¼″), Lg. 7.3 m. (23′11″), Ht. 2.66 m. (8′9″)
WEIGHT: Empty 520 kg. (1144 lb.), Gross 730 kg. (1606 lb.)
PERFORMANCE: Speed—Max. 150 km/hr (93 mph), Climb 1000 m./4 min. (3280′/4 min.) 3000 m./15 min. (9840′/15 min.)

The Halberstadt single-seaters trickled to the front in 1916 and were individually scattered among the flying sections, first fighting in February 1916 during the Verdun battle. Only six D IIs and two D IIIs were at the front on June 30, 1916, but at year's end the list included 55 D IIs, 17 D IIIs and 32 D Vs, some concentrated in the new fighter squadrons like Jasta 4. When the Albatros types proved superior in climb and maneuverability, the Halberstadts were replaced at the front.

FOKKER'S D I TO D V

Anthony Fokker realized that his monoplanes were being surpassed at the front and instructed Martin Kreutzer to prepare a biplane fighter. Should it use the heavier and more powerful water-cooled inline Mercedes, or the lighter, but less potent air-cooled rotaries? Fokker followed both lines at once.

His first biplane fighter was the *Karausche* (Carp) or M 16E, using a 100 hp Mercedes in a deep body that filled the gap between the wings. A single LMG 08/15 gun was provided. The E in M 16E stood for *Einstielig* (single bay), while an M 16Z, *Zweistielig* (two bay), was a larger two-seater with a 160 hp Mercedes. Neither had ailerons, using wing warping for control. The larger type was sold to Austria.

Parallel to these was the construction of the smaller M 17E powered by the 80 hp Oberursel. While the German Army rejected this light fighter, it was modified and sent on April 13, 1916, to Austria, which purchased a batch. One was tried with an added Mannlicher gun mounted above the upper wing, à la Nieuport.

Next appeared the M 18E, using the same water-cooled 100 hp Mercedes as the M 16E, but considerably cleaned up. A larger wing was need to improve the climb, and Fokker followed with the two-bay M 18Z and ailerons. This in turn was revised to the prototype Fokker D I, submitted for testing on April 15, 1916. Here the builders reverted to the traditional Fokker wing warping and comma-shaped rudder.

Official reaction was against Fokker, since the new Albatros seemed superior. Only after new tests in July was Fokker given an order for 80 D Is, and Austria also received some. Fokker claimed that

HALBERSTADT D II (Han.)

HALBERSTADT D III

HALBERSTADT D V
Argus As II, 120 hp
DIMENSIONS: Span 8.8 m. (28'11"), Lg. 7.3 m. (23'11"), Ht. 2.66 m. (8'9"), Wing Area 24 qm. (259 sq. ft.)
WEIGHT: Empty 525 kg. (1155 lb.), Gross 737 kg. (1621 lb.), Fuel 83 liters (22 gal.)
PERFORMANCE: Speed—Max. 185 km/hr (115 mph)

FOKKER M 17E

HALBERSTADT D IV

FOKKER M 16E

FOKKER M 17E modified

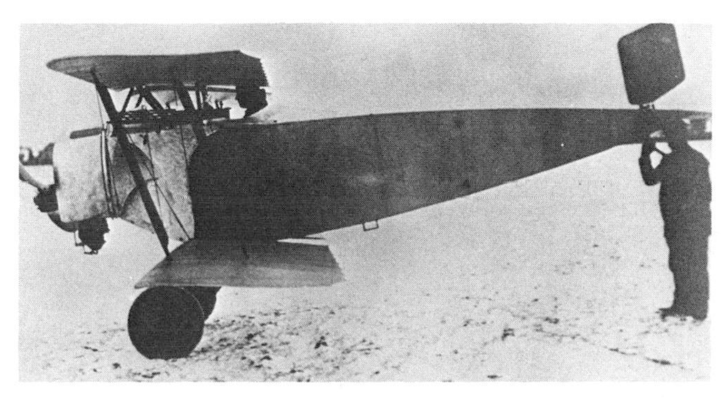

FOKKER M 18E

FOKKER M 18Z

FOKKER D II (M17 Z)
Oberursel U. I, 100 hp
DIMENSIONS: Span 8.75 m. (28′8″), Lg. 6.4 m. (21′), Ht. 2.55 m. (8′4″), Wing Area 18 qm. (193.68 sq. ft.)
WEIGHT: Empty 380 kg. (836 lb.), Gross 570 kg. (1254 lb.)
PERFORMANCE: Speed—Max. 150 km/hr (93 mph), Climb 1000 m./4 min. (3280′/4 min.), Service ceiling 4000 m. (13,120′)

FOKKER D I
Mercedes D II, 120 hp
DIMENSIONS: Span 9.05 m. (29′8″), Lg. 5.7 m. (18′8″), Ht. 2.25 m. (7′5″), Wing Area 22 qm. (236.72 sq. ft.)
WEIGHT: Empty 460 kg. (1014 lb.), Gross 670 kg. (1477 lb.)
PERFORMANCE: Speed—Max. 150 km/hr (93 mph), Climb 1000 m./5 min. (3280′/5 min.), Service ceiling 4000 m. (13,120′)

FOKKER D II (M17 Z)

FOKKER D III (M19)
Oberursel U III, 160 hp
DIMENSIONS: Span 9.05 m. (29′8″), Lg. 6.3 m. (20′8″), Ht. 2.25 m. (7′5″), Wing Area 20 qm. (215 sq. ft.)
WEIGHT: Empty 450 kg. (990 lb.), Gross 710 kg. (1562 lb.)
PERFORMANCE: Speed—Max. 160 km/hr (99 mph), Climb 1000 m./4 min. (3280′/4 min.), Endurance 1½ hours, Service ceiling 4000 m. (13,120′)

FOKKER D IV (M21)
Mercedes D III, 160 hp
DIMENSIONS: Span 9.7 m. (31′10″), Lg. 6.3 m. (20′8″), Ht. 2.45 m. (8′), Wing Area 21 qm. (226 sq. ft.)
WEIGHT: Empty 600 kg. (1320 lb.), Gross 840 kg. (1848 lb.)
PERFORMANCE: Speed—Max. 160 km/hr (99 mph), Climb 1000 m./3 min. (3280′/3 min.), Service ceiling 5000 m. (16,400′)

FOKKER D IV modified

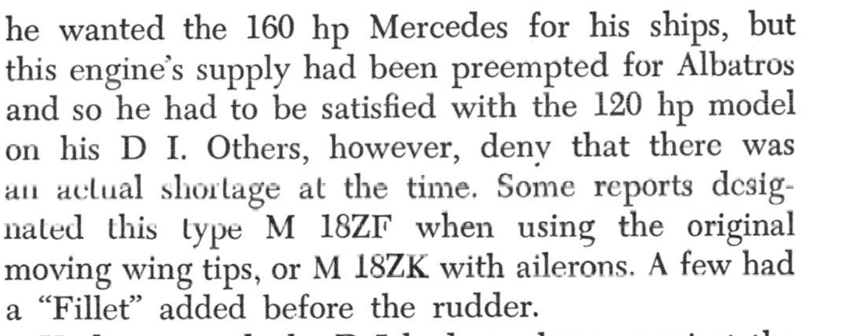

he wanted the 160 hp Mercedes for his ships, but this engine's supply had been preempted for Albatros and so he had to be satisfied with the 120 hp model on his D I. Others, however, deny that there was an actual shortage at the time. Some reports designated this type M 18ZF when using the original moving wing tips, or M 18ZK with ailerons. A few had a "Fillet" added before the rudder.

Underpowered, the D I had no chance against the opposing Nieuports, and so was soon withdrawn from the front in favor of the parallel D II. Powered by a 100 hp Oberursel rotary, the D II began as the two bay M 17Z, tested April 17, 1916. This type won an order for 170 D IIs. Armed like D I with a single LMG 08/15, they first entered service July 27, 1916. This type also proved inferior to the Albatros, and so was soon withdrawn from the West, and used mostly for training.

Concurrently, Fokker then introduced the M 19, which entered production as the D III. Powered by a 160 hp twin-row Oberursel rotary, it had the D I's larger wings and had two forward guns. Like the other Fokker types, it was built first with wing warping, and later added ailerons. Fokker built some 176 D IIIs, the most famous being the one used by Boelcke to down six enemies in September 1916.

Fokkers at the front August 31, 1916, included ten D Is, 16 D IIs and seven D IIIs, increasing by December 31 to four D Is, 68 D IIs, and 34 D IIIs. This period had seen the first *Jagdstaffeln* (single-seat fighter squadrons) or *Jastas*, each with a planned establishment of 14 D type aircraft. *Jasta* 1 formed on August 23, and Boelcke's *Jasta* 2 began August 27. The first aircraft, two Fokker D IIIs and an Albatros D I, arrived September 1, and the next day Boelcke's D III downed a DH 2. By the month's end, there were seven *Jastas* with Fokker, Halberstadt, and the new Albatros machines.

Meanwhile, Fokker had obtained some 160 hp Mercedes, installing one in the M 20 prototype. Produced as the D IV, it had two guns, and was the last Fokker with side radiators. The two-bay wings had balanced ailerons and the scalloped trailing edge typical of Fokker biplanes. Some of the later examples had a prop spinner.

Forty Fokker D IVs were built, in February–May 1917. These had been ordered solely as trainers since the Fokker types had been rejected at the front for both inferior performance and poor construction. All of the earlier D IIIs were relegated to the Home Defense units.

Fokker continued trying to produce a rotary-powered fighter that might match the Nieuport in maneuverability. Since Kreutzer had been killed on a test flight June 27, 1915, Reinhold Platz had assumed

FOKKER D V
Oberursel U I, 100 hp
DIMENSIONS: Span 8.75 m. (28'8½"), Lg. 6.05 m. (19'10"), Ht. 2.3 m. (7'), Wing Area 15.5 qm. (164.3 sq. ft.)
WEIGHT: Empty 360 kg. (792 lb.), Gross 560 kg. (1232 lb.)
PERFORMANCE: Speed—Max. 170 km/hr (105 mph), Climb 3000 m./19 min. (9840'/19 min.)

ALBATROS D I
Mercedes D III, 160 hp or Benz Bz III, 150 hp
DIMENSIONS: Span 8.50 m. (27'11"), Lg. 7.40 m. (24'3"), Ht. 2.95 m. (9'8"), Wing Area 22.9 qm. (246.4 sq. ft.)
WEIGHT: Empty 647 kg. (1423 lb.), Gross 898 kg. (1976 lb.)
PERFORMANCE: Speed—Max. 175 km/hr (109 mph), Climb 1000 m./6 min. (3280'/6 min.), Endurance 1½ hours, Service ceiling 5000 m. (16,400')

charge of design. A sweptback upper wing had been tried on an M 21 prototype, which was followed by a pair of M 22s; one with a 100 hp Oberursel and one gun, and the other with a 110 hp Siemens Sh I and two guns. The M 22Z was basically a cleaned up D III, with two bays, a circular cowl and prop spinners.

The circular cowl and prop spinner and shorter, single-bay wings were used on the D V prototype tested October 1916, along with the D IV. The powerplant was the 100 hp Oberursel rotary; perhaps one should mention that Fokker had become majority stockholder of that engine firm. Armament was limited to one gun, but the D V was quite maneuverable, and a "joy to fly." Production of 300 began in January 1917, but few went to the front, most serving as trainers, or with the Navy. Ten were sold to Holland in July 1917. By October 1917, only nine Fokker D planes remained at the front, where the Albatros types predominated.

ALBATROS D I TO D V

Albatros dominated the German fighter field from 1916 thru 1917. The trim single-seaters produced by chief designer Robert Thelen were distinguished by their streamlined plywood-covered fuselage with metal nose and rounded empennage.

The usual powerplant was a six-cylinder Mercedes of 160 hp, and from the very beginning two Spandau guns were mounted. Although later Fokker monoplanes had had similar armament, they were too underpowered to be effective. The Albatros single-seaters combined speed and firepower to be the most dangerous opponents the Allies yet faced.

The Albatros D I first reached the front in August 1916, and on September 17, Oswald Boelke's *Jasta* 2 scored several victories with the new type. On this first model the upper wing was held high above the fuselage by two inverted Vee struts, and joined to the equal-chord lower wings by a single pair of steel struts on each side.

Realizing that upward visibility could be improved, Albatros quickly introduced the D II, which lowered the top wing eight inches, and utilized N struts on

ALBATROS D II
Mercedes D III, 160 hp
DIMENSIONS: Span 8.50 m. (27'11"), Lg. 7.40 m. (24'3"), Ht. 2.95 m. (9'8"), Wing Area 24.5 qm. (263.62 sq. ft.)
WEIGHT: Empty 637 kg. (1401 lb.), Gross 888 kg. (1954 lb.)
PERFORMANCE: Speed—Max. 175 km/hr (109 mph), Climb 1000 m./5 min. (3280'/5 min.), Endurance 1½ hours, Service ceiling 5000 m. (16,400')

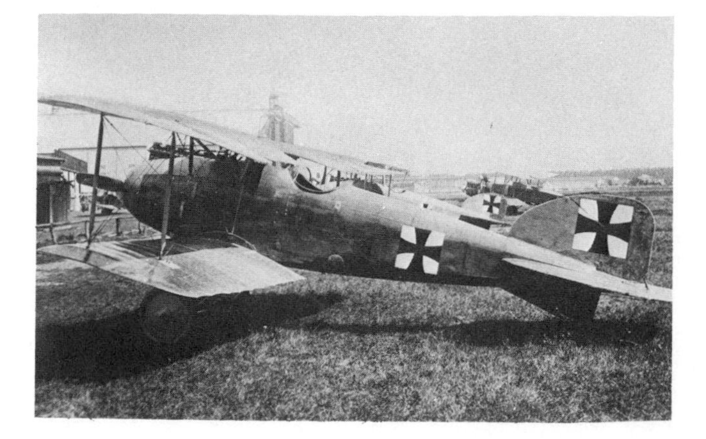

ALBATROS D III
Mercedes D II, 160 hp
DIMENSIONS: Span 9.05 m. (29'8"), Lg. 7.33 m. (24'), Ht. 2.98 m. (9'9"), Wing Area 20.5 qm. (230.58 sq. ft.)
WEIGHT: Empty 661 kg. (1454 lb.), Gross 880 kg. (1949 lb.)
PERFORMANCE: Speed—Max. 165 km/hr (103 mph), Climb 1000 m./3.3 min. (3280'/3.3 min.), Endurance 2 hours, Service ceiling 5500 m. (18,040')

each side of the center section. Later, the water radiators on each side were replaced by a single cooler built into the upper wing's center section. Seventy-five were also built under license as the LVG D I, later Alb. D II (LVG), and in Austria by Oeffag with 185 hp Austro-Daimler engines.

There were 50 Albatros D Is and 28 D IIs at the Western front October 31, 1916 and as the best fighters at the front, they soon replaced rival types. At the year's end, there were 39 D Is and 214 D IIs at the front, compared to 108 Fokker and 104 Halberstadt biplanes.

A further advance was made with the appearance of the D III in December 1916. This model had a new wing layout inspired by the Nieuport's fine downward visibility! Instead of the nearly equal-sized two-spar lower wing, a narrow one-spar lower wing was used, joined by steel V struts to the top wing, which added graceful tips.

The same Mercedes powerplant was used, but the radiator was later moved to the starboard side of the center section; so a bullet puncture would not send scalding water into the pilot's face.

Although climb was greatly improved, the new single-spar wing design suffered from the same twisting effect that endangered the Nieuport. German pilots had to be warned not to dive these planes too steeply, hardly reassuring advice to fighter pilots.

ALBATROS D III

Nevertheless, the *Jastas* largely standardized the Albatros biplanes, and their growing combat success culminated in "Bloody April," 1917. Thirteen D IIIs were at the front at the year's start, and 327 on April 30, 1917. Along with 20 D Is, 107 D IIs and 47 license-built LVG D Is, they comprised most of 686 D type aircraft at the front when America entered the war.[1]

The Albatros D IV was an experimental type utilizing the D II style wing struts, a more rounded (instead of flat-sided) fuselage, added a pilot's headrest, and had the geared Mercedes D III completely buried within the nose. It did not reach production, but the rounded fuselage and headrest were adapted for the D V.

Appearing at the front in May 1917, the Albatros D V was actually little improved over the D III, despite the more streamlined appearance of the new rounded fuselage, headrest and rudder. High compression increased the Mercedes D IIIa's best altitude to 2000 meters (6560′); where 160 hp was equivalent to 180 hp, but the engine could not be run full power at sea level.

Production overlapped that of the last batch D IIIs, which also changed to round rudders. Since the D V's headrest was removed during its service, the most positive difference in appearance was the D V's forward-slanting tail skid fairing piece.

The same structural weakness of the wings plagued the D V, which was known to lose wing tips, or even the entire lower wing, in a dive. Iron fittings were added to strengthen the lower wing's main spar, and an additional bracing wire was run from the V strut's base to the upper wing tip. This strengthened version also shifted the aileron's control cables back from the lower to the upper wing (where they had been on earlier models) and was known as the D Va by the Army, although the factory made no differentiation in designation.

Of 1224 D type fighters at the front on October 31, 1917, Albatros contributed 446 D III, 526 D V and 53 D Va biplanes. On April 30, 1918, they comprised 174, 131 and 928 respectively, of 1751 frontline Ds. By that time, the Albatros design had been surpassed by enemy types, and replacement by the Fokker D VII had been ordered. The number of *Jastas* rose from six at the end of 1916 to 51 at the end of 1917, and to 89 in the summer of 1918.[2]

In Austria, Oeffag built the Albatros D II and D III with the 185 to 220 hp Austro-Daimlers. After the war, Albatros D IIIs went to the new Polish Air Force. Seventeen American pilots of the Kosciuszko squadron flew these D IIIs in the Russo-Polish war from April to October 1920.

ROLAND D I AND D II

LFG Roland produced a single-seater along the lines of designer Tantzen's C II *Walfisch*, using the same *Wickelrumpf* (warped fuselage). That construction, developed by Hans Roever, used the plywood ribbons rolled around a wooden frame.

[1] The remainder included 99 Rolands, 44 Fokkers, 38 Halberstadts, and two Siemens D Is.

[2] For detailed lists see H. J. Nowarra, *op. cit.* p. 40–45.

ALBATROS D IV
Mercedes D III, 160 hp
DIMENSIONS: Span 9 m. (29′6″), Lg. 7.33 m. (24′½″), Ht. 2.98 m. (9′9″), Wing Area 20.5 qm. (230.58 sq. ft.)
WEIGHT: Not available
PERFORMANCE: Speed—Max. 165 km/hr (103 mph), Climb 5000 m./32 min. (16,400′/32 min.)

ALBATROS D V
Mercedes D IIIa, 160 hp
DIMENSIONS: Span 9 m. (29′6″), Lg. 7.33 m. (24′½″), Ht. 2.7 m. (8′10″), Wing Area 20.32 qm. (219 sq. ft.)
WEIGHT: Empty 680 kg. (1496 lb.), Gross 915 kg. (2013 lb.), Fuel 83 liters (22 gal.)
PERFORMANCE: Speed—Max. 165 km/hr (103 mph), Climb 1000 m./4 min. (3280′/4 min.) 5000 m./35 min. (16,400′/35 min.), Endurance 2 hours, Service ceiling 5500 m. (18,040′)

ALBATROS D Va

LFG ROLAND D I
Mercedes D III, 160 hp
DIMENSIONS: Span 8.9 m. (29'2"), Lg. 6.8 m. (22'4"), Ht. 2.9 m. (9'6"), Wing Area 23 qm. (247.48 sq. ft.)
WEIGHT: Empty 699 kg. (1538 lb.), Gross 932 kg. (2050 lb.)
PERFORMANCE: Speed—Max. 165 km/hr (103 mph), Climb 4000 m./24 min. (13,120'/4 min.), Endurance 2 hours

This work had to be done very carefully and took much time, but produced a streamlined fuselage filling the gap between the wings. A 160 hp Mercedes was nearly buried behind the large metal prop, and two Spandau guns were carried.

Sometimes called the *Haifisch* (Shark), the first Roland fighter was flown as the D I in July 1916. By October, it had been joined by the Roland D II, which replaced the original side "ear" radiators with a pair in the upper-wing center section, turned the exhaust pipe downward, and had other refinements. It was followed in 1917 by the D IIa, which had a 180 hp Argus and a longer fuselage.

Three hundred of these Roland fighters were built, about two-thirds of them by the Pfalz company. In service, they were less popular than the Albatros types because of the Roland's poor forward view and spinning tendency. The first Roland D I arrived at the front in October 1916, and by February 28, 1917, the front had 12 D Is and 22 D IIs. Two D Is and 97 D IIs were on hand the following April 30, with one D I, 41 D IIs and 128 D IIas at the front on June 30.

GERMAN "NIEUPORTS"

The next German fighters to appear at the front were frank copies of the French Nieuport 11 fighters that were proving very successful in 1916. Albatros, Euler, and Siemens-Schuckert produced biplanes incorporating the Nieuport's V strut and smaller lower wing. The Albatros D III, described before, retained the usual Albatros fuselage, but the Euler D I was nearly identical to the French aircraft. Powered by a 100 hp Oberursel rotary and armed with a single

ALBATROS D Va

Spandau gun, the Euler received an order for 50 to be used mainly for training. Two were at the front on October 31, 1916.

The Frankfurt firm completed some of these as modified D II models with the upper wing moved forward. Front-line lists included 11 Euler D IIs at 1916's end, and 16 on February 28, 1917.

Siemens-Schuckert had built an experimental D type in 1916, utilizing a 110 hp Siemens-Halske Sh I, tail and plywood fuselage from their E series and tapered wings with steel-tube spars and steel I struts. This design was abandoned in favor of an outright Nieuport copy using the same Sh I rotary and single Spandau gun as the earlier Siemens E types.

After successful tests in August 1916, 150 Siemens-Schuckert D Is were ordered in November. Deliveries were delayed because of a lag in engine production. A prop spinner was added to a standard D I which appeared at the front in small numbers by April 1917. Since they were now obsolete, they were mostly retained at training fields. Production halted in July 1917 with 94 D Is completed, and the rest delivered as uncovered airframes.

This contract's last aircraft emerged as the D Ia with two guns and larger 15.7 square meter wings. One hundred more Siemens fighters had been ordered in March 1917, but only two were completed before the order was canceled. Known as the D Ib, they had a high-compression 130 hp Sh Ia engine, and 16.2 square meter wings on one, and 19.2 square meters on the other.

Another rotary-powered fighter of this period was the almost unknown Alter biplane shown here with an Oberursel rotary and I struts. No further information is available.

ROLAND D II
Mercedes D III, 160 hp
DIMENSIONS: Span 8.94 m. (29′4″), Lg. 6.93 m. (22′9″), Ht. 3.11 m. (10′2″), Wing Area 21.78 qm. (246.25 sq. ft.)
WEIGHT: Empty 715 kg. (1573 lb.), Gross 925 kg. (2035 lb.)
PERFORMANCE: Speed—Max. 180 km/hr (112 mph), Climb 5000 m./27 min. (16,400′/27 min.)

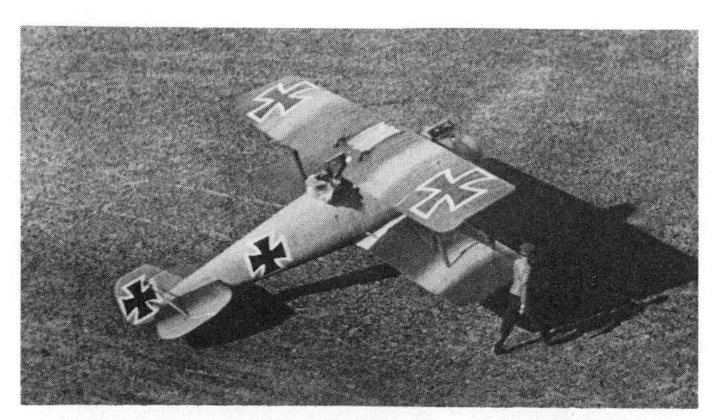

EULER D I
Oberursel U I, 100 hp
DIMENSIONS: Span 7.5 m. (24′7″), Lg. 5.8 m. (19′¼″), Ht. 2.4 m. (7′10½″), Wing Area 13 qm. (140 sq. ft.)
WEIGHT: Not available
PERFORMANCE: Speed—Max. 140 km/hr (87 mph)

EULER D II
Oberursel U I, 100 hp
DIMENSIONS: Span 7.47 m. (24′6″), Lg. 5.94 m. (19′6″), Ht. 2.75 m. (9′)
WEIGHT: Empty 380 kg. (836 lb.), Gross 615 kg. (1353 lb.)
PERFORMANCE: Speed—Max. 145 km/hr (91 mph), Climb 2000 m./9.5 min. (6560′/9.5 min.)

SIEMENS-SCHUCKERT DD5

SIEMENS-SCHUCKERT D I
Siemens Sh I, 110 hp
DIMENSIONS: Span 7.5 m. (24′7″), Lg. 6 m. (19′8″), Wing Area 14.4 qm. (154.94 sq. ft.)
WEIGHT: Empty 444 kg. (976 lb.), Gross 654 kg. (1439 lb.)
PERFORMANCE: Speed—Max. 155 km/hr (97 mph), Climb 1000 m./35 min. (3280′/35 min.)

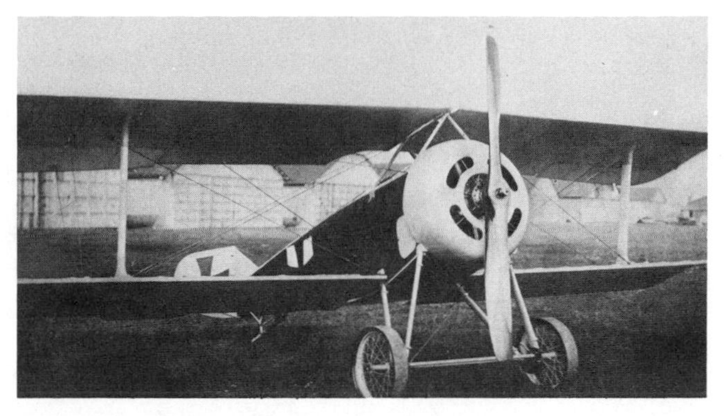

ALTER Fighter

HANSA-BRANDENBURG KD
Austro-Daimler, 160 hp
DIMENSIONS: Span 8.5 m. (27′10½″), Lg. 6.35 m. (20′10″), Wing Area 23.95 qm. (257.7 sq. ft.)
WEIGHT: Empty 672 kg. (1478 lb.), Gross 920 kg. (2024 lb.)
PERFORMANCE: Speed—Max. 187 km/hr (115 mph), Climb 1000 m./3 min. (3280′/3 min.)

THE BRANDENBURG "STAR-STRUTTERS"

One well-known German fighter design of 1916 was never used by German squadrons. Ernst Heinkel actually designed the Hansa-Brandenburg KD (*Kampf Doppeldecker*) for the Austrian Army. "Star-struts," four V struts joined in the middle, braced the square-cut wings.

This single-seater became the standard Austrian fighter type when it was produced by the Austrian Phoenix and the Hungarian UFAG factory and powered by an 160 hp Austro-Daimler. While not adopted by the German Army, a seaplane version, the KDW, served with the German Navy.

A Schwarzlose machine gun in a pod atop the wing was mounted to fire over the propeller on standard Austrian Brandenburg D Is. A larger 1917 version, the Brandenburg L 14, had a simpler bracing arrangement with W struts on each side and another strut from the V's base slanting upward; at first to the upper center section, and then later to the second prototype's fuselage.

HANSA-BRANDENBURG L 14

EXPERIMENTAL FIGHTERS 1916–17

The year following the Albatros fighters' appearance brought would-be rivals from a dozen German firms. Nearly all were unsuccessful, but they do show the numerous configurations available to wartime designers.

One of the earliest efforts was the Germania JM single-seater, whose deep fuselage's flat plywood sides completely filled the gap between the wings. Side radiators cooled the engine, a 150 hp Benz. A similar deep body, with a nose radiator and staggered wings, was used on a Pfalz 1916 design called the D 4, apparently an E V built as a biplane. A Benz powerplant was used, but the later addition of a tail fin still did not make it an acceptable flyer.

More unusual was the Dornier (Zeppelin-Lindau) V 1 designed by Dr. Claudius Dornier as a pusher of metal construction with an aluminum nacelle, steel tail booms, and fabric-covered wings and tail. The plane crashed on November 13, 1916, killing a Lieutenant von Hallerstein, who had failed to fasten his belt and was thrown out of the cockpit.

The most advanced prototype of 1916 was the Fokker V 1 designed by Reinhold Platz. The V originally stood for *Verspannungslos* (no external bracing) but later came to signify *Versuchs* (experimental).

The thick cantilever wings were built with two

BRANDENBURG-PHOENIX D I (Austria)

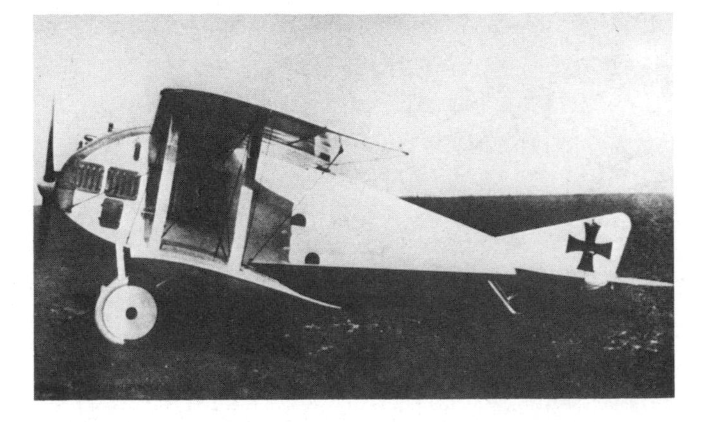

GERMANIA JM

PFALZ D 4

ZEPPELIN-LINDAU V 1
Mercedes D III, 160 hp
DIMENSIONS: Span 10.55 m. (34′7¼″), Lg. 7.10 m. (23′3½″), Ht. 2.05 m. (8′8″), Wing Area 24.6 qm. (264.69 sq. ft.)
Other data not available

FOKKER V 1
Oberursel U I, 100 hp
DIMENSIONS: Span 7.87 m. (25′9½″), Lg. 4.99 m. (16′4″), Ht. 2.74 m. (9′), Wing Area 15 qm. (161.46 sq. ft.)
WEIGHT: Not available
PERFORMANCE: Speed—Max. 178 km/hr (110 mph)

FOKKER V 2

AVIATIK D II
Mercedes D III, 160 hp
DIMENSIONS: Span 8.84 m. (29′), Lg. 6.82 m. (22′4″), Ht. 2.87 m. (9′5″)
WEIGHT: Not available
PERFORMANCE: Speed—Max. 150 km/hr (93 mph)

FRIEDRICHSHAFEN D I

LVG D 12

LVG D III
NAG III, 190 hp
DIMENSIONS: Span 10 m. (32′10″), Lg. 7.53 m. (24′8″), Ht. 2.92 m. (9′7″), Wing Area 26.2 qm. (283 sq. ft.)
WEIGHT: Empty 816 kg. (1795 lb.), Gross 1071 kg. (2356 lb.)
PERFORMANCE: Speed—Max. 175 km/hr (109 mph), Climb 5000 m./25 min. (16,400′/25 min.), Endurance 2 hours

pine-box spars and birch ply covering, with the top wing erected on steel center-section struts. No interplane struts joined it to the smaller tapered lower wing. A 100 hp Oberursel rotary set the diameter of the fabric-covered, steel-tube fuselage, and unique one-piece tail surfaces were used for control along with rotating tips on the upper wing. The wing-shaped axle fairing between the wheels became a standard Fokker feature, but the large spinner and twin guns originally fitted were deleted during flight tests.

Platz also designed the Fokker V 2, which appeared in January 1917 with an inline 120 hp Mercedes, larger wings, and conventional tail surfaces. Although these planes were a great step forward to cleaner design, they were too underpowered for combat applications.

More conventional designs used the standard 160 hp Mercedes D III. Aviatik had been building Halberstadt fighters under license, but its own D II design with a ply-covered fuselage failed late in 1916

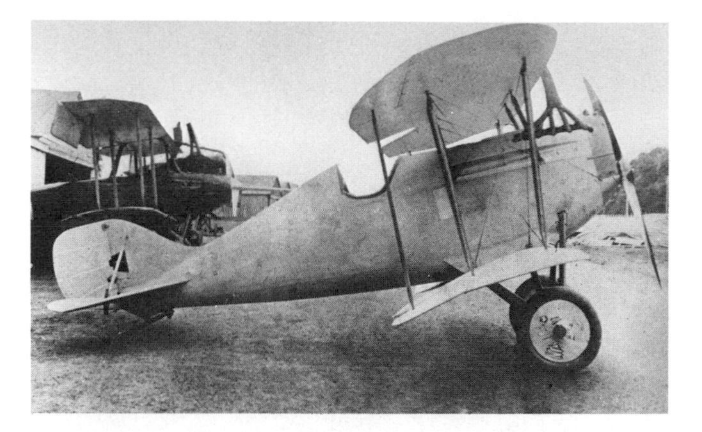

DFW D I

DFW D I modified

AEG D I
Mercedes D III, 160 hp
DIMENSIONS: Span 8.5 m. (27'10½"), Lg. 6.12 m. (20'1"), Ht. 2.65 m. (8'8"), Wing Area 16.14 qm. (176.46 sq. ft.)
WEIGHT: Empty 685 kg. (1507 lb.)Gross 940 kg. (2068 lb.)
PERFORMANCE: Speed—Max. 200 km/hr (124 mph), Climb 1000 m./2 min. (3280'/2 min.) 5000 m./25 min. (16,400'/25 min.)

AEG D I modified

to win acceptance. The same engine was used on the Friedrichshafen D I, which appears so like the Albatros that it could have offered little improvement. On the other hand, LVG, who had been building that Albatros type as their D I, attempted a radical fighter with a 120 hp Mercedes and a unique plywood fuselage filling the wide gap between the wings. Known as the D 10, it proved an unsatisfactory flier, and so LVG followed late in 1916 with the clean-looking D 12. Powered by a 160 hp Mercedes, it was said to do 200 km/hr (124 mph), but after accidental damage was not further developed.

Although an LVG D II visited the front in February 1917, it is uncertain just what the aircraft looked like. An LVG D III was built and made its type test in May 1917. This experimental biplane had an equally experimental 190 hp NAG III engine and wide wings braced by N struts and added interplane struts. Details of later Benz-powered LVG fighters are unavailable.

A flat car-type nose radiator distinguished the DFW D I, which emerged with a ply-covered fuselage, and ailerons on all four wing tips. Later on, it was rebuilt, first with a larger rudder, and then a taller tail and the lower ailerons deleted. It is uncertain how many prototypes were built, but a DFW fighter was reported at the front in June 1917.

Three examples of the little I-strutted AEG D I were built, the first appearing in May 1917 with a small radiator over the nose ahead of the Mercedes, until thin side coolers were added. In August 1917 the first D I went to the front for *Jasta* 14's leader Lieutenant Walter Hoehndorf, who had cooperated in its development. He was killed in this aircraft on September 5, when the wings failed.

This period's smallest fighter was the Rex D 17. This company began with a single-seater biplane in 1915 that was developed into the Rex 6/16 with an 80 hp Oberursel rotary and conventional wings. In 1917, a Rex D 17 was specially built for a German ace with a 100 hp Hansen seven-cylinder rotary, V struts, and a small bottom wing movable for use as ailerons or as a braking flap. After its sponsor's death, the Rex was abandoned.[3]

PFALZ D III

The only new fighter biplane of 1917 to reach large-scale production was the Pfalz D III. Previously, the Eversbusch brothers had concentrated on Morane-type monoplanes and the license-built Roland D I

[3] The ace involved was either Karl Schaefer of *Jasta* 28, killed June 5, 1917, or Werner Voss, *Jasta* 10, killed September 23, 1917.

REX D 17

PFALZ D VI

PFALZ D III prototype

LFG ROLAND D III prototype

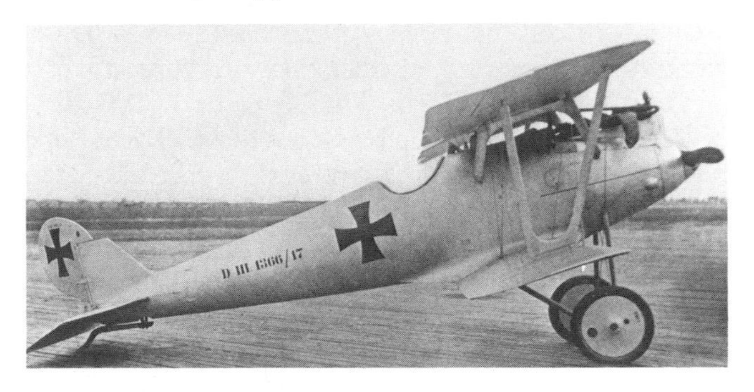

PFALZ D III
Mercedes D III, 160 hp
DIMENSIONS: Span 9.38 m. (30'9"), Lg. 6.95 m. (22'10"), Ht. 2.67 m. (8'9"), Wing Area 22.14 qm. (238.45 sq. ft.)
WEIGHT: Empty 695 kg. (1529 lb.), Gross 932 kg. (2050 lb.)
PERFORMANCE: Speed—Max. 165 km/hr (103 mph), Climb 1000 m./3.25 min. (3280'/3.25 min.) 3000 m./11.75 min. (9840'/11.75 min.), Range 400 km. (248 miles), Service ceiling 5200 m. (17,056')

LFG ROLAND D III

PFALZ D IIIa

LFG ROLAND D V

ALBATROS D VII
Benz Bz III, 200 hp
DIMENSIONS: Span 9.30 m. (30′6″), Lg. 6.61 m. (21′8″), Ht. 2.68 m. (8′9″), Wing Area 20.5 qm. (230.58 sq. ft.)
WEIGHT: Empty 630 kg. (1386 lb.), Gross 855 kg. (1881 lb.)
PERFORMANCE: Speed—Max. 180 km/hr (112 mph), Range 350 km. (217 miles), Service ceiling 6000 m. (19,680′)

and D II, but for its D III an original design of chief engineer Rudolf Geringer was used.

Powered by the reliable 160 hp Mercedes, the D III had a clean fuselage of plywood skin covered by fabric. The wings followed the Nieuport-Albatros style of narrow lower wings, but a heavier two-spar construction avoided the weakness of these types.

In June 1917, the prototype passed its type tests, and the first production aircraft emerged in August. On these planes the original rectangular rudder was replaced by a round balanced surface, and balances added to the ailerons.

Hi-compression D IIIa Mercedes were available late in 1917 for the Pfalz D IIIa. This model may be recognized by the twin guns relocated ahead of the windshield for easy sighting, instead of being housed within the fuselage as before. Another version tested an Austrian-Daimler engine, while the 185 hp Benz Bz III and 200 hp Adler Ad IV were tested on the Pfalz D IV and D V. There were 276 Pfalz D IIIs and 114 Pfalz D IIIas at the front on December 31, 1917, and by April 30, 1918, production was completed and 13 D IIIs and 433 D IIIas were there. These front-line statistics suggest, when attrition rates are considered, a total production of 900 aircraft of these types.

Pfalz also produced a parallel design using a 110 hp Oberursel Ur II rotary, the smaller Pfalz D VI. Tested by Lieutenant Wilhelm Frankl as early as beginning April 1917, it took its acceptance tests in September, but won no contracts.

MORE 1917 BIPLANES

Small-scale production was achieved by the LVG Roland D III, which used the *"Wickelrumpf"* (wrapped fuselage) of the Roland D II, but introduced a gap between the fuselage and top wing, and a narrower lower wing. Powered by the 160 hp Mercedes, the D III prototype appeared in 1917 with its predecessors' small tail fin, but a larger fin was used on the production batch. One was tested by von Richthofen, and not until February 28, 1918, are nine Roland D IIIs included in the front-line list, with only 14 in April. Roland's last effort with its wrapped fuselage was the quite similar D V, but only three were built.

While Albatros dominated the German front-line fighter picture during 1917, the company did study ways to improve its product. The D VI project was a pusher biplane powered by an 180 hp Argus, but no photograph has survived. The D VII, on the other hand, was rather modern-looking for August 1917. This single-seater had equal chord wings with a strut linking ailerons on all four tips. Outstanding feature, however, was the vee-eight Benz Bz IIIb of 195 hp.

This same engine was used in the Aviatik D III, two examples of which were built late in 1917. This design's distinction was the mounting of the lower wing slightly below the fuselage on a small keel. Uncertainty about the Benz's availability prevented orders for either of these types, although the Aviatiks remained around for the D type competition in 1918.

AVIATIK D III
Benz Bz IIIb, 195 hp
DIMENSIONS: Span 9 m. (29′6″), Wing Area 21 qm. (226 sq. ft.)
WEIGHT: Gross 864 kg. (1900 lb.)
PERFORMANCE: Climb 5000 m./20.5 min. (16,400′/20.5 min.)

AVIATIK D III

RICHTHOFEN'S FOKKER F I, 102/17

6.

Triplane Fighters

The first three-winged fighter used in the war was the Sopwith triplane; upon its first appearance in April 1917 the Germans immediately recognized its threat to their air superiority. Engineering studies of the triplane configuration had been made previously in Germany.

A captured specimen was shown to Anthony Fokker late in April, and he was asked by von Richthofen to provide an answer in a hurry. Fokker went back to Schwerin and told Platz to design a triplane with a rotary engine.

Powerplant choice was a matter of availability. Water-cooled Mercedes were in short supply, but Germany had a stock of 110 hp Le Rhone rotaries built under license in Sweden by Thulin.[1] Besides, Fokker was the sole owner of Oberursel, who was shifting production from the U.O model (Gnome copy) to the superior Le Rhone copy the Ur II and III.

Platz quickly turned out the Fokker V 3 with the rotary engine heading a flat-sided short fuselage of fabric-covered welded steel tubing. The lower wing was attached to the fuselage bottom, the second wing to the fuselage top, and the wider-span top wing had ailerons and was erected on inverted steel V struts. Narrow of chord, the wings were unconnected by struts.

After Fokker tried out his new fighter, he wanted to eliminate wing vibration, and asked for a second aircraft with redesigned wings and controls. This became the V 4, which added more span to the middle wing, balances on the ailerons and elevators, and thin interplane struts. Wing span and area was increased from 6.73 m. (22'1") and 16 sq. m. (172 sq. ft.) to 7.1 m. (23'7") and 18.66 sq. m. (201 sq. ft.).

The new design was promptly given a contract in July for 320 triplanes, including three prototypes. The V 4 was accepted as the first, numbered 101/17, and tested to destruction on August 11. Two further prototypes were accepted on August 16, 1917, and sent to *Jagdgeschwader* 1, the new fighter group composed of *Jastas* 4, 6, 10 and 11,[2] and called the Flying Circus because of its frequent moves and the pilots' fondness for garish individual color schemes.

The first two at the front had been labeled Fok. F I, although the official category was Dr (*Dreidecker*) for single-seat fighter triplanes. Werner Voss scored the triplane's first victory flying aircraft 103/17 on August 30, and Manfred von Richthofen used 102/17 when he downed his own 60th on September 1. While slower than the standard Albatros biplanes, the short little triplanes were greatly preferred by the German aces for their rapid climb,

[1] According to Weyl, but Grosz believes these engines were really *Beute,* captured engines. No proof of Swedish deliveries has been found.

[2] With 14 a/c each *Jasta.*

FOKKER V3
Oberursel U I, 100 hp
DIMENSIONS: Span 6.73 m. (22'1"), Lg. 5.73 m. (18'10"), Ht. 2.94 m. (9'8"), Wing Area 16 qm. (172 sq. ft.)
Other data not available

FOKKER V 4

instant response to control and splendid maneuverability. Like nearly all German fighters of this period, the Dr I had two LMG 08/15 guns and 1000 rounds.

The first 24 production Dr Is were delivered in October, but were grounded at the end of the month when two pilots were killed because their top wing broke up during aerobatics. Poor workmanship at Fokker proved to be the cause, and necessary reworking of the top wings reduced November deliveries to six. Front-line Dr I strength amounted to 35 at the end of 1917 and 171 on April 30, 1918, after which production ended and arrival of the famous D VII relegated the colorful triplanes to home-defense units.

Most Dr Is had Le Rhones until the Oberursel copies became available, although superior materials and work caused the service to prefer the imports. The eighth triplane was fitted with a 160 hp Goebel Goe III in October 1917 and was the V 5. The Fokker V 6 had a lengthened fuselage, larger wings and a 120 hp Mercedes, but was a less satisfactory aircraft.

Nearly identical with the Dr I, the Fokker V 7 tried a new 160 hp Siemens-Halske Sh 3 eleven-

FOKKER Dr I
Le Rhone or Oberursel Ur II, 110 hp
DIMENSIONS: Span 7.19 m. (23'7"), Lg. 5.77 m. (18'11"), Ht. 2.95 m. (9'8"), Wing span 18.66 qm. (207 sq. ft.)
WEIGHT: Empty 406 kg. (894 lb.), Gross 586 kg. (1290 lb.), Fuel 73 liters, (19 gal.)
PERFORMANCE: Speed—Max. 165 km/hr (103 mph) at 4000 m. (13,120'), Climb 1000 m./2.9 min. (3280'/2.9 min.) 4000 m./15.15 min. (13,120'/15.15 min.) Endurance 2 hours max., Service ceiling 6000 m. (19,680')

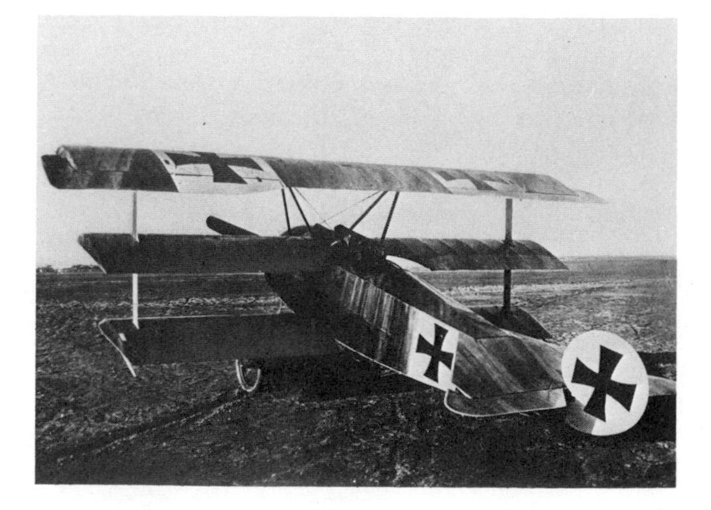

FOKKER V. 6

AEG Dr I
Mercedes D III, 160 hp
DIMENSIONS: Span 9.4 m. (30′10″), Lg. 6.1 m. (20′)
WEIGHT: Empty 710 kg. (1562 lb.), Gross 970 kg. (2134 lb.)
PERFORMANCE: Speed—Max. 170 km/hr (106 mph)

FOKKER V. 7

FOKKER V. 8

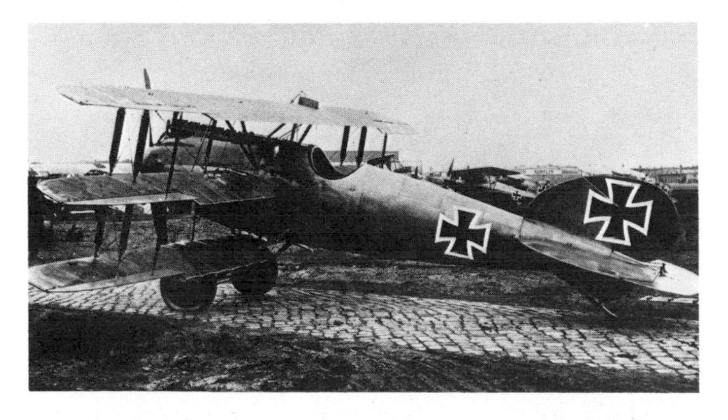

ALBATROS Dr I

cylinder counter-rotating engine with a big four-bladed propeller. Less extreme Dr variants were three fitted with captured 130 hp Clerget engines in April 1918, several with the 110 hp Goebel Goe II, and one with a 145 hp Oberursel Ur III that was said to have a 9500 m. (31,160′) ceiling.

Fokker's success with his triplane had briefly inspired an idea that five wings would be even better. Platz was pained by the idea, but dutifully produced the freakish V 8 triplane which had a 120 hp Mercedes and a pair of biplane wings added amidships. Weyl's book on Fokker describes the results:

> When the V. 8 was completed, Fokker made a short hop in it; His intimates dignified this exercise by calling it a flight. He demanded some modifications; when these were completed he made another exploratory hop. After this, Fokker decided to scrap the aircraft. He realized that Platz was right; but he did not tell him so.
>
> The V. 8 was, of course, entirely a private venture; no type-test commission was confronted with the alarming experience of evaluating it.
>
> Platz confesses that he was immensely relieved when the quintuplane proved such a convincing failure. If it had not been, Fokker would have insisted on aircraft with more and more wings, and Platz would never again have been able to revert to simple and practical aeroplanes.[3]

Fokker had produced the only really successful German *Dreidecker*, but many other efforts were made, with much less success. These were inspired by a circular sent on July 27, 1917, to all aircraft manufacturers, inviting them to inspect the captured Sopwith, and propose answers.

A dozen firms responded with prototypes of some sort, yet except for Fokker's, these designs were failures. Little is known of them except through the accompanying photos, which are usually the only evidence extant. Their inspiration, the Sopwith, was

[3] A. R. Weyl, *Fokker: The Creative Years.* Putnam & Co., London, 1965, by permission of publisher.

DFW Dr I

SCHUTTE-LANZ Dr I

withdrawn from the front by the British in November 1917.

Albatros, it can be seen, met the 1917 requirement by fitting a standard D V fuselage with three 8.7 m. (28′7″) wings with ailerons on all six tips. AEG, DFW, Pfalz and Schutte-Lanz also produced Dr Is by adding three wings to the fuselage of their D fighter prototypes. All used water-cooled 160 hp Mercedes, although the DFW's nose radiator may have cooled instead an experimental 195 hp Koerting.

Euler built no less than six vaguely known triplanes. Their first was a big Mercedes-powered 1916 two-seater with side by side placement, presumably for training. Late in 1917, Euler completed a triplane fighter with a two-row 160 hp Oberursel and V struts. About November 1917, Euler also produced a triplane with a 160 hp Mercedes and I struts and followed with a quadraplane whose top surface was actually full-span ailerons and whose engine was a 100 hp Oberursel.

Next Euler offered a triplane version of the D II with a 180 hp Goebel Goe III rotary. This aircraft was tested in 1918, along with, apparently, another triplane with a 160 hp Oberursel. All these aircraft are very obscure private ventures, with no authentic official designation available.

The next triplanes shown are the Hansa-Brandenburg L 16 designed by Ernst Heinkel with an Austrian engine, and the LFG Roland; which was designated D IV (probably before the Dr form was adopted) and introduced the new "Klinker" construction later successful on the D VI biplane fighter.

Pfalz first attempted to provide a triplane by fitting three wings to a D III fuselage in September 1917. Then they came out with the better known Dr I,

EULER Dr #1

EULER Dr #2

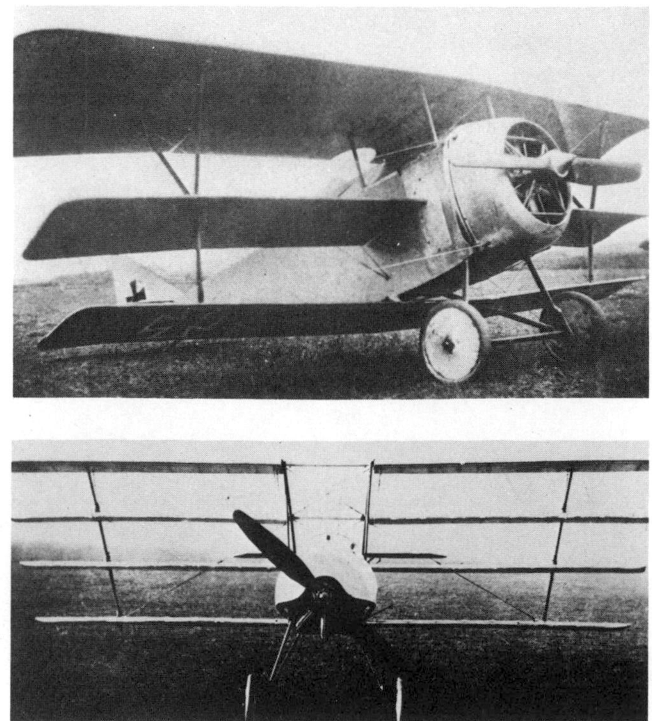

EULER Dr #4

EULER Dr #3

EULER Dr #5

LFG ROLAND D IV
Mercedes D III, 160 hp
DIMENSIONS: Span 13 m. (42'8"), Lg. 7.4 m. (24'3¼")
WEIGHT: Empty 930 kg. (2046 lb.), Gross 1390 kg. (3058 lb.)
PERFORMANCE: Speed—Max. 170 km/hr (105 mph), Service ceiling 6000 m. (19,680')

HANSA-BRANDENBURG L16
Austro-Daimler, 185 hp
DIMENSIONS: 9 m. (29'6"), Lg. 7.21 m. (23'8"), Ht. 3.7 m. (12'2"), Wing Area 33.50 qm. (360.46 sq. ft.)
WEIGHT: Empty 740 kg. (1628 lb.), Gross 935 kg. (2057 lb.)
PERFORMANCE: Speed—Max. 190 km/hr (118 mph), Climb 1000 m./4 min. (3280'/4 min.)

PFALZ Dr I
Siemens Sh III, 160 hp
DIMENSIONS: Span 8.55 m. (28'½"), Lg. 5.5 m. (18'½"), Ht. 2.76 m. (9'½"), Wing Area 17.2 qm. (185 sq. ft.)
WEIGHT: Empty 510 kg. (1020 lb.), Gross 705 kg. (1551 lb.)
PERFORMANCE: Speed—Max. 160 km/hr (99 mph), Climb 1000 m./2 min. (3280'/2 min.) 3000 m./6.2 min. (9840'/6.2 min.)

PFALZ Dr II (Dr I in rear)
Oberursel Ur II, 110 hp
DIMENSIONS: Span 7.2 m. (23'7¼"), Lg. 6 m. (19'8"), Ht. 2.9 m. (9'6")
WEIGHT: Empty 400 kg. (880 lb.), Gross 596 kg. (1311 lb.)
PERFORMANCE: Climb 1000 m./3 min. (3280'/3 min.) 3000 m./10.2 min. (9840'/10.2 min.), Endurance 1½ hours

SIEMENS D Dr I
Siemens-Halske Sh Ia, 2 X 130 hp
DIMENSIONS: Span 10.9 m. (39'9"), Lg. 5.8 m. (19'), Wing Area 30 qm. (322.80 sq. ft.)
WEIGHT: Empty 680 kg. (1496 lb.), Gross 910 kg. (2002 lb.)
Performance data not available

FRIEDRICHSHAFEN D II

NAGLO QUADRAPLANE

designed around the 160 hp Siemens Sh III rotary. Ten of these were ordered for evaluation after type tests in October 1917, and went to the front in April 1918, when engines finally became available. In the meantime, Pfalz developed a lighter Dr II with a 110 hp Oberursel Ur II, and Dr IIa with a 110 hp Siemens Sh I, but neither was satisfactory.

Easily the most unusual triplane was the Siemens-Schuckert D Dr I, which had two 130 hp Siemens Sh Ia rotaries arranged push-pull style on a central nacelle, with twin rudders on an outrigger frame. It crashed on its maiden flight in November 1917.

Vierdecker, or four-winged, fighters were also tried at this time, the first being the Friedrichshafen D II, which had a 160 hp Mercedes D III and also crashed on its first flight in 1917. It was later rebuilt as a triplane. The only aircraft by the Naglo Bootswerft of Berlin had three main wings braced by N struts, and a smaller fourth surface added on a keel below

AEG PE
Benz Bz IIIb, 195 hp
DIMENSIONS: Span 11.2 m. (36'9"), Lg. 6.6 m. (21'8")
WEIGHT: Empty 1182 kg. (2600 lb.), Gross 1412 kg. (3106 lb.)
PERFORMANCE: Speed—Max. 166 km/hr (103 mph), Climb 1000 m./5.8 min. (3280'/5.8 min.)

ALBATROS Dr II
Benz Bz IVb, 180 hp
DIMENSIONS: 10 m. (32'10"), Lg. 6.18 m. (20'3"), Ht. 3.34 m. (10'11½"), Wing Area 26.6 qm. (287 sq. ft.)
WEIGHT: Empty 676 kg. (1487 lb.), Gross 915 kg. (2013 lb.)
PERFORMANCE: Speed—Max. 165 km/hr (102 mph), Range 330 km. (205 miles)

the Albatros-style fuselage. It had a 150 hp Benz and was officially type-tested on May 24, 1918, as the D II, but no more information is available.

The AEG PE (*Panzer-Einsitzer*) of early 1918 is in a class by itself, because this triplane was an armored single-seater made for ground attack work. Powered by a 200 hp Benz vee-eight, the PE had an aluminum-covered fuselage and tubular spars for the I strutted wings. The two guns were supplemented by racks for small bombs.

The Albatros Dr II was perhaps the last German triplane fighter; one can surmise that because it is photographed in the straight cross (*Balkenkreuze*) form adopted May 16, 1918. Essentially it was a D X with Benz vee-eight and three staggered wings with wide I struts and ailerons on all tips.

7.

Fighters in 1918

THE FOKKERS

Germany began 1918 with 1608 fighters at the front, including 1136 Albatros and 390 Pfalz biplanes and 35 Fokker triplanes, but this force was finding its task getting more difficult. On the Western front the Allied air squadrons grew steadily larger and better, and were looking forward to reinforcements from America.

Facing this situation, *IdFlieg,* as the Inspectorate of Aviation troops was known, called a competition to select new fighters. At Berlin's Adlershof airfield, samples of new and old designs would be demonstrated by the aircraft companies and evaluated by combat pilots for the front. The intention was to select the best type with a water-cooled engine, the 160 hp Mercedes being the only one in mass production; and the best with an air-cooled rotary, should the Mercedes supply not hold up. Powerplant production set the primary limit on fighter performance at the time.

About 30 aircraft turned up for the competition, which began with flight trials on January 21, 1918. Albatros had four D Vs to defend the status quo; including one with the still-experimental BMW IIIa engine. The Aviatik D III and Schutte-Lanz D III were there, as well as new offerings from Kondor, Pfalz, Roland, Rumpler, and Siemens-Schuckert.

But without a doubt the key name at Adlershof, and in fact for the rest of 1918's fighter story, would be Fokker. The aggressive Dutchman turned up with eight aircraft, including four biplanes, three triplanes and a monoplane, adding another monoplane later.

Fokker had pursued his usual policy of parallel development of two fighters, one with an air-cooled rotary and the other with the standard water-cooled Mercedes. The first step was the V 9, designed by Reinhold Platz as a biplane with cantilever wings fitted with V struts to reduce flexing. Powered by the

FOKKER V 9

Oberursel, originally of 80 hp and then a 110 hp Ur II (Le Rhone), it used a Dr I fuselage. Dimensions were about 7.5 m. (24′7″) span and 5.9 m. (19′6″) length.

The larger V 11 with a 160 hp Mercedes behind a nose radiator was flown in December 1917 with N strut bracing. It retained the usual Fokker comma-shaped rudder, but in other respects was the first step toward the Fokker D VII. Wing span was originally 8.88 m. (29′1″) and length 6.73 m. (22′). A larger version known as the Fokker V 18 was also built at this time. It was longer (6.93 m. or 22′9″) and distinguished by a curved fin added before the rudder, but was said to be inferior to the V 11.

The N struts were also used on two new rotary-powered prototypes known as the V 13. With a 7.65 m. (25′1″) span and 6.19 m. (20′3″) length, the first had the usual 110 hp Le Rhone type rotary, while the second the new 160 hp Siemens-Halske

FOKKER V 11
Mercedes D III, 160 hp
DIMENSIONS: Span 8.88 m. (29′1½″), Lg. 6.73 m. (22′1″), Ht. 2.91 m. (9′6½″)
WEIGHT: Empty 655 kg. (1445 lb.), Gross 845 kg. (1860 lb.)
PERFORMANCE: Data not available

FOKKER V 13
Le Rhone, 110 hp
DIMENSIONS: Span 7.65 m. (25'1"), Lg. 6.19 m. (20'3½"), Ht. 2.91 m. (9'6½")
WEIGHT: Data not available
PERFORMANCE: Speed—Max. 190 km/hr (118 mph)

FOKKER D VI
Oberursel Ur II, 110 hp
DIMENSIONS: Span 7.7 m. (25'3"), Lg. 5.9 m. (19'4"), Ht. 2.8 m. (9'2"), Wing Area 17.1 qm. (184 sq. ft.)
WEIGHT: Empty 390 kg. (858 lb.), Gross 580 kg. (1276 lb.), Fuel 90 liters (24 gal.)
PERFORMANCE: Speed—Max. 185 km/hr (115 mph), Climb 1000 m./2.5 min. (3280'/2.5 min.) 5000 m./19 min. (16,400'/19 min.), Range 300 km. (186 miles), Service ceiling 5000 m. (16,400')

FOKKER V 18
Mercedes D III, 160 hp
DIMENSIONS: Span 8.91 m. (29'2½"), Lg. 6.93 m. (22'9"), Ht. 2.79 m. (9'2")
WEIGHT: Data not available
PERFORMANCE: Speed—Max 180 km/hr (112 mph)

FOKKER V 33

Sh III. The former engine was replaced by a 145 hp Oberursel Ur III during tests.

All those with prototypes ready came to Adlershof in January, and every company did all that could be done to persuade the pilots to favor their aircraft. Manfred von Richthofen, who was unmoved by any persuasion but performance, tried the V 11 on January 23, 1918. He told Fokker that he liked its performance and maneuverability, but its unstable flying qualities were unsatisfactory. That weekend Fokker had two welders make some quick changes in the aircraft. The fuselage was lengthened, a triangular fin added, and the ailerons modified. After a trial flight showed that the changes had worked, Richthofen was invited to try flying it again. He did, and his enthusiastic endorsement made the Fokker the major winner of the competition, and the modified V 11 became the D VII.

Not only did Fokker win the Mercedes-powered category, but his V 13 was considered by Richthofen the best all-around air-cooled type. While better rates of climb had been achieved by his triplanes and the new Siemens-powered biplanes, the triplanes were too slow and the Siemens engines far from production status. As a safeguard against a shortage of Siemens types and to utilize Dr I parts, limited production was ordered of the D VI (ex-V 13) with the available 110 hp Oberursel (Le Rhone) Ur II rotary.

Sixty were built, the first being delivered April 26, 1918. Twelve replaced the Le Rhone with a Goebel Goe III rotary. Twenty-one were at the front June 30, and 27 two months later. Some served with training units and seven were sold to Austria in August. A revised version of the D VI with a new rudder and unbalanced ailerons was known as the V 33 and used by Fokker as a personal plane.

FOKKER D VII
Mercedes D III, 160 hp
DIMENSIONS: Span 8.9 m. (29′3″), Lg. 6.95 m. (22′10″), Ht. 2.75 m. (9′), Wing Area 20.5 qm. (221 sq. ft.)
WEIGHT: Empty 670 kg. (1474 lb.), Gross 960 kg. (2112 lb.), Fuel 90 liters (24 gal.)

PERFORMANCE: Speed—Max. 189 km/hr (117 mph), Climb 1000 m./4.25 min. (3280′/4.25 min.) 3000 m./13.8 min. (9840′/13.8 min.), Endurance 1½ hours, Service ceiling 5000 m. (16,400′)

The massive success of the Mercedes-powered Fokker D VII dominated the fighter picture. Fokker had received an initial order for 300 D VIIs at a cost of 25,000 marks (about $6250) each, plus a 5 percent royalty on 400 to be built under license by his now chastened rival, Albatros. This firm found that Fokker had no workshop drawings, and so they had to produce their own drawings. Consequently, parts for the Albatros-built D VIIs were not usable on Fokker-built examples, nor were those of the OAW branch any more compatible.

Production deliveries began in April 1918, the first going to *Jagdgeschwader* 1. Von Richthofen himself never flew it in combat, and was killed April 21 in his usual Dr I. The first production D VII had the traditional Cross Patee (Iron Cross) but the others had the new standard *Balkenkreuz* (straight-armed) cross.[1] Front-line D VIIs increased in number from 19 on April 30, 1918, to 828 on August 31, (out of 1691 D types).

Sturdy and maneuverable, the D VII was popular with its pilots and became a familiar sight all along the Western front. Its armament was standard for German fighters; two LMG 08/15 guns from Spandau, each with a 500 round belt. The ammunition was a bit too close to the engine and on hot days incendiary ammunition exploded. When his D VII so ignited accidentally, a *Jasta* 4 pilot bailed out on July 16, 1918, and became one of the first wartime pilots to save his life with a parachute.

Construction was typically Fokker, with a fuselage of steel tubing and wooden wings.[2] Except for the metal engine covering and plywood leading edge, the airframe was covered with fabric. The fuel tank behind the engine had enough to last for 1½ hours at full power, also typical for the period.

A weak point was the 160 hp Mercedes used on most examples, for Allied fighters like the Spad 13 and S.E. 5a had a 220 hp Hispano-Suiza. A 185 hp BMW III installed in the second D VII production ship provided much improved performance, and Fokker got a priority for his fighters, but the engines were slow coming. BMWs were fitted in just 13 of 118 D VIIs delivered by Fokker in May, and 28 of 83 delivered in June. Sometimes the BMW Fokker was called the D VIIF.

Several efforts were made to improve the D VII, including a V 21 of June 1918 which tried tapered wings. Another VII modified by upper wing dihedral and Austrian engine, guns and four-bladed propeller became the V 22. The V 24, however, was the standard airframe tested in April 1918 with a 200 hp

[1] Standardized by April 15, 1918, in the first form, revised May 16, and finalized June 25.

[2] One Albatros example, illustrated here, had a plywood fuselage.

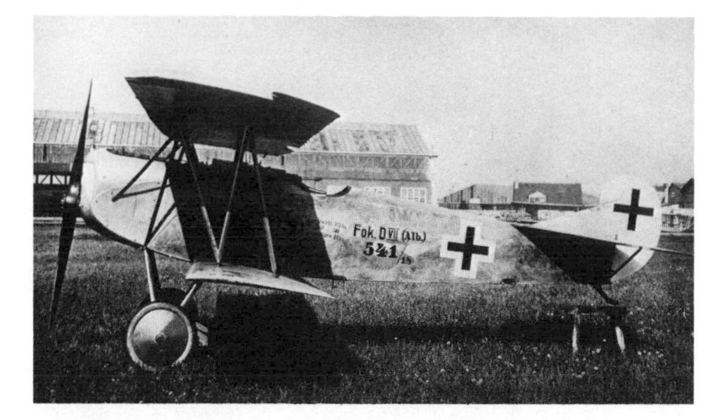

FOKKER D VII (Alb)

FOKKER D VIIF
BMW IIIa, 185 hp
DIMENSIONS: As standard D VII
PERFORMANCE: Speed—Max. 200 km/hr (124 mph), Climb 1000 m./1.75 min. (3280′/1.75 min.) 3000 m./7 min. (9840′/7 min.)

FOKKER V22
Mercedes D IIIau, 160 hp
DIMENSIONS: Span 8.9 m. (28′2″), Lg. 7 m. (23′), Ht. 2.75 m. (9′)
WEIGHT: Empty 700 kg. (1540 lb.), Gross 850 kg. (1870 lb.)
PERFORMANCE: Speed—Max. 186 km/hr (116 mph), Climb 1000 m./3.8 min. (3280′/3.8 min.)

FOKKER V 24
Benz Bz IV U, 200 hp
DIMENSIONS: As V 22
WEIGHT: Gross 1006 kg. (2213 lb.)
PERFORMANCE: Climb 1000 m./3.1 min. (3280′/3.1 min.)
5000 m./23.5 min. (16,400′/23.5 min.)

FOKKER V 34
BMW IIIa, 185 hp
DIMENSIONS: Span 9.01 m. (29′6½″), Lg. 6.93 m. (22′9″),
Ht. 2.79 m. (9′2″)
Weight and performance data not available

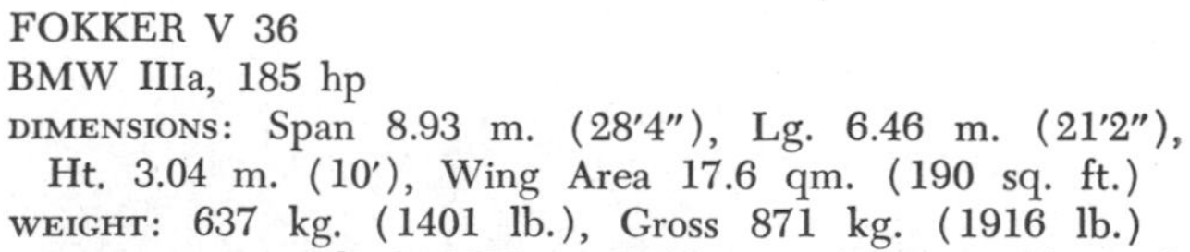

FOKKER V 36
BMW IIIa, 185 hp
DIMENSIONS: Span 8.93 m. (28′4″), Lg. 6.46 m. (21′2″),
Ht. 3.04 m. (10′), Wing Area 17.6 qm. (190 sq. ft.)
WEIGHT: 637 kg. (1401 lb.), Gross 871 kg. (1916 lb.)
PERFORMANCE: Climb 1000 m./1.75 min. (3280′/1.75 min.)
6000 m./18.25 min. (19,680′/18.25 min.)

SIEMENS-SCHUCKERT D IIc
Siemens Sh III, 160 hp
DIMENSIONS: Span 9 m. (29'6"), Lg. 6 m. (19'8"), Wing Area 18.02 qm. (195 sq. ft.)
WEIGHT: Empty 500 kg. (1100 lb.), Gross 750 kg. (1650 lb.)
PERFORMANCE: Not available

SSW D III
Siemens Sh III, 160 hp
DIMENSIONS: Span 8.4 m. (27'6½"), Lg. 5.6 m. (18'4"), Ht. 2.8 m. (9'2"), Wing Area 20 qm. (215 sq. ft.)
WEIGHT: Empty 520 kg. (1144 lb.), Gross 750 kg. (1650 lb.)
PERFORMANCE: Speed—Max. 180 km/hr (112 mph), Climb 1000 m./1.1 min. (3280'/1.1 min.) 4000 m./8 min. (13,-120'/8 min.), Service ceiling 8100 m. (26,575')

Benz Bz IVu. The next step was the V 34 and V 36, both with the 185 hp BMW IIIa behind a new rounded radiator and cowl. The former had the unusual oval tail seen on the rotary-powered V 33, while the V 36 kept the standard D VII tail but introduced a new safety feature; the main fuel supply being carried in the axle fairing. The V 35 variant was simply an unarmed BMW D VII with an additional passenger cockpit added ahead of the pilot. It should not be confused with the V 38, the two-seat observation version described in Chapter 1.

Nothing shows the importance of the D VII more than its being singled out in the armistice agreement that required all D VII aircraft to be turned over to the Allies. Not all were, for Anthony Fokker himself smuggled 120 to the Netherlands, where he resumed manufacturing operations. After the war, D VIIs were widely flown by the Dutch, Swedes, and Swiss, while 142 were shipped to the United States Army. Postwar aviation movies helped establish the D VIIs in the public mind as the symbol of German fighter planes.

SIEMENS-SCHUCKERT FIGHTERS

Fokker's success overshadows the efforts of three firms, Siemens, Roland, and Pfalz, which also had fighters in action in 1918.

The Siemens-Halske Sh III was a unique 160 hp eleven-cylinder rotary in which the crankshaft rotated in one direction at 900 rpms, while the cylinders and crankcase spun in the opposite direction at the same speed. Harold Wolff, as chief designer of the Siemens-Schuckert aircraft affiliate, prepared a barrel-shaped biplane fighter as a test-bed for the new powerplant. The first prototypes were built before the arrival of the engines in June 1917, and were known as the D II, D IIa and D IIb. No photos survive of these, but two more D IIc machines were completed. The first, D7550/17, was flown on October 22, 1917, with short 8.5 m. (27'11") span wings.

It was the next aircraft, D7551/17, that became the production ship's prototype. This D IIc (later D III) had larger 9 m. (29'11") span wings with a narrow chord and spruce near-V struts. The circular fuselage was covered with plywood, and the wings with fabric.

Twenty production D IIIs were ordered in Decem-

SSW D IV
Seimens Sh IIIa, 210 hp
DIMENSIONS: Span 8.35 m. (27'5"), Lg. 5.65 m. (18'6"), Ht. 2.72 m. (8'11"), Wing Area 15.10 qm. (163 sq. ft.)
WEIGHT: Empty 525 kg. (1155 lb.), Gross 750 kg. (1650 lb.)
PERFORMANCE: Speed—Max. 190 km/hr (118 mph), Climb 1000 m./1.9 min. (3280'/1.9 min.) 3000 m./6.4 min. (9840'/6.4 min.), Range 380 km. (235 miles), Service ceiling 6300 m. (20,665')

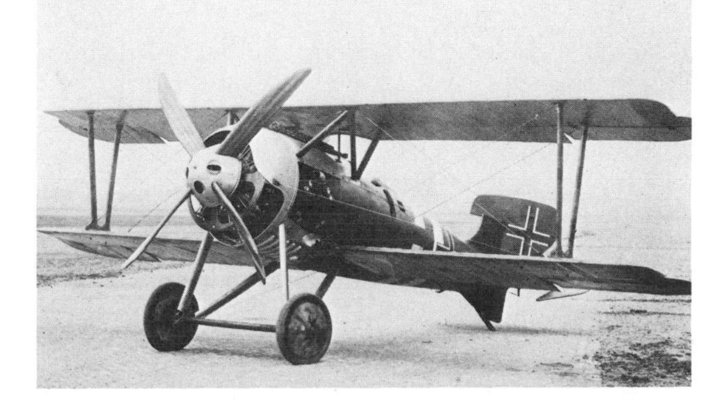

ber 1917 and featured a smaller four-blade propeller, modified tail, ailerons and N center-section struts. They first appeared on January 21, 1918, at the Adlershof competition, and displayed a remarkably fast climb. Despite tricky landing characteristics that caused several crashes, 60 D IIIs were added to 1918 orders.

The Siemens D III went to the front line in April, but had to be withdrawn the following month because the new engines had suffered piston seizure due to overheating and poor quality lubrication. These aircraft were returned to the factory where, along with those still on the assembly line, they were fitted with improved Sh IIIa engines and had the lower half of the metal cowl cut away for better cooling. These D IIIs returned to service, beginning in July, with the home-defense squadrons.

Improved performance was offered by the Siemens-Schuckert D IV, which had a new upper wing with a different airfoil section and the chord reduced to that of the lower wing. The Sh IIIa was now rated at 200 hp and four cooling holes had been cut into the prop spinner. After demonstrating rather spectacular high-altitude climb at Adlershof in June 1918, the D IV was scheduled for quantity production. Another version of the Siemens fighter shown at that time was the D V, with double-bay wing bracing, but nothing more was heard of this type.

Although 260 D IVs were ordered, only 119 were actually completed, of which less than half saw combat service. The first three to arrive at the front went to *Jasta* 14 on August 23, 1918, and made a favorable impression. The leader of the next squadron getting these ships reported on Ocober 5, that the "SSW D IV is without any doubt superior by far to all single-seaters at the front today. This superiority is shown in its climbing and turning ability and particularly in maximum level speeds at altitudes above 4000 m." (13.120′).

LFG ROLAND D VI prototype

LFG ROLAND D VIa prototype

LFG ROLAND D VIb
Benz Bz IIIa, 200 hp
DIMENSIONS: Span 9.4 m. (30′10″), Lg. 6.2 m. (20′4″), Ht. 2.84 m. (9′3″), Wing Area 23 qm. (247.48 sq. ft.)
WEIGHT: Empty 670 kg. (1474 lb.), Gross 820 kg. (1804 lb.), Fuel 83 liters (22 gal.)
PERFORMANCE: Speed—Max. 182 km/hr (114 mph), Landing speed 93 km/hr (58 mph), Climb 1000 m./2.5 min. (3280′/2.5 min.) 3000 m./9 min. (9840′/9 min.) Range 400 km. (248 miles), Service ceiling 6400 m. (21,000′)

ROLAND 1918 FIGHTERS

Although considered inferior to Fokker's designs in the January 1918 competition, the Roland D VI was ordered into small-scale production in case the Fokker D VII supply fell short.

LVG Roland's D VI *Klinkerrumpf* fuselage was covered with spruce planks "clinker" fashion, something like that used in small boats. Powered by a standard 160 hp Mercedes D III, the prototype had unbalanced controls, and a rounded tail with vertical struts. Large balances were added to the ailerons and rudder of the D VIa version.

LFG ROLAND VIb (I struts)

A Family of Roland 1918 prototypes

ROLAND D VII (224/18)

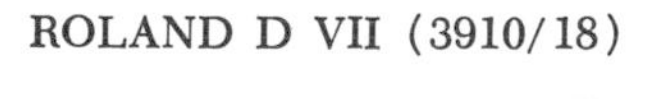

ROLAND D VII (3910/18)

ROLAND D IX (225/18)

ROLAND D IX (3001/18)

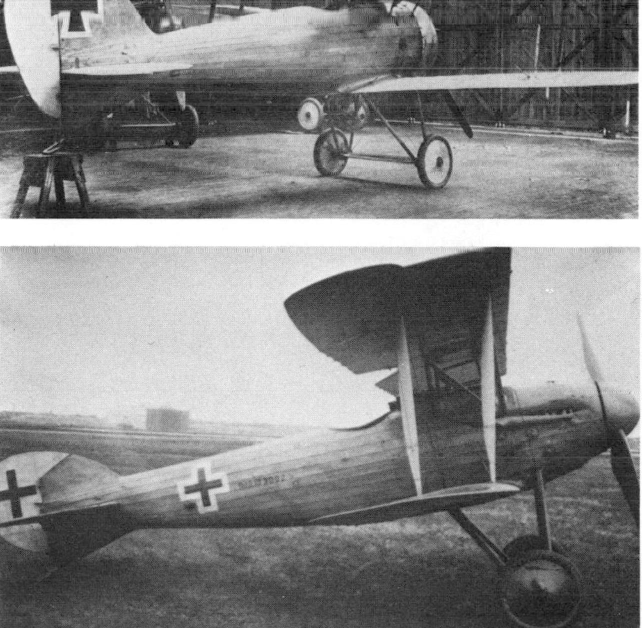

ROLAND D XIII

ROLAND D XIV

ROLAND D XV (3004/18)

ROLAND D IX (revised)

ROLAND D XV (3006/18)

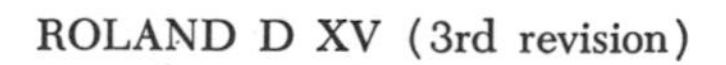

ROLAND D XV (3rd revision)

An elegantly curved and balanced rudder was used along with balanced ailerons on 100 production aircraft. These were designated D VIa with the 160 hp Mercedes, or D VIb when a 200 hp Benz Bz IIIa was used. There were 38 D VIas and 17 D VIbs at the front June 30, 1918 and 58 D VIas and 12 D VIbs on August 30.

Parallel to this production, Roland tested many variations in powerplant and design detail. For example, one photograph here shows a D VI modified by two bays of I interplane struts. A 195 hp eight-cylinder Benz Bz IIIb with direct drive, a larger vertical tail, and unbalanced ailerons distinguished the first Roland D VII of early 1918. A second D VII was built later with a geared Benz, balanced ailerons and the standard D VI tail.

No D VIII version has been identified, but the Roland D IX had the 160 hp Siemens rotary and two-bladed prop. One version had the unbalanced tail and ailerons of the first D VII, and another ler was used on the Sh III, together with the standard added larger control balances.[3] A four-bladed propel-Roland tail on a D IX which appeared in May 1918 with the number 3001/18. This aircraft was the first of a Roland batch trying varied powerplants: 195 hp Koerting Kg III vee-eight on the D XIII (3002/18), a 170 hp Goebel Goe IIIa rotary on the D XIV (3003/18), and a 160 hp Mercedes D IIIa on the D XV (3004/18), the latter with a new wing rigging that added more stagger and deleted bracing wires. Another D XV, Nr. 3006/18, had new wings braced by I struts, no wires, and a 185 hp BMW.

[3] It is questionable whether these preceded or followed No. 3001/18, but the control surfaces and wing crosses suggest the former. The D VIII was supposed to have a Bz IIIb engine.

No explanation of the missing D numbers is available, but D XV is also painted on the flat plywood sides of an entirely different Roland single-seater with a 200 hp Benz Bz IIIa and steel N struts of Fokker D VII style. No further information on this machine is available.

PFALZ 1918 FIGHTERS

Although Pfalz was unsuccessful in the first Adlershof competition, they did succeed in getting their D XII design into widespread use at the front before the war's end.

Four Pfalz aircraft had been presented at the January 1918 trials; two standard Mercedes-powered D IIIas, the 110 hp Oberursel-powered D VI of 1917, and the new D VII with a 160 hp Siemens-Halske rotary. This single-seater differed from preceding Pfalz types in having stronger double struts, rather than V struts. No contract was won, but in the spring Pfalz produced a second version with an Oberursel rotary in a Fokker-shaped cowling and balanced ailerons. The D VII was also tried with a Goebel rotary.

More success was obtained with the double-bay Pfalz D VIII which first appeared with a 160 hp Siemens-Halske Sh III, and in that form received orders for 120. Production machines added a spinner to the four-bladed propeller. One example is shown here with a 160 hp Goebel Goe III in a Fokker-style cowl, balanced ailerons, and double-bay N struts, while another tried an Oberursel rotary.

Water-cooled fighters were more popular with service pilots, however, so Pfalz developed a new type

PFALZ D VII
Siemens Sh III, 160 hp
DIMENSIONS: Span 7.52 m. (24′8″), Lg. 5.65 m. (18′6″), Ht. 2.85 m. (9′4″), Wing Area 17.12 qm. (184 sq. ft.)
WEIGHT: Empty 520 kg. (1144 lb.), Gross 715 kg. (1573 lb.)
PERFORMANCE: Speed—Max. 165 km/hr (103 mph), Climb 5000 m./14 min. (16,400′/14 min.)

PFALZ D VII (2nd version)
Oberursel Ur III, 145 hp
DIMENSIONS: Span 8.1 m. (26′7″), Lg. 5.55 m. (18′3″). Ht. 2.7 m. (8′10″), Wing Area 17.2 qm. (186 sq. ft.)
WEIGHT: Empty 483 kg. (1064 lb.), Gross 678 kg. (1624 lb.)
PERFORMANCE: Climb 5000 m./15 min. (16,400′/15 min.), Endurance 1½ hours

PFALZ D VIII
Siemens-Halske Sh III, 160 hp
DIMENSIONS: Span 7.52 m. (24′8″), Lg. 5.65 m. (18′6″), Ht. 2.75 m. (9′), Wing Area 17.2 qm. (186 sq. ft.)
WEIGHT: Empty 543 kg. (1195 lb.), Gross 738 kg. (1624 lb.)
PERFORMANCE: Speed—Max. 180 km/hr (112 mph), Climb 5000 m./15 min. (16,400′/15 min.), Endurance 1½ hours

PFALZ D VIII (with Goe III)

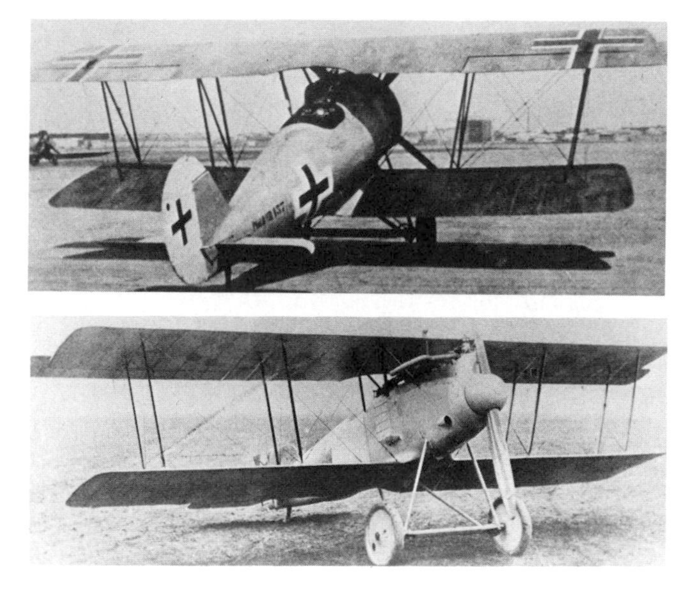

PFALZ D XI

PFALZ D XII
Mercedes D IIIaw, 180 hp, BMW IIIa, 195 hp
DIMENSIONS: Span 9 m. (29′6″), Lg. 6.35 m. (20′10″), Ht. 2.7 m. (8′10″), Wing Area 21.7 qm. (236 sq. ft.)
WEIGHT: Empty 722 kg. (1588 lb.), Gross 902 kg. (1985 lb.)
PERFORMANCE: Speed—Max. 180 (185) km/hr (112/115 mph), Climb 1000 m./2.5 min. (3280′/2.5 min.) 3000 m./11.3 min. (9840′/11.3 min.)

PFALZ D XIV
Benz Bz IVa, 195 hp
DIMENSIONS: Span 10 m. (32′10″), Lg. 6.32 m. (20′9″), Ht. 2.7 m. (8′10″), Wing Area 25.43 qm. (275 sq. ft.)
WEIGHT: 842 kg. (1853 lb.), Gross 1032 kg. (2270 lb.)
PERFORMANCE: Speed—Max. 190 km/hr (118 mph), Climb 1000 m./2.2 min. (3280′/2.2 min.) 3000 m./11 min. (9840′/11 min.)

in that category. This design first appeared with a 160 hp Mercedes and ear-type side radiators on a D III style fuselage and double-bay D VIII wings. Apparently known as the D XI, it appeared in the spring, 1918, with large balances on the ailerons and rudder.

This led to the famous Pfalz D XII, which used double N struts and a car-type nose radiator. A small batch was begun in March 1918, and appeared in time for the second Adlershof fighter competition begun May 27. The original bulky tail was soon replaced with a gracefully curved vertical surface.

The D XII appeared at Adlershof with different engines; a 170 hp Mercedes D IIIa, 180 hp Mercedes D IIIau, 195 hp BMW IIIa and the 195 hp Benz Bz IIIbou (for D XIIa). In addition, there was the slightly larger Pfalz D XIV with a 200 hp Benz Bz IVu. This did not reach production. While the BMW D XII had the best performance, availability dictated use of the standard Mercedes D III in most production ships.

On June 30, 1918, Pfalz had five D XII, 14 D VIII and 302 older D III and D IIIa fighters at the front. By August 31, there were 168 D XII, 19 D VIII, and 166 D IIIa single-seaters. Although a satisfactory type, the D XII was never as popular as the Fokker D VII, although some 800 are estimated to have been built.

The last Pfalz fighter was the D XV, which was tested in October 1918. Powered by a 185 hp BMW IIIa, it had its fuselage erected above the lower wings on N struts. The first example had I struts, but these were replaced by a single pair of N struts, without bracing wire. Rectangular lower wing tips were rounded in a later version. Two experimental ships made were to be followed by a production series, although it appears that few of these were completed.

PFALZ D XV (prototype)

PFALZ D XV
BMW IIIa, 185 hp
DIMENSIONS: Span 8.6 m. (28′3″), Lg. 6.5 m. (21′4″), Ht. 2.7 m. (8′10″), Wing Area 20 qm. (215 sq. ft.)
WEIGHT: Empty 745 kg. (1639 lb.), Gross 925 kg. (2035 lb.)
PERFORMANCE: Speed—Max. 200 km/hr (124 mph), Climb 3000 m./10.5 min. (9840′/10.5 min.)

OTHER 1918 EXPERIMENTAL FIGHTERS

Some 13 different companies offered single-seat biplanes in 1918, and the accompanying photos show the great variety of design configurations attempted. They have in common their failure to displace the dominant Fokkers.

Once the leader of German fighter development, Albatros completely failed in its 1918 efforts. The

ALBATROS D IX
Mercedes D IIIa, 180 hp
DIMENSIONS: Span 10.4 m. (34′1¼″), Lg. 8.65 m. (28′4″), Ht. 2.75 m. (9′¼″), Wing Area 24 qm. (258 sq. ft.)
WEIGHT: Empty 677 kg. (1489 lb.), Gross 897 kg. (1973 lb.)
PERFORMANCE: Speed—Max. 155 km/hr (96 mph), Climb 1000 m./4 min. (3280′/4 min.), Range 230 km. (140 miles)

ALBATROS D X
Benz Bz IIIb, 195 hp
DIMENSIONS: Span 9.9′ (32′6″), Lg. 6.18 m. (20′3″), Ht. 2.74 (9′), Wing Area 20.9 qm. (225 sq. ft.)
WEIGHT: Empty 661 kg. (1454 lb.), Gross 900 kg. (1980 lb.)
PERFORMANCE: Speed—Max. 180 km/hr (112 mph), Range 350 km. (217 miles)

ALBATROS D XI
Siemens Sh III, 160 hp
DIMENSIONS: Span 8 m. (26′3″), Lg. 5.58 m. (18′4″), Ht. 2.86 m. (9′5″), Wing Area 18.5 qm. (199 sq. ft.)
WEIGHT: Empty 494 kg. (1087 lb.), Gross 686 kg. (1516 lb.)
PERFORMANCE: Speed—Max. 190 km/hr (119 mph), Climb 5000 m./18 min. (16,400′/18 min.), Range 275 km. (170 miles)

first 1918 design was the Mercedes-powered Albatros D IX with Spad-style double-bay wing struts and a flat-sided and -bottomed fuselage easier to produce, but lacking the good-looking streamlined effect of the previous Albatros. Speed was, in fact, inferior to older types, and its story ended with a wing failure on January 18, 1918.

Albatros next built a prototype batch with the flat-bottomed fuselage, beginning with the D X, serial Nr. 2206/18. Powered by a 195 hp Benz IIIb vee-eight, the D X came out in April 1918 with a pair of wide I struts between the wings. It is uncertain whether the next serial number in this batch was assigned to a second D X or to the very similar Albatros Dr II triplane.

First Albatros designs to use a rotary engine were the two D XI fighters powered with the 160 hp Siemens-Halske Sh III in a metal cowl specially formed to improve cooling. Again I struts were used, but bracing wires were replaced by a pair of struts connecting the fuselage and lower wing. A four-bladed propeller and balanced ailerons were used on the first D XI, 2208/18, while the second used a two-bladed propeller and plain ailerons.

Standard 160 hp Mercedes D IIIs were used on both Albatros D XIIs, very conventional-looking aircraft. The first example had plain ailerons, but the second, Nr. 2211/18, had balanced controls and was the last Albatros fighter ever built. Like the D X and D XI, it participated in the second D-type competition in June 1918, but failed to win a contract. Albatros also planned a Mercedes-powered D XIII and BMW-powered D XIV, but neither was completed.

ALBATROS D XII
Mercedes DIII, 160 hp
DIMENSIONS: Span 8.2 m. (26′11″), Lg. 5.785 m. (19′), Ht. 2.8 m. (9′2″), Wing Area 19.84 qm. (213.47 sq. ft.)
WEIGHT: Empty 580 kg. (1276 lb.), Gross 760 kg. (1672 lb.)
PERFORMANCE: Speed—Max. 180 km/hr (112 mph), Climb 1000 m./2 min. (3280′/2 min.), Service ceiling 8000 m. (26,240′)

ALBATROS D XI (2209/18)

KONDOR D I

KONDOR D II
Oberursel Ur II, 110 hp
DIMENSIONS: Span 7.6 m. (24'11"), Lg. 4.86 m. (15'11"), Ht. 2.41 m. (7'11"), Wing Area 13.84 qm. (148.9 sq. ft.)
WEIGHT: Empty 368 kg. (812 lb.), Gross 548 kg. (1208 lb.)
PERFORMANCE: Speed—Max. 165 km/hr (103 mph), Climb 5000 m./33 min. (16,400'/33 min.)

KONDOR D II

With an experienced firm like Albatros so unsuccessful, it is not surprising that a smaller firm like Essen's Kondor Flugzeug-Werke was no more fortunate. Late in 1917, Kondor began two fighter designs; a light D I biplane with a 110 hp Oberursel rotary, ply-covered round fuselage, and V struts, and a triplane powered by a 160 hp Mercedes. When triplanes seemed *passé,* the aircraft was rebuilt as a biplane with an unusual strut arrangement. Labeled D 7 by the company, it received no official recognition.

Instead Kondor proceeded with a development of the D I with new wings. Retaining the 110 hp Oberursel, designer Walter Rethel's new D II project had ailerons on all four wing tips and used conventional double struts. Both the D I and D II competed in the second Adlershof meet without success. Another effort was made with the Kondor D 6 with a 140 hp Oberursel Ur III, whose distinctive feature was omission of the upper wing's center section to improve the pilot's visibility.

KONDOR D 6
Oberursel Ur III, 140 hp
DIMENSIONS: Span 8.25 m. (27'1"), Lg. 5.8 m. (19'), Ht. 2.53 m. (8'4"), Wing Area 13.8 qm. (149 sq. ft.)
WEIGHT: Empty 420 kg. (924 lb.), Gross 645 kg. (1419 lb.)
PERFORMANCE: Data not available

KONDOR D 7
Mercedes D III, 160 hp
DIMENSIONS: Span 8.5 m. (27'11"), Lg. 6.2 m. (20'4"), Ht. 2.3 (7'6"), Wing Area 15.7 qm. (169.5 sq. ft.)
WEIGHT: Empty 590 kg. (1298 lb.), Gross 785 kg. (1727 lb.)
PERFORMANCE: Data not available

Strong-looking N struts were used with the standard 160 hp Mercedes on the Schutte-Lanz D III built for the first fighter competition in January 1918, but its slow climb did nothing to improve its experimental status. A Benz-powered D IV was constructed, but it offered no improvement. May 1918 saw the Schutte-Lanz D VII, like the D III with Mercedes D IIIa, four ailerons and a nose radiator. It reappeared later with minor changes.

Euler also offered experimental fighters in the spring of 1918, beginning by rebuilding its Mercedes D III-powered triplane as a biplane with I struts. Later, V struts were fitted to this aircraft, but in May 1918 Euler also tested a biplane with I struts, no fin, and a four-bladed propeller on a 160 hp Siemens Sh III rotary. Like nearly all Euler designs, these fighters received neither official acceptance or designations.

At the Adlershof trials in both January and June, attention was attracted to Rumpler's first fighter. Powered by the standard Mercedes D III, it went thru a lengthy evolution. The Rumpler 7D 1 first emerged with a highly streamlined fuselage, I struts and its engine hidden by a cowl that ran back to the top wing. Visibility was not helped by that arrangement, so later machines had the conventional gap between top wing and fuselage, and left the engine cylinders open for easier maintenance. The next version shown has conventional double struts,

SCHUTTE-LANZ D III

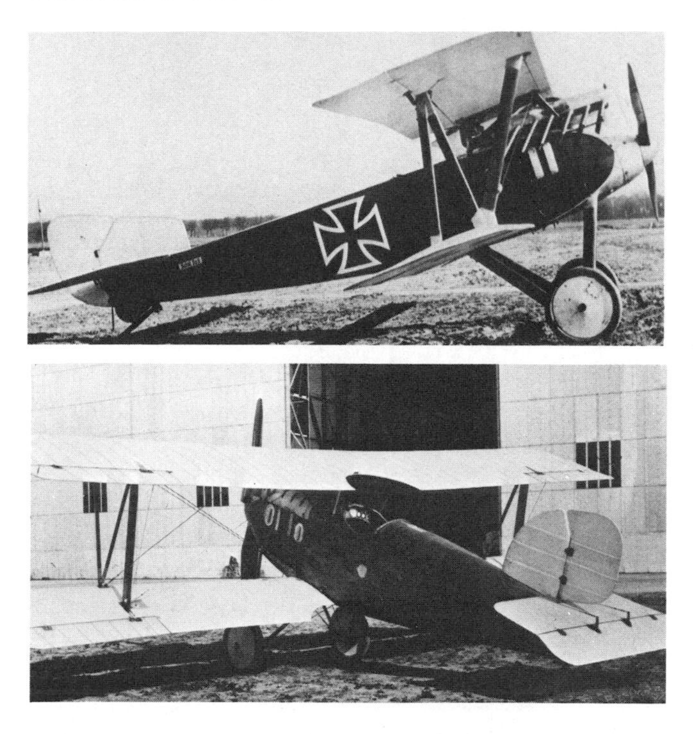

SCHUTTE-LANZ D VII (May 1918)

EULER D with Mercedes

SCHUTTE-LANZ D VII (October 1918)

EULER D with Sh III

RUMPLER 7D 1
Mercedes D III, 160 hp
DIMENSIONS: Span 8.2 m. (26'11"), Lg. 5.9 m. (19'4"), Ht. 2.6 m. (8'6")
WEIGHT: Not available
PERFORMANCE: Speed—Max. 175 km/hr (109 mph), Service ceiling 7000 m. (22,960')

RUMPLER 7D 7

RUMPLER 7D 8

as the prototype series rose from 7D 1 to 7D 6.

Then came the 7D 7, which reverted to single struts but with a narrow width, and replaced the center-section radiator with two side coolers. It was followed in May by the 7D 8, which differed only in wire bracing. Fifty Rumplers were then ordered as the D I (8D 1), differing only by balanced ailerons and a triangular vertical tail. Two participated in the June D-types competition, and another got a 185 hp BMW IIIa and demonstrated the highest ceiling of any fighter at the third Adlershof competition, October 1918.

The June 1918 competition also saw the first appearance of the LVG fighters of 1918, all of which used the 195 hp Benz Bz IIIb vee-eight. The LVG D IV came out early that year with a single-spar lower wing and V struts. It was followed by the odd LVG D V, one of the ugliest fighters ever introduced. It featured a wide wing at the bottom braced with thick struts. The narrow top surface acted as ailerons, pivoting outboard of the center section. Little more attractive was the LVG D VI, whose features are better seen than described.

The same Benz engine was used by the Aviatik D VI tested in July 1918. It featured double-bay wings, four-bladed propeller, and nose radiator. A higher tail was added to the similar Aviatik D VII.

Daimler Motoren-Gesellschaft's first design by Hans Klemm was a streamlined fighter using the new 185 hp Mercedes D IIIb vee-eight. Appearing in May 1918 as the D I, the 20 built also had the company label of L 6. They were followed by a single two-seat fighter prototype called the L 8. The next Daimler biplane was the L 9, an experimental with new struts and tail.

RUMPLER 7D 4 (designation uncertain)

This section concludes with the last remaining 1918 D types. Three obscure aircraft were of such conventional design that few words need be added to their photos. Nothing original is seen on the DFW F 34 (probably officially a D II), or on the MFW D I designed by Hillmann for Markische Flugzeug-Werke and powered by the 195 hp Benz Bz IIIb vee-eight. LVG's former chief designer, Franz Schneider, built an Oberursel-powered single-seater said to have good climb and maneuverability, yet its only innovations were placing the ailerons on the lower wings and changing incidence in flight.

Credit for originality goes to Rudolf Geringer's design for Hanseatische Flugzeug-Werke (HFW). The world's first twin-engine single-seat fighter biplane, and therefore an ancestor of the famous P-38 and Me 262, it had a 20 mm. gun and two 100 hp Oberursel rotaries. On a ground test an engine broke out of the strut framework, destroying the aircraft.

Of more immediate significance was the first all-

RUMPLER D I (8D 1)
Mercedes D IIIa, 170 hp
DIMENSIONS: Span 8.42 m. (27′7″), Lg. 5.75 m. (18′10″), Ht. 2.56 m. (8′5″), Wing Area 16 qm. (173 sq. ft.)
WEIGHT: Empty 615 kg. (1353 lb.), Gross 805 kg. (1771 lb.)
PERFORMANCE: Speed—Max. 180 km/hr (112 mph), Climb 5000 m./13.2 min. (16,400′/13.2 min.), Range 360 km. (223 miles), Service ceiling 8000 m. (26,240′)

LVG D V

AVIATIK D VI
Benz Bz IIIb, 195 hp
DIMENSIONS: Span 9.66 m. (31′8″), Lg. 6 m. (19′8″)
WEIGHT: Empty 750 kg. (1650 lb.), Gross 940 kg. (2068 lb.)
PERFORMANCE: Speed—Max. 185 km/hr (115 mph), Climb 5000 m./17 min. (16,400′/17 min.)

LVG D IV
Benz Bz IIIb, 195 hp
DIMENSIONS: Span 8.5 m. (27′11″), Lg. 6.28 m. (20′7″), Ht. 2.7 m. (8′10″), Wing Area 18.06 qm. (195 mph)
WEIGHT: Empty 680 kg. (1496 lb.), Gross 935 kg. (2057 lb.)
PERFORMANCE: Climb 5000 m./28 min. (16,400′/28 min.)

LVG D VI

AVIATIK D VII
Benz Bz IIIb, 195 hp
DIMENSIONS: Span 9.66 m. (31′8″), Lg. 2.5 m. (8′2″)
WEIGHT: Empty 745 kg. (1639 lb.), Gross 945 kg. (2079 lb.)
PERFORMANCE: Speed—Max. 190 km/hr (118 mph), Climb 6000 m./24 min. (19,680′/24 min.)

DAIMLER D I (L 6)

DAIMLER L 8

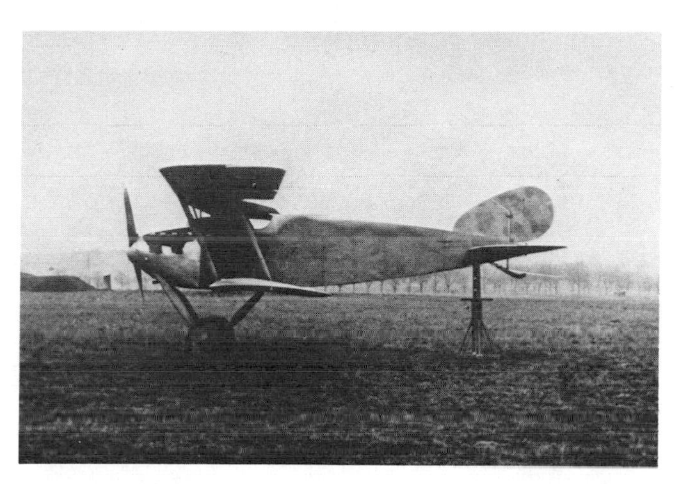

DAIMLER D II (L 9)

DFW F 34
Mercedes D III, 160 hp
DIMENSIONS: Span 9.08 m. (29′9″), Lg. 5.5 m. (18′½″), Wing Area 23 qm. (248 sq. ft.)
WEIGHT: Data not available
PERFORMANCE: Speed—Max. 177 km/hr (110 mph), Climb 1000 m./2 min. (3280′/2 min.) 5000 m./20 min. (16,400′/20 min.)

MFW D I

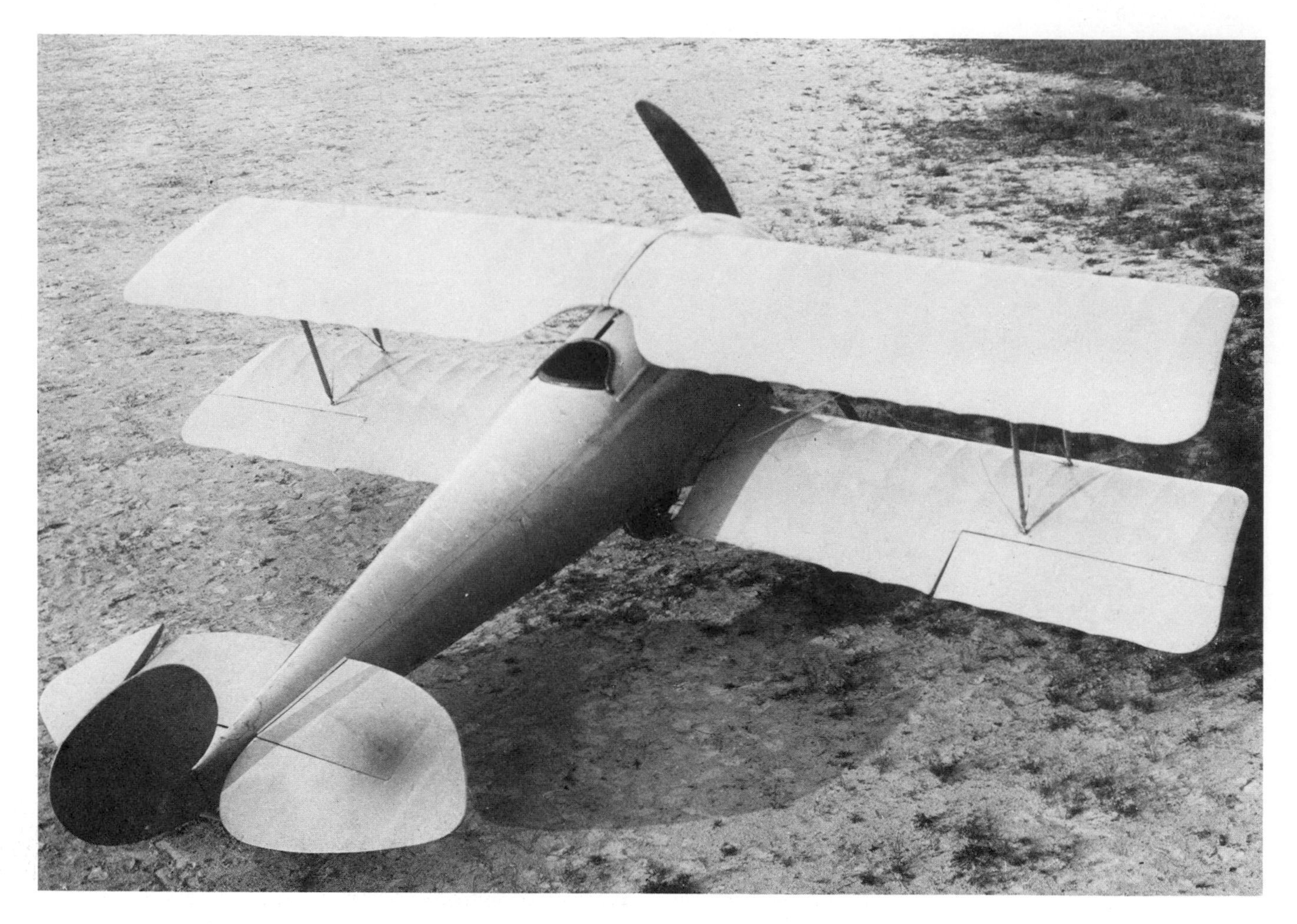

SCHNEIDER Fighter

HFW Fighter

HFW (under construction)

DORNIER (ZEPPELIN-LINDAU) D I
BMW IIIa, 185 hp
DIMENSIONS: Span 7.8 m. (25'7"), Lg. 6.4 m. (21'), Ht. 2.6 m. (8'6"), Wing Area 18.6 qm. (200 sq. ft.)
WEIGHT: Empty 725 kg. (1600 lb.), Gross 885 kg. (1915 lb.)
PERFORMANCE: Speed—Max. 200 km/hr (124 mph), Landing Speed 80 km/hr (50 mph), Service ceiling 8100 m. (26,575')

AEG DJ I
Benz Bz IIIb, 195 hp
DIMENSIONS: Span 10 m. (32'10"), Lg. 6.6 m. (21'8"), Ht. 3 m. (9'10")
WEIGHT: Empty 1185 kg. (2607 lb.), Gross 3014 kg. (6631 lb.)
PERFORMANCE: Speed—Max. 180 km/hr (112 mph)

metal biplane fighter designed by Claudius Dornier for Zeppelin-Lindau. The Duralumin structure was covered by sheet metal, except for fabric on the control surfaces and rear third of the fully cantilever wings. No struts at all were used between the wings, and only one for each wheel, while the fuel tank below could be dropped if a fire began.

This D I first flew June 4, 1918, but on July 3 a test ship lost a wing at Adlershof, killing JG 1 leader, Hauptmann Reinhardt. After the war, two examples went to the United States for tests by the Army and Navy.

Only one DJ-class aircraft—armored single-seat ground-attack biplane—was built. Developed from the PE triplane, the large AEG DJ I was first flown in June 1918 with double-bay I struts, aluminum-covered fuselage, and four-bladed propeller for its Benz. Like the previous types in this section, it saw no production.

8.

Monoplane Fighters of 1918

If inspiration for future fighter progress is valued, then Germany's most important wartime aviation contribution was the new monoplanes that were used in 1918.

The first of these to appear was the Junkers J 7, which may be considered the prototype of the world's first all-metal cantilever monoplane fighter in service, the Junkers D I. Constructed of riveted Duralumin tubing covered by corrugated metal, this low-wing single-seater was powered by a 160 hp Mercedes D III. When first flown September 17, 1917, the J 7 had a high headrest for safety, a long exhaust pipe down the right side, a radiator atop the cylinder top, and pivoting wing tips for control, instead of ailerons.

Hoping to combine the engineering talent of Junkers with Anthony Fokker's practical experience, the German government promoted a merger in October 1917 called the Junkers Fokker-Werke AG (Jfa). In fact, there was really little real collaboration between those two very different personalities, and Fokker's aid seemed limited mainly to occasional test flying. On one of these flights, the J 7 crashed. It was then rebuilt with normal balanced ailerons, a nose radiator, and short exhaust pipe. In this form it was flown by Fokker at the first Adlershof fighter competition on January 22, 1918. The propeller broke during flight, eliminating the J 7 from the competition later won by the Fokker D VII.

The Jfa J 7 was rebuilt again and was seen in its final form in April 1918 with rounded wing tips and slightly taller rudder. It was followed in May by the J 9 which had modified landing gear, uncovered turnover bars, and was armed with two Spandau guns ahead of the cockpit.

This J 9 appeared at the June Adlershof competition, and went into small-scale production as the Junkers D I, since the D designation, previously applied to biplane fighters, now stood for any fighter. While early examples had the J 7's Mercedes and short fuselage, the remainder were longer, and used a 185 hp BMW IIIa. Forty-one Junkers D Is were built, yet it is uncertain whether any were used in

JUNKERS J 7
Mercedes D III, 160 hp
DIMENSIONS: Span 9 m. (29′6″), Lg. 6.7 m. (22′), Ht. 3.31 m. (10′11″), Wing Area 11.7 qm. (126 sq. ft.)
WEIGHT: Empty 578 kg. (1272 lb.), Gross 765 kg. (1683 lb.)
PERFORMANCE: Speed—Max. 206 km/hr (128 mph), Range 310 km. (192 miles)

JUNKERS J 7 (original form)

JUNKERS D I (J 9)
BMW IIIa, 185 hp
DIMENSIONS: Span 9 m. (29′6″), Lg. 7.25 m. (23′9″), Ht. 2.6 m. (8′6″), Wing Area 14.8 qm. (159.25 sq. ft.)
WEIGHT: Empty 654 kg. (1439 lb.), Gross 835 kg. (1920 lb.)
PERFORMANCE: Speed—Max. 240 km/hr (149 mph), Climb 1000 m./2.3 min. (3280′/2.3 min.) 6500 m./25 min. (21,320′/25 min.), Range 480 km. (298 miles), Service ceiling 7600 m. (21,980′)

FOKKER V 17

combat on the Western front, although they were flown in 1919 by *Geschwader Sachsenberg* in the Baltic countries.

FOKKER MONOPLANES

Anthony Fokker built a number of cantilever monoplanes designed by Reinhold Platz, using his customary fabric-covered steel-tube fuselages and wooden wings. The first of these was the Fokker V 17, which resembled a mid-wing monoplane version of the Dr I triplane. It had the same 110 hp Oberursel Ur II rotary, a similar fuselage and tail, and a 9.5 m. (31′4″) span wing constructed of two wooden box spars covered with plywood.

Fokker demonstrated this single-seater at Adlershof on January 27, 1918, but felt better performance might be achieved with the 160 hp Mercedes D III. It is said that he phoned Platz on a Saturday night to tell him he wanted such a monoplane, and that Platz designed and built the Fokker V 20 and had it ready for its first flight the following Saturday. Surely this must be a record of some sort! The V 20 had squared-off lines like the V 11 (prototype D VII), with balanced ailerons and fabric covering behind

FOKKER V 20

FOKKER V 23

FOKKER V 26

FOKKER V 25

the rear wing spar, and a nose radiator and upward-turned exhaust pipe. It was not, however, ever submitted for official tests.

The next step was the Fokker V 23, which also used the Mercedes, but had rounded tips and inset ailerons on its two-spar, ply-covered wing. The exhaust pipe was turned downward, a pilot's head-rest added and the usual Fokker "comma" rudder retained.

Fokker offered five different monoplanes at the June 1918 Adlershof meet, where a dozen companies turned out some 20 other designs to rival the champion, the Fokker D VII. Along with the V 23 mid-wing monoplane, Fokker had the low-wing V 25, and the V 26, V 27 and V 28 high-wing parasol aircraft.

The mid-wing configuration of earlier designs had handicapped visibility, so Fokker's V 25 moved the V 23's wing down to the low position used on Junker's D I. For a powerplant, it reverted to the 110 hp Oberursel rotary, and a vertical fin was added to make a D VII-style tail. Comparing the earlier water-cooled V 23 to the air-cooled V 25's test results, one finds the 848 kg. (1866 lb.) V 23 taking three minutes to climb 1000 m. (3280′), while the 564 kg. (1241 lb.) V 25 required only 1.7 minutes.

A parasol wing was used on the other three Fokker prototypes, a wood cantilever surface like that of the V 23, but placed high enough to give the pilot excellent visibility. The standard 110 Oberursel nine-cylinder Ur II got the 605 kg. (1331 lb.) V 26 to 1000 m. in two minutes. Originally, the V 26 had unbalanced elevators and plain ailerons, but elevator balances were later added, and the ailerons inset, as on the V 25.

FOKKER D VIII (E V)
Oberursel Ur II, 110 hp
DIMENSIONS: 8.4 m. (27′7″), Lg. 5.86 m. (19′3″), Ht. 2.82 m. (9′3″), Wing Area 10.7 qm. (115 sq. ft.)
WEIGHT: Empty 384 kg. (848 lb.), Gross 563 kg. (1238 lb.), Fuel 72 liters (19 gal.)
PERFORMANCE: Speed—Max. 183 km/hr (114 mph), at 2000 m. (6560′), 185 km/hr (115 mph) at sea level, Landing speed 104 km/hr (65 mph), Climb 500 m./1 min. (1500′/1 min.) 2000 m./5 min. (6500′/5 min.), Service ceiling 6300 m. (20,650′)

FOKKER D VIIIe (as V 28 shown)
Oberursel Ur III, 145 hp
DIMENSIONS: As D VIII
WEIGHT: Empty 400 kg. (880 lb.), Gross 600 kg. (1320 lb.)
PERFORMANCE: Speed—Max. 200 km/hr (124 mph), Climb 5000 m./15 min. (16,400′/15 min.), Service ceiling 6000 m. (19,680′)

FOKKER V 27

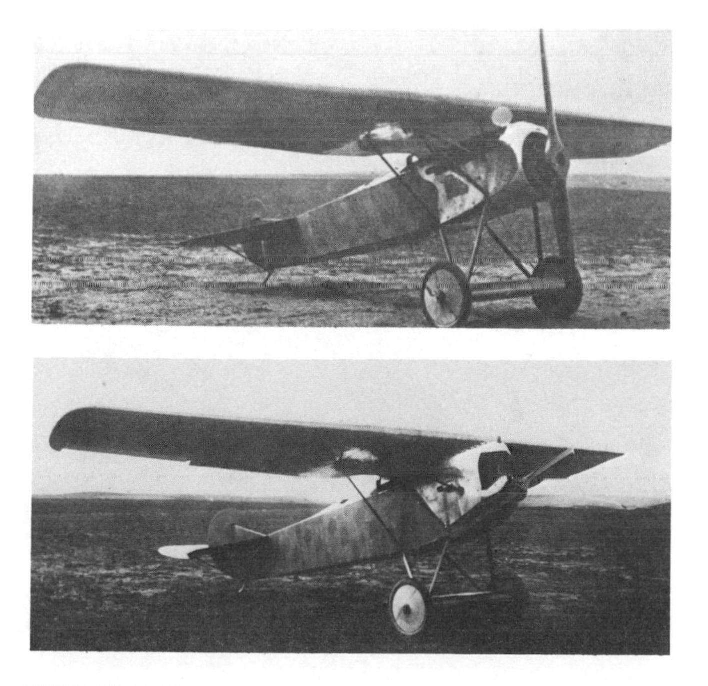

FOKKER V 29

A 145 hp eleven-cylinder Oberursel Ur III powered the V 28, whose wider diameter cowl was the only major distinction from the V 26. For experienced pilots, the V 28 seemed a masterpiece that climbed fast and could almost turn on a wing tip. The same aircraft was also tested that June with a 140 hp Goebel Goe III, and reappeared in October with a 160 hp Siemens Halske Sh III.

A water-cooled vee-eight, the 195 hp Benz Bz IIIb with a circular nose radiator, was used on the slightly larger Fokker V 27. This may be considered a prototype for the F VI, sold to the U. S. Army in 1922 as the PW-5. In 1918, however, the Germans preferred the lighter rotary-powered parasols.

An order was placed for 400 Fokker monoplanes then designated E V. While the 145 hp rotary powerplant was preferred, it had not reached mass production, and so the E V would use the 110 hp Swedish Le Rhones or their Oberursel Ur II copy. These engines were, in fact, fitted to nearly all of the 381 production ships built before the war's end. Armament was the usual two 7.9 mm. LMG 08/15 guns.

Fokker promised quick delivery, and indeed delivered the first 20 by the end of July 1918. Front-line pilots began familiarizing themselves with the E V, but before it could be introduced to combat, tragedy struck. In one week beginning August 19, three pilots were killed when their wings failed. All E Vs,

FOKKER V 37

including 60 at the front, were grounded, production acceptances ceased, and a special Crash Commission opened its investigation on August 24.

This investigation found Platz's design sound, but a victim of poor manufacturing practices. Criminal proceedings against Fokker were even recommended, but his monoplane was cleared and restored to production by September 24.[1] All existing aircraft had their wings replaced and the modified aircraft were designated D VIII. Redesignation meant the end of the old E category, and was intended to free the monoplane of the E V's dangerous reputation.

When the D VIII returned to the front on October 24, its fast climb and maneuverability made it popular. The "Flying Razor" was a tricky, but excellent plane, in hands of experienced pilots. There were 85 with the *Jastas* by November 1, plus some with the Navy.

After the war, Holland got 20 shipped out by Fokker, plus others gained from escaping pilots. Poland used a squadron, still called E Vs, in her war with the Ukraine, and on April 29, 1919, an E V pilot scored the first Polish air victory. The performance data here comes from an example tested by the U. S. Army in 1921.

Modifications of the Fokker monoplane appeared at the third and last Adlershof competition opened October 15, 1918. Fokker offered a D VIIIe with a 145 hp Oberursel Ur III, an VIIIg with the 160 hp Goebel Goe III, the V 28 fitted with a 160 hp Siemens-Halske Sh III, and the new BMW-powered V 29 monoplane and V 36 biplane.

The V 29 looked like a parasol D VII, began with a Mercedes D III, and competed with the 185 hp BMW IIIa. Of over 15 types at the October meet, the Junkers D I was the fastest, yet handicapped by poor flying qualities, while the Rumpler D I made the best climb. A close second in speed, Fokker's V 29 had the best flying qualities, and would probably have won a contract had not the war come to an end.

Fokker's last wartime single-seater was the V 37, an armored parasol monoplane for ground attack. Developed from the V 27 with the 195 hp Benz Bz IIIb, it had steel plate on the sides, bottom and back of the engine and cockpit section. To protect the frontal radiator, a circular plate was added ahead of the propeller and faired by a large spinner. Like the AEG DJ I of the same class, it was too late for serious consideration.

MONOPLANE PROTOYPES

Other companies attempted experimental high-wing monoplanes in this period. The Schutte-Lanz D VI had a standard Mercedes D III and a winglike covering on the bracing struts that gave it a mixed mono-biplane look. The only available photo shows it after a crash on its first flight, May 25, 1918.

About the same time BFW produced a monoplane with a peculiar swept-forward wing. This obscure

SCHUTTE-LANZ D VI

BFW Experimental

[1] Fokker's own explanation in his autobiography is contradicted by A. R. Weyl's account. Another problem was that moisture condensed within the wing warped and rotted the wood. Interior paint was added to prevent this.

DAIMLER L 11

DAIMLER L 14

aircraft may have been a test vehicle, not actually intended as a combat design. Little more is known of the parasol fighters Daimler produced with its 185 hp Mercedes D IIIb. The first was called the L 11, while the two-place L 14 was not completed until after the war.

Kondor produced a pair of parasol single-seaters for the October competition; the E III with a 140 hp Oberursel Ur III in a cutaway cowl, and the E IIIa with a 200 hp Goebel Goe IIIa in a circular cowl. The latter was successfully demonstrated at Adlershof by Ritter von Schleich, who wished it dispatched to the front for his personal use. The revolution at the war's end prevented this, and afterward it appeared in Switzerland for acrobatic displays.

LVG Roland also offered parasol single-seaters at Adlershof, the D XVI being like the Fokker D VIII but of reverse construction, with a ply-covered fuselage and fabric-covered wing. The first example had a 160 hp Siemens-Halske Sh III and was the best climber among the air-cooled designs. A second version had the Goebel Goe III, two-bladed propeller and a higher tail. Last Roland fighter was the D XVII,

KONDOR E III (E IIIa shown)
Oberursel Ur III, 145 hp (Goebel Goe IIIa, 200 hp)
DIMENSIONS: Span 9 m. (29′6″), Lg. 5.7 m. (18′8″), Ht. 2.74 m. (9′), Wing Area 12.4 qm. (134 sq. ft.)
WEIGHT: Empty 465 kg. (1023 lb.), Gross 660 kg. (1452 lb.)
PERFORMANCE: Speed—Max. 195 km/hr (121 mph), Climb 5000 m./16 min. (16,400′/16 min.). For E IIIa: Speed —Max. 200 km/hr (124 mph), Climb 5000 m./11 min. (16,400′/11 min.)

LFG ROLAND D XVI

LFG ROLAND D XVI (Goe III)

LFG ROLAND D XVII

with the 185 hp BMW III favored for German fighters at the war's end.

Siemens used its own Sh IIIa rotary in the last of these monoplanes, the Siemens-Schuckert D VI. Two aircraft taken from the Siemens line in October 1918 were not completed and flown as parasol monoplanes until February 1919. The performance cited is good, and the bulge below the fuselage is a droppable fuel tank.

Pfalz also constructed a parasol fighter, but it is not known if it reached any official competitions. It utilized an elongated D VIII fuselage with twin-strut braced high wing.

SSW D VI
Siemens Sh IIIa, 160 hp
DIMENSIONS: Span 9.37 m. (30'9"), Lg. 6.5 m. (21'4"), Ht. 2.72 m. (8'11"), Wing Area 12.46 qm. (134 sq. ft.)
WEIGHT: Empty 540 kg. (1188 lb.), Gross 710 kg. (1562 lb.)
PERFORMANCE: Speed—Max. 220 km/hr (136 mph), Climb 6000 m./16 min. (19,680'/16 min.), Range 350 km. (217 miles), Service ceiling 7200 m. (23,616')

Part 3 The Bombers

GOTHA G V loading bombs

9.

G Types 1915–18

Twin-engined bombers have played a role in German air power since the first Gothas appeared over London. This chapter describes the "G" class biplanes that did most of Germany's long-distance bombing in World War I.

The first of these were originally named *Kampfflugzeug* (battleplane) for their mission was to fight enemy aircraft. The K designs utilized two engines so they would have the power to carry armament. The gunner sat in an open cockpit in the bow with plenty of room to aim his weapon. In 1915, twin-engined aircraft were redesignated as G types (*Grossflugzeug*), and used as bombers.

The first of these twin-engined biplanes was actually built in 1914 for the German Navy. Designed by Hillman, the Schutte-Lanz G I had two 160 hp Mercedes D IIIs with pusher propellers and fuel for about six hours of flight. Prominent features were the overhanging upper wing, doubled landing wheels, and comma-shaped rudder, but the aircraft crashed during tests and was not rebuilt.

The first G plane for the Army's Flying Corps was the LFG Roland G I, whose two pusher propellers were driven by a powerplant in the fuselage behind the pilot. Side radiators cooled the Basse & Selve engines, and twin nose wheels were added to protect the bow gunner from noseovers. A Parabellum gun was provided. No further examples were made.

A German aviation magazine editor, Oskar Ursinus, and an Army major by the name of Friedel, had designed a large biplane with the fuselage attached to the upper wing and two Benz engines on the lower wing. Numbered B 1092/14, the Friedel-Ursinus FU was built by the military aviation workshop at Darmstadt, where it made its first flight in January 1915. There were three cockpits, and 200 kg. (440 lb.) of chrome-steel armor protected the crew. Normal armament was a machine gun on the bow gun ring, but one photograph shows Ursinus and a 20 mm. Becker gun in the front seat, and a Parabellum gun in the second seat. Small bombs could be attached on the bow and dropped by hand.

This prototype was flown on the Eastern front by Fl. Abt. 28, and was successful enough to warrant further development. In March 1915, Gothaer Waggonfabrik was licensed to produce the Ursinus design as the Gotha G I.

Gotha built a first batch of six, beginning with G 9/15 finished on July 27, 1915, and followed by six from September to November 1915, and six more from January to March 1916. They were distinguished from their prototype by various refinements, including the omission of the outer diagonal strut. Six at the front on December 31, 1915, were scattered among several units.

The most widely used G types of 1915 were the AEG biplanes, which appeared at the front in June. Somewhat smaller than its Gotha rivals, the AEG G I had two 100 hp Mercedes between the wings, driving tractor propellers. Originally known as the K I, it carried three crewmen and a gun, and double pairs

SCHUTTE-LANZ G I
Mercedes D III, 2 X 160 hp
DIMENSIONS: Span 22 m. (72′2″), Lg. 12 m. (39′4″), Ht. 4.2 m. (13′9″), Wing Area 100 qm. (1076 sq. ft.)
WEIGHT: Empty 1850 kg. (4070 lb.), Gross 3100 kg. (6820 lb.)
PERFORMANCE: Speed—Max. 125 km/hr (78 mph), Landing speed 68 km/hr (42 mph), Endurance 6 hours

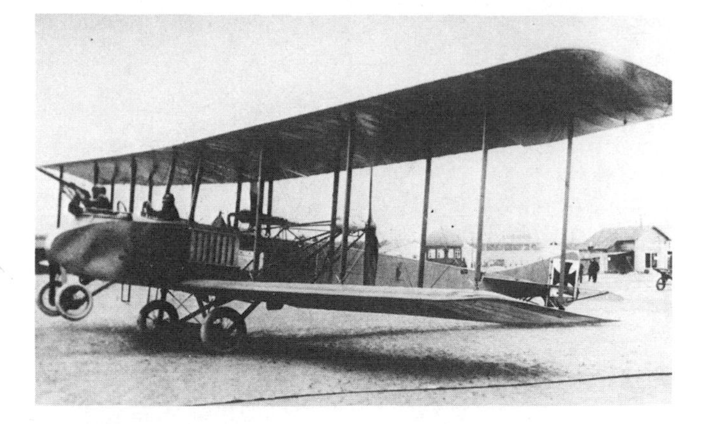

LFG ROLAND G I
Basse & Selve, 2 X 150 hp
DIMENSIONS: Span 20.1 m. (65′11″), Lg. 15.9 m. (52′2″)
WEIGHT: Empty 2750 kg. (6050 lb.), Gross 4300 kg. (9460 lb.)
PERFORMANCE: Speed—Max. 160 km/hr (99 mph)

FRIEDEL-URSINUS FU
Benz Bz III, 2 X 150 hp
DIMENSIONS: Span 20.3 m. (66′7″), Lg. 12.1 m. (39′8½″), Ht. 4 m. (13′1½″), Wing Area 82 qm. (882.64 sq. ft.)
WEIGHT: Empty 1800 kg. (3960 lb.), Gross 2600 kg. (5720 lb.)
PERFORMANCE: Speed—Max. 130 km/hr (81 mph), Service ceiling 540 m. (335′)

FRIEDEL-URSINUS FU

GOTHA G I (GUH)
Benz Bz III, 2 X 150 hp
DIMENSIONS: as FU
WEIGHT: Empty 1800 kg. (3960 lb.), Gross 2800 kg. (6160 lb.)
PERFORMANCE: Speed—Max. 130 km/hr (81 mph), Range 540 km. (335 miles), Endurance 4 hours, Service ceiling 2750 m. (9020′)

AEG G I (K I)
Mercedes D I, 2 X 100 hp
DIMENSIONS: Span 16 m. (52′6″), Lg. 8.65 m. (28′4″), Wing Area 74 qm. (796 sq. ft.)
WEIGHT: Empty 1160 kg. (2552 lb.), Gross 1954 kg. (4299 lb.)
PERFORMANCE: Speed—Max. 125 km/hr (78 mph) at sea level

AEG G II
Benz Bz III, 2 X 150 hp
DIMENSIONS: Span 16 m. (52′6″), Lg. 9.1 m. (29′10″), Wing Area 74 qm. (796 sq. ft.)
WEIGHT: Empty 1450 kg. (3190 lb.), Gross 2470 kg. (5434 lb.)
PERFORMANCE: Speed—Max. 140 km/hr (87 mph) at sea level, Climb 1000 m./11 min. (3280′/11 min.)

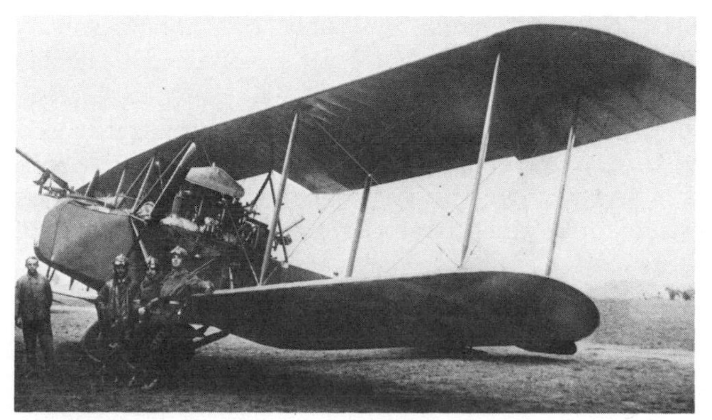

AEG G III
Mercedes D IV, 2 X 220 hp
DIMENSIONS: Span 18.44 m. (60′6″), Lg. 9.2 m. (30′2″), Wing Area 67 qm. (721 sq. ft.)
WEIGHT: Empty 2000 kg. (4400 lb.), Gross 3075 kg. (6765 lb.)
PERFORMANCE: Speed—Max. 155 km/hr (96 mph), Range 650 km. (403 miles), Service ceiling 3500 m. (11,480′)

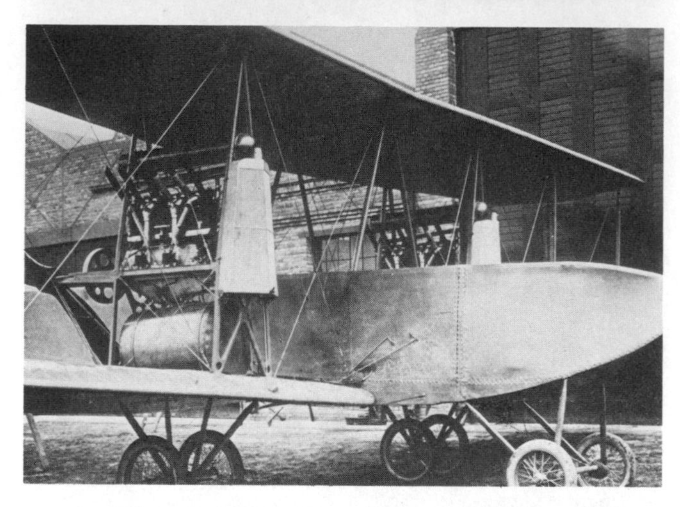

RUMPLER 4A 15
Benz Bz III, 2 X 150 hp
DIMENSIONS: Span 18.75 m. (61′6″), Lg. 11.8 m. (38′8½″), Ht. 4 m. (13′1½″)
WEIGHT: Empty 960 kg. (2112 lb.), Gross 1280 kg. (2816 lb.)
PERFORMANCE: Speed—Max. 150 km/hr (93 mph)

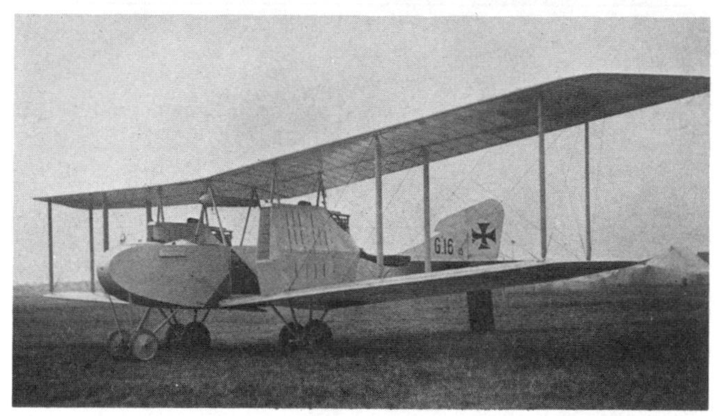

RUMPLER G I (5A 15)
Benz Bz III, 2 X 150 hp
DIMENSIONS: Span 19.3 m. (63′3½″), Lg. 11.8 m. (38′8½″), Ht. 4 m. (13′1½″), Wing Area 78.7 qm. (847.59 sq. ft.)
WEIGHT: Empty 1998 kg. (4395.6 lb.), Gross 2938 kg. (6463 lb.)
PERFORMANCE: Speed—Max. 150 km/hr (93 mph), Cruising speed 145 km/hr (90 mph), Climb 2000 m./21 min. (6560′/21 min.) Range 600 km. (372 miles), Service ceiling 4000 m. (13,120′)

of landing wheels were set between the fuselage and engine mounts.

Slightly heavier with 150 hp Benz engines, the AEG G II appeared in June 1915 with two flexible guns. The first batch, probably six, had a single rudder like the G I, but later G IIs had a triple vertical tail. There were five G Is and ten G IIs, along with five Gotha G Is, at the front on October 31, 1915. At year's end, 13 of 20 front-line G types were AEG G IIs. Since the High Command still made no distinction between bombers and fighters, they served in general "combat" roles, protecting unarmed B types.

Two 220 hp Mercedes in new nacelles with front radiators and four-bladed props were used on the AEG G III. Appearing in December 1916, the G III had balanced ailerons, elevators and high single rudder. As the number at the front rose from six on June 30, 1916, to 22 on October 31, 1916, they served with KG 1 in the Rumanian and Macedonian campaigns.

Rumpler began its *Grossflugzeug* family with the 4A 15 prototype, for the Navy, which on March 15, 1915, carried ten persons to 3200 m. height and 16 persons to 1800 meters. Two 150 hp Benz engines drove pusher propellers, and three pairs of wheels were positioned under the nose and engines.

A fire destroyed that aircraft on April 17, 1915, but development proceeded to the Rumpler G I (5A 15) with refined tail and wider span wings. Armed with one machine gun and 150 kg. (330 lb.) of bombs, this three-seater was said to have a takeoff

RUMPLER G II (5A 16)
Benz Bz IV, 2 X 220 hp
DIMENSIONS: Span 19.3 m. (63′3½″), Lg. 11.8 m. (38′8½″), Ht. 4 m. (13′1½″), Wing Area 78.7 qm. (847 sq. ft.)
WEIGHT: Empty 1990 kg. (4378 lb.), Gross 2990 kg. (6578 lb.)
PERFORMANCE: Speed—Max. 170 km/hr (105 mph)

RUMPLER G III (6G 2)
Mercedes D IVa, 2 X 260 hp
DIMENSIONS: Span 19.3 m. (63′3½″), Lg. 12 m. (39′4″), Ht. 4.5 m. (14′9″), Wing Area 73 qm. (785.5 sq. ft.)
WEIGHT: Empty 2365 kg. (5203 lb.), Gross 3620 kg. (7964 lb.)
PERFORMANCE: Speed—Max. 165 km/hr (102 mph), Climb 3000 m./22 min. (9840′/22 min.), Range 660 km. (409 miles), Service ceiling 5000 m. (16,400′)

run of only 100 m. (321′). The example in the photo, G 16/15, went to KG 1.[1] Only a few (six?) were built.

The Rumpler G II (5A 16) was the same design fitted with 220 hp Benz engines. It is reported at the front in June 1916, and eight were on hand October 31, 1916. The 260 hp Mercedes in cleaner nacelles, and balanced ailerons distinguished the Rumpler G III (6G 2). Armed with two guns and 225 kg. (495 lb.) bombs, this last twin-engined Rumpler came to the front in December 1916, and ten were on hand by October 31, 1917.

Several experimental twin-engined types were attempted in 1915 by other German aircraft builders. Their prototypes reflected the current concept of a general "combat" type, rather than a specialized bomber.

Anthony Fokker's only twin-engined wartime project was the unique M 9, or K I of April 1915. Two M 7 fuselages were joined on biplane wings with no link between the tail surfaces. A central nacelle contained the pilot's cockpit between two 80 hp Oberursel rotaries arranged push-pull fashion. Two gunners were accommodated in cockpits in the fuselage bows. After Fokker made a few test flights, he gave up on the project, and it was dismantled.

Friedrichshafen offered its first G type in 1915.

FOKKER K 9

[1] *Kampfgeschwader* 1 was a combat group attached directly to the Army's High Command. Most of its 36 planes were C type two-seaters until 1916.

LVG G I

FRIEDRICHSHAFEN FF 30 (G I)
Benz Bz III, 2 X 150 hp
DIMENSIONS: Span 20 m. (65′7″), Lg. 11 m. (36′1″)
WEIGHT and PERFORMANCE: Data not available

HALBERSTADT G I
Mercedes D III, 2 X 160 hp
DIMENSIONS: Span 15.5 m. (50′10″), Lg. 9 m. (29′6″), Ht. 3.2 m. (10′6″)
WEIGHT: Empty 1220 kg. (2684 lb.), Gross 1895 kg. (4169 lb.)
PERFORMANCE: Speed—Max. 152 km/hr (94 mph), Climb 1000 m./7 min. (3280′/7 min.) 3000 m./37.5 min. (9840′/37.5 min.), Range 550 km. (340 miles)

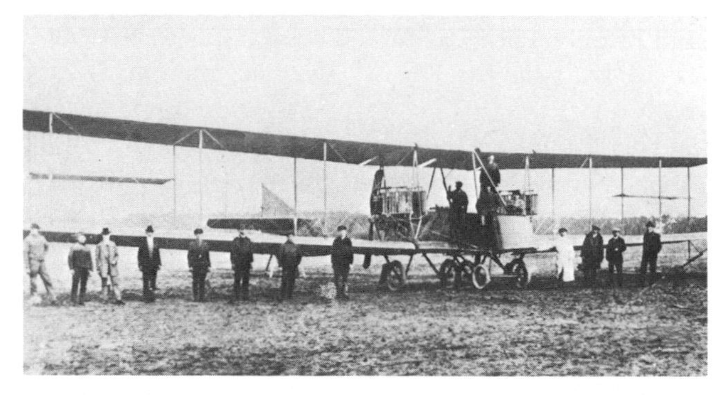

HANSA-BRANDENBURG ZM
Maybach Mb III, 2 X 160 hp
DIMENSIONS: Span 27.5 m. (90′2½″), Lg. 15.7 m. (51′6″), Wing Area 144 qm. (1550 sq. ft.)
WEIGHT and PERFORMANCE: Data not available

HANSA-BRANDENBURG GF
Austro-Daimler Dm, 2 X 160 hp
DIMENSIONS: Span 18 m. (59′1″), Wing Area 69.7 qm. (750 sq. ft.)
WEIGHT: Empty 1760 kg. (3872 lb.), Gross 2640 kg. (5808 lb.)
PERFORMANCE: Speed—Max. 140 km/hr (87 mph), Climb 1000 m./8 min. (3280′/8 min.), Range 800 km. (500 miles)

GOTHA G II prototype

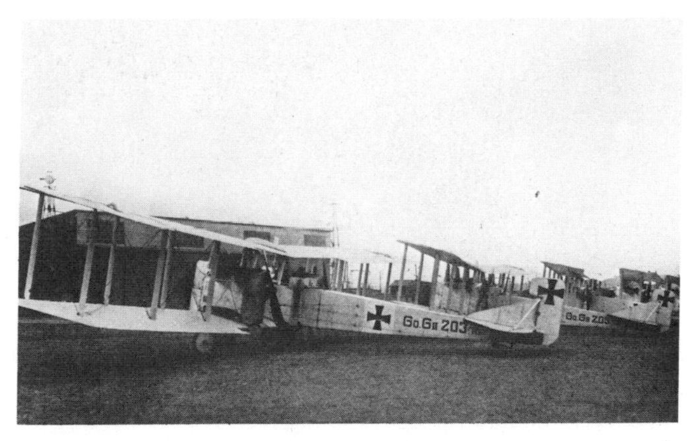

GOTHA G II
Mercedes D IV, 2 X 220 hp
DIMENSIONS: Span 23.7 m. (77'9"), Lg. 12.2 m. (40'), Ht. 3.9 m. (12'9½"), Wing Area 89.5 qm. (963 sq. ft.)
WEIGHT: Empty 2180 kg. (4769 lb.), Gross 3190 kg. (7018 lb.)
PERFORMANCE: Speed—Max. 135 km/hr (84 mph)

As the C I (FF 30) it had two 150 hp Benz as pushers, and a biplane tail. LVG's G I (KD VII) had the Benz engines arranged in tractor fashion with wide three-bay wings. Its most conspicuous feature was a front gunner's basket built high enough for him to fire over the top wing.

Halberstadt's only twin-engined type was the smallish G I. Completed in the winter of 1915–16, it had two 160 hp Mercedes D III tractor engines and only two landing wheels. Just one example was built, as in the case of the preceding experimental types.

Ernst Heinkel designed twin-engined bombers with his Austrian market in mind, the first being 1915's Hansa-Brandenburg ZM. Powered by two 160 hp Maybach pusher engines, it carried two guns and 250 kg. (550 lb.) of bombs, but this rather cumbersome effort did not pass the prototype stage.

Smaller and considerably cleaner looking was the Hansa-Brandenburg GF, which was produced in Budapest as the Brandenburg G I (UFAG) of 1916. Two 160 hp Austro-Daimler tractor engines were fitted along with triple rudders and a simplified landing gear. The pilot and rear gunner sat in a single cockpit behind the wings, while the short nose had a gun turret. Only a dozen seem to have been built.

THE GOTHAS

Without doubt, the most famous German bombers of the war were the Gothas. These twin-engined three-place biplanes became the symbol of the threat to cities far behind the Allied lines.

Hans Burkhard, Gotha's Swiss engineer, was told late in 1915 to design a twin-engined biplane to carry a 300 kg. (660 lb.) bomb load for some four hours duration. His first G II prototype was completed in March 1916 with short two-bay wings, a finless rudder, and a level landing gear with four wheels under each engine nacelle.

Test results soon proved that wider three-bay wings were required to improve climb, and a conventional tail-down landing position the best way to brake the landing run. Production G IIs had the wide wings, four wheels, tail fin, and balanced rudder and ailerons. The pusher powerplants were 220 hp eight-cylinder geared Mercedes mounted in bulky nacelles with radiators in front and fuel tanks underneath the engines. Fabric covered the wooden structure except for the plywood nose section. Two Parabellum guns were mounted at the front and rear cockpits. Small (10 kg. or 22 lb.) bombs could be carried internally, but larger bombs were carried below the fuselage.

Ten Gotha G IIs (nr. G 200/16 to 209/16) were produced, the first delivered on August 24, 1916. They were issued to KG 4, Staffel 20, and in October were joined by the Gotha G III, 25 of which had been ordered beginning with G 375/16. Two 260 hp Mercedes powered the G III, and a third gun was added at an opening in the rear cockpit floor.

The G II served KG 1 in the Balkans during the successful Rumanian campaign. At 1916's end, front-

GOTHA G III
Mercedes D IVa, 260 hp
DIMENSIONS: as G II
WEIGHT: Empty 2383 kg. (5255 lb.), Gross 3618 kg. (7978 lb.)
PERFORMANCE: Speed—Max. 135 km/hr (84 mph) at sea level, Climb 3000 m./28 min. (9840'/28 min.)

line strength in G types included 14 G III and three G II Gothas, 23 AEGs, and five Rumplers. Early in 1917, Gotha IIIs of KG 2 operated on the Western front.

Most famous of Gotha raids were those made by the G IV against England. As far back as October 1914, there had been preparations to bomb England from Belgian air bases, but this task was beyond the capacity of the single-engined types. Since October 1914, Germany had experienced many raids by British and French aircraft, and had struck back with her Zeppelin fleet.

As Zeppelin raids became too costly for the Germans, a plan was made to attack England with the Gothas. KG 3 was organized to carry out the attacks from Belgium as soon as enough G IVs became available. In August 1916, 52 Gotha G IVs had been ordered (beginning G 401/16) and license-production orders for 80 from Siemens-Schuckert and 150 from LVG were added in December.

A stronger, all-plywood fuselage, and ailerons added to the lower wings with a connecting strut to the upper pair, distinguished the G IV from its predecessors. These had suffered from a blind spot under the tail, which the new model tried to correct. On the prototype G IVs, seen in November 1916, the rear fuselage was cut in triangular shape to give the rear gunner a bigger field of fire. Production aircraft had a more ingenious system retaining the normal squared fuselage. A hollow tunnel from a top deck opening to under the tail enabled the rear gunner to fire downward, without changing to the lower gun.

In March 1917, KG 3 got its first Gotha G IVs, while deliveries began from Siemens in April and LVG in June. On June 30, 36 G IVs were in front-line service, peak strength for this model. Each was normally operated by three men; the commander in the bow acting as navigator-bombardier, the pilot, and the rear gunner. Three machine guns and six 50 kg. (110 lb.) bombs were usually carried, with heavier loads possible on occasion.

Twenty-three G IVs set out on May 25, 1917, for the first of eight daylight raids against England. The most damaging attack was on London on June 21, when 162 persons were killed and 432 injured, with no losses to the 20 Gothas starting.

Actual military damage from these raids was rather small because of the small bomb load and very poor accuracy. The High Command had also hoped for a psychological effect; that fearful civilians would demand an early end to the war. Despite the German fliers' orders to hit military targets, most victims were civilians.

On that first London raid, a 110 lb. bomb hit a nursery school and killed 16 infants; how many children, English and German, Chinese and Japanese, have since died by bombs! Even a technical book must remember the innocent victims, for they largely account for bombing's failure as a psychological weapon. Historically, in war after war, aerial bombing has always aroused more hate and desire for revenge rather than fear.

The Gotha raids' chief material result was diversion of some British war resources from the front to home defense. These defenses, far out of proportion to actual German attack strength, did make daylight raids too costly, but used British forces needed more urgently at the front.

In September 1917, the Germans turned to night bombing, in which the Gothas were joined by a few giant multiengined bombers. Nineteen night raids were made before the attacks ended in May 1918, so the German bombers could concentrate on helping their own armies.

GOTHA G IV prototype

GOTHA G V
Mercedes D IVa, 2 X 260 hp
DIMENSIONS: as G II
WEIGHT: Empty 2570 kg. (5654 lb.), Gross 3890 kg. (8558 lb.)
PERFORMANCE: Speed—Max. 140 km/hr (87 mph) Climb 3000 m./28 min. (9840′/28 min.), Range 840 km. (520 miles), Service ceiling 6500 m. (21,320′)

GOTHA G IV
Mercedes D IVa, 2 X 260 hp
DIMENSIONS: as G II
WEIGHT: Empty 2413 kg. (5321 lb.), Gross 3648 kg. (8044 lb.), Fuel 620 liters (164 gal.)
PERFORMANCE: Speed—Max. 135 km/hr (84 mph) at sea level, Endurance 3¾ to 6 hours, Service ceiling 5000 m. (16,400′)

GOTHA G Va

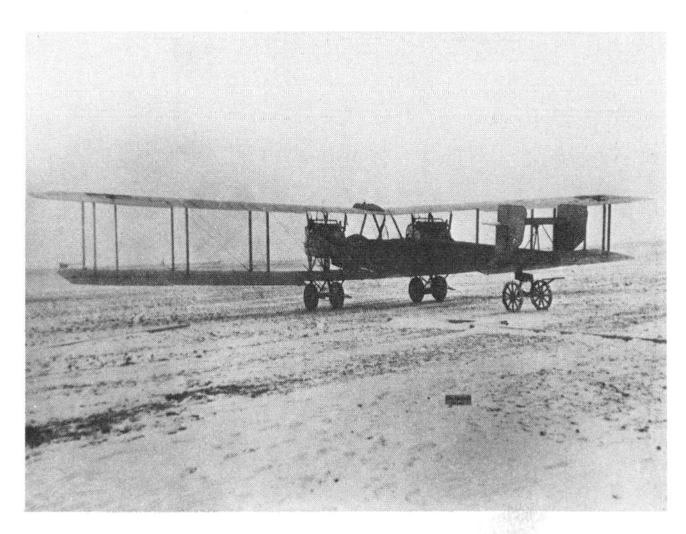

Development of the Gothas proceeded with the G Vs introduced on the night raids. While the Siemens continued its license-built G IVs, most of the Siemens machines went to training bases where more economical 180 hp Argus or NAG engines were sufficient. Several SSW-built Gothas were used for test rigs, including two examples powered by 245 hp Maybach Mb IVa high-compression engines with tractor propellers. LVG-built Gotha G IVs were used both as trainers and at the front and about 30 went to Austria in February 1918 with Austrian 230 hp Hiero engines and Schwarlose guns.

The newer Gotha G V appeared in August 1917 with the main fuel tanks moved from the nacelles to the fuselage for safety. This left the gap between engine and wing that identifies the G V model. A double tail improved single-engine flight stability on the G Va appearing in April 1918, and the G Vb in June. The G Vb added a pair of nose wheels to prevent the noseovers on night landings that had wrecked more Gothas than had enemy action. Gotha delivered 100 G V, 25 G Va and 65 G Vb by October 1918, with a final 15 G Vb aircraft produced by December.

Gotha front-line strength was 35 G IV and 20 G V bombers on October 31, 1917, eight G IVs, 36 G Vs and 11 G Vas on April 30, 1918, and on August 31, the *Kampfgeschwader* listed five G IV, eight G V, four G Va, and 21 G Vb models. A small force to have achieved such notoriety! The raids on Britain were over, but Gothas were still very active over France.

OTHER TWIN-ENGINED BOMBERS

While Gothas got the most publicity, the most widely used German bombers of the war's last year were the Friedrichshafens. This company's Fdh. G I of 1915 did not reach production, but about October 1916, designer Theodor Kober offered the Fdh. G II which did have limited production.

Powered by two 215 hp Benz engines with pusher props, the G II was a three-seater rather like the Gothas, but smaller, with two-bay outer wing panels. It was reported at the front in February 1917 and by June 30 there were 17 G IIs along with nine of the new G IIIs. The Daimler GD 5 was rather similar to the Friedrichshafen designs, but the GD 5 was rejected and Daimler built Fdh. G IIIs.

Larger, three-bay wings and a nose wheel distinguished the Friedrichshafen G III whose pusher propellers were powered by 260 hp Mercedes. Except for the inset balances on the rudder and ailerons, it resembled the Gothas but had a heavier bomb load; up to 800 kg. (1760 lb.). Two Parabellum guns were mounted in the usual positions.

Many of these bombers were built under license by Daimler (225) and by Hansa (93). Most of the license-built aircraft had biplane tails, beginning in June 1918, and were known as G IIIa.

Friedrichshafen bombers were used by KG 1, 2 and 5 and are praised highly by old veteran pilots as very reliable. G types at the front on April 30, 1918, included 96 Fdh. G IIIs, 55 Gothas, and 54 AEG G IVs. On August 31, there were 24 Fdh.

GOTHA G Vb
Mercedes D IVa, 2 X 260 hp
DIMENSIONS: as G II
WEIGHT: Empty 2950 kg. (6505 lb.), Gross 4550 kg. (10,033 lb.)
PERFORMANCE: Speed—Max. 135 km/hr (84 mph) at sea level

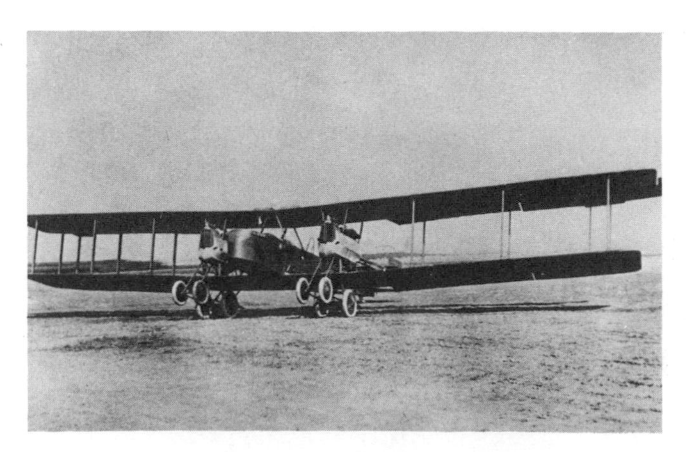

FRIEDRICHSHAFEN G II (FF 38)
Benz Bz IV, 2 X 215 hp, or Mercedes D III, 2 X 160 hp
DIMENSIONS: Span 20.3 m. (66'7"), Lg. 11.05 m. (36'3"), Ht. 3.6 m. (11'10"), Wing Area 70 qm. (764 sq. ft.)
WEIGHT: Empty 2200 kg. (4840 lb.), Gross 3171 kg. (6976 lb.)
PERFORMANCE: Data not available

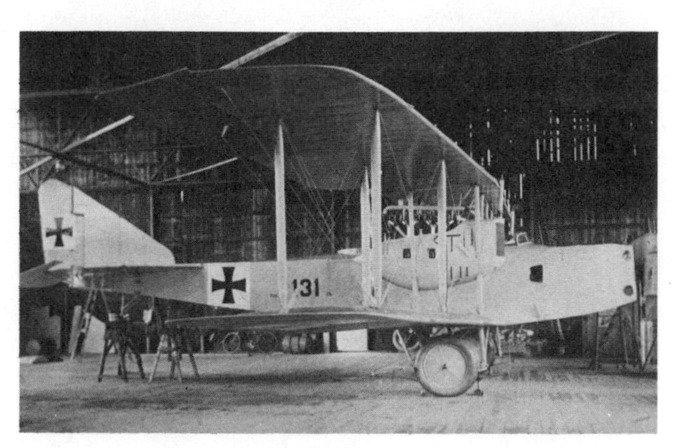

FRIEDRICHSHAFEN G III (FF 45)
Mercedes D IVa, 2 X 260 hp
DIMENSIONS: Span 23.7 m. (77′9″), Lg. 12.8 m. (42′), Wing Area 86 qm. (925 sq. ft.)
WEIGHT: Empty 2700 kg. (5940 lb.), Gross 3940 kg. (8668 lb.)
PERFORMANCE: Speed—Max. 130 km/hr. (81 mph)

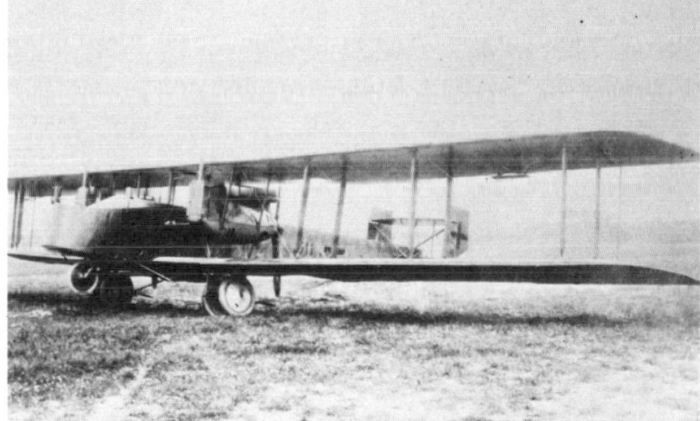

FRIEDRICHSHAFEN G IIIa (FF 61)

FRIEDRICHSHAFEN G III (Daim)

DAIMLER G D 5

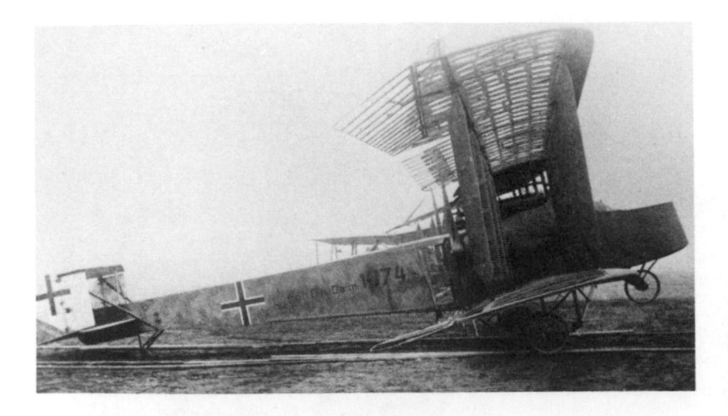

FRIEDRICHSHAFEN G IV (Daim)

FRIEDRICHSHAFEN G V (FF 55)
Mercedes D IVa, 2 X 260 hp
DIMENSIONS: Span 22.6 m. (74′1½″), Lg. 12 m. (39′)
WEIGHT: Empty 2880 kg. (6336 lb.), Gross 4980 kg. (10,956 lb.)
PERFORMANCE: Speed—Max. 135 km/hr (84 mph)

ALBATROS G II

AEG G IV
Mercedes D IVa, 2 X 260 hp
DIMENSIONS: Span 18.4 m. (60′4″), Lg. 9.7 m. (31′10″), Ht. 3.9 m. (12′10″), Wing Area 67 qm. (721 sq. ft.)
WEIGHT: Empty 2400 kg. (5280 lb.), Gross 3630 kg. (7986 lb.)
PERFORMANCE: Speed—Max. 165 km/hr (102 mph), Climb 1000 m./5 min. (3280′/5 min.) 4000 m./40 min. (13,120′/40 min.), Range 700 km. (435 miles), Service ceiling 4500 m. (14,760′)

ALBATROS G III (L 21)
Benz Bz IVa, 2 X 200 hp
DIMENSIONS: Span 18 m. (59′½″), Lg. 11.89 m. (39′), Ht. 4.2 m. (13′9″), Wing Area 79 qm. (850 sq. ft.)
WEIGHT: Empty 2064 kg. (4540 lb.), Gross 4050 kg. (8910 lb.)
PERFORMANCE: Speed—Max. 150 km/hr (93 mph), Climb 1000 m./9 min. (3280′/9 min.), Range 550 km. (340 miles)

G III and 95 G IIIa with eight new G IV and six G IVa types. The G IV was a G IIIa with four-bay wings, and provision for a 1000 kg. (2200 lb.) bomb on the G IVa.

Kober's last bomber design had the bow cut back, eliminating the front gunner and using just two crewmen. The May 1918 version shown in our photo with a 1000 kg. (2200 lb.) bomb is labeled FF 55 and is probably the first Friedrichshafen G V.

Another design made an appearance at the front in 1917. The Albatros G II designed by Madelung was unique in having a thick wing braced by a single pair of W struts. A single pair of main wheels was used, with a smaller pair under the downward sloping nose. Two pusher props were driven by 150 hp Benz engines.

A more refined G III followed with the 200 hp Benz and double paired landing wheels without the nose gear. The front-line list reports a single Albatros G II in February and in December 1917, and two G IIIs from June to October.[2] The G III is known to have been flown by KG 6.

Along with the Friedrichshafen and Gotha bombers, the AEG G IV played a very active role, the number at the front rising from five on April 30, 1917, to 74 on June 30, 1918. In action with KG 2, 4, and 5, it had the same Mercedes engines as its rivals, but had tractor propellers instead of their pusher style.

Smaller than the others, with two-bay wings, it was the fastest German service bomber. Construction was the usual AEG system of fabric-covered steel

[2] The list also reports 9 G IIs in April, and one in June and in August, but the April figure may be in error.

AEG G IVb
Mercedes D IVa, 2 X 260 hp
DIMENSIONS: Span 24 m. (78′8½″), Lg. 9.7 m. (31′10″), Ht. 3.9 m. (12′9½″), Wing Area 78.5 qm. (845 sq. ft.)
WEIGHT: Empty 2453 kg. (5396 lb.), Gross 3700 kg. (8140 lb.)
PERFORMANCE: Speed—Max. 160 km/hr (99 mph) at sea level

AEG G IV K
Mercedes D IVa, 2 X 260 hp
DIMENSIONS: As G IV
WEIGHT: Not available
PERFORMANCE: Speed—Max. 160 km/hr (99 mph), Range 700 km. (434 miles), Service ceiling 4000 m. (13,120′)

tubing, and three crewmen and two Parabellum guns were accommodated. Racks were provided for four 50 kg. (110 lb.) bombs, and 10 kg. bombs could be carried inside the fuselage.

One 1917 example modified with wider three-bay wings became the G IVb, while several standard-sized examples were tested in ground attack configuration early in 1918. Known as the G IVK (for Kanone) they had a 20 mm. Becker gun in the nose, armor and a biplane tail.

Last of the AEG bomber family was the much larger G V, intended for longer ranges than the G IV. The prototype first flew in May 1918, and several were completed and modified after the war for use

AEG G V
Mercedes D IVa, 2 X 260 hp
DIMENSIONS: Span 27.3 m. (89′7″), Lg. 10.8 m. (35′5″), Ht. 4.5 m. (14′9″)
WEIGHT: Empty 2700 kg. (5954 lb.), Gross 4800 kg. (10,584 lb.)
PERFORMANCE: Speed—Max. 145 km/hr (90 mph) at sea level, Climb 1000 m./6 min. (3280′/6 min.), 4000 m./34 min. (13,120′/34 min.)

GOTHA GL VII
Maybach Mb IVa, 2 X 245 hp at 2000 m. (6560′)
DIMENSIONS: Span 19.27 m. (63′2½″), Lg. 9.6 m. (31′6″), Ht. 3.5 m. (11′6″), Wing Area 64 qm. (689 sq. ft.)
WEIGHT: Empty 2420 kg. (5324 lb.), Gross 3140 kg. (6908 lb.)
PERFORMANCE: Speed—Max. 180 km/hr (112 mph), Climb 6000 m./38 min. (19,680′/38 min.), Range 630 km. (390 miles), Service ceiling 6000 m. (19,680′)

GOTHA G VI

GOTHA G VII
Maybach Mb IVa, 2 X 245 hp at 2000 m. (6560′)
DIMENSIONS: Span 19.3 m. (63′3½″), Lg. 9.63 m. (31′7″), Ht. 3.5 m. (11′6″), Wing Area 64 qm. (688 sq.ft.)
WEIGHT: Empty 2420 kg. (5324 lb.), Gross 3140 kg. (6908 lb.)
PERFORMANCE: Speed—Max. 180 km/hr (112 mph), Range 540 km. (335 miles)

GOTHA G VIII
Maybach Mb IV, 2 X 245 hp at 2000 m. (6560′)
DIMENSIONS: Span 21.7 m. (71′2″), Lg. 9.8 m. (32′2″), Ht. 3.5 m. (11′6″), Wing Area 79 qm. (850 sq. ft.)
WEIGHT: Empty 2676 kg. (5887 lb.), Gross 3706 kg. (8153 lb.)
PERFORMANCE: Speed—Max. 180 km/hr (112 mph), Range 480 km. (298 miles)

GOTHA G VII

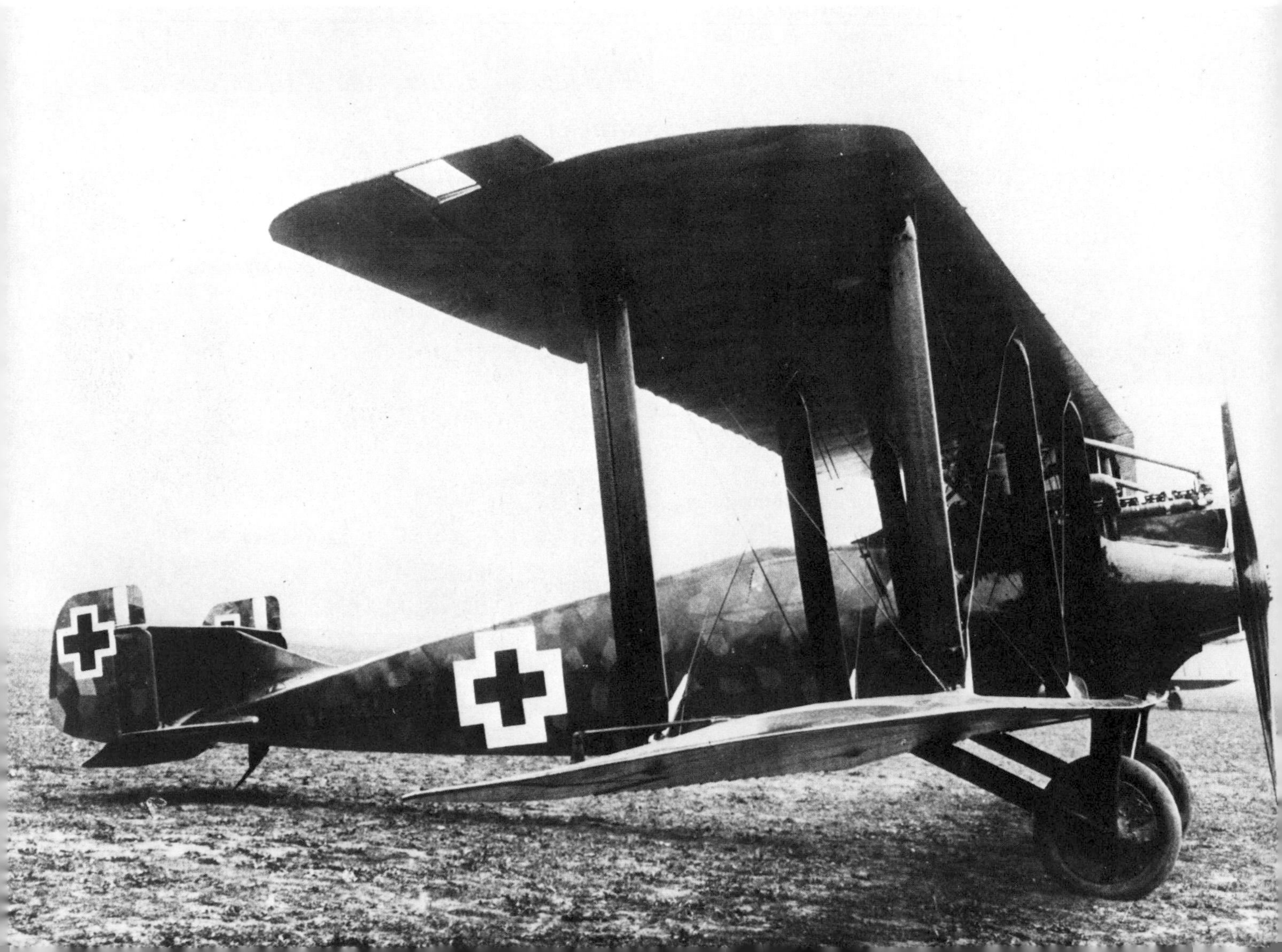

on the first German air line. Wartime armament was two guns and 600 kg. (1320 lb.) of bombs.

Discussion of wartime twin-engined bombers may conclude with experimental machines that never reached combat status. Strangest of these was the world's first asymmetric aircraft, Burkhard's Gotha G VI.

This aircraft used a standard G V's wings, tail and main fuselage, but the fuselage was attached left of center with a 260 hp Mercedes D IVa and tractor propeller in the nose. To the right, a nacelle contained a second Mercedes, mounted pusher style behind the observer's cockpit. The G VI crashed on a test in the winter of 1917–18, but another example was built later, with three-bay wings and the radiators moved from the upper wings to above the engines. Unfortunately, further details are lacking, except that the project was abandoned by April 1918.

Gotha's other designer, Karl Roesner, was usually occupied with seaplanes, but in 1917 he joined with Schleiffer to produce a new approach to G types. The GL VII (L for photo.*) was a smaller twin-engined type without a bow cockpit. The nose was cut back to the wings where the pilot sat, while the rear gunner sat behind the wings with the short fuselage curving down to a single balanced rudder. Thrust came from the two tractor propellers of the 245 hp Maybach Mb IVa engines in neat nacelles with the radiators on the upper wing. Four GL VII prototypes were built for long-range reconnaissance, but the third, G 552/17, had the double tail, increased wing span, and added pair of interplane struts used on production aircraft.

Fifty-five production aircraft were ordered from Gotha in January 1918, and the first, designated Gotha G VII 300/18, went to the front May 18, 1918. Armed with a fixed gun ahead of the pilot's cockpit and a Parabellum flexible gun behind the wings, it had three-bay wings and a double tail. An example modified with extended upper wings and bracing struts was designated G VIII 307/18 and sent to Doeberitz October 23, 1918.

Aviatik and LVG also received orders for 30 each of Gotha's GL VII design in July 1918, but it's uncertain how many short-nosed Gotha types were actually completed. LVG did produce a version with four-bay wings designated Gotha G IX (LVG) 257/18.

Last of the Gotha family were three G X prototypes ordered in August 1918. Powered by two 185 hp BMW engines, they were light recon aircraft on the GL VII pattern.

The only triplane in the G class was the big LVG G III, originally designed as the Schutte-Lanz G V.

* Lichtbild.

LVG G III
Maybach Mb IVa, 2 X 245 hp at 2000 m. (6560′)
DIMENSIONS: Span 24.5 m. (80′4″), Lg. 10.25 m. (33′7¼″), Ht. 3.9 m. (12′9½″)
WEIGHT: Empty 2960 kg. (6512 lb.), Gross 4100 kg. (9020 lb.)
PERFORMANCE: Speed—Max. 130 km/hr (81 mph), Stalling speed 60 km/hr (37 mph), Climb 3000 m./20 min. (9840′/20 min.), Range 450 km. (279 miles)

SIEMENS-SCHUCKERT L I
Maybach Mb IVa, 3 X 245 hp at 2000 m. (6560′)
DIMENSIONS: Span 32 m. (105′), Lg. 14.65 m. (48′½″), Ht. 4.4 m. (14′5″), Wing Area 169 qm. (18,184 sq. ft.)
WEIGHT: Empty 4400 kg. (9680 lb.), Gross 6400 kg. (14, 080 lb.)
PERFORMANCE: Speed—Max. 125 km/hr (78 mph) at sea level, Endurance 5½ hours, Service ceiling 5000 m. (16,400′)

GOTHA G IX (LVG)

GOTHA G X

Powered by two Maybach IVa, it flew about September 1918 with double tail and landing wheels. It appears that G III was the designation applied by the company, not the Army.

Last, we show the Siemens-Schuckert three-engined bomber. Six were ordered in October 1917 as the SSW G III, but were redesignated L I on April 1, 1918, as a type half-way between the Gs and the R giants. They had Caproni-style twin fuselages with 245 hp Maybach Mb IVa engines in their nose, and a third was a pusher behind a central nacelle. Guns were mounted in cockpits in the nose and on each boom.

The first example flew August 5, 1918 and crashed August 22, but the second was flown October 14. Despite the Armistice, a third unarmed example was completed in February 1919.

Giant Bombers, 1915–18

SIEMENS FORSSMAN "R" (modified)

Riesenflugzueg, or giant aircraft is what Germans called their multi-engined bombers. Designed for long distance raids or for large bomb loads on short trips, these big biplanes were the largest aircraft used in combat in World War I. No German bombers built in World War II were as large.

When the war began in 1914, the only four-engined aircraft in the world were Russian; the Sikorsky "Ilya Mourometz" giants that began their bombing operations on February 15, 1915.

Shortly after the war's beginning three German firms, Siemens-Schuckert (SSW), Union Flugzeug-werke, and Versuchsbau GmbH Gotha-Ost (VGO) began construction of "R" planes, although that designation was not yet officially established. It was SSW that sent the first example to the front, but its first effort in this class was quite unsuccessful.

A Swedish designer, Villehad Forssman, projected a four-engined biplane along the lines of Sikorsky's giants, and in October 1914 construction began on the Forssman R. Four 110 hp Mercedes were mounted on the lower wing. Originally the nose was a stubby pilot's enclosure in line with the propeller, but then an open observer's cockpit was added. The aircraft was completed early in 1915, but was unable to pass its tests.

Forssman left SSW, and Harold Wolff redesigned the aircraft with 220 hp engines in the inner mounts and an enclosed bow. A flight test was again attempted in September 1915, but nosed over on a landing run. Once again it was rebuilt and not until April 1916, was *Idflieg* persuaded to accept it. Soon after, the SSW Forssman R broke its back on a ground engine run.[1]

The Union G I was a four-engined biplane of R size, but with a G designation, because its 110 hp inverted Mercedes mounted back to back in enclosed nacelles on the lower wing were not serviceable in flight. Featuring a three rudder tail, it was flown in May 1915.

[1] Its misfortunes are detailed in the fine study of R types by Haddow and Grosz.

SIEMENS FORSSMAN "R"
Mercedes, 4 X 110 hp
DIMENSIONS: Span 24 m. (78'9"), Lg. 16.5 m. (54'2"), Wing Area 140 qm. (1506 sq. ft.)
WEIGHT: Empty 3250 kg. (7150 lb.)
PERFORMANCE: Speed—Max. 115 km/hr (71 mph)

SIEMENS FORSSMAN "R" (final form)
Mercedes, 2 X 220 hp and 2 X 110 hp
DIMENSIONS: Span 24 m. (78'9"), Lg. 16.5 m. (54'2"), Wing Area 140 qm. (1506 sq. ft.)
WEIGHT: Empty 4000 kg. (8820 lb.), Gross 5200 kg. (11,440 lb.)
PERFORMANCE: Speed—Max. 120 km/hr (74 mph), Climb 2000 m./28 min. (6560'/28 min.)

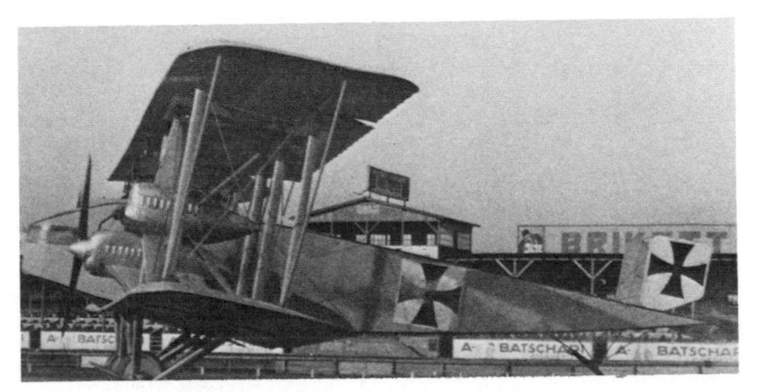

UNION G I
Mercedes Fh 1256, 4 X 110 hp
DIMENSIONS: Span 21 m. (68′10½″), Lg. 18.2 m. (59′8½″), Ht. 3.74 m. (12′3″), Wing Area 72.4 qm. (779 sq. ft.)
WEIGHT: Empty 1960 kg. (4321 lb.), Gross 2765 kg. (6096 lb.)
PERFORMANCE: Speed—Max. 128 km/hr (79 mph), Cruising speed 115 km/hr (71 mph), Climb 1000 m./14.5 min. (3280′/14.5 min.), Service ceiling 3500 m. (11,480′)

DAIMLER R I (G I)
Mercedes D III, 4 X 160 hp
DIMENSIONS: Span 21.08 m. (69′2″), Lg. 18.35 m. (60′20″), Ht. 3.8 m. (12′6″), Wing Area 73.62 qm. (792 sq. ft.)
WEIGHT: Empty 2512 kg. (5538 lb.), Gross 3630 kg. (8000 lb.)
PERFORMANCE: Speed—Max. 120 km/hr (74 mph), Cruising speed 114 km/hr (71 mph), Climb 1000 m./16.8 min. (3280′/17 min.), Service ceiling 3000 m. (9840′)

When Daimler-Motoren-Gesellschaft, makers of the Mercedes engines, decided to begin aircraft production, they chose this bomber design, and had a second G I built by Union. This aircraft broke apart during a September 1, 1915, test.

Nevertheless, Daimler went ahead with its own version, strengthening the airframe, and installing four 160 hp Mercedes. As the Daimler R I, it flew late in 1915 and was followed by a modified second example. In 1916, Daimler added two Daimler R IIs, similar but for improved nacelles. These aircraft were redesignated G I and G II in 1916.

When these aircraft were unsuccessful in obtaining further orders, Daimler concentrated on license production of Friedrichshafen G III twin-engined bombers.

DAIMLER R II
Mercedes D III, 4 X 160 hp
DIMENSIONS: Span 21.15 m. (69′4″), Lg. 18 m. (59′8½″) Ht. 3.75 m. (12′3½″), Wing Area 70.6 qm. (760 sq. ft.)
WEIGHT: Empty 2510 kg. (5534 lb.), Gross 3700 kg. (8157 lb.)
PERFORMANCE: Speed—Max. 119 km/hr (74 mph), Cruising speed 114 km/hr (71 mph), Climb 1000 m./17 min. 3280′/17 min.), Service ceiling 3000 m. (9840′)

SIEMENS-STEFFEN DESIGNS

More success was enjoyed by the Siemens three-engined bombers designed by Bruno and Franz Steffen and the parallel VGO bombers by Alexander Baumann. The engines on the Steffen types were all centralized within the fuselage, while the VGOs utilized outboard nacelles.

Along with the ill-fated Forssman design, Siemens-Schuckert had proceeded with the central-engine concept of the Steffen brothers. An agreement with the brothers in December 1914 began the work in Berlin. For secrecy, parts were shipped to Neumuenster for assembly.

Three 150 hp Benz Bz III engines were in the fuselage, two in the nose and the other behind the gear box from which transmission shafts ran to a

SIEMENS-SCHUCKERT R I
Benz Bz III, 3 X 150 hp
DIMENSIONS: Span 28 m. (91′10″), Lg. 17.5 m. (57′5″), Ht. 5.2 m. (17′1″), Wing area 138 qm. (1485 sq. ft.)
WEIGHT: Empty 4000 kg. (8820 lb.), Gross 5200 kg. (11,466 lb.)
PERFORMANCE: Speed—Max. 110 km/hr (68 mph), Climb 2000 m./35 min. (6560′/35 min.), Range 520 km. (322 miles), Endurance 4 hours, Service ceiling 3700 m. (12,136′)

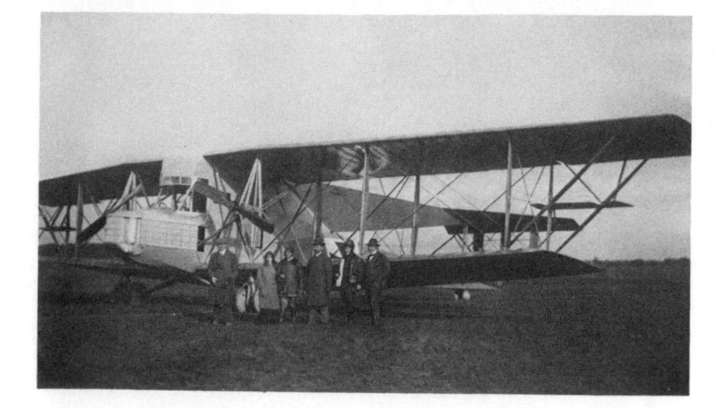

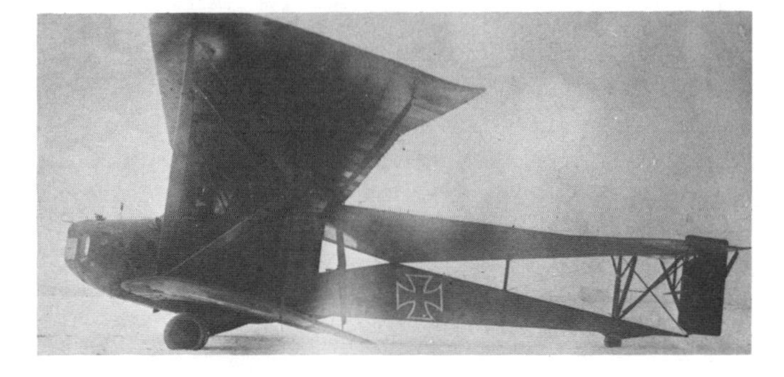

SSW R II 2/15
Mercedes D IVa, 3 X 260 hp
DIMENSIONS: Span 38 m. (124'8"), Lg. 18.5 m. (60'8"), Ht. 4.6 m. (15'1"), Wing Area 233 qm. (2507 sq. ft.)
WEIGHT: Empty 6150 kg. (13,560 lb.), Gross 8460 kg. (18,654 lb.)
PERFORMANCE: Speed—Max. 110 km/hr (68 mph), Climb 2000 m./23 min. (6560'/23 min.), Range 450 km. (280 miles), Service ceiling 3800 m. (12,465')

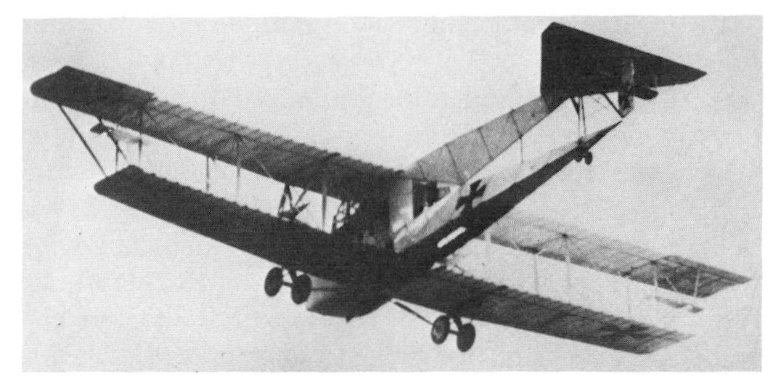

SSW R III 3/15
Benz Bz IV, 3 X 220 hp
DIMENSIONS: Span 34.33 m. (112'7"), Lg. 17.7 m. (58'1"), Ht. 4.6 m. (15'1"), Wing Area 177 qm. (1905 sq. ft.)
WEIGHT: Empty 5400 kg. (11,907 lb.), Gross 6820 kg. (15,038 lb.)
PERFORMANCE: Speed—Max. 132 km/hr (82 mph), Climb 2000 m./35 min. (6560'/35 min.), Range 450 km. (280 miles), Service ceiling 3000 m. (9840')

SSW R IV 4/15
Maybach HS, 3 X 240 hp, later Benz Bz IV, 3 X 240 hp
DIMENSIONS: Span 28.22 m./37.6 m. (92'7"/123'4"), Lg. 17.7 m./18 m. (58'/59'½"), Ht. 4.6 m. (15'1"), Wing Area 156 qm./201 qm. (1679 sq. ft./2163 sq. ft.)
WEIGHT: with Benz, Empty 5450 kg. (12,017 lb.), Gross 6900 kg. (15,214 lb.)
PERFORMANCE: Speed—Max. 130 km/hr (81 mph), Climb 2000 m./36 min. (6560'/36 min.), Range 450 km. (279 miles), Service ceiling 3050 m. (10,000')

SSW R V 5/15
Benz Bz IV, 3 X 220 hp
DIMENSIONS: Span 34.33 m. (112'7"), Lg. 17.7 m. (58'1"), Ht. 4.6 m. (15'1"), Wing Area 177 qm. (1905 sq. ft.)
WEIGHT: Empty 5300 kg. (11,686 lb.), Gross 6766 kg. (14,920 lb.)
PERFORMANCE: Speed—Max. 132 km/hr (82 mph), Climb 2000 m./35 min. (6560'/35 min.), Range 450 km. (280 miles), Service ceiling 3000 m. (9840')

tractor propeller between the wings on each side. The fuselage split backward into upper and lower tapering tail booms, a feature providing beam-mounted guns a wide field of fire. A third gun mount was planned on top, but it does not appear that weapons were actually fitted. Construction consisted of wire-braced steel tubing in the fuselage and wire-braced wood for the three-bay wings; all with the usual fabric covering.

When the Steffen brothers made the maiden flight on May 24, 1915, the aircraft was designated SSW G I 31/15. After successful trials, the five-place prototype was delivered in July, and by October 13, it was on the Eastern front with Flt. Abt. 31. On November 6, 1915, it became SSW R I, 1/15, first of the series.

Experience showed the type unready for actual combat operations, so the R I was shipped back home and was used for training future R crews at Doeberitz. Six improved versions ordered on June 10, 1915, were originally designated G 32–37/17, but on November 6 became R II–R VII, 2–7/15, and in service were labeled R 2 to R 7.

Three 240 hp Maybach HS engines powered the new ships, which otherwise had the R I's layout; the choice of these airship units was to prove a mistake. The specifications called for a 500 kg. (1100 lb.) bomb load, six hours flight duration and 135 km/hr

(103 mph). Protection was to include a 20 mm. Becker gun and 200 kg. of armor, although neither were actually provided on complete machines. The outstanding service feature was the accessibility of all engines for inflight maintenance.

The R 2 flew on October 26, 1915, the R 3 was delivered on December 30, and the R 4 the following January 29. None proved acceptable in their original form. The Maybach engines were unreliable and had to be replaced, and the wing span increased. During lengthy rebuilding the R 2 received 260 hp Mercedes engines and was accepted in June 1917, while R 3 was accepted in December 1916 with 220 hp Benz powerplants.

Both R 2 and R 3 served only as trainers, but the R 4 was flown with the Benz engines on March 14, 1917, and on April 27 flew to the Eastern front. There it joined the "giant" squadron, Rfa 501 at Vilna, where the R 6 and 7 models were already in service. These machines had profited by earlier experience and utilized the new engines and wider wings.

The R 5 was delivered with Benz engines on August 13, 1916, went to Vilna in September and made several bombing missions before being put out of action by a February 14, 1917, night landing. First SSW giant actually in combat, however, was the R 6, tested in April 1916 and delivered to Rfa 501 on August 7. It was joined on February 26, 1917, by the Mercedes-powered R 7, and in April by the renovated R 4.

These three bombers made numerous raids against Russian bases and railways, until August 1917, when Rfa 501 was transferred to the Western front and re-equipped with Staaken giants. The SSW R planes, despite their innovations and size, had served both in operations and training without any lives lost in them. Normally, they carried four or five men, and three machine guns, and up to 500 kg. (1100 lb.) of bombs; 750 kg. on the R 7.

THE VGO GIANTS

Parallel to Siemens development were the giants designed by Professor Alexander Baumann for VGO (*Versuchsbau Gotha Ost*), which later became the Staaken firm. Sponsored by Count Ferdinand von Zeppelin, whose lighter-than-air pioneering did not blind him to the potential of airplanes, design work began in September 1914 and was finished in December. Powered by three 240 hp Maybachs, the big (138′5½″ span) VGO I biplane made its first flight on April 11, 1915.

One engine was in the bow, and the others were set as pushers in nacelles between the wings. There were four rudders in the biplane tail, while three pairs of double wheels were set under the engines and the nose. Continuing difficulties with the Maybach HS engines delayed the program until an engine failure on December 15, 1915, caused a crash into a forest, and the plane had to be reconstructed.

Meanwhile a second example, the VGO II, was flown on October 25, 1915, and delivered to the Army's Doeberitz testing field the following month with serial number R 9/15. Similar to the first one in

SSW R VI 6/15
Benz Bz IV, 3 X 220 hp
DIMENSIONS: Span 33.36 m. (109′5″), Lg. 17.7 m. (58′1″), Ht. 4.6 m. (15′1″), Wing Area 171 qm. (1840 sq. ft.)
WEIGHT: Empty 5250 kg. (11,576 lb.), Gross 6800 kg. (14,994 lb.)
PERFORMANCE: Speed—Max. 132 km/hr (82 mph), Climb 2000 m./36 min. (6560′/36 min.), Range 600 km. (372 miles), Service ceiling 2950 m. (9680′)

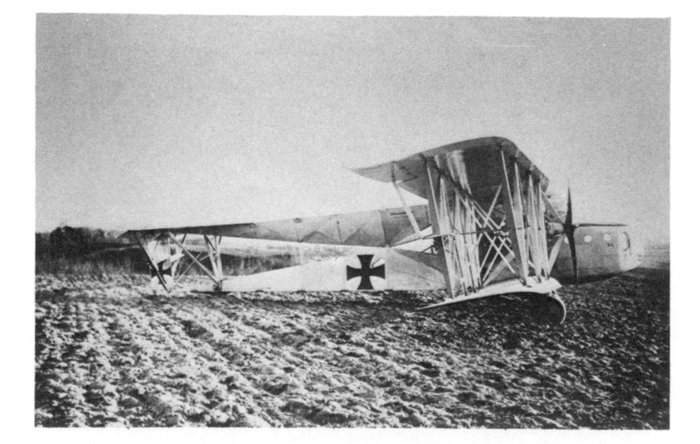

SSW R VII 7/15
Mercedes D IVa, 3 X 260 hp
DIMENSIONS: Span 38.44 m. (126′1″), Lg. 18.5 m. (60′8″), Ht. 4.6 m. (15′1″), Wing Area 210′ qm. (2262 sq. ft.)
WEIGHT: Empty 5700 kg. (12,568 lb.), Gross 7960 kg. (17,552 lb.)
PERFORMANCE: Speed—Max. 130 km/hr (81 mph), Climb 2000 m./27 min. (6560′/27 min.), Range 550 km. (341 miles), Service ceiling 3200 m. (10,500′)

ZEPPELIN-STAAKEN VGO I (RML I)
Maybach HS, 3 X 240 hp
DIMENSIONS: Span 42.2 m. (138'5½"), Lg. 24 m. (78'9"), Ht. 6.6 m. (21'7½"), Wing Area 332 qm. (3572 sq. ft.)
WEIGHT: Empty 6520 kg. (14,377 lb.), Gross 9250 kg. (20,396 lb.), Fuel 1500 liters (3960 gal.)
PERFORMANCE: Speed—Max. 110 km/hr (68 mph), Climb 2000 m./39 min. (6560'/39 min.), Service ceiling 3000 m. (9840')

ZEPPELIN-STAAKEN VGO II
Maybach HS, 3 X 240 hp
DIMENSIONS: Span 42.2 m. (138'5"), Lg. 23.78 m. (78'), Ht. 7 m. (22'11½"), Wing Area 332 qm. (3572 sq. ft.)
WEIGHT: Empty 6637 kg. (14,635 lb.), Gross 10,203 kg. (22,498 lb.), Fuel 1812 liters (4784 gal.)
PERFORMANCE: Speed—Max. 110 km/hr (68 mph), Climb 2000 m./39 min. (6560'/39 min.), Service ceiling 3000 m. (9840')

layout, it had just two rudders, and was protected by machine gunners in each nacelle's bow, and above and below the fuselage behind the wings.

In February 1916, the VGO II was flown to Rfa 500, a new unit in Latvia, and flew night raids before it was retired to Doeberitz as a trainer in 1917. By then VGO I had been rebuilt with twin rudders and four gun stations, and was accepted by the German Navy as the RML 1. Flown to the same Latvian base as its twin, it made the first of four bombing attacks on August 15, 1916. The bomb load ran from 500 to 894 kg. (1100–1967 lb.) depending on the target. Another crash interrupted its operations, and it was once again returned for reconstruction. This time, two engines were placed in each nacelle for a total of five, but the first trial flight on March 10, 1917, ended in a fatal crash.

The third aircraft was begun in October 1915 with a new powerplant. Instead of the unreliable Maybachs, six 160 hp Mercedes D IIIs were installed in pairs coupled to each propeller. Two were side by side in the nose, and two in tandem in each nacelle, with transmission shafts back to the pusher propellers. A gunner-mechanic sat in front of each nacelle, and another mechanic was in the extremely noisy nose engine compartment.

The crew of seven included the commander, two pilots, three mechanics, and a wireless operator. Some seven missions were flown before VGO III (R 10/15) was destroyed on January 24, 1917, in the first fatal R plane accident.

The VGO plant in Staaken, west of Berlin, was on August 1, 1916, renamed officially Zeppelin Werke Staaken GmbH. Nevertheless, the British press inaccurately referred to these giants as "Super-Gothas," although they had no connection with the more famous types.

ZEPPELIN-STAAKEN VGO III
Mercedes D III, 6 X 160 hp
DIMENSIONS: Span 42.2 m. (138'5½"), Lg. 24.5 m. (80'4½"), Ht. 6.8 m. (22'3½"), Wing Area 332 qm. (3572 sq. ft.)
WEIGHT: Empty 8600 kg. (18,963 lb.), Gross 11,600 kg. (25,578 lb.), Fuel 3500 liters (924 gal.)
PERFORMANCE: Speed—Max. 120 km/hr (74 mph), Climb 1000 m./16 min. (3280'/16 min.), Range 700 km. (435 miles), Service ceiling 3000 m. (9840')

EXPERIMENTAL GIANTS

Several experimental multi-engined bombers developed by other firms appeared at this time, but they were all unsuccessful. For example, the Albatros G I retained the G designation, but had four 120 hp Mercedes on the lower wing. Built by OAW at Schneidemuehl, it first flew on January 31, 1916, with a 4319 kg. (9502 lb.) gross weight. Nothing further, however, is known of its fate.

Hermann Dorner designed the DFW R I with outboard propellers connected to four 220 hp Mercedes within the center of the plywood fuselage.

ALBATROS G I

DFW R I (T 26)
Mercedes D IV, 4 X 220 hp
DIMENSIONS: Span 30.5 m. (100′), Lg. 17.6 m. (57′9″), Ht. 6 m. (19′8″), Wing Area 186 qm. (2002 sq. ft.)
WEIGHT: Empty 6800 kg. (14,994 lb.), Gross 9400 kg. (20,733 lb.)
PERFORMANCE: Speed—Max. 120 km/hr (75 mph) at sea level, Climb 1000 m./10 min. (3280′/10 min.), Endurance 6 hours, Service ceiling 3300 m. (10,820′)

DFW R II (T 26)
Mercedes D IVa, 4 X 260 hp
DIMENSIONS: Span 35.06 m. (115′), Lg. 20.93 m. (68′8″), Ht. 6.4 m. (21′), Wing Area 266 qm. (2862 sq. ft.)
WEIGHT: Empty 8634 kg. (19,038 lb.), Gross 11,693 kg. (25,783 lb.), Fuel 2450 liters (647 gal.)
PERFORMANCE: Speed—Max. 135 km/hr (84 mph), Climb 2000 m./58 min. (6560′/58 min.)

Two propellers just below the upper wing were driven by the upper engines, while two pusher props mounted on the lower wing were run by the lower powerplants. A pair of nose wheels were added to the main gear, and a nose, rear and lower gun positions were provided along with a double tail.

The only example, R I 11/15, first flew on September 5, 1916. Tests showed strengthening was needed, and so it was modified and the span and weight increased. On April 31, 1917, the DFW was flown to Rfa 500 in Latvia, where it served until an accidental crash in September.

LINKE-HOFMANN R I (8/15, also 40/16)
Mercedes D IVa, 4 X 260 hp
DIMENSIONS: Span 32 m./33.2 m. (105′½″/108′11″), Lg. 15.6 m. (51′2″), Ht. 6.78 m. (22′3″), Wing Area 264 qm./265 qm. (2840 sq. ft./2850 sq. ft.)
WEIGHT: Empty 5800 kg./8000 kg. (12,790 lb./17,640 lb.) Gross 9000 kg./11,200 kg. (19,845 lb./24,696 lb.)
PERFORMANCE: Speed—Max. 140 km/hr/130 km/hr (87 mph/ 81 mph)

DAIMLER R III

ZEPPELIN-STAAKEN R IV (12/15)
Mercedes 2 X 160 hp and Benz 4 X 220 hp
DIMENSIONS: Span 42.2 m. (138′5½″), Lg. 23.2 m. (76′1″), Ht. 6.8 m. (22′3½″), Wing Area 332 qm. (3572 sq. ft.)
WEIGHT: Empty 8772 kg. (19,342 lb.), Gross 13,035 kg. (28,742 lb.), Fuel 2080 liters (550 gal.)
PERFORMANCE: Speed—Max. 125 km/hr (77.5 mph), Climb 1000 m./10 min. (3280′/10 min.) 3000 m./89 min. (9840′/89 min.), Range 750–800 km. (465–498 miles), Service ceiling 3700 m. (12,140′)

By then, the larger R II, 15/16, was ready for its first flight on September 17. This bulky aircraft used 260 hp Mercedes arranged like those on R I, but never went to the front because it had been surpassed by the Staaken types. Two more examples were completed in 1918 numbered R 16/17 and R 17/17. The former flew July 22 with turbo-superchargers driven by an added 120 hp Mercedes D II. A plan to finish three others after the war as transports was abandoned.

Strangest looking of the giants was the Linke-Hofmann R I. The deep fuselage actually had three layers; the pilot's cabin on top, four 260 hp Mercedes, and on the bottom the bombardier and the fuel tanks. Two tractor propellers were mounted on outriggers, and the first example (LiHo R I 8/15) had transparent "Cellon" covering on the rear fuselage. This attempt at partial invisibility proved futile. On May 10, 1917, the R 8 crashed and a similar fate met 40/16, a second machine with three-bay wings and fabric-covered fuselage.

Another experimental bomber was the little known Daimler R III. It is apparent that the four propellers were turned by engines within the fuselage.

ZEPPELIN-STAAKEN BOMBERS

The most successful multi-engined bombers were the Zeppelin giants built at Staaken. Shortly after the firm moved from its VGO facility, the Staaken R IV was flown on August 16, 1916. Constructed at the older factory, it was similar in size and layout to the VGO layouts, but was powered by six 260 hp Mercedes.

Two engines were coupled to the front propeller, and two were coupled in each nacelle to a pusher propeller. Seven machine guns were mounted; one in the front of each nacelle, one in each wing above the nacelle, two at the rear cockpit, and one at a ventral position. This particular aircraft (12/15) had a remarkable service, operating in the East with Rfa 500 from May to September 1917, and for the rest of the war with Rfa 501 against Britain and France. After the war, the giant was seen on a tour of German cities.

No pusher propellers were used in the Staaken R V, powered by five 245 hp Maybach high-compression engines. One engine was in the nose, the others were coupled in nacelles. Gun posts were placed at the back of each nacelle, two more at the wide rear cockpit, a ventral post, and another in a pod in the center of the top wing's leading edge. For communication, a difficult problem on these noisy machines, there was a pneumatic-tube message system. Crew numbered eight men, who operated R V

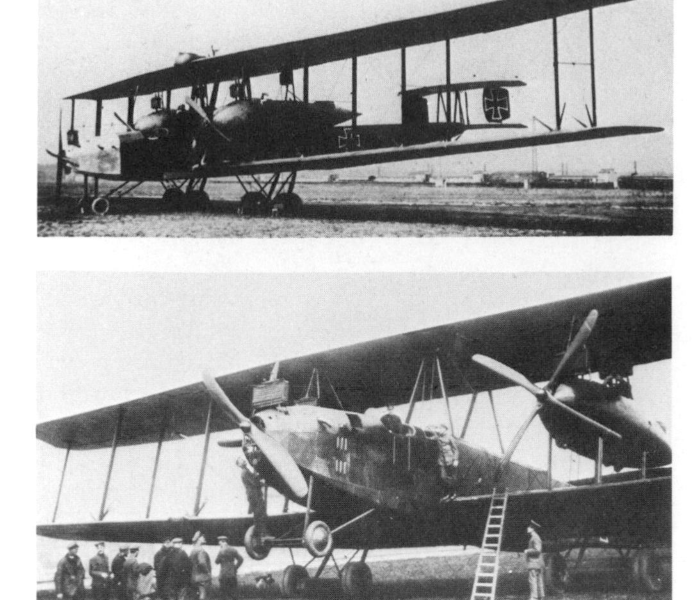

STAAKEN R V (13/16)
Maybach Mb IVa, 5 X 245 hp at 2000 m. (6560′)
DIMENSIONS: Span 42.2 m. (138′5½″), Lg. 23 m. (75′5½″), Ht. 6.8 m. (22′3½″), Wing Area 332 qm. (3572 sq. ft.)
WEIGHT: Empty 9450 kg. (20,837 lb.), Gross 13,010 kg. (28,687 lb.)
PERFORMANCE: Speed—Max. 135 km/hr (84 mph), Climb 1000 m./10 min. (3280′/10 min.), Service ceiling 4500 m. (14,760′)

STAAKEN R VI (25/16)
Mercedes D IVa, 4 X 260 hp
DIMENSIONS: Span 42.2 m. (138′5½″), Lg. 22.1 m. (72′6″), Ht. 6.3 m. (20′8″), Wing Area 332 qm. (3572 sq. ft.)
WEIGHT: Empty 7680 kg. (16,934 lb.), Gross 11,460 kg. (25,269 lb.), Fuel 2115 liters (558 gal.)
PERFORMANCE: Speed—Max. 130 km/hr (81 mph), Climb 1000 m./11 min. (3280′/11 min.) 3000 m./55 min. (9840′/55 min.), Range 1000 km. (620 miles), Service ceiling 3800 m. (12,490′)

on the Western front from December 1917 to the war's end.

The only giant bomber built in quantity was the Staaken R VI. Eighteen were built; six by Staaken, six by Aviatik, three by OAW and three by Schutte-Lanz. They served on the Western front, from September 1917 to the war's end.[2]

Four engines were used on the R VI, mounted in tandem pairs in the nacelles. Ten used the 260 hp Mercedes, but eight had 245 hp Maybach Mb IVa high-compression units giving their best at 2000 meters (6560′). Lack of a nose motor permitted an open bombardier-gunner's pit ahead of the enclosed pilot's cabin. There were few flight instruments, but an electric telegraph gave signals to the seven-man crew and a wireless set was provided. Unlike previous models, the R VI sat tail down, with only small nose wheels for safety.

Gun positions were provided in the nose, rear and ventral opening, with three captured Lewis guns being favored for their light weight. A few added the two upper wing positions seen on the R IV. Internal racks held up to 18 100 kg. (220 lb.) bombs, but 300 kg. (660 lb.) were carried externally. On three occasions, a 1000 kg. (2200 lb.) bomb was dropped on London. Bomb load varied with fuel load, but 750 kg. (1650 lb.) and 3200 liters (798 gal.) permitted a 900 km. (560 mile) range.

Our photos show the first R VI (25/16) delivered June 1917 with Mercedes engines, the R VI (Av.) 52/16 of June 1918 with Maybachs and modified nose, and 30/16, which in April 1918 attained 5900 m. (19,350′) using adjustable pitch propellers and a

[2] The combat record, as well as the construction of R types is detailed in Haddow and Grosz, *The German Giants.*

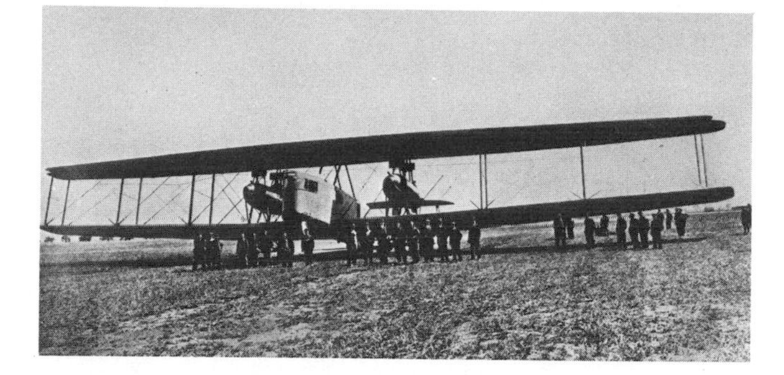

STAAKEN R VI (Av.) 52/16
Maybach Mb IVa, 4 X 245 hp
DIMENSIONS: As R VI
WEIGHT: Empty 7921 kg. (17,465 lb.), Gross 11,848 kg. (26,125 lb.), Fuel 3000 liters (792 gal.)
PERFORMANCE: Speed—Max. 135 km/hr (84 mph), Climb 1000 m./10 min. (3280'/10 min.), 3000 m./43 min. (9840'/43 min.), Range 1000–13000 km. (620–800 miles), Service ceiling 4320 m. (14,170')

turbo-supercharger powered by a 120 hp Mercedes D II added behind the pilot.

Parallel to the later R VI series was a series of Staaken giants that reverted to the engine mounted in the nose. On the first of these, R VII 14/15, the level landing and six engine arrangement of the R IV was used with the slightly shorter R VI fuselage. Delivered on July 3, 1917, the R VII crashed on the way to the front on August 16.

The next Staaken model was supposed to use four 350 hp Daimler engines, but when this powerplant failed to meet service reliability standards, five 245 hp Maybachs were fitted. One was in the nose, and the others in tandem in the nacelles.

Three examples, designated R XIV 43, 44 and 45/17 were delivered from April to August 1918, and all were on the Western front with Rfa 501. On August 10, 1918, R 43/16 was attacked by night-flying Camels, and became the first R plane known to be destroyed by Allied fighters, the only other was R 31/16 on September 16, 1918.

Nine crewmen were carried on the R XIV, and gun positions were provided in the dorsal, ventral and two upper wing pits. Unlike the enclosed cabins of its predecessors, the pilots sat in an open cockpit ahead of the wings. On the third example, this cockpit was placed behind the wings.

The next three Staaken were designated R XV 46 to 48/17 and were delivered August and September 1918. These appeared nearly identical to the R XIV, and were followed by a lighter, and refined version designated R XIVa 69/17. This aircraft was delivered on October 19, 1918, and after the war was used to fly money to a Ukrainian provisional government.

STAAKEN R VI 30/16
Mercedes D IVa, 4 X 260 hp (plus 120 hp D II for supercharger)
DIMENSIONS: As R VI
WEIGHT: Empty 8600 kg. (18,963 lb.), Gross 11,590 kg. (25,556 lb.)
PERFORMANCE: Speed—Max. 160 km/hr (99 mph), Climb 1000 m./10 min. (3280'/10 min.) 3000 m./35 min. (9840'/35 min.), Service ceiling 5900 m. (19,350')

STAAKEN R VII
Mercedes D III, 2 X 160 hp and Benz Bz IV, 4 X 220 hp
DIMENSIONS: Span 42.2 m. (138'5½"), Lg. 22.1 m. (72'6"), Ht. 6.8 m. (22'3½"), Wing Area 332 qm. (3572 sq. ft.)
WEIGHT: Empty 8923 kg. (19,675 lb.), Gross 12,953 kg. (28, 560 lb.), Fuel 3295 liters (870 gal.)
PERFORMANCE: Speed—Max. 130 km/hr (81 mph), Climb 1000 m./12 min. (3280'/12 min.) 3000 m./50 min. (9840'/50 min.), Service ceiling 3850 m. (12,628')

STAAKEN R XIV
Maybach Mb IVa, 5 X 245 hp
DIMENSIONS: Span 42.2 m. (138'5½"), Lg. 22.5 m. (73'10"). Ht. 6.3 m. (20'8"), Wing Area 334 qm. (3594 sq. ft.)
WEIGHT: Empty 10,350 kg. (22,822 lb.), Gross 14,450 kg. (31,862 lb.), Fuel 3150 liters (832 gal.)
PERFORMANCE: Speed—Max. 130 km/hr (81 mph), Climb 3000 m./70 min. (9840'/70 min.), Range 1300 km. (800 miles), Service ceiling 3700 m. (12,136')

STAAKEN R XIVa
Maybach Mb IVa, 5 X 245 hp
DIMENSIONS: as R XIV
WEIGHT: Empty 10,000 kg. (22,050 lb.), Gross 14,250 kg. (31,420 lb.)
PERFORMANCE: Speed—Max. 135 km/hr (84 mph), 1000 m./7 min. (3280'/7 min.) 3000 m./45 min. (9840'/45 min.), Range 1300 km. (800 miles), Service ceiling 4500 m. (14,760')

STAAKEN R XVI (Av.)
Benz Bz IV Tractor, 2 X 220 hp and Benz Bz VI Pusher, 2 X 530 hp
DIMENSIONS: Span 42.2 m. (138'5½"), Lg. 22.5 m. (73'10"), Ht. 6.5 m. (21'4"), Wing Area 340 qm. (3658 sq. ft.)
WEIGHT: Empty 10,400 kg. (22,932 lb.), Gross 14,650 kg. (32,300 lb.)
PERFORMANCE: Speed—Max. 130 km/hr (81 mph), Service ceiling 3710 m. (12,172')

Two sister ships, the last Staaken built for the war, were also completed and used in these operations.

Aviatik, who had produced six R VIs under license, had a contract to build three similar giants powered by two 220 hp Benz engines in the nacelle's front, and two new 530 hp Benz Bz VI pushers in the rear. Designated R XVI (Av.) 49/17, the first was completed in June–July 1918, but was wrecked in a test landing. A sister ship was flown without armament provisions in 1919. Hopes for civilian application were dashed by postwar conditions.

This review of German wartime bombers concludes with three experimental giants whose development came too late for wartime use. The AEG R I was built with a steel-tube framework and four 260 hp Mercedes in the fuselage coupled to two large propellers between the wings. The pilot's cockpit was on the top of the fuselage behind the wings. Nose, dorsal and ventral guns were provided. This prototype was flown on June 14, 1918, but crashed on September 3, when a propeller disintegrated, and no further examples were completed.

Four Mercedes also powered the Linke-Hofmann R II, but all four were in the front fuselage geared to just one 23' two-bladed propeller. The crew of six comprised two pilots, navigator, radio operator and two gunner mechanics. Two gunner's pits were placed side-by-side atop the rear fuselage, and future planes projected a retractable belly gun position.

This striking aircraft was perhaps the largest flown on one propeller, but was not tested until January 1919. Later, its layout was copied by the Breguet Leviathan.

AEG R I 21/16
Mercedes, 4 X 260 hp
DIMENSIONS: Span 36 m. (118'1½"), Lg. 19.5 m. (63'11½"), Ht. 6.35 m. (20'10"), Wing Area 260 qm. (2798 sq. ft.)
WEIGHT: Empty 9000 kg. (19,845 lb.), Gross 12,700 kg. (28,000 lb.), Fuel 2750 liters, (726 gal.)
PERFORMANCE: Data not available

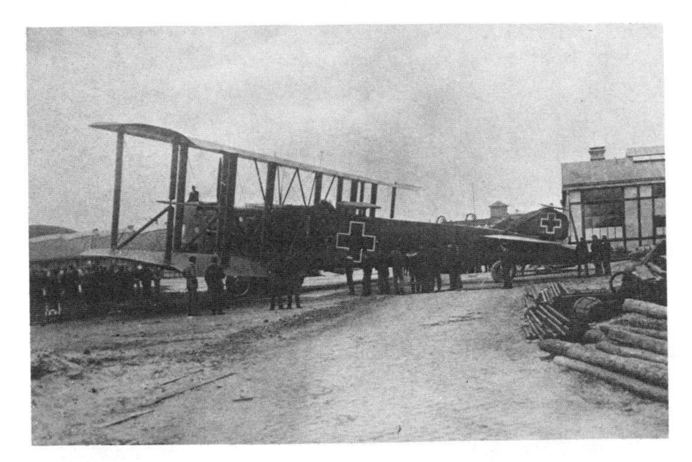

Finally, there is this war's largest aircraft, the Siemens-Schuckert R VIII. Designed in 1917 by Harold Wolff, it was powered by six 300 hp Basse and Selve engines within the fuselage. Transmission shafts from the forward powerplant pair turned two outboard two-bladed tractor propellers, while the remaining four were coupled to two four-bladed pusher propellers.

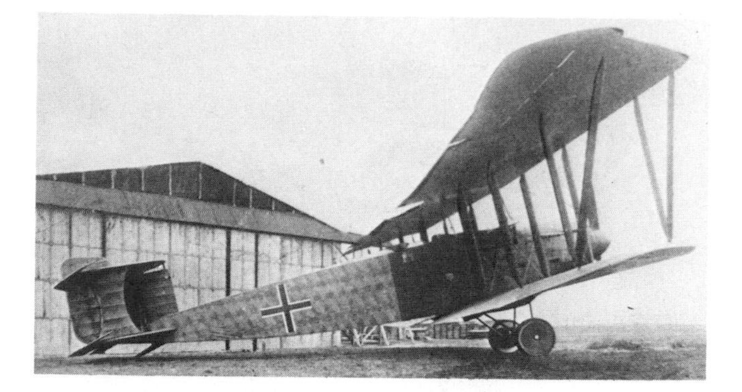

LINKE-HOFMANN R II
Mercedes D IVa, 2 X 260 hp
DIMENSIONS: Span 42.16 m. (138′4″), Lg. 20.32 m. (66′8″), Ht. 7.1 m. (23′3½″), Wing Area 320 qm. (3444 sq. ft.)
WEIGHT: Empty 8000 kg. (17,460 lb.), Gross 12,000 kg. (26,460 lb.)
PERFORMANCE: Speed—Max. 130 km/hr (81 mph), Climb 1000 m./8 min. (3280′/8 min.) 3000 m./45 min. (9840 m./45 min.), Endurance 7 hours, Service ceiling 3200 m. (10,500′)

The four-bay wings were of wooden construction and spanned 48 m. (157′6″) while the fuselage was of steel tubing with metal covering for the nose and engine room. Gun mounts were provided in the nose, rear cockpits (2) and floor; with a cockpit in the top wing's center.

Although the R VIII was supposed to be finished on March 1, 1918, it was not ready in time for the war. On March 1, 1919, it taxied out of its hangar for ground tests, for the firm hoped to find commercial application. A propeller malfunction damaged the aircraft on June 6, and the government canceled the project on June 26. The war's largest plane never flew.

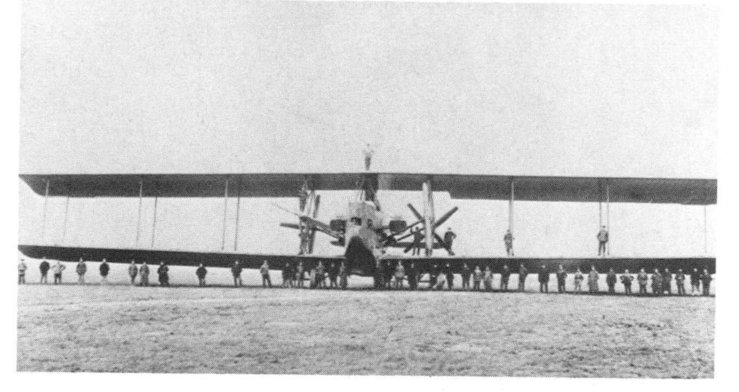

SSW R VIII 23/16
Basse & Selve BaS IVa, 6 X 300 hp
DIMENSIONS: Span 48 m. (157′6″), Lg. 21.6 m. (70′10″), Ht. 7.4 m. (24′3″), Wing Area 440 qm. (4734 sq. ft.)
WEIGHT: Empty 10,500 kg. (23,150 lb.), Gross 15,900 kg. (35,060 lb.)
PERFORMANCE: (estimated) Speed—Max. 125 km/hr (78 mph), Range 900 km. (560 miles), Service ceiling 4000 m. (13,120′)

Part 4 Marine Aircraft

FRIEDRICHSHAFEN FF 19

11.

General Purpose Seaplanes

German naval seaplanes in 1914 were single-engined, twin-float biplanes with a crew of two. Like the Army's B types, they were unarmed, with the observer sitting in the front cockpit ahead of the pilot.

Of some 35 Navy airplanes on hand when the war began, only 12 seaplanes were available for active service; six at Helgoland in the North Sea, four at Kiel and two at Putzig in the Baltic. These aircraft were assigned to coastal defense patrols when weather permitted.

New seaplane stations were opened on the sea coast islands of Borkum, Norderney, and Sylt (List) as more aircraft became available. Improved models were provided with small bombs, which were first used against an enemy cruiser on November 24, 1914. During 1915, the B-type seaplanes were joined by BFT types which added radio transmitters in April 1915, and C types with a flexible machine gun. Other categories added during the war were:

CHFT––two-seater with one gun plus wireless receiver and transmitter
C2MG and C3MG––two-seaters with two or three guns
E––single-seat flying boat with fixed guns
ED––single-seat floatplanes with fixed guns
T––twin-engined torpedo floatplanes

Landplane stations used the B, C, CL, D, E and G types used by the Army. Total seaplane deliveries amounted to some 2500–3000 aircraft, compared to over 47,000 Army aircraft produced in Germany during the war.

The most active seaplanes early in the war were the Friedrichshafen two-seaters designed by Theodor Kober. A 100 hp water-cooled Mercedes, three-bay wings and a third float under the tail were seen on five FF 19 biplanes delivered before the war, numbered 25 to 29.[1]

Ten more FF 19s were delivered, beginning September 1914, and joined in November by the first FF 29s, powered by the 120 hp Mercedes. The 14 first-line Navy floatplanes serviceable on December 14, 1914, comprised nine FF 19s, three FF 29s, and two Albatros W two-seaters.

Friedrichshafens were the first floatplanes sent to the German base at Zeebrugge on the Belgian coast in December 1914. Armed with their little 11 lb. bombs, they troubled enemy shipping along the Channel. One is shown in our photo perched on the U 12 on January 6, 1915, in an experiment to see if the aircraft's reach across the Channel could be extended by carrying it partway by submarine. The idea had tactical disadvantages, and was abandoned.

Twenty-five FF 29s were delivered with 120 hp Mercedes, while a 100 hp Mercedes powered the 12 parallel FF 29As. Seven more FF 29s were completed with Argus engines by September 1915. Ten FF 29s and all FF 29As had an unbalanced rudder, while a low balanced rudder was used on the rest of the FF 29s.

Among the first two-seaters active was the Albatros W 1, a float version of the widely used B I Army biplane. Designed by Ernst Heinkel before the war as the WDD, it was of very conventional three-bay layout. Six W 1s were delivered from July to November 1914, and one attacked the British submarine E 11 with small bombs on April 17, 1915. Ten more W 1s built in 1915 also had 150 hp Benz engines, while another was accepted with a Mercedes.

[1] Numbers assigned to seaplanes are listed in H. J. Nowarra, *op. cit.* p. 51–53, and are from 1918's *Atlas Deutscher Seeflugzeuge,* as are the delivery dates given in this section.

FRIEDRICHSHAFEN FF 29 on U 12

FRIEDRICHSHAFEN FF 33H

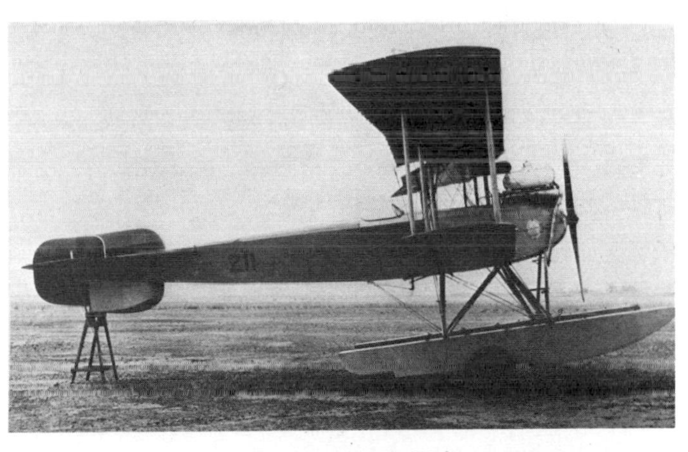

FRIEDRICHSHAFEN FF 29
Mercedes D II, 120 hp
DIMENSIONS: Span 16.8 m. (55′1¼″), Lg. 10.2 m. (33′6″), Wing Area 60 qm. (646 sq. ft.)
WEIGHT: Data not available
PERFORMANCE: Speed—Max. 95 km/hr (59 mph) at sea level

Rumpler's compact two-bay biplanes, the 4 B series were twin-float versions of the Army's B I two-seater. Wartime deliveries began in August with three aircraft using the 150 hp Benz, but the 100 hp Mercedes was on four Rumpler 4 B 11 seaplanes delivered November–December 1914. Thirty Benz-powered Rumpler 4B 12s delivered from April 1915 to March 1916 were unarmed except for a few 11 lb. bombs.

Hansa-Brandenburg's two-seaters of this class were designed by former Albatros designer Heinkel. Except for the balanced rudder, they resembled their three-bay progenitors. The Hansa-Brandenburg W was a pre-war civil design with a 150 hp Benz or Maybach engine. About 26 were delivered December 1914 to February 1916 including one fitted with a machine gun in August 1915.

FRIEDRICHSHAFEN FF 29a

RUMPLER 4B 12
Benz Bz III, 150 hp
DIMENSIONS: Span 14.5 m. (47′7″), Lg. 9.6 m. (31′6″), Ht. 3.6 m. (11′10″)
WEIGHT: Empty 960 kg. (2112 lb.), Gross 1280 kg. (2816 lb.)
PERFORMANCE: Data not available

HANSA-BRANDENBURG NW
Mercedes D III, 160 hp
DIMENSIONS: Span 16.27 m. (53′4½″), Lg. 9.85 m. (32′4″), Wing Area 55 qm. (593 sq. ft.)
WEIGHT: Empty 1020 kg. (2244 lb.), Gross 1648 kg. (3625 lb.)
PERFORMANCE: Speed—Max. 122 km/hr (76 mph), Climb 1000 m./9.5 min. (3280′/9.5 min.), Endurance 5 hours

ALBATROS W 1
Benz Bz III, 150 hp
DIMENSIONS: Span 14.3 m. (46′11″), Lg. 8 m. (26′3″), Wing Area 40 qm. (430 sq. ft.)
WEIGHT: Data not available
PERFORMANCE: Speed—Max. 120 km/hr (75 mph), Range 500 km. (310 miles), Service ceiling 1000 m. (3280′)

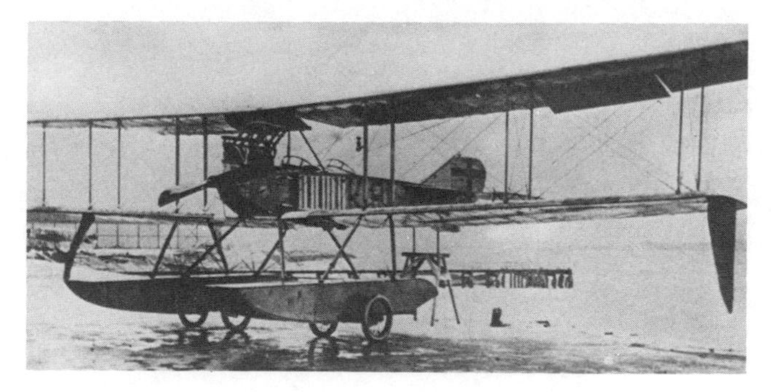

The next model had a 160 hp Mercedes and became the Hansa-Brandenburg NW. The first five NWs arrived on the North Sea coast in December 1915, and carried ten 11 lb. bombs. Eighteen more delivered by June 1916 added radio transmitters and could patrol some five hours. Eight delivered later lacked this equipment, so were probably intended only as trainers. Similar were the 16 smaller GNW aircraft, which also carried radio and bombs.

Guns were unnecessary for aircraft patrolling the North Sea and Baltic coasts beyond the range of early Allied aircraft, but English Channel operations demanded machine gun armament, leading to the next generation of two-seaters.

HANSA-BRANDENBURG GNW
Mercedes D III, 160 hp
DIMENSIONS: Span 16.2 m. (53'2"), Lg. 9.65 m. (31'8"), Wing Area 55.15 qm. (593 sq. ft.)
WEIGHT: Empty 1100 kg. (2420 lb.), Gross 1743 kg. (3835 lb.)
PERFORMANCE: Speed—Max. 115 km/hr (71 mph), Climb 1000 m./9.5 min. (3280'/9.5 min.), Range 600 km. (370 miles)

GOTHA WD I prototype

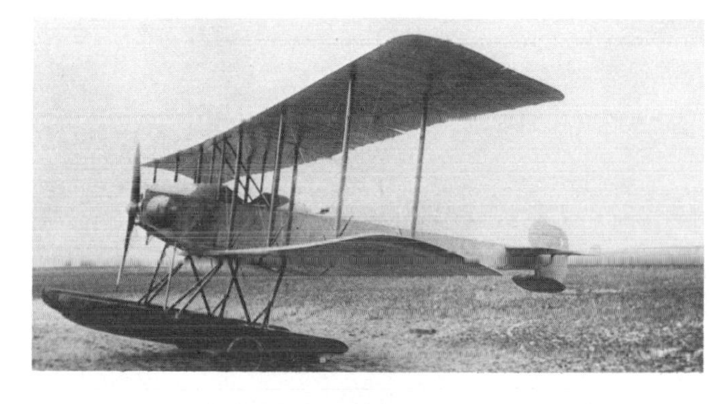

GOTHA WD 1
Mercedes D I, 100 hp
DIMENSIONS: Span 14.1 m. (46'3"), Lg. 10.3 m. (33'9½"), Wing Area 50 qm. (538 sq. ft.)
WEIGHT: Empty 900 kg. (1980 lb.), Gross 1220 kg. (2684 lb.)
PERFORMANCE: Speed—Max. 90 km/hr (56 mph) at sea level, Range 540 km. (335 miles), Service ceiling 2500 m. (8200')

Gothaer Waggonfabrik produced a successful line of seaplanes designed by Karl Roesner. As no lake or river was near Gothaer's factory in central Germany, there seaplanes had only a pool for flotation tests, and had to be flight tested at Warnemuende, the Navy's test station.

A 100 hp Gnome rotary had been used on the original Gotha WD 1 in April 1914, but the WD 2 had a water-cooled 150 hp Benz, with radiators on each side of the front cockpit. They were three-bay biplanes based on the pre-war Avro style. The German Navy acquired the WD 2 in July 1914, as its seaplane ⋇60, and the original WD 1 on August 8, (as ⋇59) while another WD 2 with a 150 hp Rapp engine (⋇61) was received December 10, 1914.

Five WD floatplanes ordered in August 1914 (⋇254–258) with the 150 hp Benz were delivered to Warnemuende from December 24, 1914, to April 7, 1915. Five WD 1 floatplanes (⋇285–289) delivered February 17 to April 24, 1915 were powered by the 100 hp Mercedes.[2]

The 160 hp Mercedes D III powered five WD 2s (⋇236–240) delivered June 29 to August 28, 1915. These WD 2s had been delivered without armament, but another (⋇424) appeared November 12, 1915, with a machine gun on a ring atop the upper wing. The observer had to stand on his seat thru a hole in the wing to aim his weapon. Since Nos. 424 and 425 were intended for Turkey, wheels were tem-

[2] The Gotha company records loaned by Peter M. Grosz provided the data in this section. Since it contradicts older accounts, dates and numbers are given in more detail. Aircraft delivery dates usually preceded by a few days the official Navy acceptances given in the *Atlas*.

GOTHA WD 2
Benz Bz III, 150 hp
DIMENSIONS: Span 15.6 m. (51′2″), Lg. 10.5 m. (34′5½″), Wing Area 56 qm. (603 sq. ft.)
WEIGHT: Empty 1065 kg. (2343 lb.), Gross 1630 kg. (3586 lb.)
PERFORMANCE: Speed—Max. 90 km/hr (56 mph) at sea level, Range 540 km. (335 miles), Service ceiling 2500 m. (8200′)

porarily attached below the floats for overland flight delivery.

Five more unarmed, Benz-powered WD 2s were delivered in February–March 1916 for a German Black Sea unit, but the gun and a Mercedes D III were fitted to eight Turkish WD 2s; six from March 22 to April 15, 1916, and the last two in August.

Several experimental seaplanes were also developed by Gotha. The small WD 5 delivered August 7, 1915, was a WD 2 with cut-down, two-bay wings, a 160 hp Mercedes and no guns. As ✠118, it was Lieutenant Walter Friedensburg's favorite aircraft.

A pusher layout offered a clear view forward for the observer, and so the Gotha WD 3 had its engine facing backward, the propeller behind regular WD 2 wings. Graceful tail booms supported twin rudders,

GOTHA WD 2 (✠424)

GOTHA WD 2 (for Turkey)

GOTHA WD 3
Mercedes D III, 160 hp
DIMENSIONS: Span 15.6 m. (51′2″), Wing Area 54 qm. (581 sq. ft.)
WEIGHT: Empty 1105 kg. (2431 lb.), Gross 1710 kg. (3762 lb.)
PERFORMANCE: Speed—Max. 112 km/hr (69 mph) at sea level, Range 670 km. (415 miles), Service ceiling 3000 m. (9840′)

GOTHA WD 5
Mercedes D III, 160 hp
DIMENSIONS: Span 12.5 m. (41′), Lg. 10.3 m. (33′9½″), Wing Area 42.5 qm. (457 sq. ft.)
WEIGHT: Empty 900 kg. (1980 lb.), Gross 1465 kg. (3223 lb.)
PERFORMANCE: Speed—Max. 126 km/hr (78 mph) at sea level, Range 440 km. (273 miles), Service ceiling 2000 m. (6560′)

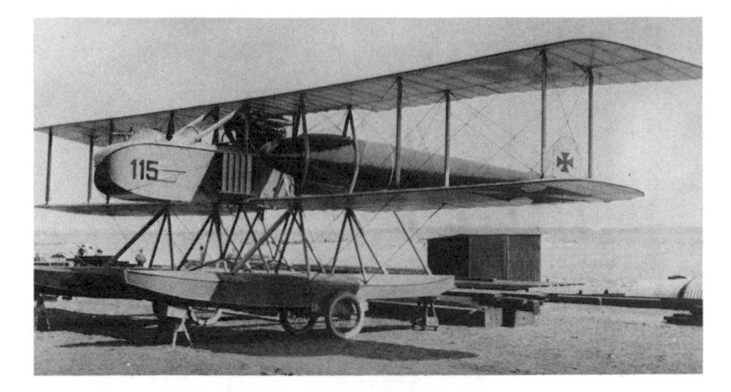

AGO C I (※115)

FRIEDRICHSHAFEN FF 31
Maybach Mb III, 160 hp
DIMENSIONS: Span 16.85 m. (55′3″), Lg. 10.15 m. (33′3½″), Wing Area 60 qm. (646 sq. ft.)
WEIGHT: Empty 1040 kg. (2288 lb.), Gross 1530 kg. (3366 lb.)
PERFORMANCE: Speed—Max. 98 km/hr (61 mph) at sea level

and a gun ring was placed on the glass-protected bow cockpit. Delivered September 14, 1915, the WD 3 (※259) was accepted in December.

The twin-boomed layout was also used on Ago two-seat pushers for the Army, and an Ago C I fitted with twin floats was the Navy's ※115. A three-bay version appeared in 1916, with a 150 hp Benz and bow gun, and a 220 hp Mercedes powered a C II seaplane version in July 1916.

Friedrichshafen also produced pushers designed for a forward flexible gun. The FF 31 had a 160 hp Maybach, pusher propeller, and the tail on a lattice strut frame (*Gitterschwanz*), but the wings and floats were those of the conventional FF 29. Performance was adequate for a seaplane, but not for an aircraft intended to attack enemy planes. Only two examples ordered in August 1914 were built, the first delivered in May 1915, the other in August.

Twin tail booms and rudders, a 240 hp Maybach and a radio transmitter were provided on the FF 34, which appeared at Warnemuende in January 1916, and returned to the factory in April. The same ※117 was used the following year for the conventional-looking FF 44.

Pusher aircraft were not accepted for production by the German Navy because they had inadequate qualities, and no defense against attacks from the rear, and tractor aircraft like the FF 33 were selected for general use.

The most widely used seaplane of World War I was the conventional-looking Friedrichshafen FF 33 two-seater, which evolved from an unarmed patrol type to a true combat aircraft.

In its original form, this three-bay biplane had the pilot in the rear cockpit, differed from the earlier FF 29 only in the absence of a tail float, and had different engines interspersed on the production line. The 100 hp Mercedes D I powered the first three FF 33A patrol aircraft delivered March 1915. From

AGO C II W
Benz Bz IV, 220 hp
DIMENSIONS: Span 18.3 m. (60′½″), Lg. 10.4 m. (34′1½″), Ht. 3.58 m. (11′9″)
WEIGHT: Empty 1316 kg. (2895 lb.), Gross 1946 kg. (3621 lb.)
PERFORMANCE: Speed—Max. 137 km/hr (85 mph) at sea level

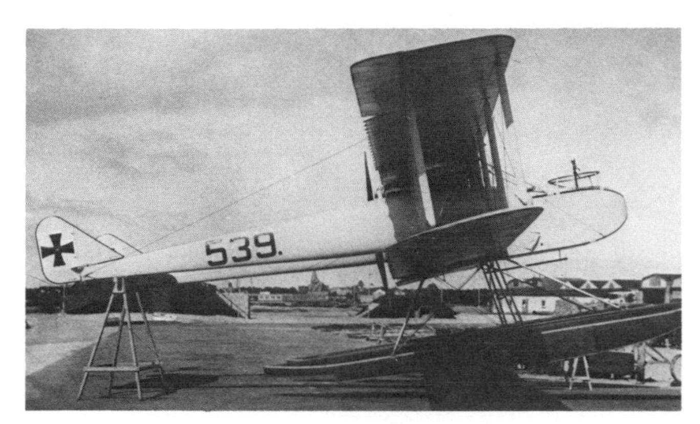

FRIEDRICHSHAFEN FF 34

April to August 1915, Friedrichshafen delivered six FF 33 models with the 120 hp Mercedes D II, three more FF 33As, five FF 33Bs with the 160 hp Maybach Mb III, and three FF 33Es with the 160 hp Mercedes and a wireless transmitter.

The main variant appeared in August 1915, also designated FF 33E, but with a 150 hp Benz Bz III and wireless transmitter. These aircraft served as the German fleet's workhorses in 1915–17, whose tasks included all patrols and reconnaissance duties that were needed. Of some 180 FF 33Es (ending February 1918), 35 were delivered as trainers with dual controls and no radios. The most famous example was FF 33E ✻841, which went on the merchant raider Wolf's cruise to the Indian and Pacific oceans. About 56 flights were made in 1917 to scout ahead of the raider, halting intended victims with warning bombs.

The first of these biplanes to put the observer in the rear seat with a flexible Parabellum gun was the FF 33B with the Mb III engine and a tail float added. It was delivered May to August 1915. Five FF 33Fs with the Bz III and rear flexible gun were delivered December 1915 through February 1916.

The most thorough combat conversion, however, was FF 33E ✻510, delivered in October 1915 with a gun ring, new tail, and its wings cut to two bays for more agility. This two-bay biplane arrangement was chosen for the FF 33H, armed with small bombs and a flexible gun to control merchant ships operating near German bases. Forty-five delivered from March to October 1916 had their radiator in front of the upper wing.

FRIEDRICHSHAFEN FF 33E (✻633)
Benz Bz III, 150 hp
DIMENSIONS: Span 16.8 m. (55′1½″), Lg. 10.27 m. (33′8½″), Wing Area 52.7 qm. (567 sq. ft.)
WEIGHT: Empty 1010 kg. (2222 lb.), Gross 1538 kg. (3383 lb.)
PERFORMANCE: Speed—Max. 126 km/hr (78 mph) at sea level

FRIEDRICHSHAFEN FF 33B (✻460)

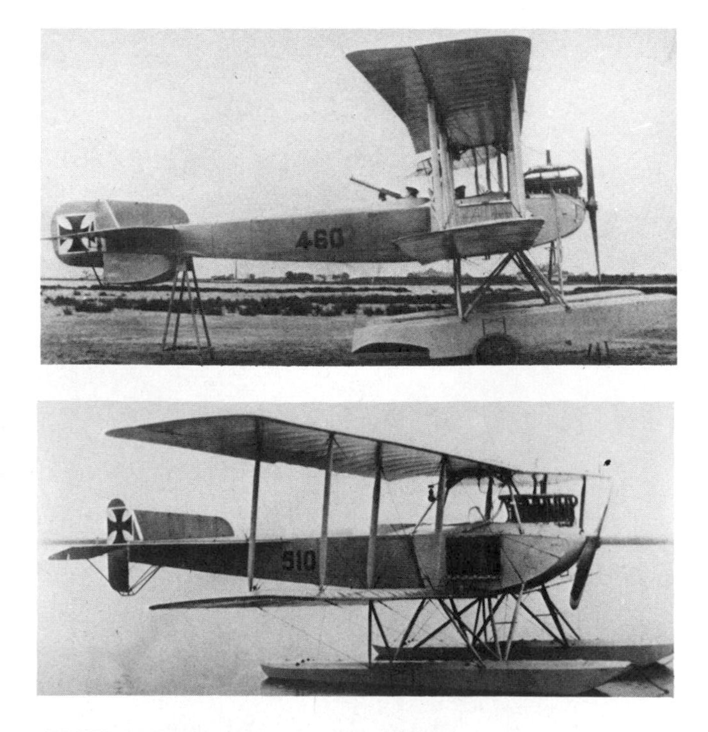

FRIEDRICHSHAFEN FF 33E (✻570)

FRIEDRICHSHAFEN F 33H
Benz Bz III, 150 hp
DIMENSIONS: Span 14.2 m. (46′7″), Lg. 9.6 m. (31′6″), Wing Area 43.4 qm. (467 sq. ft.)
WEIGHT: Empty 948 kg. (2090 lb.), Gross 1477 kg. (3256 lb.)
PERFORMANCE: Speed—Max. 123 km/hr (76 mph) at sea level

FRIEDRICHSHAFEN FF 33L (#1001, delivered March 1917)
Benz Bz III, 150 hp
DIMENSIONS: Span 13.2 m. (43′4″), Lg. 8.95 m. (29′4″), Wing Area 40.5 qm. (436 sq. ft.)
WEIGHT: Empty 940 kg. (2068 lb.), Gross 1415 kg. (3113 lb.)
PERFORMANCE: Speed—Max. 140 km/hr (87 mph), at sea level, Cruising speed 130 km/hr (81 mph), Range 450 km. (280 miles)

The next model was the unarmed FF 33J, reverting to three-bay configuration. Thirty were delivered in 1917, but it appears that these and a 1918 series were intended primarily as trainers, like 30 FF 33S models.

Among 1917's best general-purpose floatplanes was the FF 33L, which was a Benz-powered two-bay biplane like the FF 33H except for a neat prop spinner. The first appeared in January 1917 as C2MG fighters with a pilot's forward fixed gun as well as the observer's weapon. Along with 50 of these built by September 1917, Friedrichshafen made 85 more as CHFT types, in which radio equipment was added for patrol work and the forward gun deleted. The two versions worked together in service.

Our photos show four examples of the FF 33L: #1001 the first CHFT; #1262, a CHFT with

FRIEDRICHSHAFEN FF 33L (July 1917)

FRIEDRICHSHAFEN FF 33L (August 1917)

FRIEDRICHSHAFEN FF 33L (1918)

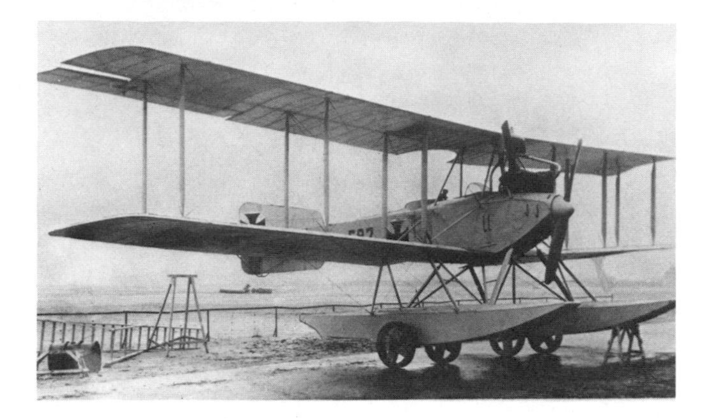

FRIEDRICHSHAFEN FF 39
Benz Bz IV, 200 hp
DIMENSIONS: 17.1 m. (56′1″), Lg. 11.4 m. (37′5″), Wing Area 68.5 qm. (737 sq. ft.)
WEIGHT: Empty 2200 kg. (4840 lb.), Gross 3171 kg. (6976 lb.)
PERFORMANCE: Speed—Max. 140 km/hr (87 mph)

FRIEDRICHSHAFEN FF 40
Maybach Mb IV, 240 hp
DIMENSIONS: Span 21 m. (68′11″), Lg. 12.43 m. (40′9″), Ht. 4.4 m. (14′5″), Wing Area 88.9 qm. (957 sq. ft.)
WEIGHT: Empty 1829 kg. (4024 lb.), Gross 2539 kg. (5586 lb.)
PERFORMANCE: Speed—Max. 125 km/hr (78 mph) at sea level

balanced ailerons; #1578 a C2MG with fixed gun and new tail, and #3144, an experimental 1918 model. It may be added that one FF 33L was delivered with wheeled landing gear. While the number of FF 33s delivered as trainers is uncertain, at least 445 of all models were accepted by the Navy, the largest total for any wartime seaplane on either side.

From the FF 33, Friedrichshafen developed the larger FF 39 with a 200 hp Benz. The prototype (#587) was delivered in March 1917 with a flexible gun and radio transmitter for the observer. Thirteen production FF 39s, delivered from April to September 1917, had both sending and receiving equipment. No further examples were made, the Navy turning instead to the more advanced FF 49.

Friedrichshafen also tested two large prototypes utilizing a 240 hp Maybach engine. The radical three-place FF 40 had the Maybach inside the fuselage behind the pilot, with drive shafts to two outboard propellers behind the wings. This allowed an observer's bow cockpit with a clear view forward, but probably presented mechanical problems. The FF 40 was delivered in July 1916. More conventional was the FF 44 delivered in May 1917 with a standard fuselage, engine, and rear cockpit arrangement, but it was rejected by the Navy.

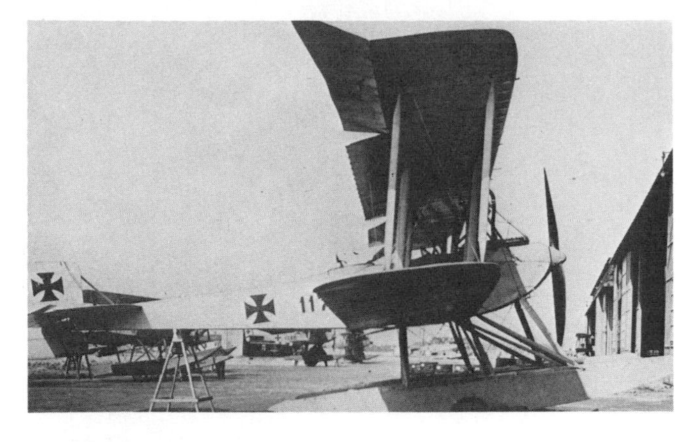

FRIEDRICHSHAFEN FF 44
Maybach Mb IV, 240 hp
DIMENSIONS: Span 18.4 m. (60′4″), Lg. 10.85 m. (35′7″), Ht. 4.25 m. (13′11″), Wing Area 68.5 qm. (737 sq. ft.)
WEIGHT: Gross 2305 kg. (5071 lb.)
PERFORMANCE: Speed—Max. 145 km/hr (90 mph), Climb 1000 m./8.8 min. (3280′/8.8 min.)

GOTHA WD 8
Maybach Mb IV, 240 hp
DIMENSIONS: Span 16 m. (52′6″), Lg. 11.2 m. (36′9″), Wing Area 59 qm. (635 sq. ft.)
WEIGHT: Empty 1250 kg. (2750 lb.), Gross 1770 kg. (3894 lb.)
PERFORMANCE: Speed—Max. 130 km/hr (81 mph), Range 480 km. (298 miles), Service ceiling 4500 m. (14,760′)

During the 1916–17 period, Friedrichshafen's success obscured the seaplanes others produced for armed reconnaissance. Gotha, for instance, built a series of single-engined biplanes designed by Karl Roesner.

The bulky Gotha WD 8 was a single engined version of the WD 7 torpedo plane, with the same three-bay wing and triple tail, but a single 240 hp Maybach. A gun ring was provided on the second cockpit, but no other examples were made. The prototype was delivered February 9, 1916, as a comparison with the twin-engined WD 7 configuration.

Two-bay wings and a 160 hp Mercedes were used on the WD 9 delivered April 19, 1916. A gun ring was also fitted to #572, the only example purchased by the German Navy. This was further developed into the WD 12 delivered February 19, 1917. While the only one (#944) built for the German Navy was unarmed, it led to the armed WD 13 for Turkey.

GOTHA WD 9
Mercedes D III, 160 hp
DIMENSIONS: Span 12.5 m. (41′), Wing Area 42.5 qm. (457 sq. ft.)
WEIGHT: Empty 968 kg. (2130 lb.), Gross 1470 kg. (3234 lb.)
PERFORMANCE: Speed—Max. 132 km/hr (82 mph) at sea level, Service ceiling 3000 m. (9840′)

GOTHA WD 12
Mercedes D III, 160 hp
DIMENSIONS: Span 15 m. (49′2½″), Lg. 10 m. (32′10″), Ht. 3.82 m. (12′6″), Wing Area 54 qm. (581 sq. ft.)
WEIGHT: Empty 1000 kg. (2200 lb.), Gross 1550 kg. (3410 lb.)
PERFORMANCE: Speed—Max. 140 km/hr (87 mph), Climb 1000 m./7.5 min. (3280′/7.5 min.), Range 770 km. (478 miles), Service ceiling 4200 m. (13,780′)

The Gotha WD 13 is not included in German Navy records for all 24 were produced December 24, 1917, to June 1918 as the standard Turkish patrol type.[3] Powered by a 150 hp Benz and armed with a flexible Parabellum gun, the WD 13 appeared with two different rudder shapes, and had the fuel tank placed on the right upper wing. Most Turkish aircraft were flown by German pilots, whose story remains untold to this day.

[3] These aircraft are also called WD 12 on Gotha records, but the WD 13 label of earlier books is continued here for convenience.

GOTHA WD 13
Benz Bz III, 150 hp
DIMENSIONS: Span 15.1 m. (49′6½″), Lg. 10 m. (32′10″), Wing Area 53 qm. (570 sq. ft.)
WEIGHT: Empty 970 kg. (2134 lb.), Gross 1530 kg. (3366 lb.)
PERFORMANCE: Speed—Max. 130 km/hr (81 mph) at sea level, Cruising speed 110 km/hr (68 mph), Range 750 km. (465 miles), Service ceiling 3800 m. (12,460′)

GOTHA WD 15
Mercedes D IVa, 260 hp
DIMENSIONS: Span 17.2 m. (56′5″), Lg. 11.2 m. (36′9″), Wing Area 64.5 qm. (694 sq. ft.)
WEIGHT: Empty 1545 kg. (3399 lb.), Gross 2300 kg. (5060 lb.)
PERFORMANCE: Speed—Max. 152 km/hr (94 mph), Range 900 km. (560 miles), Service ceiling 4200 m. (13,780′)

ALBATROS W 2

Gotha's last single-engined seaplane was its largest, the WD 15, powered by a 260 hp Mercedes. Two delivered on April 30 and September 19, 1917, were unarmed and apparently not ordered because Gotha was told to concentrate on *Grossflugzeug*.

Albatros and Hansa-Brandenburg also offered seaplane prototypes based on Army reconnaissance designs, using the 160 hp Mercedes. The Albatros W 2 (※450) delivered in June 1916 was an adaptation of the C III two-seater, while the Hansa-Brandenburg LW of August 1916 was a seaplane version of Heinkel's LDD, or C I for Austria. Both types had the armament standard for reconnaissance two-seaters; a single Parabellum gun on the observer's ring.

Three Hansa-Brandenburg KW seaplanes had been ordered in December 1915 as three-bay biplanes with a 200 hp Benz. Although armed in the usual manner, they did not appear until 1918, and were probably used only for training.

The Imperial Navy Yards (*Kaiserliche Werfte*) at Danzig, Kiel and Wilhelmshaven built a few two-seater seaplanes in 1916–17. Since these aircraft were unarmed and intended only for training, we pause only for the last Wilhelmshaven aircraft, ※947. Provided with flexible gun and radio, it was powered by a 220 hp Mercedes D IV with a four-bladed propeller. Further information is unavailable.

Dr. Josef Sablatnig established a factory in Berlin where he built seaplanes distinguished by pointed noses and overhanging upper wings. The SF 1 prototype was delivered in October 1915, and won orders for 16 SF 2s delivered, beginning June 1916, by Sablatnig, and ten each by LFG and LVG. These aircraft were unarmed two-seaters with radio transmitters and a 160 hp Mercedes and were used mainly for training.

A larger three-bay biplane armed with a flexible gun and using a radio transmitter and 220 hp Benz Bz IV was built as the SF 3. It differed from the other Sablatnigs by its plywood fuselage and balanced controls. Like the SF 4 fighter, it was unsuccessful and, after flight tests, was canceled in October 1917.

Sablatnig's most widely used type was the SF 5,

BRANDENBURG LW
Mercedes D III, 160 hp
DIMENSIONS: Span 12.4 m. (40′8″), Lg. 9.5 m. (31′2″), Wing Area 42.6 qm. (458 sq. ft.)
WEIGHT: Empty 994 kg. (2187 lb.), Gross 1555 kg. (3421 lb.)
PERFORMANCE: Speed—Max. 131 km/hr (81 mph) at sea level, Climb 1000 m./12 min. (3280′/12 min.), Range 400 km. (248 miles)

HANSA-BRANDENBURG KW
Benz Bz IV, 200 hp
DIMENSIONS: Span 16.3 m. (53′6″), Lg. 10.55 m. (34′7¼″), Wing Area 60 qm. (646 sq. ft.)
WEIGHT: Empty 1471 kg. (3236 lb.), Gross 2135 kg. (4697 lb.)
PERFORMANCE: Speed—Max. 134 km/hr (83 mph), Climb 800 m./11 min. (2625′/11 min.)

SABLATNIG SF 5
Benz Bz III, 150 hp
DIMENSIONS: Span 17.3 m. (56′9″), Lg. 9.5 m. (31′2″). Ht. 3.8 m. (12′6″), Wing Area 50.56 qm. (544 sq. ft.)
WEIGHT: Empty 1010 kg. (2222 lb.), Gross 1600 kg. (3540 lb.)
PERFORMANCE: Speed—Max. 136 km/hr (85 mph), Climb 1000 m./14 min. (3280′/14 min.)

KW WILHELMSHAFEN (※947)

SABLATNIG SF 2
Mercedes D III, 160 hp
DIMENSIONS: Span 18.35 m. (60′2½″), Lg. 9.83 m. (32′3″) Ht. 4.25 m. (13′11″), Wing Area 56 qm. (603 sq. ft.)
WEIGHT: Empty 1078 kg. (2372 lb.), Gross 1697 kg. (3733 lb.)
PERFORMANCE: Speed—Max. 130 km/hr (81 mph), Climb 1500 m./18 min. (4920′/18 min.)

SABLATNIG SF 3 (※619)

which differed from the SF 2 mainly by its 150 hp Benz and slightly smaller size. Although they had only a radio, and no armament, the SF 5 was active in the Baltic, where examples fell into Russian hands. Veteran pilots were very critical of its flying qualities.

Production amounted to 51 built by Sablatnig beginning in January 1917, plus 30 by LVG and ten by LFG to February 1918. Further trainer developments were an SF 6 landplane and the SF 8 dual-control seaplane.

Marinewerft Luebeck-Travemuende was a DFW subsidiary that built a few seaplanes for the German Navy. Its first product was the unarmed F 1, powered by a 160 hp Mercedes, but two other seaplanes were canceled. Instead, an F 2 powered by a 220 hp Mercedes was ordered March 1916, and accepted in

TRAVEMUENDE F2 (※677)

TRAVEMUENDE F 2 (production)
Mercedes D IV, 220 hp
DIMENSIONS: Span 18 m. (59′1″), Lg. 11.09 m. (36′4″), Ht. 3.55 m. (11′8″)
WEIGHT: Empty 1140 kg. (2508 lb.), Gross 2104 kg. (4629 lb.)
PERFORMANCE: Speed—Max. 141 km/hr (88 mph), Climb 3000 m./30 min. (9840′/30 min.)

LUBECK-TRAVEMUENDE F 4
Benz Bz IV, 200 hp
DIMENSIONS: Span 16.7 m. (54′9″), Lg. 11.3 m. (37′1″), Ht. 4 m. (13′1″), Wing Area 67.64 qm. (731 sq. ft.)
WEIGHT: Empty 1366 kg. (3005 lb.), Gross 1988 kg. (4396 lb.)
PERFORMANCE: Speed—Max. 138 km/hr (86 mph), Climb 1000 m./9.3 min. (3280′/9.3 min.)

FRIEDRICHSHAFEN FF 49C/49B
Benz Bz IV, 200 hp
DIMENSIONS: Span 17.15 m. (56′3″), Lg. 11.53 m. (37′10″), Ht. 4.45 m. (14′7″), Wing Area 71.16 qm. (766 sq. ft.)
WEIGHT: Empty 1485 kg/1432 kg. (3267 lb./3150 lb.), Gross 2135 kg./2097 kg. (4697 lb./4613 lb.)
PERFORMANCE: Speed—Max. 140/152 km/hr (87/91 mph), Cruising speed 130 km/hr (81 mph), Climb 1000 m./8 min. (3280′/8 min.), Range 700 km. (435 miles)

December. Number 677's outstanding feature was the *four* sets of N struts on each side of the 19 meter (62′4″) wings. A flexible gun and radio transmitter were standard.

Sixteen production F 2s built from July 1917 to May 1918 differed by having three-bay wings one meter shorter. The first one, 1147, had the prototype's tail form, but the rest had a modified tail design. Equipped with two-way radio and flexible gun, they were used on North Sea patrols.

The Luebeck-Travemuende F 4 had a flexible gun, two-way radio, 200 hp Benz and three pairs of ordinary struts. The first three were completed in March 1918, a fourth example was ordered in June. Thirty production aircraft were ordered, but it is doubtful if all were built. One was used after the war by the famous Christiansen to find herring for Norwegian fishermen; quite a different occupation for this Navy ace!

During the war's last year, the most active German reconnaissance seaplane was Friedrichshafen's FF 49 series. Basically this was a stronger version of the FF 33 with the same three-bay wings and twin floats, but the Benz powerplant was increased to 200 hp.

The first batches delivered, beginning in September 1917, included 28 FF 49Cs with standard CHFT equipment of one flexible gun and a two-way radio, and 22 FF 49Bs with only a transmitter and no guns. Further orders provided 120 more FF 49Cs, plus 30 built by June 1918 as C2MG/HFT models that added a fixed gun for the pilot; unusual among naval reconnaissance aircraft.

Forty more CHFTs were on order, plus 45 built under license by Sablatnig, and 20 ordered from LFG, but there is no data on how many of these were

FRIEDRICHSHAFEN FF 59c
Benz Bz IV, 200 hp
DIMENSIONS: Span 17.8 m. (58′5″), Lg. 11.3 m. (37′1″), Ht. 4.25 m. (13′11″), Wing Area 71.5 qm. (769 sq. ft.)
WEIGHT: Empty 1580 kg. (3476 lb.), Gross 2240 kg. (4928 lb.)
PERFORMANCE: Speed—Max. 142 km/hr (88 mph), Cruising speed 130 km/hr (81 mph), Climb 1000 m./8.9 min. (3280/8.9 min.), Range 900 km. (560 miles)

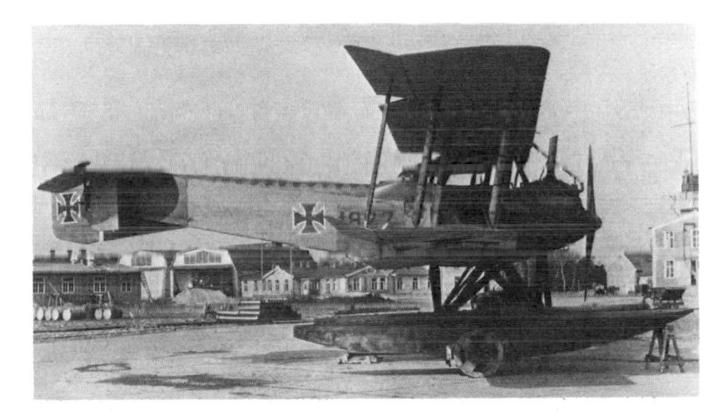

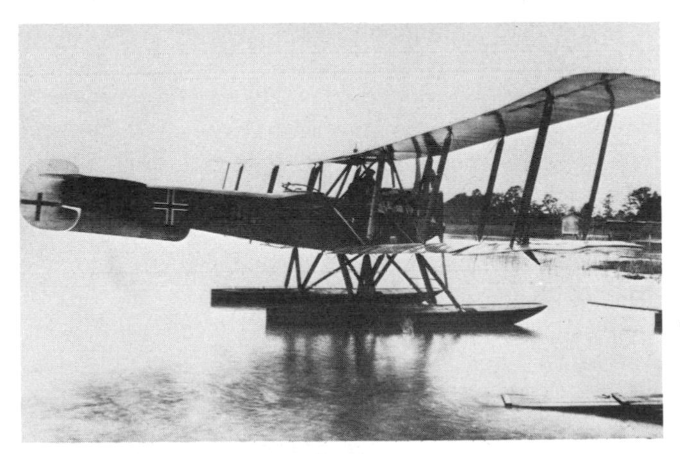

FRIEDRICHSHAFEN FF 64

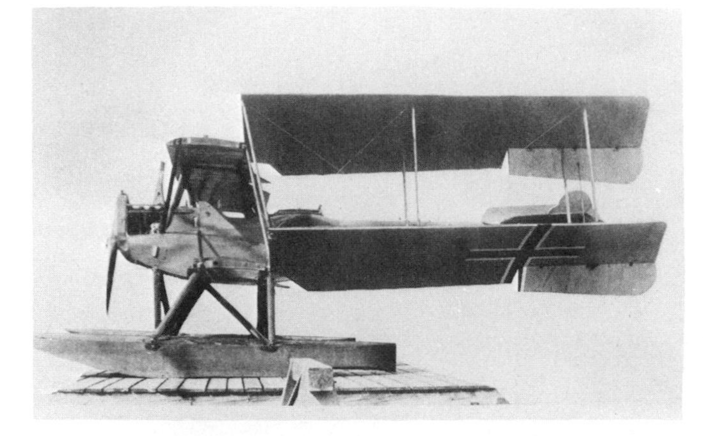

FRIEDRICHSHAFEN FF 64 with wings folded

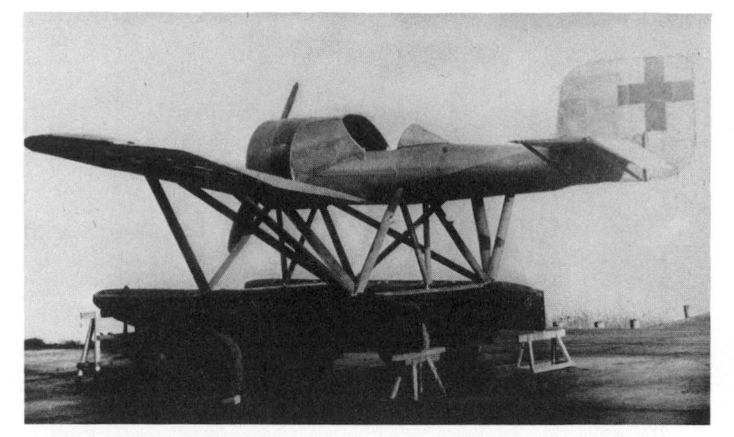

LFG V 19
Oberursel 110 hp
DIMENSIONS: Span 9.56 m. (31'4½"), Lg. 6.6 m. (21'8"), Ht. 3.1 m. (10'2")
WEIGHT: Empty 480 kg. (1056 lb.), Gross 690 kg. (1518 lb.)
PERFORMANCE: Speed—Max. 180 km/hr (112 mph), Range 360 km. (224 miles)

delivered before the war's end. The FF 49 became the Navy's workhorse on the North Sea, patrolling mine fields, controlling shipping by forcing merchant ships to German ports, and rescuing crews of downed aircraft.

Last Friedrichshafen seaplane in service was the FF 59, whose prototype, ※1822, was a rebuilt FF 49C. The same engine was used, along with a new set of larger wings with only two bays of bracing struts and another pair of struts connecting the four ailerons. It was hoped to provide a tail section like the Hansa-Brandenburg's, which gave the gunner a clear field of fire. At least two arrangements were tried before they settled on a single rudder two-thirds below the fuselage. Twenty Friedrichshafens ordered in June 1918 with CHFT equipment (one flexible gun and two-way radio) may have been FF 59s, but deliveries are uncertain.

Friedrichshafen also designed a FF 64 two-seater to be carried aboard a surface raider as had the FF 33E ※841, "Wolfchen." Powered by a 160 hp Mercedes D III and fitted with radio and flexible gun, the FF 64s had three-bay wings that folded back for easy storage. Three examples were ordered in March 1918, but photos exist only of ※3061, seen in October 1918.

The Hansa-Brandenburg W 26 was designed as a long-range patrol seaplane with two-way radio and fuel for some eight hours of flying; a long day in open cockpits. Originally there was no armament, but then the three 1918 prototypes were fitted for both fixed and flexible guns, and some 11 lb. bombs. No production order was won.

This chapter concludes with the unusual LFG Roland V 19. During the war, LFG built SF and FF seaplanes under license, having no luck with its own seaplane prototypes. These included a two-place reconnaissance type (※509) based on the Albatros C I, a single-seat fighter (※750), and a W 16 (※943) three-bay two-place patrol type with a 220 hp Mercedes, which wasn't accepted, but was returned to the factory December 1, 1917.

Its only all-metal aircraft was the V 19, a tiny single-seat scout intended, like the Hansa-Brandenburg W 20, to be carried on a submarine. This low-wing monoplane had a 110 hp Oberursel rotary and Duralumin structure, and could be folded into a deck container.

While the unarmed seaplane was finished just before the Armistice, it never reached the Warnemuende test center. Instead, it was offered as a civil sportsplane. The name "Putbus" was applied when LFG named their postwar planes after Pomeranian towns.

When the war ended, the German Navy had 673 first-line seaplanes and 11 first-line landplanes; the latter standard army fighter and reconnaissance types. Except for 11 experimental seaplanes, the rest of the Navy's 1478 aircraft were sea and land trainers. The peace treaty's Article 198 allowed Germany to keep only 100 seaplanes to help clear mine fields, and even these had to be given up after 1919.

HANSA-BRANDENBURG W 26
Mercedes D IV, 260 hp
DIMENSIONS: Span 18.8 m. (61'8"), Lg. 12.7 m. (41'8"), Wing Area 86.3 qm. (929 sq. ft.)
WEIGHT: Empty 1675 kg. (3685 lb.), Gross 2490 kg. (5478 lb.)
PERFORMANCE: Speed—Max. 140 km/hr (87 mph), Cruising speed 135 km/hr (84 mph), Landing speed 75 km/hr (47 mph), Range 1000 km. (620 miles)

12.

Torpedo Seaplanes

German torpedo-carrying aircraft were first used in combat in the Gulf of Riga, on the Baltic. Three twin-engined seaplanes attacked the Russian cruiser *Slava* September 12, 1916, sinking an escorting destroyer, but missing their main target.

When this attack method was introduced by the British in August 1915 at the Dardanelles, single-engined Short seaplanes were used, but the less powerful engines available in Germany led that Navy to prefer twin-engined types. The first German aircraft tested in this role had been single-engined, an LVG D 4 with a 150 hp Benz. Derived in 1915 from the B II landplane, it was a single-place three-bay biplane with strengthened landing gear and a torpedo rack designed by Franz Schneider.

Gotha received orders in February 1915 for two twin-engined seaplanes by different designers: #119 was Karl Roesner's WD 7, and #120 was the UWD of Oscar Ursinus. Both planes were seen as armed reconnaissance, rather than torpedo types.

The Ursinus design was a seaplane version of the G I bomber, with its fuselage attached to the top wing, and two 160 hp Mercedes on the bottom wing. Begun in April, the UWD was delivered on December 30, 1915, and accepted in February 1916. After a test flight, six passengers emerged from the fuselage, causing an official to exclaim, "That's a real Trojan Horse." It served as a bomber at Zeebrugge in 1916.

More successful was the WD 7, delivered December 8, 1915, with two 120 hp Mercedes, and the floats were placed directly under the engines. A gunner rode in the nose ahead of the pilot's cockpit, and twin balanced rudders were used.

After the prototype was accepted in January 1916, seven more WD 7s were ordered and delivered from May 16 to July 13, 1916, although only the 100 hp Mercedes model was used. The WD 7 became the first of the twin-engine seaplanes developed by Roesner into the WD 11, 14 and 20 types.

LVG D 4

Friedrichshafen also received a prototype order in February 1915, for the FF 35 with two 160 hp Mercedes mounted pusher style. Only the one example was completed in May 1916, equipped with a flexible gun and radio for armed recon patrols.

The first Navy aircraft actually ordered for torpedo carrying was the Hansa-Brandenburg GW. Designed by Ernst Heinkel as a twin-float, torpedo-carrying version of his GF bomber for the Austrian Army, the prototype (#528) was ordered September 1915 and accepted in January 1916. Ten production ships delivered from April to October had twin rudders and modified nacelles for the tractor 160 hp Mercedes. A 1600 lb. torpedo, three crewmen and a flexible gun, could be flown for four hours. It is likely that these were the Angersee-based torpedo planes that attacked the Russians on September 12.

A single rudder was used on five more GWs added beginning in November 1916, while a final batch of five more appeared September 1917 with a short, round nose omitting the bow cockpit. Com-

GOTHA UWD
Mercedes D III, 2 X 160 hp
DIMENSIONS: Span 20.3 m. (66'7"), Lg. 14.2 m. (46'7"), Wing Area 82 qm. (882.64 sq. ft.)
WEIGHT: Empty 1860 kg. (4092 lb.), Gross 2830 kg. (6229 lb.)
PERFORMANCE: Speed—Max. 120 km/hr (75 mph)

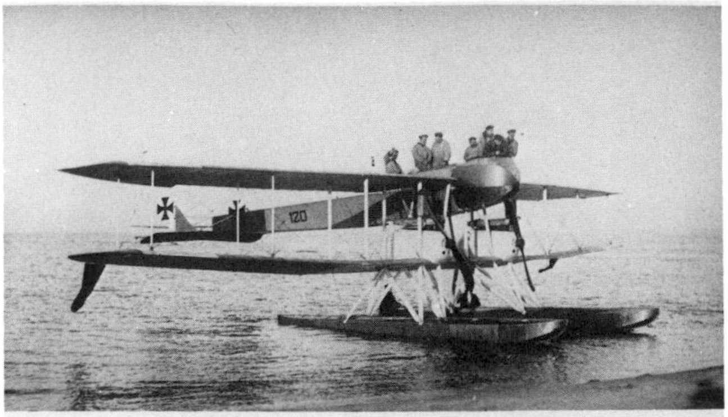

GOTHA WD 7
Mercedes D II, 120 hp
DIMENSIONS: Span 16 m. (52′6″), Lg. 11.3 m. (37′1″), Ht. 3.585 m. (11′9″), Wing Area 55.5 qm. (597 sq. ft.)
WEIGHT: Empty 1440 kg. (3168 lb.), Gross 1970 kg. (4334 lb.)
PERFORMANCE: Speed—Max. 136 km/hr (85 mph) at sea level, Cruising speed 110 km/hr (68 mph), Range 475 km. (295 miles), Service ceiling 4000 m. (13,120′)

FRIEDRICHSHAFEN FF 35
Mercedes D III, 2 X 160 hp
DIMENSIONS: Span 23.74 m. (77′11″), Lg. 13.5 m. (44′3½″), Wing Area 100 qm. (1076 sq. ft.)
WEIGHT: Empty 2292 kg. (5042 lb.), Gross 3543 kg. (7794 lb.)
PERFORMANCE: Speed—Max. 114 km/hr (71 mph) at sea level

HANSA-BRANDENBURG GW (※646, twin tail)

HANSA-BRANDENBURG GW (※700, single tail)

HANSA-BRANDENBURG GW prototype

HANSA-BRANDENBURG GW (final form)
Mercedes D III, 2 X 160 hp
DIMENSIONS: Span 21.56 m. (70′9″), Lg. 11.74 m. (38′6″), Ht. 4.14 m. (13′7″), Wing Area 103.4 qm. (1113 sq. ft.)
WEIGHT: Empty 2374 kg. (5223 lb.), Gross 3856 kg. (8483 lb.)
PERFORMANCE: Speed—Max. 127.5 km/hr (79 mph), Climb 1000 m./29 min. (3280′/29 min.), Endurance 4 hours

HANSA-BRANDENBURG GDW
Benz Bz IV, 2 X 220 hp
DIMENSIONS: Span 24.3 m. (79′9″), Lg. 15.8 m. (51′10″), Ht. 5 m. (16′5″), Wing Area 134 qm. (1442 sq. ft.)
WEIGHT: Empty 2950 kg. (6490 lb.), Gross 4865 kg. (10,703 lb.)
PERFORMANCE: Speed—Max. 130 km/hr (81 mph), Climb 1000 m./17.5 min. (3280′/17.5 min.), Range 750 km. (465 miles)

pleted in November 1917, these single-tailed versions served the North Sea stations. A single, larger, prototype was ordered April 1916 to handle a full-sized 4015 lb. torpedo. Known as the Hansa-Brandenburg GDW, it had 200 hp Benz engines, a short nose and large single rudder, and was not accepted until December 1917.

Albatros produced its first twin-engined floatplane as the VT (*Versuchs-Torpedoflugzeug*) with two 150 hp Benz pushers and a plywood fuselage that partially enclosed the torpedo. Ordered in October 1915, and later redesignated W 3, ⋇527 appeared in July 1916 and won an order for five improved W 5 aircraft. The first W 5 (⋇845) appeared with cleaner engine nacelles in May 1917, while the rest were also finished with straight cut rudder and ailerons on all

ALBATROS VT (W 3)
Benz Bz III (pusher), 2 X 150 hp
DIMENSIONS: Span 19.10 m. (62'8"), Lg. 15.6 m. (51'2"), Ht. 4.2 m. (13'9")
WEIGHT and PERFORMANCE: Data not available

four wings. Completed by January 1918, the Albatros floatplanes operated at the Baltic stations, instead of the more active North Sea stations.

Friedrichshafen and Gotha were each ordered to produce single prototypes and later eight production torpedo floatplanes. Designed by Kober and Eisenlohr, the Friedrichshafen FF 41A had two 150 hp Benz engines with tractor propellers and metal nacelles. Two men operated the aircraft with the observer in the bow cockpit releasing the torpedo and aiming the flexible gun. The prototype, ✠678, was delivered August 1916 with a triple tail, but a large single rudder was used on the eight aircraft delivered from May to August 1917.

Friedrichshafen received an order in June 1917 for three FF 53 prototypes with 260 hp Mercedes and twin rudders, but the example completed in July 1918 may have been the only one built.

The most widely used torpedo floatplanes were those built by Gotha. Developed from the smaller WD 7, the WD 11 had two 160 hp Mercedes with pusher propellers and carried one or two flexible guns, a torpedo, or 1100 lb. bomb load. The prototype ✠679 ordered March 9, 1916, and delivered August 11, was followed by eight WD 11s built from March 17 to April 28, 1917, and eight more added

FRIEDRICHSHAFEN FF 53

ALBATROS W 5
Benz Bz IV, 2 X 220 hp
DIMENSIONS: Span 22.7 m. (74'6"), Lg. 13.1 m. (43'), Ht. 4.25 m. (13'11"), Wing Area 100 qm. (1076 sq. ft.)
WEIGHT: Empty 2263 kg. (4979 lb.), Gross 3665 kg. (8063 lb.)
PERFORMANCE: Speed—Max. 133 km/hr (83 mph) at sea level, Climb 1000 m./20 min. (3280'/20 min.)

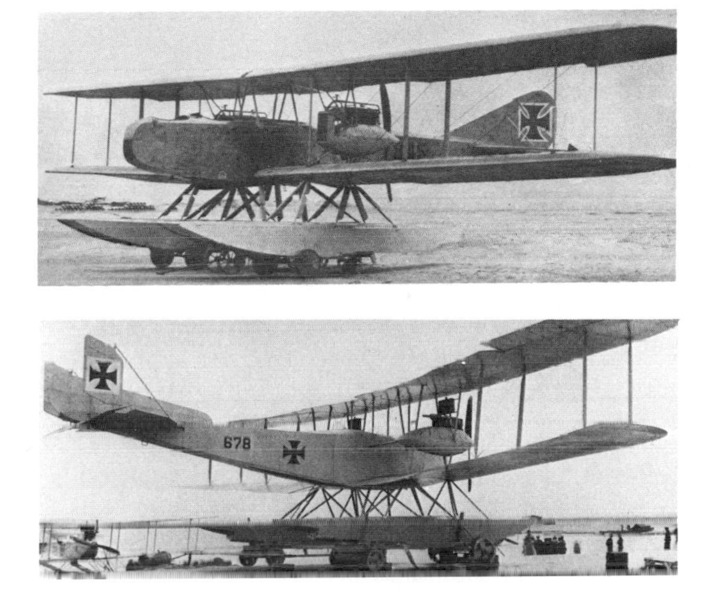

FRIEDRICHSHAFEN FF 41A prototype

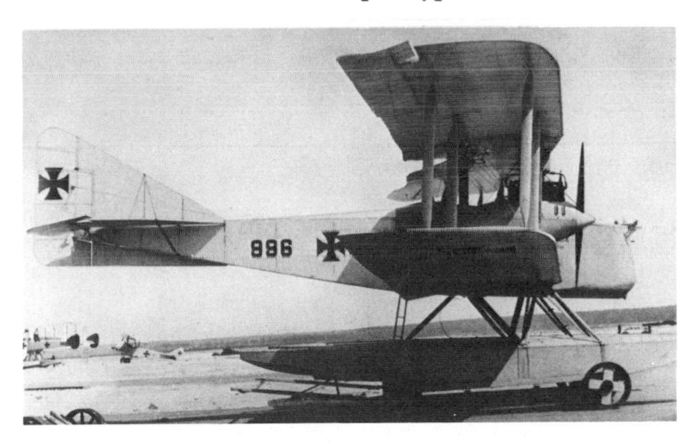

FRIEDRICHSHAFEN FF 41A
Benz Bz III, 2 X 150 hp
DIMENSIONS: Span 22 m. (72'2"), Lg. 13.7 m. (44'11"), Ht. 4.65 m. (15'3"), Wing Area 112.5 qm. (1211 sq. ft.)
WEIGHT: Empty 2300 kg. (5060 lb.), Gross 3670 kg. (8074 lb.)
PERFORMANCE: Speed—Max. 125 km/hr (78 mph), Cruising speed 115 km/hr (71 mph), Range 575 km. (355 miles)

GOTHA WD 11
Mercedes D III, 2 X 160 hp
DIMENSIONS: Span 22.5 m. (73'10"), Lg. 13.5 m. (44'3½"), Wing Area 108.4 qm. (1166 sq. ft.)
WEIGHT: Empty 2175 kg. (4785 lb.), Gross 3615 kg. (7953 lb.)
PERFORMANCE: Speed—Max. 120 km/hr (75 mph) at sea level, Cruising speed 100 km/hr (62 mph), Range 500 km. (310 miles), Service ceiling 3200 m. (10,500')

GOTHA WD 14 prototype

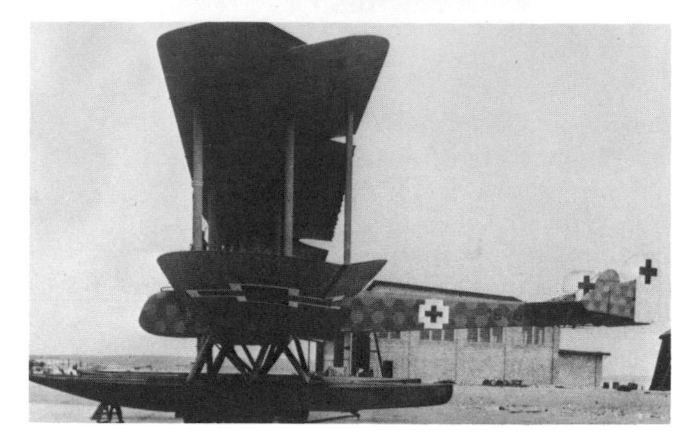

by August 14. They served in the Baltic, and after Germany and Russia made peace in March 1918, they continued to fight on behalf of Finland's General Mannerheim against the Bolsheviks.

Two 200 hp Benz engines were used on the Gotha WD 14, which also had twin rudders like the WD 7. The WD 14 prototype also had its rudder balances underneath, but had a sloping nose with a gunner placed behind the pilot and the wings. Production models, however, added a bow cockpit and gun for the torpedo man, and had their rudder balances on top. Speed was reduced from 133 km/hr (83 mph) in the prototype to 125 km/hr (77 mph) with torpedo, two guns and three crewmen.

The WD 14 prototype was ordered May 12, 1916, and delivered to Warnemuende January 16, 1917. Forty production WD 14s were delivered July 8, 1917, to May 15, 1918, by which time an additional 25 were on order. Eight were delivered by September, and the rest sent half-complete to the Navy on November 9, 1918. Gotha also delivered three similar WD 20s from May 2 to June 27, 1918. Powered by 260 hp Mercedes, they replaced the torpedo with a long-range tank for patrol work. The photo shows how the Gotha seaplanes folded their wings for storage.

German torpedo planes based on Zeebrugge attacked British merchant shipping in the Channel from April 19 to September 9, 1917. Although three ships were sunk, most of the torpedos missed, and the low altitude necessary for torpedo dropping (20–30 feet) made the aircraft easy targets for the ship's guns.

After the torpedo missions ended, these floatplanes were used for long-range reconnaissance. The Gotha's range was increased from 465 miles with torpedo to some 620 miles with a long-range tank. Should an engine fail, the seaplane had to alight on seas often too rough for floats. Nevertheless, these Gothas served until the war's end, and their tradition was revived in World War II by the Luftwaffe's Heinkel He 59.

GOTHA WD 14
Benz Bz IV, 2 X 220 hp
DIMENSIONS: Span 25 m. (82'), Lg. 14 m. (45'11"), Ht. 4.8 m. (15'9"), Wing Area 132.9 qm. (1429 sq. ft.)
WEIGHT: Empty 2430 kg. (5346 lb.), Gross 4540 kg. (9988 lb.)
PERFORMANCE: Speed—Max. 125 km/hr (78 mph), Range 750 km. (465 miles), Service ceiling 3000 m. (29,520')

GOTHA WD 20
Mercedes D IVa, 2 X 260 hp
DIMENSIONS: Span 25 m. (82'), Lg. 14.4 m. (47'3"), Wing Area 131.7 qm. (1418 sq. ft.)
WEIGHT: Empty 3030 kg. (6666 lb.), Gross 4540 kg. (9988 lb.)
PERFORMANCE: Speed—Max. 126 km/hr (78 mph)

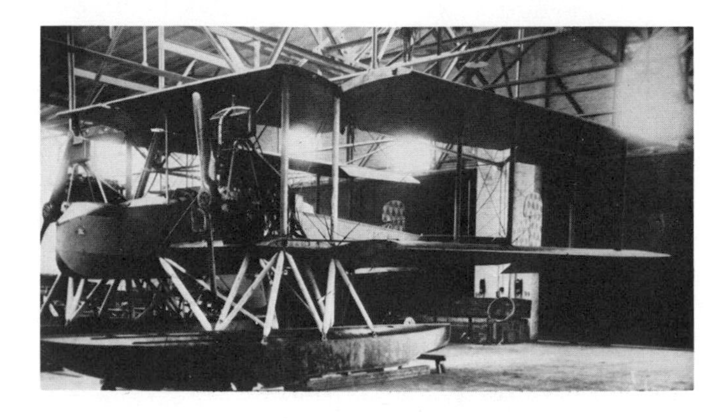

13.

Flying Boats and Giant Aircraft

Flying boats did not win the wartime popularity in Germany they had in foreign countries. Apparently the flier's dislike of pusher aircraft carried over to this class of aircraft, and only a few were accepted by the German Navy.

The first of these were the flying boats purchased from Max Oertz, a yacht builder for the Kaiser, Czar, and other royalty. His FB 3 was acquired by the Navy in July 1914, and although unarmed, was used at Zeebrugge in 1915. Its streamlined hull contained an open cockpit and an exposed Mercedes engine with an extended gear shaft to a pusher propeller near the upper wing.

It was followed in November 1914 by the similar Oertz W 4 with a 160 hp Mercedes and in January 1915 by another W 4 with a 115 hp Argus. Five more flying boats were ordered as the W 5 with two crewmen, a 240 hp Maybach, and a flexible gun. Although the first example was delivered in May 1916, the next three were delayed until 1917, and the last until February 1918.

OERTZ FB 3

OERTZ W 4

The water performance of these boats was considered excellent, but they were not as maneuverable in the air as other aircraft of their size. As the menace of land-based Allied fighters grew, they were withdrawn from the Channel to the German coast.

Strangest of the Oertz boats was the W 6 *Flugschooner,* which had two pairs of biplane wings and two 240 hp Maybachs turning two pusher props with gear shafts. The first pair of wings were set at the center of gravity over the engines and the second over the hull's stern. Although this funny bird was flown to Warnemuende and accepted in June 1917, it was impractical for service.

Two Oertz W 7 boats accepted May–June 1916 returned to the usual single-engined style with a 150 hp Maybach and single gun. A single W 8 was delivered in September 1916 with a 240 hp Maybach and a new V strut arrangement.

Hansa-Brandenburg began producing flying boats based on the Austrian Lohner boat. Their first was a

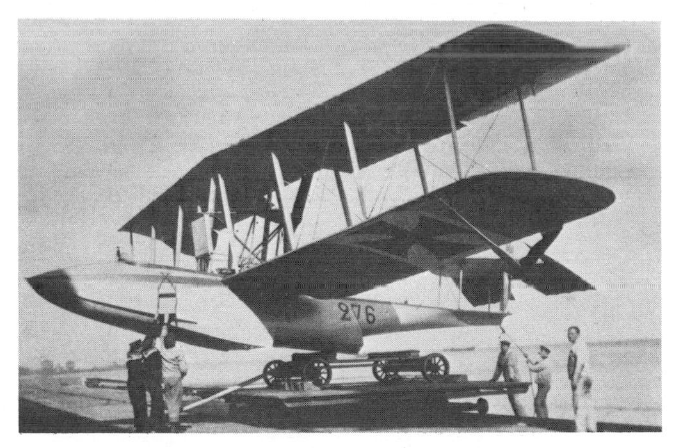

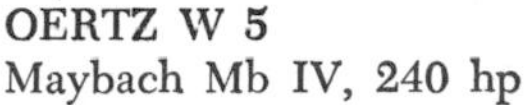

OERTZ W 5
Maybach Mb IV, 240 hp
DIMENSIONS: Span 18 m. (59′½″), Lg. 11.7 m. (38′4½″), Ht. 4.25 m. (13′1½″), Wing area 77 qm. (829 sq. ft.)
WEIGHT: Empty 2018 kg. (4440 lb.), Gross 2638 kg. (5804 lb.)
PERFORMANCE: Speed—Max. 120 km/hr (75 mph) at sea level, Endurance 5 hours, Range 500 km. (310 miles)

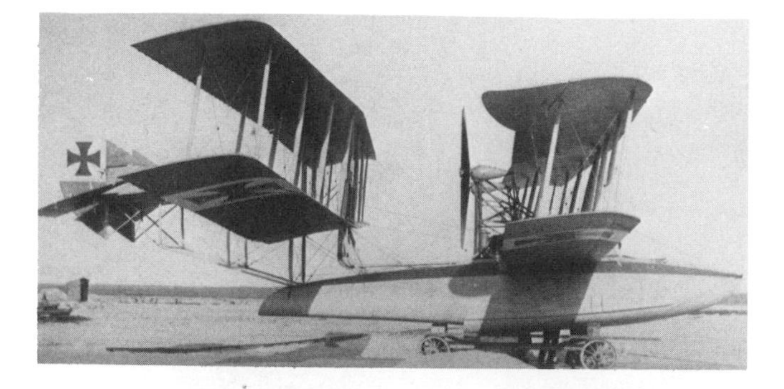

OERTZ *Flugschooner*
Maybach Mb IV, 2 X 240 hp
DIMENSIONS: Span 20 m. (65′7½″), Lg. 14.5 m. (47′8″), Ht. 4.78 m. (15′8″), Wing Area 163 qm. (175 sq. ft.)
WEIGHT: Empty 3780 kg. (8316 lb.), Gross 5030 kg. (11,066 lb.)
PERFORMANCE: Speed—Max. 115 km/hr (72 mph) at sea level

OERTZ W 8
Maybach Mb IV, 240 hp
DIMENSIONS: Span 19.6 m. (64′4″), Lg. 10.7 m. (35′1″), Ht. 3.54 m. (11′7″), Wing Area 70 qm. (753 sq. ft.)
WEIGHT: Empty 1580 kg. (3476 lb.), Gross 2250 kg. (4950 lb.)
PERFORMANCE: Speed—Max. 140 km/hr (87 mph), Climb 2000 m./20 min. (6560′/20 min.)

single Hansa-Brandenburg AE, the three-bay biplane delivered in April 1915. The same 150 hp Benz and fewer struts were used on six Hansa-Brandenburg FB two-seaters delivered April to June 1916 armed with a machine gun in the bow cockpit.

A larger development was the W 13 delivered to Austria beginning in February 1917. Designated K boats, they used the 350 hp Austro-Daimler and were produced by Phoenix in Austria and Ufag in Hungary.

While most flying boats were for reconnaissance, the Hansa-Brandenburg CC was a single-seat fighter, a rare configuration among boats actually used in combat. It was designed for the Austrian Navy by Ernst Heinkel, who named it the CC after Camillo Castiglione, the firm's owner, who financed Heinkel's wartime career.

Between the wings of the CC were the distinctive star struts of the D I, and a 150 hp Benz with a radiator in front and the propeller behind. An example ordered by the German Navy in May 1916 was delivered the following February with a single Spandau poking thru the windshield of the pilot's cockpit ahead of the wing. Small floats were attached under the wing tips.

The CC boat was also produced for the Austrian

HANSA-BRANDENBURG FB
Benz Bz III, 150 hp
DIMENSIONS: Span 16 m. (52′6″), Lg. 10.18 m. (33′5″), Wing Area 45 qm. (484 sq. ft.)
WEIGHT: Empty 1140 kg. (2508 lb.), Gross 1620 kg. (3564 lb.)
PERFORMANCE: Speed—Max. 140 km/hr (87 mph) at sea level, Climb 1000 m./12.5 min. (3280′/12.5 min.), Range 1000 km. (620 miles)

HANSA-BRANDENBURG CC
Benz Bz III, 150 hp
DIMENSIONS: Span 9.1 m. (29'10½"), Lg. 9.15 m. (30'¼"), Wing Area 26.5 qm. (285 sq. ft.)
WEIGHT: Empty 801 kg. (1762 lb.), Gross 1081 kg. (2318 lb.)
PERFORMANCE: Speed—Max. 160 km/hr (99 mph), Climb 800 m./4 min. (2625'/4 min.), Range 500 km. (310 miles)

HANSA-BRANDENBURG CC (※1144)

HANSA-BRANDENBURG CC (※1348)

HANSA-BRANDENBURG W 17

Navy, which needed a fighter to oppose Italian aircraft over the Adriatic. An Austrian ace, Gottfried Banfield, used the first Austrian CC (the A 12) to down a Caproni on December 4, 1916. Austrian Hiero engines were used on 38 CCs received by June 1917, one of them rigged as an experimental triplane.

Thirty-five CCs were acquired by the German Navy itself from April to August 1917 and had the Benz engine, radiator in the top wing and two guns. Some were modified with the extra V strut or the engine covering seen in our pictures.

Hansa-Brandenburg then produced the larger W 18 single-seat fighter. Fitted with two guns and a 200 hp Hiero, 47 went to Austria from September 1917 to May 1918, followed by 14 license-built by Phoenix. One example with a 150 hp Benz went to the German Navy in December 1917.

Other single-seat flying boats tested by Hansa-Brandenburg included the small W 17, and the W 22, a CC modified with wide hull extensions, but both of these crashed. The W 23 fighter had a 160 hp Mercedes and was armed with a 20 mm. cannon and a machine gun in the nose. Although three W 23s ordered June 1917 are said to have been delivered in January 1918, no photograph is available.

The smallest German flying boat was the Hansa-Brandenburg W 20 single-seater designed to operate from submarines. Such an aircraft was intended to be carried in a deck container on a larger submarine such as the U 139 or 155, and hastily assembled, after the U-boat surfaced, to search for enemy shipping.

The May 1917 contract called for three unarmed aircraft which could be folded into a container 6 by 1.9 meters (19'8"×6'3"). Powered by an 80 hp Oberursel and pusher propeller, the first little biplane (※1551) was only 5.8 by 5.91 meters (19'×19'5"), but a crash during tests showed the skimpy strut arrangement too weak.

The second example, ※1552, was tested in April 1918 with larger wings and more struts. Tests on this and the third W 20 went satisfactorily, and showed

HANSA-BRANDENBURG W 18
Benz Bz III, 150 hp
DIMENSIONS: Span 10.7 m. (35′1″), Lg. 8.15 m. (26′9″), Ht. 3.45 m. (11′4″), Wing Area 34.38 qm. (370 sq. ft.)
WEIGHT: Empty 875 kg. (1925 lb.), Gross 1145 kg. (2519 lb.)
PERFORMANCE: Speed—Max. 160 km/hr (99 mph), Climb 1000 m./5 min. (3280′/5 min.)

HANSA-BRANDENBURG W 22

that the aircraft could be assembled or stowed in only three minutes. Germany was unable to spare a U-boat to be modified for this purpose, and the work went for naught.

After the war, Heinkel sold submarine planes to both the U. S. and Japanese Navy, and the British lost the giant submarine M-2 testing a similar type. Only Japan carried on submarine-based flight operations in World War II.

GIANT SEAPLANES

The largest flying boats built for the German Navy in World War I were the four Dornier giants built to patrol the North Sea on missions of 10 to 12 hours duration. Although the first never flew, the second never entered service, and the last was finished too late, they stand as historic steps toward the all-metal flying boat of the World War II period.

Claudius Dornier had been employed by Count

HANSA-BRANDENBURG W 20
Oberursel U. 0o, 80 hp
DIMENSIONS: Span 6.8 m. (22′4″), Lg. 5.93 m. (19′5½″), Wing Area 15.82 qm. (170 sq. ft.)
WEIGHT: Empty 395 kg. (870 lb.), Gross 567 kg. (1248 lb.)
PERFORMANCE: Speed—Max. 117 km/hr (73 mph), Climb 800 m./11.4 min. (2625′/11.4 min.), Endurance about 75 minutes

HANSA-BRANDENBURG W 20 (revised)

Zeppelin to develop all-metal aircraft, and was given a facility at Seemoos on Lake Constance known as Zeppelin-Werke Lindau, hereafter given its more common name of Dornier. Design of a flying boat using mixed steel and Duralumin construction was begun shortly after the war started, and assembly began in January 1915, using the firm's own funds. No Navy number was ever assigned.

The largest aircraft in the world at that time, it originally had two 240 hp Maybach HS engines in the hull turning two pusher propellers on the lower wings thru an extended drive system, and a third engine between the biplane wings. The pilot sat on the nose behind a Cellon canopy.

When the extended transmission system proved unsuitable during taxiing trials, the buried engines were removed and all three engines were arranged between the wings. Still the Rs I never flew, for it was destroyed in a sudden storm on December 21, 1915.

Undaunted, Dornier went ahead with his second flying boat, Rs II. This time he used a short broad hull, high twin rudder tail on steel tail booms, and a wide high wing, with only small stubs remaining of the lower wings. All three engines were buried in the hull turning pusher propellers between the wings, and biplane elevators were added at the tail's end. Pilot and copilot sat in an open cockpit, with two mechanics behind them in the hull.

DORNIER Rs I
Maybach Mb IV, 3 X 240 hp
DIMENSIONS: Span 43.5 m. (142'9"), Lg. 29 m. (95'1½"), Ht. 7.2 m. (23'7½"), Wing Area 328.8 qm. (3538 sq. ft.)
WEIGHT: Empty 7500 kg. (16,500 lb.), Gross 10,500 kg. (23,100 lb.)
PERFORMANCE: Data not available; aircraft was never flown

DORNIER Rs I (orginal form)

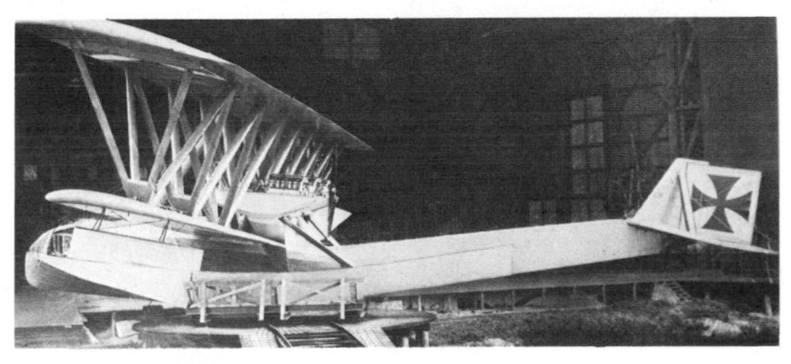

DORNIER Rs II
Maybach Mb IV, 3 X 240 bp
DIMENSIONS: Span 33.2 m. (108′11″), Lg. 23.88 m. (78′4″), Wing Area 257 qm. (2765 sq. ft.)
WEIGHT: Empty 7100 kg. (15,620 lb.), Gross 9300 kg. (20,460 lb.), Fuel 2000 liters (528 gal.)
PERFORMANCE: Test incomplete

Rs II modified

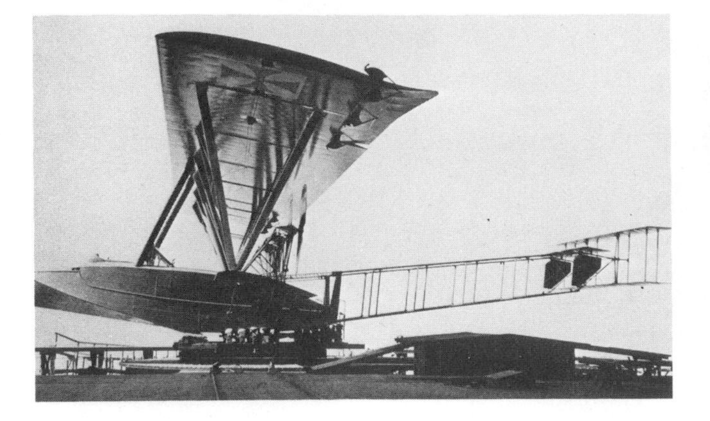

Rs II final form

On June 30, 1916, the Rs II had its maiden flight, but the powerplant still presented problems and the aircraft had to be completely rebuilt. This time, four Maybachs were used in two tandem nacelles between the wings with two pusher and two tractor propellers. In this form, the Rs II was flown again on November 16, 1916. Flight tests continued, and the tail was redesigned, but the aircraft continually suffered minor engine failures. It was supposed to go to the North Sea for Navy trials, but after a forced landing, in September 1917, the aircraft was scrapped.

In the meantime, Dornier had designed the Rs III for a Navy contract signed April 25, 1917, using an entirely new monoplane layout. There was a short dural hull, four 245 hp Maybach engines in tandem nacelles, and atop the wide wing was a long fuselage reaching back to the biplane tail. Wire cables supported the wing. Crew accommodations included a bow gun pit, pilot's cockpit, and mechanic's cockpit in the hull, and a ladder led up to the fuselage with its wireless operator's cabin and open pit with two guns.

Rs II with four engines

The Rs III made its first flight November 4, 1917, and after successful tests was transferred to the North Sea. Flying from Lake Constance northward across Germany, it reached Norderney in seven hours. After acceptance by the Navy on June 13, 1918, it was used on active service. Even after the war's end, the Dornier remained among the 100 seaplanes Germany was permitted to keep for mine spotting. It was finally destroyed by Allied order on July 30–31, 1921.

Last of the Dornier boats was the four-engined Rs IV, two examples of which were ordered in January 1918. All-metal stressed-skin construction was used, and the Dornier sponson was used for the first time. These "water wings" allowed a narrower and lighter hull while improving stability on the water. There was an open cockpit in the hull bow, and two mechanics sat in the hull between the engines among the ten

DORNIER Rs III
Maybach Mb IVa, 4 X 245 hp
DIMENSIONS: Span 37 m. (121'4½"), Lg. 22.75 m. (74'8"), Ht. 8.2 m. (26'11"), Wing Area 226 qm. (2432 sq. ft.)
WEIGHT: Empty 7200 kg. (15,840 lb.), Gross 10,670 kg. (23,474 lb.), Fuel 3140 liters (829 gal.)
PERFORMANCE: Speed—Max. 135 km/hr (84 mph), Climb 1000 m./15.5 min. (3280'/15.5 min.), Range 1400 km. (870 miles), Service ceiling 2700 m. (8850')

300 liter fuel tanks. The upper metal fuselage had an enclosed pilot's cabin between two open gunner's pits.

The Rs IV was flown on October 12, 1918, but the war's end prevented its use and completion of an improved second version. The Navy had ordered two further Dornier boats of a more modern configuration, but they did not pass the drawing board stage.

Nevertheless, the Dorniers were remarkable steps in flying boat design and from them descended 1929's marvelous 12-engine Do X and the ideas for the Pan-American "clippers" of the '30s.

FOUR-ENGINED FLOATPLANES

Along with the flying boats, the German Navy developed a series of four-engined reconnaissance planes

STAAKEN #8301
Mercedes D IVa, 4 X 260 hp
DIMENSIONS: Span 42.2 m. (138'5½"), Lg. 21 m. (68'10½"), Ht. 6.8 m. (22'3½"), Wing Area 340.5 qm. (3663 sq. ft.)
WEIGHT: Empty 9000 kg. (19,800 lb.), Gross 12,500 kg. (27,500 lb.), Fuel 3600 liters (951 gal.)
PERFORMANCE: Speed—Max. 130 km/hr (81 mph), Climb 3000 m./54 min. (9840'/54 min.)

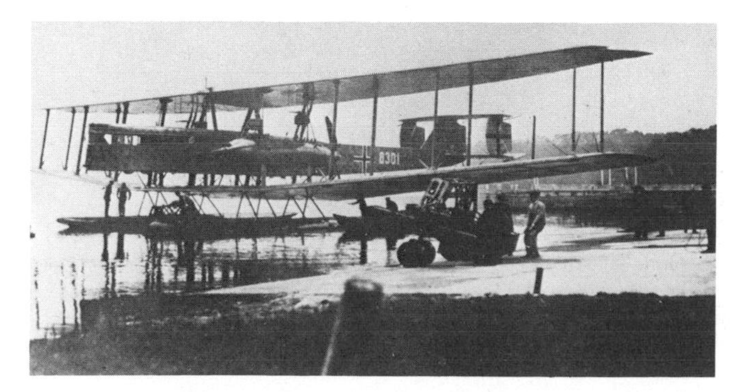

DORNIER Rs IV
Maybach Mb IV, 3 X 245 hp
DIMENSIONS: Span 37 m. (121'4½"), Lg. 22.3 m. (73'2"), Ht. 8.55 m. (28'), Wing Area 226 qm. (2432 sq. ft.)
WEIGHT: Empty 7000 kg. (15,400 lb.), Gross 10,700 kg. (23,540 lb.), Fuel 3000 liters (792 gal.)
PERFORMANCE: Speed—Max. 145 km/hr (90 mph), Landing speed 80 km/hr (50 mph), Range 1400 km. (870 miles), Service ceiling 2000 m. (6560')

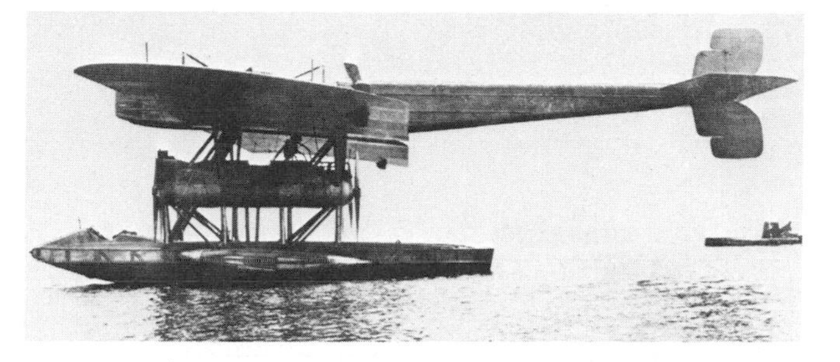

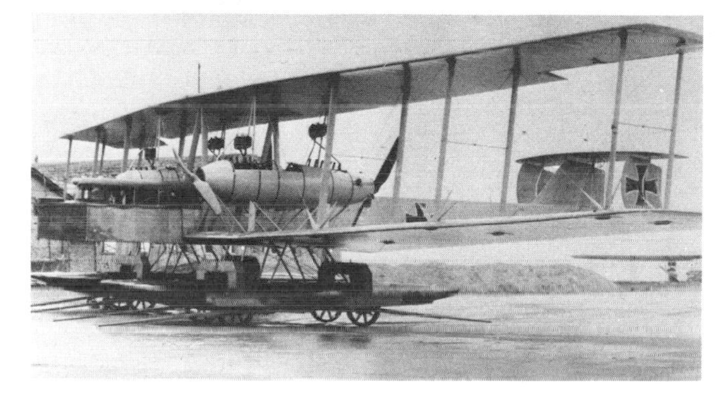

STAAKEN L
Mercedes D IVa, 4 X 260 hp
DIMENSIONS: Span 42.2 m. (138'5½"), Lg. 22.2 m. (72'10"), Ht. 7.38 m. (24'2½"), Wing Area 360 qm. (3874 sq. ft.)
WEIGHT: Empty 8400 kg. (18,522 lb.), Gross 11,800 kg. (26,019 lb.)
PERFORMANCE: Speed—Max. 125 km/hr (78 mph), Landing speed 85 km/hr (53 mph), Climb 1000 m./23.7 min. (3280'/23.7 min.), Service ceiling 2500 m. (8200')

with twin floats. The first of these was the Staaken L, built by another branch of the Zeppelin combine.

Basically, this giant biplane was a floatplane version of the Staaken R VI, and was powered by four 260 hp Mercedes in tandem nacelles. There was an enclosed pilot's cabin with an open cockpit for a gunner in the nose, and another cockpit for two gunners in the rear. Radio transmitting and receiving gear was also provided in the cabin, and fuel for ten hours flight was provided.

Ordered February 15, 1917, the Staaken L was delivered November 14, and was tested until it crashed at Warnemuende on June 3, 1918. The largest floatplane ever constructed, it was not as seaworthy as the Dornier flying boats.

Six more Staaken four-engined, five-place seaplanes were ordered, numbered 8301 to 8306. Essentially

GOTHA WD 22

Mercedes D III, 2 X 160 hp, Mercedes D I, 2 X 100 hp
DIMENSIONS: Span 26 m. (85'4"), Lg. 14.4 m. (47'3"), Wing Area 147 qm. (1582 sq. ft.)
WEIGHT: Empty 3800 kg. (8360 lb.), Gross 5170 kg. (11,374 lb.)
PERFORMANCE: Speed—Max. 131 km/hr (81 mph), Range 750 km. (465 miles)

they were similar to the L, but had a new fuselage raised above the lower wing to avoid wave spray. Cellon windows ran around the nose, which had gear for ten 22 lb. bombs. A gun ring was provided on the nose top, two flexible machine guns were provided on the upper wing above the engine nacelles, and two 20 mm. Becker guns in the cockpit behind the wings.

Number 8301 was ordered in December 1917 and first flew as a landplane in summer 1918. Then the twin Duralumin floats were added when the aircraft was tested at Warnemuende. The Allies also found the 8303 and 8304 after the war, but 8302 may have been destroyed during tests, and the last two aircraft ordered were not completed. At least one of these Staakens was used as a passenger plane for a short time before being destroyed at Allied insistence.

Gotha also built four-engined seaplanes for the German Navy, which actually enlarged developments of the twin-engined WD 20 types. Two WD 22 long-range reconnaissance biplanes ordered October 9, 1917, were delivered on May 12 and August 21, 1918, carrying a crew of four and three guns. Nacelles on the lower wings held two 160 hp Mercedes with tractor propellers, and behind them were two 100 hp Mercedes with pusher propellers. The WD 22 was said to be reliable, but had little performance advantage over twin-engined types.

Gotha's last seaplane type was the larger WD 27, using four 160 hp Mercedes in tandem mounts, and carrying four men, two guns, and radio. Three WD 27s were ordered in April 1918, but it seems that only the first was actually completed.

Competing with these Gothas was the unique Friedrichshafen FF 60 triplane. Four 160 hp Mercedes were used with tractor propellers, two on the lower wing, and two on the center wing. Four men and three guns were carried. Although two of these long-range seaplanes were ordered in February 1918, only one was completed and that never flew.

GOTHA WD 27
Mercedes D III, 4 X 175 hp
DIMENSIONS: Span 31 m. (101'8½"), Lg. 17.6 m. (57'9"), Wing Area 193 qm. (2077 sq. ft.)
WEIGHT: Empty 4500 kg. (9900 lb.), Gross 6690 kg. (14,718 lb.)
PERFORMANCE: Speed—Max. 135 km/hr (84 mph), Range 810 km. (503 miles)

FRIEDRICHSHAFEN FF 60

ALBATROS W 4 prototype

14.

Fighters on Floats

As air fighting over the English Channel and North Sea increased, the German Navy realized that fighters were needed to protect its floatplane patrols from Allied attack, as well as for offensive patrols. In June 1916, single prototypes were ordered of five single-seat, twin-float biplane fighters: the Albatros W 4, Hansa-Brandenburg KDW, Friedrichshafen FF 43, Roland (LFG) W 1 and Rumpler 6B 1, numbered 747 thru 751. Soon afterward, additional pairs of the W 4, KDW and 6B 1 aircraft were added.

The most successful of these fighters was the Albatros, which was similar to the land-based Albatros D IIs except for the twin floats and another meter added to the wing span. Two Spandau guns on the cowl fired thru the propeller, and construction was the usual Albatros plywood fuselage and fabric-covered wings.

After two prototypes were accepted in September 1916, and the third in December, production went ahead on 115 W 4s delivered from February to November 1917. The later examples had ailerons on all four wing tips and replaced the side radiators with one in the upper wing. These Albatros fighters were issued to all naval flying stations within reach of enemy aircraft. Eight went to Austria in July 1918.

The Hansa-Brandenburg KDW was a float version of Heinkel's D I for Austria, so it is distinguished by its "star struts"; eight steel tubes meeting in between the wings on each side. The deep fuselage was of wood, and a single fixed gun on the right side was joined by a twin on later ships.

A 150 hp Benz with a frontal radiator was used on the three prototypes completed in September 1916 and on ten production aircraft delivered in March–April 1917. Forty-five other KDWs built by February 1918 used instead the 160 hp Maybach with a radiator in the upper wings. Additional V struts and an upper fin were added to the last batch of these.

Hansa-Brandenburg also produced a heavier version with the 200 hp Benz and two guns known as the W 11, but only three were completed; February–March 1917. Next, the firm offered a new single seater with a 160 hp Oberursel rotary and simplified strut arrangement. Armed with two fixed guns, the W 16 again omitted bracing wires, using a single strut running from the V struts' base to the fuselage top. Although three W 16s were ordered in November, it seems that only two, the first tested in February 1917, was actually delivered.

Largest of the seaplane single-seaters was the Rumpler 6B 1, recognized by its wide double-bay wings and "rhino horn" exhaust stack. Based on the company's C I type, it had a 160 hp Mercedes and two fixed guns. The three prototypes were accepted in July–August 1916, and 40 6B 1s were delivered from November 1916 to May 1917, followed by 50 6B 2s made by January 1918 with modified tails.

ALBATROS W 4
Mercedes D III, 160 hp
DIMENSIONS: Span 9.5 m. (31'2"), Lg. 8.26 m. (27'1"), Ht. 3.65 m. (12'), Wing Area 31.6 qm. (340 sq. ft.)
WEIGHT: Empty 790 kg. (1738 lb.), Gross 1070 kg. (2354 lb.), Fuel 146 liters (39 gal.)
PERFORMANCE: Speed—Max. 160 km/hr (99 mph) at sea level, Climb 1000 m./5 min. (3280'/5 min.), 3000 m./23 min. (9840'/23 min.), Range 450 km. (280 miles), Service ceiling 3000 m. (9840')

HANSA-BRANDENBURG KDW
Maybach Mb III, 160 hp
DIMENSIONS: Span 9.3 m. (30′6″), Lg. 7.86 m. (25′9½″), Wing Area 29.15 qm. (313 sq. ft.)
WEIGHT: Empty 759 kg. (1670 lb.), Gross 1039 kg. (2286 lb.) Fuel 160 liters (42 gal.)
PERFORMANCE: Speed—Max. 172 km/hr (124 mph), Climb 1000 m./4 min. (3280′/4 min.), Range 500 km. (310 miles)

HANSA-BRANDENBURG W 11
Benz Bz IV, 200 hp
DIMENSIONS: Span 10.1 m. (33′2″), Lg. 8.1 m. (26′7″), Wing Area 31.42 qm. (338 sq. ft.)
WEIGHT: Empty 933 kg. (2052 lb.), Gross 1233 kg. (2712 lb.)
PERFORMANCE: Speed—Max. 176 km/hr (109 mph), Climb 1000 m./4 min. (3280′/4 min.), Range 350 km. (217 miles)

HANSA-BRANDENBURG KDW, final form

HANSA-BRANDENBURG W 16
Oberursel U III, 160 hp
DIMENSIONS: Span 9.11 m. (29′11″), Lg. 7.35 m. (24′1″), Ht. 2.925 m. (9′10″), Wing Area 23 qm. (247 sq. ft.)
WEIGHT: Empty 659 kg. (1450 lb.), Gross 935 kg. (2057 lb.)
PERFORMANCE: Speed—Max. 170 km/hr (106 mph), Climb 1000 m./5 min. (3280′/5 min.), Endurance 2 hours

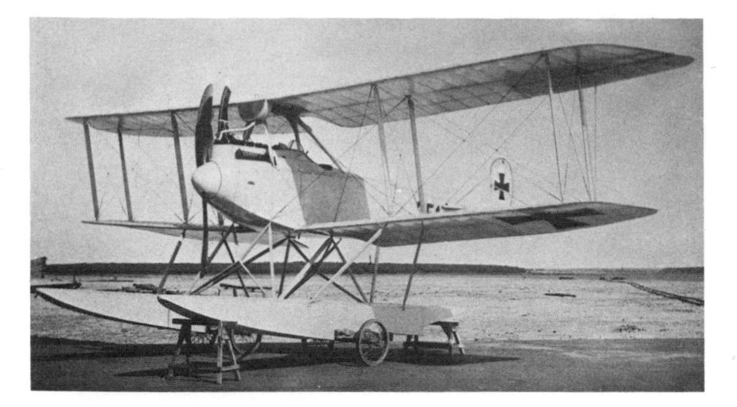

RUMPLER 6B 1
Mercedes D III, 160 hp
DIMENSIONS: Span 12.15 m. (39'10½"), Lg. 7.85 m. (25'9"), Wing Area 35.7 qm. (384 sq. ft.)
WEIGHT: Empty 790 kg. (1738 lb.), Gross 1140 kg. (2508 lb.)
PERFORMANCE: Speed—Max. 135 km/hr (84 mph) at sea level

LFG W I #750
Mercedes D III, 160 hp
DIMENSIONS: Span 10.1 m. (33'2"), Lg. 9.9 m. (32'6"), Ht. 3.2 m. (10'6"), Wing Area 29.9 qm. (321 sq. ft.)
WEIGHT: Empty 868 kg. (1910 lb.), Gross 1148 kg. (2526 lb.)
PERFORMANCE: Data not available

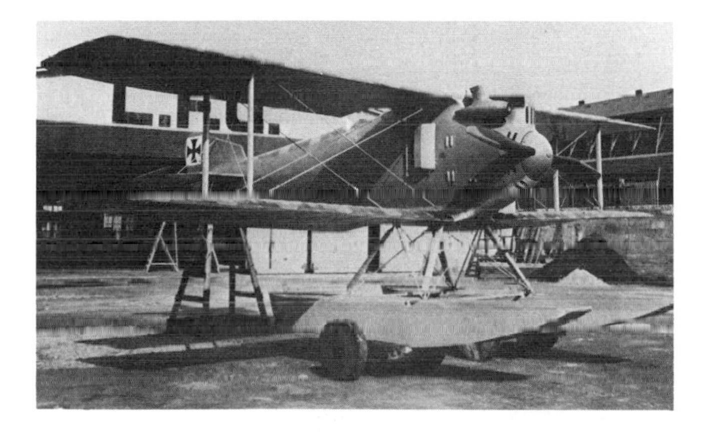

The two other single-seat seaplanes in the original design group never passed the initial aircraft prototype stage. Both the Friedrichshafen FF 43 and LFG Roland W 1 used a 160 hp Mercedes and two fixed guns, but the FF 43 was designed by Roland Eisenlohr with very conventional layout, while the Roland design had the top wing lowered to the "wrapped" wooden fuselage seen on the Roland D II. Friedrichshafen never did have success with its fighter designs, while the Roland's flight test was delayed to June 1917, too late to interest the Navy.

Several other seaplane single-seaters were begun, but none were successful. Most advanced was the aircraft designed for Gotha in 1916 by Oskar Ursinus,

FRIEDRICHSHAFEN FF 43
Mercedes D III, 160 hp
DIMENSIONS: Span 9.92 m. (32'6½"), Lg. 8.5 m. (27'10½"), Ht. 3.39 m. (11'1"), Wing Area 31 qm. (333.68 sq. ft.)
WEIGHT: Empty 790 kg. (1738 lb.), Gross 1070 kg. (2354 lb.)
PERFORMANCE: Speed—Max. 160 km/hr (99 mph) at sea level

Navy serial #782 (no official designation is known).[1] The twin floats on this remarkable aircraft were retractable, being wound up by hand, and the 150 hp Benz between the wings had an extension shaft to the propeller in the streamlined nose. Top speed was hoped to be over 200 km/hr (124 mph), but there was too much trouble with the gear, which lacked high-quality steel, and the aircraft was destroyed. This German aircraft was ahead of its time.

[1] Neither the Gotha records or the Navy type list include #782.
Its reported Gotha origin is based on the designer's connection with that firm, and that fact that numbers 752–781 were Gotha-built aircraft.

URSINUS #782
Benz Bz III, 150 hp
DIMENSIONS: Span 9 m. (29'6"), Lg. 8.65 m. (28'4"), Ht. 2.9 m. (9'6")
WEIGHT: Empty 748 kg. (1646 lb.), Gross 1000 kg. (2200 lb.)
PERFORMANCE: Untested

SABLATNIG SF 4
Benz Bz III, 150 hp
DIMENSIONS: Span 12 m. (39′4″), Lg. 8.3 m. (27′3″), Ht. 3.73 m. (12′3″), Wing Area 28.26 qm. (304 sq. ft.)
WEIGHT: Empty 790 kg. (1738 lb.), Gross 1070 kg. (2354 lb.)
PERFORMANCE: Speed—Max. 156 km/hr (97 mph), Cruising speed 140 km/hr (87 mph), Climb 1000 m./5½ min. (3280′/5½ min.)

Sablatnig received an order for two floatplane fighters in July 1916, and delivered the first single-seater in February 1917. Known as the SF 4, it had a large upper wing joined to the small lower wing by a pair of X struts covered with fabric, along with inverted V struts above them to anchor extensive bracing wire. A 150 hp Benz and a single fixed gun were used.

While the speed was not bad for a seaplane, the climb was inferior to the other fighters, and the upper wing's wide span made for very poor maneuverability. Therefore, Sablatnig finished his second single-seater with new triplane wings to get better climb. Span was reduced from 39′4″ to 30′4″, ailerons fitted to all wings, and I struts used for bracing.

An obscure little Johannisthal company called Luft-Torpedo-Gesellschaft received an order for three fighters on February 8, 1917. The first LTG SD 1, with the top wing joined to the fuselage, was delivered in May 1917, and was load tested to de-

SABLATNIG SF 4 triplane

LUFT-TORPEDO-GESELLSCHAFT LTG SD 1
Benz Bz III, 150 hp
DIMENSIONS: Span 10 m. (32′10″), Lg. 9.2 m. (30′2″), Ht. 4.8 m. (15′9″)
WEIGHT: Empty 895 kg. (1969 lb.), Gross 1165 kg. (2563 lb.)
PERFORMANCE: Speed—Max. 145 km/hr (90 mph)

LTG SD I (1918)

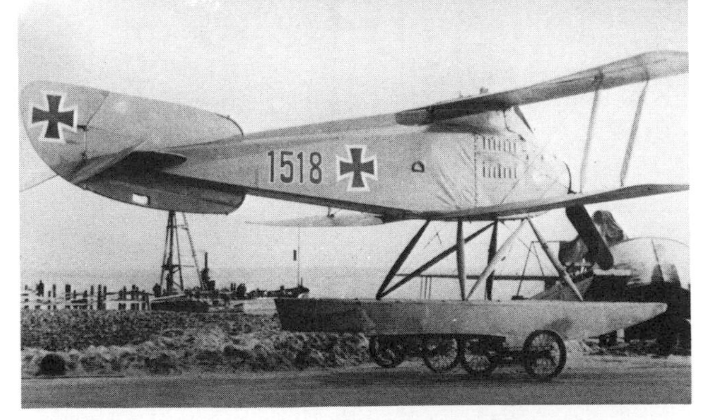

HANSA-BRANDENBURG W 25
Benz Bz III, 150 hp
DIMENSIONS: Span 10.4 m. (34′1¼″), Wing Area 30.53 qm. (229 sq. ft.)
WEIGHT: Empty 912 kg. (2006 lb.), Gross 1182 kg. (2600 lb.)
PERFORMANCE: 160 km/hr (99 mph), Climb 800 m./4.7 min. (2625′/4.7 min.)

HANSA-BRANDENBURG W 12 prototype

W 12 with Benz Bz III, 150 hp

struction, while the second was completed in July and returned to the factory in September. The third aircraft's fate is unreported. Three more with enlarged tails had been ordered in May 1917, one being delivered in March 1918, and two in June.

These were the last of the wartime single-seat seaplanes, along with the single Hansa-Brandenburg W 25 received in February 1918. With a 150 hp Benz and two guns, the W 25 had a KDW style fuselage and ordinary single-bay struts. Ailerons were fitted only to the upper wings at first, but were later also added to the lower wings to improve maneuverability. Since the two-seater fighters being produced at this time had more firepower and endurance, the W 25 was abandoned.

The single-seat fighter seaplane's weakness was that it could never match its landplane rivals in speed, climb or maneuverability. Since the Navy persisted in demanding seaplanes, the next step was the two-place fighter whose rear gun could hit an enemy behind him. As the two-seaters became available, the single-seat seaplanes were withdrawn from the West. Survivors continued to operate in the Aegean, Baltic, and Black Seas.

TWO-SEAT SEAPLANE FIGHTERS

Despite the heavy losses of seaplanes to land-based Allied fighters like the Sopwith Camel, the Navy still wanted seaplanes. To meet this requirement, Ernst Heinkel, Hansa-Brandenburg's Technical Director, chose a compact two-seat layout that became the most popular German seaplane fighter.

The Hansa-Brandenburg W 12 was a single-bay biplane whose unusual rear fuselage and tail shape was intended to give the gunner more clear space to fire. The elevators were mounted atop the rear fuselage, clear of water spray, while the rudder's balance below the fuselage became a feature of several Hein-

HANSA-BRANDENBURG W 12
Mercedes D III, 160 hp
DIMENSIONS: Span 11.2 m. (36′9″), Lg. 9.6 m. (31′6″), Ht. 3.3 m. Wing Area 36.2 qm. (390 sq. ft.)
WEIGHT: Empty 1000 kg. (2200 lb.), Gross 1463 kg. (3219 lb.)
PERFORMANCE: Speed—Max. 160 km/hr (99 mph), Climb 800 m./6 min. (2625′/6 min.), Endurance 3½ hours

kel seaplane designs. A 160 hp Mercedes, with a radiator on the top wing's leading edge, powered six W 12s ordered October 1916. They first appeared in February 1917, armed with a fixed synchronized pilot's gun and a flexible rear gun.

The 150 hp Benz with a car-type front radiator powered 50 more W 12s ordered in 1917. The first was delivered in August 1917, and quantity production got underway in September 1917. These planes were forwarded to the most active German seaplane station, Zeebrugge, where they won immediate popularity. They were followed from February to June 1918 by 30 armed with two forward and one flexible rear gun. At the same time, 60 more were built with two guns and the original Mercedes powerplant, the last 20 of these adding radio equipment.

KW WILHELMSHAFEN (#945)

HANSA-BRANDENBURG W 19
Maybach Mb IV, 260 hp
DIMENSIONS: Span 13.8 m. (45′3″), Lg. 10.65 m. (34′11″), Ht. 4.1 m. (13′5″), Wing Area 57.8 qm. (622 sq. ft.)
WEIGHT: Empty 1435 kg. (3157 lb.), Gross 2100 kg. (4620 lb.)
PERFORMANCE: Speed—Max. 151 km/hr (94 mph), Climb 1000 m./8.4 min. (3280′/8.4 min.), Endurance 5 hours

Altogether, 145 W 12s were built by June 1918. One was flown by station commander Friedrich Christiansen when he shot down the British airship C 27 on December 11, 1917. With good performance for a seaplane, they were active over the Channel through 1918. One disadvantage was the difficulty that pilot had in escaping from his cockpit under the wing.

When the need arose for a Navy fighter with greater endurance, Hansa-Brandenburg produced the larger W 19 with the 260 hp Maybach and double-bay wings. A larger fuel supply increased endurance from 3½ to five hours, and full radio equipment was provided.

Three prototypes were ordered; the first was destroyed during static tests, the second was accepted in November 1917 and the third in January 1918.

FRIEDRICHSHAFEN FF 48c
Maybach Mb III, 240 hp
DIMENSIONS: Span 16.25 m. (53′4″), Lg. 11.2 m. (36′9″), Ht. 4.4 m. (14′5″), Wing Area 68 qm. (732 sq. ft.)
WEIGHT: Empty 1591 kg. (3500 lb.), Gross 2216 kg. (4875 lb.)
PERFORMANCE: Speed—Max. 153 km/hr (95 mph), Climb 1000 m./6.4 min. (3280′/6.4 min.)

HANSA-BRANDENBURG W 27
Benz Bz IIIb, 195 hp
DIMENSIONS: Span 11.20 m. (36′9″), Lg. 8.32 m. (27′3½″), Ht. 3.057 m. (10′), Wing Area 36.6 qm. (394 sq. ft.)
WEIGHT: Empty 1109 kg. (2440 lb.), Gross 1619 kg. (3562 lb.)
PERFORMANCE: Speed—Max. 140 km/hr (87 mph)

SABLATNIG SF 7

These aircraft had one flexible and one fixed gun, while another forward gun was added to 51 production W 19s ordered by June 1918. One of these was tested in April with a 20 mm. Becker gun at the observer's station.

These designs were successful enough to eclipse other efforts to produce two-seater float fighters. The Imperial Navy Yard at Wilhelmshaven assembled a biplane known only by its serial number, 945. Powered by a 150 hp Benz and utilizing I struts, it resembled the W 12 layout, but no further information is available. The markings on the photo herewith are those used in April–May 1918.

When the Navy ordered the Hansa-Bradenburg W 19 prototypes in April 1917, it also ordered three examples each of the Friedrichshafen FF 48 and Sablatnig SF 7 two-seaters. Designed for the same long-range fighter requirement, they were also two-bay biplanes and utilized the 240 hp Maybach Mb IVa, with one fixed and one flexible gun. The FF 48, delivered in October 1917, was big for a fighter.

The first SF 7, distinguished by I struts, was seen in September 1917, but it is uncertain if the rest were delivered. The only data remaining gives a top speed of 162 km/hr (101 mph) and a climb of 1000 m. (3280′) in eight minutes at 2120 kg. (4664 lb.) gross weight.

Early in 1918, it became apparent an improved successor to the W 12 biplane would be needed, and so Hansa-Brandenburg produced six fighters using the new eight-cylinder 195 hp Benz Bz 111A in the W 12 fuselage, with a new wing arrangement. Three of these were completed as low-wing monoplanes designated W 29, while the others became the W 27 biplane with the same span as the W 12, but with new I struts.

Since the biplane version proved less satisfying than the monoplane, it was decided to relegate them to

HANSA-BRANDENBURG W 32
Mercedes D III, 160 hp
DIMENSIONS: Span 11.2 m. (36′9″), Lg. 8.37 m. (27′5½″)
WEIGHT: Empty 1063 kg. (2344 lb.), Gross 1544 kg. (3404 lb.)
PERFORMANCE: Climb 800 m./8.9 min. (2625′/8.9 min.), Endurance 4 hours

trainers. For this purpose, the new Benz was unneeded, so it was replaced by a 160 hp Mercedes with a prop spinner and new radiator. These three planes were redesignated W 32, given new serial numbers, and delivered to Kiel-Holtenau in summer 1918.

When the monoplane W 29 designed by Hans Klemm entered production in May 1918, the 150 hp six-cylinder Benz Bz 111 was standardized. A Parabellum observer's gun, a pilot's Spandau fixed on the right side, and radio equipment was provided on 40 production W 29s, but 30 more had two forward guns and no radio. A 185 hp Benz Bz 111a and three guns was specified for another batch of six. Just how many W 29s were actually built is unknown, since Navy delivery records are unavailable for the second half of 1918.

Operating from Zeebrugge, Borkum, and Norderney, these monoplanes gained fame, especially thru the flying of Christiansen, who led the Zeebrugge pilots. Among their successes was disabling the British submarine C 25 with machine gun fire on July 6, 1918, sinking three torpedo boats on August 11, and downing various British flying boats.

As the W 19 biplane had been an enlarged W 12, so the Hansa-Brandenburg W 33 was an enlarged W 29 with a 260 hp Maybach. Three prototypes ordered in April 1918 had two forward guns and one observer's gun, and were to be followed by three aircraft equipped with a radio and just one gun forward and another aft. One example had a 20 mm. Becker gun for the observer, but missing records prevent us from knowing how many more W 33s were produced. There was also a larger W 34 version, utilizing a 300 hp Basse & Selve, finished after the war, and shown here in French markings.

These seaplane designs won such a wartime reputation that, after the war, they were license-built abroad. Forty W 12 biplanes were produced by Van

HANSA-BRANDENBURG W 29
Benz Bz III, 150 hp
DIMENSIONS: Span 13.5 m. (44'3½"), Lg. 9.35 m. (30'9"), Ht. 3 m. (9'10"), Wing Area 31.6 qm. (340 sq. ft.)
WEIGHT: Empty 1000 kg. (2200 lb.), Gross 1463 kg. (3218 lb.)
PERFORMANCE: Speed—Max. 178 km/hr (111 mph), Climb 1000 m./5.9 min. (3280'/5.9 min.), Endurance 4 hours

W 29 over Norderney

Berkel for Netherlands East Indies service, and 30 W 33 monoplanes were the most important type in the Norwegian Navy. In November 1922, a W 33 with a Fiat engine was the first aircraft built in Finland by the state aircraft factory, which then built 120 from 1923–26 as Finland's general purpose type.

Experimental floatplane fighters were also made in 1918 by Albatros, Dornier, Friedrichshafen and Junkers. All were low-wing monoplanes except the Albatros W 8, a biplane completed in July 1918 with a 195 hp Benz Bz 111b. The first had a prop spinner, but the second did not and it is uncertain whether a third aircraft was actually delivered.

The same Benz engine was used in the Zeppelin-Lindau (Dornier) Cs I, a low-wing monoplane built of Duralumin except for the fabric covering on the wings and tail. Wire bracing was used on both the wings and floats. The frontal radiator was later re-

HANSA-BRANDENBURG W 33
Maybach Mb IV, 260 hp
DIMENSIONS: Span 15.85 m. (52′), Lg. 11.10 m. (36′5″), Ht. 3.37 m. (11′), Wing Area 44.6 qm. (480 sq. ft.)
WEIGHT: Empty 1470 kg. (3234 lb.), Gross 2100 kg. (4620 lb.)
PERFORMANCE: Speed—Max. 170 km/hr (106 mph), Climb 1000 m./5.4 min. (3280′/5.4 min.)

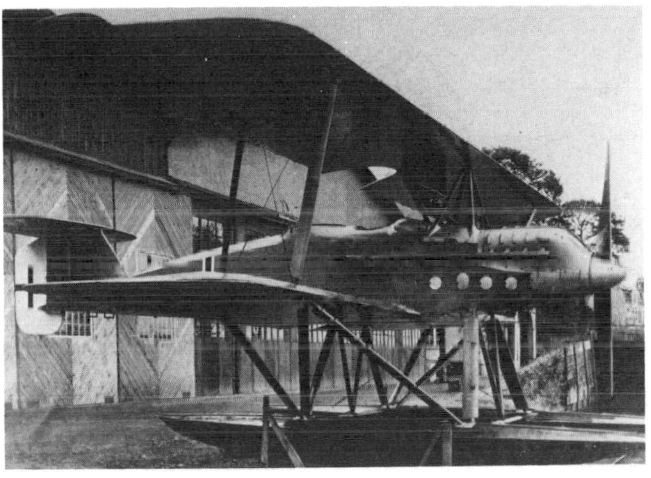

ALBATROS W 8
Benz Bz IIIb, 195 hp
DIMENSIONS: Span 11.46 m. (37′7″), Lg. 9.59 m. (11′6″), Ht. 3.39 m. (11′1″)
WEIGHT: Data not available
PERFORMANCE: Speed—Max. 150 km/hr (93 mph), Climb 1000 m./6.5 min. (3280′/6.5 min.), Range 500 km. (310 miles)

HANSA-BRANDENBURG W 34
Fiat, 300 hp
DIMENSIONS: Span 16.6 m. (54′5½″), Lg. 11.1 m. (35′8½″), Wing Area 49 qm. (527 sq. ft.)
WEIGHT: Empty 1534 kg. (3375 lb.), Gross 2270 kg. (4994 lb.)
PERFORMANCE: Speed—Max. 180 km/hr (148 mph)

ALBATROS W 8 (#2)

DORNIER (ZEPPELIN-LINDAU) Cs I
Benz Bz IIIb, 195 hp
DIMENSIONS: Span 13.28 m. (43′7″), Lg. 9.6 m. (31′6″), Wing Area 31.6 qm. (340 sq. ft.)
WEIGHT: Empty 960 kg. (2112 lb.), Gross 1479 kg. (3254 lb.)
PERFORMANCE: Speed—Max. 150 km/hr (93 mph), Range 600 km. (372 miles), Service ceiling 3000 m. (9840′)

FRIEDRICHSHAFEN FF 63

JUNKERS Ju 11
Benz Bz III, 185 hp
DIMENSIONS: Span 12.75 m. (41′10″), Lg. 8.8 m. (28′10½″), Ht. 3.05 m. (10′), Wing Area 26.6 qm. (286 sq. ft.)
WEIGHT: Empty 914 kg. (2010 lb.), Gross 1420 kg. (3124 lb.)
PERFORMANCE: Speed—Max. 180 km/hr (112 mph) at sea level, Range 720 km. (447 miles), Service ceiling 5200 m. (17,061′)

placed by two rectangular side ones before the aircraft was transferred to Warnemuende. Twin Spandaus were atop the cowl, and a gun ring was provided for the observer's weapon. Only the one example was made, first flown from Lake Constance on May 11, 1918.

The low-wing layout was also used on the very obscure Friedrichshafen FF 63, built with conventional wood and fabric frame and a 200 hp Benz. LFG also designed a similar fighter, the ME 8, but it was not completed.

The seaplane fighter story ends with the Junkers Ju 11, a naval version of the Ju 10. Officially designated C3MG, it had a 185 hp Benz and the typical Junkers all-metal, cantilever construction, and was armed with three guns. Although the original tail design was unsatisfactory, and the aircraft was overweight, it was the most advanced design concept seen among seaplanes. Three were built for the Navy, the first flying shortly before the war's end.

Rearmament and World War II

Part 5 Reconnaissance and Ground Attack Types

15.

Reconnaissance Aircraft, 1922–32

Since the Treaty of Versailles had forbidden construction of military aircraft in Germany, the manufacturers and the Defense Ministry resorted to secret programs for warplanes.

The general strategy was for the manufacturers to establish branches, with the help of government subsidies, in foreign countries. In these subsidiary plants, combat aircraft designed in Germany could be built and tested to keep Germany abreast of design progress. The most important of these opportunities came after the Treaty of Rapallo with the Soviet Union in 1922. It was natural for the nations offended by the Versailles Treaty and excluded from the League of Nations to include a secret military clause in the bargain.

This was followed in December 1923 by an agreement to establish an airbase at Lipetsk, about 180 miles southeast of Moscow. Russia would provide the land and buildings, Germany the aircraft and equipment. Here at Lipetsk, until Hitler closed the base in 1933, Germany trained hundreds of airmen and tested a new generation of equipment.

Junkers established a factory in the Moscow suburb of Fili, and the first product was the Junkers A 20. This all-metal low-wing monoplane was the most advanced product of German wartime experience, and first appeared in 1923 as a "mailplane" although its resemblance to the wartime CL I two-seater was apparent. Powered with a 160 hp Mercedes, the fast reconnaissance type was tested at Lipetsk and then went into production at Fili as the R 2 with a 300 hp Hispano-Suiza. A great improvement over the first Soviet-built military type, the R I (DH 9a) biplane, the Junkers was flown by the Germans at Lipetsk, and by the Soviet air force. Turkey also used the A 20, as the accompanying photo shows.

The next Junkers product was the smaller H 21, this time a *high-wing* monoplane of all-metal construction. This arrangement gave the two crewmen better visibility to observe the ground. Either a 185 hp BMW III or the 195 hp Junkers L 2 could be the powerplant. Designed in 1924, the H 21 went into production at Fili, and our photo shows the 100th example completed in Russia.

Junkers had also established a subsidiary factory in Sweden,[1] and there were developed military versions of the A 32 and A 35 "mailplanes" of 1926. Both were low-wing all-metal monoplanes of typical Junkers layout. The three-place A 32 became the K 39 when fitted with twin Lewis guns on the rear cockpit, a ventral bomb-aiming and gun position, and twin

[1] *Aktiebolaget Flygindustri,* at Linhamn, Malmo, most of whose aircraft were assembled from German parts.

JUNKERS A 20
Mercedes D IIIa, 160 hp
DIMENSIONS: Span 15.34 m. (50′4″), Lg. 8.35 m. (27′5″), Ht. 3.6 m. (11′10″), Wing Area 28.1 qm. (302 sq. ft.)
WEIGHT: Empty 940 kg. (2068 lb.), Gross 1500 kg. (3300 lb.)
PERFORMANCE: Speed—Max. 170 km/hr (106 mph), Cruising speed 150 km/hr (93 mph), Landing speed 95 km/hr (59 mph), Climb 1000 m./4.5 min. (3280′/4.5 min.), Service ceiling 4000 m. (13,120′)

JUNKERS H 21
Junkers L 2, 195 hp, or BMW III, 185 hp
DIMENSIONS: Span 10.77 m. (35′4″), Lg. 6.7 m. (21′11½″), Ht. 2.5 m. (8′2½″)
WEIGHT: Empty 945 kg. (2079 lb.), Gross 1145 kg. (2519 lb.)
PERFORMANCE: Speed—Max. 220 km/hr (137 mph), Cruising speed 170 km/hr (106 mph), Landing speed 95 km/hr (59 mph), Climb 1000 m./4.8 min. (3280′/4.8 min.), Service ceiling 5500 m. (18,045′)

JUNKERS K 53
Junkers L 5, 310 hp
DIMENSIONS: Span 15.94 m. (52′4″), Lg. 8.21 m. (27′), Ht. 3.5 m. (11′6″), Wing Area 29.8 qm. (320 sq. ft.)
WEIGHT: Empty 1075 kg. (2365 lb.), Gross 1500 kg. (3300 lb.)
PERFORMANCE: Speed—Max. 208 km/hr (129 mph,) Cruising speed 185 km/hr (115 mph), Landing speed 90 km/hr (56 mph), Climb 1000 m./4.5 min. (3280′/4.5 min.), Endurance 4½ hours, Service ceiling 6400 m. (20,998′)

JUNKERS K 39
BMW VI, 450 hp
DIMENSIONS: Span 17.82 m. (58′6″), Lg. 11.1 m. (36′5″), Ht. 3.38 m. (11′1″), Wing Area 40 qm. (430 sq. ft.)
WEIGHT: Empty 1950 kg. (4290 lb.), Gross 3200 kg. (7040 lb.), Fuel 710 liters (187 gal.)
PERFORMANCE: Speed—Max. 220 km/hr (137 mph), Cruising speed 185 km/hr (115 mph), Landing speed 98 km/hr (61 mph), Endurance 5 hours, Service ceiling 5000 m. (16,400′)

CASPAR C 30
Hispano-Suiza, 500 hp
DIMENSIONS: Span 10 m. (32′10″), Lg. 7.6 m. (24′11½″)
WEIGHT: Gross 1700 kg. (3740 lb.)
PERFORMANCE: Speed—Max. 225 km/hr (140 mph), Cruising speed 200 km/hr (124 mph), Landing speed 85 km/hr (53 mph), Range 1000 km. (620 miles), Service ceiling 7000 m. (22,960′)

ALBATROS L 65

Vickers nose guns. This aircraft could be used as a light bomber or reconnaissance type.

Smaller and more compact, the A 35 two-seater became the K 53 when fitted with two forward guns and flexible twin Lewis guns. Suitable for reconnaissance or fighting with twin float or wheeled landing gear, it was built in both Sweden and the U.S.S.R.

Other firms with foreign facilities included Caspar, whose Danish plant had turned out the C 30 in 1924. An unattractive biplane with N struts and a gap between the lower wing and fuselage, the C 30 did not go into quantity production.

Albatros had established a subsidiary, *Allgemeine Flug-Gesellschaft* in Memel, which had become a self-governing area outside of Germany. There several training and reconnaissance biplanes were produced, including the Albatros L 65 of 1924, a two-seater with tapered wings, I struts and a 450 hp Napier Lion inline engine.

Albatros also produced the L 76, a conventional two-seat biplane of 1926 with the 580 hp BMW VI. A metal fuselage was used for the first time on an Albatros type, and the original neat tail was replaced by a balanced rudder. While flying an L 76 to Lipetsk, the 32-victory ace, Lieutenant Emil Thuy, was killed near Smolensk on June 11, 1930.

The same BMW engine was used in 1927 on the Albatros L 78, but only one example was built. After Robert Thelen, the Technical Director of Albatros, had left the firm after the war, designer Rudolf Schubert seemed unable to reproduce his wartime success, and so the company was finally eclipsed and absorbed by Focke-Wulf in 1932.

Ernst Heinkel had established factories in Warnemuende and also in Sweden, and in 1924 produced for the secret Reichswehr the very conventional HD 17 two-seater with a 450 hp Napier Lion engine. Since German civil aircraft manufacture had been allowed since May 1922, the HD 17 could be described as a "sports" plane. The example in the photo here shows how they appeared at Lipetsk, where they were used for training in reconnaissance and bombing. A modified version was also tested in the U.S. as the Cox-Klemin CO-2.

HEINKEL HD 17
Napier Lion, 450 hp
DIMENSIONS: Span 12.8 m. (42'), Lg. 9.18 m. (30'1¼"), Wing Area 40.6 qm. (437 sq. ft.)
WEIGHT: Empty 1380 kg. (3036 lb.), Gross 2200 kg. (4840 lb.)
PERFORMANCE: Speed—Max. 220 km/hr (137 mph), Cruising speed 200 km/hr (124 mph), Landing speed 90 km/hr (56 mph), Service ceiling 6500 m. (21,325')

ALBATROS L 76

ALBATROS L 78

In 1925, Heinkel improved the type with a 660 hp BMW VI and slight refinements. With the usual provisions for a fixed gun on the cowl and flexible gun for the observer, the HD 33 was hardly different from 1918 types, or for that matter, from the He 45s that became the principal Luftwaffe reconnaissance type ten years later. The HD 33 was built in Warnemuende, the components then sent to Sweden for assembly by Svenska Aero, and the aircraft officially delivered to Germany.

Professor Claudius Dornier established a second factory in Switzerland, and there on September 25, 1924, he flew his first Do C, an all-metal, high-wing monoplane with a deep body and a choice of the Napier, BMW or Rolls-Royce engines. The small ventral radiator and balanced rudder used originally were replaced by a nose radiator and unbalanced vertical surface. Tested at Lipetsk in the reconnaissance role with different armaments, it failed to satisfy the Germans, but the Do C found other purchasers and was manufactured in Switzerland, Italy and Japan (by Kawasaki).

Junkers' Swedish branch produced a reconnaissance and light-bomber version of the W 34 civil transport in 1928, which was designated K 43. Using the low-wing all-metal layout typical of Junkers, this

HEINKEL HD 33

DORNIER Do C with ventral radiator

HEINKEL HD 33
BMW VI, 660 hp

DIMENSIONS: Span 12.8 m. (42′), Lg. 9.4 m. (30′10″), Ht. 4.35 m. (14′3″), Wing Area 43.3 qm. (466 sq. ft.)

WEIGHT: Empty 1600 kg. (3520 lb.), Gross 2730 kg. (6006 lb.)

PERFORMANCE: Speed—Max. 246.5 km/hr (153 mph), Cruising speed 200 km/hr (124 mph), Landing speed 90 km/hr (56 mph), Service ceiling 6200 m. (20,340′)

DORNIER Do C
Rolls-Royce Eagle, 360 hp, later BMW 6, 460 hp

DIMENSIONS: Span 19.6 m. (64′4″), Lg. 12.65 m. (41′6″), Ht. 3.4 m. (11′2″), Wing Area 63 qm. (678 sq. ft.)

WEIGHT: Empty 2000 kg. (4400 lb.), Gross 3400 kg. (7480 lb.)

PERFORMANCE: Speed—Max. 163 km/hr (101 mph), Landing speed 85 km/hr (53 mph), Climb 1000 m./7.5 min. (3280′/7.5 min.), Service ceiling 6500 m. (21,320′)

JUNKERS K 43
Bristol Jupiter, 500 hp
DIMENSIONS: Span 18.48 m. (60′7½″), Lg. 10.27 m. (33′8″), Ht. 3.53 m. (11′7″), Wing Area 44 qm. (473 sq. ft.)
WEIGHT: Empty 1100 kg. (2420 lb.), Gross 1600 kg. (3520 lb.)
PERFORMANCE: Speed—Max. 265 km/hr (165 mph), Cruising speed 233 km/hr (145 mph), Landing speed 116 km/hr (72 mph), Range 900 km. (560 miles), Service ceiling 6300 m. (20,670′)

three-seater added two gunners' cockpits in the cabin roof and wing racks for six 110 lb. bombs and used wheels or floats. Powered by a Bristol Jupiter radial engine, the K 43 was tested at Lipetsk. Finland bought six in 1930 with Pratt & Whitney Hornets, Argentina five with Wright Cyclones, Portugal five seaplanes with Armstrong Siddeley Panthers, and several K 43s went to Bolivia.

Fastest two-seater of this period was the Junkers K 47, which also appeared in Sweden. Designed by Karl Plauth in 1928 as a fighter-reconnaissance type, this mid-wing monoplane had twin rudders, a Siemens-built Jupiter, and turn-over guard between the cockpits, and was seen in Germany as the A 48 "sport" plane with a 425 hp Pratt & Whitney Hornet.

Armament for the K 47 included two forward guns, a flexible gun in the rear cockpit, and provision for 100 kg. (220 lb.) of bombs. The rear gunner faced aft in a seat that rocked back to point his weapon 90 degrees upward. Successful dive-bombing tests at Lipetsk provided much useful experience for the later development of the Ju 87. Work at the Russian base was conducted in absolute secrecy, of course, and to this day it has not been possible to determine the exact numbers of aircraft operated there.

Two K 47 prototypes, SE-ADL (Hornet engine) and SE-ABW (Jupiter), were tested at Lipetsk and reappeared in Germany by 1935 as D-2012 and D-2284, the former still flying in 1942. One batch of K 47s went to China, where 13 remained in July 1932; then the best combat planes in Chiang's air force.

Meanwhile, Heinkel continued to offer biplanes from his Swedish factory. For army reconnaissance, the Heinkel HD 19L of 1928, was powered by a 410 hp Siemens Jupiter. Quite similar was the 1929's

JUNKERS K 47 (1928)
Bristol Jupiter, 500 hp, also P & W Hornet of 500 hp
DIMENSIONS: Span 12.4 m. (40′8″), Lg. 8.55 m. (28′), Ht. 2.9 m. (9′6″), Wing Area 22.8 qm. (245 sq. ft.)
WEIGHT: Empty 1050 kg. (2310 lb.), Gross 1650 kg. (3630 lb.), Fuel 344 liters (90 gal.)
PERFORMANCE: Speed—Max. 285 km/hr (177 mph) at 3000 m. (9840′), 242 km/hr (150 mph) at sea level, Cruising speed 230 km/hr (143 mph), Landing speed 105 km/hr (65 mph), Climb 8000 m./32 min. (26,240′/32 min.), Range 570 km. 350 miles), Service ceiling 8500 m. (27,900′)

JUNKERS K 47 (1935)

JUNKERS K 47 (1939)

HD 41, which used either a BMW VI or a 500 hp Bristol Jupiter. The resemblance of these conventional two-place biplanes to the Luftwaffe's He 45 is evident.

Last of the manufacturers attempting reconnais-

HEINKEL HD 19L
Siemens-Jupiter, 410 hp
DIMENSIONS: Span 11 m. (36′1″), Lg. 7.8 m. (25′7″), Wing Area 31.6 qm. (40 sq. ft.)
WEIGHT: Empty 1010 kg. (2222 lb.), Gross 1560 kg. (3432 lb.)
PERFORMANCE: Speed—Max. 228 km/hr (142 mph), Cruising speed 190 km/hr (118 mph), Landing speed 84 km/hr (50 mph), Service ceiling 7700 m. (25,200′)

HEINKEL HD 41a
BMW VI, 750 hp
DIMENSIONS: Span 11.5 m. (37′9″), Lg. 10.1 m. (33′1½″), Ht. 4 m. (13′1½″), Wing Area 34.57 qm. (372 sq. ft.)
WEIGHT: Empty 1750 kg. (3860 lb.), Gross 2650 kg. (5842 lb.)
PERFORMANCE: Speed—Max. 270 km/hr (168 mph), Landing speed 110 km/hr (68 mph), Climb 1000 m./2.2 min. (3280′/2.2 min.) 3000 m./8 min. (9840′/8 min.), Service ceiling 5800 m. (19,000′)

sance aircraft during this clandestine period was Focke-Wulf, of Bremen. In 1931 this firm produced prototypes of the Focke-Wulf W 7 and S 39 two-seaters. The former was an undistinguished biplane, with a 650 hp BMW VI and four-bladed propeller, whose specifications have not been passed down. On the other hand, the S 39 was a high-wing monoplane with a neat streamlined cowl on its Siemens Jupiter. Neither type entered production, but massive rearmament was soon to change the aviation scene.

HEINKEL HD 41b
Siemens-Jupiter, 500 hp
DIMENSIONS: as HD 41a
WEIGHT: Empty 1700 kg. (3740 lb.), Gross 2435 kg. (5357 lb.)
PERFORMANCE: Speed—Max. 232 km/hr (144 mph), Cruising speed 200 km/hr (124 mph), Landing speed 85 km/hr (53 mph), Service ceiling 5800 m. (19,030′)

FOCKE-WULF W 7

FOCKE-WULF S 39
Siemens-Jupiter, 510 hp
DIMENSIONS: Span 20 m. (65′7¼″), Lg. 15.4 m. (50′6″), Ht. 5.3 m. (17′4½″), Wing Area 18.8 qm. (202 sq. ft.)
WEIGHT: Empty 2700 kg. (5940 lb.), Gross 4400 kg. (9680 lb.)
PERFORMANCE: Speed—Max. 204 km/hr (127 mph), Cruising speed 200 km/hr (124 mph), Service ceiling 3500 m. (11,480′)

16.

Luftwaffe Reconnaissance, 1933–45

HEINKEL HE 45 AND HE 46

After the Nazis came to power in 1933, a new Air Ministry (RLM)* under Goering was established to begin building the new Luftwaffe. At first the emphasis was on quantity production of the types then available, so the new Luftwaffe could be built up as quickly as possible for political and for training purposes.

The production program planned in 1934 by Erhard Milch, Goering's deputy, called for 656 two-seat reconnaissance types, (compared to 292 fighters). All were of Heinkel design: 305 He 45 biplanes for short-distance work, 279 He 46 high-wing monoplanes for artillery spotting, and 72 He 70 low-wing monoplanes for long-distance missions. These aircraft were to be built in a new Heinkel factory at Rostock-Marienehe and by several subcontractors.

First of the Luftwaffe's reconnaissance types, the He 45 was ordered in larger numbers than any type but the Ju 52. In design and function it was like the C planes of World War I, with only the minor refinements developed in the Heinkel types of the 1920s. Armament was the traditional fixed gun, a 7.9 mm. MG 17, and a flexible 7.9 mm. MG 15 gun.

The standard production versions, HE 45C and D, had a 750 hp BMW VI 7.3 inline engine and two-bladed wooden propeller, and could be distinguished from the 1932 prototype by long exhaust pipes and a larger tail. Experimental versions tested the BMW 116, Jumo 210, and Daimler DB 600 engines with three-bladed props, and the He 61 was a version for China with the 650 hp BMW VI-U.

* *Reichsluftfahrtministerium*—German Air Ministry.

HEINKEL He 45 prototype

Production deliveries began in autumn 1933, so the He 45 was probably the first type to join the still secret Luftwaffe squadrons, and 150 had been delivered by the end of 1934, as the BFW, Focke-Wulf, and Gotha factories joined the delivery schedules. Orders rose to 426 aircraft for delivery by April 1937.

There were 21 Luftwaffe reconnaissance squadrons in the summer of 1936, with 12 aircraft each. Each of the 11 long-range units (*Fernaufklaerungstaffeln*) had nine He 45 biplanes and three He 70 monoplanes, while each of the ten short-range Army units (*Heeresaufklaerungstaffeln*) had three He 45 and nine He 46 machines.[1] Forty He 45Cs went to Spain with A/88, the Condor Legion recon group. On September 2, 1939, 21 He 45s still lingered with Luftwaffe units, including 4(H)AGr 21.

Heinkel's He 46 was built at the same time for artillery observation, but had a 450 hp Siemens Jupiter radial engine. The prototype He 46a (D-1028) appeared in 1932 as a biplane, but the He 46b and all remaining ships were high-wing monoplanes. The production ships were mostly the He 46c, with seven civil He 46ds, while the He 46e and the He 46f trainer had NACA cowls on imported Armstrong-Siddeley Panther engines.

Focke-Wulf had also tried a parasol two-seater, the Fw 40 of 1933, but was eclipsed by Heinkel's ship.

Production of the He 46 by Heinkel, Siebel, Fieseler and MIAG began in February 1934, with 84 by the end of the year, and came to 424 aircraft by December 1936. Twenty were sent to Spain in September 1936, and in 1937–38 Bulgaria got 18 and Hungary 36 new He 46es with Panther and Gnome-Rhone engines. The He 46 was replaced in 1938–39 by the Hs 126 and only five Staffeln remained on September 2, 1939, with 64 He 46c aircraft.

Excessive vibration from the Siemens engine earned the nickname of *Ruttelfalke*. Only one gun, the 7.9 mm. MG 15 for the observer, was fitted. Twenty 22 lb. bombs could be carried inside the fuselage in vertical chutes.

[1] Long-range (F) squadrons: 1/121, 1–3/122, 1–2/123, 1–2/124, 1–3/125. Short-range (H) squadrons: 1/111, 1–2/112, 1–2/212, 1–3/114, 1–2/115.

HEINKEL He 45
Daimler DB 600, 880 hp
DIMENSIONS: as He 45C but Ht. 4.3 m. (14′1¼″)
WEIGHT: Empty 1985 kg. (4367 lb.), Gross 3000 kg. (6600 lb.)
PERFORMANCE: Speed—Max. 362 km/hr (225 mph), Landing speed 105 km/hr (65 mph), Climb 1000 m./2 min. (3280′/2 min.), Service ceiling 9000 m. (29,530′)

HEINKEL He 45C
BMW VI 7.3, 750 hp
DIMENSIONS: Span 11.5 m. (37′9″), Lg. 10 m. (32′10″), Ht. 3.6 m. (11′10″), Wing Area 34.59 qm. (372 sq. ft.)
WEIGHT: Empty 2105 kg. (4631 lb.) Gross 2745 kg. (6039 lb.), Fuel 580 liters (153 gal.)
PERFORMANCE: Speed—Max. 290 km/hr (180 mph) at sea level, Cruising speed 220 km/hr (136 mph), Landing speed 105 km/hr (65 mph), Climb 1000 m./2.4 min. (3280′/2.4 min.), Range 1200 km. (745 miles), Service ceiling 5500 m. (18,040′)

HEINKEL He 45 (Jumo 210)

HEINKEL He 45 (BMW 116)

HEINKEL He 61
BMW VI U, 650 hp
DIMENSIONS: Span 11.5 m. (37′9″), Lg. 10 m. (32′10″), Wing Area 34.6 qm. (372 sq. ft.)
WEIGHT: Empty 1695 kg. (3729 lb.), Gross 2580 kg. (5676 lb.)
PERFORMANCE: Speed—Max. 270 km/hr (168 mph) at sea level, Cruising speed 225 km/hr (140 mph), Landing speed 95 km/hr (59 mph), Service ceiling 6000 m. (19,-680′)

HEINKEL He 46A
Siemens Jupiter, 450 hp
DIMENSIONS: Span 11.5 m. (37′9″), Lg. 9.4 m. (30′8″), Ht. 4.2 m. (13′9″), Wing Area 34.6 qm. (372 sq. ft.)
WEIGHT: Empty 1600 kg. (3528 lb.), Gross 2170 kg. (4785 lb.)
PERFORMANCE: 198 km/hr (121 mph) at sea level

HEINKEL He 46C
Bramo 322B (formerly Siemens 22B), 600 hp
DIMENSIONS: Span 14 m. (45'11"), Lg. 9.5 m. (31'2"), Ht. 4.2 m. (13'9"), Wing Area 32.2 qm. (346.66 sq. ft.)
WEIGHT: Empty 1765 kg. (3891 lb.), Gross 2300 (5071 lb.)
PERFORMANCE: Speed—Max. 260 km/hr (161 mph) at 800 m. (2625'), 250 km/hr (155 mph) at sea level, Cruising speed 220 km/hr (137 mph), Landing speed 95 km/hr (59 mph), Climb 1000 m./2.6 min. (3280'/2.6 min.) Range 1000 km. (620 miles), Service ceiling 6000 m. (19,680')

HEINKEL He 46F

FOCKE-WULF Fw 40

HEINKEL HE 70

While the He 45s looked like their World War I ancestors, with strut-braced wings, exposed undercarriages, open cockpits and fabric-covered surfaces, the He 70 introduced the revolutionary appearance that became typical of World War II aircraft. Heinkel's *Blitz* (Lightning) was the first European production low-wing monoplane with retractable wheels.

Design of this type was begun in May 1932 by Siegfried and Walter Guenter, twin brothers at Heinkel's Warnemuende factory. Inspired by threatened competition from the Lockheed Orion, the He 70 carried a pilot, radio operator, and four passengers. The carefully streamlined fuselage had metal skin with countersunk rivets, and the enclosed pilot's cockpit was offset to the left behind the liquid-cooled 630 hp BMW VI. The landing gear retracted into elliptical wooden wings.

When first flown on December 1, 1932, the He 70 prototype transport was faster (377 kmph–234 mph) than any fighter in Europe. Production began with delivery in 1934 of four He 70A transports to Lufthansa. There were 28 commercial He 70s made, including He 70B and 70D, but mostly the heavier He 70G. One of the latter was sold to Britain as a test-bed for the Rolls-Royce Kestrel engine.

Military versions began with the He 70C (D-UHYS), He 70E (D-UBEQ) and He 70F (D-UNYS) prototypes. The latter became the service version, joining reconnaissance units from 1935 to 1937. A two or three-place long-range recon type, the He 70F was armed with a single flexible 7.9 mm. MG 15 with 450 rounds of ammunition. Internal racks for six 50 kg. (110 lb.) bombs provided on the He 70E could presumably have been added to the He 70F, if necessary.

HEINKEL He 70C

HEINKEL He 70E

HEINKEL He 170A (He 70L)
Gnome-Rhone 14K (Weiss blt.), 910 hp for takeoff
DIMENSIONS: Span 14.8 m. (48′7″), Lg. 11.5 m. (37′5″), Ht. 3.1 m. (10′2″), Wing Area 36.5 qm. (392.88 sq. ft.)
WEIGHT: Empty 2300 kg. (5072 lb.), Gross 3540 kg. (7806 lb.)
PERFORMANCE: Speed—Max. 435 km/hr (270 mph), at 4000 m. (13,120′), Landing speed 107 km/hr (66 mph), Range 450–920 km. (280–570 miles)

HEINKEL He 70F
BMW VI 7, 3Z, 750 hp at takeoff
DIMENSIONS: Span 14.8 m. (48′7″), Lg. 11.3 m. (37′½″), Ht. 3.1 m. (10′2″), Wing Area 36.5 qm. (392.88 sq. ft.)
WEIGHT: Empty 2360 kg. (5192 lb.), Gross 3370 kg. (7414 lb.), Fuel 420 liters (111 gal.)
PERFORMANCE: Speed—Max. 362 km/hr (224 mph) at sea level, Cruising speed 326 km/hr (202 mph), Landing speed 110 km/hr (68 mph), Climb 1000 m./2.6 min. (3280′/2.6 min.) 5000 m./25.4 min. (16,400′/25.4 min.), Range 1000 km. (620 miles), Service ceiling 5700 m. (18,700′)

Air Ministry reports list 196 He 70s ordered by 1936 for the reconnaissance units, as well as 74 for courier, transport and test assignments. Eighteen He 70Fs went to Spain late in 1936 for the Condor Legion's A/88 unit. When replaced by twin-engined Do 17Fs, the Heinkels went to Spanish Nationalist fliers in April 1937. When the civil war ended in April 1939, eleven remained in service.

Hungary purchased 18 aircraft for its long-range reconnaissance group in 1937. This version used a 910 hp Gnome-Rhone 14K air-cooled radial built under license in Budapest, and became known as the He 170A (formerly He 70L). Carrying three men and twin 7.8 mm. Gebauer flexible guns, they were used when Hungary joined the war against the U.S.S.R. in June 1941.

Last of this line was the single He 270 of 1938 with an 1175 hp Daimler-Benz DB 601A, three crewmen, one mg. and 300 kg. (600 lb.) of bombs.

HENSCHEL HS 126

Germany, which had a dozen different two-seat recon types at the end of World War I, began World

HEINKEL He 270
Daimler-Benz DB 601A, 1175 hp
DIMENSIONS: Span 14.8 m. (48′7″), Lg. 11.9 m. (39′), Ht. 3.1 m. (10′1″), Wing Area 36.5 qm. (392.88 sq. ft.)
WEIGHT: Empty 2670 kg. (5874 lb.), Gross 4150 kg. (9130 lb.), Fuel 420 liters (111 gal.)
PERFORMANCE: Speed—Max. 460 km/hr (285 mph) at 4000 m. (13,120′), Cruising speed 410 km/hr (254 mph), Landing speed 115 km/hr (71 mph), Climb 1000 m./2.2 min. (3280′/2.2 min.), Range 1000 km. (620 miles), Service ceiling 9000 m. (29,520′)

War II with just one such type in full production. The Henschel Hs 126 was an example of the standardization of types adopted to speed production and avoid chaotic maintenance situations.

Friedrich Nikolaus had designed the high-wing parasol monoplane which was the first aircraft to come from Henschel's new Schonefeld factory. The Henschel Hs 122V-1 (D-UBYN) short-range recon two-seater appeared in 1935 with open cockpits, wheel pants and imported 580 hp Rolls-Royce Kestrel inline engine. The second and third prototypes had a 600 hp air-cooled Siemens SAM 22B radial.

While 76 of a production version were included in the 1935 program, only a small He 122A-0 batch (7?) were completed, for performance was disappointing and Henschel's facilities were devoted mainly to the Hs 123 single-seater dive-bomber.

A redesigned Hs 126V-1 was converted from the fourth Hs 122A-0, introducing cantilever legs on the landing gear, and powered by a 600 hp Junkers Jumo inline with a three-bladed propeller. An 830 hp Bramo 323A-1 radial and an enclosed cockpit was used on the V-2 and V-3 prototypes in 1937, the latter establishing the final tail and landing gear configuration for production.

Production models included the Hs 126A-0 with the Bramo radial, the Hs 126A-1 with a BMW 132Dc giving 870 hp at 8700 ft. and the definitive Hs 126B-1, again with the Bramo 323A-1 of 830 hp at 13,120 ft. Armament of all these two-seaters included a fixed 7.9 mm. MG 17 with 500 rounds, a flexible MG 15 with 975 rounds, and ten 10 kg. (22 lb.) bombs in containers behind the cockpit, or a 50 kg. (110 lb.) bomb on a rack attached to the port side.

HENSCHEL Hs 122V-1

HENSCHEL Hs 122V-2

HENSCHEL Hs 122A
SAM 22B, 600 hp
DIMENSIONS: Span 14.5 m. (47′6½″), Lg. 10.25 m. (33′ 7¼″), Ht. 3.4 m. (11′2″), Wing Area 34.7 qm. (373 sq. ft.)
WEIGHT: Empty 1650 kg. (3630 lb.), Gross 2530 kg. (5560 lb.)
PERFORMANCE: Speed—Max. 270 km/hr (167 mph) at sea level, Cruising speed 240 km/hr (149 mph), Landing speed 85 km/hr (53 mph), Climb 1000 m./3.2 min. (3280′/3.2 min.), Range 500 km. (310 miles), Service ceiling 5600 m. (18,370′)

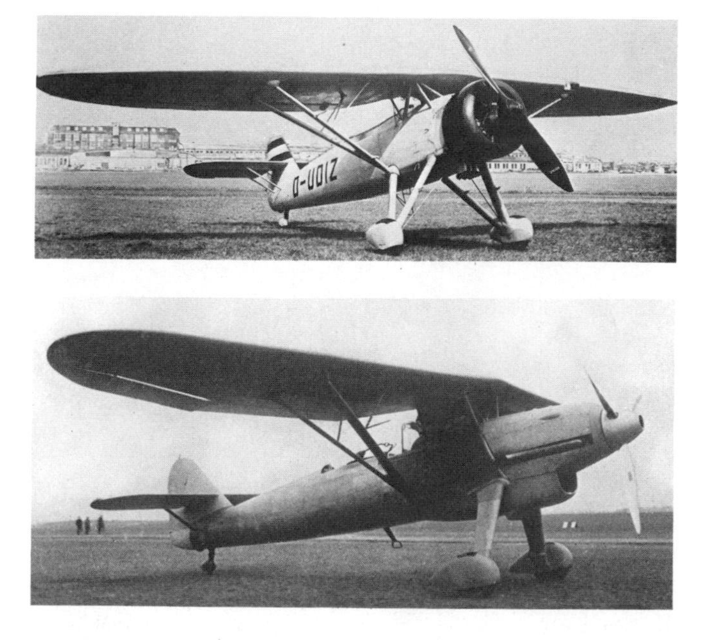

HENSCHEL Hs 126V-1

Production accelerated during 1938 and 1939, and six Hs 126As were sent to Spain and 16 to Greece. Luftwaffe Hs 126 stocks rose from 42 on September 19, 1938 to 257 on September 2, 1939; equipping 24 of the 30 short-range recon staffels, which possessed 342 two-seaters at the war's beginning.

By the end of 1939, 534 Hs 126s had been delivered, while 368 were added in 1940, with the last five added in January 1941, to bring the total to 907. This production enabled the Luftwaffe stocks to increase despite 1940 losses. On April 30, 1940, there were 344 two-seaters in short-range recon *staffeln,* with a total of 698 when aircraft in training, storage or repair status were added. By December 31, the total was 752, with 402 in the first-line units. For the first two years of the war, the Hs 126 carried the burden of short-range recon work, but even after it was replaced in 1941–42 by the Fw 189, some soldiered on until the war's end in 1945.

HENSCHEL Hs 126V-2

HENSCHEL Hs 126B
Bramo 323A-1, 830 hp
DIMENSIONS: Span 14.5 m. (47'7"), Lg. 10.85 m. (35'7"), Ht. 3.75 m. (12'3½"), Wing Area 31.6 qm. (340 sq. ft.)
WEIGHT: Empty 2030 kg. (4466 lb.), Gross 3090 kg. (6798 lb.)
PERFORMANCE: Speed—Max. 353 km/hr (219 mph) at 3000 m. (9840'), Cruising speed 290 km/hr (180 mph), Landing speed 95 km/hr (59 mph), Range 710 km. (440 miles), Service ceiling 9000 m. (29,520')

EXPERIMENTAL PROJECTS

During the years preceding the war, there were several experimental projects that offered unique solution to reconnaissance requirements. For example, the Gotha Go 147 was an odd tail-less two-seater whose twin rudders were at the end of wings swept back 40 degrees. A light test model with a 240 hp Argus was flown in 1936, but development was discontinued.

Siegfried and Walter Guenter designed a replacement for the He 70 long-range reconnaissance type that used a radical design to achieve high speed. The Heinkel He 119 was an almost perfectly streamlined low-wing monoplane with a Daimler-Benz DB 606A (actually two DB 601s coupled together) buried in the fuselage. A long extension shaft ran forward between the pilot and co-pilot to a four bladed propeller. Transparent panels covered the nose to give the pilots good visibility forward, and the fuselage was smoothly streamlined, except for a semi-retractable radiator, back to the retractable tail wheel.

The first Hs 119V-1 was finished at Rostock in the summer of 1937, and its 2350 hp DB 606A gave it a speed of 575 km/hr (351 mph), faster than any fighter plane of the day. No armament was fitted, but the second prototype, Hs 119V-2 of September 1937, had internal racks for three 250 kg. (550 lb.) bombs. The third example, however, was a pure reconnais-

GOTHA Go 147B
Argus As 10c, 240 hp
DIMENSIONS: Span 11 m. (36'1"), Lg. 5.4 m. (17'8½"), Ht. 2.54 m. (8'4")
WEIGHT: Empty 945 kg. (2079 lb.), Gross 1145 kg. (2519 lb.)
PERFORMANCE: Speed—Max. 220 km/hr (137 mph), Climb 1000 m./4.8 min. (3280'/4.8 min.), Service ceiling 5500 m. (18,040')

sance version with no armament, two crewmen, a slightly reduced span, and 590 km/hr (366 mph) top speed.

No guns were fitted to these aircraft originally, for Heinkel believed their high speed would enable them to elude hostile interceptors. The RLM insisted that weapons be fitted, however, and finally settled for a single flexible MG 15 under a sliding panel atop the radio operator's cabin behind the wing.

A new cooling system, in which the radiator was entirely retracted in flight and surface evaporation took over, was employed on the He 119 V-4. On November 22, 1937, this aircraft (D-AUTE) established a record of 505 km/hr (314 mph) for the 1000 km. (621 miles) run with a 1000 kg. (2200 lb.) payload, but a December attempt to better that mark ended with a crash landing. Nevertheless, the record run was publicized by the Propaganda Ministry as made by a Heinkel He 111U, in order to promote the entirely unrelated He 111 standard bomber!

Heinkel then produced a twin-float maritime version, the He 119V-5 which attained 570 km/hr (354 mph), but was not accepted for production. Three more landplanes were completed in 1938 as the V-6, V-7 and V-8 fitted for 1000 kg. (2200 lb.) of bombs,

HEINKEL He 119V-3 (V-2 in photo)
Daimler-Benz DB 606A-1, 2350 hp
DIMENSIONS: Span 15.9 m. (52′2″), Lg. 14.73 m. (48′4″), Ht. 5.4 m. (17′8½″), Wing Area 50 qm. (538 sq. ft.)
WEIGHT: Empty 5200 kg. (11,440 lb.), Gross 7565 kg. (16,-643 lb.)
PERFORMANCE: Speed—Max. 590 km/hr (366 mph) at 4500 m. (14,760′), 490 km/hr (304 mph) at sea level, Cruising speed 510 km/hr (316 mph), Range 3120 km. (1935 miles), Service ceiling 8500 m. (27,880′)

HEINKEL He 119V-4

HEINKEL He 119V-5

ARADO Ar 198
Bramo 323A, 900 hp at takeoff
DIMENSIONS: Span 14.9 m. (48′10½″), Lg. 11.8 m. (38′8½″), Ht. 4.6 m. (15′1″), Wing Area 35.2 qm. (379 sq. ft.)
WEIGHT and PERFORMANCE: Data not available

one MG 15 and a crew of three. Plans for further production of an He 119A reconnaissance and He 119B bomber were dropped apparently because of political intrigues in the RLM. The last two aircraft were returned to Heinkel and sold to the Japanese Navy in 1940 for development as the Yokosuka R2Y1 Keiun.

For the short-range mission performed by the Hs 126, Arado offered the Ar 198 in late 1937. A three-place midwing monoplane with an observer's enclosure in the belly between the panted landing gear, the Ar 198 had a 900 hp Bramo radial, and was armed with four 50 kg. (110 lb.) bombs, two MG 17 fixed in the wings, an MG 15 for the rear gunner, and another for the observer to fire under the tail. Only the prototype was built, as the Hs 126 seemed adequate for its mission.

BLOHM & VOSS BV 141

The same short-range requirement also inspired the most peculiar German plane of this period, the Blohm & Voss BV 141, a three-place single-engined monoplane. Dr. Richard Vogt, technical director of the Hamburg firm's aircraft division and former technical director of Japan's Kawasaki firm, conceived an asymmetrical configuration with the crew in a separate nacelle to the right of the engine and tail structure. Believing that this shape would provide the best all-around vision for reconnaissance and would cancel out propeller torque, Vogt began the project as a private venture, and a mockup was ready by June 1937. Actually, it was not the world's first asymmetrical aircraft, since that honor belongs to 1918's Gotha G VI.

BLOHM & VOSS BV 141V-1
BMW 132 N, 960 hp at 3000 m. (9840′)
DIMENSIONS: Span 15.1 m. (49′6″), Lg. 11.4 m. (37′5″), Ht. 3.2 m. (10′6″), Wing Area 41.8 qm. (450 sq. ft.)
WEIGHT: Empty 3090 kg. (6798 lb.), Gross 3829 kg. (8424 lb.)
PERFORMANCE: Data not available

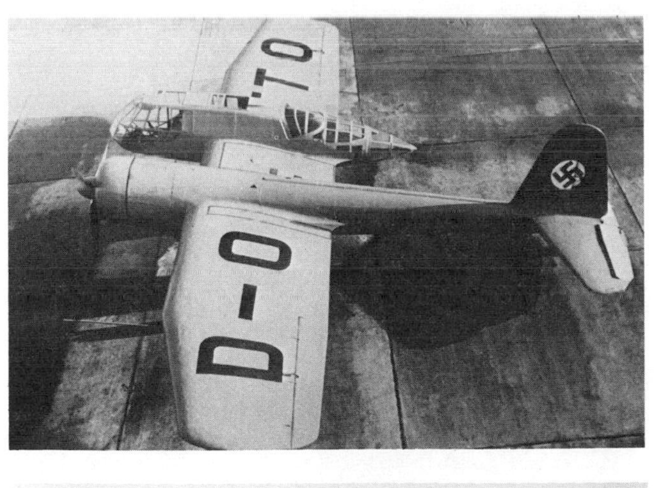

BV 141V-4

BLOHM & VOSS BV 141V-2
BMW 132a, 960 hp at 3000 m. (9840′)
DIMENSIONS: Span 15 m. (49′2″), Lg. 11.1 m. (36′5″), Ht. 3.3 m. (10′10″), Wing Area 41.5 qm. (446.7 sq. ft.)
WEIGHT and PERFORMANCE: Data not available

BLOHM & VOSS BV 141A-03 (V-6)
BMW 132N, 960 hp at 3000 m. (9840′)
DIMENSIONS: Span 15.45 m. (50′8″), Lg. 12.15 m. (39′10″), Ht. 4.1 m. (13′5″), Wing Area 42.85 qm. (461 sq. ft.)
WEIGHT: Empty 3167 kg. (6982 lb.), Gross 3900 kg. (8598 lb.), Fuel 540 liters (143 gal.)
PERFORMANCE: Speed—Max. 400 km/hr (248 mph) at 3800 m. (12,460′), 340 km/hr (211 mph) at sea level, Cruising speed 365 km/hr (227 mph), Landing speed 100 km/hr (62 mph), Range 1140 km. (708 miles), Service ceiling 9000 m. (29,520′)

On February 25, 1938, the first BV 141, registered D-ORJE, made its maiden flight. After successful test flights, including one by RLM technical chief Ernst Udet, three of the strange aircraft were ordered. The first of these introduced a new nacelle, with many flat glazed panels like the Fw 189, and was slightly larger. Designated BV 141V-1, D-OTTO, was flown in September 1938, while the original aircraft, D-ORJE, was accepted as BV 141V-2.

Although D-OTTO was wrecked in October, the third prototype, BV 141V-3 (D-OLGA) was ready and was the first to have weapons actually fitted. These included wing racks for four 50 kg. (110 lb.) bombs, two fixed 7.9 mm. MG 17 forward guns, a 7.9 mm. MG 15 in a conical Focke-Wulf tail turret, and another flexible gun for the middle crewman, pointing aft. All three prototypes used the BMW 132 radial, giving 960 hp at 9840 ft.

A "zero series" of five trial aircraft was ordered as the BV 141A-01 to BV 141A-05. Slightly larger than their predecessors, they also received *Versuchs* (experimental numbers). The first appeared early in 1939 as BV 141V-4 with civil markings D-OLLE, while the second had Luftwaffe call letters BL+AB. The BV 141A-03 (V-6) appeared in January 1940 marked BL+AC, the next in April as BL+AD and the last was BL+AE. Despite their odd looks, flying qualities were satisfactory. Nevertheless, the Luftwaffe preferred the competitive twin-engined Fw 189, and a production program was canceled April 4, 1940.

Five examples of a further development with the 1560 hp BMW 801A-0 were ordered as the BV 141B-0. This first flew on January 9, 1941, and had the right tailplane removed to improve the rear gunner's effectiveness. Numerous mechanical difficulties delayed the project, and so the last BV 141B was not delivered until May 1943.

BLOHM & VOSS BV 141B-02
BMW 801A-0, 1560 hp
DIMENSIONS: Span 17.46 m. (52′3″), Lg. 13.95 m. (45′9″), Ht. 3.6 m. (11′10″), Wing Area 52.9 qm. (569 sq. ft.)
WEIGHT: Empty 4700 kg. (10,340 lb.), Gross 5800 kg. (12,-760 lb.)
PERFORMANCE: Speed—Max. 438 km/hr (272 mph) at 5000 m. (16,400′), 369 km/hr (229 mph) at sea level, Range 1200–1900 km. (745–1180 miles), Service ceiling 10,000 m. (32,800′)

FIESELER Fi 156C-1
Argus As 10C-3, 240 hp
DIMENSIONS: Span 14.25 m. (46′9″), Lg. 9.9 m. (32′6″), Ht. 3.05 m. (10′), Wing Area 26 qm. (279.86 sq. ft.)
WEIGHT: Empty 930 kg. (2046 lb.), Gross 1320 kg. (2904 lb.), Fuel 150 liters (40 gal.)
PERFORMANCE: Speed—Max. 175 km/hr (109 mph) at sea level, Cruising speed 150 km/hr (93 mph), Landing speed 51 km/hr (32 mph), Climb 1000 m./4 min. (3280′/4 min.), Range 385 km. (238 miles), Service ceiling 5090 m. (17,300′)

BLOHM & VOSS BV 141B-02

FOCKE-WULF Fw 189V-2 prototype

FOCKE-WULF Fw 189V-1b prototype

FIESELER FI 156

Turning from experimental types to aircraft built in quantity, we find the Fieseler Fi 156 *Storch* (Stork), which began as a non-combat type, but was soon armed for front-line service.

Dr. Hermann Winter designed this aircraft to a 1935 RLM specification for a small army cooperation and liaison monoplane capable of operating from the smallest airfields. The first prototype, Fi 156V-1 (D-IKVN) appeared in 1936 and soon proved superior to its competitors, the similar Messerschmitt Bf 163, Siebel Si 201 pusher and Focke-Wulf Fw 186 autogyro. By 1937, five Fieseler prototypes were followed by the Fi 156A production series.

The *Storch* had wide high-lift wings with fixed slots across the leading edge, long landing gear struts, two or three seats in a cabin with bulging windows, and an air-cooled, inverted-vee eight cylinder Argus As 10c of 240 hp. With a minimum speed of only 51 km/hr (32 mph) it could take off and land in a very small space; almost vertically if a wind prevailed.

The little plane made itself very useful to the German Army in liaison, staff and observation work, and an example served the Condor Legion in 1937. A commercial model, the Fi 156B, was stillborn, but in 1939 Fieseler introduced the armed Fi 156C which had a single flexible 7.9 mm. MG 15 in a raised rear cabin mounting.

By the end of 1939, 332 *Storchs* had been produced, and wartime needs accelerated production from 170 in 1940 to 874 in 1943. At the war's end in 1945, some 2835 production aircraft had been delivered with many going to Germany's allies.

The *Storch* served in a great variety of roles during the war, carrying staff officers in and out of tight spots, occasionally carrying 50 kg. (110 lb.) bombs, or a 200 liter (53 gal.) extra tank, or loud speakers. The Fi 156D was a casualty evacuation version with large doors to handle a litter, while ten Fi 156Es had a caterpiller type undercarriage for rough fields. The *Storch* was also built under license by Morane-Saulnier in France and by LBB and Mraz in Czechoslovakia, both of whom continued production after the war.[2]

FOCKE-WULF FW 189

The standard Hs 126 was replaced in service by the Focke-Wulf Fw 189, a twin-engined three-place monoplane whose twin-boom layout reminded Americans of their own P-38. Designed by Kurt Tank, the Fw 189 was used for short-range, low-altitude reconnaissance.

Three prototypes were ordered in April 1937, and the Fw 189V-1 (D-OPVN) first flew in July 1938 with two 430 hp Argus As 410 inverted-vee air-cooled engines and an extensively glazed cabin for three crewmen, but no armament. Guns and bomb racks were fitted on Fw 189V-2 (D-OVHD) in August, while the third (D-ORMH) appeared the next month with automatic variable-pitch propellers.

The first aircraft was returned to the factory for conversion to an attack plane. It reappeared in 1939, as the Fw 189V-1b, with a new, smaller fuselage nacelle in which pilot and gunner sat back to back and had only tiny windows thru surrounding armor. This machine was accidentally demolished after tests with the competing Henschel Hs 129 single-seater.

A pre-production series of six Fw 189A-0s was built in 1939, but were used as V types for further development. The Fw 189V-4 (D-OCHO) was the production prototype for the A recon series, while the V-5 had a new two-seat crew nacelle developed for the B trainer model. The armored V-1b nacelle, two 20 mm. and four 7.9 mm. fixed guns, and a pair of 7.9 mm. flexible guns were used on the V-6, prototype for a stillborn Fw 189C attack series. A

[2] Morane built 784 Fi 156s and the Czechs 137 from 1942–44.

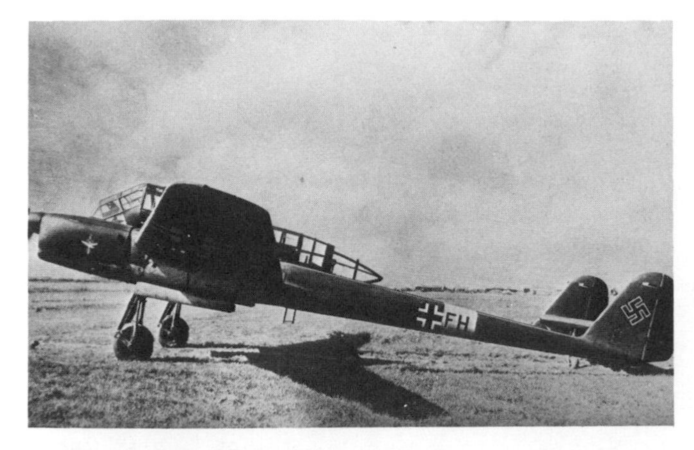

FOCKE-WULF Fw 189A-1
Argus As 410A-1, 2 X 465 hp at takeoff, 2 X 415 hp at 2400 m. (7875′)
DIMENSIONS: Span 18.4 m. (60′4½″), Lg. 12.03 m. (39′5½″), Ht. 3.1 m. (10′2″), Wing Area 38 qm. (409 sq. ft.)
WEIGHT: Empty 2830 kg. (6239 lb.), Gross 3950–4170 kg. (8708–9193 lb.)
PERFORMANCE: Speed—Max. 350 km/hr (217 mph) at 2400 m. (7875′), Cruising speed 325 km/hr (202 mph), Landing speed 120 km/hr (74 mph), Climb 4000 m./8.3 min. (13,120′/8.3 min.), Range 670–940 km. (416–580 miles), Service ceiling 7300 m. (23,950′)

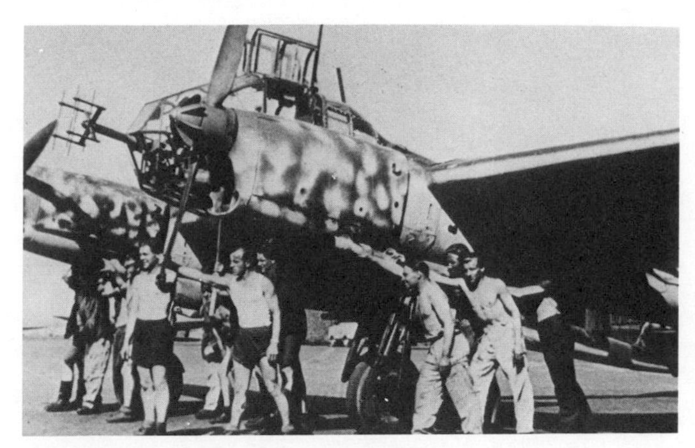

FOCKE-WULF Fw 189F
Argus As 411, 2 X 575 hp
DIMENSIONS: as Fw 189A
WEIGHT: Empty 2805 kg. (6171 lb.), Gross 4250 kg. (9350 lb.)
PERFORMANCE: Speed—Max. 380 km/hr (236 mph) at 4000 m. (13,120′), Cruising speed 330 km/hr (205 mph), Landing speed 120 km/hr (74 mph), Climb 480 m./1 min. (1575′/1 min.), Range 690 km. (425 miles), Service ceiling 7500 m. (24,600′)

canceled V-7 project was a prototype for a twin-float Fw 189D seaplane trainer.

Production deliveries began in summer of 1940 on the three-place Fw 189A recon and the two-place Fw 189B trainer. Thirty-eight were delivered in 1940, including three Fw 189B-0s, and ten Fw 189B-1s.

The Fw 189A-1 had 465 hp Argus A-1s, strengthened landing gear, two fixed 7.9 mm. MG 17s in the wing roots, a flexible MG 15 atop the second crewman's cabin, another in the conical tail turret, wing racks for four SC 50 (110 lb.) bombs, and two cameras.

Other variants included the A-2 of 1941 with twin 7.9 mm. MG 18 guns for each gunner, an A-3 dual-control trainer, and the A-4 of late 1942, which added light armor and two 20 mm. fixed FF guns in the wing roots.

In order that Focke-Wulf's Bremen plant could concentrate on fighter production, new assembly lines were set up at the Prague's Aero company in 1941 and by SNCASO at Bordeaux, France, in 1942. Deliveries for 1941 were 250 Fw 189As, including 99 from Bremen and the rest from Prague. In 1942 there were 327; 57 from Bremen, 183 from Prague, and the rest from Bordeaux, while 1943 production was 208; 11 from Bremen, three from Prague, and the rest from France. Altogether, about 816 Fw 189As were delivered from 1940 to 1943.

When Germany invaded Russia in June 1941, operational squadrons were still using the Hs 126, but the Fw 189 *Eule,* or *Uhu* (Owl) soon replaced it at the front. Except for a staffel in North Africa, these planes saw all their combat on the Eastern front. Hungary and Slovakia also operated the Fw 189A at the front.

The Fw 189E was designed in France by SNCASO to utilize 700 hp Gnome-Rhone 14M radials, but a converted Fw 189A-1 crashed while being ferried to Germany, and the project was abandoned. A pair of 600 hp Argus 411MA-1s were used on the Fw 189F-1, and 17 were made in France in 1944, before production ended.

Since the traditional low-speed recon types could not survive in the increasingly risky combat environment, the burden of tactical reconnaissance was later carried by modified Messerschmitt Bf 109G fighters.

HEINKEL He 50 modified

17.

Ground Attack, 1935–45

HEINKEL HE 50

Stuka became a notorious word early in World War II, and deservedly so, for the *Sturzkampfflugzeug* (dive-bomber) was the best example of the carefully directed air support of German ground forces that made the *blitzkrieg* so deadly.

The *Stuka* story can be begun when Ernst Udet, then the greatest living German fighter pilot, received permission to purchase two Curtiss Hawks in September 1933. The still secret Luftwaffe had provided the funds to buy these export versions of the U. S. Navy's trim F11C-2 single-seat biplanes. Udet's brilliant demonstrations of dive-bombing with these planes promoted the dive as the best way to precisely aim bombs dropped in support of ground troops.

Despite some official resistance, dive-bomber units were organized early by the Luftwaffe, and by 1936 its strength included three *Stukagruppen,* each with 39 Heinkel He 51 single-seaters and 12 Heinkel He 50 two-seaters.[1] The former were the standard biplane fighters with wing racks for 10 kg. (22 lb.) bombs, but the He 50s were Germany's first specialized dive-bombers.

Designed in 1932, the He 50 was a robust double-bay biplane with two open cockpits and a 600 hp Siemens SAM 22B radial engine. A 7.9 mm. gun (MG 17) was provided for the pilot, and another (MG 15) on the observer's ring. The first prototype (D-2471) had a Siemens Jupiter, another (D-IMOE) an NACA cowl, D-IMAA tried a BMW 132 radial, while the He 66 was a version for Japan. Japan, for whom the type may have been designed in the first place, manufactured it under license as their Navy's Aichi D1A1 and D1A2. These were the planes that sank the U.S. gunboat *Panay* in December 1937.

Eighty production He 50s were delivered from spring 1935 to the end of 1936. They served the Luftwaffe until replaced by the Ju 87 and relegated to training bases. Nevertheless, as late as 1943, these aging aircraft were used on the Russian front by night-attack units.

[1] I/162 at Schwerin, II/162 at Lubeck, and I/165 at Kitzingen.

HEINKEL He 50
Siemens SAM 22B, 600 hp
DIMENSIONS: Span 11.5 m. (37′8½″), Lg. 9.6 m. (31′6″), Ht. 4.5 m. (14′9″), Wing Area 34.8 qm. (374 sq. ft.)
WEIGHT: Empty 1600 kg. (3520 lb.), Gross 2620 kg. (5764 lb.)
PERFORMANCE: Speed—Max. 235 km/hr (146 mph), Cruising speed 200 km/hr (124 mph), Landing speed 95 km/hr (58 mph), Climb 1000 m./3 min. (3280′/3 min.), Range 850 km. (527 miles), Service ceiling 6400 m. (21,000′)

HEINKEL He 50 BMW engine

HEINKEL He 66 for Japan

FIESELER Fi 98
Bramo 322H-2, 650 hp
DIMENSIONS: Span 11.5 m. (37'8½"), Lg. 7.4 m. (24'3"), Ht. 3 m. (9'10"), Wing area 25.5 qm. (274 sq. ft.)
WEIGHT: Empty 1450 kg. (3190 lb.), Gross 2160 kg. (4752 lb.), Fuel 710 liters (187 gal.)
PERFORMANCE: Speed—Max. 295 km/hr (183 mph), Cruising speed 270 km/hr (167 mph), Landing speed 95 km/hr (59 mph), Climb 1000 m./1.7 min. (3280'/1.7 min.), Range 470 km. (290 miles), Service ceiling 9000 m. (29,-520')

HENSCHEL Hs 123V-1
BMW 132, 660 hp
DIMENSIONS: as Hs 123A-1
WEIGHT: Empty 1400 kg. (3080 lb.), Gross 2110 kg. (4642 lb.)
PERFORMANCE: Speed—Max. 310 km/hr (192 mph), Cruising speed 270 km/hr (167 mph)

HENSCHEL HS 123

The Luftwaffe's next ground attack type became the last German biplane used in wartime combat. An open cockpit single-seater with wheel pants, a pair of streamlined main struts, and a 650 hp BMW 132 radial with three-bladed propeller, the Henschel Hs 123V-1 was demonstrated to Luftwaffe chiefs by Udet himself on May 8, 1935.

A smaller cowl, with blisters for the valve gears, was introduced on the Hs 123V-2 (D-ILUA), while the third prototype (D-IKOU) was the first with a two-bladed Hamilton-license propeller and armament. After two prototypes crashed in dive tests, strengthened wings and landing gear were used in the Hs 124V-4 production prototype (D-IZXY).

HENSCHEL Hs 123V-2

HENSCHEL Hs 123V-4

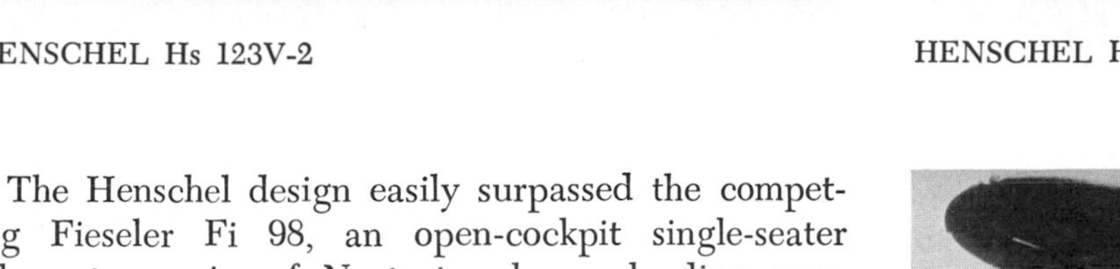

The Henschel design easily surpassed the competing Fieseler Fi 98, an open-cockpit single-seater whose two pairs of N struts, clumsy landing gear, and small second stabilizer atop the fin caused too much drag.

Production Henschel Hs 123A-1s had 870 hp and two 7.9 mm. MG 17 cowl guns, four SC 50 (110 lb.) bombs under the wings, and a rack below the fuselage for a 250 kg. (550 lb.) bomb or drop tank. Henschel began production deliveries in September 1936, and by the year's end had finished 41 of the 235 on order, including five sent to the Condor Legion for combat trials. Later, 16 were turned over to the Spanish Nationalists, while in Germany they served St.Gr. I/162 and II/162. When these groups re-equipped with Ju 87A two-seaters in 1938, the Henschels went to new battle groups (*Schlachtfliegergruppen*-SFG).

More advanced versions appeared in 1937 as the Hs 123V-5 (D-INHA) with a 960 hp BMW 132K, new cowl, and three-bladed propeller, and the Hs 123V-6 (D-IHDI), which added an armored headrest and two MG 17s in the lower wings. These were prototypes for proposed Hs 123B and C models, but no orders were placed, and Henschel ended biplane production in 1938. Group SFG 10 (later II/LG 2) at Tutow, continued to use the Hs 123A-1, which now had the new headrest added. Twelve Hs 123s were purchased by China in 1938.

On September 1, 1939, the Luftwaffe's first direct support mission of World War II was flown by

HENSCHEL Hs 123A-1
BMW 132Dc, 870 hp
DIMENSIONS: Span 10.5 m. (34′5″), Lg. 8.33 m. (27′4″), Ht. 3.21 m. (10′6″), Wing Area 24.85 qm. (267 sq. ft.)
WEIGHT: Empty 1504 kg. (3310 lb.), Gross 2217 kg. (4877 lb.)
PERFORMANCE: Speed—Max. 342 km/hr (212 mph) at 1200 m. (3940′), 333 km/hr (207 mph) at sea level, Cruising speed 317 km/hr (197 mph), Climb 900 m./1 min. (2950′/1 min.), Range 800 km. (533 miles), Service ceiling 9000 m. (29,520′)

BLOHM & VOSS Ha 137A

BLOHM & VOSS Ha 137B
Jumo 210C, 640 hp
DIMENSIONS: Span 11.15 m. (36′7″), Lg. 9.5 m. (31′2″), Ht. 4 m. (13′1¼″), Wing Area 23.5 qm. (253 sq. ft.)
WEIGHT: Empty 1800 kg. (3960 lb.), Gross 2400 kg. (5280 lb.)
PERFORMANCE: Speed—Max. 340 km/hr (210 mph), Landing speed 105 km/hr (65 mph), Climb 1000 m./1.5 min. (3280′/1.5 min.), Range 600 km. (372 miles), Service ceiling 8000 m. (26,240′)

ARADO Ar 81V-1
Junkers Jumo 210C, 610 hp
DIMENSIONS: Span 11.2 m. (36'9"), Lg. 11.65 m. (38'2½"), Ht. 3.57 m. (11'8½"), Wing Area 35.6 qm. (383 sq. ft.)
WEIGHT: Empty 1925 kg. (4235 lb.), Gross 3070 kg. (6754 lb.)
PERFORMANCE: Speed—Max. 330 km/hr (205 mph) Landing speed 97 km/hr (60 mph), Climb 4000 m./11 min. (13,-120'/11 min.), Range 700 km. (434 miles), Service ceiling 6000 m. (19,680')

ARADO Ar 81V-3
Junkers Jumo 210C, 610 hp
DIMENSIONS: as Ar 81V-1
WEIGHT: Empty 2069 kg. (4551 lb.), Gross 3198 kg. (7035 lb.)
PERFORMANCE: Speed—Max. 345 km/hr (214 mph), Landing speed 97 km/hr (60 mph), Climb 4000 m./11 min. (13,120'/11 min.), Range 700 km. (434 miles), Service ceiling 7000 m. (22,960')

II/LG 2 to aid German troops attacking Panki, Poland. This group's Henschel Hs 123As fought thru the Polish campaign, although they were the only biplanes, other than seaplanes, in the first-line Luftwaffe. German inventories show 165 *Schlacht* planes still on hand April 30, 1940; 49 were with II/LG 2 and the rest at training and storage bases.

These reserves enabled the Hs 123A to operate thru the invasions of Belgium and France and be called back to the front in 1942, when things began going badly in Russia. Modified with a headrest behind the cockpit, and with the wheel fairings sometimes removed for rough airfields, the Henschels continued their ground support. So useful were they that in January 1943, General Wolfram von Richthofen, as chief of ground attack units, asked that the venerable biplanes be restored to production. But the usefulness of such slow types was ended by increasing Soviet fighter strength.

Another single-seat dive-bomber was produced in 1935 by Hamburger Flugzeugbau, aircraft division of Blohm & Voss. The Ha 137 was a modern-looking low-wing monoplane designed by Dr. Richard Vogt with an open cockpit and the wings bent upward from deep wheel pants.

The first powerplant was an imported 525 hp Rolls-Royce Kestrel, but then it appeared as the Ha 137A with a 650 hp BMW 132E-1 radial and as the Ha 137B with a 640 hp Jumo 210C inline engine. Armament comprised of two 7.9 mm. cowl guns, a pair of 20 mm. guns in the wing joints above the wheels, a 250 kg. (550 lb.) bomb under the fuselage and four 50 kg. (110 lb.) bombs under the wings. The fuel was contained in the tubular wing spar.

There was a plan in 1935 to build 350 Ha 137s, but it was ended by the decision to concentrate on two-seat dive-bombers like the Ju 87. A rear gunner was felt essential to protect the plane during its diving attack.

HEINKEL He 118 V-2

HEINKEL He 118V-4
Daimler-Benz DB 601, 1070 hp
DIMENSIONS: Span 15 m. (49'2½"), Lg. 11.8 m. (38'8½"), Wing Area 37.7 qm. (405.8 sq. ft.)
WEIGHT: Empty 2730 kg. (6006 lb.), Gross 4150 kg. (9130 lb.)
PERFORMANCE: Speed—Max. 420 km/hr (260 mph), Cruising speed 370 km/hr (220 mph), Landing speed 115 km/hr (71 mph), Climb 1000 m./2.5 min. (3280'/2.5 min.), Range 1050 km. (651 miles), Service ceiling 9500 m. (31,160')

JUNKERS JU 87

Three two-seaters had been launched by a competition begun January 1935. Along with the single-seat Ha 137, the Arado Ar 81, Heinkel He 118 and Junkers Ju 87 were rivals for the *Stuka* production contracts. Wolfram von Richthofen, then Technical Office Chief, opposed dive-bombers as too slow and vulnerable to enemy gunfire, but Ernst Udet's demonstrations with a Focke-Wulf Fw 56 trainer indicated that dive-bombers could have twice the accuracy of horizontal bombing.

Walter Blume's Arado was the only biplane offered. Powered by a Junkers Jumo 210C, the Ar 81 had enclosed cockpits and wheel pants. The first two prototypes had twin rudders, but the third had a single tail. A 500 kg. (1100 lb.) bomb and a flexible MG 15 were carried.

This biplane was soon eliminated from competition by the Heinkel and Junkers low-wing monoplanes. The Heinkel He 118 resembled the He 70 recon type, with its elliptical wing and retractable landing gear. The controllable-pitch propeller was connected with dive brakes by an automatic dive recovery device, and a fork swung the 500 kg. bomb from the internal bay down to clear the propeller.

The first two prototypes had imported 695 hp Rolls-Royce Kestrels, but the He 118V-3 had a 910 hp Daimler-Benz DB 600C. Despite its higher speed, the Heinkel proved less satisfactory than the Junkers in pulling out from dives. Ernst Udet, who had replaced Richthofen in the Technical Office, favored the Heinkel, but on June 27, 1936, he crashed the He 118V-1 by incorrect use of the propeller pitch control. This ended Luftwaffe interest in the design, but Heinkel persisted.

An He 118V-4 with a 1070 hp Daimler-Benz DB 601A and enclosed cockpits was shipped to the Japanese Navy in February 1937, while the Japanese Army received the He 118V-5 in October. No further sales were made, so it is not clear what was done with eight preproduction examples said to have been finished in 1938.

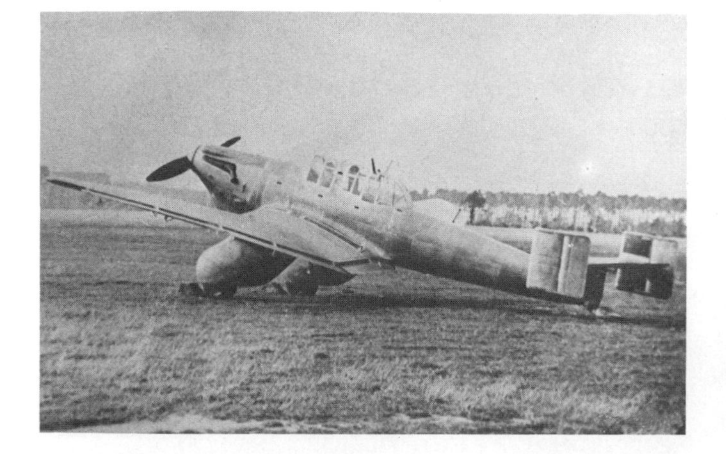

JUNKERS Ju 87V-1

JUNKERS Ju 87V-2

Competition winner was the plane that dropped the first bombs of World War II, and made *Stuka* an international word. Junkers actually had a head start from experience with its K 47 two-seat monoplane of 1928. In fact, the Ju 87 was first intended to have the earlier design's twin rudders.

Designer Karl Pohlmann prepared a monoplane with the wing bent up from the deep fairings enclosing the landing gear. The Ju 87V-1 appeared late in 1935, with a Rolls-Royce Kestrel, two-bladed wooden prop, and square-shaped twin vertical tail. This machine crashed after its tail fluttered in a dive, so the Ju 87V-2 was completed with a new single tail and larger radiator below the Kestrel.

A 610 hp Junkers Jumo 210A and three-bladed propeller was introduced on the Ju 87V-3, but the production prototype, V-4, was the first with the fork to swing the bomb clear of the propeller, and an automatic pull-out control to enable recovery from a dive, even if the pilot had blacked out. Tests of this device, incidentally, had been made by a lady *Flugkapitän,* Melitta Schiller.

After this design bested its rivals in the competition at Rechlin in June 1936, the production program was increased to 250 planes, the first appearing in 1937. As the Junkers Ju 87A, they were issued first to *Sturzkampfgeschwader* Immelman (St.G 163, later St.G 2). Three went to the Condor Legion in Spain, where pilots were rotated for combat experience. These planes had a pig insignia inspired by the animal comedy star, Jolanthe.

Powered by the 640 hp Jumo 210C, the Ju 87A had a 7.9 mm. MG 15 in the rear cockpit and an MG 17 in the right wing. The normal bomb size of 250 kg. (550 lb.) could be doubled if the plane operated as a single-seater. Production consisted of the small Ju 87A-0 "zero series," the standard A-1 and the A-2 with new propeller, and ended in 1938. One example was sold to Japan.

Since the Ju 87A was underpowered, Pohlmann prepared a Ju 87B design utilizing a 1210 hp Jumo 211. This was Pohlmann's last design for Junkers, as he went to Blohm & Voss, and further work on the Ju 87 became the Weserflug firm's responsibility. The new Ju 87B became the most famous Stuka version, fighting in all of the war's first air battles.

This model was armed with two MG 17s in the wings, and an MG 15 in the rear of an improved canopy. One 500 kg. (1100 lb.) bomb, or one 250 kg. and four 50 kg. bombs could be carried, the latter under the wings. The dive brakes remained under the wings, outboard of a new landing gear.

Five of the first ten Ju 87B-0s completed in summer 1938, were sent to the Condor Legion in October. Deliveries on the Ju 87B-1 accelerated until all nine of the first-line *Stuka* groups had been equipped, and 597 Bs delivered by the end of 1939.[2]

The Luftwaffe's first World War Two sorties were by Ju 87Bs of 3/St.G 1. Six Ju 87B groups were sent against Poland in September 1939, and the two weeks' combat cost only 31 of the 366 *Stukas* operated by the first-line units at the war's start.

[2] Including 134 from September to December.

JUNKERS Ju 87V-4

JUNKERS Ju 87A-1
Jumo 210C, 640 hp
DIMENSIONS: Span 13.8 m. (45′3″), Lg. 10.8 m. (35′5″), Ht. 3.91 m. (12′9″), Wing Area 31.9 qm. (343 sq. ft.)
WEIGHT: Empty 2270 kg. (4994 lb.), Gross 3400 kg. (7480 lb.)
PERFORMANCE: Speed—Max. 320 km/hr (199 mph) at 3700 m. (12,140′), 294 km/hr with 250 kg. bomb (183 mph with 550 lb. bomb), Cruising speed 280 km/hr (174 mph), Range 1000 km. (620 miles), Service ceiling 7000 m. (22,960′)

A tenth group was formed in September from a separate squadron originally intended for naval work, 4 (St.)/186, and these *Stuka Gruppen* remained the basic ground attack element until 1943.[3] Dive-bombers available by April 30, 1940, were 720 aircraft; 419 in the first-line groups and the remainder (including some obsolete Ju 87As and He 50s) at training and storage bases.

In May 1940, the *Stukas* once more supported an advancing German Army. Again, a special device helped increased the Ju 87's reputation as a terror weapon. On an undercarriage leg was the "Jericho Trumpet," a prop-driven siren which, added to the usual howl of the diving plane, had a demoralizing effect on enemy troops. The continuous success of these attacks against the Allies obscured the fact that they had been permitted by German dominance of the air. Heavy losses to British fighters in August 1940 made it clear that the Ju 87 could not survive without good fighter protection.

A special carrier version, the Ju 87C, was designed in 1938 for the carrier Graf Zeppelin. An arrestor hook, jettisonable undercarriage and folding wings were planned, but only a small Ju 87C-0 batch went to 4(St.)/186, and the Ju 87C-1 was canceled when it became apparent the Navy's only carrier would never operate.

The next version to actually appear was the Ju 87R (R for *Reichweite*—range). It was simply a Ju 87B with larger fuel capacity and provision for a 300 liter (79 gal.) drop tank under each wing, increasing range to 875 miles with a 250 kg. (550 lb.) bomb. The first 20 Ju 87Rs were delivered in January 1940, so this model was built alongside the Bs and comprised nearly half of the 603 Ju 87s built in 1940.

Some of the Ju 87Bs were supplied to German allies: Italy, Hungary, Rumania and Bulgaria. There were several sub-variants, such as the Ju 87B-1/Trop with desert filters and various B-2 models with differing equipment.

Combat experience brought about a redesigned model in 1940, the Ju 87D flown as prototypes in spring 1941, and in production in the fall with a 1400 hp Jumo 211J, streamlined canopy and two smaller radiators under the wing to replace the big frontal cooler. The oil cooler was moved from the top of the cowl to under the engine. Twin 7.9 mm. MG 81Z

[3] After July 1940, there were three groups each in St.G I, 2 and 77, plus IV/LG 1. Another, I/St.G 3, was added later in this period.

JUNKERS Ju 87B-1
Jumo 211Da, 1210 hp at takooff, 1100 hp at 1020′
DIMENSIONS: Span 13.8 m. (45′3″), Lg. 10.82 m. (35′5″), Ht. 3.84 m. (12′7″), Wing Area 31.9 qm. (343 sq. ft.)
WEIGHT: Empty 2760 kg. (6072 lb.), Gross 4250 kg. (9350 lb.)
PERFORMANCE: Speed—Max. 387 km/hr (240 mph), at 4400 m. (14,435′), Cruising speed 340 km/hr (211 mph), Landing speed 108 km/hr (67 mph), Climb 1000 m./2 min. (3280′/2 min.), 600 km./500 kg.; max. 800 km. (370 miles/1100 lb.; max. 500 miles), Service ceiling 8100 m. (26,560′)

guns were provided for the observer, along with extensive armor, four to ten mm. armor on the cockpit's back, sides and floor. Bomb load could include 1800 kg. (3960 lb.) on the center rack, or two 500 kg. (1100 lb.) below the wings.

The Ju 87D-1 entered combat in Russia in January 1942 and was joined in May by the heavier-armored Ju 87D-3. Post-delivery modifications were the D-2 with a glider towing device, and the D-4 ground support model had a WB 81 weapons pod under each wing. This was called a *Giesskanne* (watering can); since the six MG 81s, four firing forward and two backward, sprinkled 7.9 mm. bullets like water!

A larger, 15 meter (49′2″) wing span, an undercarriage jettisonable for emergency landing and modified dive brakes distinguished 1943's Ju 87D-5. For ground attack, a pair of 20 mm. MG 151/20s replaced the wing guns.

These guns were still too small for tough Soviet T-34 tanks, so the next step was the Ju 87G-1 whose fixed armament consisted of two 37 mm. *Flak* 18 guns in pods with six rounds each, slung under the wings. The first *Stuka* with 37 mm. guns had been a Ju 87D-1 tested in December 1942, but the standard models were the Ju 87G-1 and Ju 87G-2, modified from D-3 and D-5 aircraft, respectively. A special tank-fighting unit first used the Ju 87G in combat near Bryansk on March 18, 1943.

The most famous *Stuka* pilot, Hans Rudel, made effective use of the new weapons. During his front-line career, which amounted to 2530 sorties, Rudel is said to have destroyed enough Soviet tanks to outfit a complete armored division. This *Stuka* pilot won the highest decoration awarded a German in World War II.

A projected Ju 87F never reached production, and the dual-control Ju 87H trainers were conversions of standard models. A far more advanced Ju 187 was designed in 1941 with retractable landing gear, a 1750 hp Jumo 213 and a remote-controlled gun turret aft of the two cockpits. No prototype was completed.

JUNKERS JU 87D-1
Jumo 211J-1, 1410 hp at takeoff
DIMENSIONS: Span 13.8 m. (45′3″), Lg. 11.13 m. (36′6″), Ht. 3.84 m. (12′7″), Wing Area 31.9 qm. (343 sq. ft.)
WEIGHT: Empty 3207 kg. (8598 lb.), Gross 5724 kg. (12,592 lb.), Fuel 780 liters (206 gal.)
PERFORMANCE: Speed—Max. 408 km/hr (253 mph), at 4200 m. (13,780′) without bomb load, Cruising speed 370 km/hr (229 mph), Landing speed 110 km/hr (68 mph), Climb 4500 m./10 min. (14,760′/10 min.), Range 1000 km. (620 miles), Service ceiling 7320 m. (24,009′)

Germany produced 4144 Ju 87s from 1941 to 1944.[4] Deliveries peaked at 192 in March 1943, and ended in September 1944. Yet the *Stuka* continued in service as a night attack type, so surviving D-3 and D-5 aircraft were rebuilt as D-7 and D-8 models with 1500 hp Jumo 211P engines and flame-damped exhaust pipes.

The *Stuka* units were redesignated *Schlachtgeschwader* (SG) on October 10, 1943, and gradually equipped with Fw 190Fs modified for ground attack, and the Hs 129. Ground attack strength rose from 525 aircraft in June 1943 to 1005 a year later. By January 1945, there were 16 Fw 190 attack groups, five Ju 87 night attack groups, one Hs 129 group, and the three night groups with a miscellaneous trainer collection.

[4] 500 in 1941, 960 in 1942, 1672 in 1943 and 1012 in 1944, according to Baumbach, but Green gives 476, 917, and 1844 for the years 1941–43. Total production was 5709 from 1937–44, says one report, with 583 by Junkers and the rest by Weserflug.

JUNKERS Ju 87R

JUNKERS Ju 87G

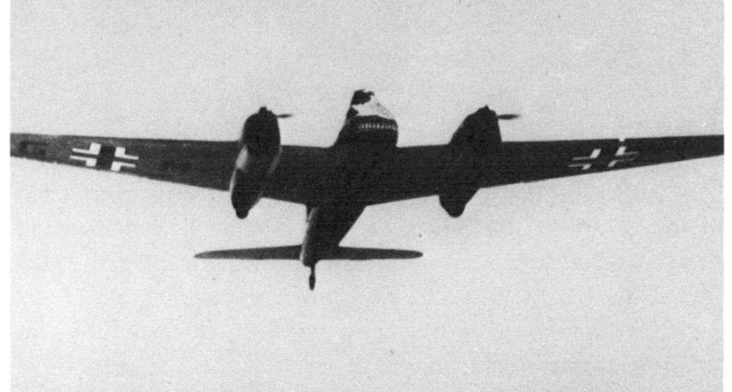

HENSCHEL Hs 129A

The Ju 87 ended its career in the hopeless struggle against the resurgent Soviet Army. During its first two years of war it was among the war's most formidable and successful weapons. If we exclude the carrier-based Douglas SBD Dauntless of the Pacific War, the Ju 87 becomes the outstanding dive-bomber of the war in Europe.

HENSCHEL HS 129

The last ground attack design to see widespread Luftwaffe service was the Henschel Hs 129, an armored single-seater powered by two air-cooled engines, the powerplant arrangement that seemed least vulnerable to anti-aircraft fire. The Henschel was chosen over a rival Focke-Wulf project in October 1937.

Designed by Friedrich Nicolaus, three Hs 129V prototypes appeared in 1939, followed by a few Hs 129A-0 preproduction aircraft. Powered by two 465 hp, air-cooled, inline Argus As 410s, the low-wing monoplane had about 1000 lb. of welded six to 12 mm. armor protecting the cockpit. On the cockpit's sides were two 20 mm. MG/FF and two 7.9 mm. MG 17 guns.

Tests by II/LG 2, alongside of that unit's Hs 123s, were unfavorable, for the pilots complained of poor visibility and insufficient power. The Hs 129A-0s were eventually passed to Rumania.

Nevertheless, the need for a ground attack type persisted, and it was hoped that the use of captured Gnome-Rhone radials would ease the powerplant problem. A preproduction batch of ten Hs 129B-0s had the 740 hp Gnome-Rhone 14M 04/05 with two MG 151/20 (250 rds) and two 7.9 mm. MG 17 (1000 rds) guns.

The first Hs 129B-0 was completed in December 1941, while the Hs 129B-1 emerged early in 1942 and was first used against the Russians by 4/Sch.G 1

HENSCHEL Hs 129B-1
Gnome-Rhone 14 MO4/05, 2 X 740 hp
DIMENSIONS: Span 14.2 m. (46'7"), Lg. 9.75 m. (32'), Ht. 3.25 m. (10'8"), Wing Area 29 qm. (312 sq. ft.)
WEIGHT: Empty 4050 kg. (8910 lb.), Gross 4960 kg. (10,912 lb.), Fuel 610 liters (161 gal.)
PERFORMANCE: Speed—Max. 408 km/hr (253 mph) at 3800 m. (12,500'), Cruising speed 320 km/hr (198 mph), Landing speed 145 km/hr (90 mph), Climb 7900 m./23 min. (25,912'/23 min.), Range 880 km. (545 miles), Service ceiling 9000 m. (29,520')

HENSCHEL Hs 129B-1

in May. Several Hs 129B variants were made available by conversion kits. Hs 129B-1/R1 had the same four guns, but added two 50 kg. (110 lb.) bombs on wing racks, while B-1/R2 added a 30 mm. MK 101 cannon with 30 rounds under the fuselage.[5] This tank-killer was the favorite version, but there was also the B-1/R3 which substituted four 7.9 mm. guns and 1000 rounds under the belly, the B-1/R4 with a belly rack for one 250 kg. or four 50 kg. bombs, and the B-1/R5 with an Rb 20/50 camera for recon work.

Although one *staffel* was tried, unsuccessfully, in North Africa, the majority of the Henschels were used on the Eastern front. They proved especially useful in July 1943 at the Kursk salient. One unit, IV (Pz) *Gruppe*/SG 9, roamed about the front to strike at enemy tank formations wherever they appeared, aiming their attacks at the tank's thinner side and rear armor. Poor engine reliability was the Henschel's weakness.

Heavier firepower was introduced on the Hs 129B-2 series. Two MG 151/20 and two MG 131 (13 mm.) guns armed the B-2/R1, which eliminated bomb racks. A 30 mm. MK 103 was added under the B-2/R2's belly, while on the B-2/R3, both MG 131s were deleted and a 37 mm. *Flak* 38 carried underneath. The experimental B-2/R4 had the two 20 mm. guns, plus a big 75 mm. Pak 40 cannon. The production version, the Hs 129B-3, appeared in June 1944 with a 75 mm. BK cannon and twelve rounds. An even more radical arrangement was that on three B-2s fitted with a six-barreled SG 113A rocket mortar that fired 77 mm. shells directly downward when triggered by a photoelectric cell's reaction to an enemy tank.

The foremost German tank-buster on the Russian front, the Henschel Hs 129B was produced until September 1944, for a total of 859.

[5] The R indicated *Ruestsatz* or conversion kit.

Part 6 Fighters

18.

Fighter Development, 1922–31

A fighter cannot easily be disguised as a civil aircraft. Reconnaissance types could be introduced in the mail carrier or aerial photography roles without difficulty, but a fighter can be little else. When the Allies allowed resumption of German civil aircraft production in 1922, strict definitions limited aircraft to a 4000 m. (13,120′) ceiling, and prohibited single-seaters entirely.

These limitations meant that any German fighter designs would have to be built abroad. Dornier's Swiss factory, for instance, would provide the first post-war fighter design, the Dornier H *Falke* (Falcon). First flown on November 1, 1922, this all-metal cantilever parasol monoplane owed most design features to 1918's Zeppelin D I. Clean lines and a 240 hp Hispano-Suiza with a neat belly radiator gave the *Falke* more speed (252 km/hr or 156 mph), than contemporary types.

Perhaps the design was too advanced for the times, because it won no large orders. An example with a license-built Wright-Hispano was tested by the U. S. Army in April 1923, and later by the Navy as the WP-1. In Japan, Nakajima offered a seaplane version with twin floats and a 350 hp BMW.

In Denmark, Caspar built a little biplane designed in 1924 by von Loessl. The first was the CI-14, with a 350 hp radial and highly tapered tail and wings, whose wide gap was joined by I struts. A second version with N struts and another British engine, the 450 hp inline Napier Lion, was known as the CS 14. Neither model was made in quantity.

Ernst Heinkel built the HD 23 biplane for the Japanese Navy in 1924; perhaps its order by a (then) Allied power made its construction possible in Germany. This single-seater's unique feature was a fuselage bottom built like a boat hull. Should failure of the Napier Lion engine force a landing at sea, the

DORNIER H SEEFALKE
BMW IVa, 350 hp
DIMENSIONS: Span 10 m. (32′10″), Lg. 8.42 m. (27′7¼″), Ht. 3.05 m. (10′), Wing Area 20 qm. (215 sq. ft.)
WEIGHT: Empty 1050 kg. (2310 lb.), Gross 1320 kg. (2904) lb.)
PERFORMANCE: Speed—Max. 240 km/hr (149 mph), Climb 5000 m./18 min. (16,400′/18 min.)

CASPAR CI-14
Armstrong-Siddeley, 350 hp
DIMENSIONS: Span 9 m. (29′6″), Lg. 5.4 m. (17′9″)
WEIGHT: Empty 800 kg. (1760 lb.), Gross 1200 kg. (2640 lb.)
PERFORMANCE: Speed—Max. 270 km/hr (167 mph), Range 1000 km. (620 miles)

DORNIER H FALKE
Hispano-Suiza, 340 hp
DIMENSIONS: Span 10 m. (32′10″), Lg. 7.43 m. (24′4″), Ht. 2.66 m. (8′9″), Wing Area 20 qm. (215 sq. ft.)
WEIGHT: Empty 840 kg. (1848 lb.), Gross 1200 kg. (2640 lb.), Fuel 272 liters (72 gal.)
PERFORMANCE: Speed—Max. 252 km/hr (156 mph), Landing speed 110 km/hr (68 mph), Climb 1000 m./2.6 min. (3280′/2.6 min.), 5000 m./23 min. (16,400′/23 min.), Service ceiling 6000 m. (19,680′)

CASPAR CS 14
Napier Lion, 450 hp
DIMENSIONS: Span 10 m. (32′10″), Lg. 6.58 m. (21′7″)
WEIGHT: Empty 1130 kg. (2486 lb.), Gross 1780 kg. (3916 lb.)
PERFORMANCE: Speed—Max. 250 km/hr (155 mph), Range 1000 km. (620 miles)

prototype shown suspended in our photo illustrates how the landing gear could be released, and the aircraft cleared to float on water.

These prototypes did not meet the need for a fighter practical for training pilots at the secret Russian base at Lipetsk. Some Fokker D VIIs and D VIIIs had been hidden away after the Armstice, but deterioration made them unusable in a few years. With great secrecy, 50 Fokker D XIII biplanes with Napier Lion engines were purchased in the Netherlands, allegedly for export to South America. In fact, they were shipped to Lipetsk in 1925, and trained German fighter pilots. Fokker had also previously supplied the Soviets with about 324 aircraft, under the auspices of the German military mission aiding the Red Air Fleet's organization.

The Junkers Fili factory at Moscow produced a new fighter in 1926. The H 22 was a cantilever parasol monoplane single-seater like the H 21 two-seater. Powered by the wartime favorite, the 185 hp BMW, it had the typically Junkers corrugated metal covering. The Russians evidently preferred their native designs, for the H 22 did not enter production.

Last of the foreign-produced prototype single-seat fighters was the Rohrbach Ro IX "Rofix" built in Denmark. Another parasol monoplane, this obscure aircraft crashed on July 15, 1927, near Copenhagen, killing wartime ace Paul Baumer.

In 1928, the Defense Ministry felt able to encourage home construction of single-seat prototypes to

HEINKEL HD 23
Napier Lion, 450 hp
DIMENSIONS: Span 10.8 m. (35′5″), Lg. 7.55 m. (24′9″), Wing Area 36 qm. (387.36 sq. ft.)
WEIGHT: Empty 1470 kg. (3234 lb.), Gross 2070 kg. (4554 lb.)
PERFORMANCE: Speed—Max. 249 km/hr (154 mph), Landing speed 88 km/hr (55 mph), Service ceiling 7900 m. (25,-912′)

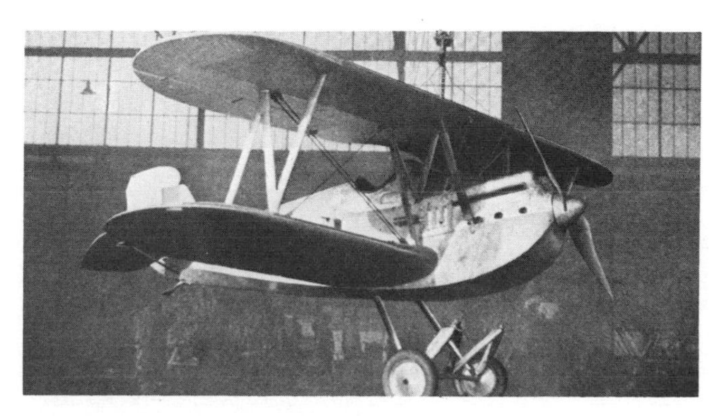

JUNKERS H 22
BMW III, 185 hp
DIMENSIONS: Span 10.77 m. (35′4″), Lg. 6.7 m. (22′)
WEIGHT: Gross 850 kg. (1870 lb.)
PERFORMANCE: Speed—Max. 250 km/hr (155 mph)

ARADO SD 1
Bristol Jupiter, 425 hp
DIMENSIONS: Span 8.4 m. (27′6½″), Lg. 6.75 m. (22′2″)
WEIGHT: Empty 850 kg. (1870 lb.), Gross 1230 kg. (2706 lb.)
PERFORMANCE: Speed—Max. 275 km/hr (170 mph)

ARADO SD 3
Siemens Jupiter, 550 hp
DIMENSIONS: Span 9.9 m. (32′6″), Lg. 7.75 m. (25′5″)
WEIGHT: Data not available
PERFORMANCE: Speed—Max. 228 km/hr (141 mph), Service ceiling 6400 m. (21,000′)

ROHRBACH Ro IX "Rofix"
BMW VI, 600 hp
DIMENSIONS: Span 14 m. (45′11″), Lg. 9 m. (29′6″), Wing Area 28 qm. (301 sq. ft.)
WEIGHT: Empty 1450 kg. (3200 lb.), Gross 1950 kg. (4300 lb.)
PERFORMANCE: Speed—Max. 270 km/hr (168 mph), Landing speed 94 km/hr (58 mph), Climb 1000 m./2 min. (3280′/2 min.) 2000 m./4.3 min. (6560′/4.3 min.), Service ceiling 7400 m. (24,300′)

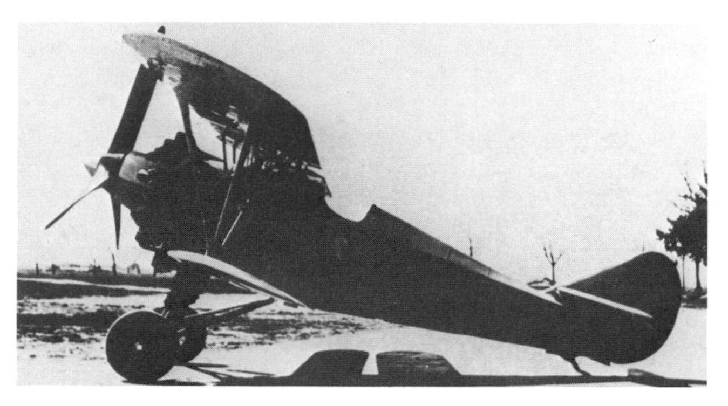

ARADO SD 2
Siemens Jupiter, 530 hp
DIMENSIONS: Span 9.9 m. (32′6″), Lg. 7.4 m. (24′3″)
WEIGHT: Empty 1445 kg. (3179 lb.), Gross 1770 kg. (3894 lb.)
PERFORMANCE: Speed—Max. 239 km/hr (148 mph), Service ceiling 7000 m. (22,960′)

HEINKEL HD 37
BMW VI, 750 hp at takeoff
DIMENSIONS: Span 10 m. (32′9½″), Lg. 7 m. (22′11½″), Wing Area 26.71 qm. (287 sq. ft.)
WEIGHT: Empty 1267 kg. (2787 lb.), Gross 1685 kg. (3707 lb.)
PERFORMANCE: Speed—Max. 312 km/hr (193 mph), Landing speed 96 km/hr (60 mph), Service ceiling 9400 m. (30,830′)

HEINKEL HD 38
BMW VI, 750 hp
DIMENSIONS: Span 10 m. (32'9½"), Lg. 8.1 m. (26'), Ht. 3.65 m. (11'11"), Wing Area 30.15 qm. (325 sq. ft.)
WEIGHT: Empty 1415 kg. (3120 lb.), Gross 1840 kg. (4057 lb.)
PERFORMANCE: Speed—Max. 285 km/hr (177 mph), Landing speed 99 km/hr (61 mph), Climb 1000 m./1.8 min. (3280'/1.8 min.) 3000 m./6.4 min. (9840'/6.8 min.), Service ceiling 7500 m. (24,600')

HEINKEL HD 43
BMW VI, 500 hp
DIMENSIONS: Span 10 m. (32'9½"), Lg. 7.1 m. (23'3"), Ht. 3.3 m. (10'9½"), Wing Area 26.56 qm. (286 sq. ft.)
WEIGHT: Empty 1280 kg. (2816 lb.), Gross 1700 kg. (3740 lb.), Fuel 310 liters (82 gal.)
PERFORMANCE: Speed—Max. 322 km/hr (200 mph), Cruising speed 290 km/hr (180 mph), Landing speed 95 km/hr (59 mph), Climb 3000 m./4.9 min. (9840'/4.9 min.) 5000 m./9.4 min. (16,400'/9.4 min.), Service ceiling 8400 m. (27,600')

DORNIER Do 10
BMW VI, 650 hp
DIMENSIONS: Span 15 m. (49'2½"), Lg. 10.5 m. (34'5½"), Ht. 4.3 m. (14'1¼"), Wing Area 32.85 qm. (353 sq. ft.)
WEIGHT: Empty 2200 kg. (4851 lb.), Gross 2680 kg. (5896 lb.)
PERFORMANCE: Speed—Max. 285 km/hr (177 mph), Cruising speed 250 km/hr (155 mph), Climb 1000 m./1.9 min. (3280'/1.9 min.), 5000 m./12.8 min. (16,400'/12.8 min.), Service ceiling 7500 m. (24,600')

Do 10 with engine tilted up

keep Germany abreast of current design practices. Of conservative pattern, they included a trio of Arado biplanes using British-designed air-cooled radials.

Walter Rethel, formerly with Kondor and Fokker, designed the Arado SD 1 with a 425 hp Bristol Jupiter and V struts. The larger SD 2 of 1929 had a 530 hp Jupiter license-built by the Siemens, and the similar SD 3 was added later. These experimental fighters led directly to the Arado 64, first fighter ordered when rearmament began in 1933.

Ernst Heinkel contributed a husky prototype trio using the liquid-cooled BMW VI, a 750 hp vee-twelve that would power a whole generation of German combat types. The first Heinkel HD 37 appeared in 1928 as a short, fast, businesslike biplane with N struts and ailerons on all four wing tips. This design was sold to the U.S.S.R. and built there as the I-7. Closely following in 1929 was the HD 38 designed to a Navy specification with equal-span wings, a curved rudder and an undercarriage stressed for catapulting with either floats (see HD 38a in Chapter 26) or wheels. The steel-tube fuselage and spruce wings were fabric covered. Similar construction, with a smaller lower wing and simplified landing gear, was seen on the HD 43. These Heinkels set the pattern that led to the Luftwaffe's He 51.

Less successful was the Dornier Do 10 parasol monoplane, a two-seat fighter derived from the C type seaplanes. First flown July 24, 1931, it was experimentally fitted with a movable engine mount to turn the BMW's thrust line upward for better climb.

19.

The Luftwaffe's First Fighters

When German rearmament began in secret after Hitler came to power, Arado Flugzeugwerke was the first to turn out fighters in quantity. Walter Rethel's experience with the SD prototypes had evolved into the Ar 64, a conventional single-seat biplane of 1930 with a 530 hp Siemens Jupiter radial, four-bladed propeller, and N struts between the wings.

This prototype was joined the following year by the Arado 65; the same size, but with a 600 hp inline BMW VI U, two-bladed prop, and wider tail fin. Firepower was the same as in 1918; two 7.9 mm. nose guns. The old Spandaus, however, were replaced by the more efficient MG 17. Top speed was about 240 km/hr (149 mph) on the Ar 64 and 300 km/hr (186 mph) on the Ar 65. Only greater horsepower made any speed improvement over 1918's biplanes.

Why did a Germany that ended the First World War with such progressive designs as the Fokker D VIII and Junkers D I monoplanes, begin its rearmament with such conservative fabric-covered, strut and wire biplanes? The new Air Ministry (RLM) wanted a lot of planes in a hurry for pilot training and for political impact, and their advisers were veteran pilots of Iron Cross days who felt that only biplanes were really maneuverable, reliable, and strong. Time enough for innovations later, but now real aircraft were needed.

Production began late in 1933, and although the Luftwaffe was officially non-existent, 19 Ar 64s and the first 80 Ar 65s were delivered by 1934's end. They were given civilian registration letters and issued to flying schools to train pilots for the secret fighter squadrons being formed. Ar 65 production ended about October 1935 with 170 aircraft.

When the Luftwaffe's first fighter formation was publicly identified March 14, 1935, as *Jagdgeschwader* Richthofen (JG 132, later to be JG 2), their base at Doeberitz displayed a line of Heinkel He 51 biplanes. With squared-off lines reminiscent of 1918's Fokkers, this He 51 became, with the Ju 52, the early Luftwaffe's most-produced combat type.

This type actually began with the Heinkel He 49a of November 1932. Like the preceding Heinkel HD

ARADO Ar 64
Siemens Jupiter, 530 hp
DIMENSIONS: Span 10 m. (32'9½"), Lg. 7.8 m. (25'7")
WEIGHT: Data not available
PERFORMANCE: Speed—Max. 240 km/hr (149 mph), Service ceiling 6000 m. (19,680')

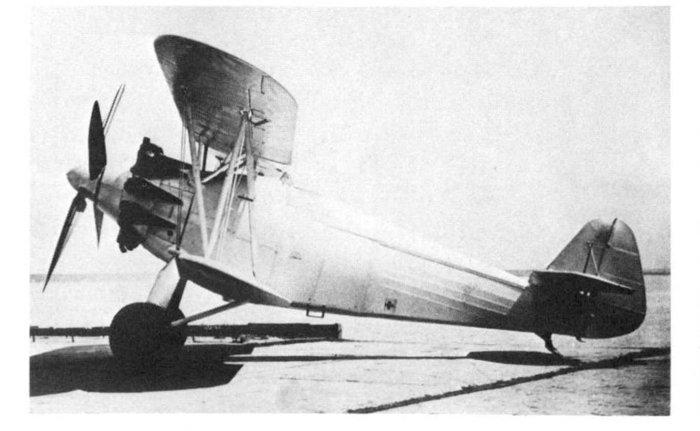

ARADO Ar 65

HEINKEL He 49
BMW VI, 650 hp
DIMENSIONS: Span 11 m. (36'1"), Lg. 8.24 m. (27')
WEIGHT: Gross 1950 kg. (4290 lb.)
PERFORMANCE: Speed—Max. 325 km/hr (202 mph), Landing speed 90 km/hr (56 mph), Service ceiling 8000 m. (26,-240')

38 and 43 biplanes, it had a 650 hp BMW VI, but utilized double-struts and wire bracing. A second prototype tried twin floats, and a third, the He 49c, had a cleaned up landing gear.

The first He 51, registered in 1933 as D-ILGY, had streamlined wheel pants and a pilot's headrest, while another prototype had double-bay wing struts. Neither the headrest nor the extra struts were used on nine "zero series" He 51A-0 preproduction aircraft (beginning with D-IQEE) built beginning July 1934 and powered by a BMW VI 7.3Z of 750 hp at takeoff. Construction was the traditional fabric-covered steel-tube fuselage and wood frame wings.

Quantity production began in February 1935 and illustrates the RLM's use of subcontractors. Of 150 in the original program, 114 He 51A-1s were to be delivered by Heinkel by July 1935, when Arado and Fieseler would start deliveries on their initial orders of 24 and 12, respectively. AGO and Erla were to add deliveries by August, and 311 were added to the program to increase the totals to 145 by Heinkel, 114 by Arado, 82 by Fieseler, 75 by AGO and 45 by Erla.

Despite some slippage, 45 He 51s were delivered by May 1, 1935. A 45 gallon drop tank was added to the He 51B-1, and although Heinkel itself was out of the program, by January 1936 the subcontractors were providing the He 51C-1 with wing racks for six 22 lb. bombs. Two 7.9 mm. MG 17 guns were provided under the cowl. The first Heinkels went to JG 132,

HEINKEL He 51 (first prototype)

HEINKEL He 51 (second prototype)

HEINKEL He 51A-1
BMW VI 7.3Z, 750 hp at takeoff
DIMENSIONS: Span 11 m. (36′1″), Lg. 8.4 m. (27′6½″), Ht. 3.2 m. (10′6″), Wing Area 27.2 qm. (292.67 sq. ft.)
WEIGHT: Empty 1465 kg. (3223 lb.), Gross 1900 kg. (4180 lb.), Fuel 210 liters (55 gal.)
PERFORMANCE: Speed—Max. 330 km/hr (205 mph) at sea level, 310 km/hr (193 mph) at 4000 m. (13,120′), Cruising speed 280 km/hr (174 mph), Landing speed 95 km/hr (59 mph), Climb 6000 m./16.5 min. (19,680′/16.5 min.), Range 400 km. (248 miles), Service ceiling 7700 m. (25,250′)

HEINKEL He 51A-0

HEINKEL He 51C in Spain

with the original civil registration replaced by a 21 (for Luftkreis II's first *Geschwader*), Balkenkreuz, and the aircraft identification, with red cowls brightening the usual Luftwaffe grey finish. Each of the Richthofen unit's groups received 39 He 51s, plus 9 Ar 65s for reserve; plus three He 51 staff planes, making a *Geschwader* strength of 120 He 51 and 27 Ar 65 fighters.[1] The first Luftwaffe ground attack unit, *Sturzkampfgeschwader* Immelmann (St.G 162) had two groups, each with 39 He 51C and 12 He 50 two-seaters.[2]

According to RLM records, 458 He 51s were built as landplanes, the last in October 1936. In addition, 14 twin-float He 51B-2 seaplanes went to the naval fighter staffel at Kiel in September 1935, plus 15 more added in October. The Heinkel became the first Luftwaffe single-seater to fight in Spain's civil war.

After Hitler agreed to Franco's request for aid, the first six Heinkel He 51s left Hamburg by ship with 85 men on July 31, 1936 and arrived in Cadiz August 5. At first the Germans were to be a training contingent, but then J/88 was formed as the Condor Legion's fighter *gruppe*. Altogether, 135 He 51Cs went to Spain for German and Spanish Nationalist pilots, 46 surviving at the war's end.

These Heinkels were naturally better than the 1927-pattern Nieuports then comprising Spanish fighter equipment. Before long, Fiats and Dewoitines had arrived from Italy and France, and Soviet I-15s joined the Republican forces in November. These types were all superior to the Heinkels in speed and manueverability, and after the Messerschmitt Bf 109Bs arrived for J/88, the Heinkels were usually limited to ground attack operations.

By 1936, the Heinkels were joined in service by very similar Arado biplanes that replaced the antiquated Ar 65s. Wheel pants, a high tail atop the fuselage and an imported Rolls-Royce Kestrel were introduced in 1933 on the Arado Ar 67. Rethel then followed with the Ar 68, which looks like an He 51 until the N struts, high rudder and one-piece elevator are noticed.

A 750 hp BMW VId powered D-IKIN, the first prototype flown in 1934 at Arado's Warnemuende factory near the Baltic Sea. The new Junkers Jumo 210A, an inverted vee-twelve supercharged to yield 610 hp up to 11,155′, was introduced on the second

[1] JG I/132 at Doeberitz, II/132 at Damm, and I/232 at Barnburg, along with JG 134, comprised the 1936 German fighter force.
[2] I/162 at Schwerin and II/162 at Lubeck.

ARADO Ar 67
Rolls-Royce Kestrel, 450 hp
DIMENSIONS: Span 9.68 m. (31'9"), Lg. 7.9 m. (25'11"), Ht. 3.1 m. (10'2"), Wing Area 25.06 qm. (268 sq. ft.)
WEIGHT: Empty 1270 kg. (2794 lb.), Gross 1660 kg. (3652 lb.)
PERFORMANCE: Speed—Max. 340 km/hr (211 mph), Landing speed 95 km/hr (59 mph), Climb 1000 m./1.5 min. (3280'/1.5 min.)

and third prototypes. Originally known as the Ar 68b (D-IVUS) and Ar 68c (D-IBAS), they became Ar 68V-2 and Ar 68V-3 when the *Versuchs* designations were adopted. The third aircraft was the first with armament, appearing in 1935 with the standard two 7.9 mm. guns and 500 rounds each under the cowl.

While the fourth prototype, Ar 68d (D-ITAR) reverted to a BMW VI, the Ar 68V-5 (D-ITEP) was the Ar 68E's production prototype, using a Jumo 210Da giving 690 hp at takeoff and 640 hp at altitude. This engine, however, was not available in sufficient quantity when production got underway, so Arado had to use the BMW VId on production ships. Designated Ar 68F, they resembled the original Ar 68a prototype.

Jagdgeschwader Horst Wessel's three groups[3] received the first 120 Arado Ar 68Fs in 1936, and found them more maneuverable and easier to handle than the He 51s, with nearly identical performance. When the Jumo 210Ea became available, the Ar 68E could appear in quantity with this Junkers powerplant. Whereas the Ar 68F's BMW provided a 330 km/hr

[3] I/134 at Dortmund, II/134 at Werl, and III/134 at Lippstadt.

ARADO Ar 68V-1

ARADO Ar 68V-5

ARADO Ar 68F
BMW VId, 750 hp at takeoff
DIMENSIONS: as Ar 68E
WEIGHT: Empty 1580 kg. (3476 lb.), Gross 2020 kg. (4440 lb.), Fuel 200 liters (53 gal.)
PERFORMANCE: Speed—Max. 310 km/hr (193 mph) at 4000 m. (13,120'), 330 km/hr (205 mph) at sea level, Landing speed 97 km/hr (81 mph), Climb 6000 m./10 min. (19,680'/10 min.), Range 500 km. (310 miles), Service ceiling 7400 m. (24,280')

ARADO Ar 68E
Junkers Jumo 210Da, 640 hp (690 hp at takeoff)
DIMENSIONS: Span 11 m. (36'1"), Lg. 9.5 m. (31'2"), Ht. 3.3 m. (10'10"), Wing Area 27.3 qm. (293.75 sq. ft.)
WEIGHT: Empty 1600 kg. (3520 lb.), Gross 2020 kg. (4440 lb.), Fuel 200 liters (53 gal.)
PERFORMANCE: Speed—Max. 335 km/hr (208 mph) at 2650 m. (8695'), 306 km/hr (190 mph) at sea level, Landing speed 97 km/hr (81 mph), Climb 775 m./1 min. (2480'/1 min.), 6000 m./10 min. (19,680'/10 min.), Range 415 km. (265 miles), Service ceiling 8100 m. (26,568')

(205 mph) speed at sea level and 310 km/hr (193 mph) at 4000 m. (13,120′), the Ar 68E did 306 km/hr (190 mph) at sea level and 335 km/hr (208 mph) at 2650 m. (8695′), with a higher ceiling.

By the end of 1936, 303 of 492 Arado Ar 68s on order had been delivered. Appearance of the fast Messerschmitt monoplanes soon made biplanes quite obsolete, however. Only in the role of night interceptor, where mild landing characteristics were desirable, did the Arados retain some interest. Two Ar 68Es were sent to Spain for night trials, but there was little enemy activity to combat.

Arado did attempt an improvement with 1937's Ar 68H. This prototype (D-ISIX) had an 850 hp BMW 132Da radial, enclosed cockpit, and added two more 7.9 mm. guns in the top wing. It was no match for monoplanes, although it was a step toward the Ar 197 carrier-based fighter described in Chapter 27.

By the time war broke out in September 1939, German *Jagdgruppen* were equipped with Messerschmitts, except for the 28 Ar 68Fs of 10 and 11. (Nacht)/JG 53 (originally JG 72). Stationed at Oedheim/Heilbronn, they flew night missions against the British Whitleys that cruised over Western Germany, dropping only leaflets at that early stage. No interceptions were recorded, however, so the Arados were retired from service without ever fighting an air battle.

THE PRE-WAR MESSERSCHMITT FIGHTERS

Only one single-seat fighter type was used in combat by Germany for the Second World War's beginning two years. The contrast with the variety of 1917–18 types emphasizes a determination to standardize production to achieve an easily serviceable volume at a relatively low cost.

Selection of the fighter type to carry this burden began with a design competition in October 1935 at Travemuende. Four companies submitted monoplanes intended to have the new Junkers Jumo inverted vee-twelve engine, although imported Rolls-Royce Kestrels had to be substituted on the first prototypes.

Walter Blume designed the Arado Ar 80, an open cockpit single-seater with a bent low wing. Powered by a 695 hp Rolls-Royce Kestrel V, its fixed landing gear kept it the slowest competitor. When a 610 hp Jumo 210C did become available in 1936, the top speed was only 410 km/hr (255 mph) instead of the 425 km/hr (264 mph) expected.

The Luftwaffe lost interest and canceled the remainder of the seven prototype order, but Arado used its own funds to complete another example that had a straight wing, second cockpit, sliding canopy, and a Jumo 210C with provision for a 20 mm. *Motorkanone* firing thru the crankshaft.

ARADO Ar 80

Jumo 210C (originally Rolls-Royce Kestrel V), 610 hp (695 hp)

DIMENSIONS: Span 11.8 m. (38′8″), Lg. 10.10/10.27 m. (33′1″/33′8″), Ht. 2.95 m. (9′8″), Wing Area 21 qm. (226 sq. ft.)

WEIGHT: Empty 1645/1630 kg. (3619/3586 lb.)

PERFORMANCE: Speed—Max. 410 km/hr (255 mph) at 4000 m. (13,120′), Landing speed 96 km/hr (60 mph), Climb 6000 m./9.5 min. (19,680′/9.5 min.), Range 600 km. (372 miles), Service ceiling 9000 m. (29,520′)

ARADO Ar 80V-2

FOCKE-WULF Fw 159

Jumo 210G, 610 hp

DIMENSIONS: Span 12.4 m. (40′8″), Lg. 10 m. (32′9½″), Wing Area 20.2 qm. (217 sq. ft.)

WEIGHT: Empty 1875 kg. (4125 lb.), Gross 2250 kg. (4950 lb.)

PERFORMANCE: Speed—Max. 385 km/hr (239 mph) at 4000 m. (13,120′), Service ceiling 7200 m. (23,600′)

FOCKE-WULF Fw 159V-2

MESSERSCHMITT Bf 109B-0

The Focke-Wulf Fw 159 was the last parasol monoplane fighter built in Germany, or anywhere else. Fitted with an enclosed cockpit and a landing gear that retracted into the fuselage, the Fw 159V-1 had one of the first 610 hp Jumo 210A engines and a two-bladed propeller. A second prototype was flown, but crashed when the landing gear failed to lock down, while the Fw 159V-3 had a 670 hp Jumo 210G and three-bladed propeller.

Both the Arado and Focke-Wulf designs were clearly inferior to the low-wing monoplanes built by BFW and Heinkel. Willy Messerschmitt, Technical Director of Bayerische-Flugzeug-Werke at Augsburg, had developed the Bf 109 low-wing monoplane. It was of all-metal construction with straight lines and an enclosed canopy.

The first prototype Bf 109V-1 (D-IABI) was flown in September 1935 with a Rolls-Royce Kestrel V, although Jumo 210s did become available for six more prototypes completed in 1936. No good photograph of the first aircraft has survived, although its top speed was reported at 480 km/hr (298 mph) at 4500 m. (14,765′), compared to the Heinkel He 112V-1's 465 km/hr (289 mph) at that altitude with the same Kestrel (695 hp for takeoff and 640 hp at 14,000′).

One reason for the Messerschmitt's speed was the small wings, which introduced automatic leading edge slots to improve stalling characteristics. The Bf 109's smaller size and lighter weight; 1900 kg. (4189 lb.) made it more maneuverable and easier to manufacture, which were winning points to RLM leaders. On the other hand, the Bf 109's weakness was its higher landing speed and narrow wheel track, handicaps which became increasingly apparent after the fighter went into service.

A 610 hp Jumo 210A was used on the Bf 109V-2 (D-IUDE) in January 1936, and on the V-3 (D-IHNY) in June. Prototypes for a projected Bf 109A series, they originally provided for two 7.9 mm. MG 17s under the cowl. Meanwhile, German intelligence services had learned that increased firepower was being provided for the Hurricane and other new foreign fighters, so more guns were needed for German fighters.

A 20 mm. *Motorkanone* like those on new French fighters seemed the way to out-range and out-punch the enemy. Such a gun was not available in Germany, so a license to produce the Swiss Oerlikon gun was obtained. This weapon was actually of German origin; the Becker gun of World War I which had been sold to Oerlikon. Now it returned to Germany as the MG/FF, which was the German designation for a free-firing version, and MG/FFM, the engine-mounted gun.

Until the 20 mm. gun became available, a third 7.9 mm. MG 17 was fitted to the next four aircraft, V-4

MESSERSCHMITT Bf 109V-4

to V-7, (Jumo 210B) which were prototypes for the Bf 109B series. Later the Bf 109V-4, D-IOQY, did try the first MG/FFM, but excessive vibration made the weapon unusable in flight. Three 7.9 mm. guns then, remained the Bf 109B's armament.

Production orders amounted by October 1936 to 740 aircraft, the largest fighter program then underway.[3] Deliveries began in March 1937 with a Bf 109B-0 preproduction batch closely followed by the B-1, which replaced the Richthofen *Geschwader*'s He 51 biplanes. Powerplants were the 610 hp Jumo 210B on the B-0, 635 hp Jumo 210D on the B-1, and 640

[3] Probably the U.S.S.R.'s fighter program was larger even then.

hp Jumo 210E with a metal variable-pitch Hamilton-license propeller on the B-2.

Previously the world's fastest fighter in squadron service had been Soviet, the 455 km/hr (283 mph) Polikarpov I-16 which joined combat in Spain November 5, 1936. In December, the Bf 109V-4, V-5 and V-6 were forwarded to the Condor Legion for operational trials. As soon as Bf 109Bs became available they were dispatched to Spain for J/88, which received 40 Bf 109Bs to replace its Heinkel biplanes.

With a top speed of 470 km/hr (292 mph), the Bf 109B was now the world's fastest service type, but combat in Spain showed it still necessary to strengthen the three 7.9 mm. gun armament. The next step was a Bf 109V-8 with two more 7.9 mm. guns in the wings, and a V-9, which was another B-2 with a 20 mm. MG/FF in each wing root. The latter, however, caused too much wing vibration.

This led to the next production model, the Bf 109C introduced late in 1937. Armed with two 7.9 mm. MG 17s in the nose and two in the wings, it was powered by the 675 hp Jumo 210G used on later B-2s. Twelve C-1s went to Spain, where one was used by Moelders to down 14 enemy fighters from July 15 to November 3, 1938. Ten Cs were sold to Switzerland in December 1938. A fifth MG 17 firing thru the crankshaft was used on a few C-2s, the C-3 was to have the V-9's wing guns, and a C-4 got an MG/FFM instead of the fifth MG 17.

The new 960 hp Daimler-Benz 600A with a three-bladed propeller was fitted to four aircraft designated Bf 109 V-10 thru V-13. The V-10 and V-13 appeared at the Zurich air meet in July 1937 along with three B-2s, for now the Germans wanted to publicize their new aircraft. Ernst Udet had an unlucky crash on V-10, but a B-2 won the speed dash, and V-13 the climb and dive competition.

To further publicize the Luftwaffe, Messerschmitt prepared the Bf 109V-13 for an attack on the world's landplane speed record. A Daimler-Benz DB 601 specially boosted to 1650 hp was installed, and on November 11, 1937, Dr. Herman Wurster beat the 100 km. closed circuit record with a 643 km/hr (379 mph) speed. The engine had to be scrapped after that flight, but the world was given the false impression that a standard fighter had set the mark.

Standard DB 600As became available in 1938 for the Bf 109D series, which was armed with two 7.9 mm. guns and one 20 mm. MG/FFM *Motorkanone*. Foreign visitors like Charles A. Lindbergh, Al Williams, General Victor Vuillemin of France, and British

MESSERSCHMITT Bf 109B-1
Jumo 210 Da, 640 hp
DIMENSIONS: Span 9.9 m. (32′4″), Lg. 8.7 m. (28′6″), Ht. 2.45 m. (18′½″), Wing Area 16.4 qm. (176 sq. ft.)
WEIGHT: Empty 1580 kg. (3476 lb.), Gross 2200 kg. (4840 lb.)
PERFORMANCE: Speed—Max. 470 km/hr (292 mph) at 4000 m. (13,120′), Climb 6000 m./9.8 min. (19,680′/9.8 min.), Range 750 km. (470 miles), Service ceiling 8150 m. (26,-730′)

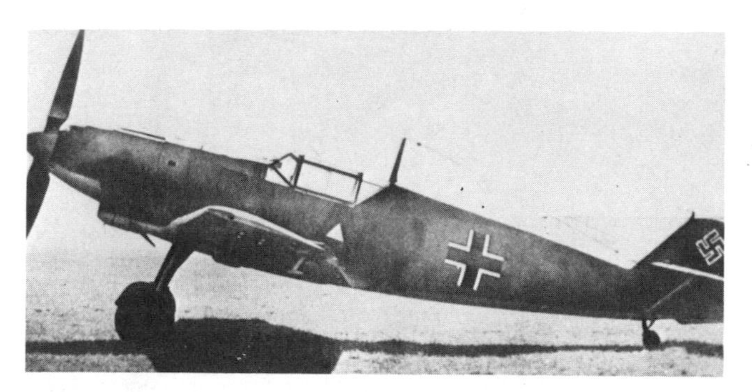

MESSERSCHMITT Bf 109D
Daimler-Benz DB 600Aa, 910 hp at 4000 m. (13,120′)
DIMENSIONS: as Bf 109B
WEIGHT: Gross 2420 kg. (5340 lb.)
PERFORMANCE: Speed—Max. 518 km/hr (322 mph) at 4000 m. (13,120′), Service ceiling 10,000 m. (32,800′)

MESSERSCHMITT Bf 109C
Jumo 210G, 675 hp

MESSERSCHMITT Bf 109V-13

HEINKEL He 112V-1
Rolls-Royce Kestrel V, 695 hp at takeoff, 640 hp at 14,000′ (4750 m.)
DIMENSIONS: Span 12.6 m. (41′4″), Lg. 8.9 m. (29′2″), Wing Area 23.2 qm. (250 sq. ft.)
WEIGHT: Gross 2310 kg. (5082 lb.)
PERFORMANCE: Speed—Max. 465 km/hr (289 mph) at 4500 m. (14,765′)

editor C. G. Grey were shown the new aircraft and impressed with Germany's new power.

Because of wartime record destruction, it's not possible to say how many B, C and D model aircraft were delivered, but one authority gives September 19, 1938, front-line strength in Bf 109s as 112 B or C series, and 471 Ds. Along with the inventory of He 51 and Ar 68 biplanes, it was a force that weighed heavily in the crisis ending with the Munich agreement.

HEINKEL'S MYSTERY FIGHTERS

Messerschmitt's rival in this period was Heinkel's He 112 fighter, a low-wing monoplane whose elegant curves showed the style of the Guenter twins. The same Luftwaffe program of June 1935 that projected the first seven Bf 109 prototypes also provided for seven He 112 and seven He 113 fighters. The He 113 project was dropped and the designation was not used again until 1940.

Like the first Bf 109, the He 112V-1 (D-IADO) appeared with a 695 hp Rolls-Royce Kestrel V and two-bladed propeller in late summer 1935. The design had an open cockpit and long headrest running back to a curved rudder atop the fuselage's end, while the

HEINKEL He 112V-2

HEINKEL He 112V-3

HEINKEL He 112V-4
Jumo 210D, 670 hp at 3900 m. (12,795′)
DIMENSIONS: Span 11.5 m. (37′9″), Lg. 9 m. (29′6″), Ht. 3.7 m. (12′2″), Wing Area 21.6 qm. (232.5 sq. ft.)
WEIGHT: Empty 1600 kg. (4189 lb.), Gross 2230 kg. (4906 lb.)
PERFORMANCE: Speed—Max. 485 km/hr (301 mph) at 3600 m. (11,800′), Service ceiling 8000 m. (26,250′)

wing had a wide chord and straight leading edge.

A 640 hp Jumo 210C with three-bladed propeller was used on the He 112V-2 (D-IHGE) appearing in November 1935, and the V-3 prototype, D-IDMO, was the first with armament; a pair of 7.9 mm. guns in troughs alongside the engine, and provision for a third firing through the propeller hub.

The Heinkels had a better climb than the Bf 109, but were heavier and more complicated to manufacture. Heinkel's technical director, Dr. Heinrich Hertel, began an extensive redesign effort whose first effects were seen with changes made on the V-3. A curved leading edge, sliding cockpit canopy, and exhaust collector were added.

The next three prototypes appeared in 1936 with the smaller, elliptical wing shape proposed for an He 112A series, and used the 670 hp Jumo 210D. Retaining an open cockpit, the He 112V-4 (D-IZMY) was the first publicly exhibited around Europe. The V-5 was similar, but V-6 replaced the long headrest with a bubble canopy.

These Heinkels were rejected by the Luftwaffe, but four prototype aircraft were used in a pioneer rocket-propulsion project. Heinkel's autobiography describes how Wernher von Braun interested him in von Braun's primitive rocket engine. Two He 112 fuselages, probably those of the V-1 and V-2, were fitted with the rocket units at Kummersdorf.

Both were destroyed in tests, but in March 1937 a "brand-new" prototype, probably the V-4, was tested with an auxiliary rocket engine. Before it left the ground, it also expoded, tossing Erich Warsitz, the pilot, out. Unhurt, he volunteered to try again with the V-5. This time he took off with the Jumo engine, and turned on the rocket. Once again he came close

HEINKEL He 112V-8

HEINKEL He 112V-7

HEINKEL He 112V-9

to disaster, but managed to return to the ground. Finally, in the summer of 1937, Warsitz succeeded in taking off, flying, and landing by use of the auxiliary rocket alone; the first controlled rocket-powered flight in history.

Meanwhile, more conventional efforts to improve the Heinkels continued. The last of the original air-frames appeared as the He 112V-8 (D-IROX). Unarmed and retaining the open cockpit, it was a test-bed for the 910 hp Daimler-Benz DB 600A, and provided with a deep radiator.

Still trying to surpass Messerschmitt, Hertel had designed a new, lighter airframe for the He 112B series; a smaller wing, bubble canopy, and a new tail with the rudder behind the fuselage was introduced on two prototypes. A DB 600A in a blunt nose was used on He 112V-7 (D-IKIK), while the He 112V-9 (D-IGSI) was flown in July 1937 with a Jumo 210E in a neatly pointed nose. While these aircraft seemed to surpass Bf 109s with the same powerplants, the Luftwaffe was committed to the Messerschmitt, and Heinkel had to try for export sales.

Thirty Heinkel He 112B-0 fighters were ordered by the Japanese Navy as shore-based interceptors, and Spain ordered 15. Similar to the V-9, they had the 670 hp Jumo 210E, two 7.9 mm. cowl guns, and two 20 mm. guns in the wings. While the He 112B was not very satisfactory for Japanese service conditions, the armament was adopted as standard for the new "Zero" fighters.

The first 26 were forwarded in 1938, but in August the Sudeten crisis caused the Luftwaffe to requisition the remaining Heinkels to replace Ar 68Es then used by III/JG 132 at Fuerstenwalde. After the Munich agreement, the Heinkels were returned to the builders for export.

By then, Japan decided against accepting the remainder of the aircraft, since the contract delivery dates had passed. Seventeen were sent instead to Franco's forces and made their first Spanish combat sortie on January 19, 1939. The last example remained with Heinkel to be fitted with a 675 hp Jumo 210G with direct fuel injection, and was designated He 112V-11. Spain continued its He 112B-0s in service during the World War II period, basing them with *Gruppe* 27 in Spanish Morocco.

Rumania purchased 24 Heinkels in 1939, the first 13 being the He 112B-0 with a Jumo 210E, and the rest were He 112B-1s with the Jumo 210G. Completed in August 1939, they participated in operations against the U.S.S.R. in 1941. Three more He 112B-1s, along with the V-9, were sold to Hungary in 1939.

Two new prototypes had been built in 1938 with the new 1100 hp Daimler-Benz DB 601A. The He 112V-10 (D-AQMA) was offered as an export model, while the similar V-12 (D-IRXS) was sold to Japan in 1939. By that time, Heinkel was concentrating on the newer He 100.

Rejection of the He 112 only provoked Heinkel into a greater effort to produce a winning fighter, and this new project became a strange episode in history. The Heinkel He 100 was the fastest plane of its time, yet never saw combat, and is remembered today mostly for the propaganda hoaxes perpetrated with it.

In May 1937 Heinkel launched the design of a single-seater intended to be the world's fastest. Powered by the then new 1100 hp Daimler-Benz DB 601A, it was designated He 100, dropping the He 113 label of 1935 to avoid arousing superstitions. First flown on January 22, 1938, the highly streamlined He 100V-1 was easy to manufacture; only 969 parts compared to 2885 of the He 112; and less than half as many rivets.

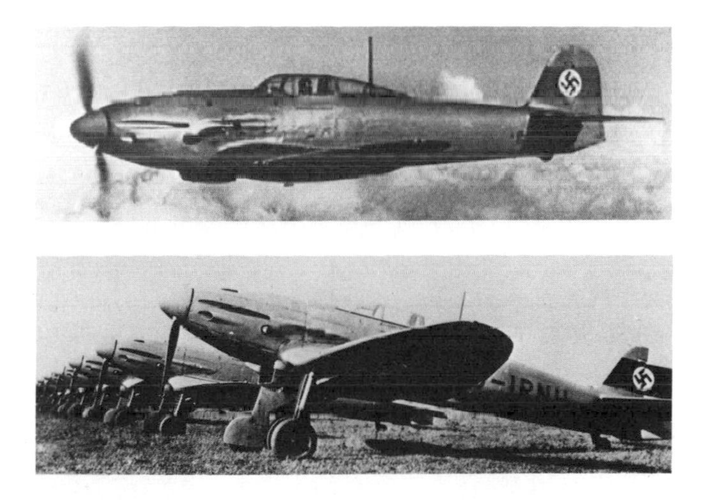

HEINKEL He 112B-0
Jumo 210E (B-0) or 210G (B-1), 670 hp
DIMENSIONS: Span 9.1 m. (29'10"), Lg. 9.3 m. (30'6"), Ht. 3.85 m. (12'7"), Wing Area 17 qm. (183 sq. ft.)
WEIGHT: Empty 1850 kg. (4070 lb.) Gross 2250 kg. (4950 lb.), Fuel 320 liters (84 gal.)
PERFORMANCE: Speed—Max. 510 km/hr (317 mph) at 4000 m. (13,120'), 430 km/hr (267 mph) at sea level, Cruising speed 425 km/hr (264 mph), Landing speed 135 km/hr (84 mph), Climb 1000 m./1.2 min. (3280'/1.2 min.), 4000 m./6 min. (13,120'/6 min.), Range 900 km. (560 miles), Service ceiling 9500 m. (31,160')

A wide-track undercarriage folding inward was used to avoid the Bf 109's frequent difficulties, although the high wing loading still made it a "hot" aircraft. Most unique was the cooling system of surface evaporation. Instead of using a drag-producing radiator, the heated water was pumped out of the engine, and circulated as steam under the wing skin, where it condensed and was recirculated back to the engine. While difficult to construct, it was less liable to damage than high pressure radiators.

The He 100V-2 (D-IVOS) was prepared for an attack on the world's landplane speed record, although it had the standard engine. General Udet suddenly appeared to make the flight himself, and on June 6, 1938, established a new 100 km. course record of 634 km/hr (394 mph). The aircraft, however, was claimed to be an He 112U (U for Udet), to gain publicity for the entirely different and older He 112 fighter already in limited production.

To continue the hoax, when General Vuillemin, Chief of France's Air Staff, visited Oranienburg on August 20, 1938, an He 100 prototype was flown past. The visitor was told that it was the record plane and near mass production.

In September 1938, a special Daimler-Benz boosted to 1800 hp was supplied for He 100V-3 (D-ISUR), which was completed with a new windshield and wings cut down from the normal size to 7.60 m.

HEINKEL He 112V-10
Daimler-Benz 601A, 1100 hp at 3700 m. (12,140′)
DIMENSIONS: as He 112B
WEIGHT: Empty 1562 kg. (4188 lb.), Gross 2100 kg. (5620 lb.)
PERFORMANCE: Speed—Max. 570 km/hr (354 mph) at 3700 m. (12,140′), 296 km/hr (285 mph) at sea level, Climb 4000 m./5 min. (13,120′/5 min.), Range 1150 km. (715 miles), Service ceiling 9500 m. (31,160′)

HEINKEL He 112V-11

HEINKEL He 112V-12

HEINKEL He 100V-1

HEINKEL He 100V-8

(24'11") span and 11 m. (118 sq. ft.) wide. A landing gear failure caused the aircraft's destruction before the record attempt.

Prototypes V-4 to V-7 were finished in the standard configuration, but the He 100V-8 (D-IDHG) was another record-breaker, with the small wing and special 1800 hp Db 601R. On March 30, 1939, twenty-three-year-old Hans Dieterle achieved a new absolute world's speed record at Oranienburg of 746.6 km/hr (463.92 mph).

Again, propaganda presented a false picture. The Heinkel company announced the record plane was an He 112U, "no racer, but a fighter available for the Luftwaffe . . . no special engine, but a normal Daimler-Benz." Even a faked newsreel with a standard He 100 was made, and the "He 112U" exhibited in Munich's Deutsches Museum. Ironically enough, the Heinkel record was to be smashed on April 26 by Messerschmitt with equally dubious fakery, and Heinkel was forbidden to challenge the new mark.

Tests at Rechlin of the He 100s demonstrated higher speeds than any rival fighter, but the fast landings were disliked by pilots. Standard armament was two 7.9 mm. MG 17s and a 20 mm. MG/FFM in the nose, but an He 100V-9 did try two MG/FFs in the wings. It was tested to destruction, along with a V-10 for static tests.

Heinkel felt his fighter was the best, but no matter; the Luftwaffe was committed to the Bf 109 and would not change everything now. As a private venture, Heinkel began construction on 15 preproduction aircraft designated He 100D-0 and D-1.

Even the outbreak of war brought no Luftwaffe orders, and a Soviet delegation visiting Heinkel in October 1939 was sold all six existing prototypes, except for the museum's record-breaking V-8. A Japanese Navy mission purchased the first He 100D-0s, along with a production license. After the third one was finished in January 1940, the fighters went by blockade runner to Japan, where they arrived in May and were designated AX He 1. A plan to have Hitachi produce them failed when Germany was unable to supply tools and jigs.

When the first He 100D-1 was completed in April 1940, there seemed no use for it. Propaganda, however, was well served! The dozen He 100D-1s were painted in fictitious markings and publicized as the "He 113." All sorts of squadron emblems and numbers were photographed to convey the impression that a fleet of super-fighters were in service. The hoax worked so well that prewarned Allied pilots often reported encounters with the "He 113," although, in fact, none ever were used in combat!

HEINKEL He 100D-1

Daimler-Benz DB 601M, 1100 hp at takeoff, 1020 hp at 4000 m. (13,120′)

DIMENSIONS: Span 9.42 m. (30′11″), Lg. 8.18 m. (26′10″), Ht. 2.5 m. (8′2″), Wing Area 14.5 qm. (156 sq. ft.)

WEIGHT: Empty 2100 kg. (4623 lb.), Gross 2545 kg. (5600 lb.)

PERFORMANCE: Speed—Max. 670 km/hr (416 mph) at 4000 m. (13,120′), 560 km/hr (348 mph) at sea level, Cruising speed 555 km/hr (344 mph), Landing speed 150 km/hr (93 mph), Climb 6000 m./6.5 min. (19,680′/6.5 min.), Range 700 km. (435 miles), Service ceiling 11,000 m. (36,080′)

Bf 109E-1B

20.

Fighters in Battle, 1939–45

Bf 109E

When war broke out the standard German fighter model was the Bf 109E, which introduced the 1100 hp Daimler-Benz DB 601A with direct fuel introduction and a new supercharger.

The two prototypes were the V-14 and V 15. While the latter had the same armament as the D model, two MG 17s and an MG/FFM gun in the nose, the V-14 had two MG 17s over the engine and two 20 mm. MG/FFs in the wings. This heavier armament was a response to German intelligence reports of increased firepower abroad. Vibration from the heavy guns continued to be a problem, so the preproduction batch of ten Bf 109E-0s was delivered in late 1938 with four Mg 17s.

In July 1938 the BFW company had been renamed Messerschmitt A.G., although the official prefix letters for its fighter remained BF 109; never Me, which came into use only on later designs. Their expanded Augsburg and Regensburg factories were joined by license-production from AGO, Arado, Erla, Fieseler, and Wiener-Neustadter-Flugzeugwerke (WNF).

The Bf 109E-1 built in such large numbers in 1939 was faster than any foreign fighter except the Spitfire. Armament comprised two MG 17s in the nose with 1000 7.9 mm. rounds each, and two MG/FF wing guns with 60 20 mm. rounds each. An MG/FFM *Motorkanone* was added to the Bf 109E-3, which was soon produced on parallel lines in 1939, but severe firing vibrations made pilots reluctant to use it. Nevertheless, three 20 mm. and two 7.9 mm. guns made the E-3 the heaviest-armed fighter in use. The limitation presented by the short range would not become apparent until the Battle of Britain.

Forty early Bf 109E-1s went to the Condor Legion, operating with J/88. At the end of the civil war in April 1939, the Legion's aircraft were turned over to Spain. German fighter pilots had claimed 318 victories, the highest score being 14 by Captain Werner Moelders.

In order to earn foreign exchange, the Bf 109Es were sold abroad. Switzerland got 30 beginning in April 1939 and despite the war, 50 more were delivered by April 1940. Yugoslavia ordered 73, Rumania 69, Bulgaria 19, Slovakia 16 and five went to the Soviet Union after the non-aggression pact. Japan bought two, but a plan to have Kawasaki build them under license was dropped.

The Luftwaffe itself began the war with 771 aircraft in the *Jagdgruppen:*[1] 28 Arado Ar 68, 112 Bf 109D, and 631 Bf 109E fighters, according to a September 2, 1939, OKL list. Ten long-range *Zerstoerergruppen* added 408: 277 BF 109D or Cs, 36 Bf

MESSERSCHMITT Bf 109E-1
Daimler-Benz DB 601A, 1100 hp
DIMENSIONS: Span 9.9 m. (32'6"), Lg. 8.7 m. (28'6"), Ht. 3.5 m. (11'6"), Wing Area 16.4 qm. (176 sq. ft.)
WEIGHT: Empty 2010 kg. (4422 lb.), Gross 2450 kg. (5390 lb.), Fuel 400 liters (106 gal.)
PERFORMANCE: Speed—Max. 570 km/hr (354 mph), at 3750 m. (12,300'), 467 km/hr (290 mph) at sea level, Landing speed 130 km/hr (81 mph), Climb 945 m./1 min. (3100/1 min.), 5000 m./6.2 min. (16,400 m./6.2 min.), Range 660 km. (410 miles), Service ceiling 10,450 m. (34,275')

[1] Fifteen groups and eight seperate squadrons, to which should be added 24 Bf 109Bs of 5 and 6 (J) 186, the naval unit. See Appendix for Order of Battle on this date.

Bf 109E-3

Bf 109E-3 (Swiss)

109Es, and 95 of the big Bf 110 two-seaters. The older Bf 109 models were being used by *Zerstoerer* units like ZG 2 and ZG 26 until new Bf 110s arrived. To the above totals should be added a considerable number of aircraft, mostly of older models, at training, repair, and storage centers.

Eight fighter groups were deployed against Poland, the three with new Bf 110s fighting the first days' battles. Then on September 4, I/ZG 2's Bf 109Ds defeated Polish PZL P-11 fighters over Lodz, while across Germany at Brunsbuettel, a Bf 109E of II/JG 77 downed a British bomber making the first strike across the North Sea.

By the end of 1939, 718 Bf 109E-1s and 854 Bf 109E-3s had been completed, enough to replace losses (67) in Poland, meet export orders, and expand the fighter units. Monthly production rose from 27 E-1 and 73 E-3 models in January 1940, to April 1940's 94 E-1s, 90 E-3s and one He 100D-1 fighter. It is sobering to note United States single-seat fighter deliveries that same April: 83 Curtiss H-75 (P-36 for France), 12 Republic EP-1 (P-35A for Sweden) and one Brewster Buffalo (for Belgium), all quite inferior to the German types.

April 30, 1940, was the peak of Luftwaffe first-line strength that year, just before the great offensive that overwhelmed France and the Low Countries. First-line unit strength on that date was 4874 aircraft according to German records, with aircraft in repair, storage or training status making a total of over 7800. Fighters included 1369 Bf 109Es assigned to ten first-line *Geschwader,*[2] with 2300 single-seaters on hand when repair, storage and training status aircraft are totaled. About ¾ of the first-line aircraft were usually serviceable on any particular day.

[2] JG 1, 2, 3, 26, 27, 51, 52, 53, 54 and 77, plus group I(J)LG 2.

MESSERSCHMITT Bf 109E-4
Daimler-Benz DB 601Aa, 1150 hp
DIMENSIONS: as Bf 109E-1
WEIGHT: Empty 2018 kg. (4440 lb.), Gross 2509 kg. (5520 lb.)
PERFORMANCE: Speed—Max. 575 km/hr (357 mph) at 3200 m. (19,700'), Service ceiling 5800 m. (36,000')

Bf 109E-4B

MESSERSCHMITT Bf 209V-1
Daimler-Benz DB 601ARV, 1800 hp
DIMENSIONS: Span 7.8 m. (25′7″), Lg. 7.24 m. (23′9″), Wing Area 10.6 qm. (114 sq. ft.)
WEIGHT: Gross 2515 kg. (5545 lb.), Fuel 500 liters (132 gal.)
PERFORMANCE: Speed—Max. 755 km/hr (469 mph) at sea level

The story of France's defeat and Britain's survival in 1940's critical summer cannot be repeated here. We refer the reader to the bibliography, and remind the reader of H. J. Nowarra's book on the Bf 109's role in the war. For this book, it is sufficient to say that every *Jagdstaffel* that year used Bf 109Es. To the Messerschmitt can be given credit for the early victories, and the blame for not having the range necessary to protect German bombers in the Battle of Britain.

During 1940, 1193 Bf 109s were delivered, of many minor variations. The E-1 and E-3 were superseded in the summer by the E-4, which deleted the troublesome *Motorkanone*. Special fighter-bomber units like II(S)LG 2 received the E-1B with racks for one 250 kg. (550 lb.) or four 50 kg. (110 lb.) bombs, and E-4/B versions with these racks went to the staffel in each *Geschwader* assigned to bombing missions. A 1200 hp DB 601N engine was used on the E-4N used by JG 27 in the Western Desert, while the E-7 added a 300 liter (79 gal.) drop tank, and the E-7/Z tried GM 1 fuel injection. The Bf 109E-8 incorporated all the previous modifications. Twenty-six reconnaissance conversions were included in 1940; equipped with cameras and only two 7.9 mm. nose guns, they were the E-5 with a standard DB 601A, the E-6 with a DB 601N, and the E-9 with the drop tank.

Another variant of the Bf 109E was designed for the German aircraft carrier *Graf Zeppelin,* and thus known as the Bf 109T, for *Traeger* (carrier). These were based on the E-3, but had wings extended to 36′4″, manually folding wings, catapult spools and arrestor hooks. Originally begun in 1939, the project was suspended in October, but revived in July 1940, when Fieseler was ordered to modify ten airframes to a carrier configuration. Work on the carrier was again suspended, but a number of Bf 109T-0 and Bf 109T-1s were completed and issued to I/JG 77, a Norwegian-based fighter group which had good use for this slow-landing version on the short Norwegian coastal landing strips.

MESSERSCHMITT ME 209

The world was stunned by the announcement that Germany had established a new world's speed record of 755 km/hr (469 mph) on April 26, 1939, using a Messerschmitt "BF 109R." Hardly recovered from the previous Heinkel mark, world aviation was now told that Germany's first-line fighter also was the world's fastest aircraft!

While the speed mark was honest, and actually still remains the official record for piston-engined aircraft,[3] the publicity was a bluff. The aircraft was no Bf 109R, but the entirely different Me 209V-1, a research vehicle specially designed to set a new speed mark. Professor Messerschmitt had lectured on the need for "real experimental planes in which the designer must be free of all restrictions during development," so that he could use any innovation possible to advance the state of the art.

In this spirit, Messerschmitt did win an order for three high-speed aircraft begun as company project P 1059, and officially designated Me 209. The compact airframe was very different than the Bf 109, with a shorter fuselage and wings, wide-track undercarriage, and vertical tail extending below the fuselage to house the tail wheel. A surface evaporation cooling system including 220 liters (48 gal.) of water was used to cool the Daimler-Benz DB 601A.

The first prototype (D-INJR) was flown on August 1, 1938, followed by the Me 209V-2 on Febru-

[3] On August 16, 1969, a modified Grumman F8F-2 claimed a new 483 mph record.

ary 8, 1939. After the V-2 crashed on April 4, the V-1 was fitted with a specially boosted Daimler DB 601 that produced 1600 hp on the record flight, and even reached 2300 hp for one minute on a test run; after such a burst, however, the engine had to be scrapped.

For the April 26, 1939, record run, the Me 209V-1 carried 500 liters (110 gal.) of fuel and 450 liters (100 gal.) of cooling water, making the 755.138 km/hr dash on a 3 km circuit at 100 m. Fritz Wendel was the pilot, and the FAI recognized the record, which was not broken until November 7, 1945, by a jet-propelled Gloster Meteor. The earlier Heinkel record had not been certified by the FAI; probably it wasn't officially reported to prevent Heinkel from getting a success that certain RLM officials wished to reserve for Messerschmitt. Political, rather than military, favoritism was involved here.

Messerschmitt completed the similar Me 209V-3 (D-IVFP) in May 1939, along with the only fighter version, Me 209V-4. First flown on May 12, V-4 was originally marked D-IRND, but labed CE+BW in 1940, and had a redesigned, larger wing with automatic leading-edge slots, two 7.9 mm. guns and a 30 mm. MK 108 *Motorkanone*.

This version inherited the many difficulties encountered with the V-1, including poor visibility and stability, enormous pressure on the controls, and very unsatisfactory cooling. After the first eight flights, normal underwing radiators replaced the surface evaporation system, while later the span was increased and the slots replaced by new leading edges. Despite all this, the Me 209V-4 remained a "little monster," in Fritz Wendel's words. After all those modifications it had little advantage over Bf 109s, and was too difficult to fly for average pilots on wartime fields.

Messerschmitt and his design team still did not want to admit they had lost the game against the new Focke-Wulf 190s so they went ahead on the entirely new Me 309 of 1942, and a fighter design of 1943 that received the designation Me 209V-5. These planes will be described at their proper place.

MESSERSCHMITT Me 209V-4

MESSERSCHMITT Me 109F-0

BF 109F AND BARBAROSSA

Messerschmitt's next production fighter was the Bf 109F, principal Luftwaffe single-seater of 1941. Faster than the preceding E series, it was more streamlined with a larger prop spinner, cleaner cowl, modified radiators, retractable tail wheel and removal of the struts bracing the horizontal tail.

Although 15 Bf 109F-0 preproduction aircraft were scheduled for completion from January to April 1940, deliveries were delayed until the new features could be tested on prototypes. The new nose shape, tailplane, and radiators were tried on a modified Bf 109E, Nr. 5604 (VK+AB), which first flew July 10 1940, with an early DB 601E. New wings with rounded tips, Frise ailerons, and plain flaps were introduced on the V-17 and V-18 prototypes.

The BF 109F-0 batch in 1940 and the first Bf 109F-1 series in January 1941 were powered by the 1200 hp DB 601N also used in late-model E series. Armament was two 7.9 mm. MG 17s and a 20 mm. MG/FFM *Motorkanone*. Several crashed and delayed the service introduction until the new cantilever tailplane could be strengthened.

Before long the Bf 109F-2 appeared with a new weapon, a 15 mm. Rheinmetal MG 151 *Motorkanone* firing 650 rounds per minute, instead of the 520 rpm of the previous MF/FFM. Two hundred rounds were carried for this gun, along with 1000 7.9 mm. rounds for the two cowl guns. Some aircraft had dust filters and tropical kits for Africa (Bf 109-2/Trop) and others GM-1 injection (F-2/Z).

Production progressed so rapidly that by June 1941 the familiar Bf 109E Emils had been replaced by Bf 109Fs in about eight of the ten *Jagdgeschwader*, which then had 1266 aircraft, 70 per cent serviceable. JG 2 and JG 26 faced the English Channel and I/JG 27 was in Libya, but the remaining single-seat units were available for Operation Barbarossa, the invasion of the Soviet Union.

MESSERSCHMITT Me 109F-1

MESSERSCHMITT Bf 109F-3
Daimler-Benz DB 601E, 1300 hp
DIMENSIONS: Span 10.06 m. (33′), Lg. 9.04 m. (29′8″), Ht. 3.04 m. (10′), Wing Area 17.3 qm. (186 sq. ft.)
WEIGHT: Empty 1980 kg. (4356 lb.), Gross 2970 kg. (6534 lb.)
PERFORMANCE: Speed—Max. 623 km/hr (387 mph) at 6700 m. (21,980′), Cruising speed 500 km/hr (310 mph), Range 710 km. (440 miles), Service ceiling 11,300 m. (37,000′)

The Luftwaffe knew it would be outnumbered, although part of the Red Air Force must remain in Siberia to face Japan, and Finns and Rumanians would help Germany on the long front's flanks. Nevertheless, the greatest asset of the battle-tested Luftwaffe was its airmen's combat experience, and a surprise attack would win air superiority.

June 22, 1941, the war's first day, saw more Luftwaffe bomber and fighter sorties (2272) than any day in the Battle of Britain. Germany's 3:15 A.M. attack was immensely successful, hitting Soviet aircraft on the ground on every airfield in reach. Not many Soviet fighters had a chance to take off, but a wave of bombers counterattacked from bases outside the first strike's radius. Without fighter escort and disorganized, they were easy prey for the Messerschmitts.

Official Soviet history gives their losses as 1200 aircraft before noon that day, over 800 on the ground. German claims for the day were 322 air victories to fighters and flak, and 1489 on the ground. The air totals are similar, and much of the difference in the ground scores can be accounted for by aircraft with repairable damage that had to be abandoned when bases were overrun by the rapidly advancing Germans. Luftwaffe losses for the day were counted by the Germans as 35.

This victory provided the air cover and support that contributed much to the invasion's rapid progress. Nevertheless, the Soviets had sufficient reserves to continually challenge the Luftwaffe. Despite German superiority in pilots and aircraft quality, the Luftwaffe lost 1023 aircraft, plus 657 damaged, in the war's first six weeks. During this period the total *Geschwader* victory score passed 1000 for JG 51, 53, and 54. JG 51 commander Moelders became the first German pilot to achieve over 100 victories.[4]

Further progress was made at home when the 1300 hp DB 601E became available in quantity for the Bf 109F-3. This increased top speed from 595 km/hr (369 mph) in the F-1 to 623 km/hr (387 mph) in the F-3.

Many German pilots missed the 20 mm. wing guns on the older Emils, and felt the F's reduced firepower a mistake. Aces like Moelders believed a single *Motorkanone* sufficient, but they were expert marksmen quick to find the right firing position, who preferred the maneuverability lighter fighters offered. Galland was among those who realized the ordinary pilot needed more firepower.

A 20 mm. barrel had been developed for the MG 151/20 which fired 650 rpm, and was introduced in 1942 on the Bf 109F-4. Two more could be attached under the wings in the Bf 109F-4/R1 kit, which was good for hitting big bombers, but the pods reduced speed and detracted from the type's clean lines. Other modifications seen in 1942 were the BF 109-4/Trop, F-4/Z with GM-1 booster and the F-4/B with a 250 kg. (550 lb.) bomb rack for the fighter-bomber *staffels* added in March 1942; 10(Jabo)/JG 2 and 10(Jabo)/JG 26. These *Jabos* were used against British shipping, railways and other targets.

The most famous ace of this period was Marseille, who ran up a score of 158 victories, mostly in Africa with his Bf 109F-4/Trop. Gordon Gollob and Herman Graf also passed the 100 mark on Bf 109Fs while flying in Russia in May 1942.

Production of the Bf 109 was 2764 in 1941 and 2665 in 1942. Most were F fighters, but 1942 includes the first Gs and eight examples of the Bf 109F-5 and F-6 reconnaissance variants. The former had a 300 liter drop tank and only two cowl guns, while the

[4] It might be noted that JG 51, which reached this score on June 30, was the only *Geschwader* at that time to have *four* groups. Moelders downed 115 aircraft; 14 in Spain, 68 in the West and 33 in Russia before his accidental death on November 22, 1941, while flying to Udet's funeral.

F-6 had no guns, but heavier cameras. During 1942, Spain bought 15 F-3 fighters and two Italian fighter groups flew Bf 109F-4s in 1943.

THE FOCKE-WULF FW 190

For two years of war, the only German single-seaters in combat had been Messerschmitts. Not until September 27, 1941, did Spitfire pilots returning from a mission over Occupied France encounter an entirely new German fighter, a *radial*-engined single-seater that was the Spitfire's superior. The dangerous new opponent was the Fw 190A flown by II/JG 26, the first Luftwaffe group so equipped.

Focke-Wulf's technical director Kurt Tank had appointed designer R. Blaser chief of the team that in the summer of 1938 designed a fighter around a radial engine and a wide-track undercarriage. The name *Wurger* (Shrike or Butcher-bird) was chosen, for all Focke-Wulf planes had bird names, but never became widely used.

At first the Air Ministry was in no hurry, since it already had the Bf 109, but then as that type's weaknesses became apparent, they pressed Blaser so hard that he collapsed with exhaustion after the prototype's first flight. The Fw 190V-1 (D-OPZE), flown June 1, 1939, and the V-2 flown on December 1, were powered by a 1500 hp BMW 139 air-cooled by a duct in the big spinner. Four synchronized guns were provided on the V-2; two 7.9 mm. MG 17s on the cowl and two 13 mm. MG 131s in the wing roots.

When the ducted spinner proved unsatisfactory, the V-1 was given a normal cowling and spinner and flown on January 25, 1940, then marked FO+LY. In the meantime, it was decided to adopt the 1600 hp BMW 801 radial, so the V-3 and V-4 prototypes were left unfinished and the V-5 finished in spring 1940 with a BMW 801C-0. This was first flown with the prototype's 9.5 m. wing (V-5k) and later with a larger 10.38 m. wing (asV-5g) for more maneuverability.[5]

A preproduction Fw 190A-0 series followed, the first nine, beginning in February 1941, with the short wings and only two MG 17 cowl guns, while the next 21 had the larger wings with two more MG 17s in the wing roots and a pair of 20 mm. MG/FF wing guns. All had a 1600 hp BMW 801C. Comparison soon showed the larger wings best and the Focke-Wulf an excellent design, but the BMW engine pre-

[5] There is some uncertainty about the V-6 and V-7 prototypes. The V-6 (※0006) became the first Fw 190A-0/U1 but V-7 seems to be the first Fw 190A-1 (※001).

Bf 109F-4B

Bf 109F-5

FOCKE-WULF Fw 190V-1
BMW 139, 1550 hp
DIMENSIONS: Span 9.51 m. (31′2″), Lg. 8.85 m. (29′), Wing Area 14.9 qm. (160 sq. ft.)
WEIGHT: Gross 2750 kg. (6062 lb.) V-2 was 2508 kg. (5530 lb.) empty, 3151 kg. (6948 lb.) gross
PERFORMANCE: Speed—Max. 595 km/hr (370 mph)

Fw 190V-1 with original nose spinner

Fw 190V-2

Fw 190V-5k

Fw 190A-0

FOCKE-WULF Fw 190A-1
BMW 801C-1, 1600 hp

DIMENSIONS: Span 10.38 m. (34′½″), Lg. 8.79 m. (28′10″), Ht. 3.96 m. (13′), Wing Area 18.3 qm. (197 sq. ft.)

WEIGHT: Empty 3183 kg. (7003 lb.), Gross 3860 kg. (8491 lb.)

PERFORMANCE: Speed—Max. 625 km/hr (388 mph) at 5500 m. (18,040′), Cruising speed 450 km/hr (279 mph), Range 940 km. (584 miles)

sented many heating problems which even the addition of cooling fans did not solve.

One hundred similar Fw 190A-1s had been ordered and in August some of the first were sent to II/JG 26 for trials in France. Engine troubles delayed the new fighter's introduction into combat, and the A-1s were used for training or experimental work. Meanwhile, deliveries began in August 1941 on the Fw 190A-2 with the BMW 801C-2, two cowl MG 17s, two MG 151/20 and two MG/FF wing guns. So the pilot could know when his wheels were down, a rod rose from the wing as the gear dropped. Altogether, 426 A-2s were completed; 203 under license by Arado, 105 by AGO and 118 by Focke-Wulf itself.

Many Fw 190 prototypes and variations were produced, and a full account requires a whole book, like H. J. Nowarra's *The Focke-Wulf 190* cited in the bibliography. This survey can mention only major types and the most striking variants.

The Fw 190A-3 was the next model, with an 1600 hp 801D-2 engine, modified fin and new fairing along the engine cowl. Altogether 509 were built, including one whose accidental landing in Britain on July 23, 1942, gave the Allies their first close look. Firepower and speed were impressive, as was the armor protection; a 14 mm. plate behind the pilot and a 5 mm. ring built into the cowl.

Production rose from 228 Focke-Wulfs in 1941 to 1850 in 1942, as other firms joined in production deliveries. After JG 26, JG 2 received its Fw 190s in April 1942. These units operated near the English Channel. Not until August 1942 did a Russian front unit, JG 51, begin rotating groups home for transition to the Fw 190. At home in Germany, JG 1 in the northwest received Fw 190A-3s. Turkey got 72 Fw 190Aa-3 fighters beginning October 1942.

FOCKE-WULF Fw 190A-3
BMW 801D-2, 1730 hp at takeoff
DIMENSIONS: Span 10.5 m. (34'5½"), Lg. 8.85 m. (29'), Ht. 3.95 m. (13'), Wing Area 18.3 qm. (197 sq. ft.)
WEIGHT: Empty 2900 kg. (6380 lb.), Gross 3978 kg. (8751 lb.), Fuel 524 liters (138 gal.)
PERFORMANCE: Speed—Max. 676 km/hr (420 mph) at 6400 m. (21,000'), 526 km/hr (327 mph) at sea level, Climb 8000 m./12 min. (26,240'/12 min.), Range 800 km. (500 miles), Service ceiling 10,600 m. (34,780')

FOCKE-WULF Fw 190A-5
BMW 801D-2, 1730 hp
DIMENSIONS: Span 10.38 m. (34'½"), Lg. 8.95 m. (29'4¼"), Ht. 3.755 m. (12'4"), Wing Area 18.3 qm. (197 sq. ft.)
WEIGHT: Empty 3610 kg. (7942 lb.), Gross 4650 kg. (10,230 lb.)
PERFORMANCE: Speed—Max. 656 km/hr (407 mph) at 6300 m. (20,670'), Climb 8000 m./12.5 min. (26,250'/12.5 min.), Range 700 km. (435 miles), Service ceiling 10,500 m. (34,500')

A GM-1 injection device increasing power from 1600 to 2100 hp for short periods was added to the Fw 190A-4, recognizable by a pylon atop the fin for a new radio. Both the A-3 and 894 A-4s were subject to many modifications. Aside from the usual "Trop" models for Africa, there were the versions designated U for *Umbau* (rebuilt or altered). The Fw 190 A-3/U1 was issued to the *Jabo* (fighter-bomber) *staffels* in 1942 with a 550 lb. bomb rack under the fuselage, and the two MG/FF guns removed. Another *Umbau* was the Fw 190A-3/U4, a dozen aircraft modified for photo reconnaissance by adding two cameras behind the pilot and the reduced armament of the U1.

The Fw 190A-4/U1 was a fighter-bomber with only two MG 151/20 guns and racks for two 250 kg. (550 lb.) bombs. More important were 30 Fw 190A-4/U3s, appearing in October 1942 as the first of the ground attack versions. It had 793 lb. of armor around the engine and cockpit and could carry a 550 lb. bomb or a drop tank. This version led directly to the F and G models. Another variant was the Fw 190A-4/U8 fighter-bomber of 1943 which added wing and belly racks for 500 kg. bombs or 300 liter tanks.

At 1943's beginning there were 520 Fw 190s with front-line units, plus those at training or storage bases. Production was rapidly increased, for now it was apparent that Germany would need far more fighters than its leaders had ever dreamed. In January the American B-17 bombers began their heavy offensive against the homeland, while the Mediterranean positions were hard pressed and the long Russian front felt growing Soviet strength. Production rose steadily from 3354 Fw 190s of all types in 1943 to 11,767 in 1944.

FOCKE-WULF Fw 190A-6
BMW 801D-2, 1730 hp
DIMENSIONS: Span 10.5 m. (34'5½"), Lg. 8.95 m. (29'4¼"), Wing Area 18.3 qm. (197 sq. ft.)
WEIGHT: Gross 4166 kg. (9100 lb.)
PERFORMANCE: Speed—Max. 651 km/hr (405 mph) at 6300 m. (20,670'), Climb 8000 m./13.2 min. (26,250'/13.2 min.), Range 10,350 m. (34,000')

One model followed another in rapid succession. The Fw 190A-5 had its engine moved forward slightly and appeared in April 1943. There were 723 A-5s built with up to 17 different *Umbauen,* modifications offering everything from cameras to torpedos.[6] Not all those suggested were actually tried, but our photos show several prototypes that were. It was soon realized that rather than attempt quantity modifications at the factories, it was best to have a kit or *Ruestsaetz,* a set of parts sent out to air force supply centers and stocked until needed at the front.

An example is the underwing gun pans introduced on a Fw 190A-5/U12 prototype tested in July 1943. Besides the usual paired MG 17s on the cowl and the two MG 151/20 guns in the roots, a pair of

[6] See Nowarra's *Focke-Wulf 190* for lists.

A-5/U3 Trop with dust filter

A-5/U12 with 20 mm. gun tray under wings

A-8 with special fuel tank on wing

Special Fw 190A Modifications:

A-4/U8 fighter bomber

A-4/R6 with W.Gr. 21 rocket projector

A-5/U14 with torpedo

A-8 with SG 116, three vertical firing 30 mm. MK 103s

A-8/U1 two-seater

MG 151/20s were added under wing; a total fire-power of six 20 mm. and two 7.9 mm. guns. This arrangement became the *Ruestsaetz* R1, a kit applicable to the later A-6 to A-10 series, beginning with Fw 190A-6/R1.

These *Ruestsaetze* run up to R31, and included all sorts of weapons arrangements, or technical devices, adapting the Fw 190A to attack the big bombers that came by day or night. The R2 kit for A-7 to A-10 carried a 30 mm. MK 108 under each wing, and R6 was especially dangerous to bomber formations; a pair of 8 inch rocket projectors that were attached to older A-4 and A-5 models, as well as to new Fw 190A-6/R6s.

Standard armament of the Fw 190A-6 was the usual MG 17 cowl guns and four MG 151/20s in the wings; the obsolete MG/FF finally being deleted. Deliveries amounted to 569 in 1943; 280 by AGO, 234 by Fieseler and 55 by Arado, but none from the parent Focke-Wulf plant. Many were modified by R1 and R6 *Ruestsaetze.*

Two 13 mm. MG 131 cowl guns were introduced in January 1944 on 80 FW 190A-7s built by Focke-Wulf, AGO, and Fieseler. Fieseler also provided 50 A-7/R2 versions with two 30 mm. MK 108s replacing one pair of MG 151/20s in the wings.

The last widely produced A version was the Fw 190A-8, with added 30 gallons of internal fuel. Beginning in March 1944, 1334 were built. Standard armament was two MG 131 cowl guns and four MG 151/20 wing guns, but several *Ruestsaetze* were used. Neither the proposed A-9 with a BMW 801TS/TH or an A-10 was ever built.

An effort was made to have A-8 produced in France but since none were completed until the German Army had been driven out, 63 A-8s were delivered to the French Air Force from March 1945 to March 1946 as NC 900.

Focke-Wulf fighter developments included the experimental Fw 190B, C and D variations, but the Fw 190F and G *Schlacht* (ground attack) versions were mass produced in parallel with the A types. Similar to the Fw 190A-4/U3 of October 1942, in its armor protection, the Fw 190F-1 had five mm. armor beneath the engine and cockpit, two MG 17 cowl guns, two 151/20s in the wing roots and the usual 1700 hp BMW 801D-2.

Thirty F-1s were delivered late in 1942, followed by the F-2, which had a rack under the fuselage adapted for one 550 lb. or four 110 lb. bombs. The F-3 added wing racks for four 110 lb. bombs, which could be carried along with a 300 liter (79 gal.) tank under the fuselage. There were 271 Fw 190F-2s built, and Arado added 247 Fw 190F-3s by May 1943. Two 30 mm. MK 103 guns were carried below

Special Fw 190F modifications:

F-3/R1 with eight 110 lb. bombs

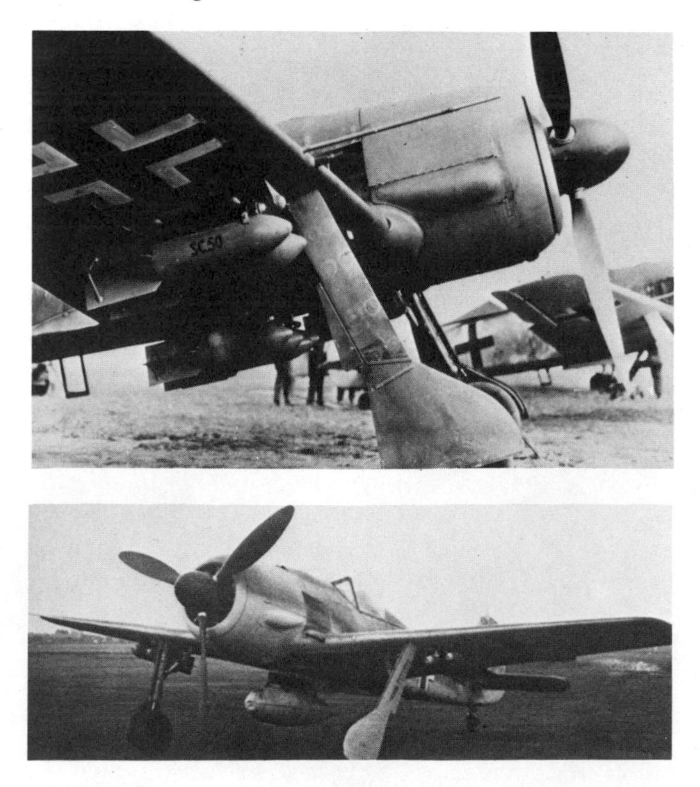

F-8/R1 with four 110 lb. bombs and drop tank

F-8/R3 with two 30 mm. guns

F-8 with SG 113 vertical guns

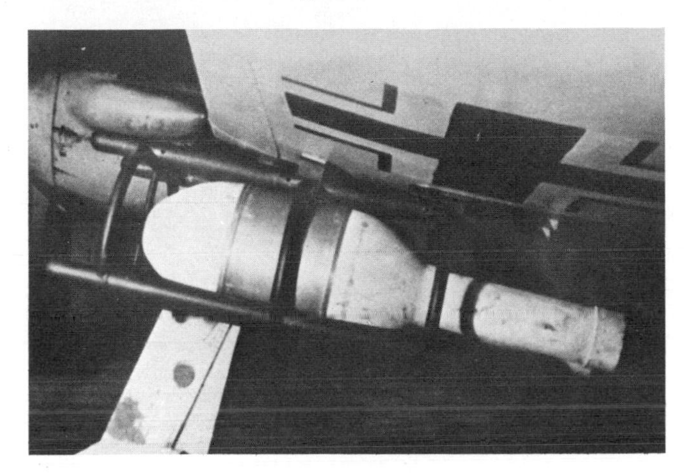

F-8 with W.Gr. 28 (28 cm. rocket projector)

Fw 190G-2

the wing on the 20 F-3/R3s whose deliveries started in December 1943.

The Fw 190G was a parallel series armed with just two MG 151/20 guns, a 500 kg. (1100 lb.) bomb under the fuselage and two drop tanks under the wing. There were 49 G-1, 468 G-2 and 150 G-3 models delivered in 1942–43 differing only in their bomb rack arrangements.

Further developments were made in 1944. The F-4, F-5 and F-6 projects were redesignated Fw 190F-8, F-9 and F-10, probably to coincide with parallel A types with similar fittings. Arado and Norddeutsche Dornier-Werke built 385 Fw 190F-8s with an added 115 liter (30 gal.) internal tank and mechanical improvements. They had several *Ruestsaetze* and *Umbau*-versions, including the F-8/U2 and U3 used to test the BT *Bomben-Torpedo,* a new weapon not ready in time for combat. A new BMW 801TS/TH and modified armor were seen on a few F-9 and the BMW 801F on the F-10, but few were actually made. Likewise, a parallel Fw 190G-8 came out alongside the A-8 and F-8, with similar fuel tank and bomb rack arrangements and *Ruestsaetze* possibilities. Altogether, 6634 ground attack Focke-Wulfs were delivered from 1942 to 1945, as well as 13,367 fighter types. Most of the latter were A series, but there were a number of new height-altitude versions described in a later section.

MESSERSCHMITT GUSTAV

Despite the Focke-Wulf's increasing popularity, the Messerschmitt Bf 190G "Gustav" was the most widely used fighter of the war's last three years. This model was designed with the new 1475 hp DB605, a cockpit pressurized for high altitudes, and was, originally armed like the F series with two MG 17s and an MG 151/20 *Motorkanone*.

When production deliveries began in May 1942, the DB605 was unready, so 12 Bf 109G-0 preproduction aircraft had to use the older DB601E. The Bf 109G-1 had the first DB605 engines with GM-1 power boost for high altitudes, and the first examples went to the newly formed II/JG 2 Staffel.[7]

Heavier armament was desired for a batch sent to Africa, so the Bf 109G-1/Trop had an intake filter and two 13 mm. MG 131 guns replacing the 7.9 mm. pair. These guns caused large humps on the cowling, and were adopted as standard on the G-5 and later models. They gave the Gs another nickname; the *Beule* (lump).

The Bf 109G-2 was a recon version with camera and drop tanks. One was tested with a belly pack carrying two *rearward* firing MG 17s, but that was not feasible and was dropped. Another experimental modification was Bf 109G-2/R1, carrying a 550 lb. bomb and two 79 gallon drop tanks. As our photo

[7] Normally a fighter *Geschwader* had nine *Staffeln,* but in 1942 JG 2 and 26 added 10 (*Jabo*) and 11 *Staffeln.*

This captured Fw 190 is flown by an American pilot; aircraft identity uncertain, but it seems to be a G-3 without bombs, or an A-8

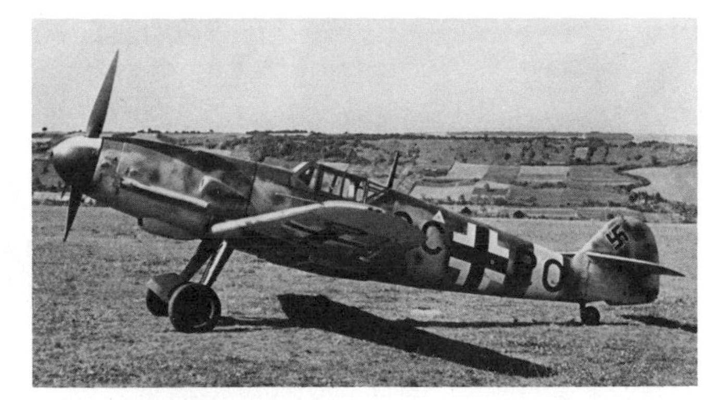

MESSERSCHMITT Bf 109G-0

Bf 109G-1

Bf 109G-2/Trop (U.S. captive)

Bf 109G-6/R1 with 550 lb. bombs

Bf 109G-2/R

Bf 109G-6/U4 with two 30 mm. guns added

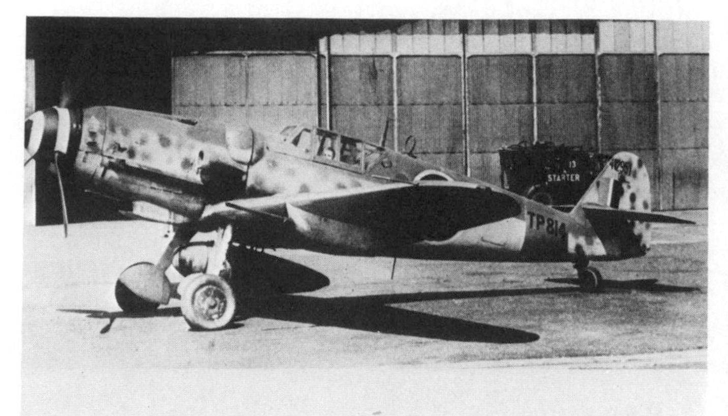

shows, a third wheel kept the bomb fins clear of the ground until takeoff, when the wheel was jettisoned.

Standard fighters like the G-1, the G-3 had a new radio, the G-4 was unpressurized and the G-5 standardized the 13 mm. cowl guns, and introduced the DB 605D engine. This was fitted with the MW 50 water-methonal injection system, in which the pilot's push button could briefly boost power from 1450 to 1800 hp. With a modified tail unit, it became the Bf 109G-5/R2.

The Bf 109G-6 was the most numerous of this series, with various DB 605 models with either GM-1 or MW 50 booster, and a 300 liter (79 gal.) drop tank. Standard armament was two 13 mm. MG 131s (300 rpg) over the engine, a 30 mm. MK 108 *Motorkanone* (100 rds), and two 20 mm. MG 151/20s (120 rpg) in fairings under the wing. The landing gear was strengthened, since gross weight had risen

MESSERSCHMITT Bf 109G-6
Daimler-Benz DB 605A-1, 1475 hp at takeoff, 1250 hp at 5800 m. (19,000′)
DIMENSIONS: Span 9.92 m. (32′6″), Lg. 9.04 m. (29′8″), Ht. 3.52 m. (11′6″), Wing Area 16.2 qm. (174 sq. ft.)
WEIGHT: Empty 2750 kg. (6050 lb.), Gross 3400 kg. (7480 lb.), Fuel 400–700 liters (105–184 gal.)
PERFORMANCE: Speed—Max. 615 km/hr (382 mph) at 7000 m. (22,960′), 540 km/hr (335 mph) at sea level, Climb 5800 m./6 min. (19,000′/6 min.), Range 720 km. (450 miles), Service ceiling 11,800 m. (38,700′)

MESSERSCHMITT Bf 109G-6/R-2
Daimler-Benz DB 605An, 1800 hp with MW 50, 1250 hp at 5800 m. (19,000′)
DIMENSIONS: as Bf 109G-6
WEIGHT: Empty 2268 kg. (4490 lb.), Gross 3320 kg. (7304 lb.)
PERFORMANCE: Speed—Max. 665 km/hr (413 mph) at 5000 m. (16,400′) MW 50, 628 km/hr (390 mph) at 6600 m. (21,650′) normal, 568 km/hr (353 mph) at sea level, Cruising speed 590 km/hr (366 mph), Landing speed 150 km/hr (93 mph), Climb 6000 m./7 min. (19,680′/6 min.), Service ceiling 11,000 m. (36,080′)

MESSERSCHMITT Bf 109G-10/R-2
Daimler-Benz DB 605D, 1800 hp at takeoff, 1150 hp at 8000 m. (26,250′)
DIMENSIONS: as Bf 109G-6
WEIGHT: Empty 2318 kg. (5100 lb.), Gross 3297 kg. (7254 lb.)
PERFORMANCE: Speed—Max. 685 km/hr (425 mph) at 7400 m. (24,200′), 550 km/hr (344 mph) at sea level, Cruising speed 628 km/hr (390 mph) at 8400 m. (27,560′), Landing speed 150 km/hr (93 mph), Climb 6000 m./6 min. (19,800′/6 min.), Range 560 km. (350 miles), Service ceiling 12,500 m. (41,000′)

from 2200 kg. (4850 lb.) in the pre-war B to 2970 kg. (6550 lb.) in the G-6.

Special modifications shown in our photos include the G-6/R1 without wing guns, but adding a rack for a 550 or 1100 lb. bomb, the G-6/R2 with 210 mm. rocket tubes instead of wing guns, and the G-6/U4 with 30 mm. MK 108s under the wing. While no G-7 or G-9 was built, many Bf 109G-8s were made in 1943 for recon, carrying only two MG 131s, a camera and belly tank.

Fastest Gustav was the Bf 109G-10, which had only two cowl guns and a DB 605D with MW 50 booster. This light weight would reach 6000 m. (19,680′) in six minutes and do 685 km/hr (425 mph) at 7400 m. (24,200′). Normal range was only 560 km. (350 miles) and often planes ran out of fuel on the way back from air battles. A tray with two MK 108s was fitted under the belly, (G-10/U4) but was later replaced by a fuel tank. Another 1944 Gustav variant was the two-seat Bf 109G-12 trainer conversion.

A new cockpit canopy, the "Galland Hood" was introduced on the Bf 109G-14, which used several DB 605 powerplant versions, the usual nose guns, and had provisions for underwing guns, bombs or rocket

Bf 109G-12 two-seaters

attachments. One variant, G-14/Ra, had a wooden tail assembly.

Germany's allies were also supplied with Gustavs. Finland purchased 35 Bf 109G-2s from March to November 1943, and added 126 Bf 109G-6s from January to August 1944. Some G-14s were acquired later when abandoned by Germans evacuating Finland.

Bulgaria received 145 Gs and Rumania 70, while I.A.R. established a production line in Brasnov. The Rumanians assembled 30 from German parts, but only 19 Gs of their own were built before an Allied air attack destroyed the factory in May 1944.

Hungary got 59 Bf 109G-6s and set up production lines in Budapest and Gyor that delivered 73 in 1943 and 344 in 1944. Caudron, in France, built a Bf 109V-24 that was intended to be the first of a French Bf 109S series with an evaporation cooling system, but the liberation of Paris ended that project. Slovakia got 15 Bf 109Gs in 1944, but production of G-14s by Avia in Prague did not begin until after the war. Avia-built Messerschmitts served the Czech Air Force, and 25 became Israel's first fighters in 1948.

Croatian and Italian squadrons attached to Luftwaffe commands flew Bf 109Gs, and neutral Switzerland got 12 Bf 109G-6s in May 1944. These were in exchange for Swiss destruction of an interned Bf 110G to protect its secret radar. Spain received 25 Bf 109G airframes for completion by Hispano Aviacon as predecessors of a Bf 109J series. No engines were received from Germany, so these aircraft were delivered in 1946 with Hispano-Suiza engines and followed by 200 aircraft of Spanish manufacture. These served thru the post-war decade and were the last Messerschmitt-designed fighters in active service. They were replaced by F-86F Sabres by 1958.

While thousands of Gs were turned out, Messerschmitt explored further developments. For high altitude operations, the Bf 109H was designed with 11.92 m. (39′1″) span wings. A few Bf 109H-0s were converted in 1943 from late Fs with the DB 601E,

Bf 109G-14 in Finland (postwar)

and a small Bf 109H-1 series was made in 1944 with a 1475 hp DB 605A and one MK 108 and two MG 17 nose guns. Despite a 750 km/hr (466 mph) speed at 14,600 m. (48,000′), wing vibration made the type impractical.

Last of the Bf 109 series was the Bf 109K, basically a G-10 with a new canopy and various engine models. The Bf 109K-0 appeared in November 1944 with a boosted DB 605D and was followed by the K-2 and K-4 with DB 605A SCM or DCM engines. Uusual armament was two MG 131s and a 30 mm. *Motorkanone*, but the Bf 109K-6 added two 30 mm. MK 103s under the wings.

Fastest version was the K-14, with a DB 605L, but only two ever reached the front. Without wing guns, they did 728 km/hr (452 mph) at 11,515 m. (37,700′). Further Bf 109 development was halted by the war's end. Stillborn projects included a Bf 109L powered by a 1750 hp Jumo 213E and a projected Bf 109Z (*Zwilling*-twin) with two G series fuselages joined on a single wing in the manner of North American's F-82 twin Mustang escort fighter.

German Bf 109 production amounted to 30,124 aircraft from 1940 to 1945, to which may be added at least 2300 in 1937–39 and license production in Hungary, Rumania, Czechoslovakia, and Spain. A total of over 33,000 built may be the highest number of any combat plane in history.

In September 1942, when German territorial gains were greatest, the Luftwaffe had 1417 single-engined

MESSERSCHMITT Bf 109K-6
Daimler-Benz DB 605D, 1800 hp at takeoff, 1150 hp at 8000 m. (26,250′)
DIMENSIONS: Span 9.9 m. (32′6″), Lg. 8.92 m. (29′3″), Ht. 3.4 m. (11′2″), Wing Area 16.2 qm. (174 sq. ft.)
WEIGHT: Empty 2346 kg. (5161 lb.), Gross 3626 kg. (7977 lb.)
PERFORMANCE: Speed—Max. 710 km/hr (441 mph) at 7500 m. (24,600′), 575 km/hr (357 mph) at sea level, Cruising speed 640 km/hr (397 mph), Climb 6000 m./9 min. (19,680′/9 min.), Service ceiling 11,800 m. (38,700′)

MESSERSCHMITT Me 309V-1
Daimler-Benz DB 603A-1, 1720 hp (DB 605B on V-2, 1475 hp)
DIMENSIONS: Span 11.04 m. (37′5″), Lg. 9.46 m. (31′¼″), Ht. 3.9 m. (12′9½″), Wing Area 16.6 qm. (178 sq. ft.)
WEIGHT: Empty 3530 kg. (7766 lb.), Gross 4250 kg. (9350 lb.)
PERFORMANCE: Speed—Max. 733 km/hr (455 mph) at 8500 m. (27,900′), Cruising speed 665 km/hr (407 mph), Climb 4000 m./4.7 min. (13,120′/4.7 min.), Service ceiling 12,000 m. (39,360′)

fighters distributed among 34 *Gruppen* and ten attached *Staffeln.* Twenty-three groups had Bf 109s and 11 Fw 190s. Despite Allied bombing, production rose from 2665 Bf 109s and 1918 Fw 190s in 1942 to a massive 13,786 Bf 109s and 11,767 Fw 190s in 1944. During June 1944 alone, German industry produced 1603 Bf 109 and 689 Fw 190 single-seaters.

Losses, however, were so great that the Luftwaffe faced the war's last battles on January 10, 1945, with 1895 (1398 serviceable) single-engine piston fighters among 28 Bf 109 and 22 Fw 190 *Gruppen.* Sixteen *Schlachtgruppen* added 677 Fw 19 ground attack aircraft. Strong as the force may seem, it was far too small to cope with the masses of Allied aircraft. Not only more, but better fighters were needed; that they were not there was not the fault of German designers.

EXPERIMENTAL FIGHTERS 1942–44

As early as 1940, Messerschmitt had been asked by the RLM to offer a replacement for the Bf 109. The new design would be the Me 309, which had several new features, including a tricycle landing gear.

At first design work went slowly, because the Messerschmitt firm still hoped a practical fighter could be redesigned from the record-setting Me 209. Several Bf 109F-1s were used to try out proposed new features, such as a retractable ventral radiator, a nose wheel, pressurized cabin, and wide-track main landing gear.

Nine protypes were ordered, the first ME 309V-1 (GE+CU) being completed in June 1942. Mechanical difficulties delayed the first flight to July 18, when overheating caused it to land after only seven minutes. The Air Ministry lost interest in the design, because it did not want to interrupt fighter production for a new type of doubtful quality.

Many accidents with the first prototype used up many parts intended for later aircraft. The Me 309V-2 (GE+CV) in fact, was the original machine rebuilt. The V-3 appeared with the letters GE+CW in March 1943, and the V-4 in May (RH+LH) was the first with armament. This consisted of two MG 151s in the wing roots, a pair of MG 131s over the engine, and a pair of MK 108/30 guns in fairings at the wing's trailing edge. A 1720 hp 603A-1 was used on the V-1, but the rest had 1475 hp DB 605Bs.

The next Messerschmitt fighter to appear was the Me 209V-5 (SP+LJ) first flown on November 3, 1943. Despite its designation, it owed little to the earlier Me 209 prototypes, and at least 65 per cent of its parts were common to the Bf 109G.

Also known as Me 209-II, the new single-seater had a 1750 hp Daimler-Benz DB 603A and wide-track landing gear. A circular nose radiator added to the impression of a cross between the TA-152 and Bf 109G. Original armament was two MG 151 and two MG 131s in the wings.

Shortly after its first flight, the aircraft was tested with a 1900 hp DB 603G, and another prototype was completed with a 1750 hp Jumo 213E. The Air Ministry rejected the new design in favor of the Fw 190D-Ta 152 series, but the prototype machines were used for further high altitude developments connected with the Bf 109H project. The proposed Me 209A production series never materialized.

MESSERSCHMITT Me 209V-5 (Me 209-II)
Daimler-Benz DB 603A, 1750 hp (or Jumo 213E)
DIMENSIONS: Span 10.95 m. (35′11″), Lg. 9.6 m. (31′6″), Ht. 3.56 m. (11′8″), Wing Area 17.15 qm. (185 sq. ft.)
WEIGHT: Empty 3283 kg.–3474 kg. (7220 lb.–7643 lb.), Gross 3870 kg.–4200 kg. (8514 lb.–9240 lb.)
PERFORMANCE: Speed—Max. 724 km/hr–738 km/hr (450 mph–458 mph), Range 480 km (200 miles), Service ceiling 12,400 m.–13,000 m. (40,700′–42,650′)

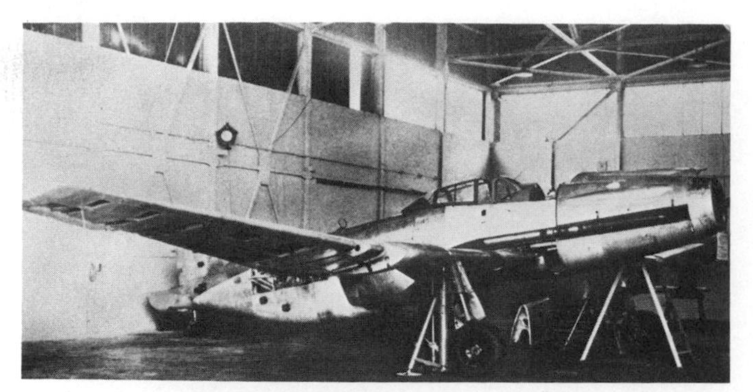

BLOHM & VOSS Bv 155
Daimler-Benz DB 603A, 1810 hp
DIMENSIONS: Span 20.33 m. (66′8″), Lg. 12.05 m. (39′6″), Ht. 3.18 m. (10′5″), Wing Area 41.5 qm. (446 sq. ft.)
WEIGHT: Empty Gross 6300 kg. (13,860 lb.)
PERFORMANCE: Speed—Max. 690 km/hr (428 mph) at 16,000 m. (52,480′), Landing speed 135 km/hr (84 mph), Range 1695 km (1050 miles), Service ceiling 16,950 m. (55,600′)

Another Messerschmitt's piston-engined fighter project began on paper as the Me 155, but was turned over to Blohm and Voss as the Bv 155V-1. The first design with this RLM number had been offered in September 1942 as a carrier-based version of the Bf 109G with a 1475 hp DB 605A. By this time, however, the carrier plan had been dropped, and the project was redone as the Me 155A single-seat bomber. Again it was rejected, only to be redone again as a Me 155B high altitude fighter.

This version appealed to the RLM, but since Messerschmitt's staff was already heavily occupied, they turned the work over to Blohm and Voss. Dr. Vogt, their chief designer, was ordered to use as many Bf 109G parts as possible, and did in fact utilize most of the fuselage and wing parts. The main differences were the addition of a large center section to the wing, a wider track landing gear and large radiators out on its wings.

Powered by a DB 603A, and armed with a 30 mm. MK 108 and two MG 151/20 guns, the Bv 155V-1 had an extremely wide wing span and prominent outboard radiators. The first flight was made on September 1, 1944, but the V-1 crashed on a later flight. Another prototype was found intact at Hamburg at the war's end. A mockup of a projected Bv 155C was also found, utilizing a laminar airfoil.

THE LONG-NOSED FOCKE-WULF

While the Focke-Wulf Fw 190A seemed superior in most qualities, its weakness was its performance at high altitudes, and new versions were prepared to correct this weakness.

A batch of Fw 190A-1s returned from the front were available for rebuilding as prototypes. Four were utilized for the Fw 190B-0 modification, which continued the 1700 hp BMW 801D-2 radial with GM-1 booster but added a pressurized pilot's cabin. The first B-0, (No. 0046) delivered without guns in January 1943, had an enlarged 20.3 qm. (218.5 sq. ft.) wing, but the rest (No. 0047–49) had the normal 18.3 qm. (197 sq. ft.) wing and two MG 17 and two MG 151 guns. Standard armament was used on the single B-1 (No. 811) converted from an A-5. No photos seem to be available for this series.

A 1750 Daimler-Benz inline DB 603 with circular radiator was the distinctive feature of the Fw 190C prototype series, all of which were also converted A-1 airframes. The first step was the Fw 190V-13, No. 0036, (SK+SJ) with a DB 603A, and the B-0's armament.

A Hirth turbosupercharger was developed for the DB 603G, offering 1740 hp for takeoff and 1390 hp at 40,000 ft. It was first installed in a scoop beneath the fuselage of the Fw 190V-18, No. 0040 (CF+OY) with a four-bladed prop, larger, wooden tail, and no guns.

Five more prototypes, V-29 to 33 (No. 0054–58) were fitted as Fw 190C-1s with turbosupercharged DB 603Gs. No. 0056 crashed on April 2, 1943, but the others survived the test program to be used later as prototypes for the Ta 152 series. Since the Hirth supercharger failed to reach serviceable reliability, the C series was abandoned.

A 1750 hp Junkers Jumo 213 and a longer fuselage

FOCKE-WULF Fw 190V-13

FOCKE-WULF Fw 190V-18 (C-0)

FOCKE-WULF Fw 190V-32 (C-1)

FOCKE-WULF Fw 190D-9
Junkers Jumo 213A-1, 1750 hp
DIMENSIONS: Span 10.5 m. (34′5″), Lg. 10.24 m. (33′5″), Ht. 3.35 m. (11′), Wing Area 18.3 qm. (197 sq. ft.)
WEIGHT: Empty 2870 kg. (7694 lb.), Gross 4309–4850 kg. (9480–10,670 lb.)
PERFORMANCE: Speed—Max. 680 km/hr (426 mph) at 7000 m. (22,960′), 571 km/hr (357 mph) at sea level, Climb 6000 m./7.1 min. (19,680′/7.1 min.), Range 850 km. (520 miles)

Fw 190V-30/U1 (Ta 152H prototype)

were seen on the Fw 190D series, which also had the C's circular nose radiator and enlarged tail. The first Jumo-powered prototype was the Fw 190V-17 (formerly A-1 No. 0039) although varied wing and gun arrangements were tried with the Jumo on V-19 to V-25. In May 1944, the modified V-17/U1 appeared in the configuration chosen for the Fw 190D-9.

Production of the long-nosed Focke-Wulfs began in August 1944. They were designated Fw 190D-9; previous D suffix numbers may have been associated with prototypes. Powered by an MW 50 boosted Jumo 213, they had two MG 131s over the engine, two MG 151/20s in the wings and a belly rack for a 300 liter (79 gal.) drop tank or 550 lb. bomb.

By the war's end, 674 Ds were completed, including several modifications. The MG 131s were replaced by a 30 mm. MK 108 *Motorkanone* on two D-10s, or by two MK 108 wing guns on seven D-11s with Jumo 213Fs. Our photo shows a D-11 flown as the Fw 190V-56 on August 31, 1944. Only a few D-12s were completed with all-weather radio equipment and D-10 armament, and only prototypes of the D-13 and D-14 variants were tested.

The last group in this fighter series was named Ta 152, to honor Kurt Tank as chief of Focke-Wulf aircraft projects. Actually, the Ta 152 was developed from the Fw 190D and its first prototypes were a further Jumo-powered reconstruction of the five A-1 aircraft that had survived the Fw 190C tests.

A new 11 m. (47′4″) wide wing was first flown with a Jumo 213E and no armament on the rebuilt Fw 190V-33/U1 (No. 0058) on July 12, 1944. It crashed the next day, but on August 9, Fw 190V-30/U1 (No. 0055) was flown with the same wing and a Jumo 213A. Bad luck continued with another crash on August 13, but by September 23, the Fw 190V-29/U1 (No. 0054) was ready with a pressurized cabin and armed with one MK 108 and two MG 151/20 guns. Other reconstructions were the V-18/U2

Fw 190V-56 (D-11) with Jumo 213F

(No. 0040) which crashed on October 8, and V-32/U1 (No. 0057) tested in November 1944 with a Jumo 213E.

Despite these misfortunes, these prototypes led to the first Ta 152 production; the 20 preproduction Ta 152H-0s. Powered by a boosted 1730 hp Jumo 213E, each had a 30 mm. MK 108 *Motorkanone* with 90 rounds, two MG 151/20s in the wing roots with 175 rpg, 150 kg. (330 lb.) of armor, and a 300 liter (79 gal.) drop tank. Internal fuel capacity was increased from 709 liters (187 gal.) to 994 liters (263 gal.) on the Ta 152H-1, with only a few completed in 1945 before the final collapse. They were used on occasion to cover the takeoff and landings of the new jet fighters.

No Ta 152A or B reached production, although many *Versuchs* models in both the Fw 190 and Ta 152 series were begun. The Ta 152C series had a smaller 11 m. (36′1″) span and a 1750 hp DB 603L with the intake on the left side, instead of the right side as on the Jumo 213. Armament included the MK 108, four MG 151/20s and a bomb rack.

The first prototype was Fw 190V-21/U1 (rebuilt No. 0039), flown November 19, 1944, with a DB 603L, and followed on February 28, 1945, with flights of the Ta 152V-6 with a DB 603L. Production was supposed to begin in March 1945 at Siebel, but it appears that only a few Ta 152C-0s were completed. Time had run out on the Luftwaffe, so the many Ta 152 variants on drawing boards or in prototype construction were forgotten. Only 67 Ta 152s had been produced before the war's end.

FOCKE-WULF Ta 152H-0 (H-1)
Jumo 213E, 1750 hp
DIMENSIONS: Span 14.4 m. (47′4″), Lg. 10.71 m. (35′1″), Ht. 3.36 m. (11′), Wing Area 23.3 qm. (250.8 sq. ft.)
WEIGHT: Empty 3921–3917 kg. (8626–8617 lb.), Gross 4730–5217 kg. (10,400–11,477 lb.), Fuel 709–994 liters (187–263 gal.)
PERFORMANCE: Speed—Max. 730–755 km/hr (453–469 mph) at 10,500 m.–12,500 m. (34,450–41,000′), Range 2010 km. (1250 miles), Service ceiling 14,800 m. (48,560′)

TANK Ta 152C-0
Daimler-Benz DB 603LA with MW 50, 2160 hp at 2200 m.
DIMENSIONS: Span 11 m. (36′1″), Lg. 10.81 kg. (35′6″), Ht. 3.38 m. (11′1″), Wing Area 19.5 qm. (210 sq. ft.)
WEIGHT: Empty 4014 kg. (8830 lb.), Gross 5322 kg. (11,798 lb.), Fuel 595–895 liters (157–236 gal.)
PERFORMANCE: Speed—Max. 730 km/hr (453 mph) at 10,500 m. (34,450′), 560 km/hr (350 mph) at sea level

21.

Twin-Engined Fighters, 1940–45

THE FIRST ZERSTOERER

When German bombers appeared over Warsaw on the war's first day, they were escorted by long-range fighters that until then had been known only by rumor. Messerschmitt's Bf 110Cs fought the war's first dogfight with the Polish defenders, driving them off.

The idea of a long-range fighter to escort bombers is credited to Hermann Goering himself. His hope was to create twin-engined two-seaters with a fighter's speed and a bomber's range. Goering became intoxicated with the concept, and design work was begun in November 1934. Messerschmitt proposed the Bf 110, and seven prototypes were ordered. Focke-Wulf and Henschel also prepared designs, but the Technical Office demanded so many modifications, including gun turrets, that their types (Fw 57 and Hs 124) finally ended as light bombers quite unable to compete with the Bf 110. Willy Messerschmitt rejected such changes, telling the RLM; "Here is my design, take it or leave it!"

The first flight of Bf 110V-1 was on May 12, 1936, and its speed of 510 km/hr (316 mph) with two new 900 hp Daimler-Benz DB 600s was the fastest of then-existing German types. The second prototype was forwarded to the Luftwaffe's Rechlin Test Center in October 1936 and the V-3 was completed in December. Pilots were impressed by the speed, but not by the limited maneuverability, yet the Luftwaffe had increased its production orders to 91 by the year's end.

The four remaining prototypes were completed from August 1937 to March 1938, designated Bf 110A-0, and armed with five 7.9 mm. guns; four in the nose and a flexible one for the second crewman. Since the Daimler had not yet reached production, two 610 hp Junkers Jumo 210Bs were used, reducing speed to only 430 km/hr (267 mph).

The first preproduction Bf 110B-0 was flown April 19, 1938, with a longer nose adding two 20 mm. MG/FFMs and deep radiators below the powerplants. Originally, these were 670 hp Jumo 210Cs with two-bladed propellers. Daimler-Benz DB 600As of 960 hp and three-bladed propellers were used on the Bf 110B-1, which was sent to Spain, but too late for action.

Meanwhile, the DB 600 had been replaced by the 1100 hp DB 601, and a preproduction Bf 110C-0 was fitted with the new powerplant. The big tunnel radiators were replaced by coolers under the wings, and the round wing tips were clipped. In January 1939, the BF 110C-1 appeared as the first operational version.

In 1939, ten Luftwaffe fighter groups were designated *Zerstoerer* (Destroyer) units,[1] but they continued to operate Bf 109C and Ds until Bf 110Cs

[1] I–II/ZG 1, I–III/ZG 2, I–III/ZG 26 and I–II/ZG 76.

MESSERSCHMITT Bf 110V-1
Daimler-Benz DB 600, 2 X 900 hp
DIMENSIONS: Span 16.81 m. (55′2″), Lg. 12 m. (39′4½″), Ht. 4.12 m. (13′6″)
PERFORMANCE: Speed—Max. 510 km/hr (317 mph)
Other data not available

Bf 110E-1

Bf 110C-0

MESSERSCHMITT Bf 110C-1
Daimler-Benz DB 601A-1, 2 X 1100 hp
DIMENSIONS: Span 16.25 m. (53′4″), Lg. 12.07 m. (39′7″), Ht. 4.13 m. (13′6″), Wing Area 38.4 qm. (413 sq. ft.)
WEIGHT: Empty 5200 kg. (11,440 lb.), Gross 6750 kg. (14,850 lb.), Fuel 1270 liters (335 gal.)
PERFORMANCE: Speed—Max. 540 km/hr (335 mph) at 6000 m. (19,680′), 475 km/hr (295 mph) at sea level, Cruising speed 350 km/hr (217 mph), Landing speed 150 km/hr (93 mph), Climb 6000 m./10.2 min. (19,680′/10.2 min.), Range 1410 km. (875 miles), Service ceiling 10,000 m. (32,800′)

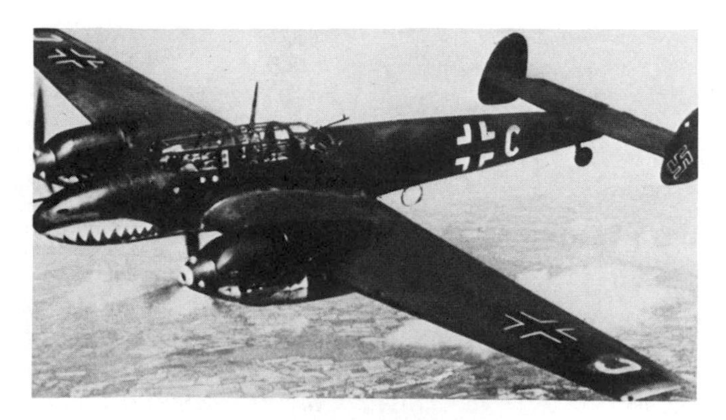

became available. The first production B 110Cs went to I/LG 1, of the elite *Lehrgeschwader* (demonstration units), then to I/ZG 1 and I/ZG 76. By September 2, 1939, these units had 68 Bf 110C-1 and 27 Bf 110B-1 fighters available.

The honor of the war's first fighter mission went to I/LG 1 at Muehlen, whose 35 Bf 110Cs escorted KG 4's Heinkel He 111Ps to Krakow on the morning of September 1, 1939. Few Polish fighters appeared then, but in the afternoon, when I/LG 1 came to Warsaw covering He 111Ps of KG 27, World War II's first big air combat took place. The Polish fighters were too slow to cope with the invaders, and were driven off, with I/LG 1 on its way to becoming the top-scoring group (28 victories) of the Polish campaign.

Losses in the Polish campaign were only 12 Bf 110Cs and as production mounted, more units were equipped with the twin-engined fighters. On December 18, 1939, I/ZG 76 scored a great success against British bombers near Wilhelmshaven. Twelve Wellingtons (34 according to German reports) were downed with the help of some Bf 109s, without any Bf 110s lost.

By the end of 1939, 264 Bf 110Cs had been delivered to the Luftwaffe, and monthly deliveries rose from 54 Bf 110Cs in January 1940 to 73 Bf 110Cs and 31 Bf 110Ds in April. By the peak of strength on April 30, 1940, 372 aircraft were with the *Zerstoerer* groups, plus about 100 in second-line status.

The various models produced that year included a Bf 110C-1/U1 glider tug, C-2 to C-4 models with radio and gun changes, and a C-4/B with racks for two 250 kg. (550 lb.) bombs. The C-5 replaced its MG/FFs with a camera for recon work, the C-6 tried

Bf 110C-5

a 30 mm. MK 101 in a ventral fairing, while the C-7 was strengthened for two 500 kg. (1100 lb.) bombs.

Increased range was built into the D series. The D-0 omitted the two 20 mm. guns, and added a 1050 liter belly tank, nicknamed *Dackelbauch,* and two 900 liter (238 gal.) tanks under the wings for a total fuel capacity of 4120 liters. In regular D-1s, however, the guns were retained and the belly tanks of the D-1/R1 were dropped in favor of 900 liter tanks under the fuselage and wing bomb racks were provided on the D-2/R2, while the D-3 could carry either bombs or drop tanks.

When Germany invaded Norway, only the Bf 110 had enough range to furnish fighter cover for the invaders, I/ZG 1 and I/ZG 76 being the groups involved. For the great battles that summer against France and Britain, the Luftwaffe used V(Z)LG 1, ZG 2, 26, and 76 and the experimental *Erprobungsgruppe* 210 fighter-bomber unit.

The Battle of Britain proved the Bf 110 was no fighter because it finally needed fighter protection itself. Spitfires were superior in speed and maneuverability, and inflicted heavy losses, the ZGs losing 235 crews in action and 11 more by accident. The Bf 110's failure meant that German bombers could not operate in daylight outside the very limited range of the lighter Bf 109s.

While the Messerschmitt failed as a long-range fighter, it was valued as an interceptor of bombers, and when the RAF turned from dropping leaflets to bombs in May 1940, German cities needed defense. Since a Bf 109 group had had little success, a night-fighter *Geschwader* (NJG 1) was formed with Bf 110s, largely of former I/ZG 1 and I/ZG 76 crewmen. They scored their first victory on July 20, 1940, but the difficulty of finding targets illuminated only by moonlight and lucky searchlights limited their success.

In June 1941, the first-line strength in twin-engined fighters included 244 aircraft with the night groups and 210 with the shrunken *Zerstoerer* groups. The night units faced West, III/ZG 2 was in Africa, and the remainder supported the invasion of Russia. By the year's end, combat losses had cut strength to 223 night fighters and only 48 more in the long-range units.

During this period Bf 110 production had dropped from 1083 (including 75 recon versions) in 1940, to 784 (190 as recon) in 1941, and 580 (79 as recon) in 1942. This reduction was due to the promised Me 210 project, which proved a failure as will be seen later.

While the Bf 110 changed little in appearance, many variants appeared. The Bf 110E-1 of 1941 could carry a 1000 kg. (2200 lb.) bomb under the fuselage and four 50 kg. (110 lb.) bombs under the wing, while the E-2 replaced the DB 601A with the 1200 hp DB 601Ns permitting a 2000 kg. (4400 lb.) bomb load. The E-3, however, omitted heavy guns and bomb racks for a camera and two 900 liter (238 gal.) drop tanks.

Installation of 1350 hp DB 601F powerplants denoted the Bf 110F of 1942, whose subtypes included an F-1 fighter-bomber armed like the E-1, an F-2 interceptor with two 210 mm. rocket projectors under each wing, and an F-3 recon version like the D-3. The Bf 110F-4 was the first version actually specialized for night fighting, with a third crewman and two 30 mm. MK 108 cannons added in a belly fairing. Further development led to the Bf 110G series, which will be discussed later.

Bf 110D-0

Bf 110D-3

Bf 110E-1

By September 1942, Bf 110s equipped three *Gruppen* and two *Staffeln* of *Zerstoerer* long-range fighters, as well as nine night fighter groups. In the latter units, they were joined by the Ju 88C and Do 217J, both improvised from successful bomber types.

In the night fighter role, these ex-bombers proved more successful than the various attempts to improve on the Bf 110 with a pure fighter design. Such types as the Fw 187, Me 210, and Ar 240 failed to either replace the Bf 110 in the "destroyer" role, or be adaptable for night work.

The first Bf 110 rival to appear was the Focke-Wulf Fw 187 *Falke* (Falcon), a twin-engined single-tailed monoplane. In 1937, the first three prototypes were completed with Junkers Jumo powerplants. The Fw 187V-1 with the 635 hp Jumo 210D and the V-2 with the 650 hp Jumo 210G were single-seaters, while a second seat was added to the V-3, also with the 210G. The third example was the first to be armed; four 7.9 mm. MG 17s and two 20 mm. MG/FF guns in the nose.

Despite V-1's crash on May 14, 1938, three more two-place prototypes were built. Two had the Jumo 210G, but Fw 187V-6 appeared in 1939 with 950 hp Daimler-Benz DB 600A engines and surface evaporation cooling. This version was credited with 600 km/hr (373 mph).

Yet Jumo 210Gs again powered three preproduction Fw 187A-0s completed in 1940. These aircraft were used to protect the builder's Bremen plant, and were briefly used at a Norwegian Luftwaffe base. At one time it was also considered as a night fighter, but was too small to accommodate the extra equipment needed.

MESSERSCHMITT Bf 110F-1
Daimler-Benz DB 601F, 1350 hp
DIMENSIONS: as Bf 110C
WEIGHT: Empty 5600 kg. (12,320 lb.), Gross 7100 kg. (15,620 lb.)
PERFORMANCE: Speed—Max. 570 km/hr (354 mph) at 5400 m. (17,700′), Cruising speed 400 km/hr (248 mph), Climb 6000 m./9 min. (19,680′/9 min.), Range 1200 km. (745 miles), Service ceiling 10,900 m. (35,760′)

FOCKE-WULF Fw 187A-0
Jumo 210Ga, 2 X 670 hp
DIMENSIONS: Span 15.3 m. (50′2½″), Lg. 11.1 m. (36′5″), Ht. 3.85 m. (12′7½″), Wing Area 30.4 qm. (327 sq. ft.)
WEIGHT: Empty 3700 kg. (8140 lb.), Gross 5000 kg. (11,000 lb.)
PERFORMANCE: Speed—Max. 525 km/hr (326 mph) 4200 m. (13,780′), Climb 6000 m./5.8 min. (19,680′/5.8 min.), Service ceiling 10,000 m. (32,810′)

FOCKE-WULF Fw 187A-0

JUNKERS Ju 88V-7

JUNKERS JU 88 FIGHTERS

Although the Junkers Ju 88 was developed as a high-speed bomber, it also became the most important German night fighter of World War II.

As early as September 27, 1938, the Ju 88V-7 with two Jumo J11Bs was flown in *Zerstoerer* form, with accommodations for three crewmen and armament in a rounded, metal nose, although no weapons were actually fitted. The first fighter version projected for the Luftwaffe was the Ju 88C-1 with two 1600 hp BMW 801A radials and two 20 mm. MG/FF and two 7.9 mm. MG 17 guns in the nose. For defense, a 7.9 mm. MG 15 fired backwards from the cabin top and another was in a gondola below the cabin.

The BMW radials were not available in quantity in 1940, so the proposed Ju 88C-1 and C-3 with modified armament were replaced in production plans by converted Ju 88A-1 bomber airframes with Jumo 211B-1 inline engines. These were completed as three-seat fighters with an MG/FF and three MG 17s fixed in the nose.

The forward guns were simply installed in the

Ju 88A-1 with fixed guns

JUNKERS Ju 88C-2
Jumo 211B, 950 hp
DIMENSIONS: Span 18.37 m. (60′3″), Lg. 14.35 m. (47′1″), Ht. 4.12 m. (13′6″), Wing Area 52.5 qm. (565 sq. ft.)
WEIGHT: Gross 11,160 kg. (24,607 lb.)
PERFORMANCE: Speed—Max. 495 km/hr (307 mph), Climb 6000 m./14.5 min. (19,680′/14.5 min.), Range 3050–4150 km. (1894–2577 miles), Service ceiling 9400 m. (30,840′)

glazed nose of the first of these, which may have been the six Ju 88As converted to long-range fighters in April 1940. Later that year the standard fighter model emerged as the Ju 88C-2, the A-1 series aircraft with the four fixed guns in a metal nose. By then Germany needed night fighters, so the C-2s went to II/NJG 1 organized in July 1940 to operate with I/NJG 1's Bf 110s.[2]

A wider, 20.5 m. (65′10″) span wing introduced on the A-5 bomber was also used on the Ju 88C-4 fighter. Sent on intruder operations against British bomber bases in 1941, the C-4 had two added MG 17 nose guns. No ventral gun was provided, but for ground attack a WB 81 pod with six 7.9 mm. guns could be added below each wing. An experimental Ju 88C-5 two-seater was built with BMW radials, an MG 151/20 and three MG 17s in the nose, two more MG 17s back under the fuselage, and an MG 15 dorsal gun.

Sixty-two Ju 88 night fighters were delivered in 1940 and 66 in 1941, with 207 added in 1942 as the bomber offensive grew. The model produced in the largest numbers was the Ju 88C-6 with 1410 hp Jumo 211J inline engines. Normal armament for day fighting (C-6a) was an MG/FF and three MG 17 nose guns, plus paired MG 81s in both dorsal and ventral positions. Airborne radar was introduced on the night fighters (C-6b), with three MG/FF and three MG 17 nose guns, two dorsal MG 81s, but no ventral guns. The Lichtenstein BC (FuG 202) radar used on early models had a 2½ mile range and its antenna array was cumbersome, but it greatly increased chances of intercepting British bombers.

Parallel to the C-6b, Junkers produced the Ju 88R-1, which appeared in 1943 with 1600 hp BMW 801A radials and similar armament and radar, and the R-2 with 1700 hp BMW 801D radials. When a Ju 88R-1 was delivered to Britain by a defecting crew on May 9, 1943, the radar system was compromised, and it became possible to jam it with "Window" metal foil dropped from bombers. The Lichtenstein SN 2 (FuG 220) radar was developed to evade jamming and increase acquisition range, and the Flensburg receiver was added to detect British tail-warning radar. These new electronic systems were added to the Ju 88C-6c.

Ju 88C-5 experimental

Ju 88C-6

[2] II/NJG 1 became I/NJG 2 in September 1940, and was assigned to long-range intruder missions.

Ju 88C-6 with *Schraege Musik* (2/20 mm.)

JUNKERS Ju 88C-6b
Jumo 211J, 1410 hp
DIMENSIONS: Span 20.08 m. (65′10″), Lg. 14.96 m. (47′1″), Ht. 4.8 m. (15′9″), Wing Area 54.5 qm. (586.64 sq. ft.)
WEIGHT: Empty 8577 kg. (18,871 lb.), Gross 11,800 kg. (25,960 lb.)
PERFORMANCE: Speed—Max. 500 km/hr (311 mph) at 6000 m. (19,680′), Cruising speed 425 km/hr (264 mph), Range 3120 km. (1950 miles), Service ceiling 9900 m. (32,500′)

JUNKERS Ju 88R-2
BMW 801D, 1700 hp
DIMENSIONS: as Ju 88C-6
WEIGHT: Data not available
PERFORMANCE: Speed—Max. 580 km/hr (360 mph), Range 3000 m. (1860 miles), Service ceiling 9000 m. (29,520′)

Ju 88G-1 (captured)

Schraege Musik (Slant music) was upward-slanting paired MG 151/20 guns mounted behind the cockpits. First used in combat on August 17, 1943, it was added to later C-6 models. Some Ju 88C-7s were delivered equipped for daytime ground attack with 500 kg. (1100 lb.) of splinter bombs in the bay and three MG/FF and three MG 17 fixed guns. Jumo 211Js were used in the C-7a and the C-7b with a 1500 kg. (3300 lb.) bomb aboard, but a few C-7cs had BMW 801 MA radials.

Junkers fighter production increased from 406 in 1943 to 2518 in 1944. Along with the Bf 110 and Do 217, they took an ever-increasing toll of the enemy bombing force. Their greatest night victory was on March 30–31, 1944, when 246 German fighters sortied against 795 four-engined British bombers and downed 95 of the foe.

Parallel to the night fighters, Junkers developed a few day fighters. For the long-range role, ten Ju 88H-2 aircraft were modified from G-1s at Merseburg by lengthening the fuselage to 17.65 m. (57′11″) to increase fuel capacity. Armament was six MG 151/20s and an MG 131 gun and range was reported at 4680 km (2900 miles).

A 1942 development was the Ju 88P series, using heavy anti-tank guns for attacks on American heavy bombers. The first version, the Ju 88P-1 powered by two 1410 hp Jumo 211Js was a rebuilt A-4 with a 75 mm. Pak 40 in a ventral fairing that also contained twin 7.9 mm. MG 81Z guns, pointing backward, and the usual MG 131 flexible dorsal gun. The gun's exhaust gases interfered with the propellers, and the project failed. Ten A-4s from the Merseburg line were completed as Ju 88P-2 with two 37 mm. Flak 38s in the ventral pod and 1200 hp Jumo 211G powerplants. The P-3 was similar, but for 1200 hp Jumo 211H engines.

In 1944, a 50 mm. BK 5 (KWK 39) gun was installed in 30 A-4s modified to a Ju 88P-4 configuration. All these big gun versions suffered a drastic speed reduction that made them unpopular in service.

The Junkers Ju 88G appeared in 1944 as the first model solely intended for night fighting. This three-seater had four MG 151/20 guns in a belly tray, where the flash would not blind the pilot, and the

Ju 88P-1 (75 mm. gun)

Ju 88P-2 (2/37 mm. guns)

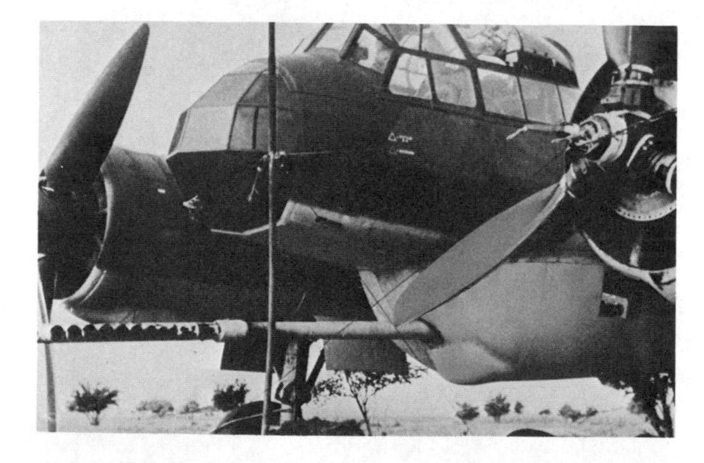

Ju 88P-4 (50 mm. gun)

Ju 88H-2 long-range fighter

Ju 388J (V-2)

Ju 88G-6 (SN 2 radar)

Ju 88G-6 (FuG 218 radar)

Ju 88G-7c (FuG 240 radar)

nose was cleared for the SN 2 radar. Powerplants were two 1700 hp BMW 801D radials on the Ju 88G-0 and G-1. The former still had two 20 mm. guns in the nose, but they were removed because they interfered with the radar antenna. A single MG 131 flexible gun was mounted in the rear of the cabin, firing past the new vertical tail also used on the Ju 188 bomber. Our photo shows a Ju 88G-1 landed by mistake in Britain on July 13, 1944, thus compromising the SN 2 and the Flensburg device. Once again new jamming techniques could be devised to frustrate the German defense.

Subtypes G-2 to 5 were only experimental rigs, but the Ju 88G-6 was built in large numbers in 1944. Inline 1750 hp Jumo 213E powerplants were the main difference with the G-1, but many had *Schraege Musik*, the paired upward-slanting 20 mm. guns, and some had twin 7.9 mm. MG 81Z guns fixed under the rudder for tail protection.

Last in this series was the Ju 88G-7, which also had the Jumo 213E. The Ju 88G-7a batch had the normal SN 2 antenna, but G-7b of 1945 had FuG 218 *Neptun* radar with the *Morgenstern* antenna partially enclosed in a wooden nose cone, while the advanced FuG 240 *Berlin* radar with an enclosed dish antenna was introduced on a few G-7c models.

The last of the Junkers night fighter types was the Ju 388J-1, *Stoertebeker,* based on the Ju 388V-2 prototype of January 1944. Powered by two 1810 hp BMW 801TJ radials, the Ju 388J-1 was armed with two MG 151/20s and two 30 mm. MK 103 fixed guns in a belly tray, and had two MG 131s in a remote-controlled tail turret. An FuG 220 radar array protruded from the nose. Only three Ju 388J-1s were completed, for the He 219 was considered a better night fighter.

From 1940 to 1945, 3964 Junkers Ju 88 fighter versions were delivered. Of 28 Luftwaffe night fighter *Gruppen* in January 1945, 16 were entirely or partially equipped with Ju 88Gs. Four groups flew Messerschmitt Bf 110G/H types entirely, and six groups shared both major types. One group had Heinkel He 219s and another was working up with Me 262 jets.

ME 210

Messerschmitt began the Me 210 two-seater in 1938 as a Bf 110 replacement with long range fighter, dive bomber and reconnaissance capabilities. The Me 210V-1 was flown September 2, 1939, with twin rudders and two DB 601As, but was later rebuilt with the single vertical tail that became an Me 210 feature.

On October 10, the Me 210V-2 was flown with a mockup of the Me 210's other innovation, two remote-controlled gun barbettes in the fuselage sides behind the cockpit. Defensive firepower was in-

MESSERSCHMITT Me 210V-1

MESSERSCHMITT Me 210A-1/A-2
Daimler-Benz DV 601F, 2 X 1395 hp at takeoff
DIMENSIONS: Span 16.34 m. (53'7"), Lg. 11.2/12.12 m. (36'9"/39'9"), Ht. 3.7/4.28 m. (12'2"/14'), Wing Area 36.2 qm. (390 sq. ft.)
WEIGHT: Empty 7070/7270 kg. (15,554/15,994 lb.), Gross 9706/10,690 kg. (21,353/23,518 lb.), Fuel 2546 liters (672 gal.)
PERFORMANCE: Speed—Max. 564/538 km/hr (350/334 mph) at 5400/5200 m. (17,700/17,060'), 463/450 km/hr (288/279 mph) at sea level, Landing speed 145/188 km/hr (90/117 mph), Climb 6000 m./12/13 min. (19,680'/12/13 min.), Range 1820/1440 km. (1130/895 miles), Service ceiling 8900 m. (29,206')

Me 210A-1/A-2

ARADO Ar 240V-3

creased from the Bf 110's single hand-operated 7.9 mm. gun to two 13 mm. power-operated MG 131s. The crew's cockpit had bulging canopy sides, and an armor apron for the gunner, with front and back pilot's armor, installed on production aircraft.

The preproduction Me 210A-0s went to Erprobungsgruppe 210 in 1940 for service tests, and in 1941 the first 92 Me 210A-1s were delivered with the 1350 hp DB 601F. Armament included two MG 151/20s and two MG 17 nose guns, the two MG 131 barbettes, and a bomb bay under the cockpit for two 500 kg. (1100 lb.) bombs. Armor weighing some 900 lb. protected the crew and engines, and external racks on the later Me 210A-2 doubled the bomb capacity.

Some of the first aircraft were tried on the Russian front by II/ZG 1, but the unit returned to Bf 110s when the Me 210 proved unsatisfactory. Serious instability caused frequent crashes, and a lengthened fuselage and other modifications failed to help. An RLM order on April 14, 1942, halted Me 210 production and reinstated further Bf 110 output.

Many Me 210s were in half-finished condition, so when leading-edge slots added in July 1942 improved flying qualities, deliveries were resumed. Besides some 15 V types and the A-0 series, 348 As were completed by 1944. Four Me 210B recon versions were rebuilt from A-0 aircraft with the MG 17 nose replaced by cameras.

Among the prototypes was the Me 210V-13, to test the pressurized cabin and four-bladed propellers planned for the projected Me 310. New 1475 hp DB 605 engines were to be used on Me 210C fighter and Me 210D recon models, but these engines were instead assigned to the Bf 110G; a more reliable choice than further Me 210 production.

ARADO 240

The twin-engined Arado Ar 240 was designed for the same fighter, dive-bomber, or recon missions as the Me 210. The Ar 240V-1 first flew on May 10, 1940, with 1175 hp Daimler-Benz Db 601As behind circular radiators and an umbrella-type dive brake behind the twin rudders.

ARADO Ar 240A-0
Daimler-Benz DB 601E, 1175 hp
DIMENSIONS: Span 14.335 m. (47′), Lg. 12.81 m. (42′), Ht. 3.95 m. (13′), Wing Area 31.3 qm. (336.79 sq. ft.)
WEIGHT: Empty 6200 kg. (13,640 lb.), Gross 9450 kg. (20,790 lb.), Fuel 2775 liters (732 gal.)
PERFORMANCE: Speed—Max. 618 km/hr (384 mph) at 6000 m. (19,680′), Cruising speed 555 km/hr (344 mph), Climb 6000 m./11 min. (19,680′/11 min.), Range 2000 km. (1220 miles), Service ceiling 10,550 m. (34,450′)

The second prototype was completed with armament, two MG 151/20s and two 7.9 mm. MG 17 nose guns. For rear defense, Arado designed remote-controlled barbettes above and below the fuselage. Fitted with twin 7.9 mm. MG 81Z guns, they were installed on the longer Ar 240V-3, which had its pressurized cockpit moved forward in the nose and replaced the tail brakes with fins.

Numerous modifications, including new ailerons, were tried to improve stability, and the V-3 was used as a recon plane in the Channel area. A dive-bomber prototype, the Ar 240V-4 had 1750 hp DB 603As, racks for four 1100 lb. bombs, and tail brakes.

Five preproduction Ar 240A-0 aircraft were made, and the first two were delivered in October 1942 with two 1350 hp DB 601Es and a redesigned wing. Both were used in Finland by JG 5, and the third went to 2(F)AGr 122 in Italy. Two more were completed with 1750 hp DB 603As and saw limited service in the reconnaissance role, but a plan for quantity production was canceled in December 1942.

Two Ar 240B-0 aircraft completed with 1475 hp DB 605As were also known as the V-7 and V-8, while four larger Ar 240C-0s had the 1750 hp DB 603A, six MG 151/20 forward guns and twin MG 131s in the turrets, and up to 2000 kg. (4400 lb.) of bombs. Finally, the DB 603G, two 30 mm. MK 108 and three MG 151/20 guns were used on the redesigned Arado Ar 440 experimental.

MESSERSCHMITT Bf 110G-2
Daimler-Benz DB 605B-1, 2 X 1475 hp
DIMENSIONS: as Bf 110F series
WEIGHT: Empty 5700 kg. (12,540 lb.), Gross 7300 kg. (16,060 lb.), Fuel 1270–1870 liters (335–494 gal.)
PERFORMANCE: Speed—Max. 595 km/hr (370 mph) at 6000 m. (19,680′), Cruising speed 450 km/hr (279 mph), Landing speed 145 km/hr (90 mph), Climb 6000 m./6.9 min. (19,680′/6.9 min.), Range 1000 km. (620 miles), Service ceiling 11,000 m. (36,090′)

BF 110G

As it became clear that the Bf 110 would continue to be the Luftwaffe's principal *Zerstoerer,* production increased from 580 in 1942 to 1580 in 1943 and 1525 in 1944. Most were Bf 110Gs; like the Bf 109G powered by the 1475 hp DB 605A.

Deliveries began late in 1942 with a Bf 110G-0 batch and the Bf 110G-1 early in 1943. Like earlier models, they had four MG 17s with 1000 7.9 mm. rpgs and two MG/FFs with 180 20 mm. rpg in the nose, and a flexible MG 15 with 750 rpg for the gunner. The widely produced Bf 110G-2, however, had the four MG 17s mounted with two MG 151/20s with 300–350 rpg and twin 7.9 mm. MG 81Zs with 400 rpg in the rear. Racks were provided for two 500 kg. (1100 lb.) bombs under the fuselage and four 50 kg. (110 lb.) bombs or two 300 liter (79 gal.) drop tanks under the wings. From five to ten mm. armor thickness protected the cockpit's front, back and bottom.

Ruestsatzen (kit modifications) for this series included;

Bf 110G-2/R1: a 37 mm. Flak 18 with 72 rds replacing the 20 mm. guns.
Bf 110G-2/R2: as R1 plus GM 1 engine booster.
Bf 110G-2/R3: with two 30 mm. MK 180 and four MG 151/20s and no bombs.
Bf 110G-2/R4: with two 30 mm. MK 108s and 37 mm. Flak 18 and no bombs.
Bf 110G-2/R5: as R4 plus GM 1, and no rear guns.

Parallel with these models was the Bf 110G-3 long-range recon model with cameras, and 150 were delivered in 1943. Normally only the four MG 17 and twin MG 81Z guns were carried, but a *backward*-firing fixed MG 151/20 was sometimes installed, and a G-3/R3 version had two MK 108 nose guns.

From early 1943 on, night fighting became the Bf 110's principal mission. Airborne radar had first been used for a Bf 110 combat victory on August 9, 1941, but was applied to Ju 88 fighters more often than to the Bf 110 in 1942. The first production

Bf 110G-4/R1 (C 1 radar)

MESSERSCHMITT Bf 110G-4/R3 (SN 2 radar)
Daimler-Benz DB 605B-1, 2 X 1475 hp at takeoff, 1250 hp at 5800 m. (19,000′)
DIMENSIONS: Span 16.25 m. (53′4″), Lg. 13.05 m. (42′10″), Ht. 4.18 m. (13′8½″), Wing Area 38.4 qm. (413 sq. ft.)
WEIGHT: Empty 5094 kg. (11,207 lb.), Gross 9888 kg. (21,754 lb.), Fuel 1270 liters (335 gal.)
PERFORMANCE: Speed—Max. 550 km/hr (342 mph) at 6980 m. (22,900′), 500 km/hr (311 mph) at sea level, Cruising speed 510 km/hr (317 mph), Landing speed 150 km/hr (93 mph), Climb 5500 m./8 min. (18,440′/8 min.), Range 900/2100 km. (560/1300 miles), Service ceiling 11,000 m. (36,090′)

MESSERSCHMITT Me 410A-1 (V-1 in photo)
Daimler-Benz DB 603A-1, 2 X 1720 hp
DIMENSIONS: Span 16.39 m. (53′9½″), Lg. 12.4 m. (40′8″), Ht. 3.7 m. (12.2′), Wing Area 36.2 qm. (390 sq. ft.)
WEIGHT: Empty 6150 kg. (13,530 lb.), Gross 10,760 kg. (23,672 lb.), Fuel 5000 liters (1320 gal.)
PERFORMANCE: Speed—Max. 624 km/hr (387 mph) at 6700 m. (22,000′), Climb 6000 m./10.7 min. (19,680′/10.7 min.), Range 2500 km. (1550 miles), Service ceiling 10,370 m. (34,000′)

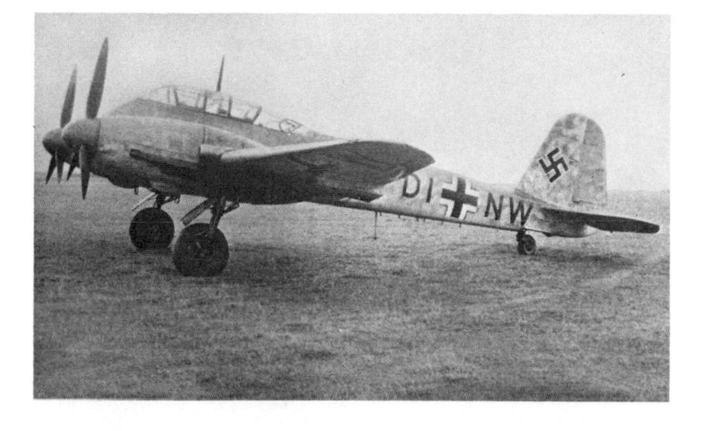

model was the Lichtenstein C 1 (FuG 212) radar whose protruding antenna offered a 24 degree angle of search and 35 cm wave length. After the British learned to jam it in July 1943, the Germans shifted to the more elaborate Lichtenstein SN 2 (FuG 220) with a 120 degree search angle and 330 cm wave length. Its cumbersome four-pole, *Hirschgeweih* (stag's antlers) antenna was seen on Bf 110G-4 and Ju 88G-6 fighters in October 1943.

As the first strictly night fighter version, the Bf 110G-4 added radar, more pilot armor, and two MG 151/20s in a belly tray, and deleted the second crewmen's armor. Two 1475 hp DB 605Bs were used, but the antenna reduced the top speed. Numerous modifications included the G-4/U7 with GM 1 booster and G-4/U8 providing two 900 liter (238 gal.) drop tanks.

The most widely used version was the Bf 110G-4/R3 three-seater with Lichtenstein SN 2 plus two MK 108 and two MG 151/20s in the nose. Other *Ruestsatzen* provided GM 1, extra fuel tanks, two more MG 151/20s in a belly tray, or combined both radar types. Five 21 cm WG 21 rocket tubes could be added under the wings for long-range attack on daylight bomber groups, or a dozen smaller tubes attached under the fuselage.

Last was the Bf 110H series, with a strengthened structure and tailwheel. Two MK 108s and a 37 mm. Flak 18 were provided on the H-2/R1, while the H-2/R2 added GM 1 boosters. The H-3 was a recon model retaining the MK 108s, and the H-4 had radar and two more MG 151/20s under the belly.

When the last 45 Bf 110s were delivered in 1945, production since September 1939 reached 5762; 3028 as long-range fighters, 2240 radar-equipped night fighters (1943–45) and 494 recon versions (1940–43). Pre-war deliveries add some 150 machines to this total.

THE LAST ZERSTOERER

After the Me 210's failure, Messerschmitt had to prepare a new heavy fighter for the same role. There was an Me 310 design with DB 603As, wider wings and pressurized cabin, but this was canceled in favor of the simpler Me 410, essentially a 210 with the 310's 1720 hp DB 603A powerplants.

After trials with seven modified 210As, an Me 410V-1 *Hornisse* (Hornet) was tested and Me 410A-1 deliveries began in 1943. Basic armament was two MG 17 (1000 rds) and two MG 151/20 (300 rds) guns in the nose, two MG 131s (450 rds) in remote-controlled barbettes, and up to 2000 kg. in the internal bomb bay below the two crewmen's cockpit.

There were several modifications: Me 410A-1/U1 had a camera in the bay and omitted the MG 17s, A-1/U2 added two more MG 151/20s in a WB 151 pod in the bay, and A-1/U4 added a long 50 mm. BK 5 gun with 21 rds to the standard armament.

Me 410A-1/U2

MESSERSCHMITT Me 410A-3 (captured)

The Me 410-2 had two MG 151/20s and two 30 mm. MK 103 nose guns, and also used the U1 and U4 modifications. Three cameras were mounted in the Me 210A-3s bulged bay, while the standard pairs of of MG 151/20 nose and MG 131 barbette guns were retained.

The armament of the Me 410B series was two MG 151/20 and two MG 131s in the nose, as well as the usual barbette guns. The B-2 added two more 20 mm. guns in a WB 151 mount in the bay, while B2/U1 had them in a WT 151 tray under the fuselage, and B-2/U2 had four MG 151/20s in the bomb bay. The B-2/U3 had FuG 200 *Hohentwiel* radar for antishipping work along with two 30 mm. MK 103 and two MG 131s in the bay, while B-2/R2 had six forward guns (two each of MG 131, MG 151/20 and 30 mm. MK 108). Similar except for MK 103s was the B-2/R3, while the B-3 had three cameras, two MG 131s in the nose, and two on the barbettes.

Production amounted to 1013 Me 410s in 1943–44, including 113 in reconnaissance configurations. They served with the last *Zerstoerer* group (IV/ZG 26) in January 1945, and with FAGr 122.

DORNIER NIGHT FIGHTERS

The first Dornier night fighter was an improvisation, the Do 17Z-6. Called the Kaus (Little Owl), this rebuilt Do 17Z-3 recon bomber had added a Ju 88C-1 nose section with a 20 mm. MG/FF and three 7.9 mm. MG 17s fixed guns.

This experiment led to nine Do 17Z-10 night fighters delivered in summer 1940 with a new cabin carrying four MG/FF and four MG 17 guns in the nose, a flexible dorsal MG 15, and a crew of three. A spanner II Anlange infrared spotlight was also tried, although it proved unsuitable and was later removed in favor of early FuG 212 airborne radar.

A few Dornier Do 215B-5s, similar but for Daimler engines, were also modified into fighter configuration, but the Dornier ships were considered inferior to the Ju 88C. Lessons learned on these aircraft were incorporated into a fighter version of the later Do 217 bomber.

The first Do 217J night fighter was flown on July 31, 1942. Essentially the Do 217Js were Do 217Es finished at Friedrichshafen as three-seat fighters and powered by 1600 hp DMW 801A radials. Four MG/FF guns were set low in the nose with four MG 17s above them, and two MG 131 flexible guns were provided in the top turret and ventral position usual to the bomber. A bay for eight 110 lb. bombs was provided on the Do 217J-1, but the more common Do 217J-2 sealed the bomb bay, replaced the MG/FF guns with MG 151/20 weapons, and had Lichtenstein C-1 (FuG 212) radar.

Parallel with the Do 217M bomber came the Do 217N fighter, which differed from the J series mainly by the 1750 hp Daimler DB 603A inline engines. Forward armament comprised the same four 20 mm. and 7.9 mm. guns with a 13 mm. gun in the rear turret, but the Do 217N-2 eliminated the ventral position retained on the N-1.

Lichtenstein radar was utilized, the C 1 of earlier ships being later replaced by improved SN 2 sets. A frequent modification was provision for *Schraege Musik;* two to four MG 151/20 guns slanted upward 70 degrees from the rear fuselage. Production of the Do 217J and N totaled 364 and ended in 1944.

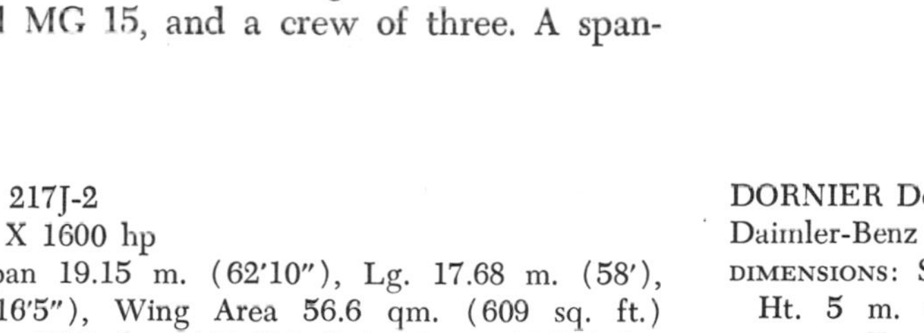

DORNIER DO 217J-2
DMW 807A, 2 X 1600 hp
DIMENSIONS: Span 19.15 m. (62'10"), Lg. 17.68 m. (58'), Ht. 5 m. (16'5"), Wing Area 56.6 qm. (609 sq. ft.)
WEIGHT: Empty 8730 kg. (19,206 lb.), Gross 15,900 kg. (34,980 lb.)
PERFORMANCE: Speed—Max. 520 km/hr (323 mph) at 4000 m. (13,120'), Cruising speed 465 km/hr (288 mph), Landing speed 148 km/hr (92 mph), Climb 1000 m./3.5 min. (3280'/3.5 min.), Range 2050 km. (1270 miles), Service ceiling 7300 m. (23,940')

DORNIER Do 217N-2
Daimler-Benz DB 603A, 2 X 1750 hp
DIMENSIONS: Span 19.15 m. (62'10"), Lg. 17.45 m. (57'3"), Ht. 5 m. (16'5"), Wing Area 56.6 qm. (609 sq. ft.)
WEIGHT: Empty 10,280 kg. (22,616 lb.), Gross 13,210 kg. (29,062 lb.)
PERFORMANCE: Speed—Max. 536 km/hr (332 mph) at 6800 m. (22,300'), Cruising speed 510 km/hr (317 mph), Landing speed 150 km/hr (93 mph), Climb 1000 m./3 min. (3280'/3 min.), Range 2050 km. (1270 miles), Service ceiling 8200 m. (26,900')

Do 217N-2 with radar added

HEINKEL HE 219

Among the most effective wartime additions to Germany's night fighters was the Heinkel He 219A, but this two-seater suffered much from the Luftwaffe bureaucracy.

Heinkel's project office began designing a multipurpose monoplane in August 1940, incorporating two Daimler-Benz engines, twin rudders, and nosewheel landing gear. At first the design aroused little RLM interest, but when their need for night fighters became evident, the project was revived and detail design began in January 1942.

A British bombing of Heinkel's Rostock-Marienehe factory destroyed the drawings and files on the He 219, but the first prototype itself escaped damage. The project was transferred to Heinkel's Vienna plant, where the He 219V-1 first flew November 15, 1942. Powered by 1750 hp DB 603As behind circular radiators, it had a speed of 440 km/hr (273 mph) at sea level and 615 km/hr (382 mph) at altitude.

Performance was considered so excellent that Major General Josef Kammhuber, night-fighter commander, urged quick formation of an operational group. Comparative tests in March 1943 showed the Heinkel superior to the Ju 88G and Do 217N, and in April, 300 were ordered.

By then four prototypes had been finished. Originally with V numbers, the first aircraft built had "zero series" designations when equipped for service testing. The He 219V-1 received a belly tray with four 30 mm. MK 108s in February 1943, adding to two MG 131s in the wing roots. A Lichtenstein C I (FuG 202) radar was first installed on He 219V-4 in March 1943. Redesignated He 219A-0/R2, the V-1 also got C I radar and MK 103 guns, and other prototypes became He 219A-0/1 to R6 with various armament and equipment changes.

These early aircraft came to NJG I's base at Venlo in the Netherlands, and on June 11, 1943, Major Werner Streib took the first He 219 on a sortie against British bombers. Five were shot down on this mission and, although his machine crashed on landing, Streib praised the plane highly.

Production aircraft were to be armed with four 30 mm. MK 103s in the ventral tray and two MG 151/20 guns in the wing roots, an arrangement installed in July 1943 on He 219A-0/R3, the A-2 series prototype. Lichtenstein SN 2 radar was first installed on the He 219A-0/R6, (originally the V-11) which became the V-16 prototype of the future A-5 series.

Eleven preproduction aircraft were completed by the end of 1943, and monthly He 219A-2 deliveries rose from five in January 1944 to 15 in June. Uneven

HEINKEL He 219A-5 (prototype in photo)
Daimler-Benz DB 603E, 2 X 1380 hp
DIMENSIONS: Span 18.5 m. (60′8″), Lg. 16.3 m. (53′5½″), Ht. 4.2 m. (13′9″), Wing Area 44.5 qm. (479 sq. ft.)
WEIGHT: Empty 8345 kg. (18,359 lb.), Gross 13,575 kg. (29,865 lb.)
PERFORMANCE: Speed—Max. 615 km/hr (381 mph) clean, 585 km/hr (363 mph) with radar and exhaust cover at sea level, Range 2850 km. (1770 miles), Service ceiling 9400 m. (30,830′)

HEINKEL He 219A-7
Daimler-Benz DB 603G, 2 X 1900 hp
DIMENSIONS: as He 219A-5
WEIGHT: Empty 8510 kg. (18,722 lb.), Gross 14,245 kg. (31,339 lb.), Fuel 2598 liters (685 gal.)
PERFORMANCE: Speed—Max. 630 km/hr (391 mph) clean, 600 km/hr (372 mph) with radar, Range 2800 km. (1736 miles), Service ceiling 10,300 m. (33,780′)

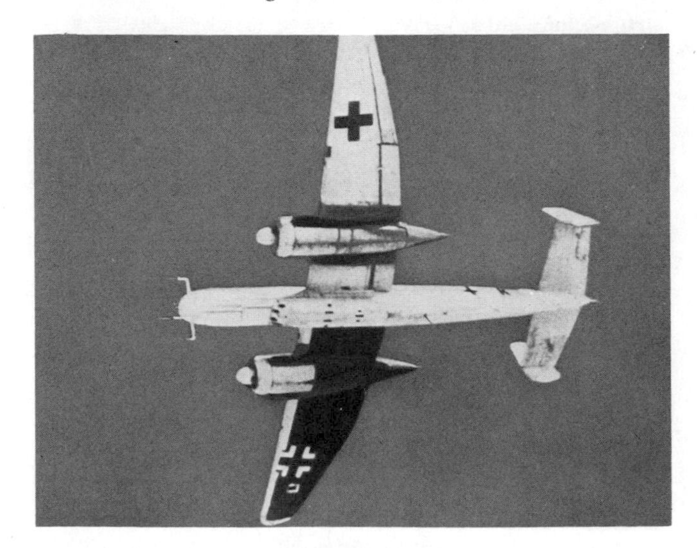

FOCKE-WULF Ta 154V-1

FOCKE-WULF Ta 154V-3

gun deliveries resulted in a variety of weapons in the belly tray, a common arrangement being two MG 151/20s and two MK 108 guns. *Schraege Musik*, two MG 151/20s slanting upward from the rear fuselage, was introduced on the V-19, and retrofitted to most production models.

State Secretary Erhard Milch of the RLM favored stopping production of the He 219A in favor of the Ju 88G, although no Ju 88Gs were yet ready. His complaint that the Heinkel carried no bombs seems unjustified in view of the immediate removal of bomb racks by the night-fighter units from BF 110, Ju 88, and Do 217 aircraft they received. Perhaps Milch was prejudiced against Heinkel because of Milch's previous close connections with Junkers. Again on April 25, 1944, the RLM decided to halt Heinkel production in favor of the Ju 388J and Ta 154, although neither was yet in production status.

In June 1944, serial production was ordered of the He 219B with a Jumo 222 engine, although raw material shortages made it impossible to expect quantity production of this engine model. However, in November 1944, the RLM terminated the production of all twin-engined aircraft but the Dornier Do 335. This order was ignored by the Heinkel works, which continued He 219 production to the war's end.

A pair of 1800 hp DB 603E engines powered the He 219A-5 which had FuG 220 radar with antenna in the rear, as well as the four nose poles. Six forward M 151/20s were accommodated in the belly tray and wing roots, but the several R versions varied. The A-5/R2 for example, used both FuG 212 and FuF 220 radar, two MK 108 *Schraege Musik* guns, two more in the tray, and the wing root MG 151/20s.

The He 219A-7 was the last production series with DB 603Gs and normally accommodated four MK 108s in the tray, with two more slanting upward, as well as the two wing root guns. Two MG 151/20s sometimes replaced two of the tray guns in the A-7/R2 to R4 modifications. Among the variants appearing in only small numbers were six A-7/R5s with Jumo 213E engines, and a single three-place He 219B-1 whose Jumo 222s failed to appear and had to be replaced by DB 603As. It crashed on its second flight, and further D and C aircraft never received the promised Jumo 222 powerplants.

Total production of the He 219 amounted to 274 aircraft, including six not built by Heinkel, but assembled from spares, by a Luftwaffe maintenance unit. I/NJG 1 was the Heinkel type's principal user.

FOCKE-WULF TA 154A-1

The British DH Mosquito's high speed had made a sharp impression on the Germans, and so in September 1942, Focke-Wulf's Technical Director Kurt Tank was asked to develop a night fighter to catch it. His answer was the Ta 154A-1, a twin-engined two-seater with tricycle gear, clean lines and wooden construction to save strategic metals.

Chief Engineer Ernst Nipp prepared the first prototype in ten months, and Ta 154V-1 (TE+FE) made

FOCKE-WULF Ta 154A-1
Jumo 213A, 2 X 1750 hp
DIMENSIONS: Span 16 m. (52'6"), Lg. 12.6 m. (41'3"), Ht. 3.67 m. (12'3⅓"), Wing Area 32.4 qm. (348.62 sq. ft.)
WEIGHT: Gross 8845 kg. (19,459 lb.), Fuel 1500 liters (396 gal.)
PERFORMANCE: Speed—Max. 632 km/hr (392 mph) at 8000 m. (26,240'), Climb 8000 m./14.5 min. (26,240'/14.5 min.), Range 1370 km. (850 miles), Service ceiling 10,920 m. (35,820')

its maiden flight July 7, 1943, at Langenhagen. Two 1500 hp Jumo 211Rs powered it and the V-2, but the 1750 hp Jumo 213 was used on the third prototype. Ta 154V-3 (TE+FG) flew on November 25, provided with two 30 mm. MK 108 and two 20 mm. MG 151 forward guns and Lichtenstein C 1 radar.

Four further prototypes, V-4 to V-7, were built in 1944, and 250 aircraft were ordered in November 1943. Eight preproduction Ta 154A-0s, also with V numbers -8 to -14, equipped with Lichtenstein SN 2 radar were built at Erfurt and Posen (now the Polish Poznan) from June to August 1944.

Two Ta 154A-1s were built at Erfurt, with the rest to be assembled at Posen. On June 28, 1944, however, the second Ta 154A-1 broke up in flight, and the first crashed some days later. Investigation proved the fault to be in the glue; the original glue used in the prototypes was unavailable, and the replacement glue's acid weakened the wooden joints.

Production was canceled after seven more A-1s were finished at Posen. This factory also built six with warhead noses and a pilot ejection seat. The idea was to fly into a bomber formation, and eject before the warhead exploded. This semi-suicide tactic, fortunately, was never tried.

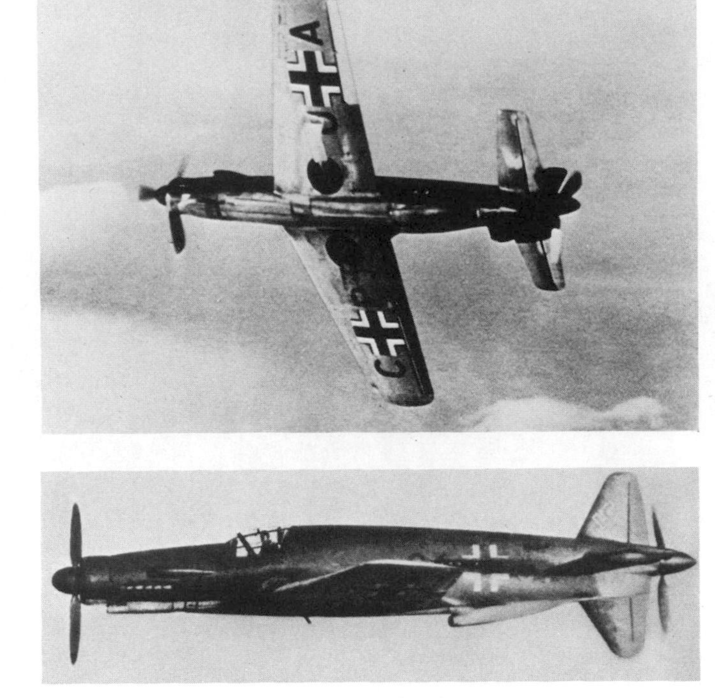

DORNIER Do 335V-1
Daimler-Benz DB 603A-2, 1750 hp
DIMENSIONS: Span 13.8 m. (45'3"), Lg. 13.85 m. (45'5"), Ht. 5 m. (16'5"), Wing Area 38.5 qm. (414 sq. ft.)
WEIGHT: Empty 7260 kg. (15,792 lb.), Gross 9150 kg. (20,130 lb.)
PERFORMANCE: Speed—Max. 732 km/hr (455 mph), Cruising speed 550 km/hr (341 mph), Landing speed 190 km/hr (118 mph), Climb 1000 m./1 min. (3280'/1 min.) 8000 m./14.5 min. (26,250'/14.5 min.), Range 2150 km. (1335 miles), Service ceiling 10,700 m. (35,100')

DORNIER DO 335 "ARROW"

Germany's last propeller-driven warplane design in production was also one of the most unusual in appearance. Dornier's Do 335 *Pfeil* (arrow) tandem "push-pull" engine arrangement was unique; the pilot sat between two Daimler-Benz engines, with the second engine's airscrew aft of the cruciform tail surfaces.

Dr. Claude Dornier had used a tandem engine arrangement on his famous flying boats, the Wal and Do 18. In 1940, he had glider designer Ulrich Hutter plan an experimental light plane with a tail propeller driven by a long extension shaft from the 80 hp Hirth HM 60R. Weighing only 720 kg. (1584 lb.) the Goeppingen Go 9 did 220 km/hr (137 mph) and proved the tail propeller a safe concept.

The RLM requested a fast bomber in 1942 as an unarmed monoplane with two engines installed in the fuselage. Such a type had existed since 1937, in the Heinkel He 119. But Heinkel was unpopular in the Air Ministry, and only Arado, Dornier, and Junkers were invited to submit designs. Dornier's Project 231 design offered inline engines in front and back, with tricycle landing gear and a four-surface tail. A 1000 kg. bomb load was carried internally.

But no interest was shown by the RLM in such a radical layout until 1943, when the Luftwaffe urgently needed new fighters. Dornier was ordered to go ahead with his single-seater as the Do 335, and the first prototype flew at Oberpfaffenhofen on October 26, 1943. Powered by 1750 hp DB 603A-2s, the Do 335V-1 differed from later models by its oil cooler inlet under the nose, circular mainwheel cover, and the lack of armament. Later aircraft incorporated the oil cooler in the nose ring radiator.

Testing went well, interrupted by an engine fire that destroyed V-2; the only accident in the prototype program. The V-3 showed a revised airframe and landing gear, while the V-5 was for armament tests with a 30 mm. MK 103 *Motorkanone* and two 15 mm. MG 151 guns over the engine. These guns had longer barrels than usual, improving muzzle velocity.

Fourteen prototypes were built eventually, including a V-4 set aside for two Jumo 222s, the powerplants intended for a projected Do 435 two-seater. The V-6, V-7 and V-9 were used for testing, the latter being the final production form. The Do 335V-8 went to Daimler-Benz to test the new DB 603E engine, while the Do 335V-10 added a new mission, night fighting. A second cockpit was added above the fuel

DORNIER Do 335A-1 (V-3 in photo)
Daimler-Benz DB 603E-1, 2 X 1800 hp
DIMENSIONS: as Do 335V 1
WEIGHT: Empty 7400 kg. (16,280 lb.), Gross 9600 kg. (21,120 lb.), Fuel 1850 liters (488 gal.)
PERFORMANCE: Speed—Max. 763 km/hr (474 mph) at 6400 m. (21,000′), Cruising speed 685 km/hr (425 mph), Landing speed 175 km/hr (108 mph), Climb 660 m./1 min. (2165′/1 min.), Range 1400 km. (870 miles), Service ceiling 11,400 m. (37,400′)

tank for a radar operator, with FuG 212 antenna on the wings. With a top speed of 688 km/hr (427 mph) at 5600 m. (18,370′), the V-10 was prototype for a projected Do 335A-6 night fighter.

A second cockpit training configuration was also provided in the V-11 and V-12, prototypes for the A-10 two-seater. A Do 335B series was also planned, the B-1 being based on the V-13 with two MG 151/20 cowl guns, and the B-2 on the V-14 with two 30 mm. MK 103s added to the wings. Although there were ambitious plans to have Heinkel join in Do 335B production, the end of war frustrated them.

Dornier did begin production in 1944 with ten Do 335A-0 series aircraft, but only eleven Do 335A-1s and one or two Do 335A-10 trainers were delivered before the final collapse in 1945.

All Do 335s except a proposed A-4 recon version had a bomb bay for one 1100 or two 550 lb. bombs. In emergencies, the pilots had an ejection seat and the vertical tails and rear propeller could be jettisoned. With a 763 km/hr (474 mph) speed, the single-seat Dornier Do 335A was the fastest propeller-driven fighter of the Second World War in Europe.

Do 335V-14

Do 335A-10

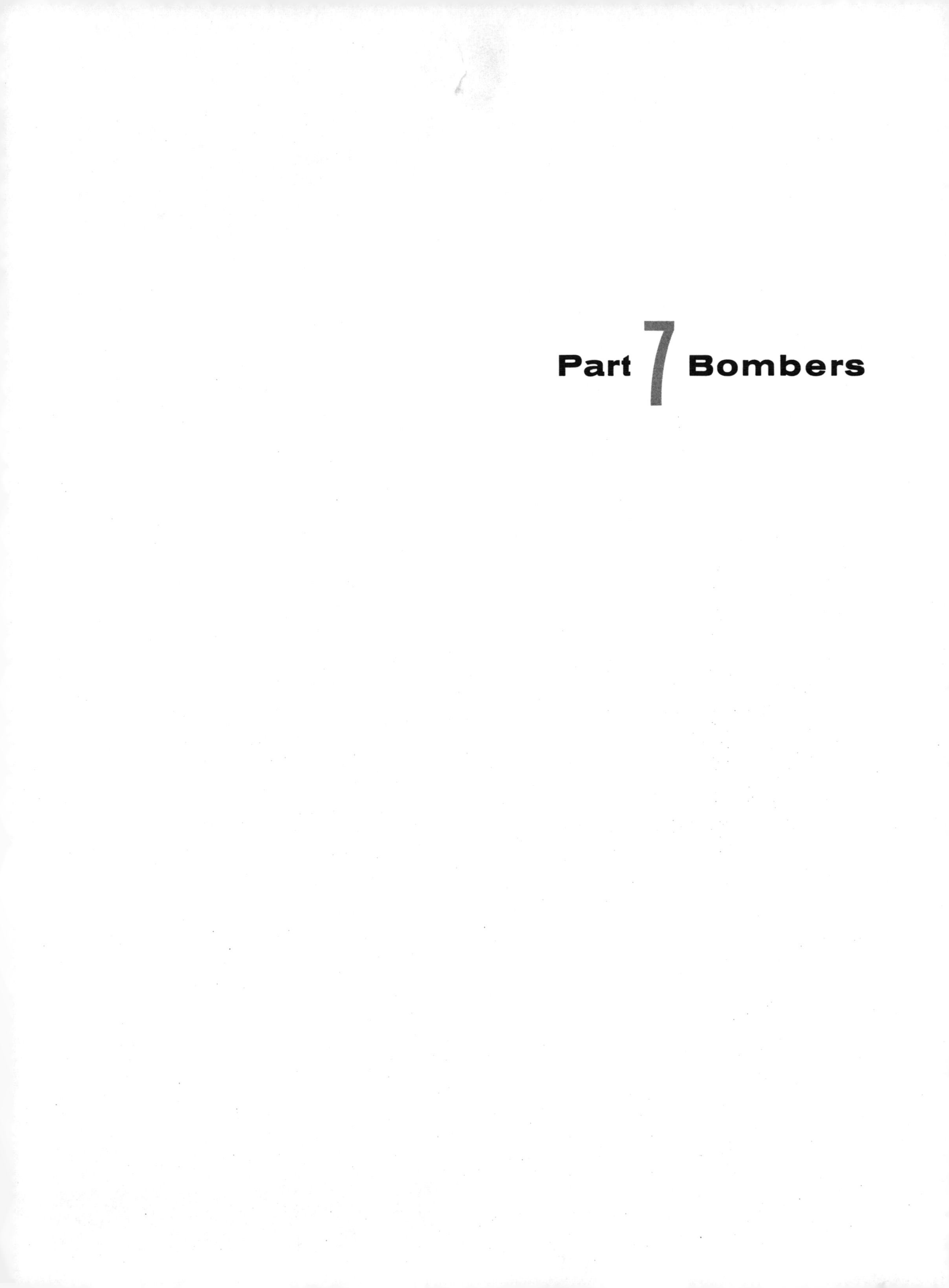

Part 7 Bombers

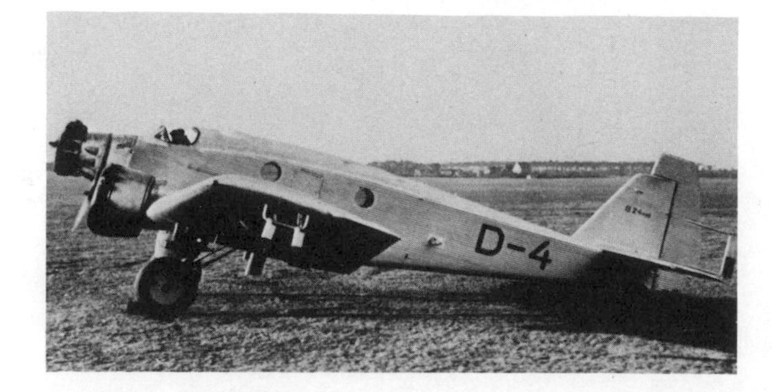

JUNKERS K 30 prototype

22.

Bomber Development in Secret, 1924–31

During the Versailles Treaty period, German bomber development was necessarily clandestine and limited. Nevertheless, utilizing facilities abroad, Germany managed a greater step forward in bomber design than those seen in other aircraft classes. The all-metal cantilever monoplane style was established first among bombers.

Pioneer in' this work was Professor Hugo Junkers, who during the war had designed a modernistic four-engined cantilever monoplane, the Junkers R I bomber. The war's end halted this giant's construction and the post-war ban on large aircraft frustrated building of a big monoplane transport. In 1924, however, Junkers offered a successful three-engined transport, the all-metal, low-wing G 24.

Junkers' Swedish affiliate, AB Flygindustri at Linhamn, quickly produced the Junkers K 30, (R 42) a bomber version. Two gunner's cockpits were cut into the cabin top and a retractable bucket turret hung below the fuselage. Twin Lewis guns were fitted at each position, and bomb racks were provided below the wings. The accompanying photos show a prototype with three 310 hp Junkers L5 incline en-
prototype with three 310 hp Junkers L5 inline engines, another with 450 hp Siemens Jupiter radials, The seaplane version was license-built in the U.S.S.R., and at least six R 42s went to Chile.

Dornier's Swiss factory built a twin-engined night bomber. First flown on February 19, 1926, the Dornier Do N owed much to the Wal design, with a boat-like metal fuselage, and two tandem inline engines mounted back to back above the strut-braced high wing. Either the 475 hp Napier Lion, 600 hp Rolls-Royce Condor or BMW VI could be used. Gunner's cockpits were placed at the bow and behind the wing. A prototype was sold to Japan, where Nakajima had arranged to produce it under license.

Dr. Adolf Rohrbach had joined Zeppelin at Staaken late in the war to design an all-metal giant bomber. When the Armistice halted that project, the Staaken works produced in 1920 his very advanced four-engined cantilever monoplane transport. As this aircraft's further development was also banned, Rohrbach went to Denmark.

In 1928, the all-metal Rohrbach Roland transport was built for Lufthansa, as a big cantilever high-wing monoplane. Three 320 hp BMW inline engines were used, one in the nose and the others under the wing. The first example, D-991, was later rebuilt as a bomber with 600 hp BMWs and flown to Lipetsk for armament tests. A bomb rack was attached below the cabin, a gunner's pit was built into the back of each engine nacelle, and a third gun mounted atop the cabin ahead of the single tail fin. Rohrbach also designed, incidentally, the big three-engined Beardmore Inflexible flown in Britain in 1928.

JUNKERS K 30 (R 42)
Junkers L 5, 3 X 310 hp
DIMENSIONS: Span 29.9 m. (98'1"), Lg. 15.23 m. (50'), Ht. 5.5 m. (18'1"), Wing Area 94.6 qm. (1018 sq. ft.)
WEIGHT: Empty 3860 kg. (8492 lb.), Gross 6500 kg. (14,300 lb.), Fuel 1250 liters (330 gal.)
PERFORMANCE: Speed 190 km/hr (118 mph) at sea level, Cruising speed 155 km/hr (96 mph), Landing speed 110 km/hr (68 mph), Climb 2000 m./14 min. (6560'/14 min.), Range 1085 km. (675 miles), Service ceiling 4500 m. (14,760')

DORNIER Do N
Napier Lion, 2 X 475 hp
DIMENSIONS: Span 26.8 m. (87′9″), Lg. 18 m. (59′½″), Ht. 6.5 m. (21′4″), Wing area 129 qm. (1388 sq. ft.)
WEIGHT: Empty 4200 kg. (9240 lb.), Gross 6300 kg. (13,860 lb.)
PERFORMANCE: Speed—Max. 190 km/hr (118 mph), Climb 1000 m./7 min. (3280′/7 min.), Service ceiling 3500 m. (11,480′)

JUNKERS K 30W (R 42W)
Junkers L 5, 3 X 310 hp
DIMENSIONS: Span 29.9 m. (98′1″), Lg. 15.5 m. (51′), Ht. 6 m. (19′8″), Wing Area 94.6 qm. (1018 sq. ft.)
WEIGHT: Empty 4390 kg. (9658 lb.), Gross 6500 kg. (14,300 lb.)
PERFORMANCE: Speed—Max. 185 km/hr (115 mph) at sea level, Cruising speed 155 km/hr (96 mph), Landing speed 110 km/hr (68 mph), Climb 2000 m./18 min. (6560′/18 min.), Service ceiling 4000 m. (13,120′)

ROHRBACH ROLAND I
BMW IV, 3 X 320 hp (600 hp BMW VI on bomber)
DIMENSIONS: Span 26 m. (85′3½″), Lg. 16.3 m. (53′6″), Ht. 4.5 m. (14′9″), Wing Area 88 qm. (947 sq. ft.)
Further bomber data unavailable, but the transport had:
WEIGHT: Empty 3365 kg. (7403 lb.), Gross 5265 kg. (11,583 lb.)
PERFORMANCE: Speed—Max. 195 km/hr (121 mph), Landing speed 100 km/hr (62 mph), Climb 1000 m./7 min. (3280′/7 min.), Range 925 km. (570 miles), Service ceiling 5500 m. (18,045′)

JUNKERS S 36
Bristol Jupiter, 2 X 480 hp
DIMENSIONS: Span 20.14 m. (66′1″), Lg. 11.4 m. (37′5″), Ht. 4.62 m. (15′2″), Wing Area 54.2 qm. (583 sq. ft.)
WEIGHT: Empty 2600 kg. (5720 lb.), Gross 4300 kg. (9460 lb.)
PERFORMANCE: Speed—Max. 245 km/hr (152 mph), Cruising speed 220 km/hr (137 mph), Landing speed 115 km/hr (71 mph), Range 1100 km. (680 miles), Service ceiling 7800 m. (25,580′)

JUNKERS K 37
Bristol Jupiter, 2 X 480 hp
DIMENSIONS: Span 20.14 m. (66′1″), Lg. 11.45 m. (37′6″), Ht. 4.5 m. (14′9″), Wing Area 54.25 qm. (584 sq. ft.)
WEIGHT: Empty 2570 kg. (5654 lb.), Gross 4300 kg. (9460 lb.)
PERFORMANCE: Speed—Max. 232 km/hr (144 mph), Cruising speed 195 km/hr (121 mph), Landing speed 115 km/hr (71 mph), Climb 1000 m./3.5 min. (3280′/3.5 min.), Range 1000 km. (620 miles), Service ceiling 7000 m. (23,000′)

K 37 in Germany

K 37 modified

HEINKEL He 34
BMW VI, 2 X 650 hp
DIMENSIONS: Span 18 m. (59′½″), Lg. 11.7 m. (38′4″), Wing Area 85.4 qm. (919 sq. ft.)
WEIGHT: Empty 3000 kg. (6600 lb.), Gross 4500 kg. (9900 lb.)
PERFORMANCE: Speed—Max. 266 km/hr (164 mph) at sea level, Landing speed 86 km/hr (53 mph), Service ceiling 7600 m. (24,930′)

MESSERSCHMITT M 22
Siemens Jupiter 2 X 500 hp
DIMENSIONS: Span 17 m. (55′9″), Lg. 13.6 m. (44′7″), Ht. 4.8 m. (15′9″), Wing Area 63.2 qm. (680 sq. ft.)
WEIGHT: Empty 2900 kg. (6380 lb.), Gross 3800 kg. (8360 lb.)
PERFORMANCE: Speed—Max. 220 km/hr (137 mph), Cruising speed 185 km/hr (115 mph), Climb 1000 m./2.4 min. (3280′/2.4 min.) 3000 m./8.5 min. (9840′/8.5 min.), Range 500 km. (310 miles), Service ceiling 6200 m. (20,340′)

The most popular bomber layout in World War II was the twin, low-wing monoplane of all-metal cantilever construction. The pioneer of this form was the Junkers S 36, introduced in 1927 as a "postal and photo" plane. Two 480 hp Bristol Jupiter radials were mounted in the low wing above the simple, sturdy landing gear. Three open cockpits were provided for the crew in the corrugated metal fuselage.

Again, the Junkers Swedish branch provided an openly military equivalent in the K 37 bomber. With another cockpit and modified twin vertical surfaces, it had two flexible gun rings and nose windows for the bombardier. Twin Lewis guns were fitted to the rings, another was in the belly, and provision was made for two Vickers or a 20 mm. gun fixed to fire forward. Japan purchased a K 37 in January 1932 and this type was manufactured by Mitsubishi as the army bomber Ki 2. Our photos also show an example on skis (D-1252) used by the secret Luftwaffe and a

Do P modified

DORNIER Do P
Siemens Jupiter, 4 X 500 hp
DIMENSIONS: Span 30 m. (98′5″), Lg. 23.4 m. (76′8″), Ht. 7.3 m. (24′), Wing Area 152.6 qm. (1642 sq. ft.)
WEIGHT: Empty 8000 kg. (17,600 lb.), Gross 12,000 kg. (26,400 lb.)
PERFORMANCE: Speed—Max. 210 km/hr (130 mph), Climb 2000 m./13.2 min. (6560′/13.2 min.), Range 1000 km. (620 miles), Service ceiling 3500 m. (11,480′)

JUNKERS K 51 (Japanese Ki 20 in photo)
Junkers L 88, 4 X 820 hp
DIMENSIONS: Span 44 m. (144′4″), Lg. 23.2 m. (76′1″), Ht. 7 m. (23′), Wing Area 294 qm. (3163 sq. ft.)
WEIGHT: Empty 14,912 kg. (32,810 lb.), Gross 25,448 kg. (56,201 lb.)
PERFORMANCE: Speed—Max. 270 km/hr (168 mph), Cruising speed 200 km/hr (124 mph), Landing speed 93 km/hr (50 mph), Climb 1000 m./6.6 min. (3280′/6.6 min.), Range 3700 km. (2,300 miles), Service ceiling 3400 m. (1115′)

modification with enclosed pilot's cockpit seen after 1935.

Despite the progress in monoplane design, the biplane configuration reappeared in two twin-engined bombers developed in the 1928–30 period. The first was the Heinkel He 34, with 650 hp BMW VI inline engines, N struts, and a short nose. Air-cooled 500 hp Bristol Jupiters, I struts, wheel pants and a fairing joining fuselage and upper wings were used on the obscure Messerschmitt M 22.

Four 500 hp Bristol Jupiters were used on the Dornier Do P monoplane, four radials paired in tandem above the wing attached to the heavy fuselage's top. The first example, CH-302, was flown in Switzerland on March 31, 1930, with twin rudders and panted landing wheels.

A second example flown on September 23, got the German registration D-1982, and had an added horizontal stabilizer and external control balances. Carrying a crew of six, three mg. and 1000 kg. (2200 lb.) of bombs for 1000 km. (620 miles) it was flown to Lipetsk for trials. After a short service the Do P was damaged beyond that base's capacity to repair and was dismantled.

Junkers had built a very large transport monoplane in 1929, the G-38 with a wing thick enough to contain passenger compartments, along with four engines. A K 51 heavy bomber version was designed for ten crewmen, four mg. and a 20 mm. gun and 2000–5000 kgs. of bombs, but the plans were sold to Japan. In great secrecy, six were built in 1931–34 as the Mitsubishi Ki 20 Type 92 Army bomber.[1]

Heinkel offered a second biplane bomber in September 1931, the He 59L with 650 hp BMW engines and four-bladed props between the fabric-covered wings. Deep wheel pants were used, and covers retained on the nose, rear, and ventral gun posts. Like the other biplanes, only one prototype was built. The He 59, however, went on as a seaplane for a long and successful Luftwaffe career.

Dornier's Do Y was a clean all-metal monoplane whose shoulder wing's leading edge swept gracefully back to the tips. Two Bristol Jupiters were mounted on the leading edges over the panted wheels, a third engine was erected above the fuselage behind the side-by-side pilot's cockpits, and external control balances were used. Crew and armament were the same as the Do P, but reduced drag made it faster with three engines than its predecessor was with four.

The first of two Bristol-powered prototypes flew on October 17, 1931. Yugoslavia ordered three Do Ys powered by 625 hp Gnome-Rhone 9Kers radials, and these had modified wing tips and internal arrangements. Experience with the Do Y led to 1932's Do 11 series, but by then the post-war period had become the Luftwaffe's prewar period.

[1] The first two were assembled in Japan from German parts, and the rest used Japanese materials.

HEINKEL He 59
BMW VI, 2 X 660 hp
DIMENSIONS: Span 23.7 m. (77'10"), Wing Area 153.2 qm. (1648 sq. ft.)
WEIGHT: Empty 5240 kg. (11,528 lb.)
PERFORMANCE: Speed—Max. 230 km/hr (143 mph) at sea level, Landing speed 85 km/hr (53 mph)

DORNIER Do Y
Bristol Jupiter, 3 X 500 hp/ or Gnome-Rhone 9Kers, 625 hp
DIMENSIONS: Span 28/26.62 m. (91'10"/87'4"), Lg. 18.2 m. (59'8"), Ht. 7.5/7.8 m. (24'7"/25'7"), Wing Area 111/108.8 qm. (1194/1170 sq. ft.)
WEIGHT: Empty 6360/5860 kg. (13,992/12,892 lb.), Gross 8500/9100 kg. (18,700/20,020 lb.)
PERFORMANCE: Speed—Max. 300 km/hr (186 mph), Cruising speed 220/240 km/hr (136/149 mph), Landing speed 90 km/hr (56 mph), Climb 4000 m./12.1 min. (13,120'/12.1 min.), Range 750/1500 km. (465/930 miles), Service ceiling 8300/8500 m. (27,220'/27,880')

DORNIER Do 11D
Siemens SAM 22B, 2 X 650 hp
DIMENSIONS: Span 26.3 m. (86'3"), Lg. 18.8 m. (61'8"), Ht. 5.4 m. (17'9"), Wing Area 107.8 qm. (1160 sq. ft.)
WEIGHT: Empty 5830 kg. (12,826), Gross 8200 kg. (18,040 lb.), Fuel 1540 liters (406 gal.)
PERFORMANCE: Speed—Max. 250 km/hr (155 mph), Cruising speed 225 km/hr (140 mph), Landing speed 102 km/hr (63 mph), Climb 1000 m./7 min. (3280'/7 min.), Range 960 km. (595 miles), Service ceiling 4100 m. (13,450')

23.

Bombers for the New Luftwaffe

When the Luftwaffe began its secret organization, only Dornier and Junkers had actual aircraft in flight status with bomber capability. Rather than wait for new designs, the Air Ministry ordered mass production of the types on hand to provide a fifteen group bomber force in 1936.

The production program underway by July 1, 1934, scheduled 792 bombers; 150 Dornier Do 11s with two Siemens radials, 180 improved Do 13s with two BMW inline engines, and 462 Junkers Ju 52s with three BMW radials. Since deliveries began before the Luftwaffe existed officially, it was convenient that these aircraft be publicized only as transports until the need for subtility ended.

The twin-engined Do 11 had been known as the Do F before the RLM began the official numbering series. First flown May 7, 1932, it had the Do Y's curved shoulder-high wing, and introduced the first German retractable landing gear. The main strut slid inward, raising the wheel up to fit flat in the nacelle behind the Siemens Jupiter.

When production deliveries began early in 1934, the aircraft was introduced as a cargo plane for a Lufthansa Air freight service, although its resemblance to a bomber was obvious. In fact, along with every Do 11 in cargo configuration, Dornier delivered crated parts for quick conversion to bomber armament.

Armament for the Do 11c service model included three 7.9 mm. guns and 1000 kg. (2200 lb.) of bombs in internal racks. Powered by 650 hp Siemens Sh 22B-2 radials with three-bladed propellers, they proved to have bad landing characteristics, and the landing gear was so unreliable that it was locked down.

Its intended successor, the Do 13, was provided with fixed, panted landing gear as well as full-span slotted flaps. The first Do 13a was flown on February 13, 1933, with the Do 11's original curved wing and radial engines, but the Do 13c production prototype had 750 hp BMW VI inline engines and four-bladed propellers.

Meanwhile, 79 Do 11s had been delivered by 1934's end, but production paused to incorporate needed modifications. The wingtips were cut short, reducing span from 28 to 26.3 meters (91'10" to 86'3"). This change was made in 1935 on the assembly line and on aircraft already delivered, changing the designation to Do 11d. Production ended in fall 1935, with 141 Do 11 bombers completed. After their replacement in service by the Do 23, some went to Bulgaria.

Similar wing revisions had been made to the Do 13 design, which also required structural strengthening and small tabs below the stabilizer. By the time production deliveries began in May 1935 to the now revealed Luftwaffe units, Dornier's four-place design

DORNIER Do 13
BMW VIU, 2 X 270 hp
DIMENSIONS: Span 28 m. (91'10"), Lg. 18.8 m. (61'8"), Ht. 5.65 m. (18'6"), Wing Area 111 qm. (1194 sq. ft.)
WEIGHT: Empty 6050 kg. (13,310 lb.), Gross 8600 kg. (18,920 lb.)
PERFORMANCE: Speed—Max. 260 km/hr (161 mph) at 1200 m. (3940'), Cruising speed 225 km/hr (140 mph), Landing speed 85 km/hr (53 mph), Range 1200 km. (744 mph), Service ceiling 4600 m. (15,088')

DORNIER Do 23G

was redesignated Do 23F and used the BMW VId. Minor revisions led to the Do 23G with the BMW VI-U also of 750 hp. Armament was three 7.9 mm. MG 15 guns at nose, dorsal and ventral mounts, and 1000 kg. (2200 lb.) in the bomb bay.

Do 23 production reached 273 when the last two were delivered in September 1936. They equipped five Luftwaffe bomber groups (36 each), with ten more groups using the Ju 52.[1] These aircraft provided bomber crews with experience until more advanced aircraft became available before the war.

The most widely used aircraft in the early Luftwaffe was the Junkers Ju 52. The 1934 program produced 196 W 33, 182 W 34, 11 Ju 160 and 462 Ju 52 aircraft. All were transports, but the Ju 52 was also a *Behelf-Bomber* (Makeshift bomber) to fill in until better types were available.

The Ju 52 began its life as a large single-engined transport monoplane first flown on October 13, 1930. Only six single-engined examples were built, however,

[1] Do 23 *gruppen* were I/KG 152 at Neubrandenburg, I/KG 153 at Merseburg, I/KG 253 at Gotha, I/KG 254 at Hanover, and I/KG 155 at Giebelstadt. The second and third groups of each *Geschwader* used Ju 52s, and nine Ju 52s supported each Do 23 unit.

DORNIER Do 23G
BMW VIU, 2 X 750 hp at takeoff
DIMENSIONS: Span 25.6 m. (84′), Lg. 18.8 m. (61′8″), Ht. 5.4 m. (18′), Wing Area 106.6 qm. (1147 sq. ft.)
WEIGHT: Empty 6400 kg. (14,080 lb.), Gross 9200 kg. (20,240 lb.), Fuel 1860 liters (491 gal.)
PERFORMANCE: Speed—Max. 260 km/hr (161 mph) at 1200 m. (3940′), Cruising speed 210 km/hr (130 mph), Landing speed 85 km/hr (53 mph), Range 1350 km. (840 miles), Service ceiling 4200 m. (13,776′)

for early in 1932 the seventh plane was redesigned by chief engineer Zindel for three Pratt & Whitney Hornet radials. This pattern was established as the principal production model. Designed Ju 52/3m (for 3 motors), they used 660 hp BMW 132As, the license-built German version of the air-cooled Hornets.

Notable for the rugged corrugated metal construction and serviceability, the Ju 52 was already flying for Lufthansa (DLH) and foreign airlines before it became the Luftwaffe's *Behelf-Bomber.* By 1934's end, 192 Ju 52s had already been completed, and 756 were delivered by December 31, 1936. Lufthansa received over 200, 29 different foreign countries were to get them, and two-thirds of the Luftwaffe's 1935–36 bomber units used the armed version. They did most of the German transport work, along with the single-engined W 34 then built in even greater numbers.

Bomber groups used the Junkers Ju 52/3m g3e model with the 760 hp BMW 132A and four-man crew. Racks for six 250 kg. (550 lb.) bombs were installed, the bombardier sitting below the fuselage in a bucket turret with a 7.9 mm. MG 15 and 750 rounds. Another MG 15 with 1050 rounds was in a gunner's cockpit back near the tail.

"Auntie Yu" and "Iron Annie" were popular names for the Junkers, which became the first German plane in the civil war that began in Spain July 18, 1936. General Franco requested Hitler's help on July 26, and soon twenty Ju 52s began night flights over France to Tetuan in Spanish Morocco.[2]

At this critical period, the Junkers by July 29 be-

[2] The first Ju 52 left Tempelhof on July 27.

JUNKERS Ju 52/3m g4e

gan history's first army air lift, flying Franco's Moorish troops to Spain. Said Hitler later, "Franco ought to erect a monument to the glory of the Junkers 52. It is this aircraft that the Spanish Revolution has to thank for its victory."

Nationalist pilots then started bombing attacks on Republican territory with armed Ju 52s. As their armies approached Madrid, they hit nearby Getafe airport with eight Ju 52s on August 23, and Madrid itself was bombed August 25. These Junkers were mostly flown by Spanish pilots until November 6, when the Condor Legion's Ju 52 group K/88 was assembled at Seville.

At least 56 Ju 52s went to Spain, including a single Ju 52w twin float seaplane used by the Condor Legion. Nationalist Ju 52s are credited with 5400 offensive missions, dropping over 6000 tons of bombs, the last on March 26, 1939.

In Germany, the Ju 52 had moved from bomber units to transport groups called KGzbV; an abbreviation for "Battle groups for special duties." Not until May 1943 were they renamed transport groups. The last bombing mission for the Ju 52 seems to be the improvised incendiary attack on Warsaw by a group on September 25, 1939.

Germany began the war with 547 Ju 52s, along with two Fw 200s, two Ju 90s and a Ju G38 in its transport units. They made possible several of the war's most remarkable operations. Twelve groups were used on the airborne invasion of Norway, flying 3018 sorties that delivered 29,280 men, 2376 tons of supplies and 311,160 gallons of fuel.

Airborne troops also led the invasion of Holland and Belgium. For the first time in war, gliders were used in combat, when 41 DFS 230s were towed by Ju 52s to seize fort Eben Emael and nearby bridges. Paratroops had been used for the first time in Norway, and then Holland, too, saw a mass descent. Fierce Dutch resistance cost 167 of 430 Ju 52s used against the Netherlands.

The largest German airborne assault was that made on Crete in May 1941. Some 22,750 men were landed by 493 Ju 52s and 80 gliders. This costly success was the last Luftwaffe airborne assault operation, the Ju

JUNKERS Ju 52/3m g3e
BMW 132A, 3 X 660 hp (725 hp at takeoff)
DIMENSIONS: Span 29.25 m. (95'11"), Lg. 18.9 m. (62'), Ht. 6.1 m. (20'10"), Wing Area 110.5 qm. (1189 sq. ft.)
WEIGHT: Empty 5720 kg. (12,584 lb.), Gross 9500 kg./10,500 kg. (20,900 lb./23,100 lb.), Fuel 2480 liters (655 gal.)
PERFORMANCE: Speed—Max. 277 km/hr (172 mph) at 915 m. (3000'), 265 km/hr (164 mph) at sea level, Cruising speed 247 km/hr (153 mph), Landing speed 101 km/hr (63 mph), Climb 1000 m./4.5 min. (3280'/4.5 min.), Range 1000 km. (620 miles), Service ceiling 5900 m. (19,350')

52s afterward finding their greatest challenges (and losses) in supply lifts to Stalingrad and Tunisia. In April 1943, 432 transports were lost flying to Tunisia, including 52 Ju 52s downed by Allied fighters in one day! Seven Ju 52 groups remained operational at the war's end.

Throughout this decade the Ju 52 remained basically the same. The Ju 52/3m g3e bomber of 1935 was followed by the strengthened Ju 52/3m g4e transport minus the bucket turret. New 830 hp BMW 132T radials were introduced on the g5e, while minor details changed g6e thru g12e, and the last model was the BMW 132Z-powered g14e of 1944. The elegant pants fitted to early model's wheels soon disappeared, and Ju 52s operated by coastal units had twin floats. A 13 mm. gun was fitted to the dorsal position on later ships, together with two 7.9 mm. guns at side windows.

German production of the Ju 52/3m amounted to 2804 after September 1939. Adding prewar production gives a total of 4835 of all types, according to a company source. In France, Amiot built 516 under license from 1942–44, and Spain's CASA built 110 as the C-352. After the war, the Czechs, French, Spaniards, and Swedes kept using the Ju 52, and some of the French series flew bombing missions in Vietnam in 1949.

JUNKERS JU 86

The next bomber in service with the Luftwaffe was the Junkers Ju 86, designed to an RLM specification for a fast twin-engined monoplane that could fit both the medium bomber and transport roles. This same requirement also produced the later and more successful He 111.

Five prototypes were ordered, three in four-place bomber configuration and the others as transports. The all-metal, low-wing monoplanes had retractable wheels that folded outward into the wings, and twin rudders. Junkers Jumo 205 Diesels were to be powerplants, but were not ready when the first prototype flew on November 4, 1934.

Known originally as Ju 86a, the Ju 86V-1 first appeared at Dessau without armament, with two 550 hp Siemens SAM 22B radials and two-bladed wooden props, and had a 300 km/hr (186 mph) top speed. The next prototype to fly in January 1935 (D-ALAL), had bomb cells and nose, dorsal and ventral gun positions, three-bladed propellers on the SAM radials, but went to Leipzig for installation of Jumo 205C diesels in March.

The next two examples were completed in April with Jumo 205s, a cabin with seats for ten passengers and civil registrations D-ABUK and A-AREV. The latter had a wider chord on the outer wing to cure poor flying qualities revealed on tests, and was designated Ju 86V-4.

The Ju 86V-5 (D-AHOE) of August 1935, prototype for the Ju 86A bomber, had 600 hp Jumo 205Cs, three-bladed props, a new transparent nose gun and bombing station, curved screen on the dorsal pit, and a retractable gun bucket behind the wing.

Early in 1936 production got underway, with the first six factory numbers being Ju 86A-0 bombers, the next six Ju 86B transports, and then three more Ju 86A-0s. The first transport (D-AXEQ) stayed with Junkers, the second went to Swiss Air in April 1936, and the rest to DLH. Jumo powerplants were used on all these early Ju 86s, but a seventh Ju 86B was modified with BMW 132Dc radials before it joined Lufthansa.

Kampfgeschwader Hindenburg (KG 152, later KG 1) received the Ju 86A-1 production ships, but were dissatisfied with their new bird. Only a 750 kg. bomb and 600 liter fuel (1650 lb. and 158 gal.) load was carried, the speed dropped 20 km/hr (12 mph) when the bottom turret was extended, and stability was still lacking. To correct this, an extended tail cone, additional bomb racks, and more fuel capacity were installed on a rebuilt Ju 86A-0 that became the V-6.

These modifications were incorporated into the Junkers assembly line and by October 1936 the Ju 86D-1 was joining KG 152. Armament included 1000 kg. (2200 lb.) of bombs and three 7.9 mm. guns. At year's end Junkers had delivered 74 Ju 86s out of

JUNKERS Ju 86V-5

JUNKERS Ju 86A-1

JUNKERS Ju 86D-1
Jumo 205C-4, 2 X 600 hp at takeoff
DIMENSIONS: Span 22.5 m. (73′10″), Lg. 17.87 m. (58′7½″), Ht. 5.06 m. (16′7″), Wing Area 82 qm. (882 sq. ft.)
WEIGHT: Empty 5150 kg. (11,330 lb.), Gross 8060 kg. (17,732 lb.), Fuel 900 liters (238 gal.)
PERFORMANCE: Speed—Max. 325 km/hr (202 mph) at 3000 m. (9840′), 300 km/hr (186 mph) at sea level, Cruising speed 275 km/hr (171 mph), Landing speed 96 km/hr (60 mph), Range 570 km. with 1000 kg.; 1500 km. max. (354 miles with 2200 lb.; 930 miles max.), Service ceiling 5900 m. (19,350′)

JUNKERS Ju 86E-1

JUNKERS Ju 86E-2
BMW 132N, 2 X 665 mph at 4500 m. (14,760′), 865 hp at takeoff
DIMENSIONS: as Ju 86D
WEIGHT: Empty 5140 kg. (11,308 lb.), Gross 8200 kg. (18,040 lb.), Fuel 1500 liters (396 gal.)
PERFORMANCE: Speed—Max. 380 km/hr (235 mph) at 4000 m. (13,120′), 330 km/hr (205 mph) at sea level, Cruising speed 340 km/hr (210 mph), Landing speed 101 km/hr (63 mph), Climb 3000 m./9.8 min. (9840′/ 9.8 min.), Range 1500 km. (930 miles), Service ceiling 7700 m. (25,250′)

Ju 86K-1

orders then at 641, including those of subcontractor Henschel. Five Ju 86D-1s were forwarded to the Condor Legion in 1937, and the new tail and fuel tanks were used on six Ju 86C transports for DLH in 1937.

These large orders were sharply cut back as the superiority of the Do 17 and He 111 then coming into service was realized. Part of the problem was the 600 hp Jumo 205Cs, which had low fuel consumption but limited power and combat reliability.

An answer to the power problem came with installation of supercharged Pratt & Whitney Hornets (SIE-G) in a Ju 86A-1k ordered by Sweden in June 1936. Successful trials with this aircraft led to use of these air-cooled radials in two more machines for Sweden and in the V-8 and V-9 conversions from D models early in 1937. These engines went into licensed production as the BMW 132 and were purchased for the Junkers Ju 86E bomber and Ju 86F transport.

These bombers entered service in 1937 as the Ju 86E-1 with 650 hp BMW 132Fs and more commonly the Ju 86E-2 with 665 hp BMW 132N radials. Parallel version for export was the Ju 86K bomber, designated B-3 in Sweden. The three Hornet-powered B-3s were followed in 1938 by 37 Ju 86Ks shipped to Sweden for completion with Swedish-built Bristol Pegasus radials. Swedish designations were B-3A for 20 with 820 hp My 111s and B-3B for 17 with 920 hp My XII engines. Sixteen more were built under license by SAAB from August 1939 to January 1941.

In 1938, Hungary received 57 Ju 86Ks fitted with 870 hp Gnome-Rhone 114Ks of their own manufacture,[3] while Portugal received ten. A Ju 86, probably the V-8, toured South America looking for sales. It lost out to the Martin 139 (B-10) in Argentina and the SM 79B in Brazil, but 1938 deliveries included 12 bombers and two transports to Chile and three transports to Bolivia.

While the Ju 86Z was a civil transport exported in small numbers, 18 built with Hornets for South African Airways in 1937–38 became wartime bombers. One had, in fact, been delivered in bomber configuration, and in 1939 all received bomb racks, a Vickers gun fixed in the nose, and two others in the dorsal and ventral positions. These Junkers served on coastal patrol, and in June 1940 flew the South African Air Force's first bombing raids on Italian East Africa.

Back in Germany, the Luftwaffe's bomber units possessed on September 19, 1938, 159 Jumo-powered Ju 86A and Ds, 43 BMW-powered Ju 86Es and 33 new Ju 86Gs. This latter model had the pilot's cockpit

[3] Including 1937 deliveries, Hungary got 66 Ju 86 K-2 bombers.

Ju 86Z of South African Air Force

moved forward, a modified-transparent nose and enlarged fuel capacity. The new nose was tested on the Ju 86V-10 converted from an E-2, and built on the last 40 production ships.

The Ju 86G-1 was used by IV/KG 1, the last group with this type, but it was retired to training schools after the Polish campaign. During the emergency at Stalingrad, 42 Ju 86s were lost transporting supplies to the doomed German Army. Other Ju 86Gs were used against Yugoslavian partisans.

It has been said in Junkers publications that 810 Ju 86s were built when production ended in 1938, but this is doubtful, since no more than some 155 were exported and the Luftwaffe apparently received less than 300. Two more models appeared in World

JUNKERS Ju 86G-1
BMW 132N, 2 X 865 hp at takeoff, 665 hp at 4500 m. (14,760′)
DIMENSIONS: Span 22.5 m. (73′10″), Lg. 17.5 m. (57′4″), Ht. 5.1 m. (16′7″), Wing Area 82 qm. (882 sq. ft.)
WEIGHT: Gross 8468 kg. (18,124 lb.)
PERFORMANCE: Speed—Max. 385 km/hr (238 mph) at 4000 m. (13,120′), 328 km/hr (205 mph) at sea level, Cruising speed 342 km/hr (211 mph), Range 460 km. with 2200 kg./650 km. with 400 kg. (286 miles with 2200 lb./404 miles with 880 lb.), Service ceiling 7700 m. (25,250′)

JUNKERS Ju 86P

JUNKERS Ju 86P
Jumo 207A-1, 950 hp
DIMENSIONS: Span 25.6 m. (84′), Lg. 16.46 m. (54′), Ht. 4.7 m. (13′4½″), Wing Area 92 qm. (990 sq. ft.)
WEIGHT: Empty 6660 kg. (15,432 lb.), Gross 10,400 kg. (22,880 lb.) on P-1 and 9500 kg. (20,900 lb.) on P-2
PERFORMANCE: Speed—Max. 360 km/hr (224 mph) at 6000 m. (19,680′), Cruising speed 3000 km/hr (186 mph), Range 1000 km. (620 miles), Service ceiling 12,500 m. (41,000′)

JUNKERS Ju 86R-1
Jumo 207B-3, 1000 hp at takeoff, 750 hp at 1200 m. (39,400′)
DIMENSIONS: Span 32 m. (105′), Lg. 16.46 m. (54′), Ht. 4.7 m. (13′4″), Wing Area 97.5 qm. (1049 sq. ft.)
WEIGHT: Empty 6780 kg. (14,942 lb.), Gross 11,530 kg. (25,366 lb.)
PERFORMANCE: Speed—Max. 420 km/hr (261 mph) at 9000 m. (29,520′), 368 km/hr (230 mph) at 14,000 m. (45,930′), Cruising speed 335 km/hr (208 mph), Climb 13,500 m./60 min. (44,300′/60 min.), Range 1570 km. (975 miles), Service ceiling 15,000 m. (49,200′)

DORNIER Do 17V-1
BMW VI, 2 X 750 hp at takeoff
DIMENSIONS: Span 18 m. (59′), Lg. 17.1 m. (56′½″), Ht. 4.62 m. (13′1″), Wing Area 55 qm. (592 sq. ft.)
WEIGHT: Empty 4200 kg. (9240 lb.), Gross 6900 kg. (15,180 lb.)
PERFORMANCE: Speed—Max. 435 km/hr (270 mph), Landing speed 110 km/hr (68 mph)

War II, but the Ju 86P and Ju 86R reconnaissance types were all converted from Ju 86D airframes.

The Ju 86P's prototype (D-AUHB) flew in February 1940, powered by two 950 hp supercharged Jumo 207A-1 diesels and carrying two men in the bow's pressurized cabin. No armament was carried, since the aircraft would operate above normal altitudes, for extended wings on the third prototype raised service to some 12,500 meters (41,000′).

Forty Ju 86D airframes were converted to Ju 86P 1 bomber or P-2 recon versions. They made their first sorties over Britain in 1940, and in 1941 flew over the Soviet Union to plan the surprise attack of June 22. Although the plane flew too high to be heard, the Russians knew they were there, but failed to draw the correct conclusions.

Co-author Nowarra noticed that during tests over Dessau, white steam trails formed over 3000 meters (9840′) and betrayed the path of the Junker Ju 86R-1. This model was rebuilt from the Ju 86P-2 in 1942, with the 1000 hp Jumo 207B-3, GM 1 injection, and extended wing span. The new model was needed, for on August 24, 1942, a Ju 86P-2 had been shot down in Egypt by a specially modified Spitfire. The high-altitude Junkers continued to operate, establishing a role that reached its greatest fame with the American U-2.

DORNIER DO 17

As the "Flying Pencil," the Dornier Do 17 became one of the Luftwaffe's first types to achieve world wide fame and was very active in the war's first year.

This design originated when the Air Ministry, impressed by the Heinkel He 70's high speed, encouraged Dornier and Heinkel to develop twin-engined aircraft of streamline form. By October 1, 1933,

Do 17V-3

nine Do 17 and seven He 111 prototype aircraft had been ordered for evaluation.

The first three Do 17s, V-1 to V-3 were completed late in 1934 with two 660 hp BMW VI engines, retractable landing gear, shoulder high wing, single tail, and the pointed nose that earned its nickname. Cabin space was provided for six passengers and mail, although accommodation was so awkward it was impractical for commercial operations.

It has been said that the prototypes languished in storage until *Flugkapitaen* Untucht urged the Do 17's adoption as a bomber. The six remaining prototypes were then completed in military form with a bomb bay and twin tail first tested on a modified Do 23. These aircraft originally also used BMW engines, except for V-5's 770 hp Hispano-Suiza imports. Do 17V-9 (D-AHAK) appeared first with a pointed nose and then introduced the round glazed nose adopted for production aircraft. Later, D-AHAK was used as an RLM official transport with the original nose. It was officially listed as owned by Lufthansa.

Production deliveries began in June 1936 with the first three Dornier Do 17E-1s. Armament of this three-seater normally comprised 750 kg. (1650 lb.) of bombs and two 7.9 mm. MG 15s, one in a dorsal turret and the other semi-fixed in the co-pilot's windshield. In December 1936, the Do 17E-1 bomber was joined by the Do 17F-1 recon version, identical except for deletion of the bomb sight protruding below the nose enclosure, and installation of cameras and flashlight bombs in the bomb bay.

By December 31, 1936, Dornier had delivered 41 Do 17Es of 481 bombers on order and three Do 17Fs of 270 recon versions on order. Twenty Do 17Es and 15 Do 17Fs went to the Condor Legion in 1937. KG 153 and KG 155 were the first bomber units with Do 17Es, while the Fs soon re-equipped the long-range recon groups attached to each of the five Luftkreis (districts).

Do 23 testing twin tail for Do 17

Do 17V-9 as transport

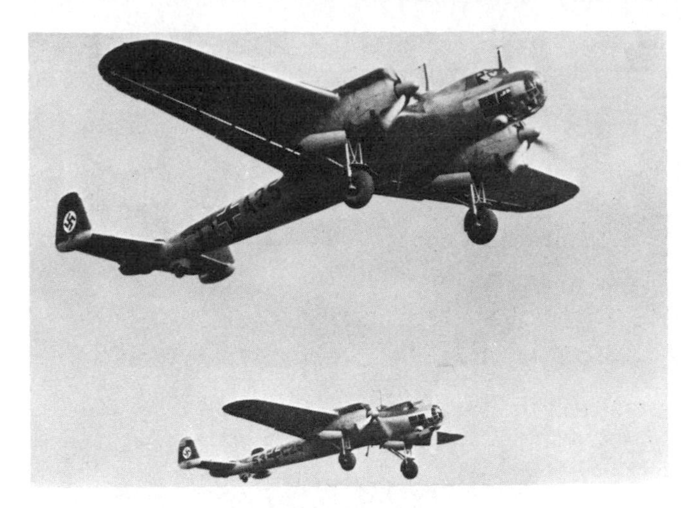

DORNIER Do 17E-1
BMW VI 7.3, 2 X 660 hp
DIMENSIONS: Span 18 m. (59′), Lg. 16.25 m. (53′4″), Ht. 4.32 m. (14′2″), Wing Area 55 qm. (592 sq. ft.)
WEIGHT: Empty 4500 kg. (9920 lb.), Gross 7040 kg. (15,520 lb.)
PERFORMANCE: Speed—Max. 310 km/hr (193 mph) at 4000 m. (13,120′), 354 km/hr (220 mph) at sea level, Cruising speed 315 km/hr (196 mph), Landing speed 121 km/hr (75 mph), Climb 1000 m./2.6 min. (3280′/2.6 min.), Range 500 km. with 750 kg.; 1500 km. max. (310 miles with 1650 lb.; 930 miles max.), Service ceiling 5100 m. (16,730′)

Do 17F-1

Do 17V-8 (MV-1)

DORNIER Do 17Ka-2
Gnome Rhone 14N1/2, 2 X 980 hp at 14,850′
DIMENSIONS: Span 18 m. (59′), Lg. 16.82 m. (55′2¼″), Ht. 4.62 m. (14′6″), Wing Area 55 qm. (592 sq. ft.)
WEIGHT: Empty 4500 kg. (9900 lb.), Gross 7040 kg. (15,490 lb.)
PERFORMANCE: Speed—Max. 415 km/hr (259 mph) at 3450 m. (11,320′), 358 km/hr (222 mph) at sea level, Cruising speed 330 km/hr (205 mph), Landing speed 121 km/hr (75 mph), Range 1590 km. (985 miles), Service ceiling 5500 m. (18,040′)

At the International Military Airplane competition in July 1937 in Switzerland, a new version appeared with 1000 hp Daimler-Benz DB 600A inline engines and a rectangular shaped nose enclosure. Known as the Do 17MV-1 (formerly the V-8), this prototype startled observers with speeds faster than those of foreign fighters. Outsiders were unaware that this was the only example of a 458 km/hr (284 mph) Dornier, the BMW-powered service model being limited to 354 km/hr (220 mph) at sea level.

Production of the Daimler engine had not reached a level sufficient to supply the Dornier line, which now added a Yugoslavian contract for 27 Do 17Ks and equipment necessary to undertake license-production at Kraljevo. Yugoslavian models used Yugoslavian-made 980 hp Gnome-Rhone radials and the MV-1's long nose with two 20 mm. MG/FF fixed guns and were designated Do 17Kb-1 in bomber form and Ka-2 and Ka-3 with recon equipment; 3 flexible 7.9 mm. guns and 1000 kg. of bombs were carried. The first example was finished in October 1937, deliveries were completed in 1938, and license production began the following year. Seventy Do 17Ks were on hand when Yugoslavia was invaded on April 6, 1941, but most were destroyed on the ground.

Bramo 323A radial engines and the standard rounded nose enclosure were seen about June 1938 on the next Luftwaffe production model, the Do 17M. The prototype, D-AYZE, was known as the MV-2, and another as MV-3. A fourth man for pathfinder services was added to two Do 17Ls also known as V-11 and V-12. Standard Do 17M-1s had three men, three MG 15s in dorsal, trapdoor and windshield positions and 1000 kg. (2200 lb.) of bombs.

More widely used was the parallel Do 17P-1 that replaced the Do 17F in recon units in 1938–39. It was identical to the Do 17M but for the BMW

DORNIER Do 17M-1
Bramo 323A-1, 2 X 900 hp at takeoff, 2 X 1000 hp at 3000 m. (9840')
DIMENSIONS: as Do 17E
WEIGHT: Gross 8000 kg. (17,640 lb.)
PERFORMANCE: Speed—Max. 410 km/hr (255 mph) at 4000 m. (13,120'), 344 km/hr (214 mph) at sea level, Cruising speed 350 km/hr (218 mph), Range 500 km. with 1000 kg.; 1360 km. max. (310 miles with 2200 lb.; 845 miles max.), Service ceiling 7000 m. (22,960')

DORNIER Do 17P-1
BMW 132N, 2 X 870 hp at takeoff, 665 hp at 4500 m. (14,765')
DIMENSIONS: as Do 17M
WEIGHT: Empty 5640 kg. (12,410 lb.), Gross 7680 kg. (16,900 lb.)
PERFORMANCE: Speed—Max. 434 km/hr (269 mph) at 4000 m. (13,120'), Cruising speed 392 km/hr (243 mph), Landing speed 125 km/hr (78 mph), Range 1700 km. (1055 miles), Service ceiling 9550 m. (31,300')

132N engines and omission of the bomb sight. Ten examples went to Spain, and nearly all of the 262 aircraft with the Luftwaffe's 23 long-range recon *Staffeln* when World War II began were Do 17Ps.[4] Production totaled 330 Do 17Ps, the last two delayed to April 1940.

Experimental work in 1938 produced the Do 17R-1 and Do 17R-2 with Daimler-Benz inline engines; 1000 hp Do 600s on the first and 1150 hp DB 601s on the other. Daimler DB 600Ns of 1050 hp were used on three Do 17s recon aircraft, the first with the *Waffenkopf* (Weapons head). This was an enlarged, deeper cabin with MG 15s at the top and lower rear, as well as the semi-flexible co-pilot's gun, and permitted four crew members with needed room and visibility. This forward section was also used on 15 Do 71U pathfinders with accommodations for five men.

The main production variant was the Do 17Z-1 powered by the Do 17M's Bramo 323A radials, and operated by four men in the *Waffenkopf*. As deliveries accelerated in 1939, Bramo 323P engines with new superchargers were used on the Do 17Z-2, and usually replaced the 323As on previous Do 17Z-1s. After the war's outbreak, there were many modifications to the Dorniers whose tactics favored low-level attacks with ten 100 kg. (220 lb.) bombs. The original three MG 15s were joined by a forward gun in the nose for the bombardier, and in 1940 a pair of guns was added to the cabin's side windows. A few Do 17Z-3s were fitted late in 1939 with cameras, the Z-4s had dual controls added for training, and another post-delivery installation was the flotation bags on the Z-5. A single Z-6 replaced the standard glazed nose with a Ju 88C-1 nose section with three 7.9 mm. MG 17 and one 20 mm. MG/FF guns. It led to nine Do 17Z-10 night fighters, with 1200 hp 323R radials, four MG/FFs and four MG 17 guns.

On September 2, 1939, the Luftwaffe had 373 Dorniers with its first-line *Kampfgeschwader* including staff planes and nine *Gruppen* of KG 2, 3, 76, and 77. Of these 212 were Do 17Zs and the rest Do 17E and Ms. Three more Do 17M-1s flew with each of the nine Stuka groups' Ju 87s as staff planes, and other Ms filled as reserves for the Do 17Ps in recon units.

Production of the Do 17Z reached 600 by 1939's end, and 269 were added in 1940. Nine of the last went to a night-fighter group as the Do 17Z-10. On May 11, 1940, the Luftwaffe's Dorniers included 422 Do 17Z bombers in 12 groups and 162 Do 17Ps, 41 Do 17Ms and 22 new Do 215s with 19 long-range recon *Staffeln*. As the superior Ju 88 came into service, it gradually replaced most of the Dorniers, and in June 1941 only KG 2 and III/KG 3 still used the Do 17Z as a bomber in Russia. A Croatian *Staffel* also appeared with this model on the Russian front, but left

[4] An exception was 1(F)124 with the Do 17F, replaced in 1940 by Do 215s.

Do 17RV-2

Do 17Z-1

DORNIER Do 17Z-2
Bramo 323P, 2 X 1000 hp for takeoff, 940 hp at 13,120′
DIMENSIONS: Span 18 m. (59′), Lg. 15.79 m. (51′10″), Ht. 4.56 m. (15′), Wing Area 55 qm. (592 sq. ft.)
WEIGHT: Empty 5230 kg. (11,532 lb.), Gross 8890 kg. (19,600 lb.)
PERFORMANCE: Speed—Max. 410 km/hr (255 mph) at 4000 m. (13,120′), 345 km/hr (214 mph) at sea level, Cruising speed 376 km/hr (233 mph), Landing speed 125 km/hr (78 mph), Range 2000 km. (1240 miles), Service ceiling 6900 m. (22,630′)

DORNIER Do 215B-1
Daimler-Benz DB 601Aa, 2 X 1175 hp
DIMENSIONS: Span 18 m. (59′), Lg. 15.79 m. (51′10″), Ht. 4.50 m. (15′), Wing Area 55 qm. (592 sq. ft.)
WEIGHT: Empty 5775 kg. (12,730 lb.), Gross 8800 kg. (19,400 lb.)
PERFORMANCE: Speed—Max. 480 km/hr (298 mph) at 4000 m. (13,120′), 385 km/hr (230 mph) at sea level, Cruising speed 455 km/hr (282 mph), Landing speed 125 km/hr (78 mph), Climb 1000 m./2.3 min. (3280′/2.3 min.), Range 380 km. with 1000 kg.; 2450 km. max. (236 miles with 2200 kg.; 1520 miles max.), Service ceiling 8800 m. (28,870′)

after heavy losses. Fifteen secondhand Do 17Z-2s went to Finland in April 1942.

The story of this Dornier family includes that of the Do 215. Originally, it was simply a Do 17Z for export. While the first example crashed shortly after its maiden flight on October 29, 1938, a preproduction Do 17Z-0 with Bramo 323A engines (D-AIIB) was designated Do 215 at RLM request and offered for export sale. A second example was demonstrated to Yugoslavian officials with Gnome-Rhone 14N radials, and a third offered Daimler-Benz DB 601A inline powerplants.

Sweden ordered 18 of the latter version as the Do 215A-1. The outbreak of war caused the Luftwaffe to take over the production line for its long-range recon units, and the aircraft were redesignated Do 215B. Powered by 1175 hp DB 601As, they were four-seaters with three MG 15s, 1000 kg. (2200 lb.) bomb load, and three cameras. The Do 215B-1 appeared in December 1939 exactly like the Do 17Z except for the inline engines, which had been delayed by a radiator problem. The B-2 differed only in equipment, and B-3 was applied to two planes delivered to the Soviets, but most were B-4s with an additional gun mount and equipment.

Do 215 deliveries reached 101 when production ended early in 1941. The Do 215Bs were used by the High Command's special *Aufklaerungsgruppe* and by 1(F)/124. The former unit was a strategic recon unit that used Do 215B, Ju 86P and Ju 88B aircraft in clandestine preparations for the invasion of Russia. Night fighter units also received about a dozen Do 215B-5 conversions utilizing the gun installation tried on the Do 17Z-10.

HEINKEL HE 111

As the Luftwaffe's standard bomber when the war began, the Heinkel 111 shared both victory and

Do 215B-4

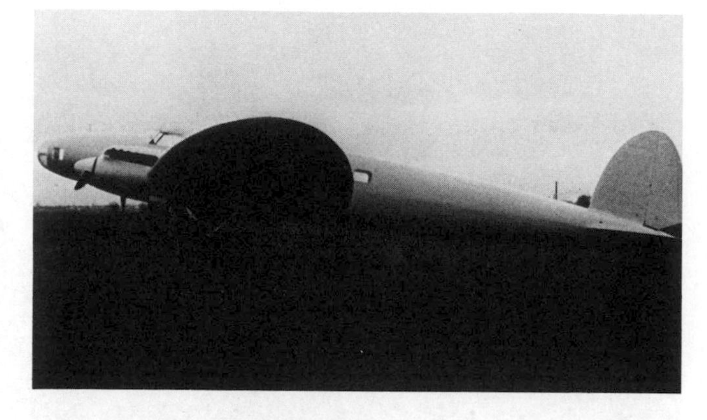

HEINKEL He 111a (V-1)
BMW VI 6.OZ, 2 X 60 hp
DIMENSIONS: Span 25 m. (82'¼"), Lg. 17.25 m. (56'7"), Ht. 3.9 m. (12'10"), Wing Area 87.6 qm. (943 sq. ft.)
WEIGHT: Empty 5800 kg. (12,764 lb.), Gross 7600 kg. (16,-755 lb.)
PERFORMANCE: Speed—Max. 350 km/hr (217 mph), Range 1500 km. (930 miles), Service ceiling 5400 m. (17,720')

defeat. They were the first bombers over Warsaw and the bombers shot down in the greatest numbers during the Battle of Britain.

Development began in 1933 when the Air Ministry ordered seven all-metal Heinkel He 111 prototypes adaptable as either bombers or transports. The first, He 111a or V-1, was designed by Siegfried and Walter Gunther with the smooth lines, retractable wheels, and elliptical wings that had given so much speed to their He 70. Powered by two 660 hp BMW VI 6.0Z inline engines, the He 111a first flew February 24, 1935, at Marienehe.

While the first prototype had both cabin windows and a glazed bombardier's nose cage, the He 111V-2 (D-ALIX) of March 1935 was fitted as a ten-place transport with modified wings. The wing tips applied to production aircraft were introduced in April on He 111V-3, D-ALES, which had a bow gun position and cabin windows. These aircraft were tested secretly, but He 111V-4 (D-AHAO) was exhibited in January 1936 as a commercial transport with new three-bladed propellers and the V-2 style wings. Both V-2 and V-4 transports were used for Lufthansa route-proving flights that actually provided photographic reconnaissance of foreign countries.

He 111V-3

HEINKEL He 111A-0
BMW VI 6.OZ, 2 X 660 hp
DIMENSIONS: Span 22.6 m. (74′2″), Lg. 17.5 m. (57′5″), 4.4 m. (14′5″), Wing Area 87.6 qm. (943 sq. ft.)
WEIGHT: Gross 8250 kg. (18,150 lb.)
PERFORMANCE: Speed—Max. 310 km/hr (195 mph) at sea level

He 111V-5

He 111B-0

No weapons had been seen on those prototypes, but in 1936 the He 111V-5, D-APYS, was the first with a gun pit atop the cabin and a retractable bucket turret underneath. Two 910 hp Daimler-Benz DB 600A engines presaged the future powerplants, while the He 111V-6, D-AXOH, served as a test bed for the 730 hp Junkers Jumo 210Ga. The seventh prototype was to introduce a new wing platform for simplified production.

Heinkel production orders rose from 102 at the beginning of 1935 to 777 He 111 bombers by December 1936. Only the first five production aircraft were delivered by the end of 1936, but deliveries accelerated, especially as the new Oranienburg factory opened.

Preproduction aircraft were the He 111A-0 with 660 hp BMWs, three-bladed props, three 7.9 mm. MG 15 guns, and 1000 kg. (2200 lb.) bomb load. Performance (including a 310 km/hr [195 mph] top speed) was not what the Luftwaffe wished, so the ten A-0s were sold to China and there fought the Japanese invasion in August 1937.

On the Luftwaffe production line, the 910 hp Daimler-Benz had become available for the He 111B series. The He 111B-0 used the DB 600A, B-1 the DB 600Aa, and the more widely used B-2, the DB 600CG. After some aileron adjustments indicated by B-0 trials, the He 111B-1 was ready in January 1937 to enter service with KG 154 (later KG 27). Thirty He 111Bs went to K/88 in Spain.

Armament included 1500 kg. (3300 lb.) of bombs carried fins down in vertical chutes and three MG 15s for the nose, dorsal and retractable bucket turrets. The latter was lowered only when enemy fighters

HEINKEL He 111B-2
Daimler-Benz DB 600CG, 2 X 950 hp at takeoff, 910 hp at 13,120′
DIMENSIONS: Span 22.6 m. (74′2″), Lg. 17.5 m. (57′5″), Ht. 4.4 m. (14′5″), Wing Area 87.6 qm. (943 sq. ft.)
WEIGHT: Gross 5840 kg. (12,877 lb.), Gross 8600 kg. (18,-963 lb.)
PERFORMANCE: Speed—Max. 370 km/hr (230 mph) at 4000 m. (13,120′), 300 km/hr (186 mph) at sea level, Cruising speed 345 km/hr (214 mph)

appeared, for it reduced speed. The Heinkels made their first sorties in Spain on March 9, 1937, and participated in the April 26 attack on Guernica.

Heinkel also delivered a ten-passenger transport series along with its bombers. Lufthansa (DLH) received six He 111Cs with BMW engines, but considered them uneconomical commercially. A new straight tapered wing simplified for easier production had been designed in 1936 for the V-7 bomber, and was applied to five transport aircraft originally labeled V-12 to V-16. BMW inline engines were fitted to the first two, which were passed to DLH in 1938 as the He 111G, along with two with BMW 132 air-cooled radials that became the He 111G-3, or He 111L. The last had DB 600G engines and became General Milch's personal transport as He 111G-4. Four copies went to Turkey as He 111G-5.

An improved engine, the Daimler-Benz BD 600G, was used on the modified He 111B-0, D-AQOX, which became the V-9, and on an He 111D-0 batch. These bombers appeared from Wismar in autumn 1937 with a cleaned-up nacelle with a deep radiator and single exhaust pipe. But quantity production never got underway, for a Daimler engine shortage

He-111D-0

forced Heinkel to shift to another powerplant.

Those were available in the new Junkers series, whose 1000 hp Jumo model was selected for the He 111E series appearing in January 1938. Basically, this series differed from the B only in the new engine nacelles and increased bomb capacity.

The He 111E-0 was followed by the He 111E-1 with 2000 kg. (4400 lb.) bomb load and 390 km/hr (242 mph) top speed. The E-3 was a larger series differing only in equipment, while the E-4 and E-5 had external racks under the fuselage for bombs too large for the internal chutes. After tests with an He 111V-17, D-ACBH, an auxiliary 853 liter (220 gal.) fuselage tank was used on the E-5.

Forty-five He 111E-1s went to the Condor Legion, beginning March 1938. Their high speed kept losses so low the Germans were misled to expect that such lightly armed bombers could operate elsewhere with similar success. This belief was soon exploded in World War Two.

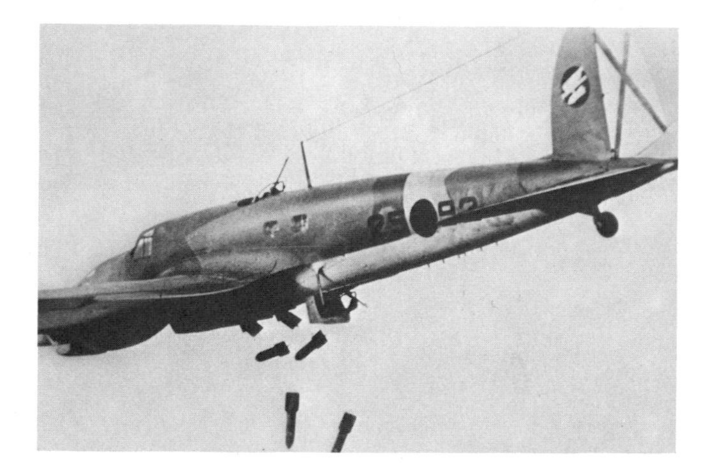

He 111-1 in Spain

The graceful curve on the Heinkel's leading edge was replaced by a straight line in the new simplified wing introduced on the V-7 and He 111G aircraft and seen in July 1937 on the He 111V-11 rebuilt from a Daimler-powered B, D-ARCG. This wing was incorporated into the bomber assembly line in summer 1938 with the He 111F-0 using the 1100 hp Jumo 211A-3. Similar to the E series, but for wing and engines, were 30 He 111F-1s sold to Turkey and 40 He 111F-4s for the Luftwaffe.

Parallel to this series were built 90 He 111J-1s using 950 hp Daimler DB 600CG engines. Originally this variant was to have an external torpedo rack tested on He 111V-18, D-ADUN, but this was abandoned on the J-1, which differed from the F only in the engines.

The Luftwaffe bomber strength on September 19,

HEINKEL He 111E-3
Junkers Jumo 211A-1, 2 X 1010 hp at takeoff, 960 hp at 1500 m. (4920′)
DIMENSIONS: as He 111B
WEIGHT: Gross 10,600 kg. (23,320 lb.)
PERFORMANCE: Speed—Max. 420 km/hr (261 mph) at 4000 m. (13,120′), 350 km/hr (218 mph) at sea level, Range 150 km. with 1000 kg.; max. 1830 km. (930 miles with 2200 lb.; max. 1140 miles), Service ceiling 7200 m. (23-620′)

He 111F-1

He 111V-18 (B with torpedo rack)

1938, during the Sudeten crisis was 1235; including 570 Heinkels: 272 He 111Bs, 171 He 111Es, 39 He 111Fs, and 88 He 111Js. When war broke out less than a year later, this force had been almost replaced by new short-nosed Heinkels, a remarkably quick modernization process.

By September 2, 1939, 21 of the 31 Luftwaffe *Kampfgruppen* used Heinkels, with 780 out of 1180 twin-engined bombers. All were short-nosed He 111H and He 111P bombers except the 38 He 111Es of I/KG 1.[5] In addition, 21 He 111Js were attached to Ku.Fl.Gr. 806 under naval command, and many older models were in reserve.

The new look in Heinkels was a transparent nose enclosure with the pilot sitting to port and the bombardier lying prone with his sight and a flexible MG 15 offset to starboard. Behind them were vertical chutes for eight 250 kg. (550 lb.) bombs, and the

[5] Heumann's count of 400 He 111Hs and 349 He 111Ps may include staff aircraft not counted above.

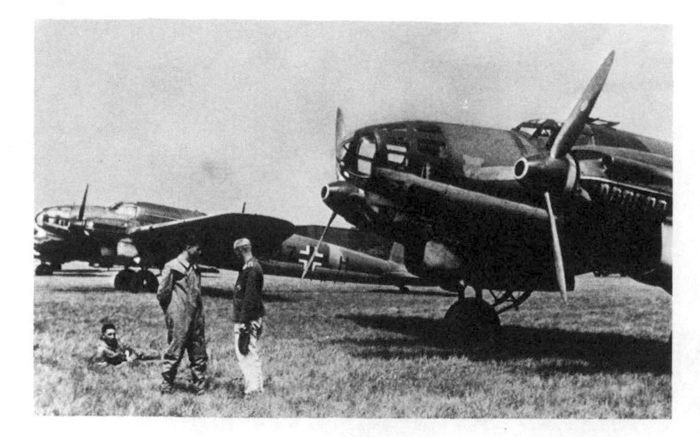

He 111J-1

He 111V-8

dorsal gun pit added a transparent hood. The lower gunner now lay prone in a gondola, since it had been realized that a well-faired emplacement caused less drag than a lowered bucket turret.

The new unbroken nose first appeared in January 1938 on a reworked B-0, He 111V-8, D-AQUO, while the new dorsal and ventral gun fairings were introduced on a modified E, He 111V-23, D-ACBH. The production prototype was D-AUKY, which seems to be the He 111V-7 rebuilt as the V-19 with Jumo 211 engines scheduled for the He 111H.

Since the Jumo 211 was needed for the Junkers Ju 87, and Daimler-Benz engines were then more available, the first short-nosed Heinkels delivered were the He 111P-0 with the 1100 hp DB 601A, seen in autumn 1938. Quantity production followed in 1939 with the He 111P-1 and the He 111P-2. The P-2 differed only by a new radio, while the P-3s were later trainer conversions with dual controls.

By May 1939, enough Jumos were available for parallel deliveries of the He 111H-1 (Jumo 211A-1) and He 111H-2 (Jumo 211A-3). They can be distinguished from the P series by the engine air intake's position; on the Jumo's left side on He 111H, but on the He 111P's Daimlers, the intakes are on the right.

In the Polish campaign, the Heinkels led the bomber offensive with attacks like the raid on Warsaw by KG 27's He 111P groups on the war's first day. Bomber losses in Poland were 78, despite the limited capacity of the defenses.

The armament of three 7.9 mm. MG 15 guns and 4400 lb. bomb load carried by the He 111H-2 and He 111P-2 at the war's start soon proved inadequate. A fifth crewman was added with a pair of MG 15 waist guns firing from side windows, and crew armor was provided. External racks for larger bombs were provided under the fuselage. These additions were made on the He 111P-4, which was followed in 1940 by the

He 111V-23

He 111V-19 (ex V-7)

HEINKEL He 111P-1
Daimler-Benz DB 601Aa, 2 X 1020 hp at 4050 m. (14,765′)
DIMENSIONS: Span 22.5 m. (73′10″), Lg. 16.4 m. (53′10″), Ht. 4.02 m. (13′2″), Wing Area 86.5 qm. (931 sq. ft.)
WEIGHT: Empty 8015 kg. (17,633 lb.), Gross 13,300 kg. (29,-260′)
PERFORMANCE: Speed—Max. 400 km/hr (248 mph) at 4500 m. (14,765′), Cruising speed 360 km/hr (224 mph), Range 960 km. with 1000 kg. (595 miles with 2200 lb.), Service ceiling 7400 m. (24,270′)

He 111H-1

He 111H-2

last Daimler-powered Heinkel, the He 111P-6 with 1175 hp DB 601N.

Corresponding to these types was the He 111H-3 with the added armament and 1200 hp Jumo 211 D-1 engines. First appearing in November 1939, it often had another gunner's mount in front of the belly gondola. A 20 mm. MG/FF could be carried here, along with five 7.9 mm. guns.

Since it had been planned to replace the Heinkels with the Ju 88, production dropped from over 110 He 111s a month in 1939 to just four He 111H machines in April 1940. Deliveries of the He 111P were suspended in March after 691 aircraft, because the limited Daimler-Benz engine supply was reserved for the fighter program. The Jumo 211 engines were for the bombers; Ju 87B, and the hastily revived He 111H program. Heinkel deliveries increased from 756 bombers in 1940 to 950 He 111Hs in 1941, 1337 in 1942 and 1405 in 1943.

During the Battle of Britain the Luftwaffe used 20 He 111 groups, along with nine Do 17 and 14 Ju 88 groups. The heavy losses suffered then should have indicated that the Luftwaffe bomber concept was outmoded, but nevertheless Heinkel's production was expanded. The increased production was necessary to replace losses, rather than for unit expansion.

Although the basic shape was unchanged, a series of improvements on the He 111H were made. Two 800 kg. (1680 lb.) torpedoes could be carried below the He 111H-4 introduced early in 1940. When torpedoes or bombs were carried externally, fuselage space permitted an extra 835 liter (220 gal.) fuel tank. Two such tanks, or up to 2500 kg. (5500 lb.) of bombs could be handled by the He 111H-5.

The most widely used version was 1941's He 111H-6, with 1340 hp Jumo 211F-1 engines and new broad-bladed propellers. Armament included a 20 mm. MG/FF in the nose, five MG 15s, and an MG 17 fixed in the tail cone in the hope its unaimed 7.9 mm. bursts would discourage an enemy directly behind. Active in Russia with KG 4, 27, 53 and 54, the He 111H-6 was also flown by KG 26 for successful torpedo attacks on Arctic convoys.

To cut barrage balloon cables, 30 earlier Heinkels were modified as He 111H-8s with a fender and cutter framework balanced by weights in the tail. Tested by the famous Hanna Reitsch, the H-8 proved too awkward for long service and so the fender was removed and the aircraft refitted as He 111H-8/R2 glider tugs.

A better cable cutter, the Kuto-nose, was used on the few He 111H-10s of 1942. These models had

He 111H-4

He 111H-6 with 3080 lb. bomb

HEINKEL He 111H-6

Junkers Jumo 211F-1, 1340 hp at takeoff, 1060 hp at 5200 m. (17,600′)

DIMENSIONS: as He 111P

WEIGHT: Empty 7720 kg. (17,000 lb.), Gross 12,030 kg. (26,500 lb.)

PERFORMANCE: Speed—Max. 415 km/hr (258 mph) at 5000 m. (16,400′), Cruising speed 358 km/hr (224 mph), Range 1200 km. with 2500 kg.; max. 2780 km. (760 miles with 5500 lb.; max. 1740 km.), Service ceiling 8390 m. (25,500′)

He 111H-8

heavier armor and a 2000 kg. (4400 lb.) bomb load, and an electric cable cutter under thin leading edges.

Heavier armament was featured on the He 111H-11: a 20 mm. MG/FF in the nose, a fully enclosed dorsal 13 mm. gun mount, twin 7.9 mm. MG 81Zs in the ventral gondola, two MG 15 waist guns, and 2250 kg. bomb load. The waist guns were replaced by two MG 81Z twins on the He 111H-11/R1 modification. An R2 glider-towing kit was also available for the H-11, as well as for the later H-14, H-16, and H-20 models.

Two Hs 293 radio-controlled missiles could be launched by the He 111H-12, which was a four-place carrier without a ventral gondola. While tests were made with missiles in 1943, it was never used operationally. Likewise, three Bv 246 glider bombs were to be carried on the H-15 but this weapon did not come in time, and the H-15 was used as a normal bomber.

For pathfinder night bombing missions the H-14 carried six men and special radios. Thirty were built for this role, and 20 more delivered with the R2 glider-towing kit.

The next large He 111 series was the H-16 of fall 1942 with the 1350 hp Jumo 211F-2 and the heavy armament associated with the H-11. The bomb and

He 111H-10

HEINKEL He 111H-16

Junkers Jumo 211F-2, 2 X 1350 hp at takeoff, 1060 hp at 17,390′

DIMENSIONS: as He 111P

WEIGHT: Empty 8700 kg. (19,140 lb.), Gross 14,000 kg. (30,800 lb.)

PERFORMANCE: Speed—Max. 435 km/hr (270 mph) at 600 m. (19,680′), 305 km/hr (227 mph) at sea level, Cruising speed 382 km/hr (239 mph), Climb 2000 m/8.5 min. (6560′/8.5 min.), Range 2050 km. with 2000 kg. (1280 miles with 4400 lb.), Service ceiling 6700 m. (21,980′)

HEINKEL He 111H-16

fuel load alternates provided allowed a maximum load of 3250 kg. (7150 lb.) for short ranges, or 1000 kg. (2200 lb.) for 2900 km. (1800 miles). The H-16/R1 had its dorsal MG 131 in a power-operated turret, (a long overdue feature) and other modifications provided glider-tug and pathfinder variants. Another pathfinder model was the H-18.

The He 111H-20 was built with four *Ruestsaetze:* R1 paratroop carrier for 16 soldiers and three crewmen, R2 glider-tug, R3 night bomber with 3000 kg. (6600 lb.), and the R4 which carried 20 50 kg. (110 lb.) bombs externally.

In 1944, the 1750 hp supercharged Jumo 213E-1 made possible the fastest variant, the He 111H-21 with a top speed of 480 km/hr (298 mph). Armament included three MG 131s in the nose, dorsal and ventral turrets, twin MG 81Zs at side windows, and 3000 kg. (6600 lb.) of bombs. Some were completed as H-22s, a model carrying a single V-1 "Buzz-bomb," the FZG 76 under the port wing. Many older Heinkels were converted to this role when the launching ramps on the Channel coast were lost. From July 7, 1944, to December 13, over 850 missiles were launched against Britain.

In the meantime, Heinkel bomber production ended in fall 1944, with the last model an He 111H-23 saboteur transport with 1776 hp Jumo 213A-1 and a drop hatch for eight parachutists. Some went to the Slovakian Air Force and others were converted to bombers by Luftwaffe workshops. No complete figures of He 111 production are available, but 5204 are reported delivered from 1940–45, with some 7400–7500 altogether.

An He 111R was designed in 1943 as a high-altitude bomber, but only an He 111V-32 prototype was actually completed. A rebuilt H-6, the V-32 had turbo-supercharged Daimler DB 601U engines with circular radiators like those on the Ju 88. The most unusual Heinkel, however, was the He 111Z twin, ten glider-tugs built in 1942 for the giant Me 321. Essentially it was two He 111H-6s joined by a middle wing section and fifth engine. The He 111Z carried seven men and mounts for four MG 131s, five MG 81s and two MG 81Zs. Actually, they proved useful on the Eastern front, towing two Gotha Go 242s. (The big Me 323s had in the meantime acquired six engines of their own.) The possibility of a bomber variant was considered, but not carried out.

Bombing, however, became less and less the Heinkel's main role as Germany had to go on the defensive. At Stalingrad, at least 165 He 111s were lost acting as transports to aid the surrounded German Army there. More and more supply, rather than bombing, became the Heinkel's role. The last big raid by the He 111s was the attack on Poltava's B-17 base on June 22, 1944, but one He 111 group remained active as bombers until the war's end.

It should be added that the Heinkel He 111 was also produced in Rumania and Spain. After receiving enough He 111H-3s in 1940 to equip a bomber regiment, the Rumanians undertook license manufacture at Bucharest. Fifty-eight Heinkels survived the Spanish Civil War, and CASA received a manufacturing license in 1938, although deliveries did not begin until 1945. The first 130 were like the He 111H-16 with Jumo 211 engines, but in 1956 Rolls-Royce 1610 hp Merlins were specified for the remainder of 236 Spanish Heinkels built as the C 2111-A to C 4111-D. They still remained in Spanish Air Force service over 20 years after World War II.

He 111V-32

HEINKEL He 111Z
Jumo 211F-1, 5 X 1340 hp
DIMENSIONS: Span 35.2 m. (115′6″), Lg. 16.6 m. (54′5½″), Ht. 4.2 m. (13′9¼″), Wing Area 148 qm. (159 sq. ft.)
WEIGHT: Empty 21,500 kg. (47,300 lb.), Gross 28,375 kg. (62,425 lb.)
PERFORMANCE: Speed—Max. 420 km/hr (261 mph), Cruising speed 395 km/hr (245 mph), Range 2400 km. (1490 miles), Service ceiling 9600 m. (31,500′)

He 111H-16/R1

In conclusion, it may be said that the He 111 was popular with its crews. They preferred it to more modern, but less reliable aircraft, such as the He 177. It was said that KGzbV 100 pilots re-equipping with He 177s deliberately crashed the new birds during training to avoid having to fly that unlucky bird. However, they still flew bombing missions in old He 111s.

EXPERIMENTAL PROJECTS, 1935–38

The first Luftwaffe bombers had doubled as transport planes, but the Air Ministry naturally pressed the development of bombers without any consideration of civilian role.

The first such specification called for the design of a *Kampfzerstoerer,* a twin-engined three-seater for bombing, fighting, recon, or close-support work. Focke-Wulf and Henschel offered the Fw 57 and Hs 124 multi-purpose types, and in 1935 each received a contract for seven prototypes, the first scheduled for delivery in December 1936.

As design work proceeded, however, the Technical Office revised its ideas and called for a more specialized type. This was the *Schnellbomber,* putting high-speed as the first consideration. Such a drastic change in mission stimulated instead the Junkers Ju 88 and Messerschmitt Bf 162.

Nevertheless, the first Focke-Wulf Fw 57 was completed with two 680 hp Jumo 210G inline engines, a single tail, and a power-operated turret. Hopelessly overweight, the project was abandoned.

The Henschel Hs 124 was also designed to carry three men, 600 kg. (1320 lb.) of bombs, and a 20 mm. gun, but this design had the power turret in the nose and twin rudders. Two 610 hp Jumo 210As powered Hs 124V-1, but Hs 124V-2 had 870 hp BMW 132Dc radials (license-built P & W Hornet). A redesigned nose on the second prototype replaced the turret with a transparent bow and hand-operated gun. A long canopy covered both the pilot and rear gunner, and the bombs, ten 50 kg. (110 lb.), were carried externally. A third prototype was to have two MG 17 and two MG/FF guns in the nose for ground attack work, but development was canceled in favor of the Ju 88.

Very little is known of another twin-engined bomber developed in Germany in 1937. The Henschel Hs 127V-1 was an all-metal twin-engined monoplane that had no armament, but relied on speed for protection. Powered by 950 hp Daimler-Benz DB 600Ds, it

FOCKE-WULF Fw 57
Jumo 210G, 2 X 680 hp
DIMENSIONS: Span 25 m. (82′), Lg. 16.4 m. (53′9″), Ht. 4.1 m. (13′4″), Wing Area 73.5 qm. (791 sq. ft.)
WEIGHT: Empty 6800 kg. (14,960 lb.), Gross 8300 kg. (18,260 lb.)
PERFORMANCE: Speed—Max. 405 km/hr (251 mph) at sea level, Service ceiling 9100 m. (29,850′)

HENSCHEL Hs 124V-2
BMW 132DC, 2 X 870 hp
DIMENSIONS: Span 18.2 m. (59′½″), Lg. 14.5 m. (47′7″), Ht. 3.75 m. (12′4″), Wing Area 54.6 qm. (587 sq. ft.)
WEIGHT: Empty 4250 kg. (9350 lb.), Gross 7230 kg. (15,906 lb.)
PERFORMANCE: Speed—Max. 435 km/hr (270 mph) at 3000 m. (9840′), Landing speed 110 km/hr (68 mph), Climb 6000 m./17.5 min. (19,680′/17.5 min.), Range 2400 km. (1490 miles)

HENSCHEL Hs 124V-1

MESSERSCHMITT Bf 162V-3

was supposed to have a 580 km/hr (360 mph) speed and carry a 1500 kg. (3300 lb.) bomb load.

Tunnel radiators on the prototype were to be later replaced by coolers in the wing's leading edge inboard of the engines. The prototype crashed, and since the Luftwaffe was turning toward heavier armament for bombers, the Hs 127 was abandoned. This Henschel greatly resembled the later DH Mosquito, whose success made the Luftwaffe wish it had not shelved the unarmed fast bomber concept.

The same requirement that inspired the Ju 88 also produced the Messerschmitt Bf 162 "Jaguar" a three-place bomber version of the Bf 110B twin-engined fighter. Three prototypes were rebuilt from Bf 110B; the Bf 162V-1 (D-AIXA) in spring 1937, the V-2 (D-AOBE) in September, and the third (D-AOVI) in August 1938. Powered by the 960 hp DB 600A, it was distinguished from its fighter sisters by a glazed bow for the bombardier. One MG 17 fixed gun and an MG 15 were carried along with 1000 kg. (2200 lb.) bomb load, and top speed was supposed to be 480 km/hr (298 mph).

Along with this bomber, Messerschmitt built two prototypes of the Bf 161 two-seater reconnaissance type. Completed in 1938, they differed from the Bf 162 by a more extended nose. Since the Air Ministry decided to have Junkers specialize on bombers and Messerschmitt on fighters, these projects were terminated. BF 161V-2, however, was used as a test-bed for remote-controlled gun barbettes.

JUNKERS JU 88

The twin-engined monoplane selected as the basic bomber for World War Two was the Junkers Ju 88, built in larger numbers than any German multiengined aircraft.

Its story begins with a Technical Office 1935 specification for a *Schnellbomber* that could do 500 km/hr (310 mph) carrying three men, one 7.9 mm. MG 15 flexible gun and a normal 500 kg. (1100 lb.) bomb load. The emphasis was clearly on a Do 17 replacement with high speed, rather than heavy armament.

Junkers assigned the task to two engineers who had just returned from the U.S.A. Alfred Gassner was an American citizen, and with W. H. Evers had experience with the smooth-skinned metal construction that replaced traditional Junkers corrugated techniques. On January 15, 1936, they began design work, preparing two projects, a Ju 85 twin rudder layout and a Ju 88 single rudder design. The latter was selected by the Luftwaffe, and ten prototypes were ordered.

The Ju 88V-1 (D-AQEN) first flew December 21, 1936, with two 910 hp Daimler DB 600A inline engines behind the circular radiators that became a Ju 88 trademark. A businesslike three-seater with clean lines and no armament yet installed, it crashed during trials. The similar Ju 88V-2 was ready on April 10, 1937, and had a 463 km/hr (289 mph) speed, 2000 km (1240 mile) range, and 6000 m. (19,680′) ceiling.

Junkers Jumo 211A engines of 1000 hp were used on the Ju 88V-3 flown September 13, 1937, with a higher cockpit roof, bomb sight and a rearward firing MG 15. Top speed reached 504 km/hr (313 mph) for 30 minutes, and 520 km/hr (323 mph) more briefly. Performance was so advanced the Luftwaffe decided on mass production, and abandoned the competitive Fw 57, Hs 124 and Bf 162 types described earlier.

The Luftwaffe decided, however, that its new bomber should have four crewmen and additional armament and be equipped and strengthened for dive-bombing. The new crew cabin was introduced on

HENSCHEL Hs 127V-1

JUNKERS Ju 88V-1

JUNKERS Ju 88V-3
Junkers Jumo 211A, 2 X 950 hp at takeoff, 1000 hp at 17,000'
DIMENSIONS: Span 18.25 m. (59'10½"), Lg. 14.25 m. (46'9"), Ht. 4.75 m. (15'7")
WEIGHT: Gross 8500 kg. (18,740 lb.)
PERFORMANCE: Speed—Max. 520 km/hr (323 mph)

the Ju 88V-4 flown February 2, 1938, with an enlarged glazed bow and a belly gondola (*Bola*) offset to starboard for a prone gunner firing backward.

This more practical bomber layout cost speed, but the RLM decided to have the Ju 88 make its first appearance in the high-speed configuration. A streamlined nose section was built on the rebuilt Ju 88V-5, first flown April 13, 1938, powered by a 1200 hp Jumo 211B. On the following March 19, the V-5 set a new world's record of 517 km/hr (321 mph) carrying a 2000 kg. (4400 lb.) load over a 1000 km (621 mile) circuit.

Thus the aviation world first learned of the new "wonder bomber," but as in the case of the Heinkel and Messerschmitt records, the record-breaking aircraft was little like the combat configuration. This was shown on the Ju 88V-6 (D-ASCY) flown June 18, 1938, with the Jumo 211B, four-bladed props, and a new landing gear which rotated the wheels 90 degrees to disappear within the engine nacelles. Three 7.9 mm. MG 15 guns and 500 kg. (1100 lb.) of bombs were carried.

Four more prototypes were completed, beginning with the Ju 88V-7 which became the first *Zerstoerer* Ju 88C prototype. Slatted dive brakes and external bomb racks gave the Ju 88V-8 (WL+008), flown October 3, 1938, the dive-bombing capability desired by the Luftwaffe. Similar were the V-9 finished that same month and the V-10 of February 1939.

Seven preproduction Ju 88A-0 bombers delivered in spring 1939 were followed by the Ju 88A-1, the first version used in combat. Three-bladed propellers were used on its Jumo 211B-1s. Four crewmen sat close together in the cabin; pilot, bombardier, flight engineer and radio-operator. An MG 15 protruded from the starboard windshield, another from the cabin's rear window and the third from the *Bola* underneath. External racks permitted dives with two 1100 lb. or four 550 lb. bombs, while 110 lb. bombs could be carried internally, providing up to 3960 lb. for horizontal bombing missions.

Due to the strong influence of Junkers Director Heinrich Koppenburg on the Technical Office's chief General Udet, Ju 88 production was widespread. Designed for very rapid production, the fuselages and one-piece wings were made in various factories and assembled by Junkers at Bernburg and under license

Ju 88V-4

Ju 88 V-5

JUNKERS Ju 88V-6
Junkers Jumo 211B, 1200 hp
DIMENSIONS: as Ju 88V-3
WEIGHT: Gross 10,200 kg. (22,590 lb.)
PERFORMANCE: Speed—Max. 485 km/hr (301 mph), Range 2450 km. (1520 miles), Service ceiling 8500 m. (27,900′)

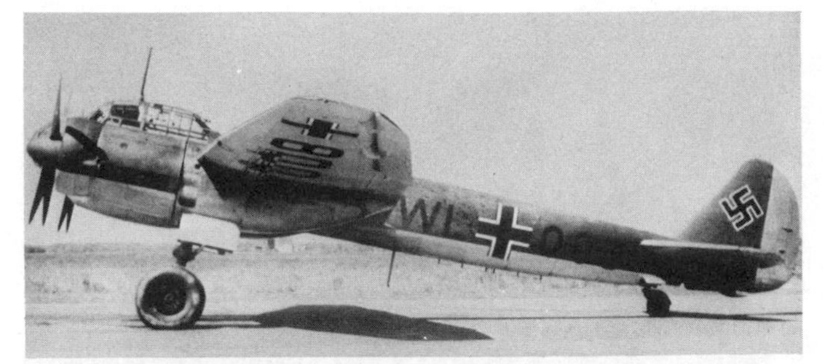

Ju 88V-8

by Arado at Brandenburg, Dornier at Wismar, Heinkel at Oranienburg, and Volkswagen-Werke at Braunschweigen-Waggum. Repair work was done by Junkers at Leipzig and Breslau and VW. Various modifications often caused much trouble. For example, shifting from electric to hydraulic landing gear, caused all of Arado's first ten planes to suffer landing gear failure.

At the war's beginning, only 18 Ju 88A's of I/KG 25, which became I/KG 30 on September 22, 1939, were available for front-line duty. On September 26, four made their first combat sortie, which resulted in the false claim that they sank Britain's then best carrier, the *Ark Royal*. In fairness, it should be stated that this claim originated with the Propaganda Office. The embarrassed pilot, Carl Francke, had reported his dive with two 1100 lb. bombs only as "near miss and possible hit. Effect not observed."

On October 16, I/KG 30 made the first German World War II raid over the British Isles, when its Ju 88s struck at warships in the Firth of Forth. On this unsuccessful attack, the group commander's Ju 88A became the first aircraft shot down by a Spitfire.

As production mounted, new groups were formed. By the end of 1939, 102 Ju 88A-1 bombers and one recon variant had been produced. Deliveries rose from 27 bombers and three recon models in January 1940 to 204 bombers and ten recon machines in April. The Ju 88A had become the Luftwaffe's most important bomber, and remained so for the rest of the war.

These aircraft were of the A-1 series, but many were modified to the A-2 or A-3 variants. These differed in the provision of the "R-Gerat" rocket-assisted takeoff device on the A-2 and dual controls on the unarmed A-3 trainer. Six of April's production were rebuilt as make-shift *Zerstoerer* aircraft with a 20 mm. MG/FF and three 7.9 mm. MG 17 guns in the transparent nose. This arrangement was later standardized in the solid-nosed Ju 88C fighters.

JUNKERS Ju 88A-1
Junkers Jumo 211B-1, 2 X 1200 hp
DIMENSIONS: Span 18.37 m. (60′3″), Lg. 14.36 m. (47′1″), Ht. 4.8 m. (15′9″), Wing Area 52.5 qm. (565 sq. ft.)
WEIGHT: Empty 7250 kg. (15,950 lb.), Gross 10,360/12,500 kg. (22,792/27,508 lb.)
PERFORMANCE: Speed—Max. 460 km/hr (286 mph) at 5500 m. (18,040′), 366 km/hr (227 mph) at sea level, Cruising speed 350 km/hr (217 mph), Range 1000 km, with 1800 kg; 2500 km. with 1000 kg. (620 miles with 3960 lb.; max. 1550 miles with 2200 lb.), Service ceiling 9350 m. (30,680′)

JUNKERS Ju 88A-5
Junkers Jumo 211G, 2 X 1200 hp
DIMENSIONS: Span 20.88 m. (65′10″), Lg. 14.36 m. (47′1″), Ht. 4.8 m. (15′9″), Wing Area 54.5 qm. (586.64 sq. ft.)
WEIGHT: Empty 8250 kg. (18,191 lb.), Gross 11,360 kg. (25,049 lb.)
PERFORMANCE: Speed—Max. 450 km/hr (279 mph) at 5500 m. (18,040′), Cruising speed 350 km/hr (217 mph), Range 2500 km. (1552 miles), Service ceiling 9000 m. (29,520′)

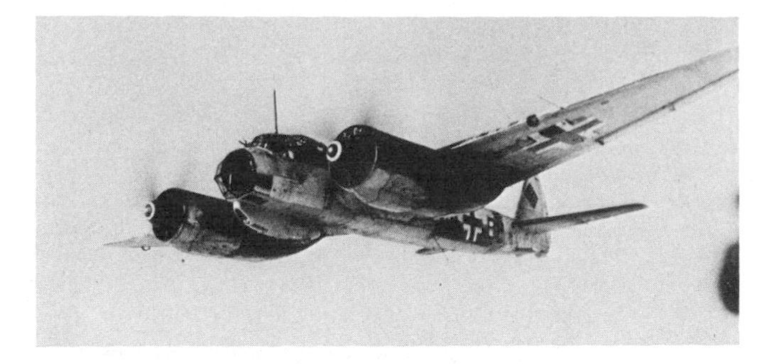

JUNKERS Ju 88A-4
Junkers Jumo 211J, 1410 hp at takeoff, 1200 hp normal
DIMENSIONS: as Ju 88A-5
WEIGHT: Empty 8620 kg. (19,007 lb.), Gross 12,122 kg. (26,-729 lb.), Fuel 1680–2900 liters (444–766 gal.)
PERFORMANCE: Speed—Max. 472 km/hr (293 mph) at 5300 m. (17,380′), Cruising speed 370 km/hr (230 mph), Climb 5400 m./23 min. (17,700′/23 min.), Range 2730 km. (1410 miles), Service ceiling 8235 m. (27,020′)

Extended wing tips with inset ailerons were introduced on the next production series. This was to be the Ju 88A-4 with improved Jumo 211J engines, but when this powerplant was delayed, the next series appeared with the new wings and Jumo 211G engines as the Ju 88A-5. This model carried four MG 15 guns, 2500 kg. (5510 lb.) bomb load, and provision for rocket-assisted takeoff or 900 liter (238 gal.) drop tanks.

This model was first used among the 14 Ju 88 equipped groups that were used in the Battle of Britain in 1940. The fighting soon proved the Junkers needed more protection.

Late in 1941, the Ju 88A-4 arrived with the 1410 hp Jumo 211J. A fixed 13 mm. MG 131 and a flexible 7.9 mm. MG 81 pointed forward, two separate MG 81s were in the dorsal position and the *Bola* retained an MG 15. Later a flexible 20 mm. MG/FF was added in the nose, and a twin MG 81Z and ten mm. armor was provided for the *Bola*. With rocket-assisted takeoff up to 3600 kg. (7940 lb.) of bombs could be lifted.

The Ju 88A-4 was the most widely used of the Junkers bombers, which equipped 25 of some 45 Luftwaffe bomber groups at the various fronts in

MG/FF (20 mm.) added

The Ju 88A-4 in detail:

Dorsal MG 81s

With open *Bola*

Captive in the U.S.

JUNKERS Ju 88B-0
BMW 801Ma, 2 X 1600 hp at takeoff, 1380 hp at 15,100′
DIMENSIONS: Span 20.08 m. (65′7″), Lg. 14.9 m. (48′11″), Ht. 4.9 m. (16′1″), Wing Area 54.5 qm. (586.64 sq. ft.)
WEIGHT: Gross 11,800 kg. (25,960 lb.)
PERFORMANCE: Speed—Max. 500 km/hr (310 mph), Cruising speed 470 km/hr (292 mph), Landing speed 145 km/hr (90 mph), Range 2500 km. (1550 miles), Service ceiling 9400 m. (30,840′)

Ju 88B-3

September 1942. Twenty-three Ju 88A-4s were dispatched to Finland, while Hungary, Italy and Rumania also got the type.

There were numerous variants on these basic models, as listed below:

Ju 88A-6––As A-5 with cable-cutting finder; later reverted to straight bomber or recon roles.
A-7––Unarmed A-5 trainer with dual controls.
A-8––As A-6, but A-4 airframe and engines.
A-9––As A-1, but with tropical equipment added.
A-10––As A-5, but with tropical equipment added.
A-11––As A-4, but with tropical equipment added.
A-12––As A-4 trainer, dual controls, no armor.
A-13––As A-4 with added armor for ground attack. Could carry two WB 81 pods with four 7.9 mm. guns firing forward and two backward.
A-14––An A-4 without dive brakes and with fixed MG/FF in front ventral fairing.
A-15––An A-4 with large wooden belly fairing for 3000 kg. (6600 lb.) bombs instead of standard bomb racks. A night bomber with only two MG 15s, weighing 12,800 kg. (28,160 lb.) gross.
A-16––A trainer based on A-14 without armament.
A-17––A torpedo-bomber; from A-4 modified by repair shops with ventral *Bola*, dive brakes, and front guns removed. Only two dorsal MG 81s remained.

The A-17 was the last of the A series. The Ju 88 had become a workhorse condemned to repeatedly take over new tasks for which it had not been designed. When a replacement type should have been ordered, about 1941, State Secretary Milch decided to continue production of this now obsolete plane, only because he feared a new type's introduction would reduce production figures.

So up to the war's end, this much too old design was still in action, repeatedly modified to try to meet the war's demands. As the man responsible for spar supply for the entire Ju 88 to 388 family, co-author Nowarra can vouch for the fact that the Ju 88 suffered over 3000 modifications and that over 60 versions were built or at least projected.

A basic improvement in the Junkers design was attempted in the Ju 88B powered by two 1600 hp BMW 801MA radials and a new streamlined nose enclosure. The prototype flown early in 1940 was otherwise like the A-1 bomber, but ten preproduction Ju 88B-0s built in the same year were finished with longer fuselages and the extended wing tips of the A-4 and A-5 series.

Armament included three pairs of MG 81 guns mounted in the nose, dorsal and ventral positions, and 5500 lb. of bombs. Although performance was better than that of the Ju 88A, the Air Ministry did not wish to disrupt production for a newer type, so no quantity orders were placed. Instead, most of the preproduction aircraft went to the High Command's special recon unit with their bomb racks replaced by cameras and extra fuel tanks. Our photo shows one example tested as a fighter with an MG 151 and three MG 17 fixed guns, and another was an armament test-bed for the future Ju 188.

Along with the bombers, Junkers provided a parallel series of reconnaissance aircraft. The first of these were Ju 88A-1s fitted with cameras, and had no separate designations, but those built parallel to the A-4 and A-5 series were designated Ju 88D. An extra fuel tank and two cameras were inserted in the bomb bay. No dive brakes were fitted, but 900 liter (238 gal.) drop tanks could be carried. The D-1 model was based on the A-4, the D-2 on the A-5 (appearing in reverse order) and D-3 was a D-1 with tropical equipment. These aircraft equipped the majority of the long-range recon units.

A special long-range version was the 20 Ju 88H-1s and 10 Ju 88H-2s built late in 1943. These three-seaters used the wings and 1700 hp BMW 801D radials of the Ju 88G with a lengthened fuselage. Extra fuel tanks provided 1600 gal. and a 3200 mile range. The Ju 88H-1 had FuG 200 radar, twin MG 81 fixed guns and a flexible MG 81 in front, and an MG 131 dorsal gun, while the Ju 88H-2 had no radar, but used six 20 mm. MG 151/20 fixed guns instead of the radar and was intended for destroyer operations.

By 1943, the majority of Ju 88 production was for the fighter units, with the Ju 88R replacing the Gs as the major model. The last bomber version was the Ju 88S, which attempted to stretch the basic design's performance to the limit.

Powered by BMW 801D radials yielding 1700 hp takeoff with 96 octane fuel, the S series reverted to the streamlined style of the early Ju 88 prototypes. A smoothly rounded glass nose replaced the multi-paneled bow, the external bomb racks were removed, and the armor and gun weight reduced.

The Ju 88V-93 prototype was a Ju 88A-4 rebuilt in 1943 in the new form, and was followed by a small Ju 88S-0 series. Armament included 800 kg. (1764 lb.) bomb load, one MG 81 forward, twin MG 81Z in the ventral gondola, and an MG 131 dorsal gun. Top speed was raised from 472 km/hr (293 mph) on the A-4 to 535 km/hr (332 mph).

Further streamlining was achieved on the Ju 88S-1 by eliminating the gondola, and 1750 hp BMW 801G engines used GM-1 booster for high altitudes. Three

JUNKERS Ju 88S-1
BMW 801D, 2 X 1730 hp at 5000′, 1430 hp at 24,000′
DIMENSIONS: Span 20.08 m. (65′7″), Lg. 14.84 m. (48′8″), Ht. 4.8 m. (15′7″), Wing Area 54.5 qm. (586.64 sq. ft.)
WEIGHT: Empty 8300 kg. (18,250 lb.), Gross 16,800 kg. (30,400 lb.)
PERFORMANCE: Speed—Max. 600 km/hr (379 mph) at 8000 m. (26,250′), Cruising speed 525 km/hr (328 mph), Range 1760 km. (1100 miles), Service ceiling 11,500 m. (37,750′)

Ju 88T-1

men, a single MG 131 dorsal gun and up to 4400 lb. of bombs could be carried at speeds of 610 km/hr (379 mph). This model was used by I/KG 66 in the West in 1944.

Turbosupercharged BMW 801 radials giving 1810 hp at takeoff and 1500 hp at 40,000′ were used on the Ju 88S-2, which had a wooden belly tray, as on the A-15, to hold up to 6600 lb. of bombs or added fuel, and two fixed MG 81s firing aft. Top speed was 595 km/hr (370 mph).

Last of the series was the Ju 88S-3 which utilized an inline Jumo 213A, whose GM-1 boosted power from 1750 to 2125 hp. The airframe was that of the S-1 and top speed was 560 km/hr at 6200 m. at 10,490 kg. gross, (382 mph, 27,900′ and 23,120 lb.). Few were finished when German bomber production came to a halt in 1944.

Parallel to the Ju 88S-1 bomber was the Ju 88T-1 reconnaissance version, similar but with cameras in the bomb bay. Plans for a Jumo-powered T-3 version to be built by Henschel were canceled in 1944, and the Ju 88 continued in production only as a fighter.

Experience with the S series suggests that the Air Ministry made a basic error when it departed from the original Ju 88 design in 1938. Had the high-speed concept of the prototypes not been distorted by the changes made as the Ju 88 went into production, Germany could have begun the war with the world's fastest bomber.

In any case, the Ju 88 had proven one of the war's most prolific types. Production totaled 9155 bombers from 1939–44, 1911 recon versions from 1940–44, and 3967 fighters or attack types from 1940–45.

THE "MISTEL" SYSTEM

A curious footnote to the Ju 88 story is the *Mistel* system, named after the Mistletoe that was so deadly in the Nordic myth. Like the Kamikaze of Japan, a complete bomber would dive on an enemy ship, but the pilot here would be in a separate aircraft. The prototype was a Ju 88A-4 with a Bf 109F riding on top attached by tripods. The fighter's pilot controlled both components with all engines running on the bomber's fuel, conserving the fighter's fuel for his return. The pilot would guide the aircraft to the target, release the *Mistel* in a dive, and return.

In July 1943, 15 old Ju 88A-4s were modified as *Mistel* I, with a detachable nose section replaceable by a 8380 lb. hollow charge. After training, five were forwarded to France to attack Allied invasion forces. The first sortie on June 24, 1944, ended in an abortion when the *Mistel* had to be released to evade a Mosquito night fighter. Four more were used later against Allied ships, with probable hits.

The Junkers repair plant at Leipzig-Mockau was ordered to rework 50 Ju 88Gs for the so-called Beethoven program, and a second 25 were added later. These aircraft were known as the *Mistel* 2, used a Fw 190 or Bf 109G pilot plane, and were first ready in November 1944. The lower components had been hastily converted on a three-shift basis from war-weary airframes and were not fitted with warheads until they reached their operational base.

Bad winter weather and flying difficulties frustrated more extensive use of the system. A plan to attack the British fleet at Scapa Flow from Danish bases in December was replaced by a plan to attack Soviet industry. The collapse of the Eastern front required II/KG 200 to commit its forces piecemeal. Attacks were made on bridges over the Neisse on March 9, 1945, and these became the *Mistel's* main duty. Junkers was asked to accelerate production, using new Ju 88G and H airframes on the assembly line, but the collapse of the German war effort intervened. The last, nearly completed, Junkers components at Leipzig were destroyed by a P-38 low-level attack witnessed by co-author Nowarra. The remaining examples fell into the hands of advancing Allies.

The *Mistel*

DORNIER Do 19

24.

Long-range Bombers

During the war, the Allies wondered why Germany had not built a force of four-engined heavy bombers comparable to the American B-17 and B-24, and the British Lancasters. Certainly such a force would have made a big difference in the war, posing a threat far greater than that of the twin-engined types. Four engines made possible a real strategic bombing capability.

The Luftwaffe's first Chief of Staff, Walther Wever, had foreseen the need for a long-distance heavy bomber, especially for attacking Russian industry beyond the Urals. In 1934, he ordered the four-engined Dornier Do 19 and Junkers Ju 89 bomber prototypes.

On October 28, 1936, the Dornier Do 19V-1 was lifted into flight by four over-burdened 650 hp BMW 322H-2 radials. A nine-place monoplane with twin rudders, it was built for ease of production. A 3000 kg. (6600 lb.) bomb load was accommodated with guns in nose, tail, dorsal, and ventral positions. The nose and tail (the first on a German bomber) turrets were spacious enough for a large-caliber weapon handled by two gunners.

The even larger Junkers Ju 89V-1 appeared in December 1936 powered by four 950 hp Daimler DB 600 inline engines and was similar in layout to the Dornier. Yet neither of these planes was further developed for the strategic bombing role. Their protagonist, General Wever, had been killed in an He 70G crash on June 3, 1936. His successor, General Albert Kesselring, as well as Generals Milch and Udet opposed the heavy bomber concept.

Luftwaffe chief Goering remarked that Hitler "will never ask me how big our bombers are, but how many we have," and on April 29, 1937, the heavy bomber program was canceled. This has been called one of the High Command's most fateful wrong decisions, since it deprived Germany of a real strategic bombing force.

This decision was still defended after the war by Kesselring, who pointed to Germany's limited raw materials and time for action. It seemed that the best investment of resources was in faster, smaller aircraft built in large numbers to directly support ground troops. Udet was Technical Office Chief, and as an ex-fighter pilot considered larger bombers "barn doors" easy to destroy, and preferred the greater accuracy of dive-bombers.

This decision can be compared with that of the U. S. Army in 1936, when twin-engined Douglas B-18s were preferred, because of their lower cost, to the early Boeing B-17s. In that case, the army generals saw no need for long-range bombing. The German situation reflected the Nazi ambition for short *Blitzkrieg* attacks against neighboring countries. Enemy industry was a prize to be captured, not a target for bombers. Bombers were seen primarily as an aid to the quick victory of the ground forces.

DORNIER Do 19
BMW 322H-2, 4 X 650 hp
DIMENSIONS: Span 35 m. (114'10"), Lg. 24.45 m. (80'2"), Ht. 5.78 m. (18'11½"), Wing Area 162 qm. (1743 sq. ft.)
WEIGHT: Empty 11,875 kg. (26,103 lb.), Gross 18,500 kg. (40,700 lb.)
PERFORMANCE: Speed—Max. 315 km/hr (195 mph), Cruising speed 250 km/hr (155 mph), Landing speed 105 km/hr (65 mph), Climb 1000 m./3.4 min. (3280'/3.4 min.) 5000 m./30.5 min. (16,400'/30.5 min.), Range 1600 km. (995 miles), Service ceiling 5600 m. (18,370')

JUNKERS Ju 89V-1
Daimler-Benz DB 600A 4 X 950 hp
DIMENSIONS: Span 35.27 m. (115'8"), Lg. 26.5 m. (86'31½"), Ht. 7.6 m. (24'11½"), Wing Area 184 qm. (1980 sq. ft.)
WEIGHT: Empty 17,000 kg. (37,485 lb.), Gross 22,800 kg. (50,274 lb.)
PERFORMANCE: Speed—Max. 390 km/hr (242 mph), Cruising speed 320 km/hr (199 mph), Range 1600 km. (995 miles), Service ceiling 6000 m. (19,680')

With the four-engined bomber program canceled, the second and third Dornier prototypes went unfinished. Junkers had finished only the second of seven Ju 89 bombers ordered in 1935, the Ju 89V-2 with modified rudders and a tail turret like the Ju 86's nose enclosure. Permission was given Junkers to finish four more prototypes as Ju 90 forty-passenger transports. The first example, Ju 90V-1, "Der Grosse Dessauer" flew August 28, 1937, also with DB 600A inline engines. Three others got 880 hp BMW 132 radials, and were to be followed by ten similar Ju 90Bs for Lufthansa. During the war, this type was developed into the Ju 290 maritime bomber to be described later.

Ju 89V-2

FOCKE-WULF CONDOR

Although Germany had no four-engined bombers on hand at the onset of the war, when Britain joined the fight it was immediately evident that long-range aircraft would be necessary to find and attack ships at sea.

Such a plane was in development as the He 177, but in the meantime the Luftwaffe improvised with adaptation of the Focke-Wulf Fw 200 and Blohm and Voss BV 142. These were four-engined transports with the endurance needed for over-water flying.

The BV 142 was developed from the four-engined, twin-float Ha 139 seaplane built in 1937 for a transatlantic mail route. The first of four landplane versions had flown October 11, 1938, as the Ha 142V-1

Ju 89V-2

BLOHM & VOSS Bv 142V-2/U1
BMW 132H-1, 4 X 880 hp
DIMENSIONS: Span 29.5 m. (96'9½"), Lg. 19.5 m. (64'), Ht. 5.05 m. (16'7"), Wing Area 130 qm. (1399 sq. ft.)
WEIGHT: Empty 11,080 kg. (24,431 lb.), Gross 16,560 kg. (36,515 lb.), Fuel 6560 liters (1732 gal.)
PERFORMANCE: Speed—Max. 374 km/hr (232 mph) at sea level, Cruising speed 355 km/hr (220 mph), Range 3900 km. (2420 miles), Service ceiling 9000 m. (29,530')

FOCKE-WULF Fw 200C-1
BMW 132H, 4 X 830 hp
DIMENSIONS: Span 32.84 m. (107'9"), Lg. 23.85 m. (78'3"), Ht. 6.3 m. (20'8"), Wing Area 118 qm. (1270 sq. ft.)
WEIGHT: Data not available
PERFORMANCE: Speed—Max. 365 km/hr (227 mph), Cruising speed 330 km/hr (205 mph), Landing speed 107 km/hr (66 mph), Range 3500 km. (2175 miles), Service ceiling 6700 m. (21,980')

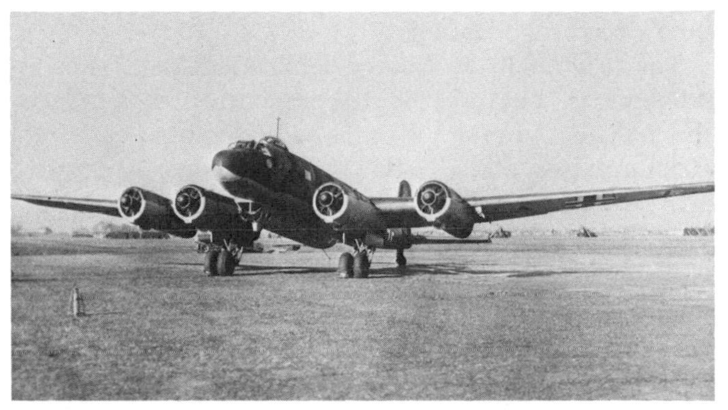

Fn 200C-2

(this was while BV was still called Hamburger Flugzeugbau). Powered by 880 hp BMW 132H radials it retained the seaplane's twin rudders and gulled wing with the fuel in the tubular wing spar.

After the war began, the second example was rebuilt as a six-place bomber with 880 lb. load and five 7.9 mm. flexible guns. One MG 15 was in the bombardier's bow enclosure, another in a top power turret, another in the ventral tray (an ex-He 111H part) and two at waist hatches.

This aircraft was designated BV 142V-2/U1 in spring 1940, and the V-1 may have been similarly reworked. The other two examples worked as transports during the Norwegian invasion. Despite trials by a special Luftwaffe OKL recon squadron, the gull-winged monoplane was not further developed. Its rival, the Fw 200, had the advantage of being already in production.

The Fw 200V-1 had first flown on July 27, 1937, with Pratt & Whitney Hornets, and made several intercontinental publicity flights before its loss. License-built Hornets, the 720 hp BMW 132G, were used on eleven similar *Kurier* 26-passenger transports built thru 1938–39. At the war's outbreak, four Fw 200As served Lufthansa and two were with the Luftwaffe (one as Hitler's personal transport, D-2600), while the others had been exported or lost.

Focke-Wulf was working, however, on eight improved Fw 200B aircraft ordered by Japan and Finland. One of the Japanese machines, in fact, was to be adapted as a maritime reconnaissance plane for the Imperial Navy. With the war's outbreak, the export license was canceled and four Fw 200Bs completed in fall 1939 were kept in Germany as transports.

The Luftwaffe purchased ten Fw 200C-0 preproduction aircraft from Focke-Wulf's Bremen plant, to be followed by quantity Fw 200C-1 production from the Cottbus factory. The first four were finished as transports from Fw 200B airframes already under construction, so two were ready by the end of 1939 and all four Fw 200C-0 transports were used to support the Norwegian invasion. While unarmed, these planes had the double-wheeled landing gear and three-bladed propellers that distinguished Cs from the earlier series.

Six more Fw 200C-0s completed with bomb racks and three flexible 7.9 mm. MG 15s were assigned to the new I/KG 40 group organized to attack British shipping. The first five armed "Condors" were delivered in April 1940, and went to a base in Denmark for operational trials. In June, I/KG 40 came to Bordeaux, France, to begin attacks with the first few Fw 200C-1 production ships.

A five-place bomber with four 830 hp BMW 132H radials, the Condor carried its 8060 liters (2150 gal.) fuel load in five fuselage and eight wing tanks. A belly gondola, offset to starboard, had a 20 mm. MG/FF in front and an MG 15 in the rear. Another MG 15 was mounted above and behind the pilots, and the third MG 15 was in the dorsal implacement near the tail. Performance included a 365 km/hr top speed (227 mph), 3500 km. (2175 mile) range and 6700 m. (21,980′) ceiling. Bomb load usually consisted of four 550 lb. bombs hung below the wings, and a fifth in the gondola, the latter usually a dummy bomb for range finding.

The Fw 200C-2 differed only in minor nacelle refinements, but in 1941 the strengthened, six-place Fw 200C-3 had BMW-Bramo 323R-2 radials rated at 1000 hp, two added MG 15 waist guns, a power-operated turret for the front dorsal gun, and a bomb load of up to 2150 kg. (4620 lb.). In practice, range requirements limited loads to the usual four 550 lb. bombs, along with one 20 mm. and five 7.9 mm. guns.

Armament modifications included the following:

Fw 200C-3/U1—15 mm MG 151 in front dorsal turret
20 mm MG 151/20 in front gondola
C-3/U2—7.9 mm MG 15 in front dorsal turret
13 mm MG 131 and Lotfe 7D bomb sight in front gondola
C-3/U3—13 mm MG 131 in front and rear dorsal position
C-3/U4—one MG 151/20 in forward gondola, two MG 15s in front dorsal and waist position
increased fuel capacity
C-4 —had FuG *Rostock* or FuG 200 surface search radar
MG 151 in front dorsal and ventral turrets, and the rest have MG 15
C-4/U1—two aircraft modified as armed transports
C-6 —C-3s modified to carry two Hs 293 missiles
C-8 —specially built for two Hs 293s.

Production never rose past a level of seven monthly in 1943, barely enough to meet attrition of those KG 40 *Staffeln* with Condors. While most of their operations were over the Atlantic, a few did appear in the Mediterranean, and two squadrons were used in the ill-fated Stalingrad emergency airlift. On December 28, 1943, a Fw 200C-6 failed in its first effort with Hs 293 missiles. When production ended in February 1944, about 263 Fw 200Cs had been delivered.

While the Condors were few in number, they made a sharp impression on the Allies. Their appearance near a convoy meant danger greater than a few bombs, for the Focke-Wulf signaled the submarine "Wolf packs" to their deadly attack. Their threat was the major reason for creating the escort carrier (CVE) class of warship. An Fw 200C shot down near Iceland on August 14, 1942, by a P-38 may have the distinction of being the first German plane lost to the AAF in World War II.

FOCKE-WULF Fw 200C-3
BMW-Bramo 323R-2, 4 X 1000 hp
DIMENSIONS: Span 33.25 m. (109′1″), Lg. 23.85 m. (78′3″), Ht. 6.2 m. (20′4″), Wing Area 118 qm. (1270 sq. ft.)
WEIGHT: Empty 14,100 kg. (31,090 lb.), Gross 22,700 kg. (49,940 lb.)
PERFORMANCE: Speed—Max. 406 km/hr (252 mph) at 5000 m. (16,400′), Cruising speed 300 km/hr (236 mph), Landing speed 116 km/hr (72 mph), Climb 6000 m./38 min. (19,680′/38 min.), Range 4100 km. (2540 miles), Service ceiling 8500 m. (27,900′)

HEINKEL HE 177

Few aircraft have as unpleasant a reputation as the Heinkel He 177, the only German four-engined bomber built in really large quantities. The story of its misadventures illustrates the technological inadequacy of German air power leadership in World War Two.

On June 3, 1936, the RLM's Chief of Technical Administration began secret discussions with representatives of several manufacturers on the requirements for a future long-range strategic bomber. The initial concept involved a 5000 km range with a 500 kg. bomb load, 500 km/hr speed, and at least a 6000 m. ceiling. This capability of 3100 miles, 1100 lb. load, 310 mph, and 19,680′ was more advanced

Fw 200C-3/U4

Fw 200C-4 with FuG 200

HEINKEL He 177V-5

than the Boeing B-17 that appeared in America in 1935.

Heinkel's 1941 project was fathered by Technical Director Heinrich Hertel and designer Siegfried Gunther. As the only strategic bomber selected by the Air Ministry it progressed to the final mockup inspection on November 5, 1937, where it was designated He 177. The name *Greif* (Griffin) later applied by the company, was seldom used in service. The most unique feature was the powerplant, two Daimler DB 603 inline engines joined on each wing in a single nacelle with a single four-bladed propeller. This compound engine was the DB 606, rated at 2600 hp and first used on the He 119.

Many changes delayed construction of the first eight prototypes. In April 1938, the Air Ministry requested a 6700 km. range with 1000 kg. and that the gun caliber be increased from 7.9 mm. to 13 mm. The original surface evaporation cooling system proved impractical when used on the He 100 fighter, and had to be replaced with circular frontal radiators, a streamlining loss. Most difficult was the demand that the big bomber be able to attack with a 60 degree dive. While diving would permit far greater accuracy, especially against moving targets, it imposed a strength requirement far beyond that really practical for a large aircraft.

Naturally, these requirements resulted in the constant weight escalation that is the airplane designer's greatest headache. Nevertheless, the He 177V-1 was first flown on November 19, 1939, at Rostock by Carl Frank. Weight was then 30,467 lb. empty and 52,734 lb. gross, but no armament was actually installed.

The new bomber displayed the transparent nose compartment typical of the German bomber, and the main landing gear had twin wheels on separate struts which folded sideways from the nacelles to fit the wheels into the wings. Dive brakes were fitted under the wings, and the internal bomb bay was doubled on the second prototype He 177V-2. The single tail had to be enlarged, and the new surfaces appeared on the V-3 and V-4 prototypes.

The He 177V-5 was the first with armament, triple bomb bays, and the production DB 606 rated at 2700 hp. Four hand-operated 7.9 mm. MG 15s were mounted in the nose, chin gondola, top of the crew cabin and in the tail turret. Weight was now up to 37,038 lb. empty and 61,883 lb. gross.

Starting with the He 177V-3's crash on April 24, 1940, all five of these prototypes were destroyed during tests. It was an ominous beginning for this unlucky bird. Nevertheless, the He 177V-6 and V-7 were forwarded to KG 40 for operational trials about September 1941. These reverted to double bomb bays and had a revised nose section. On the V-6, 13 mm. MG 131 guns were used in the gondola, top and tail positions, but 20 mm. MG/FF guns were used in V-7's gondola and top turret. Last of the pure prototypes was the V-8 used for engine trials. All later V models were reworked preproduction machines.

Despite the design's unlucky tests, production plans went ahead beginning with 15 preproduction He 177A-0 aircraft built at Rostock, 15 more at Oranienburg, and five to begin license-production at Arado's Brandenburg factory. Armament comprised a 7.9 mm. MG 81 gun in the nose, two in the top turret, and an MG 131 in the prone tail turret. The gondola below the crew's cabin accommodated an MG/FF gun in front and an MG 131 in back, but these weapons were not installed on early ships.

The first He 177A-0 appeared in November 1941, but eight of the 15 Rostock machines crashed during tests, and 17 fatalities occurred among the valuable test pilots during the He 177 development program.

HEINKEL He 177A-0
Daimler-Benz DB 606A, 2 X 2700 hp
DIMENSIONS: Span 31.44 m. (103'1"), Lg. 21.9 m. (71'10"), Ht. 6.7 m. (21'11"), Wing Area 102 qm. (1098 sq. ft.)
WEIGHT: Empty 18,500 kg. (40,700 lb.), Gross 30,000 kg. (66,000 lb.)
PERFORMANCE: Speed—Max. 515 km/hr (320 mph) at 4000 m. (13,120'), 440 km/hr (273 mph) at sea level, Cruising speed 400 km/hr (248 mph), Range 4800 km./1000 kg. (2980 miles/2200 lb.)

There were difficulties with the propellers, flaps, and cooling, but most dangerous were the repeated engine fires resulting from the crowded, and poorly designed installations. Nevertheless, no other German bomber had such performance potential.

Series production had begun in March 1942 with 130 He 177A-1s built by Arado. They had more armor and bomb capacity than their predecessors, and omitted the dive brakes, for the Luftwaffe now realized the He 177 was not strong enough for dive-bombing. Armament usually included the nose MG 81, the gondola's front MG/FF, MG 131s in the top and tail turrets and a bomb load including six 2200 lb. bombs or an equivalent load at short ranges. Modifications available included the He 177A-1/R1 with twin MG 81Z guns in the aft gondola, the R2 and R3 with an MG 131 in a remote-controlled top turret, and R4 with a manned MG 131 turret behind the wings.

A few He 177A-1s were tried by I/KG 40 at Bordeaux, but the service pilots found them unsuitable for operations. Only a few missions were attempted, including a single sortie against Bristol on August 28, 1942, that caused 45 deaths. Most He 177A-1s were limited to training and test bases, and by the time production ended in June 1943, 19 had perished in accidents not involving enemy action.

Meanwhile, Heinkel's Oranienburg factory began delivery late in 1942 on the He 177A-3, which had a lengthened fuselage and moved the engines further forward. While a few were finished with DB 606 engines, the majority had the 2950 hp DB 610, compounded from two DB 605s. By now the Air Ministry frequently complained about the production delays and accident rates, but Heinkel blamed the difficulties on the RLM's frequent and ill-considered modifications, and unsatisfactory government-furnished propellers. Heinrich Koppenberg, Udet's adviser, was reported by Heinkel to have boasted that "I killed the Do 217; now I have killed the He 177, too!"

By 1943's beginning, there had been 47 crashes; eight by engine failure, ten by airframe defects, five by engine installation defects, 20 by pilot or maintenance error, and four unknown. The Heinkel seemed too complicated and sensitive for wartime use. Some 170 major and 1395 minor modifications had had to be made.

Nevertheless, in January 1943, I/KG 50 took the He 177A-3 to Russia to participate in the Stalingrad relief operations. The type did not do badly against Soviet fighters, but powerplant fires destroyed seven.

Armament of the He 177A-3/R1 version included the usual MG/FF and MG 81 forward, twin MG 81Z ventral mount, twin MG 131s in the remote-con-

HEINKEL He 177A-5
Daimler-Benz DB 610B, 2 X 2950 hp
DIMENSIONS: As He 177A-0
WEIGHT: Empty 18,970 kg. (41,734 lb.), Gross 31,000 kg. (68,200 lb.), Fuel 5619–9610 liters (1481–2537 gal.)
PERFORMANCE: Speed—Max. 488 km/hr (303 mph), 400 km/hr (248 mph) at sea level, Cruising speed 415 km/hr (258 mph), Range 5500 km. (3417 miles) with two Hs 293, Service ceiling 8000 m. (26,250')

HEINKEL He 177A-3

trolled forward top turret, another MG 131 in the manned top rear turret, and the MG 131 in the tail turret. The A-3/R2 used the MG 151/20 in the chin and tail positions, the aft turret now being large enough for the gunner to be seated, instead of lying prone.

Further *Ruestsaetze* provided for Hs 293 missiles (R3), improved missile control installation (R4), 75 mm. fixed nose gun (R5) and various kits for torpedo and aerial mine equipment.

The next production series was the He 177A-5, appearing in February 1943. This version was an anti-shipping version developed to utilize the LT 50 torpedo, FX 1400 Fritz bomb or Hs 293 missiles. Since these had to be carried externally, the forward bomb bay was sealed off for a weapons rack and the Fowler flaps omitted to clear larger underwing stores. A shorter landing gear eased aircraft loading.

Defensive armament of the principal variant, He 177A-5/R2, was the same as the A-3/R2, and the six-place bomber could lift up to 7200 kg. (15,870 lb.). Some 826 A-5s were built by Arado and Heinkel, including a few modifications up to R8 that tested various remote-controlled gun turrets and, on the R7, a pressurized cabin. Most remarkable were five aircraft modified to *interceptors* by replacing the bomb bays with 33 rocket tubes inclined upward and 60 degrees forward. Delivered in June 1944, they were supposed to attack Allied bomber formations from below, but never seemed to have been used.

Despite the many He 177A-5s built, continued engine problems limited their combat use. On November 21, 1943, II/KG 40 at Bordeaux attacked an Allied Atlantic convoy with Hs 293 missiles, but only two ships were hit. The same unit was also used in the Mediterranean, but losses were heavy, and the Heinkels turned to night attacks.

Operation Steinbock, a series of night bombing attacks on London, began on January 21, 1944. Among the attackers were He 177s of I/KG 40 and I/KG 100, but a majority of the Heinkels launched on each mission had to abort due to engine fires or overheating. These bombers also fought the Allied invasion of France in June 1940, then had to withdraw to Norway and Germany.

By June 1944, KG 1, the famous Hindenburg *Geschwader* went into action on the Russian front with nearly 100 He 177A-5s based near Konigsberg. This unit had lost 19 planes from March 15 to June 10, before any serious air battles had begun. Although they had hoped to make strategic attacks, the Soviet summer offensive demanded the concentration of all German bombers on short-range operations. Fierce fighting soon depleted the force, and fuel shortages forced KG 1 to return to Germany where it was disbanded, along with most other bomber groups. The Luftwaffe was now fighting entirely on the defensive.

The He 177A-6/R1 had been delivered in May 1944 as a conversion of six He 177A-5/R6 bombers with pressurized cabins. Armament comprised two MG 131s under the nose and another in the gondola's rear, two MG 151/20s in the top turret, and four MG 81s in a new power-operated tail turret. Bomb load was 6600 lb. and range 3600 miles. A seventh example was completed as the He 177V-22 with redesigned nose, but series production was canceled in favor of the He 177B program.

The He 177A-7 was a high altitude version with wings extended to 36.6 m. (118′1″) and 3600 hp DB 613 engines, but only six were completed using standard A-5 fuselages and DB 610B engines. In May 1944, the third example was provided with extra fuel tanks for a flight to Japan where it would be a pattern for future Japanese production. Japan was

He 177A-5 with SG 5005 glide-bomb carrier

HEINKEL He 177B-0

unwilling to risk a flight over Soviet territory, and the project never came about. Neither did a proposed suicide raid on the United States!

On July 1, 1944, Goering himself ordered He 177 production stopped, and Heinkel's facilities turned to the Do 335 and He 162 fighter projects. The large supply of bombers still on hand were stymied by the lack of fuel; on September 15, 72 He 177A-5s of KG 40 and KG 100 were parked in Norway without any fuel supply.

It is reported by Baumbach that 1146 He 177 production aircraft were delivered, a remarkable total for a bomber seen so seldom in action. Poor powerplants frustrated the success of what might have been a great aircraft.

HEINKEL 277 AND 274

Development of improved versions of the He 177 was also stymied by official confusion. As early as 1940, Heinkel had proposed redesigning their bomber with four separate engines. While increasing drag, the separate powerplants would avoid the engine fires and service problems that plagued the coupled engines on the production He 177A-1. Separate engines seem to have been intended for the stillborn A-2 project and were joined with a pressurized cabin in the high altitude A-4 design, which later led to the He 274A project.

Four separate DB 603A engines were also used on the He 177B, which had been originally designated He 277. When Goering forbade further development, the project was disguised as under the He 177B designation until Hilter endorsed the project in May 1943. The first prototype flew late in 1943 as the He 177B-0, actually a He 177A-3/R2 converted into He 277V-1 configuration with four nacelles. A second

HEINKEL He 274

Daimler-Benz DB 603A-2 TK 11B turbosuperchargers, 1750 hp at takeoff, 1450 hp at 10,800 m.

DIMENSIONS: Span 44.1 m. (144'8"), Lg. 19.84 m. (65'), Ht. 5.58 m. (18'3"), Wing Area 170 qm. (1830 sq. ft.)

WEIGHT: Empty 21,020 kg. (46,244 lb.), Gross 36,050 kg. (79,310 lb.)

PERFORMANCE: Speed—Max. 585 km/hr (363 mph) at 6000 m. (19,680'), Cruising 485 km/hr (301 mph), Landing speed 145 km/hr (90 mph), Climb 13,000 m./30 min. (42,640'/30 min.), Range 4000 km. (2485 miles), Service ceiling 14,300 m. (46,900')

JUNKERS Ju 90V-8

prototype was converted from an A-5/R8, and flown in February 1944 officially labeled He 177B-5. Twin rudders were introduced on the third aircraft, He 277V-3.

On May 25, 1944, Goering ordered immediate production of the He 277B, but the reverses of June radically changed the situation, and on July 3, all bomber production was ended in favor of the emergency fighter program. A batch of He 277Bs with various modifications were under construction but never reached flight tests.

Last Heinkel bomber was the He 274, which was first projected October 15, 1941, as the He 177H (for Hohe or high altitude). By January 1942, it received the new designation He 274, which was to have the He 177A-4's fuselage and pressurized cabin with an extended wing with four DB 603As in separate nacelles with TK-11 turbosuperchargers. Later the fuselage was lengthened and twin rudders provided. Armament was to include twin MG 131Z guns in dorsal and ventral remote-controlled turrets, another in the nose, and up to a 7200 kg. (15,870 lb.) bomb load.

Since Heinkel's design office was overloaded, prototype detail design and construction was assigned in 1943 to the Farman (SUAF) factory in Suresnes near Paris. Since the French had little interest in building a German bomber, the two prototypes were not yet completed when Paris was liberated in July 1944. Only the engines were destroyed when the Germans left, leaving He 274V-1 and V-2 to the French. The French completed the first Heinkel after the war, flying it in December 1945 as the AAS 01A. It proved useful for high altitude tests and launching jet test vehicles.

JUNKERS Ju 90V-7

JUNKERS Ju 290A-5
BMW 801D, 4 X 1700 hp at takeoff, 1310 hp at 5800 m. (19,000′)
DIMENSIONS: Span 42 m. (137′9½″), Lg. 28.2 m. (92′6″), Ht. 6.83 m. (22′5″), Wing Area 205.3 qm. (2210 sq. ft.)
WEIGHT: Empty 33,000 kg. (72,765 lb.), Gross 45,000 kg. (99,225 lb.), Fuel 21,000 liters (3544 gal.)
PERFORMANCE: Speed—Max. 450 km/hr (279 mph) at 5500 m. (18,040′), Cruising speed 340 km/hr (211 mph), Landing speed 210 km/hr (130 mph), Climb 2100 m./10 min. (6890′/10 min.), Range 6060 km. (3760 miles), Service ceiling 6010 m. (19,710′)

JUNKERS JU 290

The only other four-engined long-range aircraft available at the war's beginning were the civil Heinkel He 116 and Junkers Ju 90. Powered by only 240 hp Hirth engines, the He 116B had no possibilities as a combat type, and was used only for photographic surveys of German-controlled territory.

The Ju 90, however, had begun its life as a bomber (Ju 89), and it was natural to revise it again to a combat version. Six of the transport models had been flown before the war, and the seventh aircraft, originally the third Ju 90B, was rebuilt to use BMW 801MA radials, instead of the civil BMW 132H engines. A longer fuselage with a hydraulic ventral loading ramp was also seen on this plane, designated Ju 90V-7, GE+GH.

Armament was introduced on the next version, Ju 90V-8 (DJ+YE), beginning with a gondola offset to port beneath the nose with an MG 151/20 firing forward and an MG 131 firing aft. A second MG 151/20 was in a power-operated dorsal turret, and the third was provided for a prone tail gunner between the twin rudders. A pair of MG 131 waist guns completed the protection. The designation of Ju 290V-1, however, was not applied until the Ju 90V-11 was rebuilt with larger wings, rectangular windows and modified tail surfaces. This aircraft was flown in August 1942, but was destroyed on an emergency supply mission to Stalingrad the following January.

Production begun in October 1942 at Bernburg with two Ju 190A-0 and five Ju 290A-1 armed transports powered by the 1600 hp BMW 801L. The first actual bombers were three Ju 290A-2s, which had a crew of seven, FuG 200 search radar, and another MG 151/20 in a second dorsal power turret near the tail. This turret acquired a low, streamlined shape on the five Ju 290A-3s, which utilized the 1700 hp BMW 801D.

Both dorsal turrets were streamlined Focke-Wulf models on the five Ju 290A-4s. The most frequently seen model was the 11 Ju 290A-5 recon-bombers with nine crewmen, heavier armor protection and 20 mm. guns in the waist. Armament now included six MG 151/20s and one MG 131 flexible gun and a 6600 lb. bomb load.

From October 1943 to August 1944, the Ju 290s

JUNKERS Ju 290A-7
BMW 801E, 4 X 1700 hp
DIMENSIONS: Span 42 m. (137′9½″), Lg. 29.12 m. (94′), Ht. 6.83 m. (22′5″), Wing Area 204 qm. (2210 sq. ft.)
WEIGHT: Empty 33,000 kg. (72,765 lb.), Gross 45,400 kg. (99,208 lb.)
PERFORMANCE: Speed—Max. 450 km/hr; or 410 km/hr with two Hs 293 (279 mph; or 255 mph) at 5500 m. (18,000′), Cruising speed 340 km/hr (211 mph), Climb 2100 m./10 min. (6890′/10 min.), Range 6000 km. (3760 miles), Service ceiling 6010′ m. (19,710′)

served FAGr 5 on search operations from Bordeaux, France, guiding U-boats to attack Allied convoys. After the opportunity for this role passed they were relegated to transport and special operations.

Only a single Ju 290A-6 was finished, this version being a 50 passenger transport intended for Hitler. In April 1945, it escaped to Spain with Nazi leaders whose actual identity is still a matter of speculation. There was also a prototype Ju 290A-7 featuring a new nose turret with a seventh MG 15/20 and external racks for three 2200 lb. bombs or missiles.

Three examples were completed as Ju 290A-9s, with increased fuel capacity and armament limited to three MG 151/20s in the gondola, front dorsal, and tail spots. Meanwhile, parallel production lines were assembling a Ju 290A-7 batch, with seven MG 151/20s in its turrets, and a Ju 290A-8 series with nine such guns in the nose, gondola, tail waist and no less than *four* dorsal power turrets. Both retained the MG 131 in the gondola's rear.

As German bomber production ended in 1944, it appears that only about six A-7 and two or three A-8 models were actually completed, but neither entered service. One of the former was flown to the United States after the war.

A more advanced version was the Ju 290B, designed to use a pressurized crew's cabin, nose and tail turrets with four MG 131 guns, two dorsal twin MG 151/20 turrets, and a third pair of 20 mm. guns in a remote-controlled belly turret. The engines were 1970 hp BMW 801E radials, but the pressurized cabin and turrets were not available when the prototype was flown in 1944.

This model was too late for production status, along with other "paper" developments. Junkers deliveries were limited to a reported 41 Ju 290A bombers.

MESSERSCHMITT Me 261
(Photo shows V-2, data for V-3)
Daimler-Benz DB 610A/B, 2 X 2950 hp at takeoff
DIMENSIONS: Span 26.87 m. (88′2″), Lg. 16.69 m. (54′9″), Ht. 4.72 m. (15′6″), Wing Area 85 qm. (915 sq. ft.)
WEIGHT: Data not available
PERFORMANCE: Speed—Max. 620 km/hr (385 mph) at 6500 m. (21,320′), Cruising speed 495 km/hr (307 mph), Range 10,000 km. (6210 miles)

THE AMERIKA-BOMBERS

It is still not generally realized that there was a German plan to bomb New York from Europe, and that prototype aircraft for this purpose were designed and built.

Design studies for that requirement had been made before the U.S. entered the war, it being supposed that the propaganda value of such raids would far exceed the limited damage possible. Focke-Wulf, Messerschmitt, and Junkers designed bombers for this mission, but the first-mentioned project was never built. The other two types, however, did fly, and were quite capable of a transatlantic round trip with a limited load.

Messerschmitt had been expected to devote its efforts solely to fighters, but its famous Director nevertheless persisted in long-range design studies. Experience with such aircraft had been gained from the Me 261V-1, designed originally to carry the Olympic fire from Berlin to Tokyo non-stop for the 1940 games, canceled by the war.

Essentially an enlarged Bf 110, the five-place Me 261 used a pair of DB 606 coupled engines, a la He 177. First flown on December 23, 1940, the Me 261V-1 monoplane's large main wheels rotated 90 degrees to retract into the nacelles. Two more prototypes were completed, the third with 2950 hp DB 610A/B engines, but none had combat armament.

MESSERSCHMITT Me 264V-1
Junkers Jumo 211J, 4 X 1400 hp
DIMENSIONS: Span 43 m. (141′), Lg. 20.93 m. (68′8″), Ht. 4.28 m. (14′½″), Wing Area 128 qm. (1378 sq. ft.)
WEIGHT: Empty 20,000 kg. (44,100 lb.), Gross 56,000 kg. (123,480 lb.), Fuel 18,400 liters (4858 gal.)
PERFORMANCE: Speed—Max. 570 km/hr (354 mph) at 6000 m. (19,680′), Cruising speed 380 km/hr (236 mph), Landing speed 130 km/hr (81 mph), Climb 5000 m./46 min. (16,400′/46 min.), Range 6200 km. (3850 miles), Service ceiling 14,000 m. (43,930′)

MESSERSCHMITT Me 264V-1

For the *Amerika-Bomber* specification, Messerschmitt offered the Me 264V-1, a four-engined monoplane designed to carry a 3960 lb. bomb load to New York. No defensive armament was provided, so the bomber depended on its speed and altitude for protection.

Seen from the front, Messerschmitt's only bomber resembled the Boeing B-29, with its circular fuselage, smooth bow and retractable nose wheels. The four 1340 hp Jumo 211J-1 engines were enclosed by the same circular radiator and nacelle used on the Ju 88A-4, while the wing had a tapered leading and straight trailing edge, and twin rudders were used. Flight tests began in December 1942.

A second prototype was built with BMW 801D radials, armor, and additional equipment, but was destroyed by an Allied bombing before it was flown. An Me 264V-3 was begun with extended wings to carry eight crewmen, 4400 lb. bomb load, and six guns. These were to include an MG 151/20 in a forward power turret, another in a ventral step, and MG 131 flexible guns in the nose, waist, and a power tail turret. Before the third version was completed, supply shortages caused the Air Ministry to curtail its plans for large aircraft types, and the Me 264 program ended.

In any case, the transatlantic mission seemed better served by a six-engined aircraft and the RLM turned to the largest landplane ever built in Germany, the Junkers Ju 390. Powered by six 1700 hp BMW 801D radials, its main landing gear comprised pairs of wheels retracting into the four inner nacelles. Many components came directly from the Ju 290 assembly line.

The Ju 390V-1 was flown at Dessau in August 1943 as an unarmed cargo plane carrying 10,000 kg. for 8000 km. (22,000 lb. for 4970 miles). Armament for maritime reconnaissance equipped the longer Ju 390V-2, which had FuG 200 radar. Four MG 151/20 guns were singly mounted in the fore and aft top power turrets, front belly gondola, and tail turret, with an MG 131 in the gondola's rear, and two more in the waist hatches.

This giant was delivered to FAGr 5 near Bordeaux

in January 1944, and used its 32 hour endurance for one particular transatlantic patrol said to have turned back only 2 km. (12½ miles) short of the U.S. coast north of New York.

Germany's increasingly difficult war situation prevented further investment in the *Amerika-Bomber,* although a Ju 390A design was prepared for production in Japan for that country's army. This project, too, ended in the paper stage.

While the Ju 390 makes an appropriate ending for this chapter on German long-range bombers, mention can be made of two large aircraft that never reached the flight stage. Focke-Wulf designed the Ta 400 as a transatlantic bomber with six 1700 hp BMW radials. Armament included up to 10,000 kg. (22,000 lb.) bomb load and 12 20 mm. guns in remote-controlled turrets.

More progress was made on Junker's last bomber, the Ju 488, which was proposed as an adaptation of the Ju 188, Ju 288, and Ju 388 designs to a heavy bomber configuration. Powered by four BMW 801TJ radials, the prototypes were to be assembled in Germany utilizing fuselages constructed in France. The fuselages were ruined by sabotage on July 16, 1944, and the project died soon after.

JUNKERS Ju 390A
(V-1 in photo)
BMW 801E, 6 X 2000 hp
DIMENSIONS: Span 50.32 m. (165'1"), Lg. 31.1 m. (102'½"), Wing Area 254.3 qm. (2737 sq. ft.)
WEIGHT: Empty 35,000 kg. (77,175 lb.), Gross 73,150 kg. (161,300 lb.)
PERFORMANCE: Speed—Max. 450 km/hr (279 mph) at 5700 m. (18,700'), Cruising speed 347 km/hr (215 mph), Climb 2000 m./10 min. (6560'/10 min.), Range 8000 km. (4970 miles)

DORNIER Do 217V-4

25.

Later Bomber Developments

DORNIER DO 217

The next twin-engined German bomber entering combat was the Dornier Do 217, which in 1941 had replaced the Do 17 and 215 in production. Despite its family resemblance to those types, it was an entirely new bomber, and took an active part in fighting in the West.

The dive-bombing tactic that bewitched the RLM's Technical Office also shadowed the Do 217's development, which began in 1937 as a Do 17 replacement with increased bombing capacity. A Do 17M had successfully tested a tail-mounted brake that opened like a parachute with four panels to limit dive speed, and this feature was built into the first seven Do 217 prototypes.

The first of these was flown in August 1938 with two 1100 hp Daimler DB 601A inline engines, but crashed a month later. Junkers 950 hp Jumo engines were used on the Do 217V-2 to V-4, the latter being the first armed example. Three flexible 7.9 mm. MG 15s were placed in the nose window, and the dorsal and ventral mounts at the cabin's rear.

The next three prototypes, however, again used the DB 601, and were designated Do 217V-1E (for *Ersatz* or replacement V-1), V-4 and V-5. Their tests revealed unfavorable handling qualities, and many failures due to the very high wing loading and the tail brakes' tendency to jam or twist the fuselage out of shape.

Nevertheless, Dornier was permitted to go ahead with 12 pre-production aircraft using DB 601 engines, but without the troublesome dive brake. Four recon versions designated Do 217A-0 had been completed by April 1940, followed by four more A-0s and four Do 217C-0 bombers. Armed with three MG 15s, the Do 217A-0 served the High Command's special recon group, along with the Do 215B, Ju 86P and Ju 88B.

A fixed 15 mm. MG 151 in the nose and a pair of MG 15s at the rear side windows were added to the Do 217C-0. Based on a Do 217CV-1 prototype which was similar but for Jumo 211 engines, the Daimler-powered C-0s were used only for bombsight and radio trials.

For mass production, the Luftwaffe had decided on the Do 217E series powered by air-cooled BMW radials giving more power than that available from the inline engines. BMW 139 radials with 1550 hp and four-bladed propellers had been used late in 1939 on the Do 217V-7 and V-8 prototypes. These were surpassed in 1940 by the Do 217V-9 which had 1600 hp BMW 801A radials, an enlarged fuselage, and 6600 lb. of bombs. Armed like the C-0, the V-9's speed was 525 km/hr (326 mph).

Production deliveries began with the first Do 217E-0 flown on October 4, 1940. The preproduction batch went to a recon *Staffel*, 2 (F)/11, but in March 1941, II/KG 40 was formed with the Do 217E-1 to attack British ships in the Atlantic. Armament included a 15 mm. MG 151 fixed in the lower left side of the nose, and five MG 15s in the nose, dorsal, ventral and side windows, while the bomb bay accommodated 2000 kg. of bombs or torpedoes, and armor plate was placed at several cabin areas.

Tail brake on Do 217V-1

Tail brake test on Do 17M

Do 217V-7

The Do 217E-2 revived the tail dive brake, and was more heavily armed. Dorsal and ventral guns were replaced by 13 mm. weapons, with the upper gun in a power-operated turret, and the bomb load could reach 4000 kg. (8800 lb.) in overload condition. Again the brake turned out to be a tricky device that could distort the fuselage and was mistrusted by the service crews. Ignoring their complaints, the Air Ministry had all E-2s completed with dive brakes. Fortunately, every plane delivered was accompanied by a boxed normal tail minus brakes. When the aircraft arrived at the front, the mechanics promptly changed tails and the brakes disappeared into the storage boxes. An attempt to provide a test aircraft with underwing dive brakes *à la* Ju 88, but inboard of the engines, was no more successful.

One hundred Do 217E-3s also went into service, utilizing a 20 mm. MG/FF as the fixed nose gun, now on the lower right side, and adding two more MG 15 guns at the side windows behind the pilot. The fact that these four side guns could be fired only if one of the three crew members (other than the pilot) were not busy with his own primary weapon, considerably limited their value.

Do 217E-0

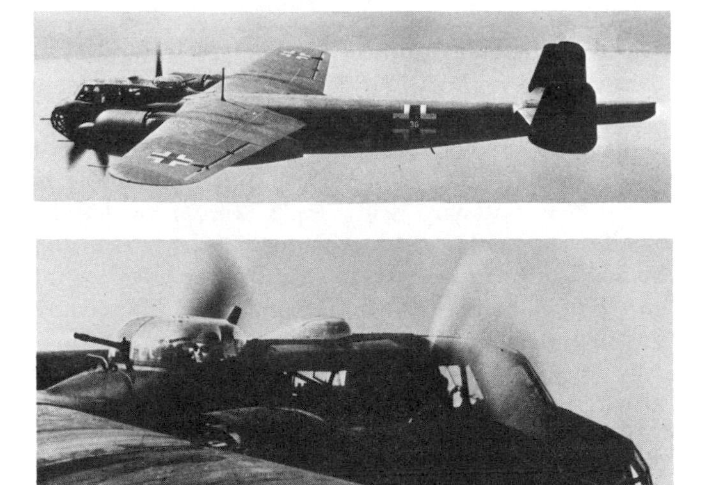

DORNIER Do 217E-2
BMW 801A, 2 X 1600 hp
DIMENSIONS: Span 19.15 m. (62'10"), Lg. 17.22 m. (56'6"), Ht. 5 m. (16'5"), Wing Area 56.6 qm. (609 sq. ft.)
WEIGHT: Empty 8855 kg. (19,481 lb.), Gross 16,465 kg. (36,-223 lb.), Fuel 6260 liters (1654 gal.)
PERFORMANCE: Speed—Max. 515 km/hr (320 mph) at 4000 m. (13,120'), Cruising speed 460 km/hr (285 mph), Landing speed 148 km/hr (92 mph), Climb 1000 m./3.5 min. (3280'/3.5 min.), Range 2300 km. (1430 miles), Service ceiling 7300 m. (23,950')

Do 217E-2/R5

Do 217E-3/R2

Do 217E-5

Numerous *Ruestsaetze* kits were provided for the E series bombers including carriers for an 1800 kg. (3940 lb.) bomb (R1), wing bomb racks (R2), a 30 mm. fixed MK 101 (R5), cameras (R6), twin 7.9 mm. MG 81Z fixed guns in the tail cone (R19), and various auxiliary fuel tank or special equipment provisions. Some of these kits also applied to the Do 217E-4 of 1942, which had the BMW 801C and Kuto-nose wing cable cutters. By then, Do 217s were standard equipment with KG 2 based in Holland, but were not generally used on the Russian front.

Dorniers were also used as pioneer missile launchers for air-to-surface missiles. Two Henschel Hs 293 missiles with 1100 lb. warheads, carried on racks below the wing center sections, were tested on the Do 217E-4/R10, and used on 65 Do 217E-5s. These were first used (without success) operationally by II/KG 100 against destroyers in the Bay of Biscay on August 25, 1943.

While several Do 217 development projects did not reach the flight stage, the Do 217H was the 21st Do 217E fitted with turbosupercharged DB 601 engines in September 1941, and the Do 217J was an experimental night fighter. The next production version was the Do 217K, first flown March 31, 1942, with an entirely new shape for its glazed bow. Two 1700 hp BMW 801Ds were used, and twin 7.9 mm. MG 81Z guns replaced the single nose gun on the E series. Two MG 131 and two MG 81s were provided in the defense positions on the top, bottom and sides.

Intended primarily as night bombers, this series consisted of a few Do 217K-0s and the Do 217K-1s used in 1943 by KG 2. The most significant version, however, was the Do 217K-2, which was history's first aircraft to sink a warship with a guided missile. The K-2 had extended outer wings increasing span to 24.5 m. (81'4") and could carry four fixed MG 81 tail guns fired by a pilot periscope, but the primary weapon was a radio-controlled SD 1400X (Fritz X) missile with a 2535 lb. armor-piercing warhead. Similar was the Do 217K-3, whose two missile racks could accommodate either SD 1400X or Hs 293 weapons.

Group II/KG 100, based near Marseille, first used the Fritz on August 23, 1943, and on September 14 sank the battleship *Roma* with a single Fritz X from 6400 m. (21,000′), when the Italians tried to defect to the Allies. Similar missiles were used against the Allies at Salerno.

The last Dornier bomber in series production was the Do 217M-1, similar to the K series, but using 1750 hp Daimler DB 603 inline engines. Armament consisted of 6600 lb. of bombs, including two 550 lb. bombs in wing racks, and two MG 131, two or four MG 81s, and the MG 81Z twin in the bow. The Do 217M-2 had the extended wings of the K-2 and the M-5 carried a single Hs 293 missile. Do 217 bomber deliveries ended in fall 1943 when the production line was entirely taken up with the Do 217N night fighter described in a previous chapter.

While there were numerous experimental versions of these Dornier bombers, including two Do 217Ks modified to Do 17Ls with rearranged cockpits, the Do 217P prototypes were the most striking. These were high-altitude models with a pressure cabin for the four crewmen and two DB 603B engines supercharged by a third DB 605T in the center fuselage, provided with extra scoops and radiators below the fuselage and wing center sections. This was the HZ system also seen on the Henschel Hs 130E.

The first Do 217PV-1 was an E-2 airframe flown in June 1942 with the powerplants giving 3500 hp for takeoff, 3240 hp at 18,700′ and 2880 hp at 45,000′. Extended wing tips like the K-2 were used on two more prototypes and three Do 217P-0 recon aircraft. The latter was a three-seater with two cameras, and three twin 7.9 mm. guns for use at low altitudes, when the cabin was not sealed. Since there was no bomb bay, outboard wing racks were provided for two 900 liter (238 gal.) tanks or 500 kg. (1100 lb.) bombs. Performance at 29,250 lb. included a top speed of 488 mph at 45,275′ and a 52,165′ ceiling. Possibly the most advanced recon type of 1943, or any other wartime year, the Do 217P did not enter production.

Total Dornier Do 217 production was 1366 bombers, 364 night fighters, and some early prototypes.

Do 217K-1/R4 with Hs 293 glide bombs

DORNIER Do 217K-2
BMW 801A, 2 X 1600 hp
DIMENSIONS: Span 24.8 m. (81′4″), Lg. 17.22 m. (56′6″), Ht. 5 m. (16′5″), Wing Area 67 qm. (721 sq. ft.)
WEIGHT: Empty 9000 kg. (19,845 lb.), Gross 16,610 kg. (36,625 lb.)
PERFORMANCE: Speed—Max. 505 km/hr (334 mph) at 4000 m. (13,120′), Cruising speed 450 km/hr (279 mph)

JUNKERS JU 288

The "Bomber B" design competition was begun in July 1939 by the RLM's Technical Office to provide a Ju 88 successor. The requirement called for a twin-engined bomber of very advanced performance, pressurized cabin, remote-controlled turrets and the projected 24 cylinder Junkers Jumo 222 or Daimler-Benz DB 604 engines.

Performance was to include a range of 3600 km. with 2000 kg. bomb load, and 600 km/hr speed at 6000 m. (2230 miles, 4400 lb., 373 mph, and 19,680′) enough to sustain attacks anywhere in the British Isles. Four companies offered designs in July 1940; the Arado Ar 340 which was rejected, the Focke-Wulf Fw 191 and Dornier Do 317 which received prototype contracts, but the RLM's favorite was the Junkers Ju 288.

Junkers' Technical Director was now Heinrich Hertel, who had been with Heinkel until May 1939. He had such confidence in the new design that

DORNIER Do 217M-1
Daimler-Benz DB 603A, 2 X 1750 hp
DIMENSIONS: as Do 217E
WEIGHT: Empty 9065 kg. (19,985 lb.), Gross 16,700 kg. (36,820 lb.)
PERFORMANCE: Speed—Max. 528 km/hr (328 mph) at 6800 m. 22,300′), Cruising speed 492 km/hr (305 mph), Climb 1000 m./3.3 min. (3280′/3.3 min.), Range 2150 km. (1335 miles), Service ceiling 8235 m. (27,000′)

DORNIER Do 217PV-1

prototype construction had begun even before mock-up inspection on May 29, 1940. The most distinctive features were the curvacious pressurized nose cabin for the three crewmen, the long fuselage running back to twin rudders, double-wheeled landing gear, dive brakes, and teardrop blisters at the cabin sides for the gunner to aim remote-controlled gun turrets.

Since the Jumo 222 was unready, the first four prototypes had 1700 hp BMW 801G radials mounted in nacelles on the short 18.35 m. (60′2″) wings. The Ju 288V-1 (D-AOTE) was finished in October 1940

JUNKERS Ju 288V-1

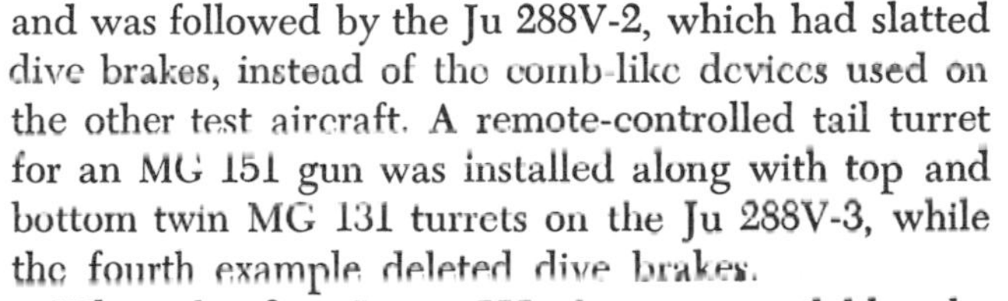

and was followed by the Ju 288V-2, which had slatted dive brakes, instead of the comb-like devices used on the other test aircraft. A remote-controlled tail turret for an MG 151 gun was installed along with top and bottom twin MG 131 turrets on the Ju 288V-3, while the fourth example deleted dive brakes.

When the first Jumo 222s became available, the Ju 288V-5 could be completed as a prototype for the Ju 288A production program. First flown on October 8, 1941, it was armed with twin MG 81 fixed guns and twin MG 131s in the turrets. The V-6 tested the 23 m. (75′5½″) wing now planned for the Ju 288B version. An enlarged tail intended for that series was used on the V-7 and V-8, the former having reverted to BMW radials as a make-shift powerplant.

JUNKERS Ju 288V-3

JUNKERS Ju 288B (V-9 in photo)
Junkers Jumo 222, 2 X 2500 hp
DIMENSIONS: Span 23 m. (75′5½″), Lg. 18.2 m. (59′8½″), Ht. 4.8 m. (15′9″), Wing Area 65 qm. (700 sq. ft.)
WEIGHT: Gross 23,000 kg. (50,715 lb.)
PERFORMANCE: Speed 670 km/hr (416 mph) at 6000 m. (19,680′), Landing speed 150 km/hr (93 mph), Climb 6000 m./14 min. (19,680′/14 min.), Range 3600 km. (2230 miles), Service ceiling 10,000 m. (32,800′)

Instead of producing the Ju 288A, Junkers was ordered as early as September 1941 to prepare for quantity productions of the larger, four-place Ju 288B. At first the Jumo 222 was the scheduled powerplant but this was never to reach quantity production status, so the Ju 288B program had to be suspended until the powerplant problems could be solved.

First of the B series prototypes was the Ju 288V-9 flown in May 1942 with 2500 hp Jumo 222 inline engines behind circular radiators, the larger wings and tail, flat gunner's windows, but no guns mounted in the chin, dorsal and tail turrets. Turbosupercharged 1810 hp BMW 801TJ radials were tried on the Ju 288V-10.

New Daimler-Benz inline powerplants were utilized on the Ju 288V-11, with two 2700 hp DB 606A/B. Periscopic sights were provided for armament; twin MG 131s in chin and dorsal turrets and an MG 151/20 in the tail. Other B series prototypes were the V-12 with Jumo 222 engines, the V-13 with DB 606s, and finally the V-14 with Jumo 222s in September 1942.

By this time, development plans had been made for a Ju 288C series with Daimler-Benz DB 610A/B engines of 2950 hp, a longer, redesigned nose, and an added MG 131Z ventral turret. Twin MG 131 guns were in each chin, dorsal and ventral turret while the tail position had an MG 151 or the new, manned four-MG 131 turret tried on one test ship.

The first eight aircraft were designated as Ju 288V-101 to V-108, probably to confuse enemy intelligence

MG 131Z turret on V-11

MG 131 (4) tail turret on V-11

JUNKERS Ju 288C (V-108 in photo)
Daimler-Benz DB 610A/B, 2 X 2950 hp at takeoff
DIMENSIONS: Span 23 m. (75′5½″), Lg. 18.25 m. (59′10½″), Ht. 4.8 m. (15′9″), Wing Area 65 qm. (700 sq. ft.)
WEIGHT: Empty 13,400 kg. (29,547 lb.), Gross 21,400 kg. (47,187 lb.)
PERFORMANCE: Speed—Max. 655 km/hr (407 mph) at 6800 m. (22,300′), Cruising speed 518 km/hr (322 mph), Landing speed 150 km/hr (93 mph), Range 2700 km. (1680 miles), Service ceiling 10,400 m. (34,120′)

reports. While the first two had DB 606A/B engines, the V-103 was flown early in 1943 with the DB 610A/B and all four gun turrets.

The whole Ju 288C program died in June 1943 when the Technical Office decided Germany could not afford a new bomber production program at that point in the war. The last Ju 288, V-108, was completed in July, and our photo shows it after a crash—the fate of nearly all of the 22 Ju 288s built. While a progressive design, the Ju 288 failed to find a wartime role.

FOCKE-WULF FW 191

The Focke-Wulf Fw 191 was designed in response to the same Bomber B requirement that produced the Ju 288. Like that bomber, it was a four-place monoplane designed for a pressurized cabin, Jumo 222, remote-controlled turrets, and twin rudders.

Since the Jumo 222s were late in arrival, the Fw 191V-1 and Fw 191V-2 were completed early in 1942 with 1600 hp BMW 801 radials. Armament included twin MG 81s in a chin turret fired by the bombardier, two more such mounts behind the engine nacelles, two MG 81s and one MG 151/20 in a dorsal turret, and another such turret behind the bomb bay. The rearward guns were fired from a transparent dome above the crew cabin and a window behind the chin turret.

Excessive weight, an overly complicated electrical system, and trouble with the combination landing and dive flaps on the trailing edge discouraged further development. The next three prototypes were left unfinished, while Fw 191V-6 was the only one completed with the 2200 hp Jumo 222 inline engines intended for the Fw 191A production model.

An Fw 191B version was designed with the coupled Daimler-Benz DB 606 or DB 610 engines used in the He 177, and heavier armament. The Luftwaffe's decision to cancel the Bomber B program ended this project and the Fw 191V-6 tests.

FOCKE-WULF Fw 191B (V-1 in photo)
Daimler-Benz DB 610A/B, 2 X 2950 hp
DIMENSIONS: Span 26 m. (85′3½″), Lg. 19.63 m. (64′5″), Ht. 5.6 m. (18′4″), Wing Area 75.5 qm. (812 sq. ft.)
WEIGHT: Empty 16,500 kg. (36,383 lb.), Gross 23,800 kg. (52,480 lb.), Fuel 6000 liters (1584 gal.)
PERFORMANCE: Speed—Max. 635 km/hr (394 mph), at 5000 m. (16,400′), Climb 1220 m./1 min. (4000′/1 min.), Range 3500 km. (2175 miles), Service ceiling 8600 m. (28,870′)
Estimated data for production model

DORNIER DO 317

Last of the "Bomber B" designs to appear was the Do 317, delayed by Dornier's preoccupation with Do 217 development. Like its rivals, the single Do 317 had its crew of four in a pressurized cabin in the bow.

The Do 317V-1 was powered by 1750 hp DB 603A inline engines and distinguished by triangular twin tail fins. First flown on September 8, 1942, it was unarmed, but the bomb bay could accommodate 6600 lb. Production Do 317As were to have a fixed MG 151 and two flexible MG 81s forward, an MG 131 in a top turret, and two flexible MG 131s aft, above and below the fuselage.

Since the Do 317V-1 showed no advantage over the Do 217P, the remaining five prototypes were completed without cabin pressurization and with external racks for Hs 293 missiles, and redesignated Do 217R. While a Do 317B with DB 610A/B engines, extended wings, and remote-controlled turrets were designed, the entire project was canceled in 1943.

DORNIER Do 317V-1
Daimler-Benz DB 603A, 2 X 1750 hp
DIMENSIONS: Span 20.64 m. (67′8½″), Lg. 16.8 m. (55′2″), Ht. 5.65 m. (18′6½″), Wing Area 68 qm. (732 sq. ft.)
WEIGHT: Empty 12,885 kg. (28,411 lb.), Gross 19,250 kg. (42,446 lb.)
PERFORMANCE: Speed—Max. 540 km/hr (355 mph), Range 3600 km. (2235 miles)

HENSCHEL Hs 128

HENSCHEL HS 130

Henschel was added to the Bomber B competitors in order to take advantage of that firm's experience with high-altitude aircraft. A bomber type was evolved by Franz Nicolaus from his twin-engined Hs 130 series originally intended as reconnaissance aircraft.

The Henschel Hs 130 was a development of the experimental Hs 128 monoplane. Designed in 1938 solely to study the problems of high-altitude flight, the Hs 128 had two crewmen in a circular pressurized cabin, a 26 m. (85′4″) wing, and fixed landing gear. Two Daimler DB 601 engines powered the first prototype and two Jumos the second. While they began tests in 1939, ten examples were ordered of a military reconnaissance version designated Hs 130A.

This type had retractable landing gear, shorter wings, two crewmen in a pressurized cabin, and a large camera bay. It was intended to use two 1475 hp DB 605s with turbosuperchargers, but since these engines were unavailable when the first three Hs 130V-1 to V-3 aircraft were completed in 1940, the DB 601R was installed. They were followed in 1941 by five Hs 130A-0s, with two more aircraft delivered in 1943 as the Hs 130A-0/U6 with further wing extension. Powerplants were the 1475 hp DB 605B with Hirth turbosupercharger and GM-1 power boost.

A mockup of a similar Hs 130B bomber was built, but since the powerplants were unready, the project was discontinued. Instead, the Technical Office encouraged a new design to the Bomber B requirement, retaining the Hs 130 designation to camouflage the development from OKL (Luftwaffe High Command) officials hostile to further expenditures along this line.

HENSCHEL Hs 130A
Daimler-Benz DB 601R or B, 2 X 1475 hp at takeoff
DIMENSIONS: Span 25.7 m. (84′4″), Lg. 15.9 m. (52′2″), Wing Area 81.5 qm. (876 sq. ft.)
WEIGHT: Empty 8150 kg. (17,930 lb.), Gross 11,200 kg. (22,640 lb.), Fuel 2580 liters (680 gal.)
PERFORMANCE: Speed—Max. 460 km/hr (285 mph) at 5800 m. (19,000′), Cruising speed 400 km/hr (248 mph), Landing speed 125 km/hr (78 mph), Climb 660 m./1 min. (2165′/1 min.), Range 1840 km. (1140 miles), Service ceiling 13,200 m. (43,300′)

The Hs 130C was actually quite different from the preceding aircraft, having a shoulder-wing layout instead of the midwing arrangement of the A types. Armament was added in three remote-controlled turrets, twin 13 mm. guns in upper and lower turrets and a 7.9 mm. MG 15 in the tail. The bomb aimer in the transparent nose could also aim either twin turret, which were normally used by the two gunners. Turbosupercharged 2000 hp BMW 801-I radials were not ready in time, so the first two prototypes had to use 1600 hp BMW 801As in 1942 and the inline 1750 hp DB 603 was used on a Hs 130V-3 in 1943. Only the latter had the turrets actually installed.

This four-place recon-bomber could handle 2000 kg. (4400 lb.), but the engines were needed for the fighter program. The project was dropped along with a planned Hs 130D with specially supercharged DB 605s.

As turbosupercharger development continued to be delayed by the Air Ministry's confused purposes, a stopgap solution was proposed in the Hs 130E. This used the so-called "Hohenzentrale" (HZ) arrangement of two Daimler-Benz DB 603As as actual propellent engines, and one DB 605T in the fuselage driving a two-stage compressor. Total power was 3500 hp for takeoff, and 2880 hp at 45,000 ft. Designer Nicolaus was ordered in 1942 to design an unarmed high-altitude recon type around this system and combined the Hs 130A fuselage and tail with the Hs 130C wings and landing gear. Wing span and length were increased, and an airscoop under the fuselage was provided for the compressor.

The first Hs 130EV-1 was flown in September 1942 without the HZ installation, and the V-2 was added in November. After the HZ was installed, and the V-3 flown, the project seemed promising enough to program seven Hs 130E-0 and 100 Hs 130E-1 bombers.

On a test flight the Hs 130EV-2's engine caught fire unnoticed by the three crewmen sitting far in the front. After this, other Hs 130Es got a plexidome on top and an additional escape hatch underneath the cabin. Provisions were made for twin MG 17 turrets on the top and bottom of the fuselage, and for 2200 lb. of bombs.

HENSCHEL Hs 130E
2 Daimler-Benz Db 603C; plus 1 DB 605T, 2 X 1750 hp; plus 1 1475 hp
DIMENSIONS: Span 33 m. (108'3"), Lg. 19.73 m. (64'9"), Ht. 5.54 m. (18'2"), Wing Area 85 qm. (914 sq. ft.)
WEIGHT: Empty 12,200 kg. (26,840 lb.), Gross 16,700 kg. (36,740 lb.)
PERFORMANCE: Speed—Max. 610 km/hr (379 mph) at 14,000 m. (45,920'), Landing speed 125 km/hr (78 mph), Climb 14,000 m./55 min. (45,920'/55 min.), Range 2250 km. (1397 miles), Service ceiling 15,100 m. (49,520')

Delivery on the seven Hs 130E-0s began in May 1943, but the HZ system was not entirely reliable, and with the downgrading of the German bomber program the E-1 series was canceled. Nicolaus proposed modification of the aircraft to a new Hs 130F layout replacing the HA system with four BMW 801-I radials on the wings. The Air Ministry rejected the design, despite predictions of improved performance. None of the Henschels were actually used on operations.

JUNKERS JU 188

The Ju 188A entered the war as a substitute for the Ju 288, whose development had been crippled by the failure of its Jumo 222 engine to reach production. The Air Ministry selected the Ju 188 as a compromise between the Ju 88's availability and the Ju 288's sophistication.

One of the rounded-nose Ju 88B-0 aircraft in 1940

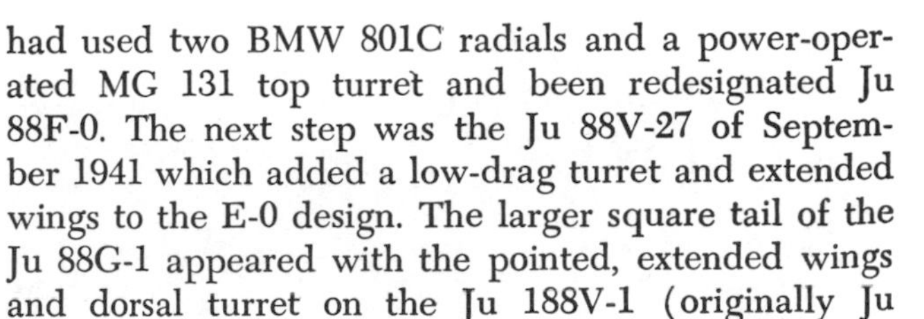

had used two BMW 801C radials and a power-operated MG 131 top turret and been redesignated Ju 88F-0. The next step was the Ju 88V-27 of September 1941 which added a low-drag turret and extended wings to the E-0 design. The larger square tail of the Ju 88G-1 appeared with the pointed, extended wings and dorsal turret on the Ju 188V-1 (originally Ju 88V-44) of December 1941.

While the V-1 had BMW 801MA radials, the Jumo 213 inline engine was selected for the Ju 188A production series, and for a Ju 188V-2 prototype. Since these engines would not be available until 1943, the first aircraft off the production line used BMW radials and were of the Ju 188E series.

The four-place Ju 188E-0 appeared in 1942 with 1600 hp BMW 801MA radials and armed with an MG 151/20 in the nose, an MG 131 in the top turret, another in the rear of the crew cabin, and two MG 81Zs in the ventral gondola. Dive brakes were provided, as on earlier Ju 88 series, along with a 6600 lb. bomb load. This series was followed by the Ju 188E-1 with the 1700 hp BMW 801D and the E-2 with provision for two torpedoes.

After a rather short production run (apparently 165), this series was succeeded in 1943 by the Ju 188F-1 recon model which replaced the bombs with three cameras and deleted the nose cannon. Later, the Ju 188F-2 got BMW 801G radials and *Hohentwiel* radar for finding ships.

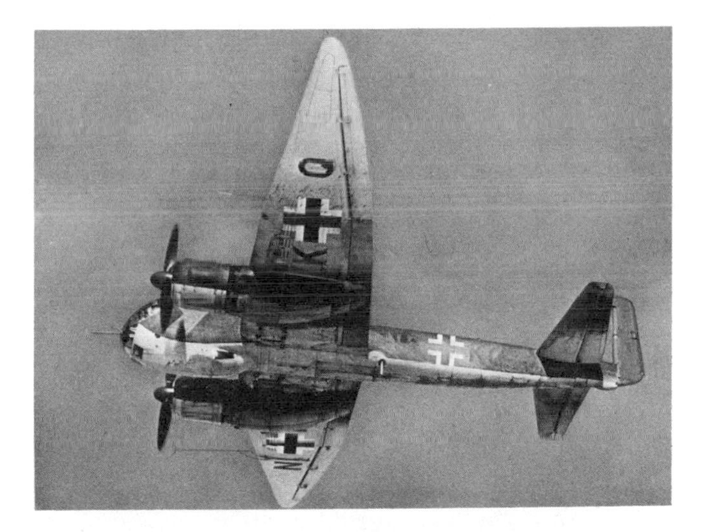

JUNKERS Ju 188E-1
BMW 801D, 2 X 1700 hp at takeoff, 1440 hp at 18,700'
DIMENSIONS: Span 22 m. (72'2"), Lg. 14.96 m. (49'½"), Ht. 4.9 m. (16'½"), Wing Area 56.6 qm. (609 sq. ft.)
WEIGHT: Empty 9860 kg. (21,740 lb.), Gross 14,510 kg. (31,994 lb.)
PERFORMANCE: Speed—Max. 500 km/hr (310 mph) at 6000 m. (19,680'), Cruising speed 375 km/hr (233 mph), Landing speed 175 km/hr (109 mph), Range 1950 km./2000 km. (1210 miles/4400 miles), Service ceiling 9450 m. (31,000')

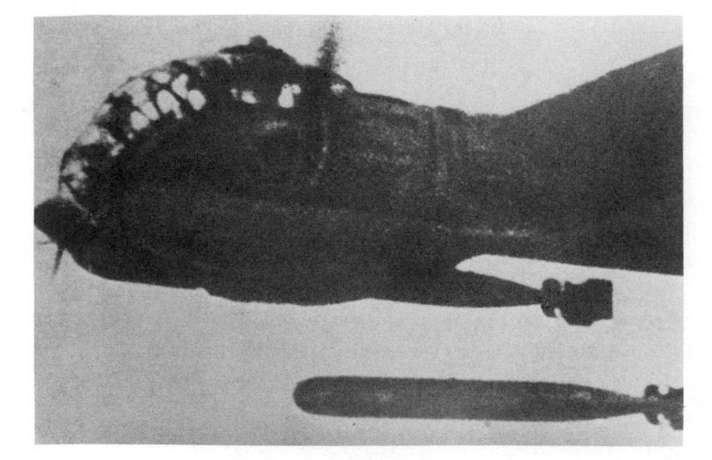

Ju 188E-2 with torpedoes

When the first Jumo 213A engines became available, the Ju 188V-2 was flown in January 1943, followed by the Ju 188A-0 series from Junkers Bernburg factory. The scheduled Ju 188A-0 series had dive brakes like the E series, but was canceled when the Luftwaffe decided against dive brakes and further overload of the Bernburg factory. Instead, ATG at Leipzig turned out the license-built Ju 188A-2. This model had two 1776 hp Jumo 213A-1 engines provided with MG 50 injection to boost power to 2240 hp at takeoff. A second MG 151/20 replaced the MG 131 in the dorsal turret, and the Ju 188A-3 was similar, but provided for two torpedoes and radar.

During 1944, the bomber version was replaced on the assembly line by the Ju 188D-1 reconnaissance model, a three-seater with cameras and full internal and external fuel capacity, which deleted the forward MG 151/20. It was joined by some Ju 188D-2s for maritime work with FuG 200 *Hohentwiel* radar.

No further large series were made, for the remaining models remained test projects. The Ju 188C was a single A model modified by a remote-controlled tail turret with twin MG 131Z guns, and a manned turret was used on the Ju 188G-0, actually the converted V-2. Three Ju 188R-0 night fighters had BMW radials, radar and four 20 mm. guns. The Ju 188J, K and L designs became part of the Ju 388 series. The high-altitude Ju 188S-1 had Jumo 213E-1, GM-1 injection, pressurized cabin and a crew of three. Few of this series were finished, because production ended in 1944 and ten were completed as Ju 188S-1/U1 attack aircraft with 50 mm. BK 5 cannon, and with altitude equipment deleted. None of the parallel Ju 188L-1 recon variants appeared.

The Ju 188s served in KG 6, 26, 66 and 200 alongside Ju 88s used by the same units. It was popular with its crews, as was the recon variants used by several long-range *Staffeln.* Total production is said to have reached 466 bombers and 570 reconnaissance aircraft.

JUNKERS JU 388

Last of the German bombers produced with two piston engines was the Ju 388. This series actually originated in September 1943 as a development of the Ju 188, and its three projected forms, the Ju 388J fighter, Ju 388K bomber and Ju 388L photoreconnaissance were originally numbered in the Ju 188 series.

All three types were powered by turbosupercharged 1800 hp BMW 801TJ radials with four-bladed propellers and had pressurized cabins. A remote-controlled

Ju 188A-3

JUNKERS Ju 188A-2
Junkers Jumo 213A-1, 2 X 1776 hp at takeoff, 2240 hp emergency
DIMENSIONS: Span 22 m. (72′2″), Lg. 14.95 m. (49′½″), Ht. 4.45 m. (14′7″), Wing Area 56 qm. (603 sq. ft.)
WEIGHT: Empty 9920 kg. (22,873 lb.), Gross 14,530 kg. (32,038 lb.), Fuel 3650 liters (964 gal.)
PERFORMANCE: Speed—Max. 520 km/hr (323 mph) at 6000 m. (19,680′), 425 km/hr (264 mph) at sea level, Cruising speed 400 km/hr (248 mph) Range 2400 km./1500 kg. (1490 miles/3300 lb.), Service ceiling 9500 m. (31,160′)

JUNKERS Ju 388K-1
BMW 801TJ, 2 X 2000 hp at takeoff
DIMENSIONS: Span 22 m. (72′2″), Lg. 14.97 m. (49′½″), Ht. 4.9 m. (16′½″), Wing Area 56.6 qm. (609 sq. ft.)
WEIGHT: Gross 14,260 kg. (31,443 lb.)
PERFORMANCE: Speed—Max. 607 km/hr (377 mph), Range 2060 km. (1010 miles), Service ceiling 13,000 m. (42,650′)

turret with twin 13 mm. MG 131s was the only defensive armament, although these turrets were not in time for the three prototypes hastily assembled late in 1943 from Ju 188 components. These led to limited production of the Ju 388J-1 described in the earlier fighter chapter, and the bomber and recon models.

Ten Ju 388K-0 bombers delivered beginning in July 1944 were rebuilt Ju 188E-1s. Like the Ju 388V-3 prototype of January 1944, it had a wooden belly tray accommodating up to 6600 lb. bomb load. They were followed by four Ju 188K-1s, which added the tail turret. Plans for further aircraft were ended by the decision to end German bomber production.

Production of the recon variant continued, however. Descended from the Ju 188V-1 of October 1943, the Ju 388L recon series began with ten Ju 388L-0s rebuilt in August 1944 from Ju 188S-1 airframes. They had three-bladed propellers and twin fixed MG 81s in a ventral pod to replace the unready tail barbette. In October 1944, delivery began on the Ju 388L-1 which had the tail barbette, four-bladed propellers and the belly tray for cameras or extra fuel.

Some 99 Ju 388L recon aircraft were delivered before production ground to a halt early in 1945. Inline Jumo 213E-1 engines with MW 50 injection were planned for the Ju 188K-2 and Ju 188L-3, neither of which seem to have been completed.

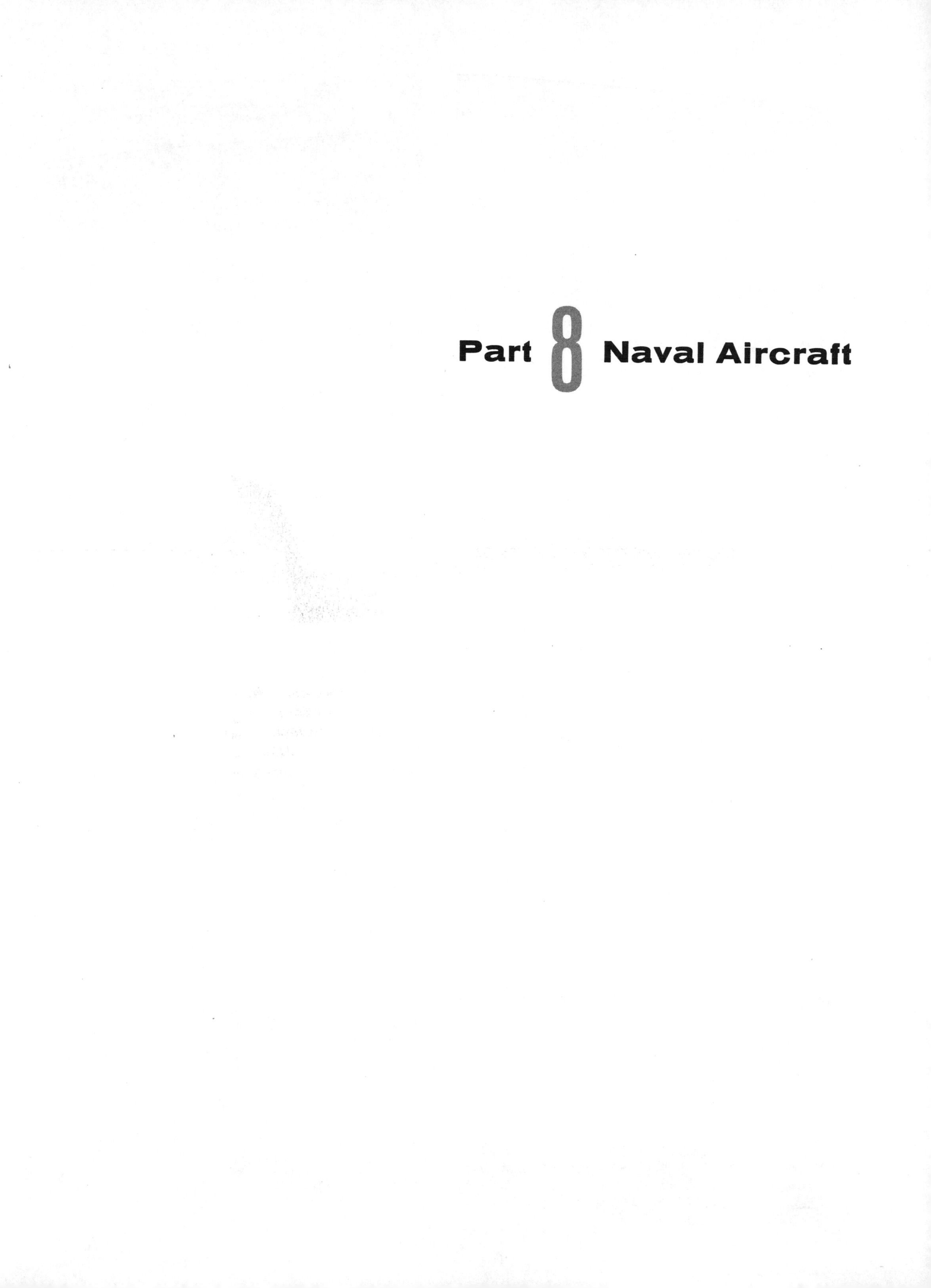

Part 8 Naval Aircraft

DORNIER WAL in Russia

26.

Flying Boats and Seaplanes, 1922–33

Between the wars, despite the Versailles Treaty, three German-owned firms built water-based military aircraft. The most successful was Dornier, whose all-metal flying boats became a familar sight over many coasts around the world.

The first of these to see a military form was the Swiss-built Do L1a, with the pilot behind a 180 hp BMW mounted above the metal bow. This design originally flew on November 24, 1920, as a five-passenger "Dolphin" civil flying boat. The all-metal structure, high wing, and sponsons became a familar feature of Dornier flying boats. A single example was purchased by the Japanese Navy in 1922 for tests with recon-bombing equipment.

Dornier's most successful design, however, was the twin-engined Wal, or Do J. First flown on November 6, 1922, this monoplane had simple, classic lines, and was to remain in production until 1937. Two 360 hp Rolls-Royce Eagle inline engines were mounted in tandem with "push-pull," four-bladed propellers above the high wing. Open cockpits were provided for an observer in the bow, pilot and co-pilot side-by-side, a mechanic within the hull, and an observer's pit in the rear.

Its military possibilities apparent, the Dornier Wal found many customers abroad. Usually equipped with rings for flexible guns at the front and rear cockpits, the five-place patrol plane could accommodate up to 2200 lb. of bombs. Such a warplane could not be made in Germany, of course, so the Wal was licensed to an Italian firm, the Societa de Construzione Aeronautique (CMASA after 1930).

Besides Italy itself, Argentina, Chile, Spain, Yugoslavia, and the Soviet Union purchased Italian-built military Wals. Other users were Norway and Portugal, while Kawasaki built the flying boat in Japan. Aviolanda built them in the Netherlands, which acquired 46 for the Dutch East Indies.

After a Wal made the first air crossing of the South Atlantic, flown by Spain's Ramon Franco on January 22, 1926, CASA procured a Dornier license. Seventeen were made at Cadiz in 1927, several lasting to serve both sides in the Civil War.

Dornier developed a single-engined version of this flying boat, the Do E of 1924. While the first had a Rolls-Royce Eagle, an example built for the Japanese Navy used a 450 hp Bristol Jupiter radial. Equipped for patrol duties, it had a four-hour endurance, two Vickers fixed guns facing forward, and a flexible rear gun. Dornier also built the Do D in Switzerland, an all-metal high-wing monoplane offered as a reconnaissance and torpedo-bombing seaplane. Powered by a 600 hp BMW VI, it had twin floats joined to the fuselage by two pairs of faired struts and the pilot's open cockpit ahead of the wing. Armament was said to include fixed Vickers guns forward and provisions for a flexible gun aft, above the cabin used for passengers on the civil version.

DORNIER Do L1a (Dolphin II)
BMW 111a, 185 hp
DIMENSIONS: Span 17.1 m. (56′1¼″), Lg. 11.57 m. (37′ 11½″), Ht. 3.1 m. (10′2″), Wing Area 51.3 qm. (552 sq. ft.)
WEIGHT: Empty 1450 kg. (3190 lb.), Gross 2200 kg. (4840 lb.)
PERFORMANCE: Speed—Max. 141 km/hr (88 mph), Cruising speed 125 km/hr (78 mph), Landing speed 90 km/hr (56 mph), Range 350 km. (217 miles), Service ceiling 4000 m. (13,120′)

DORNIER WAL
Rolls-Royce Eagle, 2 X 360 hp
DIMENSIONS: Span 22.5 m. (73′10″), Lg. 17.25 m. (56′7″), Ht. 5.2 m. (17′½″), Wing Area 96 qm. (1033 sq. ft.)
WEIGHT: Empty 3560 kg. (7832 lb.), Gross 5700 kg. (12,540 lb.)
PERFORMANCE: Speed—Max. 185 km/hr (115 mph), Range 2200 km. (1360 miles), Service ceiling 4500 m. (14,765′)

DORNIER WAL for Chile

DORNIER Do E
Rolls-Royce Eagle, 360 hp or (Bristol Jupiter, 450 hp)
DIMENSIONS: Span 17.1 m. (56′1¼″), Lg. 12.45 m. (40′10″), Ht. 3.8 m. (12′5½″), Wing Area 51.3 qm. (552 sq. ft.)
WEIGHT: Empty 1925 kg. (4235 lb.), Gross 2600 kg. (5720 lb.)
PERFORMANCE: Speed—Max. 162 km/hr (101 mph), Landing speed 85 km/hr (53 mph), Climb 1000 m./10 min. (3280′/10 min.), Endurance 4 hours, Service ceiling 3600 m. (11,800′)

Four engines were used on the Dornier Do R "Superwal 2," flown in civil form on September 15, 1928, at Altenrhein, Switzerland. A military version with 500 hp Siemens Jupiter radials had two flexible 20 mm. Oerlikons mounted at side-by-side cockpits aft of the four-bladed pusher propellers.

Ernst Heinkel's first postwar design was a tiny single-seat biplane ordered by the U. S. Navy as a submarine-based reconnaissance seaplane. Inspired by his Hansa-Brandenburg W 20 and built in Travemuende by Karl Caspar, the U.1 and a 55 hp five-cylinder radial and no struts on the cantilever folding wings. Four men could take apart the aircraft in 22 seconds for storage in the submarine's 4½′×18′ storage tank, and reassemble it for flight in only 31 seconds. The first two examples received the Navy serial numbers A6434–6435, and then the Japanese Navy purchased two powered by 80 hp Gnome radials.

When the Allies allowed civil aircraft production in Germany, Heinkel founded his own company in May 1922, opening his Warnemuende factory on December 1. The Heinkel He 1 twin-float seaplane, however, was assembled in Sweden from German parts. Similar in lines to Heinkel's famous Hansa-

DORNIER Do D
BMW VI, 600 hp
DIMENSIONS: Span 19.6 m. (64′4″), Lg. 13.45 m. (44′1½″), Ht. 4.3 m. (14′1″), Wing Area 62 qm. (667 sq. ft.)
WEIGHT: Empty 2480 kg. (5456 lb.), Gross 3830 kg. (8426 lb.), Fuel 600 liters (158 gal.)
PERFORMANCE: Speed—Max. 198 km/hr (123 mph), Cruising speed 170 km/hr (106 mph), Service ceiling 5150 m. (16,900′)

DORNIER Do R "Superwal"
Siemens Jupiter, 4 X 500 hp
DIMENSIONS: Span 28.6 m. (93'10"), Lg. 24.6 m. (80'8½"), Ht. 6 m. (19'8"), Wing Area 137 qm. (1474 sq. ft.)
WEIGHT: Empty 7780 kg. (17,116 lb.), Gross 12,600 kg. (27,720 lb.), Fuel 3800 liters (1003 gal.)
PERFORMANCE: Speed—Max. 220 km/hr (137 mph), Cruising speed 190 km/hr (118 mph), Landing speed 113 km/hr (70 mph), Range 1500 km. (930 miles), Service ceiling 3500 m. (11,480')

CASPAR U 1
Siemens, 55 hp
DIMENSIONS: Span 7.2 m. (23'7"), Lg. 6.2 m. (20'4"), Ht. 2.33 m. (7'7½"), Wing Area 14 qm. (150.7 sq. ft.)
WEIGHT: Empty 360 kg. (792 lb.), Gross 510 kg. (1122 lb.)
PERFORMANCE: Speed—Max. 148 km/hr (92 mph), Climb 1000 m./6 min. (3280'/6 min.), Service ceiling 1900 m. (6250')

HEINKEL He 2 (S 2)
Rolls-Royce Eagle, 360 hp
DIMENSIONS: Span 17.5 m. (57'5"), Lg. 12.65 m. (41'6"), Wing Area 52.5 qm. (565 sq. ft.)
WEIGHT: Empty 1700 kg. (3740 lb.), Gross 2450 kg. (5390 lb.)
PERFORMANCE: Speed—Max. 185 km/hr (115 mph) at sea level, Landing speed 84 km/hr (52 mph), Service ceiling 3800 m. (12,460')

ROHRBACH Ro II
Rolls-Royce Eagle, 2 X 360 hp
DIMENSIONS: Span 29 m. (95'2"), Lg. 16.5 m. (54'2")
WEIGHT: Empty 3700 kg. (8140 lb.), Gross 5700 kg. (12,540 lb.)
PERFORMANCE: Speed—Max. 220 km/hr (137 mph), Cruising speed 195 km/hr (121 mph), Service ceiling 4500 m. (14,765')

HEINKEL He 1 (S 1)
Armstrong-Siddeley, 240 hp
DIMENSIONS: Span 13.5 m. (44'3"), Lg. 9.3 m. (30'6"), Wing Area 31.6 qm. (340 sq. ft.)
WEIGHT: Empty 1000 kg. (2200 lb.), Gross 1460 kg. (3212 lb.)
PERFORMANCE: Speed—Max. 168 km/hr (104 mph)

Ro II by Mitsubishi

ROHRBACH Ro III
Rolls-Royce Eagle IX, 2 X 450 hp
DIMENSIONS: Span 29.1 m. (95′6″), Lg. 17.67 m. (57′11½″), Ht. 5.2 m. (17′1″)
WEIGHT: Empty 4676 kg. (10,287 lb.), Gross 6690 kg. (14,718 lb.),
PERFORMANCE: Speed—Max. 185 km/hr (115 mph), Cruising speed 170 km/hr (106 mph), Landing speed 100 km/hr (62 mph), Climb 3000 m./30 min. (9840′/30 min.), Range 2220 km. (1378 miles)

ROHRBACH RODRA
Lorraine-Dietrich, 2 X 500 hp
DIMENSIONS: Span 27.7 m. (90′10″), Lg. 17.5 m. (57′11½″), Ht. 5.2 m. (17′½″), Wing Area 73.4 qm. (790 sq. ft.)
WEIGHT: Empty 4050 kg. (8930 lb.), Gross 5800 kg. (12,789 lb.)
PERFORMANCE: Speed—Max. 205 km/hr (127 mph), Landing speed 100 km/hr (62 mph), Climb 1000 m./6 min. (3280′ 6 min.), Service ceiling 2800 m. (4180′)

Brandenburg W 29 of 1929, the He 1 was a two-place low-wing monoplane of wooden construction. A 240 hp Armstrong Siddeley had a four-bladed prop, and the rudder was balanced above and below the fuselage.

In Swedish service, the He 1 was used for coastal reconnaissance and was armed with a single fixed forward gun, and a flexible gun aft. Larger and heavier was the Heinkel He 2 built for Japan in 1923 with a 360 hp Rolls-Royce Eagle and two-bladed propeller. The Swedish version known as S 1, and using a 240 Maybach, was built by SAAB.

In Copenhagen, Denmark, Rohrbach constructed all-metal twin-engined flying boats for commercial and military purposes. The first of these was the Rohrbach Ro II of 1924, with a thick wing constructed of a Duralumin box girder above which were two nacelles for Rolls-Royce Eagles. Large side floats replaced the sponsons seen on the Dorniers.

Ten Ro IIs were purchased by the Japanese Navy, along with a manufacturing license for Mitsubishi. A license was also acquired by Kawasaki to build 1925's larger Ro III (R-3 in Japan). This six-place patrol plane had two 450 hp Eagle IX engines and two flexible guns. It was followed by the Rohrbach Rodra with two 500 hp Lorraine-Dietrich engines, built in a small series in 1925 for Turkey.

The last two flying boats in this series were two Ro IVs purchased by Great Britain. Powered by 450 hp Napier Lions, the first of these was assembled in Copenhagen from parts made in Berlin. As the N 183, it was delivered to the Royal Navy on September 18, 1925, while the second, N 184, was assembled in England as the Beardmore "Inverness." These flying boats were obtained to familiarize the British with all-metal aircraft construction.

Ernst Heinkel designed a two-place torpedo-seaplane around a 600 hp Fiat engine. The HD 14 was built at Warnemuende in secrecy, to avoid the attentions of the Allied Control Commission. It was a husky biplane with twin floats, N struts, the pilot's cockpit ahead of the wings, and the gunner's pit behind them, but was too slow.

Japan ordered two small seaplanes from Heinkel to be catapult-launched from warships. The HD 25 two-

ROHRBACH Ro IV (Inverness)
Napier Lion, 2 X 450 hp
DIMENSIONS: Span 29.1 m. (95′6″), Lg. 17.5 m. (57′11″), Ht. 5.2 m. (17′½″)
WEIGHT and PERFORMANCE: Data not available

HEINKEL HD 25
Napier Lion, 450 hp
DIMENSIONS: Span 14.85 m. (48′8½″), Lg. 9.6 m. (31′6″), Wing Area 55.8 qm. (600 sq. ft.)
WEIGHT: Empty 1550 kg. (3410 lb.), Gross 2500 kg. (5500 lb.)
PERFORMANCE: Speed—Max. 190 km/hr (118 mph), Landing speed 77 km/hr (48 mph), Service ceiling 5800 m. (19,030′)

seat biplane with a 450 hp Napier Lion was first catapult-launched at Warnemuende in June 1925, and in August Heinkel took it to Japan, where it was tested aboard the battleship *Nagato*. Smaller, and using a 300 hp Hispano-Suiza, the HD 26 single-seater was developed on the same contract. Like the HD 25, it had single-bay V struts and twin floats.

In 1926, Heinkel turned to the low-wing monoplane layout again for a single-engined recon seaplane with three open cockpits. First came the He 4, with a Rolls-Royce Eagle and airframe similar to the He 2. More successful was the modified He 5 design, whose He 5a prototype with a 450 hp Napier Lion won the June 1926 German seaplane competition.

A 420 hp Bristol Jupiter radial powered the He 5b which was sold to the Swedish Air Force and went into quantity production by Svenska Aero. Armed with one fixed and one flexible gun, this three-seater carried 440 lb. of bombs for patrol work. Various models in the Svenska S 5 series served Sweden up to World War II. The fuselage was of steel tubing and the wings of spruce, with both covered by fabric, while the twin wooden floats were braced by steel struts.

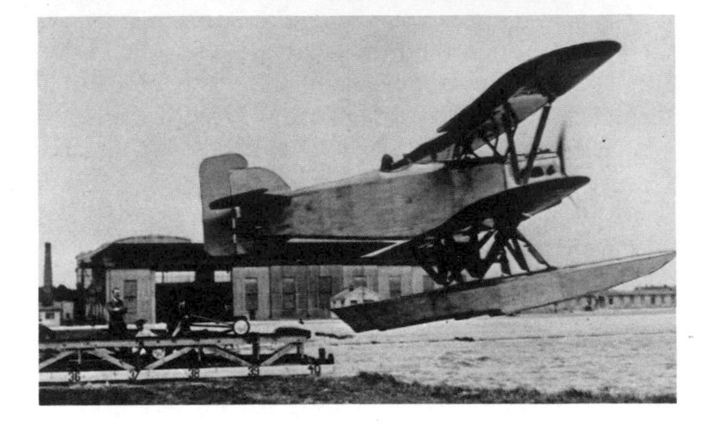

HEINKEL HD 26
Hispano-Suiza, 300 hp
DIMENSIONS: Span 11.8 m. (38′8½″), Lg. 8.3 m. (27′3″), Wing Area 37.84 qm. (407 sq. ft.)
WEIGHT: Empty 1100 kg. (2420 lb.), Gross 1677 kg. (3689 lb.)
PERFORMANCE: Speed—Max. 185 km/hr (115 mph), Landing speed 77 km/hr (48 mph), Service ceiling 5200 m. (17,060′)

HEINKEL HD 14
Fiat, 600 hp
DIMENSIONS: Span 19 m. (62′4″), Lg. 14.7 m. (48′3″), Wing Area 103.3 qm. (1112 sq. ft.)
WEIGHT: Empty 3400 kg. (7480 lb.), Gross 5600 kg. (12,320 lb.)
PERFORMANCE: Speed—Max. 175 km/hr (109 mph), Landing speed 89 km/hr (55 mph), Service ceiling 4000 m. (13,120′)

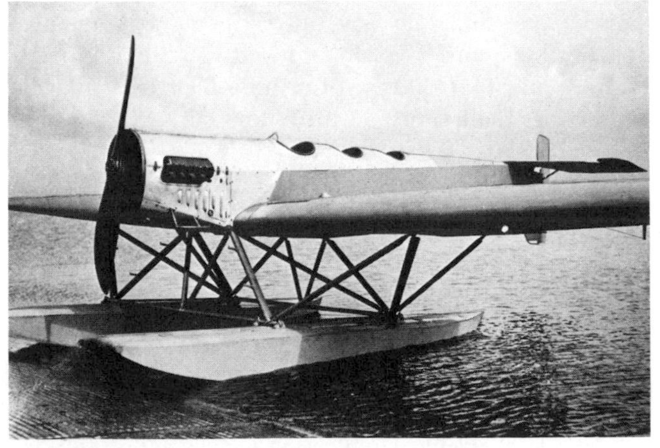

HEINKEL He 5a
Napier Lion, 450 hp
DIMENSIONS: Span 16.8 m. (55′1″), Lg. 11.8 m. (38′8½″), Wing Area 48.94 qm. (526 sq. ft.)
WEIGHT: Empty 1650 kg. (3630 lb.), Gross 2500 kg. (5500 lb.)
PERFORMANCE: Speed—Max. 209 km/hr (130 mph), Landing speed 86 km/hr (53 mph), Service ceiling 5800 m. (19,030′)

HEINKEL He 4
Rolls-Royce Eagle, 360 hp
DIMENSIONS: Span 18 m. (59'½"), Lg. 12.5 m. (41'), Wing Area 52.5 qm. (565 sq. ft.)
WEIGHT: Empty 1750 kg. (3850 lb.), Gross 2500 kg. (5500 lb.)
PERFORMANCE: Speed—Max. 180 km/hr (112 mph), Landing speed 87 km/hr (54 mph), Service ceiling 3800 m. (12,460')

HEINKEL He 5b
Bristol Jupiter, 420 hp
DIMENSIONS: as He 5a
WEIGHT: Empty 1530 kg. (3366 lb.), Gross 2500 kg. (5500 lb.)
PERFORMANCE: Speed—Max. 200 km/hr (124 mph), Landing speed 85 km/hr (81 mph), Service ceiling 5000 m. (16,400')

HEINKEL He 7a
Siemens Jupiter 2 X 450 hp
DIMENSIONS: Span 24 m. (82′), Lg. 16 m. (52′5″), Wing Area 93.42 qm. (1005 sq. ft.)
WEIGHT: Empty 3800 kg. (8360 lb.), Gross 6000 kg. (13,200 lb.)
PERFORMANCE: Speed—Max. 200 km/hr (124 mph), Landing speed 89 km/hr (55 mph), Service ceiling 2300 m. (7550′)

Two 450 hp Siemens Jupiter radials were used on the Heinkel He 7 torpedo plane of 1927. This three-place low-wing monoplane had provisions for flexible guns in the front and rear open pits. It first appeared with a plain single rudder (He 7a), but reverted to horn balances on top and bottom (He 7b). Although this type was offered thru Svenska Aero, no sales were made.

Denmark bought 22 Heinkel He 8s in 1928. Essentially, they were cleaned-up He 5s with a 385 hp Armstrong-Siddeley Jaguar radial, and in our photo the third cockpit for the gunner has been covered over. One example experimentally fitted with an 800 hp Packard inline engine was known as the He 31.

Next in this series of reconnaissance monoplanes was the He 9 delivered to the U.S.S.R. in 1929. It differed from the preceding aircraft in having a 600 hp BMW VI, metal sheet on the forward fuselage, and balanced ailerons.

Heinkel also produced several biplanes with twin floats in this same period. The HD 28 was an experimental reconnaissance three-seater sold to Japan in 1928. A 650 hp Lorraine engine and three open cockpits were used.

Designed as a three-place torpedo-bomber that could be operated either on wheels, or twin floats, the HD 16 was built for Sweden in 1928. The pilot sat ahead of the wings with a navigator at his side. A gunner could be provided in a third cockpit near the tail. The fabric-covered equal-span wings had ailerons on all four tips and were connected by a single pair of steel N struts.

The same year also saw the appearance of the smaller HD 19, whose twin-float version was tested in Sweden. A two-seat biplane with staggered wings and a 410 hp Siemens Jupiter, it was offered as a light reconnaissance type.

HEINKEL He 7b

HEINKEL He 8
Armstrong-Siddeley Jaguar, 385 hp
DIMENSIONS: Span 16.8 m. (55'1"), Lg. 11.5 m. (37'4"), Ht. 3.85 m. (12'8"), Wing Area 47 qm. (506 sq. ft.)
WEIGHT: Empty 1585 kg. (3487 lb.), Gross 2365 kg. (5203 lb.)
PERFORMANCE: Speed—Max. 216 km/hr (134 mph), Landing speed 93 km/hr (58 mph), Service ceiling 6200 m. (20,340')

HEINKEL He 9
BMW VI, 600 hp
DIMENSIONS: Span 16.8 m. (55'1"), Lg. 11.6 m. (38'1"), Ht. 4.6 m. (15'1"), Wing Area 49.49 qm. (533 sq. ft.)
WEIGHT: Empty 2130 kg. (4686 lb.), Gross 3000 kg. (6600 lb.), Fuel 590 liters (156 gal.)
PERFORMANCE: Speed—Max. 260 km/hr (161 mph), Landing speed 91 km/hr (57 mph), Climb 1000 m./2.5 min. (3280'/2.5 min.) 3000 m./8 min. (9840'/8 min.), Range 600 km. (376 miles), Service ceiling 5900 m. (19,350')

HEINKEL HD 28
Lorraine, 650 hp
DIMENSIONS: Span 15 m. (49'2½"), Lg. 11 m. (36'1"), Wing Area 59.5 qm. (645.6 sq. ft.)
WEIGHT: Empty 2365 kg. (5203 lb.), Gross 3850 kg. (8503 lb.)
PERFORMANCE: Speed—Max. 198 km/hr (123 mph), Cruising speed 175 km/hr (109 mph), Landing speed 96 km/hr (60 mph), Service ceiling 4500 m. (14,765')

HEINKEL He 31
Packard, 800 hp
DIMENSIONS: Span 16.8 m. (55'1½"), Lg. 12.2 m. (40'¼"), Wing Area 47.6 qm. (512 sq. ft.)
WEIGHT: Empty 2240 kg. (4928 lb.), Gross 3110 kg. (6842 lb.)
PERFORMANCE: Speed—Max. 250 km/hr (155 mph), Landing speed 95 km/hr (59 mph), Service ceiling 5200 m. (17,060')

HEINKEL HD 16W
Armstrong-Siddeley Leopard, 675 hp
DIMENSIONS: Span 18 m. (59'½"), Lg. 13 m. (42'8"), Ht. 5.2 m. (17'1"), Wing Area 96.9 qm. (1042 sq. ft.)
WEIGHT: Empty 2570 kg. (5668 lb.), Gross 4570 kg. (10,120 lb.)
PERFORMANCE: Speed—Max. 180 km/hr (112 mph), Landing speed 90 km/hr (56 mph), Climb 1000 m./7.5 min. (3280'/7.5 min.), Service ceiling 3300 m. (10,830')

HEINKEL HD 16L
Armstrong-Siddeley Leopard, 675 hp
DIMENSIONS: Span 18 m. (59'½"), Lg. 12.5 m. (41'), Ht. 4.6 m. (15'1"), Wing Area 96.9 qm. (1042 sq. ft.)
WEIGHT: Empty 2170 kg. (4785 lb.), Gross 4170 kg. (9195 lb.)
PERFORMANCE: Speed 190 km/hr (118 mph), Landing speed 86 km/hr (53 mph), Climb 1000 m./6 min. (3280'/6 min.), Service ceiling 4000 m. (13,120')

HEINKEL HD 19W
Siemens Jupiter, 410 hp
DIMENSIONS: Span 11 m. (36′1″), Lg. 9 m. (29′6″), Wing Area 31.6 qm. (340 sq. ft.)
WEIGHT: Empty 1175 kg. (2585 lb.), Gross 1725 kg. (3676 lb.)
PERFORMANCE: Speed—Max. 215 km/hr (133 mph), Landing speed 90 km/hr (56 mph), Service ceiling 6400 m. (21,000′)

HEINKEL HD 38W
BMW VI, 750 hp
DIMENSIONS: Span 10 m. (32′9½″), Lg. 8.8 m. (28′10″), Wing Area 30.15 qm. (325 sq. ft.)
WEIGHT: Empty 1585 kg. (3495 lb.), Gross 2000 kg. (4410 lb.)
PERFORMANCE: Speed—Max. 275 km/hr (171 mph), Landing speed 105 km/hr (59 mph), Climb 1000 m./2.2 min. (3280′/2.2 min.), 3000 m./8.5 min. (9840′/8.5 min.), Service ceiling 7000 m. (22,960′)

A single-seat fighter was developed by Heinkel late in 1928, on order of an office set up by the German Navy, the *Seeflugzeugerprobungsstelle des Reichsverbandes der Deutchen Luftfahrtindustrie.* The purpose was to provide the Navy with a variety of test combat aircraft. Heinkel's HD 38W was an equal-span single-seat biplane whose undercarriage was strengthened for catapulting from warships and could use either twin floats or wheels. The 750 hp BMW VI had a tunnel radiator below the engine on one version, and a flat frontal radiator on another.

In 1930, Russian officials called on Heinkel to request a reconnaissance airplane to be catapulted from new Soviet cruisers. The response was the Heinkel He 55, a biplane flying boat with two cockpits, and a single 500 hp Siemens Jupiter radial mounted over the pilot. Two guns were carried.

After the prototype was successfully tested, 20 were ordered by the Soviets, the largest contract for a single

HEINKEL He 55
DIMENSIONS: Span 14 m. (45'11"), Lg. 10.4 m. (34'1¼"), Wing Area 56.9 qm. (612 sq. ft.)
WEIGHT: Empty 1520 kg. (3344 lb.), Gross 2220 kg. (4884 lb.)
PERFORMANCE: Speed—Max. 194 km/hr (120 mph), Cruising speed 175 km/hr (110 mph), Landing speed 77 km/hr (48 mph), Service ceiling 4600 m. (15,092')

He 55 as the KR-1

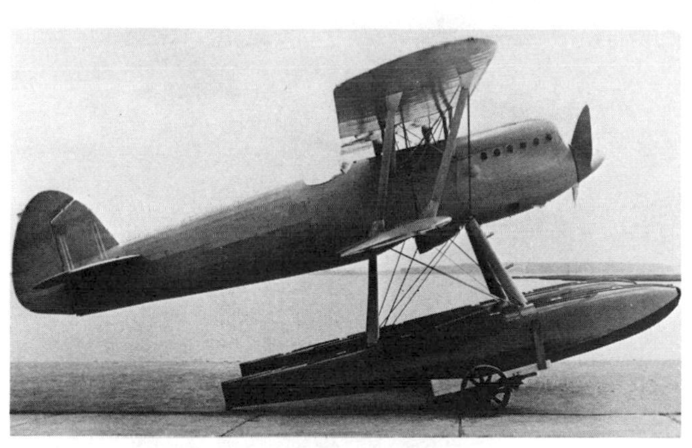

HEINKEL He 49W
BMW VI, 750 hp
DIMENSIONS: Span 11 m. (36'1"), Lg. 8.6 m. (28'2½")
WEIGHT: Gross 1970 kg. (4334 lb.)
PERFORMANCE: Speed—Max. 310 km/hr (193 mph), Landing speed 100 km/hr (62 mph), Climb 1000 m./1.5 min. (3280'/1.5 min.), Service ceiling 7500 m. (24,600')

He 50aW

type Heinkel had ever received. Production aircraft omitted the ring cowl, and had a tie rod between the ailerons paired on each side. Another order of 20 more was completed, getting Heinkel through the severe economic crisis that then depressed German industry. In Soviet service, these planes were known as the KR-1.

Heinkel tested two seaplanes in 1932 that were simply twin-float versions of the He 49 fighter and He 50 dive-bomber. The former was the predecessor of the widely built He 51 fighter, while the He 50aW two-seater had a 375 hp Junkers L5 with a front radiator. Neither of these biplanes entered service. Last of Heinkel's pre-Nazi seaplane designs was the HD 56 two-seater, which was not produced in Germany, but was built in Japan as the Aichi E3A-1. Quite similar was the HD 62 of 1933, the HD 56 airframe with the 450 hp Siemens Jupiter. Only the prototype was built for Japan; there was no series production.

Dornier offered a new design family in 1931, that included the C II reconnaissance monoplane, the C III reconnaissance biplane, and the C IV fighter monoplane, the latter described in Chapter 18.

The Dornier C II was a two-seater, twin-float monoplane whose high wing's leading edge was curved back to the tips. A four-bladed propeller was turned by a 650 hp Hispano-Suiza on the prototype, and a 740 hp Hispano engine on the modified C IIa. Colombia purchased a small batch of C IIs.

A smaller lower wing was added to the C III biplane, along with a third cockpit. The prototype was first flown on September 18, 1931, with a 650 hp Hispano-Suiza, but no sales were made.

HEINKEL HD 62
Siemens Jupiter, 450 hp
DIMENSIONS: Span 11.7 m. (39'7"), Lg. 8.48 m. (27'10"), Ht. 3.67 m. (12'½"), Wing Area 36.7 qm. (395 sq. ft.)
WEIGHT AND PERFORMANCE: Data not available

DORNIER Do C II
Hispano-Suiza, 650 hp
DIMENSIONS: Span 15 m. (49'2½"), Lg. 12.8 m. (42'), Ht. 5.1 m. (16'9"), Wing Area 32.4 qm. (448.75 sq. ft.)
WEIGHT: Gross 3300 kg. (7260 lb.)
PERFORMANCE: Speed—Max. 240 km/hr (149 mph)

DORNIER Do C IIa
Hispano-Suiza, 740 hp
DIMENSIONS: as C II
WEIGHT: Empty 2550 kg. (5610 lb.), Gross 3200 kg. (7040 lb.)
PERFORMANCE: Speed—Max. 250 km/hr (155 mph), Cruising speed 210 km/hr (130 mph), Landing speed 90 km/hr (56 mph), Climb 1000 m./3.5 min. (3280'/3.5 min.), Range 700 km. (435 miles), Service ceiling 4400 m. (14,440')

DORNIER C III
Hispano-Suiza, 650 hp (later 725 hp)
DIMENSIONS: Span 15 m. (49′2½″), Lg. 12.7 m. (41′8″), Ht. 4.7 m. (15′5″), Wing Area 44.6 qm. (478 sq. ft.)
WEIGHT: Empty 2700 kg. (5940 lb.), Gross 3300 kg. (7260 lb.)
PERFORMANCE: Speed—Max. 235 km/hr (146 mph), Climb 1000 m./2.5 min. (3280′/2.5 min.), Range 700 km. (435 mph), Service ceiling 5500 m. (18,045′)

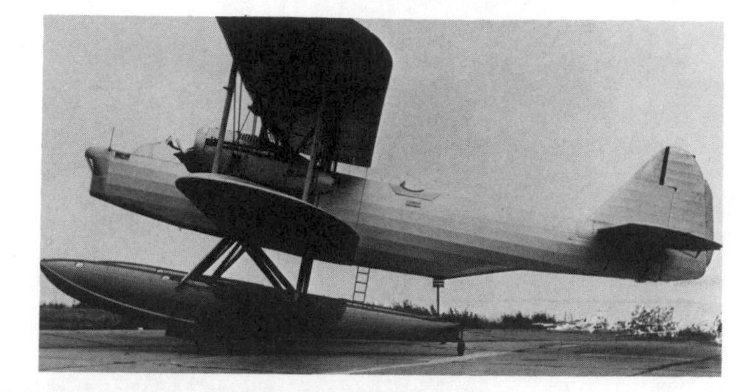

HEINKEL He 59V-2

27.

Luftwaffe Maritime Types

LUFTKREIS VI, 1934–39

During World War II, the German Navy had no air arm of its own, but had to depend on groups equipped by the independent Luftwaffe for naval operations. This system was never really satisfactory to the Navy, but Goering insisted that all aircraft should be controlled by himself.

When the Luftwaffe was officially organized in March 1935 into six district air commands (*Luftkreiskommando*), one was assigned to support the Navy. *Luftkreis* VI had its headquarters at Kiel, and was equipped entirely with water-based aircraft until late in 1938.

To equip this force, the program, by July 1, 1934, included orders for 124 aircraft: 22 Dornier Do J flying boats, 21 Heinkel He 59 torpedo-bomber seaplanes, and 81 Heinkel He 60 reconnaissance seaplanes. By May 1, 1935, 20 Do J, 21 He 59 and 42 He 60s had been delivered. These were organized into *Kuestenfliegergruppen* (Coastal groups, or Ku.Fl.Gr.) each with its first *Staffel* using He 60 reconnaissance two-seaters, the second *Staffel* with Do J patrol boats, and the third *Staffel* had He 59 four-seaters, for multi-purpose missions.

Five of these groups were operating by 1937, designated Ku.Fl.Gr. 106 to 506. Their planes carried the markings of Luftkreis VI; a 60 before the *Balkenkreuz* followed by the aircraft identity letter, and the *Gruppe* and *Staffel* numbers. For example, this chapter's first photo shows Dornier Wal 60+G12; aircraft G of the first group's second (flying boat) squadron, 2/Ku.Fl.Gr. 106.

This Dornier Do J was a development of the famous Wal flying boat of 1922. Modernized as the "8 Ton Wal," it had 600 hp BMW VI U engines on the monoplane wing in the tandem nacelle. While first flown on January 27, 1931, the new version did not go into quantity production until rearmament was ordered by Hitler in 1933.

The first patrol plane in service with the Luftwaffe, the all-metal Dornier Do J ("Military Wal 33," or Do 15) had gun rings on the bow cockpit and two gunner's pits behind the wing.[1] Thirty-three were delivered by June 1936, according to an Air Ministry schedule that also promised six more for delivery in 1937.

For the groups' multi-purpose squadrons, the Luftwaffe could turn to the He 59 torpedo-bomber built

[1] These had 7.9 mm. MG 15s, but the first MG 131s, German equivalent of the .50 caliber guns, were installed on a Do 15 Wal in July 1938. Work on this 13 mm. gun was kept secret, to give the impression only 7.9 mm. aircraft guns were available.

DORNIER J "WAL 33"
BMW VI U, 2 X 650 hp

DIMENSIONS: Span 23.2 m. (76′1″), Lg. 18.15 m. (59′6″), Ht. 5.35 m. (17′6″), Wing Area 96.2 qm. (1035 sq. ft.)

WEIGHT: Empty 5060 kg. (11,132 lb.), Gross 8000 kg. (17,640 lb.), Fuel 3150 liters (830 gal.)

PERFORMANCE: Speed—Max. 235 km/hr (146 mph) at sea level, Cruising speed 200 km/hr (124 mph), Landing speed 105 km/hr (65 mph), Climb 1000 m./7 min. (3280′/7 min.), Range 1500 km. (930 miles), Service ceiling 4500 m. (14,765′)

HEINKEL He 59A

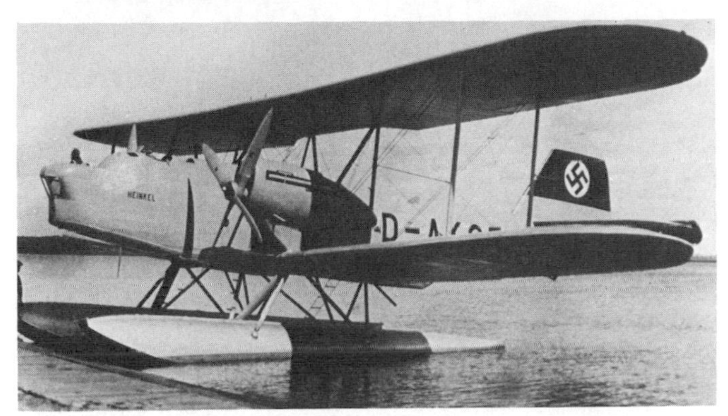

HEINKEL He 59B-2
BMW VI 6.0ZU, 660 hp
DIMENSIONS: Span 23.7 m. (77'9"), Lg. 17.4 m. (57'7"), Ht. 7.1 m. (23'3½"), Wing Area 153.2 qm. (1649 sq. ft.)
WEIGHT: Empty 6215 kg. (13,673 lb.), Gross 9000 kg. (19,800 lb.), Fuel 2700 liters (713 gal.)
PERFORMANCE: Speed—Max. 220 km/hr (137 mph) at sea level, Cruising speed 215 km/hr (133 mph), Landing speed 87 km/hr (54 mph), Climb 1000 m./4.8 min. (3280'/4.8 min.), Range 1750 km. (1087 miles), Service ceiling 3500 m. (11,480')

by Heinkel. This biplane was designed by Reinhold Mewes and first appeared with wheeled, streamlined undercarriage in September 1931. In January 1932 another prototype had twin floats beneath the two 660 hp BMW VI 6.0ZU. Four crewmen were seated in open cockpits, and no armament was installed, although its eventual location was obvious.

When rearmament got underway, the first production batch was 14 He 59As completed in 1934 for the coastal flying schools, thinly disguised as civil aircraft. Seven Heinkel He 59B-1s delivered early in 1935 had lowered engine mounts with four-bladed wooden propellers, and fuselage of steel tubing covered by fabric with a plywood nose section. On the main production variant, the He 59B-2, appearing late in 1935, the nose was of metal.

Armament included three 7.9 mm. MG 15s at the bow, dorsal, and ventral positions, and racks below the fuselage accommodated a torpedo or up to 2200 lb. of bombs. All fuel was carried in the floats. The He 59B-2's first combat service came during the Spanish

He 59C-2

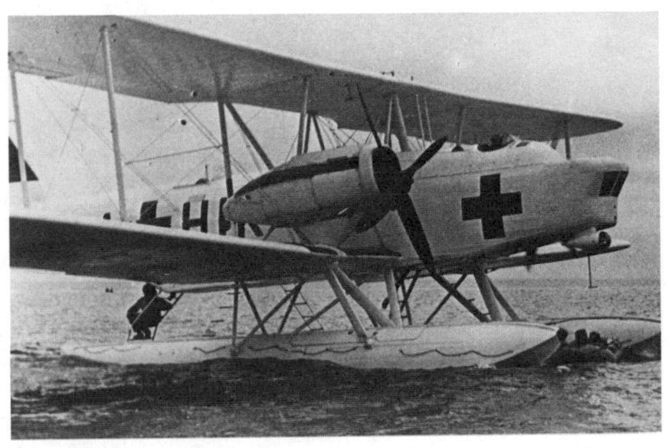

Civil War, when ten were sent to the Condor Legion. They operated from Majorca as night bombers and on anti-shipping patrols, the latter sometimes with a 20 mm. MG/FF in the bow.

Since Heinkel was preoccupied with other work, most of these seaplanes were built under license by Bachman in Ribnitz. By the end of 1936, 49 He 59s had been delivered of 105 then on order. Later models included the He 59B-3 with increased fuel capacity, He 59C-1 trainer with reduced armament and a round nose without bomber windows, and the He 59C-2 rescue seaplane, without armament. The He 59D-1 and E-1 were trainers like the C-1, except for equipment, and the last six were He 59E-2s with cameras. The He 50Ns were older models rebuilt as navigation trainers.

When the war broke out, 31 He 59s still served with the Marine Command's first-line units. They were active in patrol and mine-laying, and on May 10, 1940, 12 He 59s landed troops on the Maas River to seize bridges for the surprise attack on Rotterdam. During the Battle of Britain, He 59s painted in white with red crosses rescued German airmen down at sea. The red cross protected them only until the British decided their radioed reports guided German attacks, whereupon they were often hit by RAF fighters.

The Heinkel He 60 two-seater was another biplane inherited from the pre-Hitler period. The Navy's special office for aircraft development had in 1932 requested a seaplane to be operated from a warship. Reinhold Mewes designed the He 60 (originally HD 60) as a very conventional biplane with twin floats, open cockpits and two-bladed prop and tunnel radiators for the inline powerplant.

The first prototype, HD 60a D-2325 was flown early in 1933, with the 650 hp BMW 6.0ZU. An uprated

He 59N

750 hp model was used on the second prototype, but proved unsatisfactory, so the third prototype (D-IROL) reverted to the original engine. In April 1933, the He 60V-4 (D-IHOH) appeared with the new RLM designation system, and passed its catapult launching tests. It was the production prototype for the "A" series, along with the fifth aircraft, D-IVIX.

In 1933, work began on 12 He 60A seaplanes for the naval flying schools, and the He 60B-2 followed in 1934, still in training configuration. A 950 hp DB 600 was planned for the B-3 service version, but did not reach production in time, so the coastal groups formed in 1935 got the He 60C, still using the 650 hp BMW, but sporting a gun ring for the observer's 7.9 mm. MG 15. One example, D-IPZI, was flown with the inverted DB 600 engine for test purposes.

The Heinkel He 60C was used by Luftkreis VI coastal groups and by the *Bordfliegerstaffeln*, the two squadrons assigned to warships. Six Heinkel He 60Cs were sent to the Condor Legion. On December 31, 1936, 295 Heinkel He 60s were on order, of which 195 had been delivered.

The Luftwaffe was reorganized in 1939, and Luftkreis VI was replaced by a naval air arm under the Navy High Command. This arm possessed 240 naval aircraft on September 2, 1939, including 183 seaplanes and 57 landplanes. These comprised 81 He 60 two-seaters, 63 Do 18 patrol boats, 31 He 59 and eight He 115 multi-purpose seaplanes, while the land-based Ku.Fl.Gr. 806 had 21 He 111J bombers, and the carrier group, 186, had 24 Bf 109B fighters and 12 Ju 87C dive-bombers. Many additional seaplanes were available at training and storage bases, while the Ar 196 and He 115 monoplanes were coming off production lines to replace the aging Heinkel biplanes.

While coastal group 506 and the dive-bomber *Staffel* participated in the Polish war, most of the marine aircraft spent the war's first seven months in routine patrol of the Baltic and North Seas. In this unglamorous role, the He 60 soon faded into the obscurity its mediocre performance deserved, being replaced in more active assignments by the Ar 196 and He 114.

Since the Luftwaffe's first water-based aircraft had only modest performance, the naval arm was strengthened with a squadron of seaplane fighters. Fourteen Heinkel He 51B-2 single-seaters were completed in September 1935 for the first *Staffel* of *Kuestenjagdgruppe* 136, followed by 16 more in October. These twin-float biplanes were the only fighters directly supporting the German Navy, but after they were replaced by Bf 109Bs in 1938, the unit became a regular land-based group.

He 60a (V-1)

He 60d (V-4)

He 60b (V-2)

He 60B-2

He 60B (DB 600)

HEINKEL He 60C-2
BMW VI 6.0ZU, 660 hp

DIMENSIONS: Span 13.5 m. (44′3½″), Lg. 11.5 m. (37′9″) Ht. 5.3 m. (17′4½″), Wing Area 56.2 qm. (605 sq. ft.)
WEIGHT: Empty 2775 kg. (6105 lb.), Gross 3400 kg. (7480 lb.), Fuel 680 liters (180 gal.)
PERFORMANCE: Speed—Max. 240 km/hr (149 mph) at sea level, Cruising speed 225 km/hr (140 mph), Landing speed 90 km/hr (56 mph), Climb 1000 m./3.2 min. (3280′/3.2 min.), Range 950 km. (590 miles), Service ceiling 5000 m. (16,400′)

HEINKEL He 51B-2
BMW VI 7, 32, 750hp

DIMENSIONS: Span 11 m. (36′1″), Lg. 9.1 m. (29′10″), Ht. 3.9 m. (12′9½″), Wing Area 27.2 qm. (292.67 sq. ft.)
WEIGHT: Empty 1705 kg. (3751 lb.), Gross 1990 kg. (4378 lb.)
PERFORMANCE: Speed—Max. 318 km/hr (198 mph), Cruising speed 264 km/hr (164 mph), Landing speed 100 km/hr (62 mph), Climb 1000 m./1.5 min. (3280′/1.5 min.), Range 570 km. (354 miles), Service ceiling 7400 m. (24,280′)

DORNIER DO 18

The first German plane downed by a British fighter in World War Two was a Dornier Do 18D attacked on September 25, 1939, by a Blackburn Skua from the carrier *Ark Royal,* which the following day was itself unsuccessfully bombed by Ju 88As.

This monoplane flying boat was designed in 1933 as a replacement for the Dornier Wal, and prototypes were ordered for completion in 1935 as long-range mailplanes, although a production contract for a maritime patrol version was added before the end of 1934. Two 540 hp Jumo 205 Diesel engines were in tandem above the wing, the second turning a pusher propeller on an extended driveshaft, and the water radiators were in the front of the pylon joining the wings and fuselage. Construction was of metal except for fabric covering on the wings, and struts braced the typical Dornier sponsons.

The Do 18V-1 prototype (D-AHIS) was flown March 15, 1935, and was followed by four similar aircraft delivered to Lufthansa as the Do 18E and utilized for flights to South America. Another prototype, D-AJII, was fitted with military equipment and became the prototype Do 18D. The last prototype, D-ANHR, was delivered in 1937 with enlarged wings as the Do 18F. This machine was later rebuilt with two 960 hp BMW 132M radials, redesignated Do 18L, and flown November 21, 1939.

The four-place Do 18D naval version had flexible 7.9 mm. guns at the bow and rear cockpits, four 110 lb. bombs under the wings, and 600 hp Jumo 250C engines. Forty-four had been ordered by the beginning of 1937, with deliveries scheduled to begin that summer on the Do 18D-0, D-1 and D-2 series.

The Do 18G-1 appeared in 1939 with 880 hp Jumo 205D engines, and could be distinguished by its sharp nose from the Do 18D's rounded bow. A 13 mm. MG 131 was mounted on the bow gun ring and another was provided in the rear behind a windshield, but the rear gunner was later provided with an MG 151/20 in a power-operated dorsal turret.

At the war's beginning, 63 Do 18s were in first-line service, with 22 Do 18G and 12 Do 18H models delivered by the year's end. (The small H series were trainers with dual controls.) Production ended in 1940 with 49 more Do 18G and H aircraft. These were soon replaced in service by the Bv 138, although a number of Dorniers served on, modified as Do 18N-1 air-sea rescue boats.

FLOATPLANES FROM DO 22 TO HE 115

The Dornier Do 22 was a three-place high-wing monoplane intended for observation, bombing or torpedo missions. Powered by an 860 hp Hispano-Suiza 12Y bis, it had twin floats, with racks between them for 1100 lb. of bombs or a torpedo, and 7.9 mm. guns were provided for the gunner's Scarff ring, a ventral tunnel, and a fixed forward gun.

Two prototypes with four-bladed propellers were made in 1934 at Dornier's Altenrhein, Switzerland

DORNIER Do 18V-1

DORNIER Do 18D
Junkers Jumo 205C, 2 X 600 hp
DIMENSIONS: Span 23.7 m. (77'9"), Lg. 19.25 m. (63'2"), Ht. 5.32 m. (17'5½"), Wing Area 97.5 qm. (1049 sq. ft.)
WEIGHT: Empty 5800 kg. (12,760 lb.), Gross 10,000 kg. (22,000 lb.), Fuel 3920 liters (1035 gal.)
PERFORMANCE: Speed—Max. 245 km/hr (152 mph), Cruising speed 215 km/hr (134 mph), Landing speed 90 km/hr (56 mph), Climb 1000 m./6 min. (3280'/6 min.), Range 4225 km. (2625 miles), Service ceiling 5310 m. (17,420')

DORNIER Do 18G
Junkers Jumo 205D, 2 X 880 hp
DIMENSIONS: as Do 18D
WEIGHT: Empty 5850 kg. (12,807 lb.), Gross 10,000 kg. (22,000 lb.)
PERFORMANCE: Speed—Max. 260 km/hr (161 mph), Cruising speed 220 km/hr (137 mph), Landing speed 90 km/hr (56 mph), Climb 1000 m./5 min. 3280'/5 min.)

DORNIER Do 22V-1

factory, but none were sold to the Luftwaffe. Production was delayed until Yugoslavia ordered the Do 22Kj for its Navy, the first flying on July 15, 1938, with the Friedrichshafen factory finishing six that year and adding six more in 1939.

Greece received 12 Do 22Kgs in 1939, one being flown as a landplane (Do 22L) on March 10, 1939, and Finland received four Do 22K1 seaplanes in 1941 that had been originally ordered by Latvia. When Germany conquered the Balkan countries in April 1941, Yugoslavian pilots escaped to Egypt with others that flew with the Allies and received RAF serial numbers AX708 to 715.

The Arado Ar 95 was a general-purpose biplane built for the German Navy in 1936. The first prototype D-OLUO, was a twin-float two-seater powered by an 845 hp BMW 132 air-cooled radial, but Ar 95V-2, D-OHEO, had an inline 610 hp Jumo 210.

DORNIER Do 22W
Hispano-Suiza 12Y Br5, 860 hp
DIMENSIONS: Span 16.2 m. (53′2″), Lg. 13.12 m. (43′), Ht. 4.83 m. (15′11″), Wing Area 45 qm. (484 sq. ft.)
WEIGHT: Empty 2850 kg. (6270 lb.), Gross 3700 kg. (8140 lb.), Fuel 990 liters (261 gal.)
PERFORMANCE: Speed—Max. 350 km/hr (217 mph) at 3000 m. (9840′), Cruising speed 310 km/hr (193 mph), Landing speed 85 km/hr (53 mph), Climb 1000 m./3 min. (3280′/3 min.), Range 1500 km. (930 miles), Service ceiling 8500 m. (27,890′)

Three seats were provided on the remaining prototypes, the Ar 95V-3 and Ar 95V-5 establishing the production standard for the BMW-powered Ar 95A. The Ar 95B was to be a landplane version, so the Ar 95V-4 had wheels in streamlined pants.

Production began with six Ar 95A-0s sent to Spain in 1938 and followed by nine built for Chile, with three of the latter completed as landplanes. These three-seaters had 880 hp BMW 132Dc radials, a 7.9 mm. fixed forward gun, and a flexible gun in the rear cockpit. A rack under the fuselage accommodated a 1540 lb. torpedo, or 827 lb. bomb with six 110 lb. bombs under the wings.

After the war began, 20 more Ar 95As were ordered for completion by April 1940, but none were delivered by that date. While it is uncertain whether all of these were finished, in 1941 SAGr 125 operated Ar 95A-1s, along with He 60 and He 114 seaplanes, in the Baltic Sea.

Contemporary with the Arado was the Heinkel He 114, a two-seat reconnaissance sesquiplane, with

DORNIER Do 22L

ARADO Ar 95V-1

ARADO Ar 95A-1

BMW 132Dc, 845 hp

DIMENSIONS: Span 12.5 m. (41′), Lg. 11.1 m. (36′5″), Ht. 5.2 m. (17′1″), Wing Area 45.4 qm. (488.68 sq. ft.)

WEIGHT: Empty 2450 kg. (5488 lb.), Gross 3570 kg. (7854 lb.) Fuel 1370 liters (360 gal.)

PERFORMANCE: Speed—Max. 302 km/hr (188 mph) at 3000 m. (9840′), 275 km/hr (171 mph) at sea level, Cruising speed 260 km/hr (161 mph), Landing speed 91 km/hr (57 mph), Climb 1000 m./2.3 min. (3280′/2.3 min.), Range 2200 km. (1366 miles), Service ceiling 7300 m. (23,950′)

Ar 95V-3

ARADO Ar 95B

BMW 132Dc, 845 hp

DIMENSIONS: Span 12.5 m. (41′), Lg. 10.8 m. (35′5″), Ht. 3.9 m. (12′9″), Wing Area 45.4 qm. (488.68 sq. ft.)

WEIGHT: Empty 2235 kg. (4917 lb.), Gross 3300 kg. (7260 lb.)

PERFORMANCE: Speed—Max. 308 km/hr (191 mph) at 3000 m. (9840′), Cruising speed 268 km/hr (166 mph), Landing speed 88 km/hr (55 mph), Climb 1000 m./2.1 min. (3280′/2.1 min.), Range 1400 km. (870 miles), Service ceiling 8000 m. (26,240′)

Ar 95V-2

HEINKEL He 114V-1

HEINKEL He 114V-2

He 114V-4

its upper wing erected on sloping Y struts above a stub lower wing. The fuselage was metal-covered, and the wings of fabric, while catapult points were provided for launching from warships.

The first two prototypes appeared in 1936 with inline engines, the 670 hp Jumo 210, but BMW 132 radials were on the remaining three. Last was the He 114V-5, prototype of the A series.

Production began in 1938 with ten He 114A-0s and 33 He 114A-1s with the BMW 132D, but these models were used only for shore-based training. The He 114A-2 was the first operational version, with the BMW 132K, three-bladed propeller, catapult fittings and two 7.9 mm. guns. By 1939, export deliveries were begun on 12 He 114B-1s for Sweden and 12 He 114B-3s for Rumania, both types apparently converted from He 114A-2s. Rumania also received six He 114B-2 versions with inline engines: three with the Jumo 210, and three with the DB 600.

Last of the pre-war line were He 114C-1s with an added forward gun. The He 114s proved not sturdy enough to be a satisfactory He 60 replacement; there were in September 1939 no He 114s with the front-line groups, which still retained the elderly Heinkel biplanes. The He 114s were active with training stations, however, and were later pressed into patrol units on the Adriatic, Baltic, and Black Seas.

Seeking an He 59 replacement, the RLM in August 1935 requested design of a twin-engined general purpose toredo-bomber. After considering landplane studies, seaplanes were chosen, and Heinkel and Hamburger Flugzeugbau began prototype construction in March 1936. Both companies produced three-place, all-metal, low-wing monoplanes with twin floats and two 960 hp BMW 132K radials.

The Heinkel He 115V-1, D-AEHF, flew in July 1937 with an awkward nose enclosure for the bombardier-gunner, floats braced by struts and wires, and a single rudder. On the Hamburger (later Blohm and Voss) Ha 140V-1 the nose enclosure was smoother, large pylons supported the floats, and the tail had twin rudders. Utilizing the tubular wing spar favored by designer Vogt, it was the more streamlined of the two competitors. Both were armed with a 750 kg. (1650 lb.) torpedo and two flexible 7.9 mm. MG 15s.

A few days after its maiden flight in August 1937, the Ha 140V-1 was destroyed in a crash landing. The Ha 140V-2, D-AUTO, was completed in November 1937, but in the following January a rough sea landing bent the right float. Repair was delayed

HEINKEL He 114A-2
BMW 132K, 830 hp
DIMENSIONS: Span 13.3 m. (43'7½"), Lg. 11.9 m. (39'), Ht. 5.15 m. (16'10"), Wing Area 42.3 qm. (455 sq. ft.)
WEIGHT: Empty 2314 kg. (5102 lb.), Gross 3420 kg. (7541 lb.), Fuel 640 liters (169 gal.)
PERFORMANCE: Speed—Max. 292 km/hr (181 mph) at sea level, Cruising speed 265 km/hr (165 mph), Landing speed 95 km/hr (59 mph), Climb 1000 m./3 min. (3280'/3 min.), Range 1050 km. (652 miles), Service ceiling 4800 m. (15,750')

BLOHM & VOSS Ha 140

BMW 132K, 2 X 960 hp

DIMENSIONS: Span 21 m. (68′11″), Lg. 17.6 m. (57′9″), Ht. 5.5 m. (18′½″), Wing Area 92 qm. (990 sq. ft.)

WEIGHT: Empty 6300 kg (13,860 lb.), Gross 8500 kg. (18,700 lb.)

PERFORMANCE: Speed—Max. 320 km/hr (199 mph) at sea level, Cruising speed 295 km/hr (181 mph), Landing speed 110 km/hr (68 mph), Climb 1000 m./1.5 min. 3280′/1.5 min.), Range 2000 km. (1240 miles), Service ceiling 5000 m. (16,400′)

HEINKEL He 115V-1

He 115V-2

as the third prototype, D-AMME, was revised and strengthened for 1938 tests. When the He 115 was chosen for service, the Ha 140 was abandoned.

The He 115V-2, D-APDS, also appeared in November 1937, and differed from He 115V-1 only in the smooth engine cowlings and simplified nose. The Air Ministry now ordered a new nose shape with the gunner prone, and this nose, along with a continuous canopy running back to the rear gunner, was incorporated on the He 115V-3, D-ABAZ. Since there had been some stability trouble, a larger rudder was used on He 115A-4, D-AHME, along with strengthened float struts. In the meantime, the V-1 was stripped and modified for a speed record on March 20, 1938, in which it achieved 328 km/hr (204 mph) carrying 2000 kg. over a 2000 km. (4400 lb./1240 mile) course.

In July 1938, deliveries began on ten He 115A-0 pre-production aircraft followed in 1939 by 34 He 115A-1 seaplanes. Parallel to these came the export model, He 115A-2. Norway ordered six in August 1938, and Sweden ordered 10, with deliveries made in summer 1939. New radio and bombing equipment was used on the He 115A-3, the batch being delivered when the war broke out. Although six *Staffeln* of He 115s were supposed to be provided in 1939, aircraft deliveries were under the direction not of the Navy, but under the unsympathetic Luftwaffe High Command. At the war's beginning, only 1/106 at Norderney had He 115As, while 1/406 at List got its He 115As in September.

The fuel capacity was increased on the He 115B-0 and He 115B-1. Armament included an MG 15 in the nose with 525 rounds, another in the rear with 1500 rounds, while the bomb bay accommodated the 1650 lb. F5 torpedo, bombs, 600 liter extra fuel tank, or the 2028 lb. magnetic mine that was widely used against British shipping late in 1939. When production of this series finished at the end of 1939, 126 He 115s had been completed, 52 since September 1.

After a pause at the beginning of 1940, 76 more Heinkel seaplanes were built that year. A 20 mm. MG 151 was fixed under the nose of the Heinkel He 115C-1 and a pair of fixed 7.9 mm. MG 17s were

He 115V-4

He 115A-2 for Norway

HEINKEL He 115B-1
BMW 132K, 2 X 960 hp at takeoff, 830 hp at 850 m. (2800′)

DIMENSIONS: Span 22.28 m. (73′1″), Lg. 17.3 m. (56′9″), Ht. 6.62 m. (27′9″), Wing Area 86.7 qm. (933 sq. ft.)

WEIGHT: Empty 6715/6690 kg. (14,773/14,718 lb.), Gross 10,420 kg./10,400 kg. (22,924/22,800 lb.), Fuel 3450/4050 liters (910/1068 gal.)

PERFORMANCE: Speed—Max. 305/285 km/hr (189/177 mph) at 1000 m. (3280′), Cruising speed 295/275 km/hr (183/171 mph), Landing speed 100 km/hr (62 mph), Range Normal 1040/1190 km. Max. 2600/3000 km. (Normal 645/740; Max. 1615/1830 miles), Service ceiling 5200 m. (17,060′) Data is for torpedo/recon versions

He 115 B-2

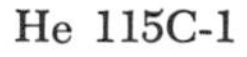

He 115C-1

sometimes added in the wing roots. Ice skids were added under the floats for Norwegian operations on the He 115B-2 and He 115C-2 modifications. Some 18 aircraft fitted with special minelaying gear became He 115C-3s, while 30 He 115C-4s were C-1s stripped for torpedo work of all guns but the single dorsal MG 15. The lone He 115D, labeled PP+ND, was an He 115A-1 with 1600 hp BMW 801 MA engines installed.

After a long suspension of production, Heinkel built 141 He 115E-1s in 1944. This model was like the C-1 with its MG 151/20 and MG 15 forward, but the rear gunner had twin 7.9 mm. MG 81Z guns mounted aft. The He 115 total seems to have been about 342, not including prototypes. These aircraft served the various coastal groups throughout the war on their varied duties, but land-based He 111s were always preferred for torpedo and bombing duties whenever available.

DORNIER Do 24V-1

DORNIER DO 24 AND 26

The Dornier Do 24 was unique among German warplanes in being designed originally for the Dutch, who in 1935 had requested a replacement for the obsolete Wals used in the Netherlands East Indies (now Indonesia). The new patrol type requested was to be a three-engined flying boat with six crewmen, three gun turrets in nose, tail and amidships positions, and a 600 kg. (1320 lb.) bomb load.

Dornier proposed a monoplane with three 600 hp Jumo 205C diesels, but the Dutch preferred using American-built Wright R-1820F-52 Cyclones giving 875 hp at takeoff and 760 hp at 5800′. While two prototypes were constructed with the diesels, the first to be finished was the Cyclone-powered Do 24V-3, D-AYWI, first flown July 3, 1937. The Jumo-powered Do 24V-1 flew January 10, 1938, followed shortly afterward by the similar V-2.

Twelve of these flying boats were purchased by the Netherlands, which organized production of a further 48 in Amsterdam by Aviolanda with De-Schelde and Fokker assisting. The Do 24V-3 was the first accepted and labeled X-1, and 11 Do 24K-1s were license-built by Weserflugzeugbau,[1] as Dornier had too much Luftwaffe work. Dutch-built boats, the Do 24K-2 models, had Wright GR-1820G radials, a 20 mm. gun amidships, and 12.7 mm. guns in the front and tail turrets.

Before the German invasion interrupted production in May 1940, 12 German and 25 Dutch-built Dorniers had been delivered to the East Indies. They were used against Japan in December 1941 to March 1942, six survivors fleeing to Australia.

Although the Luftwaffe had shown little interest in

[1] Weserflug also built a little-known amphibian, the We 271V-1 with two 240 hp Argus Ar 10Cs. Tested in fall 1938 at Lemwerder (land) and Einswaden (water landings), it resembled a Grumman Goose with twin tails.

Do 24V-2 in Norway

Do 24V-3

the prewar Dornier tri-motors, the V-1 and V-2 prototypes were pressed into service for the invasion of Norway in April 1940. When Dutch-built aircraft were captured at the Amsterdam factory, 11 were designated Do 24N-1 and used for air-sea rescue work.

Germany then decided to sponsor continued Aviolanda production, using 1000 hp BMW 323R-2 radials to replace the American engines. Designated Do 24T-1, they appeared in 1941 with 7.9 mm. MG 15s in the front and rear turrets, and a French 20 mm. HS 404 in the dorsal turret. Even rescue planes had to fight their way home now; no one bothered to wear red crosses any more. Amsterdam produced 170 Dorniers for the Germans until production ended in 1943.

A French assembly line began in 1942 at Sartrouville, where SNACAN made 48 before the liberation in 1944. The Do 24T-1 was followed in 1943 by the Do 24T-2 with improved radio, and Spain was given 12 Do 24T-3s in summer 1944, to operate a quasi-neutral Mediterranean rescue service.

So well did these Dorniers work that after the war France had 22 more built at Sartrouville for a naval transport squadron, and some Spanish boats still operated over twenty years later. Even as late as 1966, Dornier developed a modernized amphibian version as the Do 324.

Dornier's next flying boat was also not originally intended as a Luftwaffe combat type, but was armed for military service after the war began. Three Do 26s had been order for Lufthansa's transatlantic mail routes and the first flew on May 21, 1938.

The Do 26 was an advanced monoplane with gulled wings and four 600 hp Jumo 205E diesels mounted in tandem pairs, with the two rear pusher propellers on extension shafts hinged to lift the propellers clear of water spray. Instead of the traditional Dornier sponsors, the Do 26 had outboard wing floats that retracted inward into the wings.

Both the Do 26V-1, D-AGNT, and V-2, D-AWDS, were used as experimental mailplanes carrying four crewmen and 1100 lb., while the third prototype, D-ASRA, had a four-passenger cabin. After the war began the Do 26V-3 was armed for reconnaissance or military transport work. A 20 mm. MG 151 was

DORNIER Do 24K-1
Wright Cyclone R-1820F-52, 3 X 875 hp at takeoff
DIMENSIONS: Span 27 m. (88'7"), Lg. 21.95 m. (72'), Ht. 5.75 m. (18'10"), Wing Area 108 qm. (1162 sq. ft.)
WEIGHT: Empty 9200 kg. (20,240 lb.), Gross 12,400 kg. (27,280 lb.)
PERFORMANCE: Speed—Max. 300 km/hr (186 mph), Cruising speed 230 km/hr (143 mph), Landing speed 107 km/hr (66 mph), Climb 1000 m./3.1 min. (3280'/3.1 min.), 3000 m./10.5 min. (9840'/10.5 min.), Range 2120 km. (1316 miles), Service ceiling 5100 m. (16,733')

DORNIER Do 24T-1
Bramo 323R-2 Fafnier, 3 X 1000 hp
DIMENSIONS: Span 27 m. (88'7"), Lg. 22.05 m. (72'4"), Ht. 5.75 m. (18'10"), Wing Area 108 qm. (1162 sq. ft.)
WEIGHT: Empty 9400 kg. (20,680 lb.), Gross 13,700 kg. Max. 18,400 kg. (30,140 lb. max. 40,480 lb.), Fuel 5200 liters (1373 gal.)
PERFORMANCE: Speed—Max. 295 km/hr (183 mph) at 2600 m. (8500'), Cruising speed 220 km/hr (136 mph), Climb 2000 m./6 min. (6560'/6 min.), Range 2900–4700 km. (1800–2920 miles), Service ceiling 7500 m. (24,600')

WESERFLUG We 271V-1

DORNIER Do 26V-1

Do 26V-2

Do 26V-3

mounted in a bow power turret, while two waist blisters, and a hull trapdoor were each provided with a single 7.9 mm. MG 15 gun. The armed version became known as the Do 26C.

Three more prototypes completed in 1940 were also armed, and had provisions for carrying 10–12 soldiers. All six Dorniers were used as transports during the Norwegian invasion, and two were destroyed by British Hurricanes on May 28, 1940.

ARADO AR 196

The He 114 had proven unsuitable for catapulting, so another two-seat seaplane was needed to replace the He 60 aboard warships. Arado and Focke-Wulf were ordered in 1936 to produce prototypes testing both the usual twin-float landing gear and the other system favored by the U. S. Navy, a larger central float balanced by smaller floats under the wings.

The Focke-Wulf Fw 62V-1 biplane, D-OFWF, appeared first with twin floats, 870 hp BMW 132H

DORNIER Do 26C
Junkers Jumo 205D, 4 X 700 hp
DIMENSIONS: Span 30 m. (98′5½″), Lg. 24.6 m. (80′8½″), Ht. 6.85 m. (22′6″), Wing Area 120 qm. (1291 sq. ft.)
WEIGHT: Empty 10,700 kg. (23,590 lb.), Gross 20,000 kg. (44,100 lb.), Fuel 7300 liters (1927 gal.)
PERFORMANCE: Speed—Max. 345 km/hr (214 mph) at sea level, Cruising speed 305 km/hr (189 mph), Landing speed 115 km/hr (71 mph), Climb 1000 m./3 min. (3280′/3 min.), Range 7000 km. (4350 miles), Service ceiling 6000 m. (19,680′)

FOCKE-WULF Fw 62 V-1
BMW 132H, 870 hp
DIMENSIONS: Span 12.35 m. (40′6″), Lg. 11.15 m. (36′7″), Wing Area 36.1 qm. (388 sq ft.)
WEIGHT: Empty 2300 kg. (5060 lb.), Gross 2850 kg. (6270 lb.)
PERFORMANCE: Speed—Max. 280 km/hr (174 mph) at sea level, Service ceiling 5900 m. (19,350′)

Fw 62V-2

ARADO Ar 196V-1

Ar 196V-2

Ar 196V-3

Ar 196V-5

Ar 196A-2

radial, and an extra pair of N struts inboard, but Fw 62V-2, D-OHGF, also appeared in 1937 with a central float. Arado designer Walter Blume, however, produced four prototypes as low-wing monoplanes whose metal wings folded backwards for storage aboard ship.

The Ar 196V-1, D-IEHK, appeared in summer 1937 with enclosed cockpits, BMW 132K radial, two-bladed propellers and weighed 2000 kg. (4410 lb.) empty and 2900 kg. (6394 lb.) gross. The original balanced rudder was replaced by a plain surface during tests. The Ar 196V-2, D-IHQI, was similar as a prototype for the A series, but a central float was used on Ar 196V-3 and Ar 196V-4 (D-ILRE and D-OVMB), prototypes for a proposed B series. The V-4 also added a 20 mm. MG/FF below each wing, and a 7.0 mm. fixed MG 15 at the pilot's right side. A fifth prototype was added in 1938, but the Ar

ARADO Ar 196A-3 (A-4 in photo)

BMW 132K, 960 hp at takeoff, 820 hp at 1000 m. (3280′)

DIMENSIONS: Span 12.44 m. (40′10″), Lg. 10.96 m. (36′), Ht. 4.45 m. (14′7″), Wing Area 28.3 qm. (305 sq. ft.)

WEIGHT: Empty 2335 kg. (5137 lb.), Gross 3303 kg. (7267 lb.), Fuel 600 liters (159 gal.)

PERFORMANCE: Speed—Max. 320 km/hr (199 mph) at 900 m. (2950′), Cruising speed 268 km/hr (166 mph), Landing speed 106 km/hr (66 mph), Range 800 km. (500 miles), Service ceiling 7000 m. (22,965′)

ARADO Ar 231V-1
Hirth HM 501D, 130 hp
DIMENSIONS: Span 10.18 m. (33′5″), Lg. 7.81 m. (25′7½″), Ht. 3.12 m. (10′3″), Wing Area 15.2 qm. (164 sq. ft.)
WEIGHT: Empty 833 kg. (1836 lb.), Gross 1050 kg. (2315 lb.)
PERFORMANCE: Speed—Max. 170 km/hr (106 mph) at sea level, Cruising speed 130 km/hr (81 mph), Landing speed 80 km/hr (50 mph), Range 500 km. (310 miles), Service ceiling 3000 m. (9840′)

BLOHM & VOSS BV 138

BV 138V-2

BV 138A-01

BV 138MS

196V-5, D-IPOB, was a central-float version whose only visible innovation was a three-bladed propeller.

The Technical Office decided to use the twin-float Arado, abandoning the single-float configuration and the rival Fw 62. Production deliveries began in November 1938 with ten Ar 196A-0s, powered by the 960 hp (for takeoff) BMW 132K and three-bladed propeller. Armament consisted of an observer's MG 15 with 525 7.9 mm. rounds and two SC 50 (110 lb.) bombs under the wings. It is striking to note that the comparable American Vought Kingfisher seaplane had only 450 hp.

Stronger catapult fittings were used on 20 Ar 196A-1s, beginning in June 1939, but the Ar 196A-2 appeared at the end of November with fixed forward armament; a 7.9 mm. MG 17 with 500 rounds at the fuselage's right side, and two 20 mm. MG/FF guns with 60 rounds within the wings. A British submarine, the *Seal,* was captured near Sweden by two Ar 196A-2s from Ku.Fl.Gr. 706 on May 5, 1940. One Arado landed to take off the unlucky captain.

The Ar 196A-4 built in a small batch late in 1940 for the Navy's larger warships, actually preceded the Ar 196A-3 of 1941 which incorporated the A-4s improvements in structure and equipment. Last Arado seaplane was the Ar 196A-5 of 1943, whose main distinctions were a new radio and twin 7.9 mm. MG 81Z guns in the rear pit with 2000 rounds. It does appear, however, that a few Ar 196B aircraft based on the single-float V-5, were tested in 1941.

Arado produced 34 Ar 196As by the end of 1939, 98 in 1940, 97 in 1941, 94 in 1942 and 83 in 1943. To these 406 must be added license production by SNCA of 23 at St. Nazaire, and the last 69 in 1943–44 by Fokker at Amsterdam.

Arado also built a small single-seat floatplane designed to operate from U-boats. Powered by a 160 hp air-cooled, inverted inline Hirth HM 501, the Arado Ar 231 could be stowed within a two meter (6½ ft.) tube on the submarine's deck, and erected in about six minutes. After a spotting flight of up to four hours, the aircraft could be recovered.

Dismantling took about six minutes, the port side of the wing being hinged to fold over the starboard side. Six Ar 231s were produced in 1941, but the system did not meet the approval of submarine commanders, who didn't think the time on the surface a desirable risk.

BLOHM & VOSS FLYING BOATS

The last military flying boat in German production was the unusual BV 138, built by the firm originally known as Hamburger Flugzugbau, and later as Blohm & Voss.

A mockup was begun in March 1935 of a long-range patrol boat with a short hull, gulled wings and twin tail booms running back from two Junkers Jumo 206 diesels projected as 1000 hp engines. Three Ha 138 prototypes were ordered, the first to have two Jumo 206s, the second three Jumo 205s, and the third two Daimler DB 600s. While the aircraft were being constructed in fall 1936, it was decided to abandon the Jumo 206 program, and rework the flying boat to use three 600 hp Jumo 205 diesels, the third mounted atop the hull.

In this form, the Ha 138V-1, D-ARAK, made its maiden flight July 15, 1937. This six-seater had a bow turret for a 20 mm. gun, an MG 15 in a cockpit behind the top engine, and another in back of the hull. The bow turret was omitted on the Ha 138V-2, D-AMOR, but the rear gun was enclosed and the twin rudders enlarged. This aircraft was completed in August, and arrived at the Travemuende test center on November 6.

Since the hull design proved too weak and unsatisfactory, the third prototype was canceled and the aircraft completely redesigned in 1938 for a pre-production batch. The new configuration provided

BV 138B top gunner with MG 15

BLOHM & VOSS BV 138C-1
Junkers Jumo 205D Zweitakt-Diesel, 3 X 880 hp
DIMENSIONS: Span 26.94 m. (88′4½″), Lg. 19.85 m. (65′1½″), Ht. 5.9 m. (19′4″), Wing Area 112 qm. (1205 sq. ft.)
WEIGHT: Empty 11,770 kg. (25,950 lb.), Gross 14,500/17,500 kg. (31,970/38,590 lb.)
PERFORMANCE: Speed—Max. 285 km/hr (177 mph) at sea level, Cruising speed 200 km/hr (124 mph), Range normal 1250 km.; max. 4300 km. (775/2670 miles), Service ceiling 5000 m. (16,400′)

for a longer hull, straight wing, and new bow power turret. Three BV 138A-0 preproduction aircraft were built in 1939 with 605 hp Jumo 205C-1 engines, a 20 mm. gun in the bow power turret, and single MG 15s in the open top and rear pits. The first BV 138A-0, D-ADJE, is shown here.

Production began with 25 BV 138A-1s, the first five being delivered in April 1940. Pressed into rapid service, they revealed a need for structural strengthening. Along with them appeared about three BV 138B-0s, whose gross weight was increased from the A-0s 13,750 kg. (30,318 lb.) to 15,500 kg. (23,152 lb.).

The next model was the BV 138B-1, powered by three 880 hp Jumo 205D diesels and armed with an MG 151/20 in nose and stern power turrets, the MG 15 in the upper gunner's pit, and three 110 lb. bombs under the right wing. There were 24 BV 138B-1s completed in 1940–41, including three reworked from the A-0s, while the B-0 aircraft were used to test an electromagnetic ring for mine detection as the BV 138MS. Existing A-1 boats were gradually reworked to the B-1 standard.

BLOHM & VOSS Ha 139V-1 and V-2

BLOHM & VOSS Ha 139V-3
Junkers Jumo 205C, 4 X 600 hp
DIMENSIONS: Span 29.5 m. (96'9½"), Lg. 19.65 m. (64'6"), Ht. 4.8 m. (15'9"), Wing Area 129.5 qm. (1394 sq. ft.)
WEIGHT: Empty 10,750 kg. (23,700 lb.), Gross 17,550 kg. (38,700 lb.), Fuel 6560 liters (1730 gal.)
PERFORMANCE: Speed—Max. 300 km/hr (186 mph), Cruising speed 270 km/hr (168 mph) Landing speed 110 km/hr (68 mph), Range 4500 km. (2795 miles), Service ceiling 4500 m. (14,765')

BLOHM & VOSS BV 222V-1
BMW/Bramo 323R, 6 X 1000 hp
DIMENSIONS: Span 46 m. (150'11"), Lg. 36.5 m. (119'9"), Ht. 6.2 m. (20'4"), Wing Area 255 qm. (2752 sq. ft.)
WEIGHT: Empty 25,900 kg. (57,110 lb.), Gross 43,500 kg. (95,917 lb.)
PERFORMANCE: Speed—Max. 390 km/hr (242 mph), 345 km/hr (214 mph) at sea level, Cruising speed 310 km/hr (192 mph), Landing speed 125 km/hr (78 mph), Climb 6000 m./44 min. (19,680'/44 min.), Range 3100–3400 km. (1925–2110 miles), Service ceiling 6700 m. (22,000')

BV 222V-3 with MG 151/20 turret

Wing turret on BV 222V-5

The last model was the BV 138C-1 of March 1941, which had a four-bladed propeller and new radiator for the center engine, increased fuel capacity, and a 13 mm. MG 131 in the top pit. Aircraft fitted to carry six 110 lb. bombs were designated BV 138B-1/U1 or C-1/U1. By production's end in 1943, 227 BV 138C-1s had been built to provide a total of 276 production aircraft.

Blohm & Voss also contributed several other multi-engined marine aircraft to the German war effort. Among them were the three four-engined Ha 139 seaplanes built in 1937–38 for transatlantic mail runs. They were requisitioned as naval transports after the war began, but the third prototype was rebuilt for mine-sweeping with an observer's nose cage, larger vertical tail, and a peculiar magnetic de-gaussing frame draped below the aircraft. An electric motor in the cabin set up a magnetic field to detonate mines.

In this special form, the Ha 139V 3 made its first flight on January 19, 1940, after a catapult takeoff from an auxiliary ship. Together with its transport predecessors, it operated during the Norwegian campaign but the aircraft soon had to retire for lack of spare parts.

Six-engined flying boats are unusual among history's warplanes, and so the giant Blohm & Voss BV 222 *Wiking* is of special interest. Lufthansa requested a long-range flying boat and, after studying the competitive Dornier Do 20 and Heinkel He 120 designs, ordered three prototypes of Dr. Richard Vogt's then Ha 222 transport on September 19, 1937.

Powered by six 1000 hp BMW/Bramo 323R radials, the BV 222V-1, D-ANTE, flew September 7, 1940. After tests, it began flying transport test runs in July 1941 from Hamburg to Kirkenes, Norway, and later that year to North Africa. It had no armament and required escort by Bf 110s in 1941, but at the year's end it was returned to the factory to be armed as was the second prototype BV 222V-2, flown August 7, 1941.

On the cabin roof were two turrets, each with a 13 mm. MG 131, while a 7.9 mm. MG 81 was placed in a nose gunner's pit, and four more could fire from two windows on each side. The V-2 had added a gondola with two MG 131s under each wing, but that had damaged performance and had to be removed. When the third example, BV 222V-3, flew November 28, 1941, its protection was limited to the nose gun.

Carrying 92 troops, 72 litter patients, or supplies, the three giants served Rommel's Africa Korps in a special transport unit, LTS 222. The BV 222V-3 (X4+AH) joined LTS 222 in December 1941, joined by V-1 (now labeled X4+AH) in May 1942 and the reworked V-2 (X4+BH) in August 1942.

Four more BV 222A-0 aircraft produced that year received *Versuchs* numbers: V-4 delivered April 20, 1942, V-5 on July 7, V-6 on August 21, and V-8 on October 26. Joining LTS 222s Mediterranean missions, they suffered their first losses when V-6 was shot down November 24, 1942, V-8 downed on December 10 and V-1 sank after an accident at Athens in February 1943.

BLOHM & VOSS BV 222A-0 (V-8)
BMW/Bramo 323R-2 Fafnier, 6 X 1200 hp max.
DIMENSIONS: Span 46 m. (150'11"), Lg. 36.5 m. (119'9"), Ht. 10.9 m. (35'9"), Wing Area 255 qm. (2752 sq. ft.)
WEIGHT: Empty 28,550 kg. (62,950 lb.), Gross 45,600 kg. (100,550 lb.), Fuel 20,700 liters (5,465 gal.)
PERFORMANCE: Speed—Max. 311 km/hr (193 mph), Speed—Max. 297 km/hr (166 mph) at sea level, Cruising speed 254 km/hr (156 mph), Landing speed 125 km/hr (78 mph), Climb 6000 m./49 min. (19,680'/49 min.), Range 7450 km. (4626 miles), Service ceiling 6500 m. (21,320')

At this time, the four surviving giants were returned for rearmament on a pattern first completed in the V-3 in February 1943. New BMW 132R-2 radials boosted to 1200 hp each were fitted, along with three power-operated turrets. Each had an MG 151/20, and these turrets were placed behind the flight deck, and behind each of the outboard engines. An aft turret had an MG 131, and the hand-held MG 81s were retained. For naval reconnaissance over the Atlantic, FuG 200 *Hohentwiel* search radar and FuF 216R Neptun tail-warning radar was installed. They operated from Biscarosse, France, where V-3 and V-5 were destroyed by British strafing in June 1943.

As the BV 222B had been a stillborn commercial version, the BV 222C was the next naval model, and used six 1000 hp Jumo 207C diesels. The prototype was BV 222V-7, flown on April 1, 1943, with the three MG 151/20 power turrets, five MG 131s in the bow and side positions, and search radar. The V-7 was delivered to the Luftwaffe in August, and was joined in 1943 by four BV 222C-0 production boats. The first BV 222C-09 was delivered on July 23, 1943.

At the war's end, BV 222C-013 was just finished and four boats of a proposed E series were in the works. The C-013 and C-011 went to the United States after the war, while the C-012 went to Britain. The V-2, C-09 and C-010 had been destroyed in the war's last year, while V-4 and V-7 survived to be scuttled by their own crews.

The largest aircraft ever built in Germany is an appropriate conclusion for this chapter. The BV 238V-1 was a six-engined flying boat for patrol-bombing, whose design was begun in 1941, manufacturing started in July 1942, and whose first flight took place in August 1943.

The wing was built around a tubular spar which also contained all the fuel, and carried the six 1750 hp Daimler-Benz DB 603V engines and retractable floats. No armament was installed on the prototype, but it was intended that the projected BV 238A

BV 222V-7 (C series prototype)

BLOHM & VOSS BV 222C-0
Junkers Jumo 207C, 6 X 1000 hp
DIMENSIONS: as BV 222A-0
WEIGHT: Empty 30,650 kg. (67,583 lb.), Gross 50,000 kg. (110,250 lb.), Fuel 20,700 liters (5465 gal.)
PERFORMANCE: Speed—Max. 390 km/hr (242 mph), at 5000 m. (16,400′), Speed Max. 330 km/hr (205 mph) at sea level, Cruising speed 345 km/hr (214 mph), Landing speed 130 km/hr (81 mph), Climb 6000 m./52 min. (19,680′/52 min.), Range 6100 km. (3790 miles), Service ceiling 7300 m. (23,950′)

BLOHM & VOSS BV 238V-1
Daimler-Benz DB 603V, 6 X 1750 hp
DIMENSIONS: Span 60.17 m. (197′5″), Lg. 43.36 m. (142′3″), Ht. 15.5 m. (50′10″), Wing Area 362 qm. (3896 sq. ft.)
WEIGHT: Empty 54,660 kg. (120,525 lb.), Gross 94,340 kg. (208,000 lb.) Fuel 38,800 liters (10,800 gal.)
PERFORMANCE: Speed—Max. 360 km/hr (220 mph) at 4400 m. (14,430′), Cruising speed 204 km/hr (335 mph), Landing speed 125 km/hr (78 mph), Climb 6000 m./44.5 min. (19,680′/44.5 min.), Range 5000–8500 km. (3100–5280 miles), Service ceiling 6300 m. (20,670′)

BV 238A: 3-View plan of Germany's largest!

ARADO Ar 195
BMW 132M, 830 hp

DIMENSIONS: Span 12.5 m. (41′), Lg. 10.5 m. (34′5½″), Ht. 3.6 m. (11′10″), Wing Area 46 qm. (495 sq. ft.)

WEIGHT: Empty 2380 kg. (5248 lb.), Gross 3746 kg. (8260 lb.)

PERFORMANCE: Speed—Max. 282 km/hr (175 mph), at 2000 m. (6560′), Cruising speed 250 km/hr (155 mph), Landing speed 90 km/hr (56 mph), Climb 4000 m./14 min. (13,120′/5.3 min.), Range 650 km. (400 miles), Service ceiling 6000 m. (19,680′)

ARADO Ar 197V-1

production ship have four MG 131 guns in each of the power-operated turrets in the nose, tail and out behind each wing, while a fifth turret behind the flight deck held two MG 151/20s and an MG 131 was placed at windows in the side. Wing bomb bays could carry twenty 550 lb. bombs, or 150 troops could be transported in the hull.

Although carefully camouflaged and hidden on Lake Schaal, the BV 238V-1 was destroyed a few weeks before the end of the war by a strafing attack of enemy fighters. Neither the second prototype or a projected BV 250 landplane bomber development could be finished.

DESIGNS FOR THE GRAF ZEPPELIN

Only one aircraft carrier was ever launched for the German Navy, and that one was never completed. Nevertheless, a Luftwaffe group was formed for carrier operations, and aircraft were specially designed for flight deck operations.

Design of this carrier began in April 1934, the keel was laid at Kiel on December 28, 1936, and when the ship was launched December 8, 1938, it was christened *Graf Zeppelin*. With 23,200 tons normal displacement (32,600 tons full load), it was about the same size as later USN *Essex* class carriers, but accommodated less than half as many aircraft. A much greater proportion of the weight was given to armor protection and to guns; sixteen 5.9″ and twelve 4.1″ cannon, along with 22 paired 37 mm. and 28 single 20 mm. guns.

The air group's 40 planes would include two fighter *Staffeln* and a third of two-seaters for scouting, bombing and torpedo work. The latter requirement was difficult to fulfill, since it required a strong biplane with wings stressed for dive-bombing and foldable for storage on ships.

Arado and Fieseler built prototypes to this specification in 1938. Drawing upon its experience with the Ar 95 in landplane form, Arado built the Ar 195V-1 for flight deck operations. Powered by an 830 hp BMW 132M radial, this two-seater had N struts and seated the pilot ahead of the wings for better visibility. Equipment included a fixed MG 17 in the nose, a flexible MG 15 for the observer, and 1100 lb. of torpedo, bombs or two drop tanks. The three prototypes proved inferior to Fieseler's Fi 167 in performance.

Arado also produced a single-seat fighter for carriers, using the same general arrangement and wing span as the Ar 68 biplane. The Ar 197V-1 had a 900 hp DB 600A, enclosed cockpit, and four MG 17 fixed guns.

An 815 hp BMW 132J radial and arrestor hook was used on the Ar 197V-2 of 1938, while the Ar 197V-3 had two 20 mm. MG/FFs mounted in the upper wing, two 7.9 mm. MG 17s on the cowl, and could carry a drop tank or four 110 lb. bombs. Ten Ar 197A-0 biplanes with BMW 132Js were ordered, and evidence indicates the last two were delivered in January 1940.

Designed by Reinhold Mewes, the Fieseler Fi 167 had a 1175 hp DB 601 and folding double-bay wings with N struts and slots. Two prototypes were flown in 1938, and a preproduction batch of 12 was ordered when the Fi 167V-1 showed unusually good low-speed landing ability.

Ar 197V-2

ARADO Ar 197V-3
BMW 132J, 815 hp
DIMENSIONS: Span 11 m (36′1″), Lg. 9.2 m. (30′2″), Ht. 3.6 m. (11′10″), Wing Area 27.8 qm. (300 sq. ft.)
WEIGHT: Empty 1840 kg. (4048 lb.), Gross 2475 kg. (5445 lb.)
PERFORMANCE: Speed—Max. 400 km/hr (248 mph) at 2500 m. (8200′), Cruising speed 354 km/hr (219 mph) Landing speed 95 km/hr (59 mph), Climb 4000 m./5.3 min. (13,120′/5.3 min.), Range 695 km (430 miles), Service ceiling 8600 m. (28,200′)

At the war's beginning, the carrier group 186 operated 24 Jumo-powered Bf 109B fighters and 12 Ju 87C two-seaters from Danzig.[2] While they never had a flight deck to try, they did dive-bomb Polish Navy bases, and the Bf 109T batch was ordered for them. In May 1940, however, *Graf Zeppelin* construction was suspended while about 80% complete, to permit work on other projects.

The Fieseler Fi 167A-0 arrived just after its intended flight deck was stymied, and received service trials with a special test unit. Armament included a fixed MG 17 and flexible MG 17 with 500 and 600 rounds respectively, and a 1686 lb. torpedo, or 1100 lb. bomb, or even a 2200 lb. bomb could be carried. The landing gear could be released in an emergency, and a crew's dinghy was provided in the wing.

Although the Germans decided on May 13, 1942, to resume work on the *Graf Zeppelin*, the Fi 167 had been replaced by the Ju 87E in planning. As things worked out, the carrier was again suspended in 1943, and was scuttled at Stettin on April 25, 1945. The Russians later salvaged the hull, but had to scrap the ship in 1948.

[2] 4(Stuka)/186 and 6(Jagd)/186 were formed when the carrier was launched and 5(Jagd)/186 was added in August 1939. After the Polish campaign they were issued standard Ju 87B and Bf 109E models, and expanded to two separate groups. On July 6, 1940, I(Stuka)/186 and II(Jagd)/186 became III/St.G 1 and III/JG 77.

FIESELER Fi 167A-0

Daimler-Benz DB 601B, 1100 hp at takeoff, 1020 hp at 4500 m. (14,760')

DIMENSIONS: Span 13.5 m. (44'3½"), Lg. 11.4 m. (37'5"), Ht. 4.8 m. (15'9"), Wing Area 45.5 qm. (490 sq. ft.)

WEIGHT: Empty 3100 kg. (6820 lb.), Gross 4850 kg. (10,670 lb.), Fuel 1300/1600 liters (343/422 gal.)

PERFORMANCE: Speed—Max. 320/325 km/hr (199/202 mph), Cruising speed 250/270 km/hr (155/168 mph), Landing speed 95 km/hr (59 mph), Climb 1000 m./2.7 min. (3280'/2.7 min.), Range 1300/1500 km. (808/932 miles), Service ceiling 7500/8200 m. (24,600/26,900') Bomber/Recon Data

Part 9 Rockets and Jets

HEINKEL He 280V-1 at first takeoff

28.

Germany Begins the Jet Era

THE WORLD'S FIRST JETS

It is one of history's ironies that although Germans made the first rocket and the first jet aircraft, the Nazi regime was slow to recognize its opportunity to produce superior fighters. The superior performance of jet aircraft was not utilized in time to save Germany from the Allied bomber offensive.

Ernst Heinkel's experiments with rocket propulsion on He 112 prototypes have been mentioned earlier, and so it is natural that the first all-rocket-powered aircraft was the little Heinkel He 176. Built in secrecy with a Walter rocket unit, the He 176 was first flown on June 30, 1939. The rocket power lasted less than a minute, however, and barely got the machine off the ground.

Several other tests were made, but Udet exclaimed, "That's no airplane . . . I forbid any more flights." Certainly the teardrop shaped experimental bore no resemblance to the Fokker which he had flown. Its military possibilities unrealized, the He 176 was crated and sent to the Berlin Air Museum. There it was destroyed by bombing, and not even a photograph has survived.

Heinkel also began a jet-propulsion project, whose longer endurance seemed more promising. Pabst von Ohain, a twenty-four-year-old engineer hired in March 1936, had a demonstration powerplant ready by September 1937. An 1100 lb. static thrust HeS 3 was then built for the Heinkel He 178, the world's first jet aircraft.

This single-seater had a nose intake for a centrifugal-flow turbo-jet behind the pilot's cockpit. The conventional landing gear retracted into the metal fuselage, and the shoulder-mounted wing was of wood. The whining sound of jet flight was heard for the first time on August 24, 1939, when Flt.-Captain Erich Warsitz made the maiden flight.

A few days later Germany was at war in Poland, and not until November 1 were Udet and Milch persuaded to come for a demonstration flight. Heinkel was then allowed to proceed on his own initiative with the design of a single-seat fighter, the He 280.

On this, the world's first jet fighter, two 1320 lb. static thrust HeS 8 turbo-jets were mounted under the wings, leaving the fuselage clear for armament and the retracted wheels of Germany's first tricycle landing gear. Twin rudders and the world's first ejection seat were used.

Five prototypes were begun under Technical Director Robert Lusser's supervision, and the He 280V-1 airframe was completed in September 1940. The first tests were made without engines, using a Bf 110 as a tow plane. After 41 such gliding flights, the He 280V-1 was flown with jets by Fritz Schaefer on April 4, 1941. No engine covers were used on this flight.

This test preceded the first British jet flight on May 15, 1941, but neither side knew of the other's projects. Meanwhile, Heinkel went ahead with his other prototypes, flying He 280V-2 with HeS 8 turbo-jets in May 1941. The third prototype got the improved 1540 lb. s.t. HeS 8A, in July, and six Argus

HEINKEL He 178
Heinkel HeS 3B, 450 kgp (1100 lb. st.)
DIMENSIONS: Span 8 m. (26'3"), Lg. 7.48 m. (24'6"), Wing Area 7.9 qm. (85 sq. ft.)
WEIGHT and PERFORMANCE: Data not available, but an 850 km/hr (527 mph), speed was anticipated

Me 262

HEINKEL He 280V-2 before jet units installed

HEINKEL He 280V-3
Heinkel-Herth HeS 8A, 2 X 700 kpg (1540 lb. st.)
DIMENSIONS: Span 12 m. (39′4″), Lg. 10.4 m. (34′1½″), Wing Area 21.5 qm. (231 sq. ft.)
WEIGHT: Empty 3217 kg. (7093 lb.), Gross 4270 kg. (9415 lb.)
PERFORMANCE: Speed—Max. 930 km/hr (578 mph) at 6000 m. (19,680′), Landing speed 180 km/hr (112 mph), Climb 6000 m./4 min. (19,680′/4 min.), Range 700 km. (435 miles), Service ceiling 15,000 m. (49,200′)

As 014 impulse ducts were being tried on the V-1 at Rechlin when it crashed on January 13, 1942. On this occasion, the pilot escaped with the new ejection seat; the first such bailout in history.

Junkers had developed a new axial flow turbojet, the 1850 lb. s.t. Jumo 004, and in June 1942 these were installed in the He 280V-2 which also now received an armament of three MG 151/20 guns in the nose. HeS 8A units were again used on the V-4, and the V-5 had BMW 003s.

Although the new jet's superiority over conventional fighters was demonstrated in a mock dogfight with an Fw 190, no production contract was made. On September 15, 1942, Erhard Milch virtually banned the He 280 in favor of Messerschmitt's still unready Me 262. Once again, it appears that there was political favoritism in the Air Ministry. Three more prototypes were built, including the V-6 with Jumo 004 jets and armament, and the V-7, which appeared in April 1943 with a butterfly tail. After gliding tests, HeS 8A jets were later installed on the V-7 and the similar V-8 of July 1943. The V-7 was flown with its jets from November 1943 to February 1944, but the V-8 had its engines removed for further gliding tests of the butterfly tail.

MESSERSCHMITT Me 163V-2

MESSERSCHMITT ME 163 KOMET

The fastest aircraft used in World War Two combat was the Messerschmitt Me 163. With sweptback wings, no horizontal tail, and its trail of smoke, this unusual shape in the German sky worried Allied airmen far beyond its actual effect.

Actually the Me 163 had nothing to do with Messerschmitt. Designer was Dr. Alexander Lippisch, formerly with the German Research Institute for Sailplanes (DFS), Dr. Lippisch had developed a tailless series of light aircraft that seemed a suitable test-bed for a rocket powerplant. The RLM sponsored the secret DFS 194 project and, as Dr. Lippisch had no factory, he got his own design office at Messerschmitt's Augsburg factory in January 1941 so that his new designs could be constructed there.

Instead of the design's original air-cooled piston engine and propeller, the DFS 194 was completed with a 660 lb. static thrust Walter HWK RI-203 rocket engine. Flight tests early in 1941 by Heine Dittmar showed the basic design feasible, and capable of 342 mph even with such limited power.

Work went ahead on two Messerschmitt high-speed research prototypes, and the Me 163V-1 made its first flights at Augsburg in spring 1941 towed into the air by a Bf 110, and gliding back to rest. A 1650 lb. thrust Walter RII rocket was then installed, and Dittmar was flying the Me 163V-1 faster than anyone had ever flown, accelerating past 570 mph before burning up all the fuel.

To save the fuel used on takeoff, and achieve higher speeds, the prototype reverted to a towed takeoff to about 13,000′, the engine not being started until the towline was cast off. On October 2, 1941, at Peenemuende, Dittmar became the first man to fly faster than 1000 km/hr when the Me 163V-1 did 1002 km/hr (624 mph).

DFS 194
Walter HWK RI-203, 300 kpg (660 lb. st.)
DIMENSIONS: Span 9.3 m. (30′4″), Lg. 6.4 m. (21′), Wing Area 17.52 qm. (189 sq. ft.)
WEIGHT: Gross 2100 kg. (4630 lb.)
PERFORMANCE: Speed—Max. 550 km/hr (342 mph)

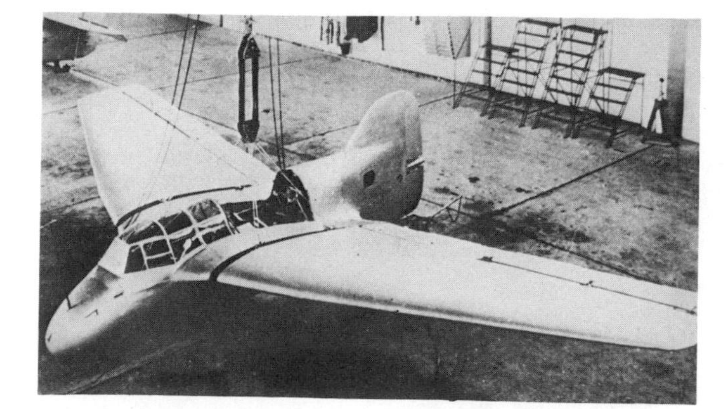

MESSERSCHMITT Me 163V-1 on early test climb

MESSERSCHMITT Me 163B-1
Walter HWK 509A-1, 1700 kpg (3750 lb. st.)
DIMENSIONS: Span 9.33 m. (30′7″), Lg. 5.85 m. (19′2″), Ht. 2.76 m. (9′½″), Wing Area 18.5 qm. (199 sq. ft.)
WEIGHT: Empty 1908 kg. (4207 lb.), Gross 4310 kg. (9500 lb.), Fuel 1028 liter *T-Stoff* (272 gal.) and 500 liter *C-Stoff* (132 gal.)
PERFORMANCE: Speed—Max. 955 km/hr (593 mph) at 9000 m. (29,520′), 830 km/hr (515 mph) at sea level, Landing speed 170 km/hr (105 mph), Climb 9000 m./2.6 min. (29,520′/2.6 min.), Normal action radius 35 km. 800 km/hr (22 miles at 500 mph), Service ceiling 12,000 m. (39,320′)

This performance led to a December 1941 order for an Me 163B operational fighter design, while ten unarmed Me 163A airframes were procured for training. These were completed first without engines as pilot training gliders, and then provided with HWK RIIs for powered practices. A 3750 lb. thrust Walter HWK 109-509B-1, using the "hot" fuel system was selected for the next three (V-3 to V-5) prototypes, designed as interceptor fighters. Although the Me 163V-3 airframe was completed in April 1942, the

JUNKERS Ju 248V-1 (Me 263 prototype)
Walter HWK 109-509C-4 2000 kgp+400 kgp (4400 lb. st.+880 lb. st.)
DIMENSIONS: Span 9.5 m. (31′2″), Lg. 7.89 m. (25′10½″), Ht. 3 m. (9′10″), Wing Area 17.8 qm. (192 sq. ft.)
WEIGHT: Empty 2200 kg. (4850 lb.), Gross 5300 kg. (11,680 lb.), Fuel 2440 liters (644 gal.)
PERFORMANCE: Speed—Max. 950 km/hr (590 mph), at 6000 m. (19,680′), Climb 15,000 m./3 min. (49,200′/3 min.), Endurance 15 min., Service ceiling 15,000 m. (49,200′)

MESSERSCHMITT Me 163V-6

improved Walter engine wasn't ready for installation until August 1943, when the first powered flight tests began.

By that time, Messerschmitt's Regensburg plant had completed the first of ten Me 163B-0 fighters, to be followed by 60 Me 163B-1 aircraft. These single-seaters were used to retrain veteran pilots for rocket flight by a special test unit, EK 16. Preferring to concentrate on his Me 262, Messerschmitt discontinued his affiliation with Dr. Lippisch, and large-scale Komet production was turned over to Klemm Flugzeugwerke at a secret Bollingen factory in the Black Forest. Acceptances rose from three in June 1944 and 12 in July to a high of 90 aircraft in December.

The first operational rocket-fighter group was I/JG 400, which flew its first sorties from Brandis, near Leipzig. According to U. S. Army Air Force records, the Komet was first encountered on July 28, 1944, shot down its first Americans on August 5, and suffered its first loss August 16.

The Me 163B-1's pilot sat behind a 15 mm. armor nose cone tipped by a little propeller for its generator. A windshield of 10 mm. armor glass and 8–13 mm. back plates further protected the pilot. While early examples had two MG 151/20 guns with 100 rpg, standard armament was a 30 mm. MK 108 with 60 rounds in each wing root. A dozen special Komets replaced the gun with five SG 500 rockets in each wing root, automatically fired by photo-electric cells when the Komet passed beneath a B-17, but it appears this system was used successfully only once.

The small rocket engine was fueled by 1028 liters (271 gal.) of *T-Stoff* (80% hydrogen peroxide plus phosphate) in the fuselage and 500 liters (132 gal.) of *C-Stoff* (30% hydrozine hydrate solution in menthol) in the wings. This fuel lasted only eight minutes, limiting the Komet to actions within some 22 miles of its base. In 2.6 minutes the Me 163B-1 could climb to 29,520′, dash after its target at 593 mph, dive to the attack, and glide back to its base.

The landing gear consisted of a retractable steel skid to which a two-wheel dolly was added to be dropped after takeoff. A tail wheel and small wing tip skids balanced the aircraft as it came to rest. The fuselage was all metal with wooden construction and plywood covering for the wings. A 23 degree sweepback enabled the control surfaces to act as both ailerons and elevators (elevons) but was insufficient to increase the critical Mach number. Fixed wing slots prevented spinning.

An Me 163C series was planned around the HWK 109-509C engine, which added a 660 lb. thrust auxiliary unit. This power supplemented the main 3750 lb. thrust element during climb, after which the main unit was turned off, and the auxiliary used for cruising. This powerplant raised ceiling a third to 52,500′, and endurance to 12 minutes, and was tested on the Me 163V-6. Production Me 163Cs were to be larger and heavier, with bubble canopy and the guns repositioned in the nose, but none were actually completed.

The most advanced development began as the Me 163D, using wheeled landing gear and an HWK 109-509C-4 offering 4400 lbs. thrust and 880 lb. for cruising. The design was turned over to Junkers' Dessau factory and the supervision of Professor Heinrich Hertel. A prototype was finished in August 1944 as the Ju 248V-1 with a longer fuselage, more fuel, pressurized cockpit with bubble canopy, and retractable tricycle wheeled landing gear. Although the design was returned to Messerschmitt for production as the Me 263A, this aircraft never materialized.

While standard Me 163B-1 production amounted to some 364 in 1944–45, the combat results were disappointing. Many Komets were destroyed when the highly dangerous fuel exploded in takeoff or landing accidents. The very limited endurance reduced opportunities for successful attacks, and the same speed that was too fast to be caught by enemy fighters or tracked by bomber's turret guns, made it difficult for Komet pilots to score hits. The only operational group, I/JG 400, claimed only nine kills during its employment; a poor record next to the jet-propelled Me 262.

MESSERSCHMITT ME 262

The most important military aircraft to come out of Germany may well be the Me 262, the world's first operational jet fighter. The most effective of today's jet fighters, like the McDonnel F-4 and MiG-21, are descendants of the Messerschmitt twin-jet single-seaters.

In 1938, the RLM had ordered BMW and Junkers to develop turbojet powerplants with a static thrust of 1320 lbs. When the first projected designs for these engines became available, Messerschmitt was ordered to design a fighter aircraft for the new powerplants and in June 1939 the design was offered as Project 1065. It is remarkable that Heinkel, who was already building the first turbojet engine and jet aircraft as a private venture, was excluded from this program.

Three prototypes designated Me 262 were ordered on December 19, 1939, to use two of the BMW engines and conventional tail-down landing gear. The Me 262 mockup was inspected on March 1, 1940, but when the BMW P 3302 (later 109-003) turbojets were test run the following summer, they yielded only 570 lb. thrust, and were unreliable.

The three airframes were completed in April 1941, but the turbojets were still unavailable. To test the aircraft's flight characteristics, Me 262V-1 (PC+UA) was fitted with a 1200 hp Jumo 211G in the nose. With its wing nacelles still empty, it was flown on April 18, 1941, powered by the Jumo and its two-bladed propeller.

Messerschmitt urged more haste with turbojet engine development, but was assured by General

MESSERSCHMITT Me 262V-1 with propeller and empty jet housings

Udet and State Secretary Milch that turbojet development wasn't urgent, for the war would be won with conventional powerplants. Finally, a pair of 1100 lb. thrust BMW 003 turbojets was available and were used on a three-engined flight made November 25, 1941. Fortunately the Jumo had been retained, for both jets jammed shortly after takeoff and the propeller in the nose was needed to return the aircraft to safety.

After these misfortunes, it was decided to abandon the BMW engine in favor of the Junkers Jumo 004. A pair of these 1850 lb. s.t. units were fitted to the Me 262V-3 (PC+UC) and flown by Fritz Wendel on July 18, 1942.

At this point, we remind the reader that the He 280 had flown with BMW jets on April 4, 1941, and with Jumos in June 1942, while the American Bell

MESSERSCHMITT Me 262 V-2

XP-59A wasn't ready until October 1, 1942, and the British Gloster Meteor until March 5, 1943. These rivals did have one great advantage over the Messerschmitt, in their tricycle landing gear, whose level position permitted better visibility during takeoff as well as safer landings.

The tail-down position's handicap was demonstrated on August 11, 1942, when Me 262V-3 taxied through a fence at Rechlin and was smashed on a trashheap. Nevertheless, Milch preferred the Messerschmitt to Heinkel's jet, but was reluctant to interrupt priorities for conventional fighters to allow quantity production of a radical new type.

As more Jumo turbojets became available, the Me 262V-2 (PC+UB) flew on October 2, 1942, the rebuilt V-1 flew with jets on March 2, 1943, followed by the similar Me 262V-4 (PC+UD) and Me 262V-5 (PC+VE). The latter was provided with a fixed nose wheel, and tests begun June 26, 1943, proved the tricycle gear's superiority.

Germany's Fighter Commander, Major General Adolf Galland, flew the Me 262V-4 on May 22, 1943, and enthusiastically welcomed the new jets as the answer to Germany's air defense problem. This would "Guarantee us an unbelievable advantage in operations, while the enemy adheres to the piston engine."

Although Goering agreed with Galland's approval, and a preproduction Me 262A-0 series was ordered June 2, 1943, Hitler's unwillingness to commit himself delayed Messerschmitt's authorization to prepare for mass production until August 27. A new prototype batch was then built as Me 262V-6 to V-10 (W.Nr. 130001 to 005, VI+AA to AE), with retractable tricycle landing gear and improved 1980 lb. thrust Jumo 004B engines. The Me 262V-6 was demonstrated before Hitler on November 26, 1943, the V-7 tried a pressurized cockpit, the V-8 was the first to be fitted with the standard four 30 mm. cannon armament, and the V-9 had more advanced radio equipment.

When Hitler saw the jet demonstrated, he astonished Galland and Messerschmitt by declaring the jet to be his long-awaited "Blitz bomber" with which he could strike the threatening Allied invasion forces. Messerschmitt then arranged for the future Me 262V-10 to be strengthened and fitted with racks under the fuselage for two 550 lb. bombs, but the Me 262 early production aircraft went unchanged. Production had already been too long delayed, and Hitler's intentions to make a bomber out of the jet was ignored. A dictatorship is not always as responsive as the dictator himself expects.

MESSERSCHMITT Me 262 V-3

A further delay occurred when construction of the nearly complete Me 262A-0 13 plane preproduction batch was disrupted by the American bombing of Augsburg on February 19, 1944. Production was hastily decentralized, and a new assembly line began deliveries in April 1944, when the Luftwaffe accepted the first 18 jets. More damage from an April 24 attack reduced May deliveries to only seven Me 262A-1s, instead of the 60 promised in the 1943 program.

All of these jets were pure fighters, for only the Me 262V-10 (VI+AE) flown on May 1 had bomb racks, as well as a special control device for high-speed rolls. When Hitler discovered that none of his "Blitz bombers" had been made, he was furious with his staff. He demanded that all jets under construction be completed as bombers, and forbade any officials to speak of the Me 262 as a fighter; only as a bomber would it be discussed!

Control of the jets' distribution and training was turned over to the bomber commanders, despite Galland's protests. Galland had declared in April that one Me 262 fighter was worth more to him than five Bf 109s, but all 28 Messerschmitt Me 262s accepted in June 1944, and the 59 accepted in July were Me 262A-2 "bombers." Though named *Sturmvogel,* instead of *Schwalbe,* they differed only in the

MESSERSCHMITT Me 262 A-1a
Junkers Jumo 004B-2, 2 X 1980 lb. st.
DIMENSIONS: Span 12.51 m. (41′), Lg. 10.605 m. (34′9″), Ht. 3.85 m. (15′9″), Wing Area 21.7 qm. (233.59 sq ft.)
WEIGHT: Empty 3800 kg. (8379 lb.), Gross 6926 kg. (15,272 lb.), Fuel 2600 liters (686 gal.)
PERFORMANCE: Speed—Max. 870 km/hr (540 mph) at 6000 m. (19,680′), Cruising speed 750 km/hr (465 mph), Landing speed 250 km/hr (155 mph), Climb 6000 m./6.8 min. (19,680′/6.8 min.) 9000 m./13.2 min. (29,520′/13.2 min.), Range 1050 km. (650 miles), Service ceiling 11,450 m. (37,560′)

provision of bomb racks and a simple aiming device.

The first aircraft from the assembly line went to a test unit at Rechlin and a tactical training command, EK 262, at Lechfeld. Attrition was heavy as the pilots learned the type's eccentricities, especially a tendency of the engines to catch fire if handled too roughly. It was probably a Lechfeld jet that made the July 25 attack on an RAF Mosquito that is the first recorded Allied encounter with the Me 262. At that time, the Me 262's top speed of 540 mph was over 100 mph faster than the American P-51D Mustang, fastest Allied fighter. In accordance with Hitler's wishes, the first operational pilots assigned to the Me 262 were bomber pilots from KG 51. These men spent the summer in transition from their twin-engined experience to the novelties of turbo engines, tricycle landing gear, and jet speeds. The most difficult problem was learning to aim their bombs at such high speeds. Horizontal bombing was impossible, and the jet was too fast for dive-bombing. A shallow dive technique was used, complicated by Hitler's orders not to fly below 4000 meters to prevent the jet's "secrets" from falling into Allied hands.

No "Blitz bombers" were ready to greet the Normandy invasion, and in fact, KG 51 didn't begin regular bombing sorties until October 1944. The inaccuracy with which its few bombs were dropped limited the raids to only nuisance value. Hitler's "Blitz bomber" foolishness had only delayed by four critical months the jet's use as a fighter.

After Hitler began to relent on his opposition to fighters, acceptances amounted to 15 bombers and five fighters in August, 72 and 19 in September, and 65 and 52 in October. This confusion about the jet's mission crushed whatever chances the Me 262 may have had of reversing the course of the air war.

Not until September 25, 1944, was the first operational fighter unit set up with 30 Me 262A-1s released because the new Ar 234 jet bomber was becoming available. This was *Kommando* Nowotny, at Achmer, lead by Major Walter Nowotny, a 250-victory ace. These few jets entered a sky crowded with Allied aircraft, fighting from October 2 on against enormous odds.

When Major Nowotny was killed on November 8, the unit was removed from combat after 26 losses and 22 victory claims. Its pilots became the nucleus of Germany's first jet fighter wing, JG 7. Now, the Luftwaffe was belatedly concentrating on jet fighters, conserving its resources for new blows at the front. Me 262A-1 fighter acceptances were 101 in November and 124 in December, making a total of 568 twin-jet Messerschmitts delivered by the year's end.

Production rose to 160 in January 1945, and 280 in February, and some 1294 Me 262s were finished before Germany's collapse. The earlier bomber versions were hastily converted back to fighters as KG 51 became a fighter wing, along with the hastily converted KGJ 6, 27, and 54. Yet shortages of fuel and skilled pilots left most of the jets sitting helplessly on the ground.

General Galland had been dismissed as Fighter Commander because of his objections to Goering's policies, and was allowed to form a special unit, Jagdverband 44, operating from Munich-Riem with the best remaining fighter pilots in April 1945. By then, it was much too late to change the war's course, for as the Germans say; "Too many dogs are the hare's death." Nazi incompetence had lost the value of the fighter force's best weapons.

Allied intelligence had had ample warnings of the jet's coming, and several bombings had been directed at disrupting production. Unaware of Hitler's own confused purposes, American commanders feared the jets might wrest air superiority from them before the advancing ground armies could put the fighter factories out of business.

A defecting German pilot delivered a new unpainted Me 262A-1, the one shown in our flight photos, to the Americans on March 30, 1945. The four MK 108s converged at 500 yards and were

Me 262A-2

Me 262A-1a/MK 14

Me 262B-1a/U1

provided with 200 30 mm. rounds for the upper pair and 160 rounds for the lower pair. Attachments were provided for two 79 gallon drop tanks beneath the A-1's fuselage, while the A-2 carried two 550 lb. bombs that cost some 120 mph in speed; sixteen mm. armor was provided.

The Me 262's general construction was a conventional dual structure, but the single spar was swept back 18½ degrees on the leading edge and had automatic slots that opened at 186 mph in a glide or 279 mph in a climb. The fuselage's triangular cross-section, blending to a circular nose, was to allow the main wheels to retract into the bottom.

Besides the main Me 262A-1a and A-2a models the following A series variants are known:

Me 262A-1a/U1: Strengthened armament of two MG 151/20s, two MK 108s and two MK 103s.
A-1a/U2: Additional FuG 25 radio for bad weather.
A-1a/U3: No guns, two cameras for recon.
A-1b: Wing racks for 24 R4M rockets, only 20 built.
A-2a/U1: Only two MK 108s, special TSA bombsight.
A-2a/U2: No guns, bomb-aimer in perspex nose with Lotfe 7H sight.
A-3a: As A-2a, but more armor for ground-support missions.
A-5a: Two MK 108s, two RB 50/30 cameras for recon.
A-1a/MK 114: Four armed with single 50 mm. MK 114 guns in the nose.

A two-place trainer version was the Me 262B-1a, which had standard armament, dual controls, reduced internal tankage to 1730 liters, but utilized two 300 liter (79 gal.) external tanks. Some of these two-seaters were converted to night fighters by provision of Lichtenstein SN 2 radar in the nose, where the forked antenna reduced top speed about 37 mph. In April 1945, 10/NJG II was the war's only jet night fighter squadron.

A single Me 262B-2 was built with a four foot longer fuselage to accommodate more fuel and an added pair of MK 108s slanted upward. Later, the SN 2 radar was replaced by FuG 224 with enclosed radar.

An additional rocket engine was proposed for an Me 262C series, but only a single Me 262C-1a was flown with a HWK 109-509 (used in the Me 163B) rocket in the tail. The fuel supply included 900 liters (238 gal.) of *T-Stoff* and 600 liters (158 gal.) *C-Stoff* for the rocket, and 1070 liters (283 gal.) of internal and 600 liters (158 gal.) of external jet fuel. On its first flight this aircraft reached 38,800′ in only 4.5 minutes.

An Me 262C-2b was completed with two BMW 003Rs, each of which was a 1700 lb. s.t. 003A-2 jet combined with a rocket unit offering 3300 lb. s.t. for three minutes. This powerplant did not work out, however. Several other more radical ideas to improve the Me 262 failed to pass the paper stage.

The standard fighter version was considered a great success by its German pilots, despite the adverse conditions in which it reached battle. Twenty-two Me 262 pilots were said to be jet aces, and Heinz Baer was first with 16 victories. On the other hand, many unfortunate pilots were shot down when its 100 mph advantage over enemy prop-driven fighters was canceled out by the enemy's maneuverability and numbers. The U. S. Eighth Air Force admitted losing at least 52 heavy bombers and ten fighters, yet claimed some 200 victories; data for the other Allied air forces is unavailable.

Certainly the captured jets were in high demand among the Allies, and they took an important role in advancing aviation in the United States, Britain, Czechoslovakia, and the Soviet Union.

ARADO AR 234

The only jet-propelled aircraft operational in World War II that was actually intended as a bomber was the Arado Ar 234. A single-seater of very simple design, it was a shoulder-wing monoplane with a turbojet under each wing. The pilot sat in the rounded transparent bow with a remarkable forward view, and fuel tanks filled most of the rest of the narrow fuselage.

The Ar 234 originated with an RLM request late in 1940 for a medium-range reconnaissance type using the revolutionary new turbojets to achieve speeds beyond those of enemy fighters. Early in 1941, the design was completed and work begun on prototypes, but the engines fell far behind schedule and examples were not available to Arado even for ground tests until February 1943.

A unique landing gear had been designed to minimize weight and space needs; a retractable skid below the fuselage and below each engine. For take-off, the aircraft rode on a three-wheel trolley which was released after liftoff, and brought to rest by parachutes.

Powered by two 1850 lb. s.t. Jumo 004A jets, the Ar 234V-1 flew at Rheine on June 15, 1943. The flight went well, except for failure of the trolley's

Me 262B-2

ARADO Ar 234V-3

ARADO Ar 234V-1

ARADO Ar 234V-6

ARADO Ar 234V-8

parachute to open as expected. Top speed was rated at 680 km/hr (423 mph), but no armament or equipment was carried. The similar Ar 234V-2 was flown July 27.

Ar 234V-3 and V-4 were intended as production prototypes for the Ar 234A service series, and were provided with ejection seat, pressurized cockpit, and takeoff rockets (*R-Geraete*) under each wing. The third prototype was ready August 25, the fourth September 15, and performance was reported to include a 750 km/hr (466 mph) speed, 12,500 m. (41,000′) ceiling and 1200 km. (745 mile) range.

Improved Jumo 004B production engines were provided on the Ar 234V-5, ready December 20, 1943, and the Ar 234V-7. The latter's fire in April 1944, was the first fatal incident in the Arado's story, causing the death of the test pilot Selle.

Seeking still more power, two prototypes were each provided with four BMW 003A jets. The Ar 234V-8 appeared on February 1, 1944 with its four powerplants paired in twin nacelles, but the Ar 234V-6 was ready April 8 with engines in four separate nacelles. The V-8's arrangement seemed more efficient, and was adopted for the later Ar 234C series.

Since the trolley and skid undercarriage had proven impractical for combat use, retractable tricycle wheels were specified for production aircraft, which were designated Ar 234B. The nose wheels retracted behind the pilot's seat, and the main wheels into the center section. Three prototypes were hastily completed with the new undercarriage, two Jumo 004B jets, and ejector seats; the Ar 234V-9 of March 1944, the V-10 of April and the V-11 of May.

While the Arado prototypes were built at Warne-

ARADO Ar 234B-1

ARADO Ar 234B-2
Junkers Jumo 109-004B, 2 X 900 kgp (1980 lb. st.)
DIMENSIONS: Span 14.41 m. (47'3"), Lg. 12.61 m. (41'4½"), Ht. 4.3 m. (14'1"), Wing Area 26.4 qm. (284 sq. ft.)
WEIGHT: Empty 5200 kg. (11,466 lb.), Gross 8410 kg. (18,544 lb.), Max. 9800 kg. (21,609 lb.) Fuel 3750/4350 liters (990/1148 gals.)
PERFORMANCE: Speed—Max. 742 km/hr (461 mph) at 6000 m. (19,680'), Landing speed 146 km/hr (91 mph), Climb 6000 m./12.8 min. (19,680'/12.8 min.), Range 1100 km./1500 kg. bombs, (680 miles/3300 lb.) 1550 km./500 kg. (960 miles/1100 lb.) 1630 km. (1000 miles) as recon, Service ceiling 10,000 m. (32,800')

muende, an Ar 234B production line was set up at Alt Loennewitz and the first example was flown on June 8, 1944. Five were accepted in July and deliveries increased to 40 in October, with 148 finished by year's end.

The first of these were pure reconnaissance aircraft, with a pair of cameras in the Ar 234B-0's rear fuselage, and an automatic pilot and two 79 gal. drop tanks added to the Ar 234B-1. The Ar 234B-2 was fitted for bombing; up to three 1100 lb. bombs could be handled on single racks beneath the fuselage and each engine.

A Lotfe 7K sight between the pilot's legs was used for level bombing in connection with the automatic pilot. A periscope in the canopy roof could be used with a bombing computer in shallow dives, or turned rearward to fire two fixed MG 151/20 guns with 200 rpg that pointed backwards under the tail. (These were often omitted in service.)

Faster than any Allied fighter at the front, the Arado jets began reconnaissance missions in September. The bomber version was issued to KG 76, striking

ARADO Ar 234V-13

Allied positions during the Ardennes offensive in December, and in March 1945 they were sent against the Remagen Bridge, that had been fortuitously captured by the Americans. Although some 210 Ar 234Bs were completed, the last machines were immobilized by fuel shortages.

A diverse development and experimental program continued with the Arado jets illustrates the remarkable vitality of German designing in the war's last year. Besides improvement of the B series, the program included a four-engine Ar 234C, two engine Ar 234D and an Ar 234P night fighter.

A series of B prototypes from V-10 to V-18 were begun in 1944 to try various ideas, but the most notable was the crescent-shaped sweptback wing on Ar 234V-16. This aircraft was not completed, but the Ar 234V-13 appeared with four 1760 lb. thrust BMW 003A 1 turbojets instead of the two Jumos usually used. This engine arrangement was that chosen for the Ar 234C series.

ARADO Ar 234C-3 (V-21 in photo)
BMW 109-003A-1, 4 X 800 kgp (1760 lb. st.)
DIMENSIONS: Span 14.41 m. (47'3"), Lg. 12.62 m. (41'5"), Ht. 4.42 m. (14'6"), Wing Area 26.4 qm. (284 sq. ft.)
WEIGHT: Empty 6500 kg. (14,332 lb.), Gross 11,000 kg. (24,255 lb.)
PERFORMANCE: Speed—Max. 852 km/hr (529 mph) at 6000 m. (19,680'), 800 km/hr (497 mph) at sea level, Climb 10,000 m./16.7 min. (32,800'/16.7 min.), Range 1215 km. (755 miles), Service ceiling 11,000 m. (36,000')

ARADO Ar 234C-1

Four-engined prototypes V-19 to V-30 were begun, and an Ar 234C assembly line began to roll out completed bombers in 1945. It is believed that 19 of the C series aircraft were completed before the war's end, although none reached service units.

The Ar 234C-1 was a four-engined recon model based on the V-19, while Ar 234C-2 was the bomber version. An Ar 234V-21 was prototype for the Ar 234C-3 bomber and Ar 234C-4 recon model, introducing a raised cabin roof and adding two forward-firing MG 151/20s.

The first two-place version was the Ar 234V-25, with the cockpit having two staggered seats as planned for the Ar 234C-5 multi-purpose series. Another two-place variant was the Ar 234D-1 recon with a pair of 2860 lb. thrust Heinkel HeS 011 engines. Just two were completed in April 1945, and none of an Ar 234D-2 bomber version appeared.

Also projected was an Ar 234P night fighter with two men, radar nose, and fixed cannon. Versions proposed included a P-1 with four BMW jets, a P-3 with two HeS jets, a P-4 with two Jumo jets, and a three-seat P-5 with two HeS jets. None passed the paper stage, including a supposed P-2 about which nothing is reported.

THE PEOPLE'S FIGHTER

The last combat type to enter production in Germany was created in a remarkably short time to meet the desperate situation at the war's end.

On September 8, 1944, as the war's sixth year began, the RLM issued a specification for a simple, low-cost fighter using one BMW 003 jet which would not weigh over 2000 kg. (4400 lb.), have a top speed of 750 km/hr (466 mph) and a 30 minute endurance. Above all, the aircraft had to be ready for production by January 1, 1945, and the preliminary designs were considered on September 15.

Of the six proposals then submitted, that of Blohm & Voss was judged the best, but Heinkel's representative was insistent on the project prepared by Siegfried Gunther. Messerschmitt had refused to submit a proposal for what they considered an unrealistic requirement. For once, however, political considerations favored Heinkel. Goering had resolved on a "people's fighter" (*Volksjaeger*) program to be flown by Hitler Youth, as a counterpart to Himmler's *Volkssturm.*

Goering's support led to Heinkel's completing design work on September 23, and preparing a mockup. After much argument, on September 30, the Heinkel was ordered into immediate production with a planned output of 1000 aircraft per month. The designation chosen was He 162; this repeated the Bf 162 number, apparently to confuse Allied intelligence.

An initial batch of ten *Versuchs* aircraft were begun at Heinkel's Vienna plant, which was responsible for developmental work and establishment of a mass production line underground in a former chalk mine at nearby Hinterbruehl. Other assembly lines were set up by Heinkel at Marienehe and Junkers at Bernburg, utilizing extensive subcontracting and even salt mines as underground fuselage assembly halls.

The He 162V-1 made its first flight on December 6, 1944, near Vienna, only 69 days after it was ordered. On December 10, while making a low altitude demonstration pass over an official party, the right wing failed, the aircraft rolled, and had a fatal crash. A still from a film of the accident is shown here, showing the right wing tip, aileron and fin breaking away.

Defective wood bonding caused the accident, which didn't interfere with continued construction. He 162V-2 was flown on December 22, while the next two aircraft were modified by enlarging the tail assembly and turning the wing tips downward. The He 162V-3 and V-4 flew on January 16, 1945.

HEINKEL He 162V-1

He 162V-1's fatal accident

Two 30 mm. MK 108s with 60 rpg had armed the first six prototypes, but the heavy guns were too much for the airframe. Two MG 151/20s and double the ammunition supply was standard on the remaining experimental and production aircraft. Incorporat-

HEINKEL He 162A-2
BMW 003E-1, 80 kgp (1760 lb. st.)
DIMENSIONS: Span 7.2 m. (23′7″), Lg. 9.25 m. (30′4″), Ht. 2.55 m. (8′4¼″), Wing Area 11.2 qm. (120 sq. ft.)
WEIGHT: Empty 1800 kg. (3970 lb.), Gross 2490 kg. (5490 lb.), Fuel 950 liters (250 gal.)
PERFORMANCE: Speed—Max. 840 km/hr (522 mph) at 6000 m. (19,680′), 784 km/hr (490 mph) at sea level, Landing speed 165 km/hr (102 mph), Climb 6000 m./6.6 min. (19,680′/6.6 min.), Range 430 km. (267 miles), Service ceiling 12,000 m. (39,360′)

ing the changes indicated by test experience, production aircraft were labeled Hs 162A-2 and replaced the BMW 003A with the 003E-1.

This engine was mounted above the fuselage in a location better for serviceability than streamlining. The fuselage was of metal, with wood used on the wings and fins, and the landing gear had tricycle wheels.

Several developments of the *Volksjaeger,* or Salamander as the company wished to call it, were projected, but none passed the paper stage. They included an He 162B-1 with two small 740 lb. thrust As 014 pulse jets, He 162B-2 with an 1100 lb. thrust As 044, He 162C with 2860 lb. thrust HeS 011 and swept-forward wings, and He 162D with HeS 011 and sweptback wings; the latter two with butterfly tail.

Production of standard Hs 162A-2s amounted to 116 before the war's end. Most went to JG 1, but none seem to have been used in combat. On VE Day, May 8, 1945, JG 1's fighters were found neatly lined up at the Lech base, near the Danish border. It was the end of the Luftwaffe's fighters.

EXPERIMENTAL JETS

German ingenuity was displayed by the many experimental projects attempted in the war's last year. Desperation became the dominant motive in the last struggle, and the variety of aircraft configurations reflected both creativity and an attitude of try anything.

Among the strangest configurations was that of the Junkers Ju 287 jet bomber, which featured the only *swept-forward* wing ever flown on a combat plane. This wing had been designed by Dr. Hans Wocke to get the speed advantage of sweep along with better stalling characteristics. The shape requires a very strong wing, and has not proven suitable for supersonic speeds, but did perform satisfactorily on some 17 flights of the Ju 287V-1.

Design work had begun on the bomber late in 1942, and the first prototype's construction was expedited by using available components, such as adapting an He 177A-3 fuselage and Ju 388 tail assembly. The main wheels were from a wrecked American B-24, and two small wheels were under the nose, with streamlined pants on all four wheels. The powerplant was four Jumo 004B-1 jets, two mounted on the forward fuselage, and another beneath each wing. Below each engine was a Walter rocket pack used for takeoffs, and parachuted for retrieval.

The Ju 287V-1 was photographed on the ground by a British reconnaissance Mosquito in April 1944, and aroused much interest. The first flight was from Brandis by *Flugkapitaen* Siegfried Holzlauer on October 16, 1944.

Further development was inhibited by the end of the Luftwaffe bomber program, but a Ju 287V-2 was begun, providing for retractable landing gear and

JUNKERS Ju 287V-1 in flight

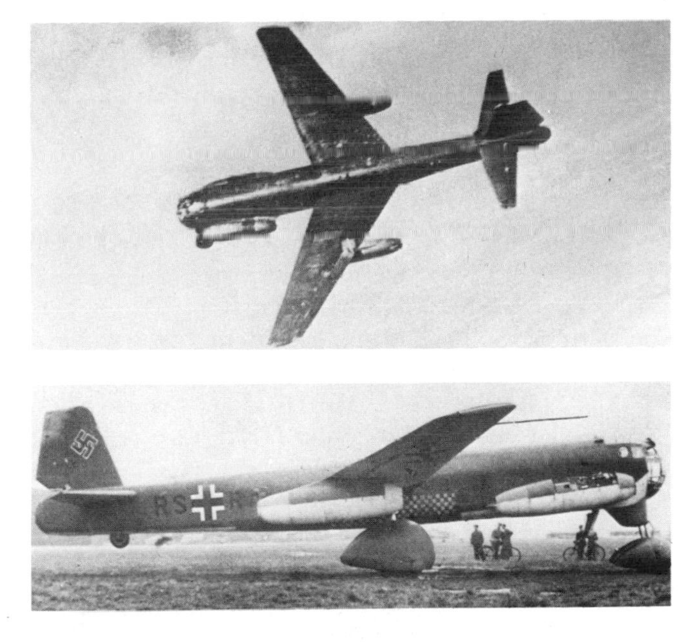

JUNKERS Ju 287V-1
Junkers Jumo 004B-1, 4 X 900 kgp (1980 lb. st.)
DIMENSIONS: Span 20.1 m. (65′11½″), Lg. 18.28 m. (60′), Wing Area 58.3 qm. (627 sq. ft.)
WEIGHT: Empty 12,500 kg. (27,557 lb.), Gross 22,550 lb. (49,723 lb.)
PERFORMANCE: Speed—Max. 814 km/hr (505 mph) at 5900 m. (19,350′) Landing speed 170 km/hr (105 mph), Range 1576 km. (980 miles), Service ceiling 10,800 m. (35,430′)

JUNKERS Ju 287V-1

four 2200 lb. thrust HeS 011 jets. A Ju 287V-3 was also designed for future production and was to have six 1760 lb. thrust BMW 003 jets, a crew of three in a Ju 388 nose, twin MG 131s in the tail, and an expected 540 mph top speed.

The world's first jet heavy bombers were in Soviet-occupied Dessau when the war ended, and the Russians removed the Ju 287V-1 and incomplete V-2, as well as Dr. Wocke and most of the Junkers organization to the Soviet Union. The Ju 287V-2 was completed with four Jumo 004B jets under the wings and flown at Ramenskoye, near Moscow.

The Gotha Go 229 fighter developed with a series of all-wing aircraft designed before the war by Reimar and Walter Horton. By 1943, these had evolved into the Horton IX V-1 begun at Gottingen as a single-seat fighter powered by two BMW 003A-1 turbojets.

Since the BMW jets proved too large for the wing, the first aircraft was flown in 1944 as a glider with fixed tricycle gear. Two 1960 lb. thrust Jumo 004B-1s were used on the Horton IX V-2, but the aircraft was destroyed by an engine fire, so frequent in the early jet days.

Gothaer Waggonfabrik of World War I fame was assigned to develop the all-wing fighter, beginning construction of five Gotha Go 229 prototypes and 20 Go 229A-0 service test examples. The Go 229V-3 was a single-seater with sweptback leading edge, twin Jumo 004B-1s, retractable tricycle gear and four 30 mm. MK 108 guns. The next two prototypes were to be two-place night fighters, while V-6 and V-7 were to be fighter-bombers.

When American troops occupied the factory in April 1945, they found the Go 229V-3 in the unfinished condition shown in the photo. The all-wing layout had some resemblance to the smaller American flying wing, the Northrop XP-79B built the same year.

The most advanced German jet fighter actually under construction was probably the Messerschmitt

GOTHA Go 229V-3
Junkers Jumo 004B-1, 2 X 890 kgp (1980 lb. st.)
DIMENSIONS: Span 16.78 m. (55'½"), Lg. 7.47 m. (24'6"), Ht. 2.81 m. (9'2½"), Wing Area 52.5 qm. (565 sq. ft.)
WEIGHT: Gross 8000 kg. (17,600 lb.)
PERFORMANCE: Speed—Max. 1000 km/hr (621 mph) at 6100 m. (20,000'), Cruising speed 900 km/hr (559 mph), Landing speed 130 km/hr (81 mph), Range 1930 km. (1200 miles), Service ceiling 15,600 m. (51,160')

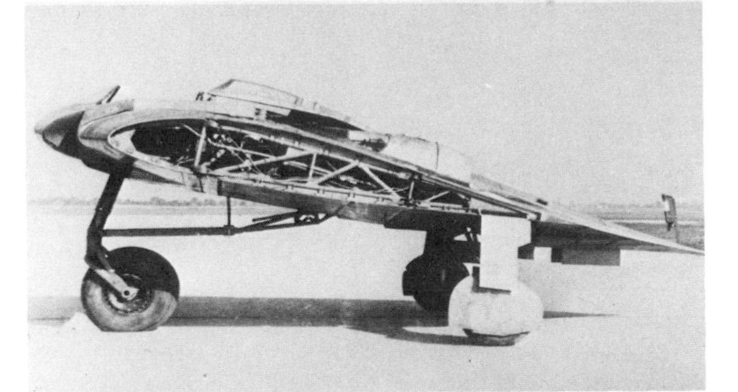

project 1101, begun in July 1944. Traces of its influence can be seen in many famous designs, like the F-86 Sabre, MiG-15, and SAAB J 29.

The Messerschmitt's outstanding feature was the sweep, 40 degrees on the wing's leading edge and 45 degrees on the tail. A nose intake drew air beneath the pilot to the 2860 lb. thrust HeS 011A turbojet built into the fuselage under the midwing. Tricycle landing gear and two 30 mm. MK 108 cannon were incorporated into the design.

The only P 1101 prototype, authorized in September 1944, was nearly finished at Oberammergau but was captured by the Americans, and inspired the Bell X-5 flown in 1951.

AN APPENDIX OF PECULIAR WEAPONS

A strange episode in German aviation is difficult to classify, for it has no powerplant. The Blohm & Voss BV 40 was conceived in late 1943 as a single-place armored glider to attack enemy bombers.

The construction was of wood, except for the nose cockpit in which the pilot lay prone on a padded bench. The small frontal area would provide only a small target to enemy gunners, as the glider attacked firing its twin 30 mm. MK 108 guns. Armor was a quarter of the gross weight, consisting of 20 mm. welded steel and 120 mm. armor-glass in front, eight mm. on the side, and five mm. on the rear.

A Bf 109G was to tow the BV 40 off the ground, dropping the glider's two-wheel dolly on liftoff, flying to one or two thousand feet above and ahead

GOTHA Go 229V-3

MESSERSCHMITT P 1101
Heinkel HeS 011A, 1300 kgp (2860 lb. st.)
DIMENSIONS: Span 8.24 m. (27'), Lg. 9.17 m. (30'1"), Ht. 2.8 m. (9'2"), Wing Area 13 qm. (140 sq. ft.)
WEIGHT: Empty 2620 kg. (5764 lb.), Gross 4070 kg. (8954 lb.), Fuel 935 liters (246 gal.)
PERFORMANCE: Speed—Max. 981 km/hr (608 mph) at 7000 m. (22,960'), 885 km/hr (549 mph) at sea level, Cruising speed 910 km/hr (564 mph), Landing speed 171 km/hr (106 mph), Climb 2000 m./1.5 min. (6560'/1.5 min.), Range 1500 km. (930 miles), Service ceiling 13,800 m. (45,265')

BLOHM & VOSS BV 40
None; this was a "battle glider"
DIMENSIONS: Span 7.85 m. (25'9"), Lg. 5.5 m. (18'1")
WEIGHT: Gross 948 kg. (2085 lb.)
PERFORMANCE: Speed—Max. under tow 550 km/hr (341 mph)

of the enemy bombers, and releasing the BV 40 for a 20 degree dive head on toward the bomber.

Seven prototypes were built, with BV 40V-1 making its first towed flight in May 1944. A crash on June 2 destroyed it, but the second example was flown on June 5. By this time, the presence of large fighter escorts with the American bomber made the scheme tactically unfeasible, and a production order for 200 soon was canceled.

Early in 1944, serious consideration was given to a suicide squadron whose pilots would dive directly into American bombers, exploding an 1100 lb. warhead on contact. The aircraft considered for this role had been begun in March 1943 as an expendable, cheap battle glider, like the BV 40. Two variants were planned as the Me 328A interceptor and the Me 328B bomber, and the development of the simple pulse jet engine for the V-1 flying bomb provided an inexpensive powerplant. Two 792 lb. thrust Argus As 014 units were to be mounted under the wings.

Construction was assigned to the Jacob Schweyer glider company and the first example was tested early in 1944, as a glider launched from a rack atop a Do 217E. Although the aircraft were considered expendable, the pilot had armor protection and was expected to bail out before contact. The Me 328A was superseded by the Me 328B in planning and Heinz Kensche and Hanna Reitsch were encouraged to form a group of would-be suicide pilots.

The concept was opposed by high German officials, and when the first powered tests suffered accidents due to excessive vibration, the project was canceled.

The Bachem Ba 349 was a curious rocket-powered interceptor that was a mixture of aircraft and missile concepts. Searching for answers to Allied bomber raids, the RLM ordered development of an *Objektschutzjaeger* (target defense fighter).

While Heinkel, Junkers, and Messerschmitt submitted proposals, the only project selected was that of Erich Bachen, an old glider pilot and Fieseler director. Development began in August 1944 under the designation Ba 349 "Natter" (Viper). The small, expendable aircraft had a small wooden structure with a cruciform tail and was powered by a 3750 lb. thrust Walter HWK 109-509 like that on the Me 163.

Boosted by four added Schmidding solid-fuel rockets, it had a total of 14,330 lb. thrust during its ten seconds. Starting from vertical guide rails, it dropped its four boosters and accelerated during the first minute to 37,000' and then had a second minute at heavy G forces during takeoff.

The climb was automatically controlled, and radio directed the aircraft to the enemy bomber. Only then would the pilot assume manual control, dropping

MESSERSCHMITT Me 328A

MESSERSCHMITT Me 328B
Argus As 014, 2 X 360 kgp (790 lb. st.)
DIMENSIONS: Span 6.9 m. (22'7½"), Lg. 7.18 m. (23'6½"), Ht. 1.6 m. (5'3"), Wing Area 8.5 qm. (91 sq. ft.)
WEIGHT: Empty 1600 kg. (3520 lb.), Gross 4500 kg. (9900 lb.)
PERFORMANCE: Speed—Max. 805 km/hr (500 mph), Range 485 km. (300 miles)

off the nose cap to expose 24 RSM 55 mm. rockets to be fired in salvo at the enemy. The pilot would then eject himself from the cockpit, while the rocket engine in the rear would break off and descend by parachute.

The first six experimental Natters were tested by being carried up to altitude by He 111s and gliding back to earth. The first self-propelled takeoff, using only the four booster rockets, was attempted December 18, 1944, but failed. On December 22, the vertical takeoff succeeded. By February 2, 1945, the whole system worked on an unmanned test mission in which the nose was smoothly jettisoned, and the dummy pilot was automatically ejected and descended by parachute.

The first piloted takeoff was made at the end of February by Lothar Siebert. The climb began fast, but suddenly the cockpit hood flew off, the Natter turned, exploded, and crashed. Investigation indicated the canopy had been damaged in transport, and that the shock of its breakaway had pushed back the pilot's head and broke his neck.

Nevertheless, development continued until April 1945, with 36 Natters built. Of these, 18 were expended in pilotless tests, four used on piloted tests, and ten more were in position, but had to be destroyed when Allied ground troops approached. Of the rest, three were captured by Americans, and the other by the Russians. While most Natters were of the Ba 349A series, one or two became improved Ba 349Bs with a 4400 lb. HWK 109-509D engine to increase speed and endurance from two to four minutes.

BACHEM Ba 349A
Walter HWK 109-509, plus four Schmidding 109-533, 6500 kgp (14,330 lb. st.)
DIMENSIONS: Span 3.6 m. (11'10"), Lg. 6 m. (19'8"), Wing Area 3.6 qm. (39 sq. ft.)
WEIGHT: Gross 2200 kg. (4840 lb.), Fuel 400 liters *T-Stoff*, (106 gal.) with *T-Stoff*, 190 liters (52 gal.) *C Stoff*
PERFORMANCE: Speed—Max. 800 km/hr (497 mph) at sea level, Climb 12,000 m./1 min. (39,400'/1 min.), Range 40 km. (25 mph), Service ceiling 16,000 m. (52,480')

Postscript

Collapse of the Third Reich in 1945 ended the creation of German combat planes. For a decade, German armed forces were banned entirely, until the 1955 decision to reconstitute German forces as an integrated part of the North Atlantic Treaty Organization.

All German combat planes used since then have been single-seaters of foreign design. They began with the arrival in November 1956 of the first of 450 Republic F-84F fighter-bombers, whose 658 mph speed demonstrated postwar jet progress. They were joined by 108 RF-84F recon jets, 225 Sabre 6 interceptors (F-86s built in Canada), 88 F-86K all-weather interceptors (built by Fiat), and 68 Hawker Sea Hawk naval fighters. The only native design produced was the Dornier Do 27, a non-combat liaison type.

The new Luftwaffe was re-equipped in the 1960s with Fiat G 91 fighter-bombers and the Lockheed F-104G Starfighter, the latter built by a European production complex including a revived Messerschmitt company. While the Starfighter's operational difficulties became notorious, its performance was unquestioned, and dramatized the enormous increase in speed since air combat began in 1915. The Fokker E I did 81 mph and the F-104G did 1328 mph and the increase in firepower is beyond comparison!

Germany's role in manned combat aircraft design may well be over, but the impact of its progress from 1915 to 1945 has had an enormous effect on history.

FIAT G 91

Appendix

The Luftwaffe Order of Battle on September 2, 1939, as World War II opened, is given below. This strength does not include the large stock of older aircraft at training, storage or test stations. Some of these, like the Hs 123 and Ju 86 stocks were later drawn upon for combat units.

Arabic numbers in the prefix were used to denote the *staffel* and Roman numerals denote a *gruppe,* as in 4 (F) AGr 14, or II/KG 4. Abbreviations include:

AGr	Recon *gruppe*
JG	Fighter *geschwader*
KG	Bomber *geschwader*
KGr	Coastal *gruppe*
LG	Demonstration *geschwader*
StG	Dive-bomber *geschwader*
ZG	Long-range fighter *geschwader*
(F)	Long-range recon *staffel*
(H)	Short-range recon *staffel*
(S)	Ground attack *staffel*
Stab	*Geschwader* staff flight

Data for this table was obtained from Vol. 3, no. 9, of *Archiv,* the magazine of Gruppe 66, the International Society of German Aviation Historians. This journal has been published by Bill Conway in London irregularly since 1966.

LUFTWAFFE BATTLE ORDER, SEPTEMBER 2, 1939

BOMBERS UNITS		Type	Nr. a/c	FIGHTERS UNITS		Type	Nr. a/c
Luftwaffe Lehrdivision							
Stab	LG1	He111	10	I(2)	LG1	BF110	32
II(k)	LG1	He111	41	Stab	LG2	BF109	3
III(k)	LG1	He111	40	I(J)	LG2	BF109	36
				II(N)	JG2	BF109	10
Luftflotte 1 (Northeast)							
Stab	KG1	He111	7	I	JG1	BF109	54
I	KG1	He111	38	I	JG2	BF109	42
I[2]	KG152	He111	37	10(N)	JG2	BF109	9
Stab	KG2	Do17	11	Stab	JG3	BF109	3
I	KG2	Do17	37	I	JG3	BF109	48
II	KG2	Do17	35	I	JG20	BF109	21
Stab	KG3	Do17	9	I	JG21	BF109	29
II	KG3	Do17	36	I	ZG1	BF110	32
III	KG3	Do17	39	II	ZG1	BF109	36
Stab	KG4	He111	6	I	ZA2	BF109	44
I	KG4	He111	31				
II	KG4	He111	32				
III	KG4	He111	33				
I[3]	KG25	JU88	18				
Luftflotte 2 (Northwest)							
Stab	KG26	He111	8	I	JG26	BF109	48
I	KG26	He111	32	II	JG26	BF109	48
II	KG26	He111	35	I	ZG26	BF109	52
Stab	KG27	He111	6	II	ZG26	BF109	48
I	KG27	He111	34	III	ZG26	BF109	48
II	KG27	He111	26				
III	KG	He111	28				
II	KG28	He111	35				
Luftflotte 3 (Southwest)							
Stab	KG51	He111	6, DO17 3	I	JG51	BF109	47
I	KG51	He111	36	I	JG52	BF109	39
III	KG51	He111	36	I	JG53	BF109	51
Stab	KG53	He111	6	II	JG53	BF109	43
I	KG53	He111	32	1-2	JG70	BF109	24
II	KG53	He111	32	1-2	JG71	BF109	39
III	KG53	He111	35	10(N)	JG72	AR68	16
Stab	KG54	He111	9	11(N)	JG72	AR68	12
I	KG54	He111	36	I	ZG52	BF109	44
Stab	KG55	He111	9				
I	KG55	He111	33				
II	KG55	He111	31				
Luftflotte 4 (Southeast)							
Stab	KG76	DO17	9	I	JG76	BF109	49
I	KG76	DO17	36	I	JG77	BF109	50
III	KG76	DO17	39	II	JG77	BF109	50
Stab	KG77	DO17	9	I	ZG76	BF110	31
I	KG77	DO17	37	II	ZG76	BF109	40
II	KG76	DO17	39				
III	KG76	DO17	34				
Oberkommando der Marine							
?	KGR806	He111	21	5-6	(J)186	BF109	24

[1] Probably includes 3 DO 17M lead ships
[2] Later became II/KG1
[3] Later I/KG30

GROUND ATTACK UNITS	Type	Nr. a/c	RECON UNITS	Type	Nr. a/c
IV(St) LG1	JU87	42[1]	7(F) LG2	DO17	12
			8(F) LG2	DO17	12
			9(H) LG2	Hs126	9, He46 2
II(S) LG2	Hs123	40	1-2(H) AGR10	Hs126	23
I St.G1	JU87	38, DO17 3	1(H) AGR11	Hs126	9, He46 3
I St.G2	JU87	38, DO17 3	1-3(H) AGR21	Hs126	35
II St.G2	JU87	38, DO17 3	4(H) AGR21	He45	9
III St.G2	JU87	40, DO17 3	1-3(H) AGR41	Hs126	32, He46 2
			3(F) AGR10	DO17	12
			2-4(F) AGR11	DO17	33
			1(F) AGR120	DO17	13
			1-4(F) AGR121	DO17	44
			1-3(H) AGR12	Hs126	33, He46 1
			4(H) AGR12	He46	9, He45 3
			1-3(F) AGR122	DO17	30
III St.G51	JU87	40, DO17 3	1-3(H) AGR13	Hs126	35
			4(H) AGR13	Hs126	9, He46 3
			5(H) AGR13	Hs126	9, He45 3
			1(H) AGR22	Hs126	12
			1(H) AGR23	Hs126	12
			2 AGR23	He46	12
			4 AGR23	He46	9, He45 3
			1-3(F) AGR22	DO17	35
			1-3(F) AGR123	DO17	37
I St.G76	JU87	39, DO17 3	1-3(H) AGR14	Hs126	30, He46 6
Stab St.G77	JU87	3	1(H) AGR31	Hs126	9
I St.G76	JU87	37, DO17 3	2(H) AGR31	He46	8
II St.G76	JU87	39, DO17 3	4 AGR31	He46	9, He45 3
			4(F) AGR14	DO17	11
			3(F) AGR31	DO17	12
			1(F) AGR124	DO17	11
4(St.) 186	JU87	12		DO18	63
				He59	31
				He60	81
				He115	8

Selected Bibliography

While original documents are beyond the reach of most American readers, the following books are suggested for additional information on German combat planes and their historical background. A brief comment has often been added to aid the reader.

BAUMBACH, WERNER, *The Life and Death of the Luftwaffe.* New York: Coward-McCann, 1960. The former commander of Hitler's bomber force reviews Luftwaffe planning, and gives useful statistics.

BEKKER, CAJUS, *Angriffshohe 4000.* Olderburg: Gerhard Stalling Verlag, 1965. Published in English as: *The Luftwaffe War Diaries,* translated and edited by Frank Ziegler, London: Macdonald & Co., Ltd., 1966; New York: Doubleday & Co., Inc., 1966. The most detailed operational history available.

CAREL, PAUL, *Hitler Moves East 1941–1943.* Boston: Little, Brown & Co., 1965. A study of Barbarossa from the German point of view.

CLARK, ALAN, *Barbarossa.* New York: William Morrow & Co., 1965. A History of the Russo-German war.

CONSTABLE, TREVOR J., and TOLIVER, COL. RAYMOND F., Ret., *Horrido! Fighter Aces of the Luftwaffe.* New York: Macmillan Co., 1968. Detailed story of Germany's aces.

CUNEO, JOHN R., *The Air Weapon 1914–1916.* Vol. II: *Of Winged Mars.* Harrisburg: Military Service Publishing Co., 1947. Documented study of the war's first two years.

FOKKER, ANTHONY, and GOULD, BRUCE, *Flying Dutchman.* New York: Henry Holt, 1931. His autobiography, much criticized by later authorities.

FREDETTE, RAYMOND H., *The First Battle of Britian 1917–18.* London: Cassel & Co., Ltd., 1966. Gothas against London.

GALLAND, ADOLF, *The First and the Last.* New York: Henry Holt & Co., 1954. The last chief of Luftwaffe fighters reviews Luftwaffe history.

GRAY, PETER, and THETFORD, OWEN, *German Aircraft of the First World War.* London: Putnam & Co., Ltd., 1962. The most thorough English book on this subject.

GREEN, WILLIAM, *War Planes of the Second World War.* London: Macdonald & Co., 1960. *Fighters.* Vol. I–IV. *Flying Boats.* Vol. V. *Floatplanes.* Vol. VI. *Bombers.* Vol. VII–X. A detailed review of wartime types.

HADDOW, G. W., and GROSZ, PETER M., *The German Giants, The German R-planes 1914–1918.* London: Putnam, 1962, (new edition 1969). Remains the definitive work on these types.

HADINGHAM, EVAN, *The Fighting Triplanes.* New York: Macmillan Co., 1969.

HEGENER, HENRI, *Fokker—The Man and the Aircraft.* Letchworth, Herts: Harleyford Publications Ltd., 1961. A favorable biography.

HEINKEL, ERNST, *Stormy Life.* New York: Dutton, 1956. The famous builder's memoirs.

Hoffschmidt, Edward J., *German Aircraft Guns.* Old Greenwich, Conn: WE Inc., 1969. Detailed coverage of armament from 1914 to 1945.

JOHNEN, WILHELM, *Battling the Bombers.* New York: Ace Books, Inc., 1958. Published in England under the title *Duel Under the Stars* by William Kimber and Co., Ltd. A night fighter's personal account.

KENS, KARLHEINZ, and NOWARRA, HEINZ, *Die deutschen Flugzeuge 1933–1945.* Munchen: J. F. Lechmann Verlag, 1961. The most comprehensive German account of the Luftwaffe warplanes.

KESSELRING, ALBERT, *A Soldier's Record.* New York: William Morrow & Co., 1954. Memoirs of Luftwaffe general.

KILLEN, JOHN, *The Luftwaffe History.* London: Frederick Muller Ltd., 1964. A short general history.

LAMBERTON, W. M., edited by Chessman, E. F., *Fighter Aircraft of the 1914–1918 War.* Letchworth, HERTS: Harleyford Publications Ltd., 1960. This series is especially distinguished by its 1/72 scale drawings.

———, edited by Chessman, E. F., *Reconnaissance and Bomber Aircraft of the 1914–1918 War.* Los Angeles: Aero Publishers Co., 1962. A general survey.

MANVELL, ROGER and FRAENKEL, HEINRICH, *Goering.* New York: Simon and Schuster, 1962. A biography of the Luftwaffe chief.

NOWARRA, HEINZ, *Eisernes Kreuz und Balken Kreuz.* Mainz: Verlag Dieter Hoffmann, 1968. Color illustration of markings, along with much organizational information.

———, *50 Jahre Deutsche Luftwaffe.* Vol. I, II, III.

Los Angeles: Aero Publishers, 1964. A pictorial history of German Air Power.

———, *The Focke-Wulf 190, A Famous German Fighter.* Letchworth, Herts: Harleyford Publications Ltd., 1965. This fighter aircraft's biography.

———, *Marine Aircraft of the 1914–1918 War.* Letchworth, Herts: Harleyford Publications, Ltd., 1966.

———, *The Messerschmitt 109.* Letchworth, Herts: Harleyford Publications, 1963. The story of the most widely used German aircraft.

OBERMAIER, ERNST, *Die Ritterkreuztrager der Luftwaffe.* Mainz: Verlag Dieter Hoffmann, 1966. The fighter pilots who won the Knight's Cross.

RIES, KARL, *Dora–Kurfurst und rote 13.* Vol. I to III, Finthen Bei Mainz: Verlag Dieter Hoffmann, 1964–65.

ROBERTSON, BRUCE, (ed.), *Air Aces of the 1914–1918 War.* Letchworth, Herts: Harleyford Publications, Ltd., 1959.

RUDEL, HANS ULRICH, *Stuka Pilot.* New York, Ballantine Books, 1963. Autobiography of an unrepentant Ju 87 specialist.

SHIRER, WILLIAM L., *The Rise and Fall of the Third Reich.* New York: Simon and Schuster, 1960. The most popular American political history of Hitler's Germany.

Suchenwirth, Richard, *Historical Turning Points in the German Air Force War Effort.* New York: Arno Press, 1968. One of a series of historical studies done by Germans for the USAF.

Tatum, W. H., and Hoffschmitt, E. H., editors, *The Rise and Fall of the German Air Force.* Old Greenwich, Conn: WE Inc., 1969. A reprint of a study done for the Royal Air Force about 1948

United States Strategic Bombing Survey, *The Effects of Strategic Bombing on the German War Economy.* Washington: Government Printing Office, 1945. Has data on German plans, policies and economics.

WEBSTER, CHARLES K., *Strategic Air Offensive Against Germany, 1939–1945.* 4 vols. London: Her Majesty's Stationery Office, 1961. The official history, with data of German production.

WEYL, A. R., *Fokker: The Creative Years.* London: Putnam & Co., Ltd., 1965. A critical study.

WOOD, DEREK, and DEMPSTER, DEREK, *The Narrow Margin.* New York: McGraw-Hill Book Co., 1961. The Battle of Britain, with much data from German side.

ZIEGLER, MARROW, *Rocket Fighter.* London: Macdonald, 1963. Development of the Me 163.

Profile Publications issued a series of booklets giving the history and markings of individual aircraft that have been bound together and offered in the U.S. as *Aircraft in Profile* by Doubleday & Co., 1968. Those dealing with German aircraft are listed here with their author and number.

Albatros DI–III *Peter L. Gray* 127
Albatros DV *Peter L. Gray* 9
Focke-Wulf Fw 190A *Martin C. Windrow* 3
Focke-Wulf Fw 190D/TA 152 *J. Richard Smith* 94
Focke-Wulf Fw 200 *J. Richard Smith* 99
Fokker D VII *Peter L. Gray* 25
Fokker D VIII *J. M. Bruce* 67
Fokker Dr I *J. M. Bruce* 55
Fokker Monoplanes *J. M. Bruce* 38
Gotha GI–GV *Peter M. Grosz* 115
Heinkel Hs 111H *Martin C. Windrow* 15
Heinkel Hs 162 *J. Richard Smith* 203
Henschel Hs 129 *J. Richard Smith* 69
Junkers Monoplanes *Hugh Corvin* 187
Junkers Ju 52 *J. Richard Smith* 177
Junkers Ju 87A & B *J. Richard Smith* 76
Junkers Ju 88A *Martin C. Windrow* 29
Junkers Ju 88 Fighter *Alfred Price* 148
Messerschmitt Bf 109E *Martin C. Windrow* 40
Messerschmitt Bf 109F *Martin C. Windrow* 184
Messerschmitt Bf 109G *J. Richard Smith* 113
Messerschmitt Bf 110 *Martin C. Windrow* 23
Messerschmitt Me 210/410 *J. Richard Smith* 161
Messerschmitt Me 262 *J. Richard Smith* 130
Pfalz D III *Peter L. Gray* 43
Pfalz D XII *Peter Grosz* 199
Roland C II *Peter Grosz* 163
Siemens-Schukert DIII/IV *Peter Grosz* 86

Aero Publishers of Fallbrook, California, published a series of paperbacks from 1965 to 1968 including several German types. The art work was by Uwe Feist, and text jointly by R. S. Hirsch, E. T. Maloney or H. J. Nowarra. Each booklet has a short text and extensive photographic coverage of the type. Titles published included:

Dornier Do 335
Focke-Wulf Fw 190
Heinkel He 112/100
Heinkel He 162
Heinkel He 177
Junkers Ju 87
Messerschmitt Bf 109
Messerschmitt Bf 110
Messerschmitt Me 163
Messerschmitt Me 262

Index

NOTE: Aircraft are listed under the company that built them.

B

C

D

E

F

G

H

I

J

K

L

M

N

O

P

R

S

T

U

V

W

Y

Z